P9-DNV-317

BACK
TO THE
LAKE

BACK
TO THE
LAKE

A READER
FOR WRITERS

Thomas
Cooley

SECOND EDITION

W · W · NORTON & COMPANY · NEW YORK · LONDON

W. W. Norton & Company has been independent since its founding in 1923, when William Warder Norton and Mary D. Herter Norton first published lectures delivered at the People's Institute, the adult education division of New York City's Cooper Union. The firm soon expanded its program beyond the Institute, publishing books by celebrated academics from America and abroad. By midcentury, the two major pillars of Norton's publishing program—trade books and college texts—were firmly established. In the 1950s, the Norton family transferred control of the company to its employees, and today—with a staff of four hundred and a comparable number of trade, college, and professional titles published each year—W. W. Norton & Company stands as the largest and oldest publishing house owned wholly by its employees.

Copyright © 2012, 2009 by W. W. Norton & Company, Inc.

All rights reserved
Printed in the United States of America

Editor: Marilyn Moller
Developmental editor: Rebecca Homiski
Associate editor: Betsye Mullaney
Editorial assistant: Erica Wnek
Production manager: Ben Reynolds
Design director: Rubina Yeh
Design: JoAnne Metsch
Marketing manager: Scott Berzon
Emedia editor: Cliff Landesman
Composition: TexTech, Inc.—Brattleboro, VT
Manufacturing: Courier—Westford, MA

Library of Congress Cataloging-in-Publication Data

Cooley, Thomas, 1942–
  Back to the lake : a reader for writers / Thomas Cooley. — 2nd ed.
    p. cm.
  Includes bibliographical references and index.

ISBN: 978-0-393-91268-5 (pbk.)
ISBN: 978-0-393-91804-5 (Instructor's Edition; pbk.)

  1. College readers. 2. English language—Rhetoric—Problems, exercises, etc. 3. Report writing—Problems, exercises, etc. I. Title.
  PE1417.C6549 2012
  808'.0427—dc23

                    2011043356

W. W. Norton & Company, Inc., 500 Fifth Avenue, New York, NY 10110
www.wwnorton.com
W. W. Norton & Company Ltd., Castle House, 75/76 Wells Street, London W1T 3QT
1 2 3 4 5 6 7 8 9 0

Preface

I first read E. B. White's classic essay "Once More to the Lake" with awe and wonder as a freshman in a college writing course. Only years later did I realize that White worked his magic with common rhetorical techniques—narration, description, comparison, and the other modes of writing discussed in this book—that good writers use every day in all kinds of texts and contexts. Far from magic, these standard techniques could be applied to my own writing, whether to structure a paragraph or an entire essay, or, even more essentially, to generate ideas and organize my thoughts throughout the writing process.

We now take it for granted that the process of writing is one we can learn—and teach. This was not the case in White's day, however, as I discovered when, as a young assistant professor of English, I rashly fired off a letter asking him to explain how he composed "Once More to the Lake." To my astonishment, White not only responded to my letter, he said he didn't really know how he wrote anything. "The 'process,'" White confided, "is probably every bit as mysterious to me as it is to some of your students—if that will make them feel any better."

Fortunately for today's students and teachers, the scene has changed; we now know a lot more than we once did about how the writing process works and how to teach it. *Back to the Lake*—which takes its title from White's essay—applies this understanding of the process to show students how to make the basic moves that seasoned writers make, whether consciously or otherwise, in their writing.

An Overview of the Book

As its subtitle announces, *Back to the Lake* is a reader for writers. It contains more than 85 readings, from the most classic ("Grant and Lee") to the most current (a blog post from a veteran of the war in Iraq) to the best-selling (*The Checklist Manifesto*)—all demonstrating that the rhetorical methods taught in this book are ones that all good writers depend on. Each mode is accompanied by 6 or 7 readings, including at least one annotated student example and one story or poem.

Chapter 1 introduces students to the principles of analytical reading, taking them through the basic steps of reading with a critical eye.

Chapter 2 gives an overview of the writing process, preparing students to analyze assignments; come up with topics and generate ideas; draft and revise an essay with a particular audience and purpose in mind; and edit and proofread.

Chapter 3 covers the basic moves of academic writing, helping students research a topic, synthesize ideas, respond with ideas of their own, consider counterarguments, and explain why their ideas matter.

Chapters 4 through 12 each focus on one of the rhetorical modes as a basic method of discovery and development. Practical guidelines lead students through the process of composing a text using that mode: generating ideas, organizing and drafting, getting feedback, and revising and editing a final draft.

Chapter 13 demonstrates how much real-world writing combines those methods.

An **appendix on using sources** offers guidance in finding, incorporating, and documenting sources MLA-style—and includes an annotated student research paper.

A **glossary / index** completes the book, providing definitions of all the key terms along with a list of the pages where they are covered in detail.

Highlights

An engaging, teachable collection of readings, from classic ("I Have a Dream") to current ("Happy Meals and Old Spice Guy") to humorous ("All Seven Deadly Sins Committed at Church Bake Sale")—all demonstrating the patterns taught in this book. Each chapter includes a student essay (annotated) and a poem or story.

Everyday examples, showing that the methods taught in this book are familiar ones—and that they are not used just in first-year writing; that a recipe, for example, relies on process analysis and that a T-shirt can make an argument.

Templates to help students get started drafting, providing language to help them make the moves needed to describe, compare, define, and so on.

Practical editing tips, to help students check for the kinds of errors that frequently occur with each of the rhetorical methods taught in this book—for instance, to check that verb tenses accurately reflect when actions occur in a narrative.

Help for students whose primary language is not English, with glosses for unfamiliar terms and cultural allusions, templates for getting started, and tips for dealing with predictable stumbling points, such as adjective order or the use of the present perfect.

User friendly, with exceptionally well written pedagogy that makes the subject matter interesting, relevant, and easy to understand. The two-color design, with all instruction printed on green pages, makes the book easy to use. A combined glossary / index provides full definitions of all key terms, along with references to pages where students can find more detail.

What's New

34 new readings: Including Laurel Thatcher Ulrich's "Well-Behaved Women Seldom Make History," Lynda Barry's "Sanctuary of School," Steven Pinker's "Mind Over Mass Media." Of the new readings, 20 are appearing in a composition reader for the first time.

Navigation features that make the book easier to use than ever. Notes in the margins explicitly link the readings with the writing instruction, leading students from the instruction to specific examples in the readings, and the reverse. A quick-reference guide inside the front cover helps students know when to use each of the rhetorical methods covered in the book, and a menu of readings inside the back cover makes specific readings easy to find.

Expanded coverage of academic writing, including a new chapter teaching the basic moves of academic argument; five student essays that use MLA or APA style; and an MLA-style citation for each of the readings, showing students how to cite them properly.

A free and open student website (wwnorton.com/write) includes exercises on editing common errors, downloadable templates for drafting, downloadable worksheets for reading with a critical eye, biographical notes on each author in the book, and tutorials on research writing and avoiding plagiarism.

Acknowledgments

For help in the preparation of a new edition of this book, I wish to thank a number of people. As always, I am most grateful to Barbara Cooley, who deals equally well with issues of water quality and murky prose. Marilyn Moller, without your inspiration and experience at the editorial helm there would be no *Back to the Lake*; I thank you for keeping us all on course during a longer voyage than anyone expected. Thanks as well to Rebecca Homiski, my wonderful hands-on editor at Norton, who took care of development, photo research, and copyediting, as well as overseeing the book's typesetting and layout. I am also grateful to Mark Gallaher and Michal Brody for their work on the glosses and instructor's notes. In addition, I wish to thank Jo Metsch for the beautiful design; Bethany Salminen and Margaret Gorenstein for clearing the many permissions; Betsye Mullaney for her advice in selecting new readings; Ben Reynolds for getting the book produced in good form despite the many deadlines some of us missed; and Marian Johnson and Julia Reidhead for their support of this ambitious project all along the way.

Thanks go as well to the following teachers who reviewed the first edition: Kellee Barbour, Virginia Western Community College; Judy Bello, Lander University; Kathleen Collins Beyer, Farmingham State College; Jonathan Bradley, Concord University; Mary Jane Brown, Miami University Middletown; Sarah Burns, Virginia Western Community College; Marian Carcache, Auburn University; Amy Cooper, St. Cloud State University; Lily Corwin, Kutztown University; MaryBeth Drake, Virginia Western Community College; Richard Farias, San Antonio College; Gabriel Ford, Penn State–University Park; Bill Gahan, Rockford College; Mary Ellen Ginnetti, Hillsborough Community College; Peggy Hach, SUNY New Paltz; Monica Hatchett, Virginia Western Community College; Jim Hilgartner, Huntingdon College; Gina L Hochhalter, Clovis Community College; Jo Ann Horneker, Arkansas State University; Laura Jensen, University of Nebraska; Sandra Kelly, Virginia Western Community College; Aaron Kimmel, Penn State; Henry Marchand, Monterey Peninsula College; Howard Mayer, University of Hartford; Scott Moncrieff, Andrews University; Bryan Moore, Arkansas State University; Angela Mustapha, Penn State; Charlene Pate, Point Loma Nazarene University; Gregg Pratt, North Country Community College/SUNY Adirondack; Lisa Riggs, Oklahoma Wesleyan University; Craig-Ellis Sasser, Northeast Mississippi Community College; Anne Taylor, North Dakota State College of Science; Julian Thornton, Gadsden State Community College; April Van Camp, Indian River State College; Karina Westra, Point Loma Nazarene University; Lea Williams, Norwich University.

I am grateful as well to the instructors who took time to share their thoughts on the new readings: Andrea Bates, Coastal Carolina Community College; Darren DeFrain, Wichita State University; Catherine F. Heath, Victoria College; James M.

Hilgartner, Huntingdon College; Sandra Kelly, Virginia Western Community College; Jacquelyn Robinson, Victoria College; Craig-Ellis Sasser, Northeast Mississippi Community College; Nann Tucker, Hillsborough Community College.

It is a great pleasure to name the teachers of writing and experts in the field of composition and rhetoric who have given advice, or otherwise assisted me, at various stages in the evolution of this book. They include my colleagues at Ohio State, particularly Beverly Moss, Sara Garnes, and the late Edward P. J. Corbett; the late Dean McWilliams of Ohio University; Roy Rosenstein of the American University of Paris; and, for his great generosity in allowing me to use the fruit of his research and experience in the appendix, Richard Bullock of Wright State University. For a clean, well-lighted place to write away from home, thanks to Ron and Elisabeth Beckman of Syracuse University and Paris.

Finally, I say a big thank you to Gerald Graff and Cathy Birkenstein for showing me—particularly in *"They Say / I Say": The Moves That Matter in Academic Writing*—how to represent sophisticated intellectual and rhetorical strategies in a shorthand, generative way that teachers can actually use to help students make those moves in their own writing. I believe, with them, that writing and reading are "deeply reciprocal activities" and that "imitating established models" is one of the best ways to learn how to write.

Contents

5 Description 121

ZAINAB SALBI, *Little House in the War Zone* 142
"The house I grew up in was nestled in a grove of eucalyptus trees at the end of a Baghdad cul-de-sac. . . . It was in this cul-de-sac, long after I went to bed, that Saddam Hussein used to park his car."

JOHN BRANCH, *Perfection in the Horseshoe Pit* 146
"Get a ringer 70 percent of the time, and you are in a shrinking class of world-class pitchers. Get one 80 percent of the time, and you are probably in the top two. Get one 90 percent of the time, and you are Alan Francis."

JUDITH ORTIZ COFER, *More Room* 152
"Though the room was dominated by the mahogany four-poster, it also contained all of Mama's symbols of power."

ZORA NEALE HURSTON, *How It Feels to Be Colored Me* 157
"I feel most colored when I am thrown against a sharp white background."

E. B. WHITE, *Once More to the Lake* 163
"I felt the same damp moss covering the worms in the bait can, and saw the dragonfly alight on the tip of my rod as it hovered a few inches from the surface of the water. It was the arrival of this fly that convinced me beyond any doubt that everything was as it always had been, that the years were a mirage and that there had been no years."

RITA DOVE, *American Smooth* 170
"We were dancing—it must have / been a foxtrot or a waltz, / something romantic but / requiring restraint"

6 Example 173

7 Process Analysis 223

"Do not stay up with someone you know will distract you with either idle chatter or sexual tension."

"But just in case you ever find yourself in a hostile situation or, God forbid, a Raiders home game, today I'm going to pass along the lessons I learned in Fright School as recorded in my notes."

"I guarantee you've done something harder than a five-page essay."

"A glass jar. About 4 1/2 inches long, about three inches in diameter, with a pinched-in neck—a large baby-food jar, perhaps. It is jammed over the skunk's head, completely covering it past the ears."

"Nobody's first drafts are good. The difference between a successful scholar and a failure need not be better writing. It is often more editing."

"'Tis first—I lock the Door—"

8 Comparison and Contrast 269

GITANGELI SAPRA, *I'm Happy with an Arranged Marriage* 288
"Such is the dance of modern-day arranged marriage, at least as I, a 24-year-old Hindu born in Britain, have experienced it."

ROGER COHEN, *The Meaning of Life* 291
"Life without death would be miserable. Its beauty is bound to its fragility. Dawn is unimaginable without the dusk."

DAVID SEDARIS, *Remembering My Childhood on the Continent of Africa* 296
"Certain events are parallel, but compared with Hugh's, my childhood was unspeakably dull. When I was seven years old, my family moved to North Carolina. When he was seven years old, Hugh's family moved to the Congo."

NICHOLAS D. KRISTOF, *Food for the Soul* 303
"Bob names all his cows, and can tell them apart in an instant. He can tell you each cow's quirks and parentage. They are family friends as well as economic assets."

BRUCE CATTON, *Grant and Lee* 307
"They were two strong men, these oddly different generals, and they represented the strengths of two conflicting currents that . . . had come into final collision."

WILLIAM SHAKESPEARE, *Sonnet 130* 313
"My mistress' eyes are nothing like the sun"

9 Classification 316

STEPHANIE ERICSSON, *The Ways We Lie* 336
"I once tried going a whole week without telling a lie, and it was paralyzing. I discovered that telling the truth all the time is nearly impossible."

AMY TAN, *Mother Tongue* 345
"Sociologists and linguists probably will tell you that a person's developing language skills are more influenced by peers. But I do think that the language spoken in the family, especially in immigrant families, . . . plays a large role."

DAVID BROOKS, *People Like Us* 352
"Many of us live in absurdly unlikely groupings because we have organized our lives that way."

ERIN MCKEAN, *Verbed! Not Every Noun Wants to Stay That Way* 359
"Almost any word can be drafted to serve as a verb, even words we think of as eternal and unchanging, stuck in their more traditional roles."

DEBORAH TANNEN, *But What Do You Mean?* 363
"Women are often told they apologize too much. The reason they're told to stop doing it is that, to many men, apologizing seems synonymous with putting oneself down."

ANNE SEXTON, *Her Kind* 371
"A woman like that is not afraid to die. / I have been her kind."

10 Definition 374

MARY ROACH, *How to Know If You're Dead* 402

"The modern medical community is on the whole quite unequivocal about the brain being the seat of the soul. . . . It is similarly unequivocal about the fact that people like H. are, despite the hoochy-koochy going on behind their sternum, dead."

FATEMA MERNISSI, *The Harem Within* 410

"A harem was about private space and the rules regulating it. In addition, Yasmina said, it did not need walls. Once you knew what was forbidden, you carried the harem within."

JACK HORNER, *The Extraordinary Characteristics of Dyslexia* 418

"But what most non-dyslexics don't know about us, besides the fact that we simply process information differently, is that our early failures often give us an important edge as we grow older."

BOBBIE ANN MASON, *Being Country* 422

"I can still see Mama emerging from that restaurant kitchen, carrying two hamburger platters and gabbing with her customers as if they were old friends who had dropped in to visit and sit a spell. In the glass of the picture window, reflections from the TV set flicker like candles at the church Christmas service."

GEOFFREY NUNBERG, *The War of Words* 432

"Broad linguistic shifts such as these usually owe less to conscious decisions by editors or speechwriters than to often-unnoticed changes in the way people perceive their world."

FLANNERY O'CONNOR, *A Good Man Is Hard to Find* 436

"The grandmother shrieked. She scrambled to her feet and stood staring. 'You're The Misfit!' she said. 'I recognized you at once!' "

11 Cause and Effect 451

HENRY LOUIS GATES JR., *The Way to Reduce Black Poverty in America* 484
"Yet it isn't a derogation of the black vernacular—a marvellously rich and inventive tongue—to point out that there's a language of the marketplace, too, and learning to speak that language has generally been a precondition for economic success, whoever you are."

HENRY L. ROEDIGER III, *Why Are Textbooks So Expensive?* 488
"Let us go back in time to what educational historians refer to as the later Paleolithic era in higher education, that is, the late 1960s, when I was in college. Here was how the used book market worked then."

DAN BARRY, *Cancer's Oddest Effect* 495
"I had a pre-existing case of fogginess that lifted during and immediately after my chemotherapy regimen: I suddenly experienced acute clarity. Then, as the effects and memory of chemotherapy faded, my confusion returned. Twice."

HAL R. VARIAN, *Analyzing the Marriage Gap* 500
"Married men make more money than single men. . . . The question is why."

SHIRLEY JACKSON, *The Lottery* 504
"Mr. Graves opened the slip of paper and there was a general sigh through the crowd as he held it up and everyone could see it was blank."

12 Argument 513

THOMAS JEFFERSON, *The Declaration of Independence* 542
"We hold these truths to be self-evident, that all men are created equal."

CHIEF SEATTLE, *Reply to the U.S. Government* 547
"Let him be just and deal kindly with my people, for the dead are not powerless.
Dead, did I say? There is no death, only a change of worlds."

MARTIN LUTHER KING JR., *I Have a Dream* 553
"I have a dream that my four children will one day live in a nation where they will
not be judged by the color of their skin but by the content of their character."

BARACK OBAMA, *A More Perfect Union* 560
"Working together we can move beyond some of our old racial wounds, and . . . in
fact we have no choice if we are to continue on the path of a more perfect union."

SOJOURNER TRUTH, *Ain't I a Woman?* 574
"If the first woman God ever made was strong enough to turn the world upside down
all alone, these women together ought to be able to turn it back, and get it right side
up again!"

MICHAEL LEWIS, *Buy That Little Girl an Ice Cream Cone* 578
"I should be sweeping her out of the pool and washing her mouth out with soap. . . .
Actually, I'm impressed. More than impressed: awed. It's just incredibly heroic, tak-
ing out after this rat pack of boys."

DEBATING THE DRINKING AGE 583

RUTH C. ENGS, *Why the Drinking Age Should Be Lowered* 584
"Because the . . . drinking-age law is not working . . . it behooves us . . . to teach responsible drinking techniques for those who choose to consume alcoholic beverages."

JACK HITT, *The Battle of the Binge* 587
"Alcohol consumption . . . is a socialized phenomenon, which if not taught, yields up
a kind of wild child."

13 Combining the Methods 649

MICHAEL LEWIS, *Liar's Poker* 653
"The code of the Liar's Poker player was something like the code of the gunslinger. It required a trader to accept all challenges."

EVERYDAY WRITING / A Book Cover 658

MELISSA HICKS, *The High Price of Butter* 660
"To me, the cost of butter is more than a price tag. The cost of butter reminds me of my childhood, and how my family struggled to be pioneers in the twentieth century."

ERIC SCHLOSSER, *What We Eat* 667
"Fast food has proven to be a revolutionary force in American life; I am interested in it both as a commodity and as a metaphor."

MALCOLM GLADWELL, *The Tipping Point* 675
"The rise of Hush Puppies and the fall of New York's crime rate are textbook examples of epidemics in action. Although they may sound as if they don't have very much in common, they share a basic, underlying pattern."

ATUL GAWANDE, *The Checklist Manifesto* 682
"Medicine . . . poses a significant challenge: What do you do when expertise is not enough? . . . We've begun to see an answer, but it has come from an unexpected source—one that has nothing to do with medicine at all."

BILLY COLLINS, *Fishing on the Susquehanna in July* 696
"I have never been fishing on the Susquehanna / or on any river for that matter / to be perfectly honest."

Appendix: Using Sources in Your Writing 699

Thematic Guide
to the Readings

Cultures and Ethnicities

Ethics and Religion

Fiction

Gender

History

Home and Family

Humor and Satire

Language and Identity

Life, Death, and Illness

Love and Marriage

Memories of Youth

Nature and the Environment

Poetry

Public Policy

Reading and Writers

Science and Technology

Sociology and Anthropology

Sports and Leisure

Student Writing

CHAPTER 1
Good Writers Are Good Readers

The more that you read, the more things you will know. The more that you learn, the more places you'll go.
—Dr. Seuss

Learning to write is similar to learning to play the piano. You have to practice daily to improve your skills. Studying good examples also helps.
—Juha Haataia

Let's start with the alphabet. By the time you learned the alphabet song, you were already proficient at what linguists call *first order* language skills—listening and speaking. We pick up these skills naturally as young children simply by hearing other people talk and by imitating the sounds we hear. The *second order* language skills, reading and writing, take much longer to learn, and they require more formal instruction—just as it took you more time and study to learn the written (as opposed to spoken or sung) alphabet. This is especially true if we are to achieve real competence with the written word. To a degree, however, we learn to write as we first learned to speak—by imitating the words of others.

Consequently, good writers are usually good readers. They may not read every book in the library; but they read critically, paying close attention to the strategies and techniques that accomplished writers use for presenting their ideas. This chapter focuses on how to engage in such close reading and provides some guidelines to help you read the essays in this book with an eye for what they can teach you about your own writing.

Reading Closely—and Critically

Like writing, reading is an active process. Even when you take a thriller to the beach and read for fun, your brain is at work translating words into mental images and ideas. When you read more purposefully, as with the essays in this book, your brain will get even more of a workout. In both instances, however, the words on the page form a text that can be analyzed and interpreted. The word *text*, like the word *textile*, derives from the Latin word for *weaving*. A text is a written fabric of words. When you read a text with a critical eye, you unravel that fabric, looking at how the words fit together to make meaning. You also question what you're reading and think more deeply about your own ideas on the subject.

Reading a text critically does not mean that you have to be judgmental. Instead, it means that you analyze the text as carefully and objectively as you can. This is why critical reading will be defined in this book as *close* reading: it sticks to the text as closely as possible and avoids reading too much (or too little) into the text.

The Reading Process

When you read any text, you engage in a number of activities. Among these are previewing, reading, and responding. *Previewing* a text means looking it over generally to get a rough sense of its subject, scope, and context. When you actually *read* the text, you comb through it systematically from beginning to end, trying to discern the author's main point, how it's supported, and whether any pertinent information is missing. As you *respond* to the text, you think about whether you agree or disagree (or both) with the author's ideas; you may reread parts of the text that you have questions about. Let's take a closer look at each of these activities.

Previewing a Text

Before you plunge into a text, it's a good idea to take a few moments to survey the territory. Get your pencil ready, but resist the urge to underline until you have a better sense of where the text is going and what you want to focus on. Here are some tips for previewing any text, including the readings in this book:

- *Look at the introduction or headnote* to find out about the author and the original context—the time, place, and circumstances in which the text was written and published. For example, a soldier's first-hand account of a battle has a far different context than a historian's account of the same battle written years later.
- *Think about the title.* What does it reveal about the topic and tone of the text? Are you expecting a serious argument, or an essay that pokes fun at its subject?
- *Skim the text for an overview*, noting any headings, boldfaced words, illustrations, charts, or footnotes.

- *Skim the introduction and conclusion.* What insight do they give into the purpose and message of the text?
- *Think about your own expectations and purpose for reading.* Are you reading to obtain information? for entertainment? to fulfill an assignment? How will your purpose and prior knowledge affect what you take from the text?

Reading a Text

Reading a text closely is a little like investigating a crime scene. You look for certain clues; you ask certain questions. Your objective is to determine, as precisely and accurately as you can, both what the text has to say and how it says it. Your primary clues, therefore, are in the text itself—the actual words on the page.

If you've previewed the text carefully, you already have some idea of what it's about. Now is the time to examine it closely. So pull out your pencil, and perhaps a highlighter, and be ready to annotate the text as you go along—to jot down questions or comments in the margins, underline important points, circle key words, and otherwise mark places in the text that you may want to come back to.

The following example shows how a student writer, Judy Vassey, annotated a paragraph from an essay reprinted later in this chapter. Notice that she has identified and underlined the author's main point, circled a few words and phrases that she wants to investigate further, and raised a key question about the many questions in the passage.

For some of us, reading (begets) rereading, and rereading begets   ⋯ begets = Bible?
writing. (Although there is no doubt which is first, and supreme; as   ⋮ main point
(Alberto Manguel) writes in his wonderful (A History of Reading,) "I could   ⋯ who's Manguel?
perhaps live without writing. I don't think I could live without read-
ing.") After a while (the story) is familiar, the settings known, the char-   ⋯ what story?
acters understood, and there is nothing left to discover but technique.
Why that sentence structure and not something simpler, or more
complex? Why that way of ordering events instead of something more   ⋯ why all the questions?
straightforward, or more experimental? What grabs the reader by the
throat? What sags and bags and fails? There are only two ways, really,
to become a writer. One is to write. The other is to read.

—ANNA QUINDLEN, *How Reading Changed My Life*

Vassey is a good close reader, but even she can't decipher all the important clues on her first run through a relatively complex passage. How does a good detective ensure that she hasn't missed any important evidence? She returns to the scene of the crime—she rereads the text.

When Vassey reread the Quindlen text, she answered her own query about the number of questions the author asks, noting that they show how a writer habitually reads with an eye for methods and technique. To discover not only *what* a text is saying but *how* and *why*—this is your goal as a writer reading the work of others.

QUESTIONS FOR READING

- *What is the writer's main point?* Is it clearly stated in a thesis? If so, where? If the main point is not stated directly, is it clearly implied?

- *What is the primary purpose of the text?* To provide information? Sell a product or service? Argue a point of view? Make us laugh? Tell a story?

- *Who is the intended audience?* Readers who are familiar with the topic? Those who know little about it? People who might be inclined to agree—or disagree?

- *What is the tone and style of the text?* Serious? Informal? Inspirational? Strident?

- *How and where does the writer support the main point?* Can you point out specific details, facts, examples, visuals, expert testimony, personal experience, or other kinds of evidence?

- *Is the evidence sufficient?* Or does the supporting evidence fail to convince you? Are sources clearly identified so you can tell where quotations, paraphrases, or summaries are coming from?

- *Has the writer fairly represented—and responded to—other points of view?* Has any crucial perspective been left out?

- *How is the text organized?* Do ideas flow logically from one to another? Where, if anywhere, is the text difficult to follow? Why?

- *What is the larger historical and cultural context of the text?* Who is the author? When was the text written and published? By whom? What other ideas or events does it reflect?

Responding to What You've Read

Once you've read a text closely—questioning point by point what it says and how—you're in a good position to judge what the text adds up to and how you feel about it, both emotionally and intellectually. That is, you're ready to respond—preferably in writing—to the text as a whole. Go back over the text once more and try the following:

- *Summarize what you've read in your own words.* If you can write a SUMMARY of the main points, you probably have a good grasp of what you've read.

- *Think about and record your own reactions.* To what extent do you agree or disagree—or both—with what the author is saying? It is usual, of course, to accept some statements in a text—including the THESIS, or main point—and still question others. And it is possible to like (or dislike) the tone and style of a text even if you reject (or accept) the argument.

- *Consider what you learned about writing.* Make note of any techniques used in the text that you might want to incorporate into your own writing. For example, does the piece have a catchy introduction, interesting and pertinent examples, or striking visuals? If the text has elements you don't want to emulate—such as a weak conclusion—you might write those down as well.

Reading Visual Texts

Almost everywhere we look these days, we are surrounded by visuals—on blogs and websites, in magazines and textbooks, on billboards and subways. It is essential, then, to be able to read visuals closely, to look at them with a critical eye.

In many ways, reading a visual is similar to reading a written text: you have to think critically about its purpose, its main point, and so on. Some visuals consist only of images—photographs, drawings, paintings—whereas other visuals—like graphs and diagrams—include words. Many advertisements, for example, combine images and words to create an explicit message, urging us perhaps to buy a Honda, support the NRA, or quit smoking. Here are some tips for reading visuals:

- *What is the specific message of the visual?* Does the message come across clearly, and does it do so with words as well as images?

- *How does the visual support its message?* For example, does it use a poignant photograph, a quotation from an expert, or relevant statistics?

- *What is the source and purpose?* Was it developed by an individual? A corporation? A government agency? Is the source reputable? What does the nature of the source tell you about the purpose of the visual? Is the purpose to sell you something? to provide information? to persuade you to support a cause?

- *Who is the intended audience?* Is it aimed at a general audience or at a more specialized one: college students, parents, sports enthusiasts, experts in a particular field? How do you think the intended audience affects the argument the text makes?

- *What is the tone of the overall design—and what does that say about the message? What word would you use to describe the design—bold? lively? tranquil? gloomy? cluttered? something else?*

This book cover has been annotated by a student writer; a passage from the book begins on the next page. After you've read the passage, look back at this cover and think about how (and how well) the illustration supports the written text.

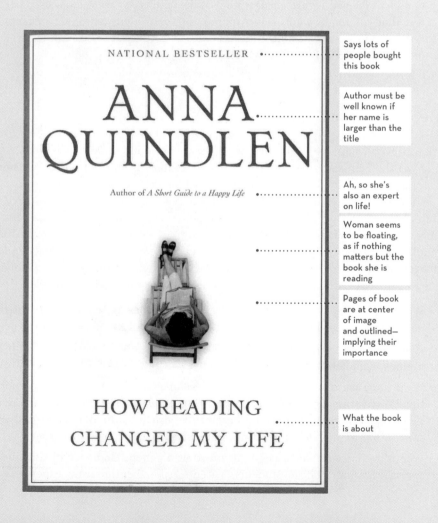

NATIONAL BESTSELLER ················· Says lots of people bought this book

ANNA QUINDLEN

Author must be well known if her name is larger than the title

Author of *A Short Guide to a Happy Life* ················· Ah, so she's also an expert on life!

Woman seems to be floating, as if nothing matters but the book she is reading

Pages of book are at center of image and outlined—implying their importance

HOW READING
CHANGED MY LIFE

What the book is about

ANNA QUINDLEN

How Reading Changed My Life

Anna Quindlen (b. 1952) grew up in the suburbs of Philadelphia in a neighborhood that was "the sort of place in which people dream of raising children—pretty, privileged but not rich, a small but satisfying spread of center-hall colonials, old roses, rhododendrons, and quiet roads." After graduating from Barnard College, Quindlen worked as a reporter, first for the New York Post *and then for the* New York Times, *where her regular column, "Public and Private," won a Pulitzer Prize in 1992. Though she still contributes a biweekly column to* Newsweek, *Quindlen gave up full-time journalism in 1995 to concentrate on writing fiction. Her novels include* Every Last One *(2010),* Blessings *(2002), and* Black and Blue *(1998).*

She is also the author of How Reading Changed My Life *(1998), from which this reading is taken. The personal story of her private life with books, Quindlen's narrative is also an account of how a writer learns the craft of writing by reading the work of other writers.*

IN 1997 KATHERINE PATERSON, whose novel *Bridge to Terabithia* has engaged several generations of young people with its story of friendship and loss—and also led to a policy in a school district in Kansas requiring a teacher to list each profanity in required reading and forward the list to parents—gave the Anne Carroll Moore[1] Lecture at the New York Public Library. It was a speech as fine as Ms. Paterson's books, which are fine indeed, and she spoke of the dedication of the children who are her readers: "I increasingly feel a sense of pity toward my fellow writers who spend their lives writing for the speeded-up audience of adults. They look at me, I realize, with a patronizing air, I who only write for the young. But I don't know any of them who have readers who will read their novels over and over again."

As someone who reads the same books over and over again, I think Ms. Paterson is wrong about that, although I know what she means. I have sat on the edge of several beds while *Green Eggs and Ham* was read, or recited more or less from memory; I read *A Wrinkle in Time* three times in a row once, when I was twelve,

---

1. *Anne Carroll Moore* (1871–1961): An author of children's books and the first supervisor of Work with Children at the New York Public Library in Manhattan. *Bridge to Terabithia* (1977): A novel about two children who create an imaginary kingdom in a forest.

SUGGESTED MLA CITATION: Quindlen, Anna. "How Reading Changed My Life." 1998. *Back to the Lake.* Ed. Thomas Cooley. 2nd ed. New York: Norton, 2012. 7–8. Print.

because I couldn't bear for it to end, wanted them all, Meg and Charles Murry and even the horribly pulsing brain called It,[2] to be alive again as they could only live within my mind, so that I felt as if I killed them when I closed the cover and gave them the kiss of life when my eyes met the words that created their lives. I still reread that way, always have, always will. I suspect there are more of us than Ms. Paterson knows. And I think I know who we are, and how we got that way. We are writers. We danced with the words, as children, in what became familiar patterns. The words became our friends and our companions, and without even saying it aloud, a thought danced with them: I can do this. This is who I am.

For some of us, reading begets rereading, and rereading begets writing. [3] (Although there is no doubt which is first, and supreme; as Alberto Manguel writes in his wonderful *A History of Reading*,[3] "I could perhaps live without writing. I don't think I could live without reading.") After a while the story is familiar, the settings known, the characters understood, and there is nothing left to discover but technique. Why that sentence structure and not something simpler, or more complex? Why that way of ordering events instead of something more straightforward, or more experimental? What grabs the reader by the throat? What sags and bags and fails? There are only two ways, really, to become a writer. One is to write. The other is to read.

2. *A Wrinkle in Time* (1962): A novel by Madeleine L'Engle (1918–2007) about three children who are transported through the galaxy by transcendental beings to fight an evil force known as It. The manuscript took a while to find a publisher because, according to L'Engle, many considered it "too different." *Green Eggs and Ham* (1960): A popular children's book written and illustrated by Dr. Seuss (Theodor Seuss Geisel, 1902–1991), who believed that children learn to read through repetition and familiarity.

3. *Alberto Manguel* (b. 1948): A writer and editor living in Buenos Aires. *A History of Reading* (1996) is his enthusiastic, thematic tour through the library imagined in a story by the Argentinean writer Jorge Luis Borges (1899–1986).

Reading the Essays in This Book

Even if reading doesn't change your life, it will change your writing. Good writers are good readers because many of the basic skills of writing can only be learned by reading the work of other writers. Before we come back to the example of Anna Quindlen and the specific methods and techniques she uses in her brief essay, let's look ahead to the rest of the essays in this book.

In *Back to the Lake*, you will be reading and analyzing numerous essays by many different writers on a variety of topics. The essays are grouped into chapters according to the principal methods they use: NARRATION, DESCRIPTION, EXAMPLE, PROCESS ANALYSIS, COMPARISON AND CONTRAST, CLASSIFICATION AND DIVISION, DEFINITION, CAUSE AND EFFECT, and ARGUMENT.

Experienced writers often employ more than one method in the same essay, so there is also a final chapter called "Combining the Methods."

Your main goal in reading the essays in this book is to master the methods of development they demonstrate so you can use those methods in your own writing. As you study these model essays in detail, however, you will encounter many other useful strategies and techniques—ways of beginning, of using transitions to move a text along, of presenting certain kinds of information in lists or charts, and so on.

Each selection in *Back to the Lake* is introduced with a headnote—like the one before the Quindlen piece—that provides information about the author of the text and its historical, social, or cultural context; and each selection is followed by study questions and writing prompts. The following questions and suggestions for writing pertain to "How Reading Changed My Life," but they are typical of the ones you will find after every other selection in this book (except they include sample answers after the questions).

READING CLOSELY

1. Anna Quindlen thinks that "Ms. Paterson is wrong about that" (2). About what? What's at issue between these two writers—one who writes exclusively for children, the other who writes both for children and adults?

   At issue is the nature of today's reading audience. Katherine Paterson claims that adult readers are too busy to reread anything. Thus, she feels "a sense of pity for my fellow writers" who do not write for children, because children read their favorite authors again and again (1).

2. In her debate with Katherine Paterson, what position does Quindlen take?

   Quindlen thinks there is at least one class of adult readers—those who are also writers—who read a favorite book over and over again. "I still reread that way," says Quindlen, "always have, always will" (2).

3. In paragraph 3, Quindlen tells how her childhood reading inspired her to become a writer. What, according to Quindlen, do writers learn from reading and rereading a familiar text?

   They learn "familiar patterns" of writing (2).

STRATEGIES AND STRUCTURES

1. Quindlen begins by disagreeing with a fellow writer. How, and how fairly, does she represent the opposing point of view?

   Before saying that Ms. Paterson is wrong, Quindlen praises her as a "fine" writer and speaker (1). She also says that she understands the opposing point of view and gives herself as an example of a repeat reader of children's books.

2. What evidence does Quindlen give to support her contention that at least some adult readers are rereaders? How convincing do you find this evidence? Why?

   Most of Quindlen's evidence comes from her own experience, particularly of rereading A Wrinkle in Time. *She might have cited the experiences of other writers to support her statement, "I suspect there are more of us than Ms. Paterson knows" (2).*

3. The chair on the cover of Quindlen's book (p. 6) looks at first like it's upside down. Why do you think the designer chose this particular angle?

   It looks like the reader is floating—and could go anywhere as she reads. The viewing angle shows the woman from above, focusing our gaze on the book in the woman's lap. From a different angle, the book becomes less central to the picture.

4. *Other Methods.* Quindlen's personal NARRATIVE not only tells the story of how reading changed her life, it analyzes the EFFECTS of a life-changing experience. What are they?

   The main effect was to make her want to be a writer as well as a reader: "I can do this" (2). But Quindlen cites other effects as well: an exciting mental life filled with imaginary companions—and rich memories to savor as an adult.

THINKING ABOUT LANGUAGE

1. Ms. Paterson pities writers who must write for an audience that is "speeded-up" (1). Why do you think she chose this word instead of *sped up* or *hurried*?

   By emphasizing the word speed, *she draws the reader's attention to how fast-paced contemporary life has become, how we are accustomed to completing daily activities— including reading—as quickly as possible.*

2. Look up "begets" in a dictionary (3). What are the CONNOTATIONS of the term? Why do you think Quindlen chose it to describe how writing comes from reading?

   Beget means "to father" or "to cause to exist." It connotes a close and natural relationship. Perhaps she is suggesting that writing is a natural progression from reading.

3. What does Quindlen mean by "technique" (3)?

   From the examples she gives, it means practically every choice—sentence structure, overall organization, audience appeal—that a writer makes to achieve the desired effect on the reader.

4. Quindlen is recalling her childhood from memory. Which particular phrases and sentences in her narrative do you find most memory-like in their flow and structure? Explain.

   Most of Quindlen's sentences are long, but when she recalls how reading enchanted her as a child—and still does—the words become almost dreamlike in the way they mimic her thought processes. The best example is the sentence beginning, "I have sat on the edge of several beds" (2).

FOR WRITING

1. Write a paragraph or two explaining how you typically read a text.
2. Write a narrative about how you learned to read or write.
3. Choose a seemingly small moment from your childhood and write a narrative about the effect it has had on your life.

CHAPTER 2

The Writing Process

Writing organizes and clarifies our thoughts. Writing is how we think our way into a subject and make it our own. —WILLIAM ZINSSER

I think I did pretty well, considering I started out with nothing but a bunch of blank paper. —STEVE MARTIN

To learn to do anything well, from baking bread to programming a computer, we usually break it down into a series of operations. Writing is no exception. This chapter introduces all the steps of the writing process that will take you from a blank page to a final draft: planning; generating ideas; organizing and drafting; revising your draft as it progresses, both on your own and with the help of others; and editing and proofreading your work into its final form.

Keep in mind, however, that writing is a recursive process—that is, it involves a certain amount of repetition. We plan, we draft, we revise; we plan, we draft, we revise again. Also, we tend to skip around as we write. For example, if we suddenly think of a great new idea, we may go back and redraft what we have already written, perhaps revising it completely. Often, in fact, we engage in the various activities of writing more or less at the same time.

Planning

Most of the writing we do—and not just in school—starts with an assignment. An English teacher asks you to analyze a poem by Billy Collins. A prospective employer wants to know, on a job application form, why he or she should hire you. A college application includes an essay question, asking you to explain why you want to go to that school. Before you plunge headlong into any writing assignment, however, you need to think about where you're going. You need to plan.

To plan any piece of writing effectively, think about your purpose in writing, the audience you're writing for, and the nature and scope of your topic. If a topic hasn't already been suggested or assigned to you, of course, you'll have to find one. You'll also need to budget your time.

Managing Your Time

When is the assignment due? As soon as you get a writing assignment, make a note of the deadline. Some teachers deduct points for late papers; some don't accept them at all. Even if your instructor is lenient, learning to meet deadlines is part of surviving in college—and beyond. And remember that it's hard to plan well if you begin an assignment the night before it's due. Especially with research papers and other long-range projects, you should begin early so you have plenty of time to do everything the assignment requires.

What kind of research will you need to do? If you are writing a personal narrative or analyzing a process you know well (such as teaching an Irish setter to catch a Frisbee), you may not need to do much research at all before you begin to write. On the other hand, if you are preparing a full-scale research paper on climate change or the fiction of Henry James, the research may take longer than the actual writing. Most college assignments require at least some research. So as you plan any piece of writing, think about how much and what kind of research you will need to do, and allow plenty of time for that research.

Finding a Topic

Though we often use the words interchangeably, a *subject*, strictly speaking, is a broad field of study or inquiry, whereas a *topic* is a specific area within that field. If you are writing a paper for an ecology class, the subject of your paper is likely to be ecology. However, if your teacher asks what you're planning to write on and you reply simply, "ecology," be prepared for a few more questions.

Even if you said "climate change" or "global warming," your teacher would still want to know just what approach you planned to take. A good topic not only narrows down a general subject to a specific area within that field, it addresses a particular aspect of that more limited area, such as what climate change is, or what causes climate change, or what effects climate change has on the environment, or how to stop climate change.

With many writing assignments, you may be given a specific topic or choice of specific topics. For example, an essay exam in Ecology 101 might ask: "Can climate change be stopped? How? Or why not?" Or it might say, more specifically: "Describe the key principles of the Kyoto Protocol." In a literature course, you might get a topic like this: "The narrator of Henry James's *The Turn of the*

Screw: heroine or hysteric?" Or in a political science course, you may be asked to compare Marx's theory of revolution with Lenin's.

When you're given such a specific topic, make sure you read the assignment carefully and know just what you are being asked to do. Pay close attention to how the assignment is worded. Look for key terms like *describe, define, analyze, compare and contrast, evaluate, argue*. Be aware that even short assignments may include more than one of these directives. For example, the same assignment may ask you not only to define climate change but to analyze its causes and effects, or to compare and contrast present-day climate conditions with those of an earlier time, or to construct an argument about what should be done to stop climate change.

Many teachers provide lists of possible topics. With longer assignments, however, you may have to work out a topic yourself, perhaps after meeting with your teacher. Start the conversation as soon as you get the assignment. Let your instructor know if there are any areas within your field of study you find particularly interesting or would like to learn more about. Ask for guidance and suggestions—and start looking on your own. If your school has a writing center, it might be useful to discuss possible topics with someone there.

Thinking about Purpose and Audience

We write for many reasons: to organize and clarify our thoughts, express our feelings, remember people and events, solve problems, persuade others to act or believe as we think they should.

For example, let's look at this passage from *Time* magazine:

> If droughts and wildfires, floods and crop failures, collapsing climate-sensitive species and the images of drowning polar bears didn't quiet most of the remaining global warming doubters, the hurricane-driven destruction of New Orleans did. Dismissing a scientist's temperature chart is one thing. Dismissing the death of a major American city is something else entirely. What's more, the heat is only continuing to rise. This past year [2006] was the hottest on record in the U.S. The deceptively normal average temperature this winter masked record-breaking highs in December and record-breaking lows in February. That's the sign not of a planet keeping an even strain but of one thrashing through the alternating chills and night sweats of serious illness.
>
> —Jeffrey Kluger, "What Now for Our Feverish Planet?"

The main purpose of this passage is to persuade the reader that global warming can no longer be dismissed as an untested theory. The planet's temperature has been definitively taken, the author asserts, and by all accounts the patient is ailing.

As you think about *why* you're writing, however, you also need to consider *who* your readers are. In his article on climate change, for example, Jeffrey Kluger speaks directly to his intended audience:

> Our feverish planet badly needs a cure. Climate change is caused by a lot of things, and it will take a lot of people to fix it. There's a role for big thinkers, power players, those with deep pockets—and the rest of us.

Kluger is speaking not to big thinkers or power players, but to "the rest of us"—ordinary folks who read *Time* magazine. Your intended audience can be yourself; someone you know, such as your roommate or your teacher; or someone you don't know. These different audiences have different needs, which you'll want to take into account. If *you* are the intended audience—as when you write in a diary or journal, or write a reminder for yourself—you can be as cryptic as you like:

> GW lecture tonight @ 8 in Denney.
> Joy @ Blue Dube, get notes, ask her to feed cat.

Once you plan to address someone else in writing, no matter what your purpose, you will need to fill in more blanks for the reader, even if you know that person well and are simply, as in the following example, leaving an informal message:

> Joy,
>
> I have to go to a global warming lecture tonight in Denney. Meet you at the Blue Danube at 6. May I borrow your ecology notes? Please feed Gen. Burnsides for me. Friskies in cabinet above fridge. Half a can. Thanks!
>
> Fred

Obviously, the writer of this message is familiar with his audience. He can assume, for example, that she knows Denney is the name of a building on campus and that General Burnsides is the name of a cat—but even Joy has to be told where the cat food is stashed and how much to serve. When you don't know your audience, or when you can't be sure they know what you're talking about, you need to supply them with even more information.

In each chapter that follows, you'll find a section that will help you think about purpose and audience as you write. For now, here is a checklist of general guidelines to help you think about your intended audience and your purpose.

THINKING ABOUT PURPOSE AND AUDIENCE

- *What is the occasion for writing?* Are you writing a research paper? Applying for a job? Responding to an email? Commenting on a blog? Planning a wedding toast?

- *What is your purpose?* Do you want to tell your readers something they may not know? Entertain them? Convince them to do something? Change their minds?

- *Who is going to read (or hear) what you write?* Your classmates? Your teacher? Readers of a blog? Guests at a wedding?

- *What do you know about your audience's background?* For example, if you are writing an argument on how to stop climate change, you can expect readers who come from coal-mining regions to be more sympathetic if you suggest reducing carbon emissions than if you propose shutting down all coal-burning power plants.

- *How much does your audience already know about your subject?* If you are writing for a general audience, you may need to provide some background information and explain terminology that may be unfamiliar. For example, if you are writing about global warming for a newsmagazine, you might note that sequestration is a promising way to reduce carbon emissions—and then define sequestration, a process by which carbon emissions are stored underground. If you're writing for an audience of environmental scientists, though, you may be able to assume that they are familiar with sequestration and you don't have to define it.

- *What should you keep in mind about the demographics of your audience?* Does the gender of your audience matter? How about their age, level of education, economic status, or religion? Once you have sized up your audience, you're in a better position to generate ideas and evidence that will support what you have to say *and* appeal to that audience.

- *Who do you want your audience to be?* The language you use can let your readers know that you are writing to them—or not. In particular, be careful how you use the personal pronouns *we, us,* and *our.* For instance, if you write, "As Christians, we need to have compassion for others," be sure you want to limit your audience to Christians, for this language is likely to exclude anyone who is not.

Generating Ideas

Once you have a topic, purpose, and audience clearly in mind, it's time to start generating ideas. Where do you look for ideas? How do you go from nothing to something in a systematic way?

Over the years, writing teachers have developed a number of techniques to help writers find ideas. Freewriting, looping, listing, and brainstorming are ways to probe what you already know; clustering can help you connect ideas and begin organizing a text around them; questioning can be particularly useful when you're trying to make a topic more specific; and keeping a journal can be helpful at any stage. All of these techniques, in fact, may come in handy at various points in the writing process, not just at the outset.

Freewriting

When you freewrite, you simply put pen to paper (or fingers to keyboard), and force yourself to jot down whatever pops into your head.

1. Write nonstop for a short period of time, say five or ten minutes. If nothing comes to mind at first, just write: "Nothing. I'm getting nothing. The words aren't coming." Eventually, the words *will* come—if you keep writing and don't stop until time runs out.
2. This is freewriting—so skip around freely and don't get bogged down.
3. Circle or underline words and ideas that you might want to revisit, but don't stop freewriting until your time is up. Then go back over what you have written and mark any passages that stand out as promising.
4. Freewrite again, using something you have marked in the previous session as your starting point. Do this over and over until you find an idea you want to explore further.

Here's an example of a five-minute freewriting session by Zoe Shewer, a first-year writing student at Vanderbilt University who was given the assignment "Write about an experience that has taught you something new about yourself."

> Write write write. Five minutes. Okay, something I learned about myself. Yikes, what a question. I'm me. Blond, not too tall—okay, looks really aren't the point here. I'm a pretty good athlete, love riding horses. I have a brother named Max and 2 dogs named Oz and Jazz. I tutor kids in Harlem—I like (volunteering.) I had a great time at Camp Robin Hood last summer. Working with all those different nonprofits was great. But did I learn anything about myself? I learned how to clean gutters, some American Sign Language, how to make spaghetti sauce. I learned that I'm not a good cook. Time.

Freewriting like this is more than a stretching exercise. It can lead to many new ideas if you take something you have just said as the point of departure for more probing. Shewer's freewriting session led her to a possible source for an essay topic: her volunteer work.

Looping

To narrow down the subject you are exploring, try the more directed form of freewriting called *looping*. Looping not only helps you turn up a specific topic, it nudges you into writing sentences about it. Later on, you may want to use some of these sentences in your essay.

1. Freewrite for five or ten minutes, focusing on a single subject or idea and putting down everything about that subject that you can think of.

2. When you've finished that first loop, look over what you've written and summarize the most important part in a sentence: "I learned a lot volunteering last summer."

3. Use this summary sentence as the point of departure for your next loop. Write for another five or ten minutes without stopping. Then reflect on what you've just written, and compose another sentence summing it up: "Volunteering last summer taught me that I have a lot to learn."

4. Do as many loops as necessary until you have a direction in mind. If you already know the final destination of your essay, so much the better; but for now you're mainly looking for ways of refining your topic along the way.

Looping can be especially useful when you are trying to make an ABSTRACT subject more CONCRETE. Shewer summed up her freewriting exercise with the sentence "I learned a lot volunteering last summer" and used that sentence as the starting point for a new loop that helped her explore what she learned about herself.

Summary sentence from freewriting: I learned a lot volunteering last summer.

Loop 1: I learned a lot volunteering last summer through Camp Robin Hood. At Ready, Willing & Able, Seymour taught me to clean gutters. At ABC, I learned some American Sign Language, and I learned how strong those kids were. Every day, they came in determined to do everything. At the homeless shelter, I learned so much from Elsie about the city and how to survive in it. But did I learn anything about *myself*? At the end of the summer I had more admiration for Seymour, Elsie, and the kids at ABC. They all had so much more experience with life—even the kids. They had a lot of hard knocks and kept getting back up. Maybe I learned just how lucky I've been. But I think I already knew that. Maybe it was mostly that I learned that I really haven't experienced all that much.

Summary sentence: Volunteering taught me that I have a lot to learn.

Loop 2: Volunteering taught me that I have a lot to learn. Seymour told me a lot of stuff that I didn't know before, not just how to drain gutters but what his life was like. Elsie didn't talk much about her personal life, but she did tell me a lot about being homeless. And just being with the kids at ABC gave me insight into what it's like to be disadvantaged. They had to have so much determination. So did Seymour and Elsie. I don't have that kind of determination.

Summary sentence: Volunteering taught me to admire the determination of Seymour, the children at ABC, and Elsie.

As these excerpts show, looping brings ideas into sharper focus. By writing out her thoughts and looping back over them several times, Shewer was able to come up with concrete ideas about what she learned through volunteering.

Keeping Lists

Most writing is better and clearer if it is detailed and specific instead of general and abstract. Keeping lists is a good way to generate ideas—and to illustrate those ideas with interesting examples and specific details.

1. A list can be written anywhere: on paper, on a computer, in a notebook, on a napkin. Keep your lists handy so you can add to them at any time.

2. Don't worry about the form of your lists. But if the lists start to get long, group related items into piles, as you would if you were sorting your laundry.

3. Look for relationships not only *within* those piles but *between* them. Later, if you decide to construct a formal outline for your essay, you can build on the loosely arranged lists you already have.

Brainstorming

Brainstorming is a form of listing, but you write down words and ideas in one sitting rather than over time.

1. If you are brainstorming by yourself, first jot down a topic at the top of your page or screen. Then make a list of every idea or word that comes to mind.

2. Brainstorming is often more effective when you do it collaboratively, as part of a team, with everyone throwing out ideas and one person acting as scribe.

3. If you brainstorm with others, make sure everyone contributes. If one person monopolizes the session, the purpose of brainstorming is lost.

Clustering

Clustering helps you to make connections among ideas.

1. Write down your topic in the center of the page, and circle it.

2. Outside this nucleus, jot down related topics and ideas, and circle each one. Draw a line from each of these satellite ideas to the central topic.

3. As you think of additional ideas, phrases, facts, or examples, group them in clusters and connect them to one another.

Zoe Shewer created the following cluster to group her ideas.

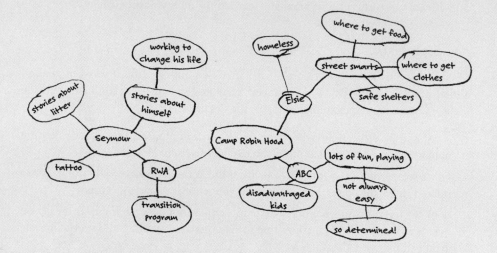

Asking Who, What, Where, When, Why, and How

Journalists ask *who, what, where, when, why,* and *how* to uncover the basic information that readers look for in a news story. These standard journalistic questions can be useful for all kinds of writing. Here is how you might use them in an essay about a car accident involving a member of your family:

1. *Who* was involved in the accident? What should I say about my sister (the driver)? About the passengers in the car (including the dog)? The police officer who investigated? The witnesses on the sidewalk?

2. *What* happened? What were the main events leading up to the crash? What did my sister do to avoid hitting the other car head-on? Should I mention that the dog got out of the car first?

3. *Where* did the accident occur? How much of the scene should I describe? The intersection itself? The hill leading up to it?

4. *When* did the accident take place? What time did my sister leave the party? Was it still raining?

5. *Why* did the accident happen? Did the other car swerve into her lane?

6. *How* could it have been avoided? Would my sister have reacted sooner if she hadn't been on her cell phone? Should I write about cell-phone usage as a contributing cause in traffic accidents?

Asking key questions like these early in the writing process will help you turn up ideas and figure out which aspects of your subject you want to write about. Later on, the questions you choose to answer will determine, in part, the methods you use to organize your essay. For example, if you decided to explain in detail what happened on the day of your sister's accident, you would draw extensively on the techniques of NARRATION. Or if you decided to focus on the scene of the accident, you would write a largely DESCRIPTIVE essay.

Keeping a Journal

A personal journal can be a great source of raw material for your writing. Here, for example, is part of a journal entry that Annie Dillard kept when she went on a camping trip in Virginia:

> Last night moths kept flying into the candle. They would hiss & spatter & recoil, lost upside down & flopping in the shadows among the pans on the table. Or—and this happened often, & again tonight—they'd burn their wings, & then their wings would <u>stick</u> to the next thing they'd touch—the edge of a pan, a lid. . . . These I could free with a quick flip with a spoon or something.

Two years after she made this journal entry, Dillard used some of those same details in an essay entitled "The Death of a Moth." In the published essay, the moth-drawn-to-the-flame becomes a vivid image of the dedicated writer who devotes all her energy to her work. Obviously, however, Dillard did not begin the writing process with a big idea like this in mind, and neither should you. She started with the homely details of pots and pans and ordinary moths as recorded in her journal. If you keep a journal regularly, as many writers do, you will have at your fingertips a world of concrete details to think and write about.

You can learn a lot about keeping a journal from an entry like Dillard's:

1. Write down your observations as close to the time of the event as possible; don't wait until you get home from a camping trip to note what happened while you were camping.

2. The observations in a journal don't have to deal with momentous events; record your everyday experiences.

3. Make each journal entry as detailed and specific as possible; don't just write "the bugs were bad" or "another beautiful day."

4. The entries don't have to be long or formally composed; they are for your eyes alone, so be as informal as you like.

5. You may not know the significance of a particular entry until months, even years, after you've written it.

Organizing and Drafting

Once you accumulate enough facts, details, and other raw material, your next job is to organize that material and develop it into a draft. The method (or methods) of development that you use will be determined by the main point you want your draft to make.

Stating Your Point

As you begin gathering materials for an essay, you probably won't know exactly what your THESIS—your main point—is going to be (unless, of course, you've been given a specific one as part of your assignment). Before you begin writing, however, try to state your thesis in one sentence. You may find as you go along that you need to revise it, but you should start with a thesis in mind.

What makes a good thesis statement? First, let's consider what a thesis statement is not. A general announcement of your topic—"in this paper I plan to write about how you can fight global warming"—is *not* a thesis statement. A thesis statement tells the reader what your topic is, and it makes an interesting CLAIM *about* your topic, one that is open to further discussion. This is why statements of fact aren't thesis statements either: "The effects of climate change were first predicted in the 1890s by a little-known Swedish chemist." Historical and scientific facts may help support your thesis, but the thesis itself should say something about your subject that requires further discussion. For example:

> The best way you can fight climate change is by reducing your personal carbon footprint.

> The fight against climate change will be won or lost in developing nations such as India and China.

> The United States is still the biggest energy hog on the planet.

When you draft an essay, make sure you state your thesis clearly, usually near the beginning. Like these examples, your thesis statement should be direct and specific, and it should let readers know what you'll be discussing in your essay.

Making an Outline

An informal outline is simply a list of your main points in the order they might appear in your draft. For example, after grouping her ideas into clusters, Zoe Shewer created this informal outline for her essay on an unexpected lesson:

Volunteering
  three nonprofits
  learned about myself
Ready, Willing & Able
  Seymour
  draining gutters
  telling stories
  his plans
Association to Benefit Children
  disadvantaged kids
  loved to play
  persevered
Homeless shelter
  Elsie
  street smarts
Learned that I have a lot to learn

For longer projects, such as a research paper, you may need a more detailed outline, indicating the order of both the main ideas and the less important ones. When you make a formal outline, you also show—by indenting and using letters and numbers—how all of your ideas fit together to support your thesis:

Thesis statement: Volunteering taught me to admire the determination of Seymour, the children at ABC, and Elsie.

  I. Camp Robin Hood
    A. Crash course in volunteering
    B. Ready, Willing & Able
    C. Association to Benefit Children
    D. Homeless shelter
  II. Ready, Willing & Able
    A. Seymour
    B. Taught me to drain gutters
    C. Told me about his own life
  III. Association to Benefit Children (ABC)
    A. Played with disadvantaged kids
    B. Read to them
    C. Admired their determination
  IV. Homeless shelter
    A. Elsie
    B. Depended on handouts and shelters
    C. Had figured out the system

V. Conclusion
    A. Wanted to give something back
    B. Hope I helped others
    C. Sure I learned a lot myself

When you construct a formal outline like this, try to keep items that are at the same level in more or less the same grammatical form. Also, include at least two items for each level, otherwise you don't need to subdivide. Whatever kind of outline you make, however, change it as necessary as you write and revise.

Using the Basic Methods of Development

Once you've accumulated enough material to write about, have narrowed your subject down to a manageable topic, and have a workable thesis, you should choose one or more methods of development.

Zoe Shewer, for example, ultimately chose to write a narrative. This method of development is appropriate for her particular topic and thesis: an explanation of what she learned from doing volunteer work. Within a narrative framework, however, she also incorporated some description and analyzed cause and effect.

Often you will want to use several methods together. Let's look at brief examples of each method.

Narration. Telling a story is one of the oldest ways of making a point. In this example, a journalist shows his mixed feelings toward his long-absent father by recalling the events of their last day together:

> He was living in a little house in Jacksonville, Alabama. . . . I knocked and a voice like an old woman's, punctuated with a cough that sounded like it came from deep in the guts, told me to come on in, it ain't locked. It was dark inside, but light enough to see what looked like a bundle of quilts on the corner of a sofa. Deep inside them was a ghost of a man, his hair and beard long and going dirty gray, his face pale and cut with deep grooves. I knew I was in the right house because my daddy's only real possessions, a velvet-covered board pinned with medals, sat inside a glass cabinet on a table. But this couldn't be him. . . .
>
> "It's all over but the shoutin' now, ain't it, boy," he said, and when he let the quilt slide from his shoulders I saw how he had wasted away, how the bones seemed to poke out of his clothes, and I could see how it killed his pride to look this way, unclean, and he looked away from me for a moment, ashamed.
>   —RICK BRAGG, *All Over But the Shoutin'*

Description. Description helps the reader to see, hear, feel, smell, or, taste whatever you're writing about. Descriptive writing uses specific details that appeal to the senses in order to create some DOMINANT IMPRESSION. In this example from a humor magazine, that impression is one of disgust and "horror" as a food critic describes how her subject looks and tastes:

> Next on the menu was a can of Kal Kan Pedigree with Chunky Chicken. Chunky chicken? There were chunks in the can, certainly—big, purplish-brown chunks. I forked one chunk out (by now I was becoming more callous) and found that while it had no discernible chicken flavor, it wasn't bad except for the texture—like meat loaf with ground-up chicken bones.
>
> In the world of canned dog food, a smooth consistency is a sign of low quality—lots of cereal. A lumpy, frightening, bloody, stringy horror is a sign of high quality—lots of meat. Nowhere in the world of wet dog foods was this demonstrated better than in the fanciest I tried—Kal Kan's Pedigree Select Dinners. . . .   —ANN HODGMAN, "No Wonder They Call Me a Bitch"

Example. Giving examples is one of the best ways to support a general statement or make a point, as in this observation about cultural differences in perception:

> University of Michigan researchers reported that Asians and North Americans see the world differently. Shown a photograph, for example, North American students of European background paid more attention to the object in the foreground of a scene, while students from China spent more time studying the background and taking in the whole scene.
> —RANDOLPH E. SCHMID, "Dyslexia Differs by Language"

Process analysis. Breaking an activity into steps is a good way to figure out and systematically explain how something works or is made. Often the purpose of a process analysis is to enable the reader to replicate the process, as in this set of instructions:

> To start juggling, you begin by tossing a ball back and forth from left to right. This is the hardest part because you must learn where your hands must be positioned. Try to throw the ball to the same place each time.
>
> Once you get this down, you are ready for the next step. . . .
>
> Two balls is easy. Once you have one down, just throw the second ball up as the first ball starts to reach its peak (the highest point before descending). Don't worry if they occasionally collide. . . .
>
> Once you have the pattern down for two balls, add a third ball. Throw the third ball when the second ball is at its peak height. At this point, the first ball should be passing your hand. Don't worry about catching it at first. Just get used to throwing all three balls at the right times.

After some practice at this, you will want to try to catch the first two balls. As you get the knack of throwing two balls and catching the first two, try to throw the first ball when the third is reaching its peak.

—CHRIS SEGUIN, "How to Juggle"

Comparison and contrast. Tracing similarities and differences tells readers how two or more subjects are alike, or different, or both. This example contrasts the experience of death in two cultures:

Once, a long time ago, living in Vietnam, we used to stare death in the face. The war, in many ways, had heightened our sensibilities toward living and dying. I saw dead bodies when I was five after a battle erupted near my house during the Tet Offensive. . . .

Though the fear of death and dying is a universal one, Vietnamese do not hide from it. We pray daily to the dead at our ancestral altar. We talk to ghosts. Death pervades our poems, novels, and sad-ending fairy tales. We dwell in its tragedy. We know that terrible things can and do happen to ordinary people.

But if agony and pain are part of Vietnamese culture, even to the point of being morbid, pleasure is at the center of American culture. While Vietnamese holidays are based on death anniversaries of famous kings and heroes, here we celebrate birth dates of presidents.

American popular culture treats death with humor. People laugh and scream at blood-and-guts movies. Zombie flicks are the rage. The wealthy sometimes freeze their dead relatives. Cemeteries are places of business, complete with colorful brochures. There are, I saw on TV the other day, drive-by funerals in some places in the Midwest where you don't have to get out of your car to pay your respects to the deceased.　　—ANDREW LAM,
"They Shut the Door on My Grandmother"

Classification. Dividing a subject into kinds helps explain a complex subject and can also suggest an outline for an entire essay. The following example subdivides conservation into three categories:

There are, as nearly as I can make out, three kinds of conservation currently operating. The first is the preservation of places that are grandly wild or "scenic" or in some other way spectacular. The second is what is called "conservation of natural resources"—that is, of the things of nature that we intend to use: soil, water, timber, and minerals. The third is what you might call industrial troubleshooting: the attempt to limit or stop or remedy the most flagrant abuses of the industrial system. All three kinds of conservation are inadequate, both separately and together.　　—WENDELL BERRY,
"Conservation Is Good Work"

Definition. To explain what something is, identify its main characteristics. The following example identifies the main characteristics that many astronomers think are important for defining a planet in the solar system:

> The issue of a clear definition for planet came to a head in 2005 with the discovery of the trans-Neptunian object Eris, a body larger than the smallest then-accepted planet, Pluto. In its 2006 response, the International Astronomical Union (IAU), recognized by astronomers as the world body responsible for resolving issues of nomenclature, released its decision on the matter. This definition, which applies only to the Solar System, states that a planet is a body that orbits the Sun, is large enough for its own gravity to make it round, and has "cleared its neighborhood" of smaller objects around its orbit. Under this new definition, Pluto, along with the other trans-Neptunian objects, does not qualify as a planet. The IAU's decision has not resolved all controversies, and while many scientists have accepted the definition, some in the astronomical community have rejected it outright. —Definition of "Planet," *Wikipedia*
> (accessed March 22, 2011)

Cause and effect. Tracing causes and effects is a fundamental way of exploring relationships. The purpose of a cause-and-effect analysis is to show that one event (in the following example, a high rate of behavioral disorders in young males) is actually the result of another event (hormones released before birth):

> Lest males of all ages feel unfairly picked upon, researchers point out that boys may be diagnosed with behavioral syndromes and disorders more often than girls for a very good reason: their brains may be more vulnerable. As a boy is developing in the womb, the male hormones released by his tiny testes accelerate the maturation of his brain, locking a lot of the wiring in place early on; a girl's hormonal bath keeps her brain supple far longer. The result is that the infant male brain is a bit less flexible, less able to repair itself after slight injury that might come, for example, during the arduous trek down the birth canal. Hence, boys may well suffer disproportionately from behavioral disorders for reasons unrelated to cultural expectations.
> —NATALIE ANGIER, "Intolerance of Boyish Behavior"

Argument. When you argue a point, you make a claim and give evidence to support it, as in the following passage from a Florida community newspaper proposing that readers speak out to protect local wildlife:

> In the real world . . . , the alligators on this sanctuary island can't speak for themselves. So maybe it's time for the rest of us to do it for them and ask if we should reevaluate our alligator policy.

In 2004, responding to two fatal attacks, the city changed how it deals with alligator complaints. Under that policy, not only nuisance alligators can be destroyed but *any* alligator in the area that exceeds four feet in length. More than 200 alligators have been killed since the 2004 policy was initiated.

Since alligators don't breed until they're about six feet long, we could be on our way to eliminating these reptiles from the island and dramatically altering the natural balance among its wildlife. Fewer alligators mean more raccoons, snakes, and other natural prey left to feed on birds' eggs and hatchlings. Is that what we want?

—BARBARA JOY WHITE,
"Speaking Up for Alligators"

The Parts of an Essay

No matter what methods of development you use, any essay you write should have a beginning, a middle, and an end. These three basic parts are usually referred to as the introduction, the body, and the conclusion.

In the introduction, you introduce the topic and state your thesis. That is, you tell the reader exactly what you're writing about and what your main point is. In the body—which may run anywhere from a few sentences or paragraphs to many pages—you offer evidence in support of your thesis. In the conclusion, you wrap up what you have to say, often by restating the thesis—but with some variation based on the evidence you have just cited.

For example, here is the alligator argument again with all its parts. The author states her thesis in the first two paragraphs. In the middle paragraph—the body of her essay—she cites facts and figures to support her thesis. And in the final paragraph, she concludes by restating that thesis—with a twist.

Introduction
States the thesis.

Body
Supports the thesis with facts, figures, and other evidence.

At the Congregational Church, Pastor John puts on puppet shows for the children. One of the star characters is Chompers, a crocodile who talks, attends church, and could go to City Hall if he wanted to.

In the real world, however, the alligators on this sanctuary island can't speak for themselves. So maybe it's time for the rest of us to do it for them and ask if we should reevaluate our alligator policy.

In 2004, responding to two fatal attacks, the city changed how it deals with alligator complaints. Under that policy, not only nuisance alligators can be destroyed but *any* alligator in the area that exceeds four feet in length. More than 200 alligators have been killed since the 2004 policy was initiated.

Since alligators don't breed until they're about six feet long, we could be on our way to eliminating these reptiles from the island and dramatically altering the natural balance among its wildlife. Fewer alligators mean more raccoons, snakes, and other natural prey left to feed on birds' eggs and hatchlings. Is that what we want?

Now that the alligator population on the island is clearly under control, perhaps even threatened, let's ask City Hall to reconsider its "targeted harvest" policy. Attend Tuesday's Council meeting and speak up for the alligators. Tell 'em Chompers sent you.

Conclusion Restates the thesis with a twist.

Any essay you write should have an introduction and a conclusion, as in this example. Usually, however, you will need more than a single paragraph in the body of your essay.

If you are writing about how individuals can combat climate change, for example, you might want to have a paragraph about the benefits of recycling old clothes. But you will likely also include at least one additional body paragraph for each way of reducing carbon consumption that you discuss, such as eating less red meat, planning a green wedding, or making fewer left turns when we drive.

THE INTRODUCTION

Because it is the first thing the reader sees, the beginning of an essay requires special care. Here are a number of effective strategies for introducing an essay—all of which are intended to make the reader want to read more.

Start with a question. The following example opens with a serious question that grabs the reader's attention:

> What's the difference between dementia and Alzheimer's? It's a common question, and doctors are some of the best at confusing us. Physicians seem to prefer the word "dementia," possibly because Alzheimer's has become such a loaded word. "Dementia" somehow sounds less frightening to many people, and now even the experts have started using the words interchangeably.
> —MOLLY SHOMER, "What's the Difference Between Alzheimer's and Dementia?"

Start with a quotation or dialogue. In this example from *Outside* magazine, the author opens with an intriguing bit of dialogue, words that get the reader's interest and make a point about the beauty of nature:

> "The thing is, there's this red dot," says Beau Turner, standing quietly in a longleaf-pine forest on his Avalon Plantation, 25,000 red-clay acres half an hour south of Tallahassee. It's 6:30 on a late-spring morning, and the humidity is rolling in like a fog; already I regret the hot coffee in my hand. One of our chores today is to band some new woodpecker chicks with Avalon identification, but then the red dot came up and I was anxious to see it. Not much bigger than the head of a pin, the red dot is a nearly Zen idea of nature's beauty. It sits behind the ear of the male red-cockaded woodpecker, an endangered species that Turner has spent the last four years trying to reintroduce to this land. —JACK HITT, "One Nation, Under Ted"

Place your subject in a historical context. In the essay from which this introduction is taken, an economist makes the point that the rate of global warming may be higher than originally estimated; but first he puts the issue in historical perspective:

> The 1995 consensus was convincing enough for Europe and Japan: the report's scientific findings were the basis for the Kyoto negotiations and the treaty they produced; those same findings also led most of the developed world to produce ambitious plans for reductions in carbon emissions. But the consensus didn't extend to Washington, and hence everyone else's efforts were deeply compromised by the American unwillingness to increase the price of energy. Our emissions continued to soar, and the plans of many of the Kyoto countries in Western Europe to reduce emissions sputtered. —WILLIAM MCKIBBEN, "Warning on Warming"

Open with an anecdote. Brief, illustrative stories work especially well at the beginning of an essay. Here, the author is preparing to discuss how African American men are sometimes misperceived in public spaces:

> My first victim was a woman—white, well dressed, probably in her early twenties. I came upon her late one evening on a deserted street in Hyde Park, a relatively affluent neighborhood in an otherwise mean, impoverished section of Chicago. As I swung onto the avenue behind her, there seemed to be a discreet, uninflammatory distance between us. Not so. She cast back a worried glance. To her, the youngish black man . . . seemed menacingly close. After a few more quick glimpses, she picked up her pace and was soon running in earnest. Within seconds she disappeared into a cross street. . . .

I was surprised, embarrassed, and dismayed all at once. Her flight made me feel like an accomplice in tyranny. It also made it clear that I was indistinguishable from the muggers who occasionally seeped into the area from the surrounding ghetto.   —BRENT STAPLES, "Black Men and Public Space"

Shock or provoke the reader—mildly. You don't want to alarm your reader needlessly, but sometimes you may want to say "listen here" by being mildly provocative or controversial:

> Let's use the F word here. People say it's inappropriate, offensive, that it puts people off. But it seems to me it's the best way to begin, when it's simultaneously devalued and invaluable.
> Feminist. Feminist, feminist, feminist.   —ANNA QUINDLEN,
> "Still Needing the F Word"

THE BODY PARAGRAPHS

The body of your essay supports and develops your thesis; it is where you give the evidence for the main point you're making. You can use many different kinds of evidence to develop paragraphs in the body of your essay:

Specific examples. Barbara Joy White supports her claim that a city wildlife policy should be reevaluated by giving an example of an imbalance in nature: "Fewer alligators mean more raccoons, snakes, and other natural prey left to feed on birds' eggs and hatchlings."

Facts and figures. White also supports her claim with mortality statistics: "More than 200 alligators have been killed since the 2004 policy was initiated."

Expert testimony. To support the point that left turns waste fuel, editors of an online marketing magazine cite an executive at United Parcel Service (UPS): "According to UPS spokesman Steve Holmes, 'It seems small, but when you multiply it across 88,0000 vehicles making nearly 15 million deliveries every day during the course of a year, it adds up.'"

Personal experience. To make the point that making left turns wastes time as well as fuel, you might cite your own personal experience: "First I made the trip through the Chicago Loop taking nothing but right turns. I travelled down Columbus Drive, took a right on Congress Parkway, and then took another right turn to my destination, the Dirksen Federal Building at Dearborn and Adams streets. Then I made the trip through the Loop to the Dirksen Building taking mostly left turns. The traffic was the same, but the left-turn trip took me three minutes and thirty seconds longer than the right-turn trip."

How much evidence is enough? That depends in part on your topic. In "Speaking Up for Alligators," for example, Barbara Joy White can adequately support her thesis in only a few sentences because her topic is so narrow in scope. A broader topic about how we can combat global warming, for example, would require more evidence to support the writer's thesis. Ultimately, however, it is the reader who determines how much evidence is sufficient to do the job. To make sure your evidence meets the reader's needs, follow these guidelines.

- *Is your evidence concrete and specific?* Have you provided details that will make your point clear and interesting to the reader?

- *Is your evidence relevant to the case?* Will the reader understand immediately why you're citing particular facts, figures, personal experience, and other evidence? Do you need to explain further? Or choose other evidence?

- *Is your evidence sufficient to prove the case?* Have you cited enough evidence, or is the reader likely to require additional—or better—support before becoming convinced?

- *Are your sources fully and adequately documented?* Have you represented your sources fairly and accurately? Can readers locate them easily if they want to check your facts or interpretation? Have you scrupulously avoided representing the words or ideas of other writers as your own? (For more information on using and citing sources, see the Appendix.)

THE CONCLUSION

The ending of an essay is your last chance to drive your point home with the reader—and to provide a sense of closure. Here are a few common approaches.

Restate your main point. But don't simply repeat it: remind the reader what you've said, and—as in the conclusion of this essay—add a little more:

> At a time when it seems that society is being destroyed by its own designs, it is good to be able to hold up a mirror that shows us the extent of our problems. Neither escapist nor preachy, *The Simpsons* provides such a satiric mirror, a metaphoric reflection of our dissolving social foundation. More than that, *The Simpsons* is therapeutic: to be able to laugh in the face of such problems is the ultimate catharsis.
> —BEN MCCORKLE,
> "*The Simpsons*: A Mirror of Society"

End with a recommendation. This strategy is especially appropriate when you are completing an ARGUMENT, as in this study of the effect of handguns on the homicide rates in Seattle and Vancouver:

> Our analysis of the rates of homicide in these two largely similar cities suggests that the modest restriction of citizens' access to firearms (especially handguns) is associated with lower rates of homicide. This association does not appear to be explained by differences between the communities in aggressiveness, criminal behavior, or response to crime. Although our findings should be corroborated in other settings, our results suggest that a more restrictive approach to handgun control may decrease national homicide rates.
>
> —JOHN HENRY SLOAN ET AL., "Handgun Regulations, Crime, Assaults, and Homicide: A Tale of Two Cities"

Show the broader significance of your argument. The following example is the last paragraph of an essay on evolution. The essay opens by noting that the effects of the "great transition of animals from water to land" can be seen, for example, when modern humans shake hands. Now, many paragraphs later, the author concludes by using the study of evolutionary biology as a tool for understanding the entire living world:

> Let's return to our opening handshake. The structures we shook with— our shoulder, elbow, and wrist—were first seen in fish living in streams over 370 million years ago. Our firm clasp is made with a modified fish fin. Actually, we carry an entire branch of the tree of life inside of us, and it does not stop there. That broad smile we give when we shake hands? The jaws that form our grin arose during another ancient "great" transition. The pair of eyes we use to make eye contact? These were the product of an even more ancient "great" transition. The list goes on and on. . . . Perhaps that is what is so profound about evolution: Everyday biological processes can explain things that seem special or mysterious about the living world.
>
> —NEIL SHUBIN, "The Great Transition"

Developing Paragraphs

Just as an essay is made up of a number of related paragraphs, a paragraph is made up of a number of related sentences. You can develop paragraphs by using the same methods—NARRATION, DESCRIPTION, EXAMPLE, CLASSIFICATION, and the others— that are also used to organize whole essays. Whatever method of development you use, however, you will need to tell the reader clearly and directly what your paragraph is about and where it's going. This is the purpose of the TOPIC SENTENCE.

WRITING TOPIC SENTENCES

Just as a thesis statement alerts readers to the main point of your essay, a topic sentence lets them know what to expect in a paragraph. A good topic sentence should not only tell the reader precisely what the topic of the paragraph is ("behavioral disorders in boys"), it should make a clear statement about that topic ("Doctors are now diagnosing behavioral disorders in boys more frequently than they used to"). Notice that each of the following topic sentences (from the passages on pp. 26–27) proposes something interesting—and arguable—about the topic:

There are, as nearly as I can make out, three kinds of conservation currently operating.   —WENDELL BERRY, "Conservation Is Good Work"

But if agony and pain are part of Vietnamese culture, even to the point of being morbid, pleasure is at the center of America's culture.
          —ANDREW LAM, "They Shut the Door on My Grandmother"

Lest males of all ages feel unfairly picked upon, researchers point out that boys may be diagnosed with behavioral syndromes and disorders more often than girls for a very good reason: their brains may be more vulnerable.
          —NATALIE ANGIER, "Intolerance of Boyish Behavior"

Each of these topic sentences appears at the beginning of a paragraph and tells the reader exactly where the paragraph is going. Sometimes, however, the topic sentence comes at the end and tells the reader where the paragraph has been:

If the first woman God ever made was strong enough to turn the world upside down all alone, these women together ought to be able to turn it back, and get it right side up again! And now they is asking to do it, the men better let them.
          —SOJOURNER TRUTH, "Ain't I a Woman?"

No matter where it appears, your topic sentence should be supported by every other sentence in the paragraph. The supporting sentences can give examples, introduce facts and figures, or even tell an illustrative story; but they all need to connect logically with the topic sentence in ways that are apparent to the reader.

LINKING IDEAS TOGETHER

Each paragraph in your essay should lead logically to the next, with clear TRANSITIONS that indicate to the reader how the paragraphs are connected. Here are some transitional words and phrases that will help you tie your ideas together.

To give examples: for example, for instance, in fact, in particular, namely, indeed, of course, such as, specifically, that is

To compare: also, as, in a similar way, in comparison, like, likewise

To contrast: although, but, by contrast, however, on the contrary, even though, on the other hand

To indicate cause and effect: as a result, because, consequently, so, then

To indicate logical reasoning: accordingly, hence, it follows, therefore, thus, since, so

To indicate place or direction: across, at, along, away, behind, close, down, distant, far, here, in between, in front of, inside, left, near, next to, north, outside, right, south, there, toward, up, above, below, elsewhere

To indicate time: at the same time, during, frequently, from time to time, in 1999, in the future, now, never, often, meanwhile, occasionally, soon, then, until, when

To indicate sequence or continuation: also, and, after, before, earlier, finally, first, furthermore, in addition, last, later, next, eventually

To summarize or conclude: in conclusion, in summary, in the end, consequently, so, therefore, thus, to conclude

Using Visuals

You may want to consider using visuals. Illustrations such as graphs and charts can be especially effective for presenting or comparing data, and photographs can help readers see things you describe in your written text.

Visuals should never be mere decoration or clip art, however. Any visuals should be directly relevant to your topic and must support your thesis in some way. For example, if you are writing about conserving energy by carrying a reusable cloth shopping bag, you might include an illustration showing the kind of bag you have in mind.

As with a written text, any visual material you include should be appropriate for your audience and purpose. A picture of a raven, for example, would not add much to an essay for a literature class on Edgar Allan

This reusable bag lets you avoid using plastic shopping bags, thereby conserving energy and reducing landfill waste. © Doug Steley B / Alamy.

Poe's famous poem—but it might be appropriate, if properly labeled, for a biology paper or a field guide to birds.

If you do decide that a visual illustration will genuinely enhance your argument, be sure to refer to it in your text and number it, if necessary, so that readers can find it ("see Fig. 1"). Position the visual as close as you can to the part of your text that it illustrates, and provide a caption that identifies and explains its point. If you found the visual in another source, identify the source and provide documentation in a Works Cited or References list.

To cite visual sources MLA-style, see p. 722.

Revising

Revising is a process of re-vision, of looking again at your draft and making necessary changes in content, organization, or emphasis. Occasionally when you revise, you discover only a few minor scrapes and bruises that need your attention. More often, however, revising requires some major surgery: adding new evidence, narrowing a thesis, cutting out paragraphs or entire sections, rewriting the beginning to appeal better to your audience, and so on.

Revising is not generally the time to focus on words or sentences, though you may change some words and smooth out awkward or unclear sentences as you go. Nor is revising a matter of correcting errors, but rather of more general shaping and reshaping. Many writers try to revise far too soon. To avoid this pitfall, put aside your draft for a few hours—or better still, for a few days—before revising.

Reading a Draft with a Critical Eye

Start by reading the draft yourself, and then try to get someone else to look it over—a classmate, a writing tutor, your roommate, your grandmother. Whoever it is, be sure he or she is aware of your intended audience and purpose. Here's what you and the person with fresh eyes should look for as you read:

AN EFFECTIVE TITLE. Is the title more than a label? How does it pique the reader's interest? Does it indicate the point of the essay—and if not, should it?

A CLEAR FOCUS. What is the main point? Is it clearly stated in a THESIS statement— and if not, should it be? Is the thesis too broad? Sufficiently narrow?

SUFFICIENT INFORMATION FOR YOUR AUDIENCE. How familiar is the topic likely to be to your readers? Is there sufficient background information? Are there clear definitions for any terms and concepts readers might not know? Will readers find it interesting?

ADEQUATE SUPPORT FOR THE THESIS. What evidence supports the thesis? Is the evidence convincing and the reasoning logical? Could the draft be strengthened by adding more facts or specific details?

ORGANIZATION. Is the draft well organized? Does it have a clear beginning, middle, and ending? Are paragraphs related to each other by clear TRANSITIONS? Does each paragraph contribute to the main point, or are some paragraphs off the topic? Does the ending give a sense of closure?

METHODS OF DEVELOPMENT. What is the main method of development—is the draft primarily a NARRATIVE? a DESCRIPTION? an ARGUMENT? Is this method effective? If not, which other methods might be introduced? For instance, would more EXAMPLES, or DEFINITIONS, or a discussion of CAUSES be beneficial?

SOURCES. Is there material from other sources? If so, how are those sources incorporated—are they quoted? paraphrased? summarized? How are they acknowledged? In other words, is it clear to the reader whose words or ideas are being used? How does the source material support the main point? Have all source materials been properly cited and documented?

PARAGRAPHS. Does each paragraph focus on one main idea and have a clear topic sentence? Does the structure of paragraphs vary, or are they too much alike? If they all begin with a topic sentence, should you consider rewriting some paragraphs to lead up to the topic sentence instead of down from it? Does every sentence in a paragraph support the point that the rest of the paragraph is making? Are there any long or complex paragraphs that should be subdivided?

The more common problem, however, is that paragraphs are too short. Are there paragraphs that should be combined with other paragraphs, or developed more fully? How well does the draft flow from one paragraph to the next? If any paragraphs seem to break the flow, look to see if you need to add transitions or to use repetition to help the reader follow the text.

SENTENCE LENGTH AND VARIETY. Check the length of your sentences. If they are all approximately the same length, try varying them. A short sentence among long sentences can provide emphasis. On the other hand, too many short sentences, one after another, can sound choppy. Try combining some of them.

VISUALS. Does the draft include any visuals? If not, is there any material in the text that would be easier to understand as a chart or table? Any descriptive passages where a photo might help readers see what you're talking about? If there are visuals, are they relevant to the topic? How do they support your thesis?

A Sample Student Essay

Here is Zoe Shewer's first draft of an essay on what she learned about herself from a summer program. It is based on her formal outline on pages 23–24.

FIRST DRAFT

How should I spend my summer vacation? Many college students have internships or summer jobs. Some travel. I spent last summer volunteering with three nonprofits through Camp Robin Hood.

Camp Robin Hood is a hands-on summer crash course in New York City nonprofit organizations. Every week, I worked at a different nonprofit: a day care center, a homeless shelter, and a transitional lifestyle program for ex-convicts and former addicts. At every organization, I learned something about working with the underprivileged, but at the end of the summer, I realized that I had also learned something about myself.

I began by working at Ready, Willing & Able, where ex-convicts and former addicts clean streets as part of a transitional lifestyle program. I'll never forget the street cleaning attendant I worked with there. Seymour was tall, tattooed, and a former addict. He was also calm and completely at ease in his RWA jumpsuit, sweeping the sidewalks and wheeling a huge blue trash can through the streets. Seymour taught me how to drain gutters by diverting the flow of water with a rolled-up towel. He also taught me to "read" the back stories in the litter. It was like he saw a story in every piece of trash: a schoolgirl who discarded a bracelet in a temper tantrum, a closet eater who ate Twinkies in the street. He talked about his family, too, and his dreams and plans. I grew to respect him and admire his perseverance and determination, despite all the setbacks in his life.

That respect and admiration was something I would come to feel at each of the nonprofits. At the Association to Benefit Children, an organization that provides services to underprivileged children, I played with and taught children who had many challenges. Like any kids, they loved singing, finger painting, and playing with toys. But there was no escaping the fact that these activities didn't always come easily to them. They worked hard for what they wanted. It was impossible not to admire their determination.

At a homeless shelter, where I handed out clean clothes and tickets for showers, I met people from every walk of life. Some had addiction problems or other illnesses, but many had simply fallen on hard times. The loss of a job or an unexpected medical problem ended up costing them their homes, and they had nowhere else to go. I spent many evenings talking to one woman in particular, Elsie. She had been homeless for several years and knew the streets of New York better than anyone I've ever met. She knew which restaurants would give out their leftover food and when you should appear at their back door for dinner. She knew which churches had the best soup kitchens, and which shelters were safest, and where to find the best cast-off clothing. I never found out how she'd become homeless, but she'd figured out the system and made it work for her. Although I grew up in New York City, her street smarts made me feel like I'd never really known the city.

I volunteered for Camp Robin Hood because I wanted to give something back. I know that my upbringing has been privileged, and I've been lucky to have never gone without. I wanted to do something for those who weren't so lucky. But I discovered that while I may have more tangible goods than those I was volunteering to help, they had a lot to teach me about the intangible: qualities like perseverance, determination, optimism and cheerfulness no matter what the circumstances. They taught me that I have a lot to learn.

Getting Response before Revising

After finishing her first draft, Shewer set it aside for a few hours and then reread it, using the guidelines for reading a draft with a critical eye (pp. 36–37). She also asked a classmate to read it, and he offered her the following comments:

> I really like the topic of your essay, and I think it meets the assignment well. But maybe it would be more effective if you picked one of the three places you worked to focus on, so that you could talk about it more in depth. I'd like to know more about them.
>
> You kind of state a thesis—"At every organization, I learned something about working with the underprivileged, but at the end of the summer, I

realized that I had also learned something about myself"—but then you state it more directly at the end of the paper—"They taught me that I have a lot to learn." That works pretty well, and the body paragraphs do support this idea.

You describe the people you meet, but it might be more interesting if there was more of a story.

Shewer agreed with her classmate's suggestions to focus on just one of the places she worked, and to incorporate more narration. She chose to write about her experience at Ready, Willing & Able, and to focus on her day working with Seymour. After some BRAINSTORMING about that day, she decided to add a NARRATIVE about one incident in particular. She then revised her THESIS to reflect her narrower focus on that specific day. She also added a title, which she hadn't included in her first draft.

SECOND DRAFT

Ready, Willing, and Able

July is stifling in New York City, and I was not looking forward to wearing an oversized jumpsuit in ninety-degree heat. I was suited up to clean streets as part of the Camp Robin Hood program. I was at the headquarters of Ready, Willing & Able. Most RWA employees are ex-convicts or former addicts for whom street cleaning is both a job and part of a transitional lifestyle program.

The program coordinator waved me toward a tall man who had apparently been waiting for me. His name was Seymour, and he was the street cleaning attendant I would be working with all day. As he reached out to shake my hand, I noticed that he had a tattoo on his forearm.

We headed out to the street, and while I fidgeted with the broom I carried, Seymour calmly wheeled a bright blue trash can behind him. As we began sweeping the sidewalks, Seymour not only showed me how to drain the gutters, he talked about who might have dropped certain kinds of trash and why and told me about his family and his desire to get his life back on track. Though I had lived in the city my entire life, I began to see things in a new light. I became so absorbed in Seymour's stories that I heard some girls laughing and almost didn't realize they were laughing at me. "I wonder what *she* did to deserve *that*!"

I looked up and saw a group of girls about my age laughing at me as they walked past. They obviously thought I was serving a juvenile court sentence. Ordinarily I may have laughed at the idea that I could be mistaken for a juvenile delinquent, but on this day I felt butterflies in my stomach.

What if Seymour thought I was just like those other girls? What if he thought I didn't want to be there and was counting down the minutes until the day would be over? I wanted to tell him that I had a lot of respect for his work and that I knew I couldn't possibly understand what he does just by shadowing him for a day. I wanted to tell him that I was not simply doing a day of community service so I could include it on a résumé.

But Seymour broke the silence, saying, "Put some muscle in it, Goldilocks."

Revising a Second Draft

After setting her revision aside for a day, Shewer came back to her essay and reread it, again following the questions for revision on pages 36 37. She liked the story of her day working with Seymour, but she thought that now there was too much narration, and she needed to have more DESCRIPTIVE details. She also decided that she needed to explain more about the incident with the girls—how she felt and how that moment taught her something. Finally, she revised some of her sentences to keep them from being the same length and tried to make some of her language more precise.

FINAL DRAFT

Ready, Willing, and Able

Wearing a canvas jumpsuit zipped up to my neck, I must have looked as though I was stepping onto the set of *ET: The Extra-Terrestrial*, but my actual destination was Madison Avenue, home to some of the fanciest boutiques in New York City. The bright blue jumpsuit I wore was far from high fashion: it was sized for a full-grown man, and it ballooned about my slender frame. My blond hair was pulled back in a ponytail, and the only label I displayed was the bold-lettered logo on my back: Ready, Willing &

Introduction

Able. I was suited up to collect trash from the sidewalks of New York.

Beginning of narrative: the first day

July is stifling in New York City, and I was not looking forward to wearing the oversized jumpsuit in ninety-degree heat. As I made my way through the Ready, Willing & Able (RWA) headquarters, I passed colorfully decorated bulletin boards bearing smiley-faced reminders: "Drug testing is on Monday!" "Curfew is midnight!" Most fulltime employees of RWA are ex-convicts or former addicts for whom street cleaning is the work-for-housing component of a transitional lifestyle program. For me, street cleaning was day one of Camp Robin Hood, a hands-on summer crash course in New York nonprofit organizations. As I selected a broom from the supply closet, I reminded myself that I had volunteered to do this. Feeling like a new kid on the first day of school, I stood nervously next to the program supervisor who would introduce me to the street cleaning attendant I would be helping.

Description of key character, with concrete details

If I was the awkward new kid, the street cleaning attendant to whom I was assigned, a tall man named Seymour, was undoubtedly the Big Man on Campus. Seymour wore his RWA cap slightly askew, and, as he reached out to shake my hand, I caught a glimpse of a tattoo under his sleeve. We headed out to the street together, and, while I nervously fidgeted with the broom I carried, he calmly wheeled a bright blue trash can behind him. Seymour began sweeping the sidewalks, and I followed his lead. He not only showed me how to drain the gutters by diverting the flow of water with a rolled-up towel, he also taught me how to "read" the back stories in the litter. To Seymour, a torn hemp bracelet on the curb was a schoolgirl's temper tantrum; a Twinkie wrapper in the street was a closet eater's discarded evidence. Though I have lived in New York my entire life, I began to see my surroundings in a new light. The streets that had always felt so familiar seemed full of surprises. As our afternoon continued, Seymour also told me stories about his sister, his desire to get his life back on track after

Fig. 1. Homeless men get back to work and self-respect by going through the Ready, Willing & Able program sponsored by the DOE Fund.

some time on the wrong side of the law, his love of Central Park, and his aspiration to travel across the country.

After several hours, I had more or less forgotten about my tent-sized RWA jumpsuit when suddenly I heard someone laughing at me: "I wonder what *she* did to deserve *that*?!"

I looked up and saw a group of girls my age looking in my direction and laughing as they walked past. My stomach tightened. They obviously thought I was being punished, perhaps serving a juvenile court sentence. Ordinarily I might have laughed at the idea that I could be mistaken for a juvenile delinquent, but on this day I felt a jumble of feelings—panic, shame, sadness, and admiration for a man whose history is suggested by his jumpsuit and the logo on his back. I will admit

Dialogue and climax of narrative

Effect of incident

that a few hours earlier I was embarrassed about my ill-fitting uniform. Halfway through the work day, however, the girls' rude comments caused an entirely different kind of shame: What if Seymour thought *I* was anything like those girls? What if he thought that I was faking a smile and counting down the minutes until the day was over?

Thesis indicated indirectly

I suddenly wanted to thank Seymour for this experience. I wanted to tell him that he was probably the best guide through these streets I had ever had, and that I knew I could not possibly understand what he does by shadowing him for a day in a borrowed uniform. I wanted to explain to him that I volunteer regularly in New York: I am committed to working with at-risk children, and have done so for years at an after-school program in Harlem. I wanted to share how much I relate to his closeness with his family, his desire to travel, and his love of Strawberry Fields in Central Park. But the girls' mocking comments and laughter had left us in an uncomfortable silence, and I felt that anything I might say would make us feel even more awkward.

Significance of narrative

It was Seymour who broke this silence. As I stood next to the trash can and tried to avoid staring off in the direction of the latte-carrying girls, Seymour caught my eye, smiled, and nodded toward my broom with one excellent piece of advice: "Put some muscle in it, Goldilocks."

Conclusion with dialogue

This final draft, Shewer felt, better blended the modes of narration and description, and it fulfilled the assignment to write about an experience that taught her something new about herself. She especially liked the concrete details she included and the dialogue that ended the essay.

Editing and Proofreading

When you finish revising your essay, you're still not quite done. You've put the icing on the cake, but you need to make sure all the candles are straight and to wipe the edge of the plate. That is, you need to edit and proofread your final draft before presenting it to the reader.

When you edit, you add finishing touches and correct errors in grammar, sentence structure, punctuation, and word choice that affect the sense and meaning of your text. When you proofread, you take care of misspellings, typos, problems with your margins and format, and other minor blemishes in the appearance of your document.

Certain types of problems are common to certain types of writing. Chapters 4–12 include sections on "Editing for Common Errors"—the kinds that are likely with the method being discussed. Here are some tips that can help you check your drafts for some common mistakes.

TIPS FOR EDITING SENTENCES

Check to be sure that each sentence expresses a complete thought—that it has a subject (someone or something) and a verb performing an action or indicating a state of being.

Check capitalization and end punctuation. Be sure that each sentence begins with a capital letter and ends with a period, a question mark, or an exclamation point.

Look for sentences that begin with it or there. Often such sentences are vague or boring, and they are usually easy to edit. For example, if you've written "There is a doctor on call at every hospital," you could edit it to "A doctor is on call at every hospital."

Check for parallelism. All items in a list or series should have parallel forms—all nouns (Lincoln, Grant, Lee), all verbs (dedicate, consecrate, hallow), all phrases (of the people, by the people, for the people).

TIPS FOR EDITING WORDS

There, their. Use *there* to refer to place or direction, or to introduce a sentence (Who was there? There was no answer.). Use *their* as a possessive (Their intentions were good).

It's, its. Use *it's* to mean "it is" (It's difficult to say what causes dyslexia). Use *its* to mean "belonging to it" (Each car has its unique features).

Lie, lay. Use *lie* when you mean "recline" (She's lying down because she's tired). Use *lay* when you mean "put" or "place" (Lay the book on the table).

TIPS FOR EDITING PUNCTUATION

Check for commas after introductory elements in a sentence

The day he disclosed his matrimonial ambitions for me, my uncle sat me at his right during lunch. —SAIRA SHAH, "Longing to Belong"

Check for commas before *and, but, or, nor, so,* or *yet* in compound sentences

They divorced when I was in junior high school, and they agreed on little except that I was an impossible child. —RICHARD RUSSO, "Dog"

Check for commas in a series

A circuit of the courthouse square took you past the grand furniture stores, the two dime stores, the shoe stores, the men's stores, the ladies' stores, the banks, the drugstores. —BOBBIE ANN MASON, "Being Country"

When you quote other people's words, be sure to put quotation marks at the beginning and end of the quotation

Instead of offering an abject apology, Ms. Hegemann insisted, "There's no such thing as originality anyway, just authenticity." —TRIP GABRIEL, "Plagiarism Lines Blur for Students in Digital Age"

Check to be sure that you've put commas and periods inside quotation marks

"Put some muscle in it, Goldilocks." —ZOE SHEWER, "Ready, Willing, and Able"

"You know," Dave told his grandmother, "I'm responsible for the lives of 40 men." —ANNE BERNAYS, "Warrior Day"

Check your use of apostrophes with possessives. Singular nouns should end in 's, whereas plural nouns should end in s'. The possessive pronouns *hers, his, its, ours, yours,* and *theirs* should not have apostrophes.

Robert Bergman's radiant portraits of strangers provoked this meditation. —TONI MORRISON, "Strangers"

Morrison's meditation was provoked by the strangers' faces.

> Theirs was the life I dreamt about during my vacations in eastern North Carolina. —DAVID SEDARIS, "Remembering My Childhood on the Continent of Africa"

Proofreading and Final Formatting

Proofreading is the only stage in the writing process where you are *not* primarily concerned with meaning. Of course you should correct any substantive errors you discover, but your main concerns when you proofread are small technicalities and the appearance of your text. Misspellings, margins that are too narrow or too wide, unindented paragraphs, missing page numbers—these are the kinds of imperfections you're looking for as you put the final touch on your document.

Such minor blemishes are especially hard to see when you're looking at your own work. So slow down as you proofread, and view your document more as a picture than as a written text. Use a ruler or piece of paper to guide your eye line by line as you scan the page; or read your entire text backward a sentence at a time; or read it out loud word by word. Use a spellchecker, too, but don't rely on it: a spellchecker doesn't know the difference, for example, between *spackling* and *spacing* or *Greek philosophy* and *Geek philosophy*.

After you've proofread your document word for word, check the overall format to make sure it follows any specific instructions that you may have been given. If your instructor does not have formatting requirements, follow these tips based on the Modern Language Association (MLA) guidelines:

TIPS FOR FORMATTING AN ESSAY

Heading and title. Put your name, your instructor's name, the name and number of the course, and the date on separate lines in the upper-left-hand corner of your first page. Skip a line and center your title, but do not underline it or put it in quotation marks. Begin your first paragraph on the next line.

Typeface and size. Use ten-, eleven-, or twelve-point type in an easy-to-read typeface, such as Times New Roman, Courier, or Palatino.

Spacing. Double-space your document.

Margins. Set one-inch margins at the top, bottom, and sides of your text.

Paragraph indentation. Indent the first line of each paragraph one-half inch.

Page numbers. Number your pages consecutively, and include your last name with each page number.

CHAPTER 3

Putting in Your Oar: Learning the Basic Moves of Academic Writing

Imagine that you enter a parlor.

—KENNETH BURKE, *The Philosophy of Literary Form*

You come late to a party. A lively conversation is going on around you. You aren't sure what it's about at first—a class, a movie, the merits of two teams? Academic writing is like this, except the discussion began long ago, and—as suggested by philosopher Kenneth Burke's famous parlor analogy—it never ends. Here's the scene as Burke describes it:

> Imagine that you enter a parlor. You come late. When you arrive, others have long preceded you, and they are engaged in a heated discussion, a discussion too heated for them to pause and tell you exactly what it is about. You listen for a while, until you decide that you have caught the tenor of the argument; then you put in your oar. Someone answers; you answer him; another comes to your defense; another aligns himself against you. . . . The hour grows late, you must depart. And you do depart, with the discussion still vigorously in progress.

Like Burke's parlor, academic writing is the site of an ongoing conversation—about ideas. The ultimate purpose of that conversation is the advancement of human knowledge. More immediately, you can learn a lot about any field of study that interests you, from physics to dance, just by listening to what knowledgeable people in that field have to say.

Academic writing, like other social activities and forms of conversation, has its own rules and conventions. Don't leave a party without properly thanking the hostess; don't turn in a paper without properly citing your sources. This chapter covers some of the basic conventions and patterns of academic writing:

- researching what's been said about your topic
- synthesizing the ideas you find with your own ideas
- presenting your ideas as a response to the ideas of others
- considering other views
- saying why your ideas matter
- using description, comparison, and the other methods taught in this book

Finding Out What's Been Said about Your Topic

Before you put in your oar, you need to get your bearings. So before you leap into a discussion on a topic that's new to you, test the waters by attending lectures, talking with your teachers and fellow students, and reading and thinking about what others have written on the topic under discussion. In short, you need to do some preliminary research.

With many kinds of academic writing—a brief answer on an essay exam, for example your research will consist mostly of thinking about your topic and figuring out what you want to emphasize. For a research paper, however, you will need to find out what experts in the field are saying. So you'll need to look for authoritative written sources of information, such as academic books and peer-reviewed articles. Remember that all the sources you consult when you write a research paper should be identified in a reference list at the end of your paper—and you'll also name many of your most important sources as you go along.

Refer to the Appendix (pp. 695–733) for information on finding, evaluating, and citing sources.

Academic writing is about much more than amassing sources, however. With even the most informal research paper, you'll be expected to show what you've learned and even to contribute ideas of your own to the discussion. Coming up with ideas, in fact, is the main reason you join in the give and take of an academic conversation in the first place.

In some cultures, it is impolite to disagree directly and openly with others, especially if they are older than you are, or are your hosts at a social event. But imagine a conversation in which every assertion ("the earth is flat," "printing new money will ease the financial crisis") is always met with polite assent ("I agree"; "yes, that's right"). Academic discourse should always be courteous, but in most U.S. academic contexts, the conversation that goes more like this: "I see what you're saying, but what about . . . ?" "No, that's not my point. My point is. . . ." In other words, this tradition of academic discourse is based on a synthesis of different—even conflicting—ideas and viewpoints.

Synthesizing Ideas

Suppose you're writing a paper on how the Internet has changed our lives. You've begun to do your research, and you're finding lots of good ideas, some of which you plan to weave into your paper—with full attribution, of course. You don't want to simply repeat what others have said on your topic, however. You want to synthesize their ideas and come up with some new ones of your own.

Here's how that process might work. As you read through your many sources, you keep running into various arguments to the following effect: "The Internet is making us stupid." You don't agree with this view; but you find it thought-provoking. You may even mention it in your paper as an idea that helped nudge you into taking a different (more positive) position on your topic.

As you mull over such negative statements about the effect of the Internet on the human brain, you come upon others that are virtually the antithesis of the first. They run, more or less, as follows: "The Internet is making us all smarter because it places more information at our fingertips more quickly than ever before."

You do not agree entirely with these ideas, either; but by bringing them together—which is what *synthesis* means—with other, opposing ideas on your topic, a spark is struck in your mind. You now have a clearer conception of what you want to say.

You jot down some notes before you forget: "Both of these positions are flawed. The Internet's not really making us smarter or dumber. Just speeding up our access to information. Conclusion: the Internet is not fundamentally changing how we think; it's simply making us more efficient."

This last statement is a synthesis of the opposing views you have encountered in your research. It will make a dandy THESIS, or main point, for the paper you want to write about the Internet. And it came to you out of the intellectual give and take that is the heart, or rather, the brain, of academic writing. As you present this proposition to your readers, you may also want to explain some of the other, contrasting ideas that inspired it.

Presenting Your Ideas as a Response to the Ideas of Others

Starting with the ideas of others is so basic to academic writing that some teachers and theorists of writing consider it to be *the* underlying pattern of much academic prose, cutting across all disciplines and majors. The following is an elegant statement of this view:

> For us, the underlying structure of effective academic writing . . . resides not just in stating our own ideas, but in listening closely to others around us,

summarizing their views in a way that they will recognize, and responding with our own ideas in kind. Broadly speaking, academic writing is argumentative writing, and . . . to argue well you need to do more than assert your own ideas. You need to enter a conversation, using what others say (or might say) as a launching pad . . . for your own ideas.

—GERALD GRAFF AND CATHY BIRKENSTEIN,
*"They Say / I Say": The Moves That Matter in Academic Writing**

In the following passage from an Op-Ed piece in the *New York Times*, for example, a psychology professor starts by summarizing the views of other writers—and then disagrees, advancing his own view:

Media critics write as if the brain takes on the qualities of whatever it consumes, the informational equivalent of "you are what you eat." As with primitive peoples who believe that eating fierce animals will make them fierce, they assume that watching quick cuts in rock videos turns your mental life into quick cuts or that reading bullet points and Twitter postings turns your thoughts into bullet points and Twitter postings. . . . Far from making us stupid, these technologies are the only things that will keep us smart.

—STEVEN PINKER, "Mind Over Mass Media"

Although Pinker disagrees completely with those who say that electronic media are making us stupid, he nonetheless puts forth his own views as a response to their views. In particular, he does so by COMPARING—a common pattern in academic writing—their respective ideas with those of "primitive peoples."

To see how well Pinker defends his thesis, read his essay on p. 640.

In any academic writing you do, there are many ways of introducing the ideas of others. Three of the most common ones are:

- *Quoting another writer's exact words:* "Media critics," says Steven Pinker, "write as if the brain takes on the qualities of whatever it consumes, the informational equivalent of 'you are what you eat.' "

- *Paraphrasing another writer's ideas:* According to Steven Pinker, critics of the new media have a faulty view of the human brain as an organ that must be fed a constant diet of intellectual red meat.

- *Summarizing another writer's ideas:* Steven Pinker attacks the views of media critics as a primitive form of superstition.

*In fact, the work of Graff and Birkenstein in demystifying the argumentative aspect of academic writing has served not only as a launching pad for this chapter but for the templates throughout the book. As these scholars demonstrate, such templates "do more than organize students' ideas; they help bring those ideas into existence."

Now let's look at a more complicated example. In the following passage, a writer both summarizes and quotes from the work of writers with whom she agrees:

> Pioneering evolutionary psychologist Robert L. Trivers has observed that having and rearing children requires women to invest far more resources than men do because of the length of pregnancy, the dangers of childbirth, and the duration of infants' dependence on their mothers (145). According to Helen Fisher, one of the leading advocates of this theory, finding a capable mate was a huge preoccupation of all prehistoric reproductive women, and for good reason: "A female couldn't carry a baby in one arm and sticks and stones in the other arm and still feed and protect herself on the very dangerous open grasslands, so she began to need a mate to help her rear her young" (Frank 85). . . . [T]hese are the bases upon which modern mate selection is founded, and there are many examples of this phenomenon to be found in our own society.
> —Carolyn Stonehill,
> "Modern Dating, Prehistoric Style"

For tips on deciding when to quote, paraphrase, or summarize, see pp. 704–6 in the Appendix.

In this passage, Stonehill is not simply reporting what she learned about human mating behavior by reading the work of experts in the field of evolutionary biology, such as Trivers and Fisher. Having synthesized their views in her own mind, she uses them as a framework to support *her* thesis, stated in the previous paragraph, about the origins of "modern mate selection": "Driven by the need to reproduce and propagate the species, these ancestors of ours formed patterns of mate selection so effective in providing for their needs and those of their off spring that they are mimicked even in today's society."

As you introduce the ideas of others into your writing, you can present you own ideas by responding to theirs in many different ways. These three are the most common: agree with what they say (as Stonehill did), disagree (like Pinker), or both. The following templates suggest some ways to structure your response.

Agree

When you agree with others, do more than just echo their arguments—point out unnoticed implications, or explain a concept that you think needs to be better understood.

▸ One of the most respected experts in the field is X, who says essentially that _____.

▸ Advocates of this view are X and Y, who also argue that _____.

▸ Thus, I agree with those who say _____.

Disagree

Don't just contradict the views of others: offer persuasive reasons why you disagree. Justify your reason for writing and move the conversation forward.

- ▸ In my view, these objections do not hold up because _____.
- ▸ Like some critics of these ideas, particularly X and Y, I would argue instead that _____.
- ▸ X's focus on _____ obscures the underlying issue of _____.

Both Agree and Disagree

This approach works well when your topic is complex. It avoids a yes/no standoff and displays your thorough understanding of the issues. You don't have to give equal weight to all aspects of the topic—just the main points under debate. This approach invites COMPARISON, for example, when you want to list pros and cons.

- ▸ Although I concede that _____, I still maintain that _____.
- ▸ Whereas X and Y make good points about _____, I have to agree with Z that _____.
- ▸ X may be wrong about _____, but the rest of her argument is persuasive.

Considering Other Views

Carolyn Stonehill's paper on mate selection is a good example of academic writing that both agrees and disagrees with the views of other writers. Stonehill is aware that evolutionary psychology is a controversial field. So after building on the work of such evolutionary psychologists as Trivers and Fisher, she anticipates other possible arguments: "There is, however," she writes, "a good deal of opposition to evolutionary theory. Some critics say that the messages fed to us by the media are a larger influence on the criteria of present-day mate selection than any sort of ancestral behavior."

You can read the complete version of this paper on p. 55.

As Steven Pinker does when he disputes critics of mass media, Stonehill introduces the views of potential opponents ("some critics") for the purpose of acknowledging other views, a rhetorical move known as *planting a naysayer*. Stonehill does not simply disagree with the naysayers' position, however; she carefully refutes it by summarizing and then directly quoting arguments on *her* side of the debate about which has the greater influence—modern media or ancestral behavior—on how we date and mate today.

First her summary: "Evolutionary psychologists argue that research has not determined what is cause and what is effect." Then the quotation (from the work of Cosmides and Tooby): "In the absence of research on the particular topic, there is no way of knowing." These arguments do not conclusively prove Stonehill's point, of course. But they may cast a reasonable doubt on the position she is challenging.

Saying Why Your Ideas Matter

Who cares? Why does it matter? Whatever you're writing about, you also need to explain the *significance* of your ideas. Stonehill does so by explicitly stating that her thesis "would explain why women of our time are preoccupied with plastic surgery, makeup, and . . . a quick hair check as a potential date approaches." Most aspects of "our mating behavior," in fact, can be better understood, she argues, if we recognize that they derive from "the complex mating strategies developed by our ancestors." These last three templates suggest some ways to explain why your ideas matter:

▶ The prevailing view has long been _____; but now we can see that _____.

▶ This conclusion is significant because _____.

▶ In particular, X and Y should be interested in this view because _____.

Using the Methods Taught in This Book

The basic purpose of most academic writing is to prove a point. The writer makes a claim in the form of a thesis and then supports that claim throughout the rest of his or her paper. The basic strategies and methods of ARGUMENT are, therefore, particularly useful in academic writing.

In addition to argument, however, the other basic methods of development taught in this book—cause and effect, classification, comparison and contrast, definition, description, example, narration, and process analysis—can also help you figure out and present what you have to say in any piece of academic writing. Carolyn Stonehill, whose paper on mating behavior we've been excerpting throughout the chapter, begins by using NARRATION to tell the story of a young woman who is attracted to her lab partner because he drives a BMW. She also DESCRIBES the young woman as having "a pearly white smile" and the young man as "tall, muscular, and stylishly dressed."

Development templates for these methods appear on pp. 519, 69, and 129.

Stonehill further COMPARES AND CONTRASTS different theories of mating behavior to each other; and she draws repeatedly upon strategies of CAUSE AND EFFECT to explain the origins and consequences of those behaviors.

DEFINING key concepts precisely is fundamental to academic writing. Stonehill uses common techniques of definition to explain what she means by such terms as "evolutionary psychologists" and "mating behavior." And she gives specific EXAMPLES of what she is talking about when she cites Jenny's instinctive attraction to Joey and his "resources."

> Development templates for these methods appear on pp. 277, 456, 380, and 178.

Useful as these methods of development can be for presenting your ideas in an academic paper, they can also serve you as ways of discovering what you have to say in the first place—as you do research and begin to write. Much of the rest of this book, in fact, is about that process of discovery and the use of these methods and patterns both as ways of thinking and as strategies for writing.

A Sample Academic Essay

In "Modern Dating, Prehistoric Style," Carolyn Stonehill draws on her research in the field of evolutionary psychology to argue that many of the dating habits of modern humans derive from behaviors developed by our ancient ancestors as they struggled to survive and reproduce in dangerous environments. Since Stonehill's paper was written for a first-year college writing class, she uses MLA style to cite her sources. Styles of documentation vary from discipline to discipline, however, so consult your instructor if you're not sure which style you should use.

Modern Dating, Prehistoric Style

Consider the following scenario: It's a sunny afternoon on campus, and Jenny is walking to her next class. Out of the corner of her eye, she catches sight of her lab partner, Joey, parking his car. She stops to admire how tall, muscular, and stylishly dressed he is, and she does not take her eyes off him as he walks away from his shiny new BMW. As he flashes her a pearly white smile, Jenny melts, then quickly adjusts her skirt and smooths her hair.

> Introduction uses NARRATION and DESCRIPTION to give an EXAMPLE of "modern dating"

This scenario, while generalized, is familiar: Our attraction to people—or lack of it—often depends on their physical traits. But

Raises a key
question about
CAUSE AND
EFFECT

why this attraction? Why does Jenny respond the way she does to
her handsome lab partner? Why does she deem him handsome
at all? Certainly Joey embodies the stereotypes of physical
attractiveness prevalent in contemporary American society.
Advertisements, television shows, and magazine articles all provide
Jenny with signals telling her what constitutes the ideal American
man. Yet she is also attracted to Joey's new sports car even though
she has a new car herself. Does Jenny find this man striking because
of the influence of her culture, or does her attraction lie in a more
fundamental part of her constitution? Evolutionary psychologists,

DEFINES the field
of evolutionary
psychology,
which may be
unfamiliar to
Stonehill's
AUDIENCE

who apply principles of evolutionary biology to research on the
human mind, would say that Jenny's responses in this situation are
due largely to mating strategies developed by her prehistoric
ancestors. Driven by the need to reproduce and propagate the

States the
main point,
or THESIS, of
Stonehill's
paper

species, these ancestors of ours formed patterns of mate selection so
effective in providing for their needs and those of their offspring
that they are mimicked even in today's society. While cultural

Anticipates
views of poten-
tial opponents

values and messages clearly play a part in the process of mate
selection, the genetic and psychological predispositions developed by
our ancestors play the biggest role in determining to whom we are
attracted.

Women's Need to Find a Capable Mate

Pioneering evolutionary psychologist Robert L. Trivers has
observed that having and rearing children requires women to invest
far more resources than men do because of the length of pregnancy,

SUMMARIZES
and QUOTES
the views of
other writers
whose ideas
Stonehill plans
to build on

the dangers of childbirth, and the duration of infants' dependence
on their mothers (145). According to Helen Fisher, one of the
leading advocates of this theory, finding a capable mate was a huge
preoccupation of all prehistoric reproductive women, and for good
reason: "A female couldn't carry a baby in one arm and sticks and
stones in the other arm and still feed and protect herself on the very
dangerous open grasslands, so she began to need a mate to help her
rear her young" (Frank 85). So because of this it became advantageous

for the woman to find a strong, capable man with access to resources, and it became suitable for the man to find a healthy, reproductively sound woman to bear and care for his offspring. According to evolutionary psychologists, these are the bases upon which modern mate selection is founded, and there are many examples of this phenomenon to be found in our own society.

One can see now why Jenny might be attracted by Joey's display of resources—his BMW. In our society, men with good job prospects, a respected social position, friends in high places, or any combination thereof have generally been viewed as more desirable mates than those without these things because they signal to women that the men have resources (Buss and Schmitt 226). Compared with males, females invest more energy in bearing and raising children, so it is most advantageous for females to choose mates with easy access to resources, the better to provide for their children.

Men's Need to Find a Healthy Mate

For men, reproductive success depends mainly on the reproductive fitness of their female counterpart: No amount of available resources can save a baby miscarried in the first month of gestation. Because of this need for a healthy mate, men have evolved a particular attraction "radar" that focuses on signs of a woman's health and youth, markers that are primarily visual (Weiten 399). Present-day attractiveness ratings are based significantly on this primitive standard: "Some researchers have suggested that cross-cultural standards of beauty reflect an evolved preference for physical traits that are generally associated with youth, such as smooth skin, good muscle tone, and shiny hair" (Boyd and Silk 625). This observation would explain why women of our time are preoccupied with plastic surgery, makeup, and—in Jenny's case—a quick hair check as a potential date approaches. As Michael R. Cunningham et al. noted, "A focus on outer beauty may have stemmed from a need for desirable inner qualities," such as health, strength, and fertility, and "culture may build on evolutionary

SYNTHESIZES the views of other writers as a basis for Stonehill's own claim

Returns to Stonehill's opening NARRATIVE and reads it in the light of ideas in evolutionary psychology that support her position

SUMMARY statement about origins of female behavior leads to COMPARISON with male behavior in next section

Introduces more expert opinion in support of Stonehill's thesis—and explains the broader significance of that thesis

dynamics by specifying grooming attributes that signal successful adaptation" (262–63).

The Influence of the Media on Mate Selection

There is, however, a good deal of opposition to evolutionary theory. Some critics say that the messages fed to us by the media are a larger influence on the criteria of present-day mate selection than any sort of ancestral behavior. Advertisements and popular media have long shown Americans what constitutes a physically ideal mate: In general, youthful, well-toned, symmetrical features are considered more attractive than aging, flabby, or lopsided ones. Evolutionary psychologists argue that research has not determined what is cause and what is effect. Leda Cosmides and John Tooby offered the following analogy to show the danger of assigning culture too powerful a causal role:

> For example, people think that if they can show that there is information in the culture that mirrors how people behave, then *that* is the cause of their behavior. So if they see that men on TV have trouble crying, they assume that their example is *causing* boys to be afraid to cry. But which is cause and which effect? Does the fact that men don't cry much on TV *teach* boys to not cry, or does it merely *reflect* the way boys normally develop? In the absence of research on the particular topic, there is no way of knowing. ("Nature and Nurture: An Adaptationist Perspective," par. 16)

We can hypothesize, then, that rather than media messages determining our mating habits, our mating habits determine the media messages. Advertisers rely on classical conditioning to interest consumers in their products. For instance, by showing an image of a beautiful woman while advertising a beauty product, advertisers hope that consumers will associate attractiveness with the use of that particular product (Weiten 684). In order for this method to be effective, however, the images depicted in conjunction with the

---

[Margin notes:]

Introduces naysayers in order to anticipate and refute views of potential opponents

Explains Stonehill's point in directly quoting two more writers with whom she agrees

Places Stonehill's views in direct opposition to those of naysayers

beauty product must be ones the general public already finds attractive, and an image of a youthful, clear-skinned woman would, according to evolutionary psychologists, be attractive for reasons of reproductive fitness. In short, what some call media influence is not an influence at all but merely a mirror in which we see evidence of our ancestral predispositions.

SUMMARIZES Stonehill's position in response to opposing views of mate selection

If Not Media, Then What?

Ian Tattersall, a paleoanthropologist at the American Museum of Natural History, offered another counterargument to the evolutionary theory of mate selection. First, he argued that the behavior of organisms is influenced not only by genetics, but also by economics and ecology working together (663). Second, he argued that no comparisons can be made between modern human behavior and that of our evolutionary predecessors because the appearance of *Homo sapiens* presented a sudden, qualitative change from the Neanderthals—not a gradual evolution of behavioral traits:

Anticipates another possible argument

> As a cognitive and behavioral entity, our species is truly unprecedented. Our consciousness is an emergent quality, not the result of eons of fine-tuning of a single instrument. And, if so, it is to this recently acquired quality of uniqueness, not to the hypothetical "ancestral environments," that we must look in the effort to understand our often unfathomable behaviors. (665)

The key to Tattersall's argument is this "emergent quality" of symbolic thought; according to his theories, the ability to think symbolically is what separates modern humans from their ancestors and shows the impossibility of sexual selection behaviors having been passed down over millions of years. Our sexual preferences, Tattersall said, are a result of our own recent and species-specific development and have nothing whatsoever to do with our ancestors.

Focuses on the key assumption of the other argument

Opponents of the evolutionary theory, though, fail to explain how "unfathomable" mating behaviors can exist in our present society for no apparent or logical reason. Though medicine has

Attacks that assumption as unfounded and draws support from additional sources

advanced to the point where fertility can be medically enhanced, Devendra Singh observed that curvy women are still viewed as especially attractive because they are perceived to possess greater fertility—a perception that is borne out by several studies of female fertility, hormone levels, and waist-to-hip ratio (304). Though more and more women are attending college and achieving high-paying positions, women are still "more likely than men to consider economic prospects a high priority in a mate" (Sapolsky 18). While cultural norms and economic conditions influence our taste in mates, as Singh showed in observing that "the degree of affluence of a society or of an ethnic group within a society may, to a large extent, determine the prevalence and admiration of fatness [of women]" (304-05), we still react to potential mates in ways determined in Paleolithic times. The key to understanding our mating behavior does not lie only in an emergent modern quality, nor does it lie solely in the messages relayed to us by society; rather, it involves as well the complex mating strategies developed by our ancestors.

> Conclusion acknowledges the validity of opposing views but stipulates that Stonehill's argument is also valid

Works Cited

Boyd, Robert, and Joan B. Silk. *How Humans Evolved.* 5th ed. New York: Norton, 2009. Print.

Buss, David M., and David P. Schmitt. "Sexual Strategies Theory: An Evolutionary Perspective on Human Mating." *Psychological Review* 100.2 (1993): 204–32. Print.

Cosmides, Leda, and John Tooby. "Evolutionary Psychology: A Primer." *Center for Evolutionary Psychology.* University of California, Santa Barbara, 1997. Web. 14 Oct. 2010.

Cunningham, Michael R., Alan R. Roberts, Anita P. Barbee, Perri B. Druen, and Cheng-Huan Wu. " 'Their Ideas of Beauty Are, on the Whole, the Same as Ours': Consistency and Variability in the Crosscultural Perception of Female Physical Attractiveness." *Journal of Personality and Social Psychology* 68.2 (1995): 261–79. Print.

Frank, C. "Why Do We Fall in—and Out of—Love? Dr. Helen Fisher Unravels the Mystery." *Biography* Feb. 2001: 85+. Print.

Sapolsky, Robert M. "What Do Females Want? Does a Male's Long Tail or Flashy Coloration Advertise His Good Genes? New Research Challenges the Old Answers" *Natural History* 110.10 (2001): 18–21. Print.

Singh, Devendra. "Adaptive Significance of Female Physical Attractiveness: Role of Waist-to-Hip Ratio." *Journal of Personality and Social Behavior* 65.2 (1993): 293–307. *PubMed*. Web. 14 Oct. 2010.

Tattersall, Ian. "Evolution, Genes, and Behavior." *Zygon: Journal of Religion & Science* 36.4 (2001): 657–66. Web. 29 Sept. 2010.

Trivers, Robert L. "Parental Investment and Sexual Selection." *Sexual Selection and the Descent of Man: The Darwinian Pivot*. Ed. Bruce G. Campbell. New Brunswick, NJ: AldineTransaction, 2006. 136–79. Print.

Weiten, Wayne. *Psychology: Themes & Variations* 8th ed. Belmont, CA: Wadsworth/Cengage, 2010. Print.

CHAPTER 4

Narration

Narrative is the oldest and most compelling method of holding someone's attention; everyone wants to be told a story. —WILLIAM ZINSSER

Narration is the storytelling mode of writing. The minute you say to someone,
"You won't believe what happened to me this morning," you have launched
into a narrative. To understand how narration works, let's have a look at the story
of a young man's arrival, after an arduous journey, in the city of Philadelphia:

> I walked up the street, gazing about till near the market-house I met a boy
> with bread. I had made many a meal on bread, and, inquiring where he got
> it, I went immediately to the baker's he directed me to, in Second-street, and
> ask'd for bisket, intending such as we had in Boston; but they, it seems, were
> not made in Philadelphia. Then I asked for a three-penny loaf, and was told
> they had none such. So not considering or knowing the difference of money,
> and the greater cheapness nor the names of his bread, I bade him give me
> three-penny worth of any sort. He gave me, accordingly, three great puffy
> rolls. I was surpriz'd at the quantity, but took it, and, having no room in my
> pockets, walk'd off with a roll under each arm, and eating the other. Thus I
> went up Market-street as far as Fourth-street, passing by the door of Mr.
> Read, my future wife's father; when she, standing at the door, saw me, and
> thought I made, as I certainly did, a most awkward, ridiculous appearance.
> Then I turned and went down Chestnut-street and part of Walnut-street, eat-
> ing my roll all the way, and, coming round, found myself again at Market-
> street wharf, near the boat I came in, to which I went for a draught of the
> river water; and, being filled with one of my rolls, gave the other two to a
> woman and her child that came down the river in the boat with us, and were
> waiting to go farther.
> —BENJAMIN FRANKLIN, *Autobiography*

Defining Narrative:
Telling What Happened

What makes Franklin's text a narrative? Like all narratives, the story of his arrival in Philadelphia is an account of events. It answers the question "What happened?"—to a particular person in a particular place and time. Young Franklin arrived in the city, shopped for bread, ate, gazed and strolled about, saw a young woman, performed an act of charity.

Narratives focus on events, but you do not have to live a life of high adventure or witness extraordinary acts in order to write a compelling narrative. The events in Franklin's story, you'll notice, are all perfectly ordinary; they could have happened to anybody. The interest, even the drama, that we all enjoy in a well-told story often comes not so much from the nature of the events themselves as from how they are presented.

> Lynda Barry builds a narrative around the ordinary events of a school day (p. 84).

In this chapter, we will examine how to come up with the raw materials for a story, how to select details from those raw materials to suit your purpose and audience, and how to organize those details as a narrative—by the use of chronology, transitions, verb tenses, and plot. We will also review the critical points to watch for as you read over a narrative, as well as common errors to avoid when you edit. But first, let's consider *why* we write narratives at all—and how they can help us to make a point.

Why Do We Write Narratives?

Everybody likes a good story, and we tell stories for many reasons: to connect with other people, to entertain, to record what people said and did, to explain the significance of events, to persuade others to act in a certain way, or to accept our point of view on an issue. Ben Franklin, for example, tells his famous story at the beginning of his *Autobiography* in order to capture the reader's attention right off the bat—and to set the scene for the rest of his life story.

Brief illustrative narratives, or ANECDOTES, appear in all kinds of writing, often at the beginning. Writers typically use them to grab the reader's interest and then lead into their main points, much as a graduation speaker opens with a humorous story or poignant tale before getting down to the serious business of talking about life after college.

Franklin's great point in his *Autobiography* is to show readers how he succeeded in life, and so he begins with the story of his humble arrival in Philadelphia as a

THE SUCCESS STORY

One common narrative pattern, which Ben Franklin practically invented in his famous *Autobiography*, is the success story. As in many fairy tales, the central event of such a narrative is the transformation of the hero or heroine. One reading in this chapter that uses a variation on this pattern is Phil Holland's "Render Unto Larry's," which tells how the author succeeded in righting a wrong he had committed almost fifty years before.

To see how you can use the success-story pattern in your own writing—and how narratives differ from the actual events on which they are based—think of a successful person you might write about and make a list of key events in that person's life. Then identify a "turning point"—a particular event or series of events that changed the fortunes of your hero or heroine forever. Divide the rest of the events on your list into "before" and "after." Imagine the story you might construct around this outline.

Now take the same person and life events and consider how you would arrange them according to some other pattern, such as a journey or a fall from grace. This time, instead of dividing your narrative into before and after, imagine a different story line—a meandering path or a downward spiral. As you can see, you would end up telling a different story about the same person.

young man from the provinces. That way, says Franklin, "you may in your mind compare such unlikely beginnings with the figure I have since made."

Toni Morrison's point in "Strangers" is "that there are no strangers" (p. 110, ¶9).

Although a good story can be an end in itself, this chapter focuses on narratives that are written to make a point or support an argument. Such a narrative can be a brief part of a longer work, or it can be used to structure an entire essay.

Suppose you are a geneticist, and you are writing about mitochondrial DNA and how it can be used to study human evolution. (Mitochondrial DNA is passed down, unaltered, from generation to generation on the mother's side.) Suppose, further, that you have isolated seven strains of mitochondrial DNA and traced them back to the seven prehistoric female ancestors of all persons presently alive. How would you convey your exciting conclusions to a general audience?

Bryan Sykes, a professor of genetics at the Institute of Molecular Medicine at Oxford University, recently had to solve this problem because his research team had isolated those seven separate lines of human descent. He decided to convey the findings by recreating the story of each of these "seven daughters of Eve," whose DNA can be identified by modern research methods.

Here is how he concludes his narrative about one of them, a woman who lived forty-five thousand years ago:

> Ursula had no idea, of course, that both her daughters would give rise, through their children and grandchildren, to a continuous maternal line stretching to the present day. She had no idea she was to become the clan mother, the only woman of that time who could make that claim. Every single member of her clan can trace a direct and unbroken line back to Ursula. Her clan were the first modern humans successfully to colonize Europe. Within a comparatively short space of time they had spread across the whole continent, edging the Neanderthals into extinction. Today about 11 percent of modern Europeans are the direct maternal descendants of Ursula. They come from all parts of Europe, but the clan is particularly well represented in western Britain and Scandinavia. —BRYAN SYKES, *The Seven Daughters of Eve*

Sykes' story about Ursula efficiently explains a number of complicated points about genetic studies and human descent. By giving each of the maternal ancestors a story, Sykes makes his findings much easier to understand—and to remember. Sometimes there's no better way to make a point than by telling a good story—*if* it really fits the subject you are writing about and doesn't go off on a tangent.

Composing a Narrative

Let's go back to the adventures of Ben Franklin for a moment. How did Franklin know, on his initial stroll around the city, that the young woman he saw standing at Mr. Read's door would one day be his wife? Obviously, he couldn't know this when he first saw her. Franklin's reference to his future wife shows us not that young Franklin was psychic but that his narrative has been carefully composed— after the fact, as all narratives are.

As the author of a narrative, you know everything that is going to happen, so you can present events in any order you please. However, if you want anyone else to understand the point you are trying to make, you need to compose your narrative carefully. Consider, first of all, your AUDIENCE and your PURPOSE for writing. Then think about which details to include and how to organize those details so that readers can follow your story and see your point in telling it. To make your story a compelling one, be sure to give it a PLOT and tell it from a consistent POINT OF VIEW.

Thinking about Purpose and Audience

The first thing to do as you compose a narrative is to think hard about the audience you want to reach and the purpose your narrative is intended to serve. Suppose you are emailing a friend about a visit to a computer store, and your purpose is simply to say what you did yesterday. In this case, your narrative can ramble on about how you got to the store, discovered it was much larger than you expected, went into the monitor section and looked around, then wandered over to the printers and couldn't get a salesperson's attention, but eventually spoke to a very helpful manager, and so on. The story might end with your emerging triumphantly from the store with a good printer at a good price. It wouldn't matter much that your story goes on and on because you're writing to a friendly reader who is interested in everything you do and has time to listen.

Now suppose you are writing an advertisement, the purpose of which is to sell printers to the general public. You could still write about your visit to a computer store, but you would tell your story differently because you now have a different purpose and audience: "When I walked into ComputerDaze, I couldn't believe my eyes. Printers everywhere! And the cheap prices! Plus they give you a ream of paper absolutely free! I went home with a printer under each arm." Or suppose you are writing a column in a computer magazine, and your purpose is to show readers how to shop for a printer by telling them about the problems you dealt with as you shopped. You might write: "The first hurdle I encountered was the numbing variety of brands and models."

Not familiar with Afghani table manners? Saira Shah fills you in, p. 99.

Whatever your purpose, you will want to think about how much your audience is likely to know about your subject—computers, for instance—so you can judge how much background information you need to give, how much technical language you can use, what terms you may need to define, and so on. If you are writing for an audience that knows nothing about computers and peripherals, for instance, you might even have to explain what an external hard drive is before you tell your readers how to buy or use one.

Generating Ideas:
Asking What Happened—and Who, Where, When, How, and Why

Before you can tell a good story, you have to have a story to tell. How do you come up with the raw materials for a narrative in the first place? BRAINSTORMING, CLUSTERING, and other methods can help you generate ideas. But a narrative is not just a kind of writing; it is also a way of thinking, one that can help you find ideas to write about. How do you get started? Let's look at an example.

Consider the following passage in which Annie Dillard tells about what happened one Saturday afternoon when her father was preparing to leave for a trip:

Getting ready for the trip one Saturday, he roamed around our big brick house snapping his fingers. He had put a record on: Sharkey Bonano, "Li'l Liza Jane." I was reading Robert Louis Stevenson on the sunporch: *Kidnapped*. I looked up from my book and saw him outside; he had wandered out to the lawn and was standing in the wind between the buckeye trees and looking up at what must have been a small patch of wild sky. Old Low-Pockets. He was six feet four, all lanky and leggy; he had thick brown hair and shaggy brows, and a mild and dreamy expression in his blue eyes.

—ANNIE DILLARD, *An American Childhood*

We can only imagine the exact process by which a superb writer like Dillard brought to light the vivid details of her past to form a passage like this. However, we do know that she wrote it many years after the fact, and so she must have probed her memory to find the details for her narrative.

As she prepared to write about her past experience, Dillard may well have asked herself the questions that journalists typically ask when developing a story: who, what, where, when, how, and why? Certainly her narrative answers most of those questions: *who* (she and her father), *what* (reading and listening to music), *where* (on the sunporch), *when* (one Saturday), *why* (to get ready for a trip).

If Dillard had stopped her questioning here, though, she would have turned up only the skeleton of a narrative, one that might read something like this:

Getting ready for his trip, Father roamed around the house listening to music while I read on the sunporch. He wandered outside and looked up at the sky. He was tall with thick hair and blue eyes.

This is the beginning of a narrative, but only the beginning, because it lacks the vivid details by which Dillard brings the past to life.

When you are planning a narrative, then, keep asking *who, what, where, when, how,* and *why*. Look for lots of particular details, both visual and auditory. "Just take a period," the writer John Steinbeck once advised a friend who was trying to write his life story. "Then try to remember it so clearly that you can see things: what colors and how warm or cold and how you got there. . . . It is important to tell what people looked like, how they walked, what they wore, what they ate." That way, instead of a generic girl with a nameless book and an anonymous man listening to unidentified music, your readers will see and hear Old Low-Pockets snapping his fingers as "Li'l Liza Jane" plays in the background and you pore over *Kidnapped*.

You will also want your readers to know *why* you're telling this particular story. In Dillard's case, the who, what, where, and when are vividly presented. We can see the scene, and everything that happens in it, clearly. But the *why*—Why is her father preparing for a trip? Why is she telling the story?—is not so obvious.

As it happens, Dillard's father is about to leave his family in Pittsburgh and his job at the American Standard Company and take off down the Ohio River, heading, ultimately, to New Orleans, birthplace of jazz. Dillard could have simply told us that her father was an impractical man who suffered from wanderlust and a romantic notion of the cool life far away from the familiar world of manufacturing and plumbing fixtures. However, by constructing a narrative in which her father snaps his fingers to a jazz tune with a "dreamy expression" in his eyes, Dillard not only makes her point, she gives evidence in support of it at the same time. Every detail in her narrative is carefully selected to make that point.

Even the title of Dillard's memoir suggests why she is telling her story (p. 90).

Organizing and Drafting a Narrative

Once you've figured out what's going to happen in your narrative, it's time to get down to the business of organizing your material and writing a draft. As you draft a narrative, your task is to turn the *facts* of what happened into a *story* of what happened. To do this, you will need to put the events in CHRONOLOGICAL ORDER, connect them with appropriate TRANSITIONS and verb tenses, give your narrative a PLOT—and somehow indicate the point you are making. The templates on page 69 can help you get started.

STATING YOUR POINT

Most of the narrative writing you do as a student will be for the purpose of making some kind of point, and sometimes you'll want to state that point explicitly. If you are writing about information technology for an economics class, for example, you might tell your story about going to a computer store; and you would probably want to explain why you were telling about the experience in a THESIS statement like this: "Go into any computer store today, and you will discover that information technology is the main product of American business."

FOLLOWING CHRONOLOGICAL ORDER

In his arrival narrative, Ben Franklin's point is to show how far he's going to go from his humble beginnings. To this end, he arranges events in chronological order. First his arrival; then breakfast, followed by a stroll around the town; next comes the encounter with Miss Read; and, finally, the return to the wharf and the dispensing of the bread—all in the order in which they occurred *in time*. There is no law that says events in a narrative have to follow chronological order, and there are times when you will want to deviate from it. As a general rule, though, arrange events chronologically so your reader doesn't have to figure out what happened when.

TEMPLATES FOR DRAFTING

When you begin to draft a narrative, you need to say who or what the narrative is about, where it takes place, and what's happening as the story opens—moves fundamental to any narrative. See how Toni Morrison makes such moves in the beginning of her essay in this chapter:

> I am in this river place—newly mine—walking in the yard when I see a woman sitting on the seawall at the edge of a neighbor's garden.
> —TONI MORRISON, "Strangers"

Morrison says who her narrative is about ("I," "a woman"); where it takes place ("in this river place"); and what is happening as the story opens ("I see a woman"). Here are two more examples from this chapter:

> This is the true story of a dyed-in-the-wool pacifist Jewish woman who recently spent two days at the Marine Corps Base at Quantico, Virginia, and survived, almost intact.   —ANNE BERNAYS, "Warrior Day"

> I closed the door to the sterile white examination room to face a thin, pale young boy, fourteen years old and sitting on the exam table with his knees pulled to his chest.   —JEFF GREMMELS, "The Clinic"

The following templates can help you make some of these basic moves in your own writing. But don't take these as formulas where you just fill in the blanks. There are no shortcuts to good writing, but these templates can serve as starting points.

▶ This is a story about _____.
▶ The time and place of my story are _____ and _____.
▶ As the narrative opens, X is in the act of _____.
▶ What happened next was _____, followed by _____ and _____.
▶ At this point, _____.
▶ The climax of these events was _____.
▶ When X understood what had happened, he / she said "_____."
▶ The last thing that happened to X was _____.
▶ My point in telling this story is to show that _____.

ADDING TRANSITIONS

Notice the many direct references to time in Ben Franklin's narrative: *then, immediately, when, again.* No doubt, you can think of countless others: *first, last, not long after, next, while, thereafter, once upon a time.* Such direct references to the order of time can be boring in a narrative if they become too predictable, as in *first, second, third.* But used judiciously, such transitions provide smooth links from one event to another, as do other connecting words and phrases like *thus, therefore, consequently, what happened next, before I knew it, as he came back to the dock.*

USING APPROPRIATE VERB TENSES

In addition to clear transition words, your verb tenses, especially the sequence of tenses, can help you to connect events in time. To review for a moment: An action in the past perfect tense (he *had arrived*) occurs before an action in the past tense (he *arrived*), which occurs before an action in the present tense (he *arrives*), which occurs before an action in the future tense (he *will arrive*). Actions in the present perfect (he *has arrived*) may start in the past and continue in the present.

Many of the verbs in Franklin's narrative are in the simple past tense: *walked, went, ask'd, thought, found, gave.* "I had made many a meal on bread," however, is in the past perfect tense because the action had already occurred many times *before* young Franklin asked for directions to the bakery.

Tense sequences mark the time of actions in relation to one another. Thus, all actions that happen more or less at the same time in your narrative should be in the same tense: "The young man got off the boat, went to the bakery, and walked around the town." Don't shift tenses needlessly; but when you *do* need to indicate that one action happened before another in time, be sure to change tenses accordingly—and accurately. Sometimes you may need to shift out of chronological order altogether. (It's called a FLASHBACK if you shift back in time, a FLASH-FORWARD if you shift into the future.) Most of the time, however, stick to chronology.

Notice how often Franklin uses *-ing* forms of verbs: *gazing, inquiring, intending, considering, knowing, having, eating, passing, standing, eating* (again), *coming, being, waiting.* Putting *-ing* on the end of a verb makes the verb progressive. If Franklin's writing seems especially vivid, part of his secret lies in those progressive verb forms, which show past actions as if they are still going on as we read about them more than two centuries later.

DEVELOPING A PLOT

Connecting events in chronological order is always better than presenting them haphazardly. Chronology alone, however, no matter how faithfully followed, is insufficient for organizing a good narrative. A narrative, yes; a good narrative, no.

Suppose Ben Franklin returned for a visit to modern-day Philadelphia and filed the following account:

I took 76 East (the Schuylkill Expressway) to 676 East, exited at Broad Street (the first exit) and continued straight on Vine Street to 12th Street. Then I turned right and proceeded two blocks to the Convention Center. There I paused for lunch (a Caesar salad with three great puffy rolls), afterward continuing my journey down 12th and back to Vine. Proceeding east for some distance, I then rounded Franklin Square, crossed the Franklin Bridge, and entered into New Jersey.

This account is, technically, a narrative, and it follows chronological order. By comparison with the original, however, it is pretty dull. If it went on like this for another paragraph or two, most readers would give up long before Franklin got back to Boston. Little more than an itinerary, this narrative moves steadfastly from place to place, but it doesn't really get anywhere because it has no plot.

Whether we read about pirates on the high seas or hobbits and rings of power, one of the most important elements that can make or break the story is how well it is plotted. It is no different when you write narratives of your own—events need to be related in such a way that one leads directly to, or causes, another. Taken together, the events in your narrative should have a beginning, a middle, and an end. Then your narrative will form a complete action: a plot.

One of the best ways to plot a narrative is to set up a situation; introduce a conflict; build up the dramatic tension until it reaches a high point, or CLIMAX; then release the tension and resolve the conflict. Consider the following little horror story, replete with a giant insect. First we set up the situation:

Little Miss Muffet sat on a tuffet
Eating her curds and whey.

Now comes the conflict:

Along came a spider

Then the climax:

Who sat down beside her

And finally the resolution:

And frightened Miss Muffet away.

You knew all along how it was going to end; but it's still a satisfying story because it's tightly plotted with a keen sense of completion at the close.

Back to Ben Franklin's narrative. One reason this story of starting out in Philadelphia is among the most famous personal narratives in American literature, even though it's just one paragraph, is that it has a carefully organized plot—a *beginning* action (the hero's arrival); a *middle* (the stroll), in which a complication is introduced and the tension rises as the young hero sees his future wife and appears ridiculous; and an *ending* (the return to the wharf), in which the narrative tension is resolved as the hero comes back to his starting point and dispenses bounty in the form of the bread.

MAINTAINING A CONSISTENT POINT OF VIEW

Such is the difference between life and a *narrative* of life: life happens, often in disorderly fashion; a narrative, by contrast, must be carefully composed—from a particular point of view. Why do you think Annie Dillard wrote that her father looked up "at what must have been a small patch of wild sky"? Why didn't she just come out and say that the sky *was* wild? The reason is that, as the NARRATOR, or teller of her story, Dillard is speaking from the vantage point of herself as a child sitting on the sunporch. From that point of view, she could not logically have seen the sky as her father saw it.

As you construct a narrative, you need to maintain a logical and consistent point of view. Don't attribute perceptions to yourself or your narrator that are physically impossible ("I lay inside on the sofa while Old Low-Pockets wandered out to the lawn. His back to the house, he stared dreamily in the direction of his impending journey. A tear came into his eye"). If you do claim to see (or know) more than you reasonably can from where you sit, your credibility with the reader will soon be strained.

In a narrative written in the grammatical FIRST PERSON (*I* or *we*), like Dillard's, the speaker can be both an observer of the scene ("I looked up from my book and saw him outside") *and* a participant in the action ("I was reading Robert Louis Stevenson on the sunporch"). In a narrative written in the grammatical THIRD PERSON (*he, she, it,* or *they*), as is the case in most articles and history books (and in Bryan Sykes' narrative about Ursula), however, the narrator is often merely an observer, though sometimes an all-knowing one.

> A writer uses *she* instead of *I* to give a nuanced view of the Marine Corps on p. 104.

ADDING DIALOGUE

In contrast to narratives told in the third person—which can have unlimited points of view—first-person narratives are *always* limited to telling us only what the narrator knows or imagines. There is a means, however, by which even first-person narrators can introduce the points of view of other people into a story. That is by the use of dialogue, or quoting their direct speech. "Lie on your back," her mother tells young Dillard elsewhere in her narrative. "Look at the clouds and figure out what they look like."

As a first-person narrator, Dillard might have written, "My mother told me to look at the clouds and figure out what they look like." But these words would be filtered through Dillard's point of view. They would be a step removed from the person who said them and so would lack the immediacy of direct dialogue.

Suppose you are a witness to an accident in which a pedestrian was hit by a turning car, and you want to tell what happened—in a police report, say. Your narrative might begin with an account of how you noticed a car stopped at a red light and then saw another car approach suddenly from the right and pause. After the light changed, the first car went straight ahead; then the second car turned left. At the same time, a pedestrian, who had been trying to cross behind the first car, moved into the middle of the street and was hit by the turning car.

Why did the pedestrian cross the street against traffic? Your narrative can't say for sure because you don't know what was going on in the pedestrian's mind. If, however, you (or the police) approached the man and started asking him questions as he pulled himself to his feet, his point of view might be revealed in the ensuing dialogue.

Then, if you incorporated that dialogue into your narrative, you would not only capture another person's motives and point of view, but your narrative would be more interesting and lively:

"Why did you cross the street?"
"The stoplight was red and the little man on the pedestrian sign was on."
"Did you see the car turning in your direction as you crossed?"
"No, the stopped car was blocking my view."
"After it started up, did you see the other car?"
"Yes."
"Why did you cross anyway?"
"The little man told me to."

You can *tell* the reader of your narrative that someone is delusional or means well or would never hurt a fly. But if you let people in your narrative speak for themselves and *show* what they are thinking, the reader can draw his or her own conclusions. Then your story will seem more credible, your characters will come to life, and your whole narrative will have a greater dramatic impact.

USING OTHER METHODS

Narratives don't take place in a vacuum. As you tell what happens in your narrative, you'll likely need to draw on other methods of writing as well. For example, to show why your characters (the people in your narrative) do what they do, you may need to analyze the CAUSES AND EFFECTS of

The main effect of Phil Holland's boyhood transgression is adult guilt (p. 95).

their actions. Or you may want to COMPARE AND CONTRAST one character with another. Almost certainly, you will want to DESCRIBE the characters and the physical setting of your narrative in some detail.

In Franklin's case, for instance, the description of his "awkward, ridiculous appearance" as he walks around the streets of Philadelphia "with a roll under each arm" is important to the story. The tattered young man may look foolish now—but not for long. This is an American success story, and already the new arrival is staking out his territory.

Reading a Narrative with a Critical Eye

Once you have drafted a narrative, it's always a good idea to ask someone else to read it. And, of course, you yourself will want to review what you have written from the standpoint of a critical reader. Here are some questions to keep in mind when checking a narrative.

PURPOSE AND AUDIENCE. Does the narrative serve the purpose it is intended to serve? Is it appropriate for its intended audience? Does it need any additional background information or definitions?

THE STORY. Does it consist mainly of actions and events? Do they constitute a plot, with a clear beginning, middle, and end? Is every action in the narrative necessary to the plot? Have any essential actions been left out?

THE POINT. Does the narrative have a clear point to make? What is it? Is it stated explicitly in a thesis? If not, should it be?

ORGANIZATION. Is the story line easy to follow? Are the events in chronological order? Are there any unintentional lapses in chronology or verb tense? Are intentional deviations from chronology, such as flashbacks, clearly indicated?

TRANSITIONS. Are there clear transitions to help readers follow the sequence of events? Have you checked over each transition to see that it logically connects the adjoining parts of the narrative?

DIALOGUE AND POINT OF VIEW. If there is no dialogue in the narrative, would some direct speech help bring it to life? If there is dialogue, does it sound like real people talking? Is the narrative told from a consistent, plausible point of view?

DETAILS. Does the narrative include lots of concrete details, especially visual and auditory ones? Does it show as well as tell?

THE BEGINNING. Will the beginning of the narrative get the reader's attention? How? How well does it set up what follows? How else might the narrative begin?

THE ENDING. How satisfying is it? What does it leave the reader thinking or feeling? How else might the narrative end?

Editing for Common Errors in Narrative Writing

As with other kinds of writing, narration calls for distinctive patterns of language and punctuation—and thus invites certain kinds of errors. The following tips will help you check your writing for errors that often appear in narratives.

Check verb tenses to make sure they accurately indicate when actions occur

Because narrative writing focuses on actions or events—what happens or happened—it relies mightily on verbs. Some writers get confused about when to use the simple past tense (Ben *arrived*), the present perfect (Ben *has arrived*), and the past perfect (Ben *had arrived*).

Use the simple past to indicate actions completed at a specified time in the past.

▶ He has completed the assignment this morning.

Use the present perfect to indicate actions begun and completed at some unspecified time in the past, or actions begun in the past and continuing into the present.

▶ The war in the north ~~goes~~ has gone on for five years now.
▶ For five years now, the insurgents have fought in the north.

Use the past perfect to indicate actions completed by a specific time in the past or before another past action occurred.

▶ The bobcats arrived next, but by then the muskrats had moved out.

Check dialogue to be sure it's punctuated correctly

Narrative writing often includes the direct quotation of what people say. Punctuating dialogue can be challenging because you have to deal with the punctuation in the dialogue itself and also with any punctuation necessary to integrate the dialogue into the text.

Commas and periods always go inside the quotation marks.

▶ "Perspective in painting is hard to define," my art history professor said.
▶ She then noted that in Western painting, "perspective means one thing."

Semicolons and colons always go outside the quotation marks.

> ▶ But "in Asian painting, it means quite another"; then she went on to clarify.

> ▶ Asian painting presents the landscape "in layers": from the tops of mountains to the undersides of leaves in the same picture.

Question marks, exclamation points, and dashes go *inside* the quotation marks if they are part of the quoted text but *outside* if they are not part of the quoted text.

> ▶ The teacher asked, "Sam, how would you define perspective in art?"

> ▶ Did you say, "Divine perspective"?

Student Example

Jeff Gremmels was a medical student at the University of Illinois College of Medicine at Rockford when he wrote "The Clinic." As part of his training, Gremmels saw patients weekly at one of the university's primary care centers. This selection centers on a particularly difficult case—one in which the novice doctor needs to look beyond physical explanations.

"The Clinic" won first prize in an essay competition sponsored by the University of Illinois College of Medicine. Why would a college of medicine promote a writing contest? "Because writing is a good way to clarify our thoughts and feelings," said Margaret Maynard, the microbiologist in charge of the contest. Also, she notes, the college "wanted to foster a compassionate, humanitarian approach to the practice of medicine . . . to graduate caring, concerned doctors, not just technically gifted ones." "The Clinic" suggests that the author, now a practicing radiologist in Illinois and Missouri, was well on his way to becoming just such a physician. First published in the *Rockford Register Star* in 1998, this essay has also appeared in *Becoming Doctors*, an anthology of essays by medical students.

The Clinic

FIRST-PERSON point of view

Every Wednesday, as part of my second-year medical student experience in Rockford, I travel north to see patients at the UIC University Primary Care Clinic at Rockton. Early this past winter, I was handed the chart of a new patient and I was told I was seeing him for "stomachaches." I closed the door to the sterile white

examination room to face a thin, pale young boy, fourteen years old
and sitting on the exam table with his knees pulled to his chest. His
head jumped as the exam door snapped briskly shut. I introduced
myself and crouched at eye-level next to him. He tightened the grip
on his knees. "What's wrong?" Silence filled the bleach-tinged air,
and his eyes stared at me, unblinking.

DESCRIPTIVE details set the scene and focus on the patient

"He's not eating anything, says his stomach hurts." The voice
came from the mother in the corner of the room. I hadn't even
noticed her as I entered, all my attention focused immediately on
the tensed figure on the bed. "For the past two weeks, it's been
nothing but cereal, and only a handful of that." I listened to the
mother sketch a history of nausea, stomachaches, and absent stares.
It gave the impression of more than the typical stomachache, and I
plied ahead, waiting to finally ask the key question that slipped the
knot on this mystery and sent the bacteria or virus or swallowed
garden flower culprit plummeting into my lap. The knot refused
to give.

2

DIALOGUE provides information narrator did not know

Narrator introduces a key conflict into the PLOT

"Where did he get the bruises?" I ventured, hoping to unearth some
bleeding disorder with a forgotten manifestation of gastrointestinal
symptoms. The mother looked at the scattered marks around the redhead's temples through her friendly librarian glasses, then up at me.

3

"He's very active, normally, and <u>gets</u> into all sorts of spots. He
<u>comes</u> in from the woods with new cuts and scrapes every night.
You <u>should have seen</u> him after the big rains, all mud and torn
jeans." With this she <u>looked</u> back at the alabaster boy huddling on
the bed and <u>smiled</u> with the memory of his past spirit.

4

Mother uses present and past perfect tenses to refer to earlier actions by her son; narrator uses past tense to describe mother's actions in the exam room

A professor teaching our physical diagnosis class told us we
should know 80 percent of the cases coming before us by hearing
the history alone. This case was quickly proving itself the undesired
20 percent. I moved to the physical exam. The boy was not keen on
the concept of my examining him, and made his desires very clear as
he refused every request to look up at me or to open his clamped
mouth. I wanted to solve this puzzle and began to insist more
forcefully until finally, with his surprisingly strong mother, I

5

Events in exam room presented in CHRONOLOGICAL ORDER

managed to pull his loose shirt over his head. Beneath that shirt lay pale doughy skin, its spongy texture belying the taut musculature beneath. On the surface of the skin was a continuation of the light bruising around his temples. As the mother sat down and the boy resumed his curled-ball posture, my eyes picked out almost one-dozen small, red "U"s, with two small bars between the uprights like a German umlaut.[1] Raised and bright, more like a rash or burn than a bruise, I hoped these would be the clues I needed to solve my mystery of the afternoon. Further examination revealed nothing more than a continuation of the pattern down to his ankles.

I combed my cloudy memories of past lectures for anything reminiscent of this strange mark <u>as</u> I walked up the hall to find a doctor. The search failed to exhume any diseases with ties to Germanic vowels.

6

<u>As</u> I explained my cryptic findings to the attending physician, I saw her eyes quickly open, contradicting my belief that she was actually asleep. Pushing insurance papers towards me, she quickly stated, "I'm going to look at him. I want you to have the mother fill these out in the waiting room." I followed her white lab coat to the exam room and completed my assigned mission. I returned from the waiting room—despite the mother's distant protests of having already completed the same forms—to find the attending physician on the phone and admitting my patient directly to hospital care.

7

<u>Twenty-five minutes later</u>, I again sat in her office, listening to the diagnosis. "The wheels of a lighter, a disposable lighter, leave those two umlaut marks—nothing else looks like it. It's almost always abuse in his age group." I couldn't think of any reply, and we spent several minutes gazing into the carpet, silent and introspective. I left the clinic alone and went directly to my apartment, missing the evening lecture on "Insulin and Diabetic Control."

8

TRANSITIONS increase suspense, then lead to CLIMAX of plot

---

1. *Umlaut*: A two-dot diacritical mark that appears over certain vowels in German (in this instance, Ü).

<u>Four days later</u>, I went to the hospital to see the boy who was once my patient. I read the psychiatrist's chart notes slowly, rereading the passages describing the boy's abuse by his stepfather and his three-year history of self-mutilation and depression. It never entered my mind, so avid for a solution, to ask for a history of hospitalizations or illness, and I felt the cavernous shadows of my own missing knowledge hinting at their depth. My focus had always been on the disease, the physiologic atrocity accosting the patient's unsuspecting organs and cells. This was my first glimpse into an arena I had utterly neglected—the patient's psyche—quietly present in everyone and in every disease.

9 · · · · More transitions lead to narrator's final understanding of events

<u>Entering the boy's room</u>, I found him asleep, an IV pole standing sentry over his frail visage. I picked up a crumpled note from the floor, smoothing it to reveal the young patient's shaky handwriting:

10

> I wish I were a paper airplane,
> Soaked in gas, shooting red flames,
> burning with an orange glow, over
> all the people below.
> I could fall through the sky
> like a comet or a meteorite.
> I could become a UFO,
> become someone I did not know.

Years of lectures, labs, and research could not match the education I received in five days with this single boy.

11 · · · · Narrator's main point in telling the story

Analyzing a Student Narrative

In "The Clinic," Jeff Gremmels draws upon rhetorical strategies and techniques that good writers use all the time when they write a narrative. The following questions, in addition to focusing on particular aspects of Gremmels' text, will help you to identify those common strategies and techniques so you can adapt them to your own writing. These questions will also help to prepare you for the analytical questions—on content, structure, and language—that you'll find after all the other selections in this chapter, along with suggestions for writing on related topics.

READING CLOSELY

1. A key question to ask about any narrative is "Whose story is it?" Would you say "The Clinic" is the boy's story or the medical student's? Or both? Why?

2. Why is Jeff Gremmels unable, on his own, to determine what is wrong with his patient? How does the attending physician figure it out?

3. When the attending physician explains the strange marks on the patient's body, Gremmels says he "couldn't think of any reply" (8). Why is the student doctor left speechless?

STRATEGIES AND STRUCTURES

1. What is Gremmels' PURPOSE in writing about this particular experience? How do you know?

2. "The Clinic" is told as a medical detective story. Why do you think Gremmels chose that genre?

3. Make a list of the main clues in this case. How does Gremmels reveal them to the reader, and how do these clues advance the narrative?

4. The last sentence of his essay, Gremmels says, "was put there because I suspected the medical school judges would like it. I, personally, think the story should end with the poem" (11). What do you think? Why?

5. *Other Methods.* As a rule, mystery stories present EFFECTS, and the detective has to figure out CAUSES. Is this true of "The Clinic"? Explain.

THINKING ABOUT LANGUAGE

1. Why does Gremmels introduce the METAPHOR of the knot in paragraph 2?

2. The DENOTATION of "exhume" is "to find or uncover" (6). What are the CONNOTATIONS of the word here, and what does the word contribute to the narrative?

3. In paragraph 9, the second-year medical student mentions the "cavernous shadows of my own missing knowledge." Is this phrase appropriate, in your opinion? Why or why not? How does it affect the TONE of the essay? Explain.

FOR WRITING

1. Write a paragraph or two narrating from your perspective a visit to a doctor—or a teacher, counselor, or someone else you've gone to for help. Put the events of the visit in chronological order, and use transitions as needed to lead your reader through the story. Pay particular attention to the first sentence; see if you can make it introduce your main point. Then, switch perspectives, and

rewrite your narrative from the POINT OF VIEW of the other person. Keep in mind how he or she might see both you and the visit differently than you do.

2. Write a narrative essay about some problem you had to diagnose and solve. The problem can be about anything—a car or computer, for example, or a friend or family member. Try to develop a PLOT that will get and hold readers' interest.

A Vanity License Plate

In only two words, the license plate of this sports car tells a story. It may not tell the whole story of the courtship and marriage *before* the divorce, but we know how the story ended: she got the Porsche. Narratives tell what happened (however briefly). To construct a compelling narrative, as this ad does, you need to set up a situation (such as a troubled marriage) in a particular time (the recent past) and place (a tree-shaded, urban neighborhood of elegant townhouses); then introduce a conflict (divorce proceedings would qualify); build up the tension (she wants his car); and resolve the conflict (she gets it). More than just a tale of conflict and revenge, however, this story has a point to make. The law firm of Sanders, Lyn & Ragonetti wants the reader's business, and it knows that narratives are a good way to attract the attention of potential clients—particularly women seeking a divorce who want to ride off into the sunset in style.

Sanders, Lyn & Ragonetti Associates, Trial Lawyers

202-195 County Court Blvd. Brampton, Ontario L6W 4P7 Tel:(905)450-1711 Fax:(905)450-7066 www.slra.com

LYNDA BARRY

The Sanctuary of School

Lynda Barry (b. 1956) is a cartoonist, novelist, and teacher of writing. Born in Wisconsin, she spent most of her adolescence in Seattle, where she began supporting herself at age sixteen as a janitor. At Evergreen State College in Olympia, Barry began drawing Ernie Pook's Comeek, *the comic strip for which she is perhaps best known. Barry's first novel* Cruddy *(2000) was about a teenager whose troubled family life "in the cruddiest part of town" resembled her own. Her more recent* Picture This *(2010)—a sequel of sorts to her Eisner Award–winning* What It Is *(2008)—is a graphic memoir and how-to book that instructs the reader in the therapeutic uses of art and drawing with the aid of a nearsighted monkey.*

In "The Sanctuary of School," which appeared in the "Education" section of the New York Times *in January 1992, Barry tells how she first discovered the therapeutic value of art—and of good teachers. Her narrative essay carries a pointed message for those who would cut costs in the public school system by removing art from the curriculum.*

I WAS 7 YEARS OLD the first time I snuck out of the house in the dark. It was winter and my parents had been fighting all night. They were short on money and long on relatives who kept "temporarily" moving into our house because they had nowhere else to go.

My brother and I were used to giving up our bedroom. We slept on the couch, something we actually liked because it put us that much closer to the light of our lives, our television.

At night when everyone was asleep, we lay on our pillows watching it with the sound off. We watched Steve Allen's mouth moving. We watched Johnny Carson's mouth moving. We watched movies filled with gangsters shooting machine guns into packed rooms, dying soldiers hurling a last grenade and beautiful women crying at windows. Then the sign-off finally came and we tried to sleep.

The morning I snuck out, I woke up filled with a panic about needing to get to school. The sun wasn't quite up yet but my anxiety was so fierce that I just got dressed, walked quietly across the kitchen and let myself out the back door.

It was quiet outside. Stars were still out. Nothing moved and no one was in the street. It was as if someone had turned the sound off on the world.

SUGGESTED MLA CITATION: Barry, Lynda. "The Sanctuary of School." 1992. *Back to the Lake.* Ed. Thomas Cooley. 2nd ed. New York: Norton, 2012. 84–88. Print.

I walked the alley, breaking thin ice over the puddles with my shoes. I didn't   6
know why I was walking to school in the dark. I didn't think about it. All I knew
was a feeling of panic, like the panic that strikes kids when they realize they are
lost.

That feeling eased the moment I turned the corner and saw the dark outline of my   7
school at the top of the hill. My school was made up of about 15 nondescript portable classrooms set down on a fenced concrete lot in a rundown Seattle neighborhood, but it had the most beautiful view of the Cascade Mountains. You could see
them from anywhere on the playfield and you could see them from the windows of
my classroom—Room 2.

I walked over to the monkey bars and hooked my arms around the cold metal. I   8
stood for a long time just looking across Rainier Valley. The sky was beginning to
whiten and I could hear a few birds.

In a perfect world my absence at home would not have gone unnoticed. I would   9
have had two parents in a panic to locate me, instead of two parents in a panic to
locate an answer to the hard question of survival during a deep financial and emotional crisis.

But in an overcrowded and unhappy home, it's incredibly easy for any child to   10
slip away. The high levels of frustration, depression and anger in my house made
my brother and me invisible. We were children with the sound turned off. And for
us, as for the steadily increasing number of neglected children in this country, the
only place where we could count on being noticed was at school.

"Hey there, young lady. Did you forget to go home last night?" It was Mr. Gunderson,   11
our janitor, whom we all loved. He was nice and he was funny and he was old with
white hair, thick glasses and an unbelievable number of keys. I could hear them jingling
as he walked across the playfield. I felt incredibly happy to see him.

He let me push his wheeled garbage can between the different portables as he   12
unlocked each room. He let me turn on the lights and raise the window shades and
I saw my school slowly come to life. I saw Mrs. Holman, our school secretary, walk
into the office without her orange lipstick on yet. She waved.

I saw the fifth-grade teacher, Mr. Cunningham, walking under the breezeway   13
eating a hard roll. He waved.

And I saw my teacher, Mrs. Claire LeSane, walking toward us in a red coat and   14
calling my name in a very happy and surprised way, and suddenly my throat got
tight and my eyes stung and I ran toward her crying. It was something that surprised us both.

It's only thinking about it now, 28 years later, that I realize I was crying from   15
relief. I was with my teacher, and in a while I was going to sit at my desk, with my

crayons and pencils and books and classmates all around me, and for the next six hours I was going to enjoy a thoroughly secure, warm and stable world. It was a world I absolutely relied on. Without it, I don't know where I would have gone that morning.

Mrs. LeSane asked me what was wrong and when I said "Nothing," she seemingly left it at that. But she asked me if I would carry her purse for her, an honor above all honors, and she asked if I wanted to come into Room 2 early and paint. 16

She believed in the natural healing power of painting and drawing for troubled children. In the back of her room there was always a drawing table and an easel with plenty of supplies, and sometimes during the day she would come up to you 17 for what seemed like no good reason and quietly ask if you wanted to go to the back table and "make some pictures for Mrs. LeSane." We all had a chance at it—to sit apart from the class for a while to paint, draw and silently work out impossible problems on 11 × 17 sheets of newsprint.

Drawing came to mean everything to me. At the back table in Room 2, I learned 18 to build myself a life preserver that I could carry into my home.

We all know that a good education system saves lives, but the people of this 19 country are still told that cutting the budget for public schools is neces- sary, that poor salaries for teachers are all we can manage and that art, music and all creative activities must be the first to go when times are lean.

When you tell a story, it should have a point (p. 68). Here's Barry's.

Before- and after-school programs are cut and we are told that public schools are 20 not made for baby-sitting children. If parents are neglectful temporarily or perma- nently, for whatever reason, it's certainly sad, but their unlucky children must fend for themselves. Or slip through the cracks. Or wander in a dark night alone.

We are told in a thousand ways that not only are public schools not important, 21 but that the children who attend them, the children who need them most, are not important either. We leave them to learn from the blind eye of a television, or to the mercy of "a thousand points of light"[1] that can be as far away as stars.

I was lucky. I had Mrs. LeSane. I had Mr. Gunderson. I had an abundance of art 22 supplies. And I had a particular brand of neglect in my home that allowed me to slip away and get to them. But what about the rest of the kids who weren't as lucky? What happened to them?

By the time the bell rang that morning I had finished my drawing and Mrs. 23 LeSane pinned it up on the special bulletin board she reserved for drawings from the back table. It was the same picture I always drew—a sun in the corner of a blue sky over a nice house with flowers all around it.

Mrs. LeSane asked us to please stand, face the flag, place our right hands over 24 our hearts and say the Pledge of Allegiance. Children across the country do it faith- fully. I wonder now when the country will face its children and say a pledge right back.

1. *"A thousand points of light"*: In his inaugural address on January 20, 1989, President George H. W. Bush used this phrase to refer to "all the community organizations that are spread like stars through- out the Nation, doing good."

READING CLOSELY

1. When she first left home in the dark in a fit of panic and anxiety, why did seven-year-old Lynda Barry instinctively head for her school?

2. What does Barry mean when she writes, "We were children with the sound turned off" (10)? Who fails to hear them? Why?

3. What's the significance of the picture that young Barry always drew when she sat at the art table in the back of Mrs. LeSane's classroom?

4. Why does Barry refer to the Pledge of Allegiance in the last paragraph of her essay?

STRATEGIES AND STRUCTURES

1. Barry characterizes Mrs. LeSane, Mr. Gunderson, and the other adults in her narrative mostly through their gestures and bits of DIALOGUE. Point out several instances, and explain what these small acts and brief words reveal about the people Barry is portraying.

2. Barry DESCRIBES her room at home, the exterior of her school, and her classroom—Room 2—with a few telling details. What are some of those details, and how do they help to set the scene for her narrative?

3. Where and how does Barry present the CAUSES of her childhood panic and sense of anxiety? Of the sense of "sanctuary" that she feels at school?

4. What role does television play in Barry's narrative? Where does she DEFINE that role most explicitly?

5. *Other Methods.* Barry uses her narrative to support an ARGUMENT about public schools in America. What's the point of that argument, and where does she state it most directly?

THINKING ABOUT LANGUAGE

1. Barry refers to children, including herself at a younger age, who "wander in a dark night alone" (20). What are the implications of this METAPHOR, and how has Barry paved the way for it by telling about "the first time I snuck out of the house in the dark" (1)?

2. Barry uses the word *light* to mean different things at different points in her narrative. What are some of them? Why does she say that the "points of light" in a child's life can be "as far away as stars" (21)?

3. Why do you think Barry characterizes her old school as a *sanctuary*—instead of, for example, a *haven* or *safehouse*? Is the term apt? Why or why not?

4. Why does Barry refer to television as having or being "a blind eye" (21)?

FOR WRITING

1. Write a brief narrative about a time when you found school to be a sanctuary (or the opposite). Be sure to describe the physical place and tell what particular people said and did there.

2. Using your narrative as a basis for your argument, write a narrative essay in which you make a point about school and education in a particular locality, such as your hometown, or in the country as a whole.

ANNIE DILLARD

An American Childhood

Annie Dillard (b. 1945) grew up in Pittsburgh with a book in her hand. Her master's thesis at Hollins College was on Thoreau's Walden, *to which her work has been compared. Dillard is known for her meditative essays on nature, collected in* A Pilgrim at Tinker Creek *(1974), which won the Pulitzer Prize for nonfiction, and* Teaching a Stone to Talk *(1982). She's published a novel,* The Maytrees *(2007), and two memoirs,* A Writing Life *(1989) and* An American Childhood *(1987), from which the following was taken.*

This selection is a narrative of childhood, an adventure through Dillard's old neighborhood—and her imagination. Her inspiration? Classic narratives of adventure, such as Robert Louis Stevenson's Kidnapped. *According to Dillard, "you have enough experience by the time you're five years old" to create your own adventure narrative. "What you need is the library. . . . What you have to learn is the best of what is being thought and said. If you [have] a choice between spending a summer in Nepal and spending a summer in the library, go to the library."*

SOME BOYS TAUGHT ME TO PLAY FOOTBALL. This was fine sport. You thought up a new strategy for every play and whispered it to the others. You went out for a pass, fooling everyone. Best, you got to throw yourself mightily at someone's running legs. Either you brought him down or you hit the ground flat on your chin, with your arms empty before you. It was all or nothing. If you hesitated in fear, you would miss and get hurt: you would take a hard fall while the kid got away, or you would get kicked in the face while the kid got away. But if you flung yourself wholeheartedly at the back of his knees—if you gathered and joined body and soul and pointed them diving fearlessly—then you likely wouldn't get hurt, and you'd stop the ball. Your fate, and your team's score, depended on your concentration and courage. Nothing girls did could compare with it.

Boys welcomed me at baseball, too, for I had, through enthusiastic practice, what was weirdly known as a boy's arm. In winter, in the snow, there was neither baseball nor football, so the boys and I threw snowballs at passing cars. I got in trouble throwing snowballs, and have seldom been happier since.

SUGGESTED MLA CITATION: Dillard, Annie. "An American Childhood." 1987. *Back to the Lake.* Ed. Thomas Cooley. 2nd ed. New York: Norton, 2012. 90–93. Print.

With this transition paragraph (p. 70), Dillard introduces the particular day she is telling about.

On one weekday morning after Christmas, six inches of new snow had ₃ just fallen. We were standing up to our boot tops in snow on a front yard on trafficked Reynolds Street, waiting for cars. The cars traveled Reynolds Street slowly and evenly; they were targets all but wrapped in red ribbons, cream puffs. We couldn't miss.

I was seven; the boys were eight, nine, and ten. The oldest two Fahey boys were ₄ there—Mikey and Peter—polite blond boys who lived near me on Lloyd Street, and who already had four brothers and sisters. My parents approved of Mikey and Peter Fahey. Chickie McBride was there, a tough kid, and Billy Paul and Mackie Kean too, from across Reynolds, where the boys grew up dark and furious, grew up skinny, knowing, and skilled. We had all drifted from our houses that morning looking for action, and had found it here on Reynolds Street.

It was cloudy but cold. The cars' tires laid behind them on the snowy street a ₅ complex trail of beige chunks like crenellated castle walls. I had stepped on some earlier; they squeaked. We could have wished for more traffic. When a car came, we all popped it one. In the intervals between cars we reverted to the natural solitude of children.

I started making an iceball—a perfect iceball, from perfectly white snow, per- ₆ fectly spherical, and squeezed perfectly translucent so no snow remained all the way through. (The Fahey boys and I considered it unfair actually to throw an iceball at somebody, but it had been known to happen.)

I had just embarked on the iceball project when we heard tire chains come ₇ clanking from afar. A black Buick was moving toward us down the street. We all spread out, banged together some regular snowballs, took aim, and, when the Buick drew nigh, fired.

A soft snowball hit the driver's windshield right before the driver's face. It made ₈ a smashed star with a hump in the middle.

Often, of course, we hit our target, but this time, the only time in all of life, the ₉ car pulled over and stopped. Its wide black door opened; a man got out of it, running. He didn't even close the car door.

He ran after us, and we ran away from him, up the snowy Reynolds sidewalk. At ₁₀ the corner, I looked back; incredibly, he was still after us. He was in city clothes: a suit and tie, street shoes. Any normal adult would have quit, having sprung us into flight and made his point. This man was gaining on us. He was a thin man, all action. All of a sudden, we were running for our lives.

Wordless, we split up. We were on our turf; we could lose ourselves in the ₁₁ neighborhood backyards, everyone for himself. I paused and considered. Everyone had vanished except Mikey Fahey, who was just rounding the corner of a yellow brick house. Poor Mikey, I trailed him. The driver of the Buick sensibly picked the two of us to follow. The man apparently had all day.

He chased Mikey and me around the yellow house and up a backyard path we   12
knew by heart: under a low tree, up a bank, through a hedge, down some snowy
steps, and across the grocery store's delivery driveway. We smashed through a gap
in another hedge, entered a scruffy backyard and ran around its back porch and
tight between houses to Edgerton Avenue; we ran across Edgerton to an alley
and up our own sliding woodpile to the Halls' front yard; he kept coming. We ran
up Lloyd Street and wound through mazy backyards toward the steep hilltop at
Willard and Lang.

He chased us silently, block after block. He chased us silently over picket fences,   13
through thorny hedges, between houses, around garbage cans, and across streets.
Every time I glanced back, choking for breath, I expected he would have quit. He
must have been as breathless as we were. His jacket strained over his body. It was
an immense discovery, pounding into my hot head with every sliding, joyous step,
that this ordinary adult evidently knew what I thought only children who trained
at football knew: that you have to fling yourself at what you're doing, you have to
point yourself, forget yourself, aim, dive.

Mikey and I had nowhere to go, in our own neighborhood or out of it, but away   14
from this man who was chasing us. He impelled us forward; we compelled him to
follow our route. The air was cold; every breath tore my throat. We kept running,
block after block; we kept improvising, backyard after backyard, running a frantic
course and choosing it simultaneously, failing always to find small places or hard
places to slow him down, and discovering always, exhilarated, dismayed, that only
bare speed could save us—for he would never give up, this man—and we were losing speed.

He chased us through the backyard labyrinths of ten blocks before he caught us   15
by our jackets. He caught us and we all stopped.

We three stood staggering, half blinded, coughing, in an obscure hilltop back-   16
yard: a man in his twenties, a boy, a girl. He had released our jackets, our pursuer,
our captor, our hero: He knew we weren't going anywhere. We all played by the
rules. Mikey and I unzipped our jackets. I pulled off my sopping mittens. Our
tracks multiplied in the backyard's new snow. We had been breaking new snow all
morning. We didn't look at each other. I was cherishing my excitement. The man's
lower pants legs were wet; his cuffs were full of snow, and there was a prow of
snow beneath them on his shoes and socks. Some trees bordered the little flat
backyard, some messy winter trees. There was no one around: a clearing in a grove,
and we the only players.

It was a long time before he could speak. I had some difficulty at first recalling   17
why we were there. My lips felt swollen; I couldn't see out of the sides of my eyes;
I kept coughing.

"You stupid kids," he began perfunctorily.   18

We listened perfunctorily indeed, if we listened at all, for the chewing out was   19
redundant, a mere formality, and beside the point. The point was that he had
chased us passionately without giving up, and so he had caught us. Now he came
down to earth. I wanted the glory to last forever.

But how could the glory have lasted forever? We could have run through every   20
backyard in North America until we got to Panama. But when he trapped us at the
lip of the Panama Canal, what precisely could he have done to prolong the drama
of the chase and cap its glory? I brooded about this for the next few years. He could
only have fried Mikey Fahey and me in boiling oil, say, or dismembered us piece-
meal, or staked us to anthills. None of which I really wanted, and none of which
any adult was likely to do, even in the spirit of fun. He could only chew us out
there in the Panamanian jungle, after months or years of exalting pursuit. He could
only begin, "You stupid kids," and continue in his ordinary Pittsburgh accent with
his normal righteous anger and the usual common sense.

If in that snowy backyard the driver of the black Buick had cut off our heads,   21
Mikey's and mine, I would have died happy, for nothing has required so much of
me since as being chased all over Pittsburgh in the middle of winter—running ter-
rified, exhausted—by this sainted, skinny, furious red-headed man who wished to
have a word with us. I don't know how he found his way back to his car.

READING CLOSELY

1. When she was growing up in Pittsburgh, says Annie Dillard, nothing that girls
   normally did "could compare with" playing football (1). What was so special to
   her about this "boys" sport?

2. How old is Dillard at the time of the big chase? Does it matter that she is the
   youngest in the game—and the only girl? Why or why not?

3. As the chase goes on, Dillard's pursuer becomes her "hero" (16). Why? How,
   according to Dillard, is true "glory" to be achieved in any pursuit (19)?

4. What do the man's appearance and behavior tell us about the America of
   Dillard's childhood?

STRATEGIES AND STRUCTURES

1. Dillard begins her narrative with an account of learning to play football and
   other boys' games. Why is this introduction necessary to the PLOT of the story?

2. As the chase unfolds, Dillard steadily increases the tension between the adversaries. How? Give examples from the text.

3. Dillard gives only the beginning of the victor's lecture, "You stupid kids" (18). Why doesn't she quote his whole speech?

4. What does the young Dillard learn by imagining different outcomes to the chase? What does this lesson reveal about her PURPOSE for writing?

5. *Other Methods.* Dillard's narrative includes vivid DESCRIPTION. Imagine the chase scene without the descriptive detail—of a perfect iceball, for instance, or of what the man was wearing. How does such description contribute to the point Dillard is making in this essay? What do you think that point is?

THINKING ABOUT LANGUAGE

1. What is "righteous anger" (20)? How does it differ from other kinds? Why is such anger "normal" in the time and place that Dillard is describing (20)?

2. What is the meaning of "perfunctorily" (18, 19)? Why is the word appropriate?

3. They were "the only players," says Dillard, when the chase comes to an end (16). In what sense(s) is she using the word *players* here? How is she using "grove" (16)?

FOR WRITING

1. Did you ever get in trouble while playing a childhood sport or game? Write a paragraph about what happened.

2. Write a narrative about an early childhood encounter in which adults did not behave as you expected them to. Be careful to establish a consistent POINT OF VIEW, whether that of a child or of an adult looking back—or both, as Dillard does.

3. Write a narrative in which the setting is your old neighborhood. Show and tell the reader about something that you and your friends typically did there. Write as an adult looking back, but try to capture your point of view as a child as well.

PHIL HOLLAND

Render Unto Larry's

Phil Holland is the chair of the English Department at Anatolia College, a secondary school in Thessaloniki, Greece. A graduate of Dartmouth College and the University of London, Holland joined the Anatolia faculty in 1996. Active in TESOL (Teachers of English to Speakers of Other Languages), a voluntary organization of English teachers, he specializes in helping Greek students of English master English pronunciation. To prospective writers and teachers, Holland offers the following advice: "You had better have an interest, not to say a passion, for the English language. . . . English is your element, immerse yourself at every opportunity."

In "Render Unto Larry's," a 2009 Op-Ed column from the New York Times, *Holland tells the story of boyhood crimes he and a friend committed many years before. Narrating the events of the story this time, he admits, was much easier than when he first confessed and tried to make amends.*

FORTY-SEVEN YEARS AGO, when I was 12, my friend Chester and I stole model 1 car paints, and even models themselves, from Larry's Variety on our way home from Saturday basketball practice in our small New England town. That is easier to say now that I have said it twice. This is the story of the first time.

The model cars came in plastic pieces. The paints, in little bottles, had names 2 like Metallic Green and Racing Blue. Why we started to steal those paints, I don't recall. They were easy to slip into our pockets when the man wasn't looking, and we paid for some, too.

Eventually we became so brazen that we concealed whole models in their boxes 3 in our gym bags. We were never caught. But once my father asked me why we were so late returning from practice. I blamed it on our coach. My father almost called him. That set the nail in my conscience, where it remained.

I have not lived in that town for 40 years, but I pass through every now and 4 then, taking a detour on my way to Vermont. Though much has changed, there's still a Larry's Variety, though it moved into larger quarters on the corner where the barber shop used to be.

In my day there had been a man in his 20s who I assumed was Larry. There was 5 also an older man, a short, white-haired man with thick glasses. He was very courteous. We did our stealing when he was on duty.

SUGGESTED MLA CITATION: Holland, Phil. "Render Unto Larry's." 2009. *Back to the Lake.* Ed. Thomas Cooley. 2nd ed. New York: Norton, 2012. 95–97. Print.

I had the idea some years ago of going into Larry's and paying for what I had stolen. I imagined confessing and making amends. 6

Once I did stop and enter. It wasn't the old Larry's, which was dark and narrow, with two aisles. Now there were four wide aisles, a bank of coolers along the wall, with snacks and groceries and other items (but no model cars). It was clean and well lit, but rather soulless. Not a place to make amends. 7

Last August, back in the States from Europe, where I now live, I drove off the highway, saw the shopping center, and again I passed by. But I needed to buy a phone card, and the only store open was Larry's Variety. I turned around and went in. 8

There were a couple of customers ahead of me and one behind me. The woman at the register looked to be in her late 30s. I looked at her face: She had the same eyes as the old man, no doubt her grandfather. 9

I told her that I had grown up in the town and used to shop at the old Larry's. She told me how the store had been started by her grandfather and passed on to her by her father (the man in his 20s). 10

The memories made her smile, even as it sharpened my guilt. I paid for the phone card and moved toward the door. My heart was racing. If I failed this time, I would never come back. I went to the cooler while the man behind me paid, and I found a cream soda like the ones I used to drink at the soda fountain next door. I took it to the register to pay. There was no one else in the store now but me and the granddaughter. 11

Franklin isn't really frowning at him; Holland is just maintaining the guilty adult's viewpoint (p. 72).

I put the soda on the counter and produced a hundred-dollar bill, with the face of Benjamin Franklin looking up at me with pursed lips. The woman looked at the bill and asked if there would be anything else. 12

I said, in an unsteady voice, "Yes. I would also like to pay for the things that I stole from your grandfather's store in 1962. Some car models and some paints. It's been bothering me all these years." 13

The woman quickly replied, in a kind voice, "Oh, you don't have to do that. Don't worry about it." 14

I said, thickly, "I want to do it. I need to do it." 15

Seeing my distress, and no doubt a bit stunned by this repentant apparition from the past, she let me leave the bill. Or rather, I simply left it, turned and left, soda in hand, compressing my lips to hold myself together. 16

In my rental car, I sipped that sweet vanilla nectar as I felt the guilt leaving me like a disease. Not only had I confessed and made some amends to the flesh and blood of the man I had wronged two generations before, I had been forgiven by someone with a generous heart before I had repaid a penny. 17

To my father, who died some years ago, I can never apologize for stealing and   18
for lying that day. Perhaps I will tell my son, who has some of his grandfather's
features, what I have done.

✠ ⸱⸱⸱⸱⸱

READING CLOSELY

1. Forty-seven years after the fact, Phil Holland confesses that he stole model cars
   and paints from Larry's Variety store back in his hometown in New England.
   Why do these boyhood misdeeds still matter to him as an adult? Should they?

2. At least once before, Holland had returned to Larry's and "imagined confessing
   and making amends" (6). Why didn't he do it then?

3. What causes Holland to change his mind and actually confess once he enters
   the store this time?

4. Why did young Holland steal only when the "older man" was on duty (5)? What
   relation does this man bear to the other people in the story?

5. Why does Holland mention his own father in the final paragraph?

STRATEGIES AND STRUCTURES

1. What is Holland's PURPOSE in telling the general public about "the first time" he
   confessed to stealing from Larry's (1)? To whom else in particular does he think
   about retelling the story? For what purpose?

2. Holland starts his narrative with a confession. Is this an effective way to begin, or
   should he have led up to the revelation, as crime narratives often do? Explain.

3. Holland can't recall why he and his friend stole the model cars and paints.
   Should he have included a motive for the theft? Why or why not?

4. Holland DESCRIBES the crime scene in some detail. Point out several examples,
   and explain how these particular details contribute to the PLOT of his narrative.

5. Holland's narrative begins with his confession and ends with his sense of relief
   as the guilt leaves him "like a disease" (17). What main actions and events constitute the middle part of his plot?

6. Holland introduces DIALOGUE at key points in his narrative. Point out several
   instances, and explain what they add to the POINT OF VIEW of the story.

7. *Other Methods.* Why does Holland feel so guilty about taking the model cars? How and where does he deal with the CAUSES of his lingering guilt?

THINKING ABOUT LANGUAGE

1. What are the implications of using "brazen" to describe the boys' theft (3)? What does this word suggest about their otherwise unexplained motives?

2. The words "Render Unto" in Holland's title are a verbal echo of the biblical passage in which Jesus is reported as saying, "Render therefore unto Caesar the things which are Caesar's; and unto God the things that are God's" (Matthew 22:20–22). What does this ALLUSION contribute to Holland's narrative?

3. Why does Holland call attention to the "pursed lips" of Benjamin Franklin on the face of the hundred-dollar bill (12)?

4. After Holland leaves Larry's and returns to his car, the soda he purchased has turned to "nectar" (17). What is the significance of this transformation, and how did it occur?

FOR WRITING

1. Write a brief confession admitting to a particular misdeed, or failure to act, at some time in the past that has since caused you to feel guilt or regret.

2. Using your "confession" as a starting place, write a narrative essay about what you have done (or would like to do) to make amends to the person or persons you feel you have wronged.

SAIRA SHAH

Longing to Belong

Saira Shah (b. 1964) grew up in Britain, listening to stories about her family's "mythological homeland" in Afghanistan. But when Shah first visited Afghanistan as a young journalist, the reality she encountered did not square with family myth. Afghanistan was at the time ruled by the fundamentalist Taliban and occupied by the Soviets. It was difficult for women to work or even to travel around the country, conditions Shah later captured dramatically in a documentary film, Beneath the Veil *(2001).*

The essay included here does not take place in Afghanistan, however, but in neighboring Pakistan, which Shah visited when she attended a family wedding at the age of seventeen. As the title suggests, it is a personal narrative about her longing to belong—in this case, to "experience the fairy tale" of her family's homeland. It was first published in 2003, in the New York Times Magazine.

THE DAY HE DISCLOSED his matrimonial ambitions for me, my uncle sat me at 1
his right during lunch. This was a sign of special favor, as it allowed him to feed me choice tidbits from his own plate. It was by no means an unadulterated pleasure. He would often generously withdraw a half-chewed delicacy from his mouth and lovingly cram it into mine—an Afghan habit with which I have since tried to come to terms. It was his way of telling me that I was valued, part of the family.

My brother and sister, Tahir and Safia, and my elderly aunt Amina and I were 2
all attending the wedding of my uncle's son. Although my uncle's home was closer than I'd ever been, I was not yet inside Afghanistan. This branch of my family lived in Peshawar, Pakistan. On seeing two unmarried daughters in the company of a female chaperone, my uncle obviously concluded that we had been sent to be married. I was taken aback by the visceral longing I felt to be part of this world. I had never realized that I had been starved of anything. Now, at 17, I discovered that like a princess in a fairy tale, I had been cut off from my origins. This was the point in the tale where, simply by walking through a magical door, I could recover my gardens and palaces. If I allowed my uncle to arrange a marriage for me, I would belong.

Over the next few days, the man my family wished me to marry was introduced 3
into the inner sanctum. He was a distant cousin. His luxuriant black mustache was

SUGGESTED MLA CITATION: Shah, Saira. "Longing to Belong." 2003. *Back to the Lake*. Ed. Thomas Cooley. 2nd ed. New York: Norton, 2012. 99–101. Print.

"I was taken aback by the visceral longing I felt to be part of this world. . . . Like a princess in a fairy tale, . . . simply by walking through a magical door, I could recover my gardens and palaces. If I allowed my uncle to arrange a marriage for me, I would belong."

generally considered to compensate for his lack of height. I was told breathlessly that he was a fighter pilot in the Pakistani Air Force. As an outsider, he wouldn't have been permitted to meet an unmarried girl. But as a relative, he had free run of the house. Whenever I appeared, a female cousin would fling a child into his arms. He'd pose with it, whiskers twitching, while the women cooed their admiration.

A huge cast of relatives had assembled to see my uncle's son marry. The wedding lasted nearly 14 days and ended with a reception. The bride and groom sat on an elevated stage to receive greetings. While the groom was permitted to laugh and chat, the bride was required to sit perfectly still, her eyes demurely lowered. I didn't see her move for four hours. 4

Watching this *tableau vivant*[1] of a submissive Afghan bride, I knew that marriage would never be my easy route to the East. I could live in my father's mythological homeland only through the eyes of the storyteller. In my desire to experience the fairy tale, I had overlooked the staggeringly obvious: the storyteller was a man. If I 5

---

1. *Tableau vivant*: French for "living picture"; a theatrical display in which costumed performers pose against a scenic backdrop.

wanted freedom, I would have to cut my own path. I began to understand why my uncle's wife had resorted to using religion to regain some control—at least in her own home. Her piety gave her license to impose her will on others.

My putative fiancé returned to Quetta, from where he sent a constant flow of lavish gifts. I was busy examining my hoard when my uncle's wife announced that he was on the phone. My intended was a favorite of hers; she had taken it upon herself to promote the match. As she handed me the receiver, he delivered a line culled straight from a Hindi movie: "We shall have a love-match, *ach-cha*?" Enough was enough. I slammed down the phone and went to find Aunt Amina. When she had heard me out, she said: "I'm glad that finally you've stopped this silly wild goose chase for your roots. I'll have to extricate you from this mess. Wait here while I put on something more impressive." As a piece of Islamic one-upmanship, she returned wearing not one but three head scarves of different colors. 6

By adding dialogue (p. 72), you can introduce new perspectives into a narrative.

My uncle's wife was sitting on her prayer platform in the drawing room. Amina stormed in, scattering servants before her like chaff. "Your relative . . . ," was Amina's opening salvo, ". . . has been making obscene remarks to my niece." Her mouth opened, but before she could find her voice, Amina fired her heaviest guns: "Over the *telephone*!" 7

"How dare you!" her rival began. 8

It gave Amina exactly the opportunity she needed to move in for the kill. "What? Do you support this lewd conduct? Are we living in an American movie? Since when have young people of mixed sexes been permitted to speak to each other *on the telephone*? Let alone to talk—as I regret to inform you your nephew did—of love! Since when has love had anything to do with marriage? What a dangerous and absurd concept!" 9

My Peshawari aunt was not only outclassed; she was out-Islamed too. "My niece is a rose that hasn't been plucked," Amina said. "It is my task as her chaperone to ensure that this happy state of affairs continues. A match under such circumstances is quite out of the question. The engagement is off." My uncle's wife lost her battle for moral supremacy and, it seemed, her battle for sanity as well. In a gruff, slack-jawed way that I found unappealing, she made a sharp, inhuman sound that sounded almost like a bark. 10

✢

READING CLOSELY

1. Why does Saira Shah's Pakistani uncle assume that a marriage must be arranged for his visiting niece? Why does she go along with his plans at first?

2. What event causes young Shah to change her mind about an arranged marriage to her distant cousin? What does she come to realize?

3. Why does Aunt Amina help Shah instead of insisting that her niece follow tradition and go through with the marriage?

4. What does the title of the narrative tell us about Shah's main point? What do you think that point is?

5. According to Shah, what's wrong with the way the marriage story is told in her homeland? How would she (and Aunt Amina) change such narratives?

STRATEGIES AND STRUCTURES

1. In many fairy tales, the central event of the PLOT is a transformation—of a frog into a prince, for example. What transformation does Shah long for? In the last paragraph, who is transformed into what?

2. If the uncle's wife is the wicked stepmother in Shah's updated fairy tale, what role does Aunt Amina play? What other aspects of the traditional fairy-tale narrative does Shah retain? How is the traditional fairy-tale plot altered?

3. Shah doesn't introduce DIALOGUE into her narrative until paragraph 6. Why do you think she waits so long? How does the dialogue help to show her disillusionment?

4. *Other Methods.* In paragraph 2, Shah explicitly COMPARES the life she imagines for herself in her ancestral homeland to a fairy tale. How is her awareness of living in such a narrative similar to and different from the heroine's perspective in an actual fairy tale?

THINKING ABOUT LANGUAGE

1. According to your dictionary, what are the DENOTATIONS of the following words: "visceral" (2), "luxuriant" (3), "putative" (6)? What does such formal language contribute to Shah's point?

2. An "inner sanctum" is the holiest of holy places in a shrine or temple (3). How is Shah's use of the phrase here IRONIC?

3. Babies are not literally flung into the arms of Shah's potential husband, nor are servants scattered "like chaff" (3, 7). What function does HYPERBOLE serve in this essay?

4. Shah says that a "cast of relatives" assembles for her cousin's wedding (4). Where else in her narrative does Shah refer to life in her uncle's household as a show or spectacle? What does such imagery imply?

FOR WRITING

1. Write a paragraph comparing real life in a place you have come to know to life in that place as you had imagined it.

2. Aunt Amina states that marrying for love is "a dangerous and absurd concept" (9). Write a narrative in which you explore the implications of this concept—or its opposite.

ANNE BERNAYS

Warrior Day

Anne Bernays (b. 1930) is a novelist and teacher of writing at Harvard. She is married to Justin Kaplan, the editor mentioned in her essay, who is the author of several biographies of major figures in American literature. Grand-niece of Sigmund Freud, the father of psychoanalysis, Bernays attended Wellesley and graduated from Barnard College in 1952. Her novels include Professor Romeo *(1989) and* Trophy House *(2005).*

In "Warrior Day," which appeared in the "Lives" feature of the New York Times Magazine *in 2009, Bernays tells the story of attending her grandson's graduation from the Basic School for young Marine officers at Quantico, Virginia. Narrating her experience in the third person, Bernays captures both the events of the visit, such as her firing an M-16 on the rifle range, and her conflicting emotions toward those events.*

THIS IS THE TRUE STORY of a dyed-in-the-wool pacifist Jewish woman who 1 recently spent two days at the Marine Corps Base at Quantico, Virginia, and survived, almost intact.

Years earlier she was a sure-footed young New Yorker with liberal convictions. 2 She married an introverted editor, moved to Cambridge, Massachusetts, and began raising three daughters. What a delightful life they led. The "best schools." No money worries. The Vietnam War was raging, and the woman roiled in opposition to it, but she didn't feel she could leave her children to protest.

Skip ahead more than a decade—during which the life of this family ran as 3 smoothly as a Rolls Royce. The oldest daughter married a man who renovated houses,

Use a flash-forward (p. 70) when you need to skip ahead.

and they bought their own near Boston. Within five years they had two sons. David, the oldest, was a solid, handsome athlete who also excelled academically. He went to a college in Maine, where he did well in his studies and played on the football team. After school, Dave took a management-track job with a construction company. Then one day he announced he was joining the Marines.

This was a blow to the first woman (now referred to as "the grandmother"). She 4 couldn't conceive of anyone wanting to do this; it seemed as exotic and unsettling as if he had joined a monastery.

Dave's graduation from the Basic School at Quantico (which the grandmother 5 referred to silently as Guantánamo) took place this spring. His mother and

SUGGESTED MLA CITATION: Bernays, Anne. "Warrior Day." 2009. *Back to the Lake*. Ed. Thomas Cooley. 2nd ed. New York: Norton, 2012. 104–06. Print.

grandparents flew down together on a Tuesday. The grandmother was filled with trepidation. The schedule: Wednesday, Warrior Day; Thursday, graduation.

Greeting them, Dave peppered his language with initials: P.O.V.; I.O.C.[1] They passed through a checkpoint, and an enlisted man saluted Dave, whose new lieutenant's bars shone. They walked along a corridor with posters and legends— reminders that marines always act in exemplary ways. Dave's "bedroom" was the size of a walk-in closet: there were bunk beds and a sink. Another room held desks and a small refrigerator. His roommates were ordinary, bright twenty-somethings, only more polite.

No time for breakfast. In a filled auditorium, a colonel welcomed them. He referred to himself as a teacher and the trainees as students. Quantico was a "campus." The course was divided into segments: leadership; academics; military skills. The men were being trained not to be soldiers or marines but "warfighters."

Next on the agenda: the firing range. Sitting on bleachers, the visitors were instructed in how to "employ the weapon system," meaning how to shoot an M-16 rifle. The grandmother was issued a flak jacket, a Kevlar helmet and two little things she first thought were candies but turned out to be earplugs. A warrior helped her hold up her M-16. She pulled the trigger and hit the target five times. She felt a rush of excitement that embarrassed her. Later they saw an amphibious tank, an "up-armored" Humvee and a captured Iraqi tank, all beat up. Someone asked Dave why his dog tag was on the tongue of his boot, under the laces. He said, "You don't want to know."

Graduation Day. At 6:30 a.m. they drove to Dave's barracks, but then he phoned his mother to say that he was delayed by an unspecified snafu. Waiting for him, the family saw one marine drop the white dress pants he was carrying onto the wet pavement. Another, in his dress uniform, dragged a vacuum cleaner. The grandmother found this almost unbearably poignant. Finally Dave appeared, smiling. It took him 45 minutes to put on his dress uniform. "There are lots of suspenders and straps and things that hold the thing together," he explained. The grandmother recaptured a moment when, as a girl, she had a brief romance with a West Point cadet; his uniform was irresistible.

P.O.I.; A.A.V.; P.A.O. The graduation ceremony was S.R.O.[2] Dave came in 11th in a class of 282, making him an honor graduate. He would be a platoon commander. How could the grandmother's heart not swell with pride? Conflicting emotions swirled within. The speeches were crisp and to the point. Marines

---

1. *I.O.C.*: Infantry officer candidate. *P.O.V.*: Privately owned vehicle. Both acronyms are used in processing visitors through the checkpoint.

2. *S.R.O.*: Standing-room only; a nonmilitary acronym. *P.A.O.*: Public affairs officer. *A.A.V.*: Amphibious assault vehicle. *P.O.I.*: Program of instruction at Basic School.

possessed the warrior spirit; had character and integrity; upheld the highest standards.

Each new second lieutenant, six platoons of them, walked straight-backed across 11 the stage to receive his or her diploma. The women, more than a sprinkling, looked smart and self-conscious. The Marine brass band played beautifully. Dispersal. Picture-taking.

"You know," Dave told his grandmother, "I'm responsible for the lives of 12 40 men."

READING CLOSELY

1. Anne Bernays begins her narrative by announcing that she is a "pacifist" (1). What bearing does this information have upon her story?

2. Why is the grandmother embarrassed by the "rush of excitement" she feels when she hits the target with an M-16 rifle (8)? Where else in her narrative does Bernays exhibit conflicting emotions? What are some of them?

3. What causes the grandmother to recall her youthful romance with a West Point cadet (9)?

4. To what extent, if any, do the grandmother's attitudes toward the military and her grandson's career choice change or develop as a result of the experience she writes about here?

STRATEGIES AND STRUCTURES

1. Whose story is this? The grandmother's? Her grandson Dave's? The Marine Corps'? Explain.

2. Throughout her narrative, Bernays speaks of herself in the THIRD PERSON as "the grandmother." Why do you think she uses this POINT OF VIEW instead for the more conventional FIRST-PERSON "I"?

3. Most of the events in Bernays' narrative are presented in CHRONOLOGICAL ORDER. Point out several examples, and note the time tags she uses—such as "next on the agenda" (8).

4. Bernays composes her narrative mostly in short sentences and phrases—like notations in a diary. What effect does this brisk style have on the pace of events in her story and on her presentation of herself as a participant in those events?

5. Bernays focuses on the two days she spent with her family at Quantico. Where and why does she use a FLASHBACK to widen the time frame of her narrative?

6. Bernays ends her narrative with a line of DIALOGUE spoken by her grandson, a new Marine Corps second lieutenant. Why do you think she gives him the last word in the story?

7. *Other Methods.* How and where does Bernays COMPARE her actual experience of military life with what she had expected it to be like?

Thinking about Language

1. Why does Bernays pepper her narrative with acronyms like "P.O.V." and "S.R.O." (6, 10)? Should she have explained what they stand for? Why or why not?

2. Bernays, a novelist, finds the pre-graduation scene in Dave's barracks to be "unbearably poignant" (9). Why? What are the implications of this phrase?

3. As a pacifist during the Vietnam War era, Bernays says she "roiled in opposition" to the conflict (2). Why might Bernays have chosen this phrase to describe her feelings instead of simply saying that she was opposed to the war?

4. Bernays compares the course of her family life to the running of a Rolls Royce (3). What are the implications of this SIMILE?

For Writing

1. Make a list, in chronological order, of the principal events leading up to a graduation or other formal ceremony that you participated in. Group the events on your list into "scenes."

2. Recount a "true story" about a ceremonial occasion—such as a graduation, wedding, or memorial service—that you witnessed or took part in. Show how and where the actual events of the experience met (or conflicted with) your expectations.

TONI MORRISON

Strangers

Toni Morrison (b. 1931) is a native of Lorain, Ohio. A graduate of Howard University and Cornell, she was a professor of humanities at Princeton when she retired in 2006. She is the author of such well-known works as The Bluest Eye *(1970),* Song of Solomon *(1977),* Tar Baby *(1981),* Beloved *(1987), and other portrayals of African American experience. In 1993, she was awarded the Nobel Prize for literature. Her acceptance speech took the form of a narrative about an old blind woman, a storyteller, who demonstrates to a skeptical audience the power of narrative.*

"Strangers" begins with an account of another old woman who tells Morrison a story. The encounter leads Morrison to meditate on how strangers help us to understand ourselves and our humanity. "Strangers" originally appeared as the introduction to A Kind of Rapture *(1998), a book of photographs by Robert Bergman.*

I AM IN THIS RIVER PLACE—newly mine—walking in the yard when I see a   1
woman sitting on the seawall at the edge of a neighbor's garden. A homemade fishing pole arcs into the water some twenty feet from her hand. A feeling of welcome washes over me. I walk toward her, right up to the fence that separates my place from the neighbor's, and notice with pleasure the clothes she wears: men's shoes, a man's hat, a well-worn colorless sweater over a long black dress. The woman turns her head and greets me with an easy smile and a "How you doing?" She tells me her name (Mother Something) and we talk for some time—fifteen minutes or so—about fish recipes and weather and children. When I ask her if she lives there, she answers no. She lives in a nearby village, but the owner of the house lets her come to this spot any time she wants to fish, and she comes every week, sometimes several days in a row when the perch or catfish are running and even if they aren't because she likes eel, too, and they are always there. She is witty and full of the wisdom that older women always seem to have a lock on. When we part, it is with an understanding that she will be there the next day or very soon after and we will visit again. I imagine more conversations with her. I will invite her into my house for coffee, for tales, for laughter. She reminds me of someone, something. I imagine a friendship, casual, effortless, delightful.

SUGGESTED MLA CITATION: Morrison, Toni. "Strangers." 1998. *Back to the Lake*. Ed. Thomas Cooley. 2nd ed. New York: Norton, 2012. 108–11. Print.

She is not there the next day. She is not there the following days, either. And I   2
look for her every morning. The summer passes, and I have not seen her
at all. Finally, I approach the neighbor to ask about her and am bewil-   Verb tenses (p. 70) can help you connect events in time.
dered to learn that the neighbor does not know who or what I am talking
about. No old woman fished from her wall—ever—and none had permission to do so. I decide that the fisherwoman fibbed about the permission and took
advantage of the neighbor's frequent absences to poach. The fact of the neighbor's
presence is proof that the fisherwoman would not be there. During the months
following, I ask lots of people if they know Mother Something. No one, not even
people who have lived in nearby villages for seventy years, has ever heard of her.

I feel cheated, puzzled, but also amused, and wonder off and on if I have   3
dreamed her. In any case, I tell myself, it was an encounter of no value other
than anecdotal. Still. Little by little, annoyance then bitterness takes the place of
my original bewilderment. A certain view from my windows is now devoid of
her, reminding me every morning of her deceit and my disappointment. What
was she doing in that neighborhood, anyway? She didn't drive, had to walk four
miles if indeed she lived where she said she did. How could she be missed on
the road in that hat, those awful shoes? I try to understand the intensity of my
chagrin, and why I am missing a woman I spoke to for fifteen minutes. I get
nowhere except for the stingy explanation that she had come into my space (next
to it, anyway—at the property line, at the edge, just at the fence, where the most
interesting things always happen), and had implied promises of female camara-
derie, of opportunities for me to be generous, of protection and protecting. Now
she is gone, taking with her my good opinion of myself, which, of course, is
unforgivable.

Isn't that the kind of thing that we fear strangers will do? Disturb. Betray. Prove   4
they are not like us. That is why it is so hard to know what to do with them. The
love that prophets have urged us to offer the stranger is the same love that Jean-
Paul Sartre[1] could reveal as the very mendacity of Hell. The signal line of *No Exit,*
"*L'enfer, c'est les autres,*" raises the possibility that "other people" are responsible
for turning a personal world into a public hell. In the admonition of a prophet and
the sly warning of an artist, strangers as well as the beloved are understood to
tempt our gaze, to slide away or to stake claims. Religious prophets caution against
the slide, the looking away; Sartre warns against love as possession.

The resources available to us for benign access to each other, for vaulting   5
the mere blue air that separates us, are few but powerful: language, image, and

---

1. *Jean-Paul Sartre* (1905–1980): French existentialist philosopher; this line from his play *No Exit*
(1944) is usually translated as "Hell is other people."

experience, which may involve both, one, or neither of the first two. Language (saying, listening, reading) can encourage, even mandate, surrender, the breach of distances among us, whether they are continental or on the same pillow, whether they are distances of culture or the distinctions and indistinctions of age or gender, whether they are the consequences of social invention or biology. Image increasingly rules the realm of shaping, sometimes becoming, often contaminating, knowledge. Provoking language or eclipsing it, an image can determine not only what we know and feel but also what we believe is worth knowing about what we feel.

These two godlings, language and image, feed and form experience. My instant 6 embrace of an outrageously dressed fisherwoman was due in part to an image on which my representation of her was based. I immediately sentimentalized and appropriated her. I owned her or wanted to (and I suspect she glimpsed it). I had forgotten the power of embedded images and stylish language to seduce, reveal, control. Forgot, too, their capacity to help us pursue the human project—which is to remain human and to block the dehumanization of others.

But something unforeseen has entered into this admittedly oversimplified menu 7 of our resources. Far from our original expectations of increased intimacy and broader knowledge, routine media presentations deploy images and language that narrow our view of what humans look like (or ought to look like) and what in fact we are like. Succumbing to the perversions of media can blur vision, resisting them can do the same. I was clearly and aggressively resisting such influences in my encounter with the fisherwoman. Art as well as the market can be complicit in the sequestering of form from formula, of nature from artifice, of humanity from commodity. Art gesturing toward representation has, in some exalted quarters, become literally beneath contempt. The concept of what it is to be human has altered, and the word *truth* needs quotation marks around it so that its absence (its elusiveness) is stronger than its presence.

Why would we want to know a stranger when it is easier to estrange another? 8 Why would we want to close the distance when we can close the gate? Appeals in arts and religion for comity in the Common Wealth are faint.

It took some time for me to understand my unreasonable claims on that fisher- 9 woman. To understand that I was longing for and missing some aspect of myself, and that there are no strangers. There are only versions of ourselves, many of which we have not embraced, most of which we wish to protect ourselves from. For the stranger is not foreign, she is random, not alien but remembered; and it is the randomness of the encounter with our already known—although unacknowledged—selves that summons a ripple of alarm. That makes us reject the figure and the emotions it provokes—especially when these emotions are profound. It is also what makes us want to own, govern, administrate the Other. To romance her, if we can, back into our own mirrors. In either instance (of alarm or false reverence), we deny her personhood, the specific individuality we insist upon for ourselves.

READING CLOSELY

1. At first, Toni Morrison is merely puzzled and annoyed by the behavior of the old woman she finds fishing on the seawall of the property next door. Then "bitterness" sets in (3). What makes Morrison bitter about the encounter?

2. Why, according to Morrison, is it "hard to know what to do with" strangers (4)?

3. In Morrison's view, what are the three main "resources" that human beings have for getting in touch with one another (5)? How are they related to each other?

4. Whose story is Morrison telling here, the fisherwoman's or her own? Why do you think so, and why does it matter whose story this is?

STRATEGIES AND STRUCTURES

1. "Strangers" begins as a series of interlocking narratives, the first of which is the story of Morrison's encounter with the fisherwoman, "Mother Something" (1). What happens in this brief narrative, and how effectively does it capture the reader's attention?

2. What is Morrison's main point about "the human project" in this essay (6)? Why do you think she uses stories to make her point? How effective do you find this strategy?

3. How does Morrison use her encounter with the fisherwoman to EXEMPLIFY what she has to say about strangers and our relation to them?

4. In Morrison's analysis, what EFFECT do the media have on our perceptions of how people, including ourselves, ought to look and be? What CAUSES does she cite for this effect?

5. *Other Methods.* Morrison wrote this essay as the introduction to a collection of photographs. How—and how effectively—does her DESCRIPTION of "Mother Something" help to lead the reader from one form of communication (language) to the other (images)?

THINKING ABOUT LANGUAGE

1. Morrison meets her stranger "at the edge, just at the fence," of the neighboring property (3). What space is she talking about when she says this is "where the most interesting things always happen" (3)?

2. Morrison does not use the term, but in what sense(s) might the old woman she meets be called a *marginal* figure? How does the concept of a "margin" relate to photographs and other images? To narratives?

3. Why do you think Morrison refers to "language and image" as "godlings" (6)? Why doesn't she just call them "gods," or even "Gods"?

FOR WRITING

1. Morrison's essay is the introduction to *A Kind of Rapture*, Robert Bergman's book of color photographs of ordinary people. Find a photograph that captures your interest and write a paragraph or two responding to it. You could look at pictures in *A Kind of Rapture*, or search the Web for images by other photographers such as Annie Leibovitz, Dorothea Lange, or Joel Sternfeld, or you could find a photo in a magazine or newspaper. You might imagine meeting the person in the photo, or imagine what he or she is thinking, or you may just want to write down your thoughts as inspired by the photo.

2. Write a narrative essay about an encounter with someone—a stranger, or even a friend or relative—that left you wanting to know that person better. Tell the story in such a way that the reader understands what attracted you to this person and why you wanted to strike up a friendship with him or her.

RICHARD RUSSO

Dog

Richard Russo (b. 1949) is a novelist. He is the author of, among other works,
Nobody's Fool *(1991) and* Empire Falls *(2002), which received the Pulitzer Prize
in fiction. His latest novel is* That Old Cape Magic *(2009). Before he turned exclusively to writing, Russo taught fiction writing at Southern Illinois University and
Colby College.*

Out of this experience came his academic novel, Straight Man *(1997), about
William Henry Devereaux Jr., the son of two English professors and himself the
chair of the English department at the mythical West Central Pennsylvania University. "Dog," which first appeared as a short story in the* New Yorker *in 1996, is
the prologue to that novel. In "Dog" we return to the narrator's childhood. His
parents are in the process of splitting up, though their son doesn't know it yet. All
he wants is a dog, and he sets out relentlessly to get one. As you'll see, though, this
is far more than a boy-meets-dog narrative.*

They're nice to have. A dog.   —F. SCOTT FITZGERALD, *The Great Gatsby*

TRUTH BE TOLD, I'm not an easy man. I can be an entertaining one, though it's   1
been my experience that most people don't want to be entertained. They want to
be comforted. And, of course, my idea of entertaining might not be yours. I'm in
complete agreement with all those people who say, regarding movies, "I just want
to be entertained." This populist position is much derided by my academic colleagues as simpleminded and unsophisticated, evidence of questionable analytical
and critical acuity. But I agree with the premise, and I too just want to be entertained. That I am almost never entertained by what entertains *other* people who
just want to be entertained doesn't make us philosophically incompatible. It just
means we shouldn't go to movies together.

The kind of man I am, according to those who know me best, is exasperating.   2
According to my parents, I was an exasperating child as well. They divorced when
I was in junior high school, and they agree on little except that I was an impossible
child. The story they tell of young William Henry Devereaux, Jr., and his first dog
is eerily similar in its facts, its conclusions, even the style of its telling, no matter
which of them is telling it. Here's the story they tell.

SUGGESTED MLA CITATION: Russo, Richard. "Dog." 1996. *Back to the Lake*. Ed. Thomas Cooley.
2nd ed. New York: Norton, 2012. 113–18. Print.

I was nine, and the house we were living in, which belonged to the university, ₃ was my fourth. My parents were academic nomads, my father, then and now, an academic opportunist, always in the vanguard of whatever was trendy and chic in literary criticism. This was the fifties, and for him, New Criticism[1] was already old. In early middle age he was already a full professor with several published books, all of them "hot," the subject of intense debate at English department cocktail parties. The academic position he favored was the "distinguished visiting professor" variety, usually created for him, duration of visit a year or two at most, perhaps because it's hard to remain distinguished among people who know you. Usually his teaching responsibilities were light, a course or two a year. Otherwise, he was expected to read and think and write and publish and acknowledge in the preface of his next book the generosity of the institution that provided him the academic good life. My mother, also an English professor, was hired as part of the package deal, to teach a full load and thereby help balance the books.

The houses we lived in were elegant, old, high-ceilinged, drafty, either on or ₄ close to campus. They had hardwood floors and smoky fireplaces with fires in them only when my father held court, which he did either on Friday afternoons, our large rooms filling up with obsequious junior faculty and nervous grad students, or Saturday evenings, when my mother gave dinner parties for the chair of the department, or the dean, or a visiting poet. In all situations I was the only child, and I must have been a lonely one, because what I wanted more than anything in the world was a dog.

Predictably, my parents did not. Probably the terms of living in these university ₅ houses were specific regarding pets. By the time I was nine I'd been lobbying hard for a dog for a year or two. My father and mother were hoping I would outgrow this longing, given enough time. I could see this hope in their eyes and it steeled my resolve, intensified my desire. What did I want for Christmas? A dog. What did I want for my birthday? A dog. What did I want on my ham sandwich? A dog. It was a deeply satisfying look of pure exasperation they shared at such moments, and if I couldn't have a dog, this was the next best thing.

Life continued in this fashion until finally my mother made a mistake, a doozy ₆ of a blunder born of emotional exhaustion and despair. She, far more than my father, would have preferred a happy child. One spring day after I'd been badgering her pretty relentlessly she sat me down and said, "You know, a dog is something you earn." My father heard this, got up, and left the room, grim acknowledgment that my mother had just conceded the war. Her idea was to make the dog conditional. The conditions to be imposed would be numerous and severe, and I would

---

1. *New Criticism*: A twentieth-century literary theory in America and Britain that stressed the close reading of texts.

be incapable of fulfilling them, so when I didn't get the dog it'd be my own fault. This was her logic, and the fact that she thought such a plan might work illustrates that some people should never be parents and that she was one of them.

I immediately put into practice a plan of my own to wear my mother down. 7 Unlike hers, my plan was simple and flawless. Mornings I woke up talking about dogs and nights I fell asleep talking about them. When my mother and father changed the subject, I changed it back. "Speaking of dogs," I would say, a forkful of my mother's roast poised at my lips, and I'd be off again. Maybe no one *had* been speaking of dogs, but never mind, we were speaking of them now. At the library I checked out a half dozen books on dogs every two weeks and left them lying open around the house. I pointed out dogs we passed on the street, dogs on television, dogs in the magazines my mother subscribed to. I discussed the relative merits of various breeds at every meal. My father seldom listened to anything I said, but I began to see signs that the underpinnings of my mother's personality were beginning to corrode in the salt water of my tidal persistence, and when I judged that she was nigh to complete collapse, I took every penny of the allowance money I'd been saving and spent it on a dazzling, bejeweled dog collar and leash set at the overpriced pet store around the corner.

During this period when we were constantly "speaking of dogs," I was not a 8 model boy. I was supposed to be "earning a dog," and I was constantly checking with my mother to see how I was doing, just how much of a dog I'd earned, but I doubt my behavior had changed a jot. I wasn't really a bad boy. Just a noisy, busy, constantly needy boy. Mr. In and Out, my mother called me, because I was in and out of rooms, in and out of doors, in and out of the refrigerator. "Henry," my mother would plead with me. "Light somewhere." One of the things I often needed was information, and I constantly interrupted my mother's reading and paper grading to get it. My father, partly to avoid having to answer my questions, spent most of his time in his book-lined office on campus, joining my mother and me only at mealtimes, so that we could speak of dogs as a family. Then he was gone again, blissfully unaware, I thought at the time, that my mother continued to glare homicidally, for long minutes after his departure, at the chair he'd so recently occupied. But he claimed to be close to finishing the book he was working on, and this was a powerful excuse to offer a woman with as much abstract respect for books and learning as my mother possessed.

Gradually, she came to understand that she was fighting a battle she couldn't 9 win and that she was fighting it alone. I now know that this was part of a larger cluster of bitter marital realizations, but at the time I sniffed nothing in the air but victory. In late August, during what people refer to as "the dog days," when she made one last, weak condition, final evidence that I had earned a dog, I relented and truly tried to reform my behavior. It was literally the least I could do.

What my mother wanted of me was to stop slamming the screen door. The 10
house we were living in, it must be said, was an acoustic marvel akin to the Whispering Gallery in St. Paul's, where muted voices travel across a great open space and arrive, clear and intact, at the other side of the great dome. In our house the screen door swung shut on a tight spring, the straight wooden edge of the door encountering the doorframe like a gunshot played through a guitar amplifier set on stun, the crack transmitting perfectly, with equal force and clarity, to every room in the house, upstairs and down. That summer I was in and out that door dozens of times a day, and my mother said it was like living in a shooting gallery. It made her wish the door wasn't shooting blanks. If I could just remember not to slam the door, then she'd see about a dog. Soon.

I did better, remembering about half the time not to let the door slam. When I 11
forgot, I came back in to apologize, sometimes forgetting then too. Still, that I was trying, together with the fact that I carried the expensive dog collar and leash with me everywhere I went, apparently moved my mother, because at the end of that first week of diminished door slamming, my father went somewhere on Saturday morning, refusing to reveal where, and so of course I knew. "What *kind*?" I pleaded with my mother when he was gone. But she claimed not to know. "Your father's doing this," she said, and I thought I saw a trace of misgiving in her expression.

When he returned, I saw why. He'd put it in the backseat, and when my father 12
pulled the car in and parked along the side of the house, I saw from the kitchen window its chin resting on the back of the rear seat. I think it saw me too, but if so it did not react. Neither did it seem to notice that the car had stopped, that my father had gotten out and was holding the front seat forward. He had to reach in, take the dog by the collar, and pull.

As the animal unfolded its long legs and stepped tentatively, arthritically, out of 13
the car, I saw that I had been both betrayed and outsmarted. In all the time we had been "speaking of dogs," what I'd been seeing in my mind's eye was puppies. Collie puppies, beagle puppies, Lab puppies, shepherd puppies, but none of that had been inked anywhere, I now realized. If not a puppy, a young dog. A rascal, full of spirit and possibility, a dog with new tricks to learn. *This* dog was barely ambulatory. It stood, head down, as if ashamed at something done long ago in its puppydom, and I thought I detected a shiver run through its frame when my father closed the car door behind it.

The animal was, I suppose, what might have been called a handsome dog. A 14
purebred, rust-colored Irish setter, meticulously groomed, wonderfully mannered, the kind of dog you could safely bring into a house owned by the university, the sort of dog that wouldn't really violate the no pets clause, the kind of dog, I saw clearly, you'd get if you really didn't want a dog or to be bothered with a dog. It'd belonged, I later learned, to a professor emeritus of the university who'd been put

into a nursing home earlier in the week, leaving the animal an orphan. It was like a painting of a dog, or a dog you'd hire to pose for a portrait, a dog you could be sure wouldn't move.

Both my father and the animal came into the kitchen reluctantly, my father 15 closing the screen door behind them with great care. I like to think that on the way home he'd suffered a misgiving, though I could tell that it was his intention to play the hand out boldly. My mother, who'd taken in my devastation at a glance, studied me for a moment and then my father.

"What?" he said. 16

My mother just shook her head. 17

My father looked at me, then back at her. A violent shiver palsied the dog's 18 limbs. The animal seemed to want to lie down on the cool linoleum, but to have forgotten how. It offered a deep sigh that seemed to speak for all of us.

"He's a good dog," my father said, rather pointedly, to my mother. "A little high- 19 strung, but that's the way with purebred setters. They're all nervous."

This was not the sort of thing my father knew. Clearly he was repeating the 20 explanation he'd just been given when he picked up the dog.

"What's his name?" my mother said, apparently for something to say. 21

My father had neglected to ask. He checked the dog's collar for clues. 22

"Lord," my mother said. "Lord, lord." 23

"It's not like we can't name him ourselves," my father said, irritated now. "I 24 think it's something we can manage, don't you?"

"You could name him after a passé school of literary criticism," my mother 25 suggested.

"It's a she," I said, because it was. 26

It seemed to cheer my father, at least a little, that I'd allowed myself to be drawn 27 into the conversation. "What do you say, Henry?" he wanted to know. "What'll we name him?"

This second faulty pronoun reference was too much for me. "I want to go out 28 and play now," I said, and I bolted for the screen door before an objection could be registered. It slammed behind me, hard, its gunshot report even louder than usual. As I cleared the steps in a single leap, I thought I heard a thud back in the kitchen, a dull, muffled echo of the door, and then I heard my father say, "What the hell?" I went back up the steps, cautiously now, meaning to apologize for the door. Through the screen I could see my mother and father standing together in the middle of the kitchen, looking down at the dog, which seemed to be napping. My father nudged a haunch with the toe of his cordovan loafer.[2]

He dug the grave in the backyard with a shovel borrowed from a neighbor. My 29 father had soft hands and they blistered easily. I offered to help, but he just looked

---

2. *Cordovan loafer*: A style of casual but expensive men's shoes made from fine horse leather.

at me. When he was standing, midthigh, in the hole he'd dug, he shook his head one last time in disbelief. "Dead," he said. "Before we could even name him."

I knew better than to correct the pronoun again, so I just stood there thinking   30
about what he'd said while he climbed out of the hole and went over to the back porch to collect the dog where it lay under an old sheet. I could tell by the careful way he tucked that sheet under the animal that he didn't want to touch anything dead, even newly dead. He lowered the dog into the hole by means of the sheet, but he had to drop it the last foot or so. When the animal thudded on the earth and lay still, my father looked over at me and shook his head. Then he picked up the shovel and leaned on it before he started filling in the hole. He seemed to be waiting for me to say something, so I said, "Red."

> A well-plotted story needs to give a clear sense of an ending (p. 70). Thud.

My father's eyes narrowed, as if I'd spoken in a foreign tongue. "What?" he said.   31
"We'll name her Red," I explained.   32

In the years after he left us, my father became even more famous. He is some-   33
times credited, if credit is the word, with being the Father of American Literary Theory. In addition to his many books of scholarship, he's also written a literary memoir that was short-listed for a major award and that offers insight into the personalities of several major literary figures of the twentieth century, now deceased. His photograph often graces the pages of the literary reviews. He went through a phase where he wore crewneck sweaters and gold chains beneath his tweed coat,[3] but now he's mostly photographed in an oxford button-down shirt, tie, and jacket, in his book-lined office at the university. But to me, his son, William Henry Devereaux, Sr., is most real standing in his ruined cordovan loafers, leaning on the handle of a borrowed shovel, examining his dirty, blistered hands, and receiving my suggestion of what to name a dead dog. I suspect that digging our dog's grave was one of relatively few experiences of his life (excepting carnal ones) that did not originate on the printed page. And when I suggested we name the dead dog Red, he looked at me as if I myself had just stepped from the pages of a book he'd started to read years ago and then put down when something else caught his interest. "What?" he said, letting go of the shovel, so that its handle hit the earth between my feet. "What?"

It's not an easy time for any parent, this moment when the realization dawns   34
that you've given birth to something that will never see things the way you do, despite the fact that it is your living legacy, that it bears your name.

---

3. *Crewneck sweaters . . . tweed coat*: Tweed coats are stereotypical clothing for professors and other academics. Crewneck sweaters worn with heavy gold chains were a macho style of the 1970s.

READING CLOSELY

1. Why does Henry want a dog?

2. How and why does young Henry earn the nickname "Mr. In and Out" (8)? How appropriate is the name?

3. What plan does Henry set into motion in paragraph 7? How well does it work?

4. Henry relents from his plan and tries hard not to slam the screen door. What does this change of heart show the reader about his character and personality? What can we make of his final screen-door slam (28)?

STRATEGIES AND STRUCTURES

1. Richard Russo's story of a boy and his dog doesn't actually begin until paragraph 4. What is the PURPOSE of the first two paragraphs of the narrative?

2. Where and why does Russo's story engage in a FLASH-FORWARD to a time in the future? How does he bring the story back to the present?

3. Besides telling a boy meets dog story, Russo's narrator is also telling the story of how he became "the kind of man I am" (2). What kind of man is he, and what are some of the CAUSES?

4. Russo does not introduce extensive DIALOGUE into his story until paragraph 16. Why do you think he waits until this particular point before letting his characters speak?

5. *Other Methods.* Russo DESCRIBES in detail the "acoustic marvel" of a house in which the Devereaux family is living (10). Why does he pay so much attention to the screen door in particular? Point out other places where Russo's descriptions support the actions of the story.

THINKING ABOUT LANGUAGE

1. Russo uses the following academic language in paragraph 1: "populist position," "much derided," "questionable analytical and critical acuity," "premise," "philosophically incompatible." Why does he use such language so early in his story?

2. Why does Henry's father refer to the new dog as "he" (19)? What does the boy's reaction to this "faulty pronoun reference" tell you about his upbringing and future (28)? Give examples of other times when Henry challenges his father.

3. When his parents tell the story of him and his first dog, says Henry, the story is "eerily similar in . . . its telling" (2). Why does he consider their mutual agreement about the story to be "eerie"?

FOR WRITING

1. Write a paragraph or two narrating your efforts to convince your family to acquire a pet or something else you've wanted.

2. Write a narrative essay about something that mattered a lot to you when you were a child—a dog, a doll, a game, etc. Your essay should tell about some memorable incident. Make sure the essay has a beginning, middle, and ending, and choose details that will bring the incident alive for the reader. Be sure to indicate why the incident was significant to you.

3. The writer Annie Proulx has praised Russo for creating characters "as real as we are," ones readers can see "coming out of doorways, lurching through life." Write a narrative essay about some real person you know. Focus on an incident (to be sure you write a narrative, not just a description). Choose details that will give readers a sense of who the person is, and arrange actions carefully to lead readers through the story.

CHAPTER 5

Description

Can you describe the vibration? Is it all the time? Certain speeds? While accelerating? While decelerating? Could be wheel bearings, warped brake rotors, improperly tightened lug nuts, out of balance driveshaft, bad U-joints. Giving a better description would help us help you!

—CHUCK H., VoyForums Message Board

In his classic essay "Once More to the Lake," E. B. White writes about going out early one morning in a rowboat with his young son:

> We went fishing the first morning. I felt the same damp moss covering the worms in the bait can, and saw the dragonfly alight on the tip of my rod as it hovered a few inches from the surface of the water. It was the arrival of the fly that convinced me beyond any doubt that everything was as it always had been, that the years were a mirage and that there had been no years. The small waves were the same, chucking the rowboat under the chin as we fished at anchor, and the boat was the same boat, the same color green and the ribs broken in the same places, and under the floorboards the same freshwater leavings and débris—the dead helgramite, the wisps of moss, the rusty discarded fishhook, the dried blood from yesterday's catch. We stared silently at the tips of our rods, at the dragonflies that came and went. I lowered the tip of mine into the water, tentatively, pensively dislodging the fly, which darted two feet away, poised, darted two feet back, and came to rest again a little farther up the rod.

You can picture the tranquil scene because this passage is a little masterpiece of descriptive writing with every detail carefully chosen to create the illusion of time standing still.

Defining Description:
Telling How Something Looks, Sounds, Feels, Smells, or Tastes

Description appeals to the senses: it gives the reader something to look at (the green boat, the rusty fishhook, the hovering dragonfly); to feel (the damp moss); to hear (the small waves); and to smell (the drying fish blood). As for taste, White appeals more directly to that sense later in his essay, when he and his young son go to a nearby farmhouse for dinner (fried chicken, apple pie). What does a subject look, feel, smell, sound, or taste like? These are the fundamental questions that descriptive writing addresses.

In this chapter we will see where to fish for the specific physical details you need for building a good description. We will examine how to select ones that best suit your PURPOSE and AUDIENCE and how to organize and present those details so they contribute directly to the DOMINANT IMPRESSION you want your description to make. Then we will review the critical points to watch for as you read back over and revise your description, as well as common errors to avoid as you edit.

Why Do We Describe?

Description is a means of showing rather than telling. We describe something—a person, a lake, a memory, a chemical reaction—so that the reader can experience it directly as we do. Description makes anything we write less ABSTRACT, or general, and more CONCRETE, referring to specific characteristics we can perceive directly with the senses. White, for example, could simply tell us that time seemed to stand still on the lake, but he makes the abstract idea of timelessness much easier to grasp by showing us such specific details as the dragonfly hovering (like time) at the end of his fishing rod.

Composing a Description

Your reader will find almost anything you write easier to comprehend if you describe your subject in vivid detail. However, in a personal essay about your grandmother's cooking, you will probably describe things differently than in a lab report on dissecting a shark.

For a journalist's objective description of an unusual star athlete, see p. 146.

There are basically two ways of describing something—objectively or subjectively. An OBJECTIVE description presents its subject impartially. Its purpose is to provide the reader with information, as in this description of a watershed in southern Alaska:

Duck Creek is a small anadromous [running upriver from the sea] fish stream located in an old outwash channel of the Mendenhall Glacier in the center of the most populated residential area of Alaska's capital, Juneau. Duck Creek supports a large over-wintering population of coho salmon juveniles that migrate into the stream each fall from the estuarine wetlands.

—ENVIRONMENTAL PROTECTION AGENCY,
"Make Way for Salmon in Duck Creek"

The EPA's description is objective not only because it uses precise scientific terms ("anadromous," "estuarine") but because it is made up entirely of factual information about its subject—the size and age of the creek, where it is located, the type of fish that inhabit it, and so on.

A SUBJECTIVE description provides information, too. But it also conveys the writer's personal response to the subject being described, as in this piece from an article about a visit to the 2008 Iowa State Fair:

And then I wound up at an open-air brick pavilion for the llama judging. Llamas are gentle, dignified beasts, and here were four of them being shown by teenagers. The animals' military bearing, heads high, their stately gait, their dark soulful eyes—they looked as if they'd walked straight out of *Dr. Doolittle*. . . . According to a poster, they are raised for "fiber, showing, carting, guardians and companionship." One girl stood by her llama and blew gently on its nose, and he looked lovingly into her eyes. A sort of conversation. If every teenager had his or her own llama, this would be a very different country. —GARRISON KEILLOR, "A Sunday at the State Fair"

This is a subjective description: the author feels or imagines that the llamas are dignified and loving—and that one is having a "conversation" with his keeper.

However, many of the other details in Keillor's description—including the physical location, the number of llamas on display, who the exhibitors are, and the exact words of the poster explaining what llamas are raised for—are rendered objectively. Most descriptions include a combination of subjective and objective elements. And even the most subjective description should be grounded in the concrete physical features of the person, place, or thing it describes—which is why E. B. White's description of the lake is so effective.

For a deeply subjective description, see "How It Feels to Be Colored Me" (p. 157).

Not all subjective descriptions are so successful, however. Consider the following passage, which refers to the same lake described by White. According to the region's official website, the area around that lake is "famous for its sparkling scenic streams and chain of seven lakes, its panoramic views of fields, hills and woodlands, its inviting towns and villages."

Sparkling streams, panoramic views. Sounds like a nice place. The same could be said, however, of a large car wash with a picture window in the waiting room. This subjective description offers no definite impression of the lakes because it merely names abstract qualities. So does the rest of the site, which says that the region is "picturesque and welcoming," providing "a retreat for peace and tranquility."

Picturesqueness and tranquility are difficult to smell or taste. The problem with this tourist-brochure prose is that it tells the reader what to think *about* the place; it doesn't capture the place itself. The fundamental purpose of descriptive writing, whether subjective or objective, is to recreate the characteristics of its subject so vividly that readers perceive it with their own eyes and ears—and mind.

Good descriptive writing is built on concrete particulars rather than abstract qualities. So don't just write, "It was a dark and stormy night"; try to make your reader see, hear, and feel the wind and rain.

Thinking about Purpose and Audience

Your purpose in describing something—whether to picture your subject as objectively as possible, capture it in a certain light or mood, express your feelings about it, persuade the reader to visit (or avoid) it, or merely to amuse the reader—will determine the details you'll want to include in your description. For example, the

PINE ISLAND, BELGRADE LAKES, ME.   51807

A postcard of Belgrade Lakes, Maine, c. 1914.

official Belgrade Lakes website describes family vacations; like E. B. White, it dwells on the beauty, peace, and tranquility of the place, as well as the fishing and boating. Its slogan—"Where Memories Last a Lifetime"—might almost have been drawn from White's essay. The website, however, aims to persuade the general public to visit the area and thus emphasizes "wholesome family fun" and "activities for all ages"—and leaves out the storm clouds that gather in White's essay.

Suppose you were describing Belgrade Lakes to friends who were thinking of going there and wanted information about the area. You might express your feelings toward the region, but your main purpose would be to inform your friends about it—as objectively as possible—so they could decide for themselves whether or not to go. You would talk about the peace and quiet, of course; but you would also include other aspects of the scene, such as the pebble beaches, touristy shops, and local restaurants—not to mention the night crawlers at the Pickled Trout Saloon. Instead of selecting details that presented only one aspect of the place, you would choose representative details that painted a fair and accurate picture of what it was like as a whole.

Whatever your purpose, you need to take into account how much your audience already knows (or does not know) about the subject you are describing. For example,

Three ways of looking at a lake. This website—like the old postcard on page 124 and E. B. White's classic essay "Once More to the Lake" on page 163—describes the Belgrade Lakes region of central Maine. All three capture the peace and tranquility of the place; but the two earlier "views" emphasize its remote, timeless qualities, while the website, which can be updated at any time, presents the region as an easily accessible tourist destination.

if you want to describe to someone who has never been on your campus the mad rush that takes place there when classes change, you're going to have to fill in the background for them: the main quadrangle with its sun worshipers in bathing suits, the brick-and-stone classroom buildings on either side, the library looming at one end. On the other hand, if you were to describe this same scene to fellow students who already know the territory well, you could skip the background description and go directly to the mob scene.

Generating Ideas:
Asking How Something Looks, Sounds, Feels, Smells, or Tastes

Good descriptive writing begins and ends with the concrete physical characteristics of whatever you are describing. To gather those details, you need to ask what your subject looks, sounds, feels, smells, or tastes like. Methods like BRAINSTORMING and LISTING can help you probe for ideas as you run through each of the five senses.

Another resource for answering these questions is direct experience and observation. Even if you are describing a familiar subject—a lake you've often visited, your old neighborhood, a person from your hometown—go back to the source. Try to see your subject objectively as well as subjectively; take notes—much like a reporter on assignment, or a traveler in a strange land.

Zainab Salbi (p. 142) draws on memories of her father's employer, Saddam Hussein.

One of your richest sources of ideas for a description, especially if you are describing something from the past, is memory. Ask others—friends, parents—to help you remember things accurately and truthfully. Let's assume you're describing your hometown. Pick a spot, maybe the main shopping street or town square. Ask yourself what it looked like, and in your mind's eye, try to see specific details: colors, landmarks, signs on the buildings. Then try to recall sounds, smells, textures—and what you did there. As sensations stand out in your memory, let them dominate your description. This example recalls a town in Kentucky:

> Food was better in town, we thought. It wasn't plain and everyday. The centers of pleasure were there—the hamburger and barbecue places, the movie shows, all the places to buy things. Woolworth's, with the pneumatic tubes overhead rushing money along a metallic mole tunnel up to a balcony; Lochridge & Ridgway, with an engraved sign on the third-story cornice: STOVES, APPLIANCES, PLOWS. . . . A circuit of the courthouse square took you past the grand furniture stores, the two dime stores, the shoe stores, the men's stores, the ladies' stores, the banks, the drugstores. You'd walk past the poolroom and an exhaust fan would blow the intoxicating smell of hamburgers in your face.
> —BOBBIE ANN MASON, "Being Country"

What makes this description so vivid is the specific details—the pneumatic tubes in Woolworth's, the engraved words on the appliance store.

For a photograph of the courthouse square at the period Mason describes, see p. 426.

How did the writer generate such details? As she searched her memory, we can imagine Mason asking herself, "What *did* the place look like exactly? What did it sound like? What did it smell and taste like?" Many writers find that tastes and smells are particularly evocative. In fact, it is the "intoxicating" smell of hamburgers from the poolroom that provides the high point of Mason's description—and that may have brought the place to life for her as she searched her memory for ideas.

The pond of memory is a rich reservoir of sensations for the writer of description. The process of recovering its treasures is a little like fishing: think back to the spots you knew well; bait the hook by asking the key sensory questions; weigh and measure everything you pull up. As you revise, you can always throw back the ones you can't use. Just the right details for capturing your subject on paper *are* lurking there, often in plain sight—or just below the surface. Your job as a writer is to bring those details to light, with the life still in them.

Organizing and Drafting a Description

Once you've gathered the specific details that capture your subject, you're ready to begin organizing and drafting. As you write, let those details speak for themselves. Give enough of them so that readers can picture your subject clearly, but select and arrange particular details so they contribute to the dominant impression you want your description to make. Maintain a consistent vantage point throughout and, of course, let readers know the point of your description. The templates on page 129 can help you get started with your draft.

STATING YOUR POINT

Description is seldom an end in itself. Ordinarily, we describe something to someone for a reason. Why are you describing a particular fishing trip, or a woman hanging out laundry, or bloody footprints in the snow? You need to let the reader know. It can be by way of an explicit THESIS statement: "This description of Washington's ragged army at Yorktown shows that the American general faced many of the same challenges as Napoleon in the winter battle for Moscow, but Washington turned them to his advantage."

Or your reasons can be stated less formally. Consider the following description of the streets of Havana, Cuba:

> Everywhere I went, there were men and women waiting in lines. There were lines to get water, lines to have cheap cigarette lighters repaired, lines to get

into the city's lone merchandise store in Miramar where a simple sledge-hammer cost fifty-six dollars. At the nationalized health care clinics, the lines wrapped away for blocks; the somber aged, the ill, the expectant young mothers, all waiting, patiently enduring.

—RANDY WAYNE WHITE, *Last Flight Out*

The point of this description is to show that everyday life is difficult in a Communist system where everything is centrally controlled, including simple consumer goods and services. Randy Wayne White is writing a descriptive travel essay, however, not a political treatise. So he states his point informally, as a personal observation: "A few weeks of living like that, and I myself—not the bravest of men—would consider worming into an inner tube and paddling north."

See how E. B. White does this with a single chilling phrase (p. 168, ¶13).

You don't always have to make a formal statement of your thesis—"Communism failed as a social system because it failed as an economic system"—when you write a description. But you *should* include a clear statement, however informal, of why you're writing the description.

BEGINNING WITH DETAILS

One way *not* to begin a description is to leap immediately into a general statement of the impression your subject is supposed to make. Instead, you should begin with specific descriptive details, and let your readers form that impression for themselves. The following statement, for example, would not be the best way to begin a description of the Grand Canyon: "As the abyss yawned at my feet, I was swept away by the beauty and majesty of the scene."

Few writers have taught us this lesson better than Ernest Hemingway, whose stories and newspaper correspondence are full of powerful descriptions that show us a place or object long before telling us what to think of it. Here's Hemingway's rendition of a father and son fishing on a lake early in the morning:

They were seated in the boat, Nick in the stern, his father rowing. The sun was coming up over the hills. A bass jumped, making a circle in the water. Nick trailed his hand in the water. It felt warm in the sharp chill of the morning.   —ERNEST HEMINGWAY, "Indian Camp"

The boy in the story, Nick Adams, has just witnessed a grisly suicide. As Nick and his father row home, the boy is soothed by the morning sun, the leaping bass, and the warm water. Nature seems kind, and the story ends with a direct statement of what the boy thinks about the scene: "In the early morning on the lake sitting in the stern of the boat with his father rowing, he felt quite sure that he would never die."

TEMPLATES FOR DRAFTING

When you begin to draft a description, you need to identify who or what you're describing, say what your subject looks or feels like, and indicate the traits you plan to focus on—moves fundamental to any description. See how Judith Ortiz Cofer makes such moves in the beginning of her essay in this chapter:

> My grandmother's house is like a chambered nautilus; it has many rooms, yet is not a mansion. Its proportions are small and its design simple.   —JUDITH ORTIZ COFER, "More Room"

Ortiz Cofer identifies what she's describing ("my grandmother's house"); says something about what her subject looks like ("a chambered nautilus"); and indicates some of the physical characteristics (the proportions and design of the house) that she plans to discuss. Here is one more example from this chapter:

> The house I grew up in was nestled in a grove of eucalyptus trees at the end of a Baghdad cul-de-sac. Built by my parents in 1969, the year I was born, it is a simple, two-story, middle-class home. I spent a lot of my childhood in my second-floor bedroom, watching the trees and the street outside. . . . It was in this cul-de-sac, long after I went to bed, that Saddam Hussein used to park his car.
> —ZAINAB SALBI, "Little House in the War Zone"

The following templates can help you make some of these basic moves in your own writing. But don't take these as formulas where you just fill in the blanks. There are no shortcuts to good writing, but these templates can serve as starting points.

▶ X is like a _____; it has _____, _____, and _____.

▶ He / she looked a lot like _____, except for _____, which _____.

▶ From the perspective of _____, however, X could be described as _____.

▶ In some ways, namely _____, X resembles _____; but in other ways, X is more like _____.

▶ X is not at all like _____ because _____.

▶ Mainly because of _____ and _____, X gives the impression of being _____.

▶ From this description of X, you can see that _____.

The purpose of Hemingway's description is to show us the boy's naïveté. However, Hemingway does not deliver the punch line—the boy's stated feeling about the scene—until he has given us the physical details on which that feeling is based. You could organize an entire descriptive essay on this model: detail (early morning), detail (lake), detail (boat), detail (boy sitting in the stern), detail (father rowing)—dominant impression (boy feeling "quite sure he would never die").

CREATING A DOMINANT IMPRESSION

Some descriptions, such as Hemingway's, appeal to several different senses—the sight of the rising sun, the sound of the jumping bass, the touch of the warm water in the chilled air. Don't feel that you have to give equal attention to all five senses when you write a description; but whether you appeal to a single sense or several, make sure they all contribute to the dominant impression you want your description to make upon the reader.

The dominant impression conveyed by Hemingway's description of fishing on the lake, for example, is that of peace and calm—the soothing tranquility of nature. Now, suppose you were to describe a similar morning scene on a freshwater lake in a rowboat. But instead of bass and sunrise, you call the reader's attention to an ominous dark cloud in the distance, drawing nearer. The wind rises. The reader hears a nasty grating sound as the little boat scrapes over a sunken log in the fast-flowing current. Instead of gently chucking the boat under the chin, the waves, now grown to white caps, flip it over with a crash, throwing you into the icy water. Nature, the reader concludes as you disappear beneath the surface, is not kind. The reader is left with the dominant impression of danger because you have chosen to build your description on particular details (mostly sounds) that contribute to a sense of danger and foreboding.

ARRANGING THE DETAILS

While the events in a NARRATIVE are usually organized chronologically, the physical elements of a description are often organized according to their location.

So as you begin to get your description down on paper, the physical configuration of whatever you're describing will often suggest a pattern of organization to you. Bobbie Ann Mason's description on page 126 of the sights and smells of her hometown in Kentucky, for example, follows the "circuit" of the courthouse square. In Mason's description, we get the furniture stores, then the dime stores, then the men's and ladies' stores and the banks and, finally, the poolroom, because that is the order in which young Mason would have seen them all, starting where she did and walking around the main square of the town.

Descriptions of places are often organized, like Mason's, by physical direction—around the block, north to south, front to back, left to right, inside to outside, near to far, top to bottom. If you were describing a room, for example, you might use an outside-to-inside order, starting with the door (don't forget the knob and other details). Next you could present the main physical features of the room as they might appear to someone just crossing the threshold (oak floors, high ceilings, ancient fireplace). Then would come the grand piano, the candle on a stand, the old lady mending a tapestry—just as these objects might appear to a person entering the room and adjusting his or her eyes to the light.

A particular object can suggest an order of arrangement as well as a place can. For instance, in the following description of a tarpon, addressed to a blind boy who has just caught it, the order of the details follows the anatomy of the fish.

> "More Room" (p. 152) traces several generations of a family by describing home renovations.

> He's mostly silver, but the silver is somehow made up of *all* the colors. . . . He has all these big scales, like armor all over his body. They're silver, too, and when he moves they sparkle. He has a strong body and a large powerful tail. He has big round eyes, bigger than a quarter, and a lower jaw that sticks out past the upper one and is very tough. His belly is almost white and his back is a gunmetal gray. When he jumped he came out of the water about six feet, and his scales caught the sun and flashed it all over the place.
> —CHEROKEE PAUL McDONALD, "A View from the Bridge"

McDonald's description begins and ends with the colors of the fish, its most noticeable feature (to a sighted person) in the glinting sun. Most of his description, however, is organized according to the parts of the subject itself, moving from the body of the tarpon as a whole to the tail, eyes, belly, and back. From whole to parts, or parts to whole: you can go either way when constructing a description. Or you can describe the most important or unusual features of your subject first, then the least important or most familiar ones (or vice versa). Or you can go from the largest to smallest, or from specific to general, or from concrete to abstract—or vice versa—so long as you maintain a consistent vantage point.

MAINTAINING A VANTAGE POINT

In McDonald's essay, as the title suggests, the vantage point is from the bridge. Here's the beginning of the essay, before the boy catches the tarpon:

> I was coming up on the little bridge in the Rio Vista neighborhood of Fort Lauderdale, deepening my stride and breathing to negotiate the slight incline without altering my pace. And then, as I neared the crest, I saw the kid.

He was a lumpy little guy with baggy shorts, a faded T-shirt and heavy sweat socks falling down over old sneakers.

Partially covering his shaggy blond hair was one of those blue baseball caps with gold braid on the bill and a sailfish patch sewn onto the peak. Covering his eyes and part of his face was a pair of those stupid-looking '50s-style wrap-around sunglasses.

Like his description of the tarpon, McDonald's description of the boy moves from the whole (lumpy little guy in shorts and T-shirt) to the parts (hair, cap, patch, eyes, face, glasses). It also presents those details in the order in which the observer perceives them from his vantage point. That is, the reader of McDonald's essay sees only what the runner sees as he comes over the bridge. For example, at this point in his description, the runner does not yet know that the boy is blind, which is why he's wearing "stupid-looking" sunglasses. As you compose a description, be careful to maintain a consistent vantage point, as McDonald does.

USING FIGURATIVE LANGUAGE

Because descriptive writing presents the reader with images of the physical world, it lends itself to the use of figurative language. The three figures of speech you are most likely to use in composing a description are similes, metaphors, and personification.

Similes tell the reader what something looks, sounds, or feels like, using *like* or *as*:

She was like a pretty kite that floated above my head.   —Maya Angelou

Suspicion climbed all over her face like a kitten, but not so playfully.
                                        —Raymond Chandler

Two policemen . . . were leaning into a third woman as if she were a stalled car.
                                        —T. C. Boyle, *Talk, Talk*

Metaphors make implicit comparisons, without *like* or *as*:

All the world's a stage.

You are my sunshine.

Papa was a rolling stone.

Metaphors have two parts: the subject of the description (*world, you, Papa*); and the thing (*stage, sunshine, rolling stone*) to which that subject is being implicitly compared.

Personification assigns human qualities to inanimate objects, as in this poetic description of a mirror:

> I am silver and exact.
> I have no preconceptions.
> Whatever I see I swallow immediately
> Just as it is, unmisted by love or dislike.   —SYLVIA PLATH, "Mirror"

USING OTHER METHODS

When you describe something, you will often have reason to use other methods as well—to DEFINE it, analyze what CAUSED it, and so on. Especially if you are describing something that is unfamiliar to the reader—as in this description of a cemetery in rural El Salvador—consider COMPARING it with something the reader already knows about:

> Plunged like daggers to the ground are the crosses, mainly a fabulous aqua color, though some are bleached white and some are unpainted. . . . It looks like the aftermath of a piñata party, with crepe-paper chains strewn like leis about the necks of the gravestone markers, plastic red roses wreathed at the feet, errant scraps of yellow paper and transparent cellophane trapped between the blades of grass.   —BETH KEPHART, *Still Love in Strange Places*

"Daggers" imply violence, of course; but the cemetery in this colorful description is far from somber. The dominant impression is a sense of festive disorder, as Kephart compares this strange scene to a more familiar one in which children have just left after hammering a piñata to release the candy and toys inside.

Reading a Description with a Critical Eye

Once you have drafted a description, try it out on someone else to get a sense of what's working and what needs revision. Then read it over yourself with a critical eye. Here are some questions to keep in mind when reviewing descriptive writing.

PURPOSE AND AUDIENCE. Who is the intended audience, and why will they be reading this description? Does it tell them everything they'll need to know, or will they need more background information?

THE POINT. Does the description have a clear point? Is that point set out in a thesis statement? If not, should it be?

SPECIFIC DETAILS. Are there enough details to give the reader a vivid impression of the subject? To which senses in particular does the description appeal—sight? sound? smell? touch? taste?

OBJECTIVE OR SUBJECTIVE? Are the details of the description presented objectively, subjectively, or does it contain elements of both? Is the degree of objectivity appropriate for the overall purpose and audience of the description? If not, how can it be made more informative and less emotional (or vice versa)?

DOMINANT IMPRESSION. What overall impression does the description give? Does every detail contribute directly to that impression? What additional details would make the dominant impression clearer or stronger? Do any details detract from that impression?

ORGANIZATION. How are the details of the description presented—by moving from part to whole? Whole to part? North to south? Most important to least important? Some other way?

VANTAGE POINT. From what perspective are the various aspects of the subject described? Near and intimate? Far and detached? Somewhere in between? Is that perspective maintained consistently throughout the description?

FIGURATIVE LANGUAGE. What figures of speech, such as metaphors, similes, or personification, does the description use? Are they appropriate for this purpose and audience?

OTHER METHODS. Has the description been expanded to include other methods of development—for example, by analyzing what caused something, or by comparing its attributes to those of other things with which the reader may already be familiar?

Editing for Common Errors in Descriptive Writing

Descriptive writing is often marred by qualifiers that are overly abstract, empty, or out of sequence. The following guidelines will help you check your description for these common problems and correct them.

Check your details to see if you can make them more concrete

▸ Great Pond is so ~~amazing and incredible~~ <u>clear and deep</u> that floating on it in a boat seems like floating on air.

Amazing and *incredible* are abstract terms; *clear* and *deep* describe the water in more concrete terms.

▸ The Belgrade region is famous for its ~~charming views~~ <u>panoramic views of fields, hills, and woodlands</u>.

The second sentence says more precisely what makes the views charming.

Check for filler words like *very, quite, really,* and *truly*

▸ The lake was ~~very much secluded~~ <u>fifteen miles from the nearest village</u>.

If you've used several adjectives together, be sure they are in the right order

Subjective adjectives (those that reflect the writer's own opinion) go before objective adjectives (those that are strictly factual): write "fabulous four-door Chevrolet" rather than "four-door fabulous Chevrolet." Beyond that, adjectives usually go in the following order: number, size, shape, age, color, nationality.

▸ The streets of Havana were lined with many ~~old, big~~ <u>big, old</u> American cars.

Check for common usage errors

UNIQUE, PERFECT

Don't use *more* or *most, less* or *least,* or *very* before words like *unique, equal, perfect,* or *infinite.* Either something is unique or it isn't.

▸ Their house at the lake was a ~~very~~ unique place.

AWESOME, COOL

Not only are these modifiers too abstract, they're overused. You probably should delete them or replace them with fresher words no matter how grand the scene you're describing.

▸ The Mississippi is ~~an awesome river~~ <u>the largest river system in the United States</u>.

Student Example

Jim Miller grew up in a small town in Arkansas. A student at Henderson State University in Arkadelphia, he wrote the following selection as an entry in a national writing contest sponsored by the editors of the *Nation* magazine, who awarded it a first prize. Contestants were asked to write an 800-word essay detailing how they and their communities had been affected by the economic downturn of 2008.

"The Natural Order of a Small Town" is Miller's response to that assignment. Published in 2009, it presents a detailed description of economic and social conditions in rural Arkansas.

Introduction promises to focus on changes in the region

Particular details show the dilapidated condition of the library

Additional details contribute to the DOMINANT IMPRESSION of the region as empty and economically depressed

States the main point of the description

Explains the meaning of the title

The Natural Order of a Small Town

1 The strangest thing about the recession if you live in Arkansas is that things seem pretty much the same as they were before with the exception of a few subtle differences. It just seems like everyone else in the country is catching up.

2 The smallest library in the entire United States resides in a rural town in Arkansas, and it has no books in it. There is a blue tarp over the roof because it started leaking a few years ago. Small towns in the area are a lot like this tiny 15-by-24-foot library. These erstwhile communities are disappearing, leaving nothing but road signs, with lonely post offices, empty parks and closed gas stations. Public school districts have gotten so spread out that it's getting more and more difficult to afford diesel for the buses to pick children up for school. These are the kids living on dirt roads an hour away from the nearest city. Their parents are the ones losing the jobs.

3 The economic life of a small town in Arkansas has always been precarious, but the recession has accelerated the decline. There are still the same number of empty houses on stretches of highway. It's just that now you see more used vehicles for sale. Older generations believe that this is the natural order of things, like when a well dries up and a new one springs up somewhere else to take its place. This is why they save their Folgers coffee cans and anything else that might help to make life easier.

4 Growing up in areas like this is becoming harder, and so the numbers of young are dwindling, and small, rural areas are drying up. A graduating class of forty students has become a class of twenty, and the only explanation is that there are no local jobs. There are no local jobs because the timber industry is no longer what it used to be. In high school, kids look forward to having an office view of the interstate while sitting behind the wheel of an eighteen-wheeler that they might be lucky enough to own one day. Or maybe they will nab a job at the Willie Nelson water-bottling factory in the next town over, where new mothers drive to renew their WIC vouchers so they

can purchase baby formula and blocks of government cheese. Some
women, like my mother, sew cuffs on firemen's gloves in a factory.
They are happy to have a job with good insurance. It's not the
type of insurance that will help you quit smoking a pack a day
unless you're clinically depressed, but all the same it's good
insurance. It numbs the realization that you are hardly getting
paid anything.

> Miller is bringing his own family into the picture

I guess that one thing almost every employable person in this
area can look forward to is applying for a job at Wal-Mart. The
company was born in Arkansas, and it is always taking applications
because it's capable of weathering the storm. This is more than
can be said for Affiliated Southwest, an Arkansas food distributor
that abruptly declared bankruptcy earlier this summer, leaving
hundreds of small-town groceries sweating bullets and damning
the economy. Most of these stores simply readjusted to the
situation by going with other food distributors in neighboring
states, but many small business owners lost their retirements in
the process.

> 5
>
> Grammatical point of view shifts from third person to first person

Students and others throughout the country are being encouraged
to continue their education, and many of them do it by taking out
school loans or maxing out their mother's credit cards so she has to
take out loans herself, either from the credit union at the Social
Security office where she works or at the bank where her husband
used to deposit the proceeds from his air-conditioning business
before it went belly up.

> 6

Here and there you might find an independent farmer who still
remembers what it's like to be self-sufficient. And then there are
people like my father, who purchased cattle as a life insurance
policy, because insurance companies won't touch a man with a pre-
existing condition. All throughout the country there are now people
resolved to live their lives simply out of necessity and not want. In
the end maybe this is a good thing. Maybe sooner or later a new
spring will bloom.

> 7
>
> Conclusion looks to individuals to bring hope and rejuvenation to natural order

Analyzing a Student Description

In "The Natural Order of a Small Town," Jim Miller draws upon rhetorical strategies and techniques that good writers use all the time when they write a description. The following questions, in addition to focusing on particular aspects of Miller's text, will help you to identify those common strategies and techniques so you can adapt them to your own writing. These questions will also help to prepare you for the analytical questions—on content, structure, and language—that you'll find after all the other selections in this chapter, along with suggestions for writing on related topics.

READING CLOSELY

1. As a result of the recession, says Jim Miller, the rest of the country is just now "catching up" with rural Arkansas (1). Why was the region he describes already in "decline" (3)?

2. Although "things seem pretty much the same as they were before," Miller notes "subtle differences" in the town since the economic downturn of 2008 (1). What are some of them, according to his description?

3. How has the recession affected Miller's family in particular? Point to specific details in the text that paint a clear picture of their situation.

STRATEGIES AND STRUCTURES

1. Miller organizes his description around the concept of a "natural order" (3). What kind of sequence does he have in mind? What phase or season does his description focus on?

2. Is Miller's description of the way the recession has affected his town more subjective or objective? Explain by citing particular details in the text.

3. Miller ends his essay with a reference to spring. How, and how well, does this conclusion fit the organizing principle of the rest of his description?

4. *Other Methods.* Miller's essay combines techniques of description with those of CAUSE AND EFFECT analysis. Which does he describe in greater detail, the causes of the recession or its effects? Why?

Thinking about Language

1. Look up the root meaning of *erstwhile* in your dictionary. Is the term a good choice for the situation Miller is describing? Explain.

2. Old-timers in the town, says Miller, explain what's happening in the region by comparing it to a well. How appropriate is this ANALOGY?

3. Explain the IRONY in Miller's reference to "an office view of the interstate" (4).

For Writing

1. In a paragraph or two describe the main differences you see in your community or family before and after the recession of 2008.

2. Contestants in the *Nation* writing contest were asked to compose an "800-word essay detailing how the recession had affected them." Write an essay giving your response to this topic.

A Nike Sneaker

When you describe something, such as a pair of classic Nike sneakers, you tell what it looks like and what characteristics distinguish it from other, similar objects. First released in 1984, the original Nike Vandals, for example, had uppers "made of thick canvas" rather than leather, the material of more mundane sneakers of the day. All editions were designed as basketball shoes. The more expensive Vandal Supremes, however, could be further distinguished from the basic model by uppers composed of nylon. They also were more visually complex, with a Velcro ankle strap that included a "three-way" color combination and two sets of laces that gave the wearer multiple options for mixing and matching. These last physical details, in particular, contribute to the dominant impression of stylishness that the writer of this description wanted to leave with the audience, sneaker fans who are told that the classic Vandal was "one of the first fashionable basketball shoes" and has never been surpassed for style and quality.

nike | vandal

NIKE VANDAL

AS FEATURED IN THE ROCK STEADY CREW'S UPROCK MUSIC VIDEO...

The Nike Vandal was made from 1984 until 1987. Its upper was made of thick canvas or nylon, rather than leather. The nylon editions were called Vandal Supreme and came with two different coloured sets of laces and a Velcro ankle support strap (with a three-way colour scheme).

The Vandal was one of the first fashionable basketball shoes. In 2003, the Vandal and Vandal Supreme returned. That year, an assortment of special editions were launched: the Jim Morrison, the Haight Street and the Geoff McFetridge. In 2004, camouflage and Premium editions were produced.

The original Vandals are rare gems: they ooze quality and look great. The reissues were not produced to the original spec, and sneaker fans tend to prefer the real thing.

SHOE DATA

FIRST RELEASED
1984
ORIGINAL PURPOSE
Basketball
EXAMPLE SHOWN
Original
NOTES
The Nike Vandal had a cameo appearance in the film *Terminator*.

VANDAL

ZAINAB SALBI

Little House in the War Zone

Zainab Salbi (b. 1969) is the founder and CEO of Women for Women International, a grassroots humanitarian organization that helps women survivors of war to rebuild their lives by distributing grants and microloans. Salbi grew up in Iraq, where her father was Saddam Hussein's personal pilot. She was sent to the United States for an arranged marriage at age 19. This marriage did not last, however, and Salbi started a new life, eventually graduating from George Mason University and the London School of Economics and Political Science. Her humanitarian work led to honors from the Clinton White House in 1995 and the Conrad N. Hilton Prize in 2005. She is the author of Between Two Worlds: Escape from Tyranny: Growing Up in the Shadow of Saddam *(with Laurie Becklund, 2005) and* The Other Side of War: Women's Stories of Survival and Hope *(2006).*

In "Little House in the War Zone," a September 2009 Op-Ed from the New York Times, *Salbi describes the rise and fall of her family home in Bagdad as it became a favored resort of the Iraqi president and his entourage in their black limousines.*

THE HOUSE I GREW UP IN was nestled in a grove of eucalyptus trees at the end of a Baghdad cul-de-sac. Built by my parents in 1969, the year I was born, it is a simple, two-story, middle-class home. I spent a lot of my childhood in my second-floor bedroom, watching the trees and the street outside. In my earliest memories, the cul-de-sac is teeming with water. While my parents bemoaned the lack of proper drainage in the city, I welcomed the floods. My brothers and I would splash through the rainwater, surrounded by enormous boats that my father lovingly constructed out of newspaper.

It was in this cul-de-sac, long after I went to bed, that Saddam Hussein used to park his car. At the time, Mr. Hussein, then vice president, was courting Baghdad society, and my parents were considered part of the "hip" crowd. My father had studied in Scotland and traveled the world as a commercial pilot, accumulating a collection of record albums; my mother was a fashionable, intelligent teacher who loved parties and dancing. Most important, they weren't interested in politics. So Mr. Hussein never viewed them as a threat to his power, and this made it safe for them to entertain him, though they never let on how hard it was to refuse any of Saddam Hussein's wishes, even then.

SUGGESTED MLA CITATION: Salbi, Zainab. "Little House in the War Zone." 2009. *Back to the Lake*. Ed. Thomas Cooley. 2nd ed. New York: Norton, 2012. 142–44. Print.

After he became president, Mr. Hussein made my father his personal pilot. The ³ president's visits to our house became official affairs. One car in the cul-de-sac morphed into an entourage of black Mercedes, and armed security guards patrolled the neighborhood. (This was during the war with Iran.) Watching from my window, I wondered about the white car hidden amidst the eucalyptus trees day and night.

The president showered us with gifts, but also monitored our every move. We ⁴ knew that our house was bugged, and we knew many family friends who had been executed for saying the "wrong thing" about his policies or his mistress. Looking back, I think of Mr. Hussein's presence in our life as a poisonous gas that leaked into our home. We inhaled it gradually.

In the summer of 1990, I left Iraq for an arranged marriage in the United States. ⁵ (My mother was adamant that I leave at any cost, and marriage was the safest way to do that with the president's approval.) I convinced myself that it wouldn't be long before I could return to my family's house.

But that August, Iraq invaded Kuwait and the country plunged into war yet ⁶ again. It took me nine years to return.

The occasion was my mother's funeral. In the intervening years, my mother had ⁷ left my father and fled to Jordan, Mr. Hussein had fired my father (thankfully, a rather lenient punishment for my mother's departure) and our house had fallen into disrepair. Its decay reflected not only our family's pain but also the suffering of a country which had endured widespread sanctions. After the funeral, I left as quickly as I could.

The second time I visited Iraq was in January 2003, on the eve of the American ⁸ invasion. After the regime fell, possibility infused the air. My younger brother decided to marry and live in the house. In preparation for the wedding, he repainted the walls and reupholstered the furniture. On the day of the celebration, friends and family, dressed in colorful clothes, danced in our cul-de-sac.

But the security situation deteriorated and my brother faced kidnapping threats. ⁹ In 2005, he, his wife and our father moved to Jordan, hoping, as I had, that they would someday return. Soon, our neighborhood, Al Mansour, was taken over by the Mahdi army—insurgents loyal to the cleric Moktada al-Sadr. Shiite families were allowed to stay, while Sunnis were driven out or killed. In the middle of the night, Sadrists barged into our house, and transformed it, according to our neighbors, into an execution center.

It is impossible to describe the sense of bewilderment I felt. All I could ¹⁰ think to tell my father was, "Let us just thank God that it is the house and not our family that is witnessing these atrocities."

To describe an abstract idea like "bewilderment," tie it to something concrete (p. 122) like a building.

By last summer, Iraqi and American troops had driven the militias out. ¹¹ In the increasing stability, a group of prostitutes moved into the house. At first I was relieved—and then I became sickened, thinking of the men using the room I'd grown up in to take advantage of women forced by circumstance into prostitution.

Just last fall, my father went back to Iraq, wanting to see for himself what had 12 become of his country. He found that our home was no longer an execution center nor a brothel; it was being used by the Iraqi Army.

Corrupt soldiers demanded $30,000 from my father before they'd leave the 13 house. He contemplated selling, giving up hope for good, but he is now waiting them out. In this respect, he is like many Iraqis—aware of the progress made, pleased that American troops have withdrawn, but worried about renewed violence and unsure of the future.

The only constant, it seems, is the house, which has witnessed the best and 14 worst of Iraq's recent history. A place that was once filled with the happiness of my childhood, the fear of Saddam Hussein, the loss of my mother, the joy of my brother's wedding, the horror of the execution center, the pain of the prostituted women and the weapons of the army, still holds my family's hopes and dreams.

Reading Closely

1. According to Zainab Salbi, why did Saddam Hussein choose her family and their home at the end of a quiet cul-de-sac in Bagdad for his frequent visits?

2. Salbi remembers a white car hidden "day and night" in the eucalyptus trees surrounding her childhood home (3). To whom does it belong? Why is it there?

3. Under what pretext did Salbi leave Iraq for the United States? For what reason did she return nine years later?

4. Despite all the pain his family has suffered there, Salbi's father wants to keep the family home. Why?

Strategies and Structures

1. Salbi opens her essay with a description of the flooded street outside her family's house in Bagdad and the delight she takes as a child playing in the water. Is this an appropriate introduction? Why or why not?

2. The focal point of Salbi's description is the house she grew up in. In describing the house and its "decay" (7), however, she is also describing her native country. What are some of the major points of comparison between the two?

3. Salbi says the sense of "bewilderment" that she felt after her childhood home was turned into an execution center is "impossible to describe" (10). Point out specific details throughout Salbi's essay that nonetheless convey to the reader an impression of bewildered innocence.

4. In the final paragraph, Salbi makes a point about the "hopes and dreams" of her family—and perhaps of her native land as a whole. What is her point and how does she sum it up here?

5. *Other Methods.* As she describes her childhood home, Salbi also tells about times when she and her family, particularly her father, returned to the house. How does Salbi use this NARRATIVE of departure and return to help organize her description?

THINKING ABOUT LANGUAGE

1. Salbi says that Sadam Hussein's presence in her family's home was like "a poisonous gas" (4). How does she enlarge and extend this SIMILE by saying that the family inhaled the poison "gradually" (4)?

2. Salbi refers to the house as a "witness" (10, 14). Is this an effective use of PERSONIFICATION? Why or why not?

3. Salbi refers to the house as a "constant" (14). What are the implications of this word, and how well does it fit her description?

4. Why has Salbi put the phrase "Little House" in her title? Explain the ALLUSION.

FOR WRITING

1. Write several paragraphs describing your childhood home. Try to capture the dominant sense—of stability, bewilderment, or some other feeling—that living there gave to your childhood (or a part of it).

2. Write an extended description of a house, store, apartment building, or other structure that, to your mind, EXEMPLIFIES the neighborhood or region in which it is located. Use specific details to give the reader a picture not only of the life or history of the structure but of its larger surroundings.

JOHN BRANCH

Perfection in the Horseshoe Pit

John Branch (b. 1968) is a sportswriter for the New York Times. *After graduating from business school at the University of Colorado in 1989, Branch went into retail sales and managed a Costco store in Denver before returning to school to study journalism in 1995. After covering several Super Bowls and other major sporting events, Branch began to look for stories in the less-traveled corners of the sports world.*

"Perfection in the Horseshoe Pit," which appeared in the Times *in July 2010, is typical of the offbeat subjects he seeks out. Almost purely descriptive, it captures the sights and sounds of warm evenings in a small Ohio town when spectators gather to watch (and listen) as a master horseshoe pitcher goes through his workout. Known only in the narrow circles of the horseshoe pit, the man at the center of Branch's descriptive essay—with a "ringer percentage" of over ninety—shows himself to be in some ways "the most dominant athlete in any sport in the country."*

Fʀᴏᴍ ʙᴇʜɪɴᴅ ᴀ ɴᴇᴀᴛ, ranch-style house on Melody Lane came the clinking and clanking rhythm of iron striking iron. 1

> Sensory details like these can help you create a dominant impression (p. 130).

Alan Francis stood more than a dozen long-legged strides from an inch-thick stake drilled deep into tacky clay. Perhaps the most dominant athlete in any sport in the country, Francis lifted his right arm, swung it behind him and forward again. 2

He launched a horseshoe toward the target 40 feet away. It weighed a little more than two and a half pounds and spun slowly, sideways. It rose and fell in an arc until its narrow open end, three and a half inches across, caught the stake with percussive perfection. 3

Clink. 4

Francis, satisfied but expressionless, pitched another. 5

Clank. 6

"Those are the sounds you want," he said, smiling. 7

Built narrow like a stake, with a mustache and a crew cut, Francis is widely considered the best horseshoe pitcher in history. He has won 15 world titles, including the past seven. He hopes to extend his streak in early August at the National Horseshoe Pitchers Association world tournament in Cedar Rapids, Iowa. 8

SUGGESTED MLA CITATION: Branch, John. "Perfection in the Horseshoe Pit." 2010. *Back to the Lake*. Ed. Thomas Cooley. 2nd ed. New York: Norton, 2012. 146–49. Print.

But the number that most impresses those whom the 40-year-old Francis routinely beats or who gather to watch him pitch is the key statistic in horseshoes: ringer percentage. 9

Get a ringer 70 percent of the time, and you are in a shrinking class of world-class pitchers. Get one 80 percent of the time, and you are probably in the top two. 10

Get one 90 percent of the time, and you are Alan Francis. 11

"Of all the guys that have pitched this game, he's the best," said Gerald Bernard, a veteran of a summer tournament circuit made up almost entirely of people with no hope of beating Francis. "No doubt." 12

In the championship game of last year's world tournament, which had more than 1,300 participants, Francis fell far behind Vermont's Brian Simmons, a two-time world champion and Francis' only viable rival. Francis pitched ringers on 25 of his final 26 shoes to win what some call the greatest match in the sport's history. 13

"When he gets on a roll, you're not going to beat him," Simmons said. 14

Francis finished the 19-game tournament with ringers on 917 of 1,016 pitches, a record 90.26 percent. 15

In late June, after a five-hour drive, Francis arrived at the Eastern National tournament in Erie, Pennsylvania. For an hour he attracted old friends and a few autograph and picture seekers. When he settled onto one of the courts to warm up, people crowded for the best view. 16

"He's the man I came to watch," one man said to another. 17

Clink. 18

"Jeez," the other said. "He's amazing." 19

Clank. 20

"I don't understand why he's practicing," a third onlooker said. "Can't get any better." 21

Francis began competing when he was 9, and won the first of four consecutive junior (under 18) world titles when he was 12. He won the men's world championship for the first time in 1989, at 19. He has won it 14 of the past 17 years. 22

"I've worked hard, honing that skill," Francis said. "At the same time, it's a gift. I think I was given the ability to do it." 23

Francis was born and raised in Blythedale, Missouri, part of a family of full-time farmers and part-time horseshoe pitchers. His earliest memory is of his father, Larry, pitching shoes in a pasture. 24

Francis attended his first world tournament in Des Moines in 1978. ("World" is a wishful misnomer in horseshoes, since few competitors come from beyond the United States and Canada.) Walter Ray Williams Jr., who gained greater fame as a professional bowler, won the first of his six world titles. 25

Also at that tournament was Amy Brown, whose family was equally enamored 26
of horseshoes. Now a three-time world runner-up, she and Francis married in
1996. They have a 6-year-old son, Alex, who tosses ringers from short distances.

Women, children and seniors pitch from 30 feet, not 40, and usually flip shoes 27
end over end. But a well-thrown flipped shoe can bounce off the stake, which is
why most top men's players spin their horseshoes horizontally. The shoes typically
rotate clockwise, one and a quarter or one and three-quarters times, virtually locking themselves onto the stake.

As a boy, Francis heaved horseshoes with a slow counterclockwise rotation. His 28
"three-quarter reverse" remains a trademark.

"I'd say there may be 1 percent or less that throw a three-quarter reverse," Fran- 29
cis said. "But that's the style that works for me, and that's the style I've tried to
perfect."

As with baseball pitchers, some windups are compact and quick, others flailing 30
and lurching. Francis has fewer moving parts than anyone—no hitches or stray
movements in his arm swing, joints or stride.

He holds the horseshoe sideways in his right hand, the open end pointed left, 31
his thumb on top. Feet nearly together, Francis gently swings his arm, then holds
the shoe in front of his face for a beat or two, using it as a frame to stare down the
target. His elbow is tight toward his belly button.

"Francis has fewer moving parts than anyone—no hitches or stray movements in his arm
swing, joints or stride."

Displaying little effort, Francis tosses each shoe as he steps with his left foot. 32
The horseshoe's arc reaches only about eight feet. ("More air, more error," said
Simmons, who also has a flat shot.)

Francis' manner is equally consistent. He tosses his two horseshoes, steps aside 33
to watch his opponent, and strides to the other end to determine the points. Even
his wife struggles to read his blank expression.

"I'm not real smart," Francis said with typical self-deprecation. "But I can focus 34
on things that are in front of me."

Francis received $4,000 for winning last year's world title. At that level, players 35
try to reach 40 points under a cancellation method, which means that a ringer by
one person (usually worth 3 points) cancels a ringer by the other.

Francis' sole sponsorship deal is with White Distributors, makers of tournament- 36
level horseshoes—including four designs stamped with Francis' name, costing up
to $81 a pair. Francis earns up to about $4,000 annually in royalties.

He buys Nike collar-less shirts to wear for the dozen or so competitions each 37
year, and tucks them into khaki shorts that are a couple of inches above his knee.
Any longer, and his hand or horseshoe might brush against them during the toss.

Francis was the first in his family to go to college, graduating from Northwest 38
Missouri State with an agronomy degree. He struggled to find an agricultural job
he liked and surprised everyone, including Amy, by moving from Missouri just
months into their romance in 1995.

"When we met, I had the better job," said Amy, the director of financial aid at 39
Defiance College.

Alan Francis is now a purchasing manager for the Hubbard Company, a family- 40
run commercial printing business. He works on the second floor in a wood-paneled
office, where the smell of ink from the printing room below hangs in the heavy air.

The office has no mementos of his alter-ego—no trophies or plaques or even a 41
lucky horseshoe tacked above the door. Most co-workers have never seen him
pitch. ("I've seen him throw on TV," said one, Ken Sanders.)

"Maybe it's the way my parents raised me," Francis said. "I don't brag, and don't 42
try to bring attention to myself if I don't have to."

His horseshoes tell most of the story, and their sound never lies. On warm eve- 43
nings in Defiance, they can be heard for blocks, emanating from a backyard up on
Melody Lane, the percussion of iron striking iron from 40 feet.

Clink. 44

Clank. 45

It is the backbeat of summer, the sound of perfection. 46

READING CLOSELY

1. How did Alan Francis get to be "the best horseshoe pitcher in history" (8)? What are some of his accomplishments in this unsung sport?

2. Why does Francis always pay close attention to how his shoes sound when they hit the stake? What does the sound tell him—and the writer who describes it?

3. What is John Branch talking about when he says that Francis "has fewer moving parts than anyone" (30)?

4. What does Francis' behavior and bearing at the office have in common with his behavior and bearing in the horseshoe pit?

5. Branch's descriptive essay includes information about how much money his subject makes in royalties. Is this information relevant? Why or why not?

STRATEGIES AND STRUCTURES

1. Branch's description of Francis in the horseshoe pit is intended to convey a sense of "perfection." How and how well do his words create that DOMINANT IMPRESSION in the reader? Through which details in particular?

2. What is the purpose of Branch's COMPARISON of his champion horseshoe pitcher with a baseball pitcher winding up (30)? How apt is the comparison? Explain.

3. How and where does Branch use the *sounds* of the sport he is describing to help tie his description together? Where does he shift the focus to the reader's (and spectators') sense of *sight*? Point out several instances where Branch pictures his subject with particular visual clarity.

4. Francis is said to exhibit "little effort" when pitching horseshoes with deadly accuracy (32). How does Branch solve the problem of describing a sportsman and a sport that display so little action?

5. *Other Methods.* Branch's essay is almost purely descriptive. Occasionally, however, he introduces elements of NARRATIVE. What are some of them, and how do they complement Branch's description of a stellar athlete?

THINKING ABOUT LANGUAGE

1. Why does Branch compare his subject to "a stake" rather than, say, a rope or a beanpole (8)?

2. A *misnomer* is an inaccurate name or description. Why does Branch say that "'World' is a wishful misnomer in horseshoes" (25)?

3. What is an *alter-ego*, and why does Branch use the term to describe Francis in his role as a champion horseshoe pitcher (41)?

4. How does Branch's reference to "the backbeat of summer" fit in with the sounds he describes as coming "from behind a neat, ranch-style house on Melody Lane" in Defiance, Ohio (46, 1)?

5. Branch DEFINES a number of terms that are unique to the sport of horseshoe pitching. Point out several, and explain what they mean.

6. Of any athlete in any sport, says Branch, Francis is the most "dominant" (2). What sort of distinction is he making here? Is it valid?

FOR WRITING

1. Observe a talented athlete engaged in his or her sport. In a paragraph or two, describe in some detail how he or she looks and sounds when making characteristic moves or plays.

2. Write a descriptive essay about an athlete, musician, or other performing artist who exhibits "perfection" in some demanding form of physical or intellectual endeavor. (A chess player would be a good example of the latter.) Try to make every detail in your essay contribute directly to that dominant impression.

JUDITH ORTIZ COFER

More Room

Judith Ortiz Cofer (b. 1952) is a native of Puerto Rico but moved to Paterson, New Jersey, as a small child. Though Ortiz Cofer grew up and went to school on the "mainland," she often returned for extended visits to her grandmother's home in Puerto Rico, the casa de Mamá *described in "More Room." This bicultural experience is the basis of much of Ortiz Cofer's writing, including her novel* The Meaning of Consuelo *(2003), which won the Americas Award, and* The Latin Deli *(1993), a collection of essays and poems that won the Anisfield-Wolf Book Award. A poet as well as a novelist, Ortiz Cofer teaches creative writing at the University of Georgia, where she is Franklin Professor of English.*

"More Room" is from Silent Dancing *(1990), a memoir of Ortiz Cofer's childhood in Puerto Rico and New Jersey. In this description, Ortiz Cofer shows how a few remembered details can bring back an entire scene and the people in it.*

Mʏ ɢʀᴀɴᴅᴍᴏᴛʜᴇʀ's ʜᴏᴜsᴇ is like a chambered nautilus; it has many rooms, 1
yet it is not a mansion. Its proportions are small and its design simple. It is a house that has grown organically, according to the needs of its inhabitants. To all of us in the family it is known as *la casa de Mamá*. It is the place of our origin; the stage for our memories and dreams of Island life.

Descriptive writing often includes figures of speech (p. 132).

    I remember how in my childhood it sat on stilts; this was before it had 2
a downstairs. It rested on its perch like a great blue bird, not a flying sort of bird, more like a nesting hen, but with spread wings. Grandfather had built it soon after their marriage. He was a painter and housebuilder by trade, a poet and meditative man by nature. As each of their eight children were born, new rooms were added. After a few years, the paint did not exactly match, nor the materials, so that there was a chronology to it, like the rings of a tree, and Mamá could tell you the history of each room in her *casa*, and thus the genealogy of the family along with it.

Her room is the heart of the house. Though I have seen it recently, and both 3
woman and room have diminished in size, changed by the new perspective of my eyes, now capable of looking over countertops and tall beds, it is not this picture I carry in my memory of Mamá's *casa*. Instead, I see her room as a queen's chamber where a small woman loomed large, a throne-room with a massive four-poster bed in its center which stood taller than a child's head. It was on this bed where her

SUGGESTED MLA CITATION: Ortiz Cofer, Judith. "More Room." 1990. *Back to the Lake.* Ed. Thomas Cooley. 2nd ed. New York: Norton, 2012. 152–55. Print.

own children had been born that the smallest grandchildren were allowed to take naps in the afternoons; here too was where Mamá secluded herself to dispense private advice to her daughters, sitting on the edge of the bed, looking down at whoever sat on the rocker where generations of babies had been sung to sleep. To me she looked like a wise empress right out of the fairy tales I was addicted to reading.

Though the room was dominated by the mahogany four-poster, it also contained 4 all of Mamá's symbols of power. On her dresser instead of cosmetics there were jars filled with herbs: *yerba buena, yerba mala,*[1] the making of purgatives and teas to which we were all subjected during childhood crises. She had a steaming cup for anyone who could not, or would not, get up to face life on any given day. If the acrid aftertaste of her cures for malingering did not get you out of bed, then it was time to call *el doctor.*

And there was the monstrous chifforobe she kept locked with a little golden key 5 she did not hide. This was a test of her dominion over us; though my cousins and I wanted a look inside that massive wardrobe more than anything, we never reached for that little key lying on top of her Bible on the dresser. This was also where she placed her earrings and rosary at night. God's word was her security system. This chifforobe was the place where I imagined she kept jewels, satin slippers, and elegant sequined, silk gowns of heartbreaking fineness. I lusted after those imaginary costumes. I had heard that Mamá had been a great beauty in her youth, and the belle of many balls. My cousins had other ideas as to what she kept in that wooden vault: its secret could be money (Mamá did not hand cash to strangers, banks were out of the question, so there were stories that her mattress was stuffed with dollar bills, and that she buried coins in jars in her garden under rosebushes, or kept them in her inviolate chifforobe); there might be that legendary gun salvaged from the Spanish-American conflict over the Island. We went wild over suspected treasures that we made up simply because children have to fill locked trunks with something wonderful.

On the wall above the bed hung a heavy silver crucifix. Christ's agonized head 6 hung directly over Mamá's pillow. I avoided looking at this weapon suspended over where her head would lay; and on the rare occasions when I was allowed to sleep on that bed, I scooted down to the safe middle of the mattress, where her body's impression took me in like a mother's lap. Having taken care of the obligatory religious decoration with a crucifix, Mamá covered the other walls with objects sent to her over the years by her children in the States. *Los Nueva Yores*[2] were represented by, among other things, a postcard of Niagara Falls from her son Hernán, postmarked,

1. *Yerba buena, yerba mala:* Literally "good herb, bad herb." *Yerba buena* usually refers to a species of mint. *Yerba mala* could be almost any "bad herb."
2. *Los Nuevas Yores:* The New Yorkers.

Buffalo, N.Y. In a conspicuous gold frame hung a large color photograph of her daughter Nena, her husband and their five children at the entrance to Disneyland in California. From us she had gotten a black lace fan. Father had brought it to her from a tour of duty with the Navy in Europe (on Sundays she would remove it from its hook on the wall to fan herself at mass). Each year more items were added as the family grew and dispersed, and every object in the room had a story attached to it, a *cuento* which Mamá would bestow on anyone who received the privilege of a day alone with her. It was almost worth pretending to be sick, though the bitter herb purgatives of the body were a big price to pay for the spirit revivals of her story-telling.

Mamá slept alone on her large bed, except for the times when a sick grandchild   7 warranted the privilege, or when a heartbroken daughter came home in need of more than herbal teas. In the family there is a story about how this came to be.

When one of the daughters, my mother or one of her sisters, tells the *cuento* of   8 how Mamá came to own her nights, it is usually preceded by the qualifications that Papá's exile from his wife's room was not a result of animosity between the couple, but that the act had been Mamá's famous bloodless coup for her personal freedom. Papá was the benevolent dictator of her body and her life who had had to be banished from her bed so that Mamá could better serve her family. Before the telling, we had to agree that the old man was not to blame. We all recognized that in the family Papá was as an *alma de Dios*, a saintly, soft-spoken presence whose main pleasures in life, such as writing poetry and reading the Spanish large-type editions of *Reader's Digest*, always took place outside the vortex of Mamá's crowded realm. It was not his fault, after all, that every year or so he planted a baby-seed in Mamá's fertile body, keeping her from leading the active life she needed and desired. He loved her and the babies. Papá composed odes and lyrics to celebrate births and anniversaries and hired musicians to accompany him in singing them to his family and friends at extravagant pig-roasts he threw yearly. Mamá and the oldest girls worked for days preparing the food. Papá sat for hours in his painter's shed, also his study and library, composing the songs. At these celebrations he was also known to give long speeches in praise of God, his fecund wife, and his beloved island. As a middle child, my mother remembers these occasions as a time when the women sat in the kitchen and lamented their burdens, while the men feasted out in the patio, their rum-thickened voices rising in song and praise for each other, *compañeros* all.

It was after the birth of her eighth child, after she had lost three at birth or in   9 infancy, that Mamá made her decision. They say that Mamá had had a special way of letting her husband know that they were expecting, one that had begun when, at the beginning of their marriage, he had built her a house too confining for her taste. So, when she discovered her first pregnancy, she supposedly drew plans for another room, which he dutifully executed. Every time a child was due, she would demand, *more space, more space*. Papá acceded to her wishes, child after child, since he had learned early that Mamá's renowned temper was a thing that grew like a monster along with a new belly. In this way Mamá got the house that she wanted, but with each child she lost in heart and energy. She had knowledge of her body and perceived that if she had any more children, her dreams and her plans would have to be permanently forgotten, because she would be a chronically ill woman, like Flora with her twelve children: asthma, no teeth, in bed more than on her feet.

And so, after my youngest uncle was born, she asked Papá to build a large room 10 at the back of the house. He did so in joyful anticipation. Mamá had asked him special things this time: shelves on the walls, a private entrance. He thought that she meant this room to be a nursery where several children could sleep. He thought it was a wonderful idea. He painted it his favorite color, sky blue, and made large windows looking out over a green hill and the church spires beyond. But nothing happened. Mamá's belly did not grow, yet she seemed in a frenzy of activity over the house. Finally, an anxious Papá approached his wife to tell her that the new room was finished and ready to be occupied. And Mamá, they say, replied: "Good, it's for *you*."

And so it was that Mamá discovered the only means of birth control available to 11 a Catholic woman of her time: sacrifice. She gave up the comfort of Papá's sexual love for something she deemed greater: the right to own and control her body, so that she might live to meet her grandchildren—me among them—so that she could give more of herself to the ones already there, so that she could be more than a channel for other lives, so that even now that time has robbed her of the elasticity of her body and of her amazing reservoir of energy, she still emanates the kind of joy that can only be achieved by living according to the dictates of one's own heart.

READING CLOSELY

1. Mamá's house in Puerto Rico was originally built on stilts to avoid high water, but the lower level got filled in when the family needed more room. How are these old additions different from the new room with shelves and a private entrance?

2. Mamá exercises "dominion" over all her house and family (5). Her grandchildren ascribe her power to the exotic items in her room, but what is the true source of her power?

3. If Mamá is the "queen" (3) of the house and household that Judith Ortiz Cofer describes, what are some of Papá's other roles (besides that of prince consort)?

4. When Papá is preparing birthday odes and patriotic hymns to be sung at annual feasts, what are the women in the family doing? Why? What is Ortiz Cofer suggesting about the culture she is describing?

5. Ortiz Cofer describes the outside of her grandmother's house before moving to the inside. What specific details does she focus upon?

STRATEGIES AND STRUCTURES

1. Why does Mamá need more room? What point is Ortiz Cofer making about women and families by describing her grandmother's home?

2. Once she moves inside the house, which room does Ortiz Cofer single out? Why? What does it contribute to her description of Mamá?

3. Ortiz Cofer is not so much describing her grandmother's house as it is today as the house as it exists in her memory. How is this "picture" different from present-day reality (3)? How does she capture the place from the viewpoint of a child?

4. Mamá's house is full of her "symbols of power" (4). What DOMINANT IMPRESSION of the place and of her do they help convey to the reader?

5. *Other Methods.* In addition to describing her grandmother's house and its contents, "More Room" tells the story of a "bloodless coup" (8). What coup? How does this NARRATIVE relate to Ortiz Cofer's description of the house?

THINKING ABOUT LANGUAGE

1. "Build three more stately mansions, O my soul. / As the swift seasons roll!" So begins the final stanza of "The Chambered Nautilus" (1858) by Oliver Wendell Holmes. How does Ortiz Cofer make use of this ALLUSION?

2. *Cuento* (6, 8) is the Spanish word for story. Why does Ortiz Cofer mention the telling of stories in her description?

3. Mamá's room, says Ortiz Cofer, is the "heart" of the house (3). What are the implications of this METAPHOR?

FOR WRITING

1. Write a paragraph or two in which you COMPARE the present-day aspects of a house, room, or other place with those of the place as you picture it in memory.

2. Write a description of a house or other place that captures the tension (or harmony) among its inhabitants by describing the physical features of the place.

How It Feels to Be Colored Me

Zora Neale Hurston (1891–1960) was a novelist and folklorist who was born in Ala-
bama but lived most of her life in Florida. After studying anthropology at Barnard
College and Columbia University, she collected folklore in the South, particularly Flor-
ida, and in Jamaica, Haiti, Bermuda, and Honduras. In the 1950s, she worked as a
maid, freelance writer, librarian, newspaper writer, and teacher. Late in life, she was a
librarian for the Library of Congress and a professor of drama at North Carolina Col-
lege. She is best known for her novel Their Eyes Were Watching God *(1937).*

"How It Feels to Be Colored Me" was first published in The World Tomorrow, *a*
Christian socialist magazine, in 1928, the year Hurston graduated from Barnard. It
opens with a description of Hurston's childhood experience in the all-black community
of Eatonville, Florida. When Hurston was thirteen, her mother died, and she was
obliged to leave Eatonville for Jacksonville, Florida. "How It Feels to Be Colored Me"
describes the difference Hurston feels between being black in an all-black community
and being black "against a sharp white background."

I AM COLORED but I offer nothing in the way of extenuating circumstances except   1
the fact that I am the only Negro in the United States whose grandfather on the
mother's side was *not* an Indian chief.

I remember the very day that I became colored. Up to my thirteenth year I lived   2
in the little Negro town of Eatonville, Florida. It is exclusively a colored town. The
only white people I knew passed through the town going to or coming from
Orlando. The native whites rode dusty horses, the Northern tourists chugged down
the sandy village road in automobiles. The town knew the Southerners and never
stopped cane[1] chewing when they passed. But the Northerners were something
else again. They were peered at cautiously from behind curtains by the timid. The
more venturesome would come out on the porch to watch them go past and got
just as much pleasure out of the tourists as the tourists got out of the village.

The front porch might seem a daring place for the rest of the town, but it was a   3
gallery seat for me. My favorite place was atop the gate-post. Proscenium box for a
born first-nighter.[2] Not only did I enjoy the show, but I didn't mind the actors

---

1. *Cane:* Sugarcane.
2. *First-nighter:* An avid theatergoer who makes a point of attending the first performances of new
plays. *Proscenium box:* Seats that are next to, and almost part of, the stage.

SUGGESTED MLA CITATION: Hurston, Zora Neale. "How It Feels to Be Colored Me." 1928. *Back to*
the Lake. Ed. Thomas Cooley. 2nd ed. New York: Norton, 2012. 157–61. Print.

knowing that I liked it. I usually spoke to them in passing. I'd wave at them and when they returned my salute, I would say something like this: "Howdy-do-well-I-thank-you-where-you-goin'?" Usually automobile or the horse paused at this, and after a queer exchange of compliments, I would probably "go a piece of the way" with them, as we say in farthest Florida. If one of my family happened to come to the front in time to see me, of course negotiations would be rudely broken off. But even so, it is clear that I was the first "welcome-to-our-state" Floridian, and I hope the Miami Chamber of Commerce will please take notice.

During this period, white people differed from colored to me only in that they 4 rode through town and never lived there. They liked to hear me "speak pieces" and sing and wanted to see me dance the parse-me-la,[3] and gave me generously of their small silver for doing these things, which seemed strange to me for I wanted to do them so much that I needed bribing to stop. Only they didn't know it. The colored people gave no dimes. They deplored any joyful tendencies in me, but I was their Zora nevertheless. I belonged to them, to the nearby hotels, to the county—everybody's Zora.

But changes came in the family when I was thirteen, and I was sent to school in 5 Jacksonville. I left Eatonville, the town of the oleanders, as Zora. When I disembarked from the river-boat at Jacksonville, she was no more. It seemed that I had suffered a sea change. I was not Zora of Orange County any more, I was now a little colored girl. I found it out in certain ways. In my heart as well as in the mirror, I became a fast brown—warranted not to rub nor run.

But I am not tragically colored. There is no great sorrow dammed up in my soul, nor 6 lurking behind my eyes. I do not mind at all. I do not belong to the sobbing school of Negrohood who hold that nature somehow has given them a lowdown dirty deal and whose feelings are all hurt about it. Even in the helter-skelter skirmish that is my life, I have seen that the world is to the strong regardless of a little pigmentation more or less. No, I do not weep at the world—I am too busy sharpening my oyster knife.

Someone is always at my elbow reminding me that I am the granddaughter of 7 slaves. It fails to register depression with me. Slavery is sixty years in the past. The operation was successful and the patient is doing well, thank you. The terrible struggle that made me an American out of a potential slave said "On the line!" The Reconstruction said "Get set!"; and the generation before said "Go!"[4] I am off to a flying start and I must not halt in the stretch to look behind and weep. Slavery is the price I paid for civilization, and the choice was not with me. It is a bully adven-

3. *Parse-me-la*: A dance popular in the southern United States in the 1890s.
4. *The terrible struggle . . . "Go!"*: Hurston is comparing the U.S. Civil War (1861–1865) and the period immediately following to the beginning of a race.

ture and worth all that I have paid through my ancestors for it. No one on earth ever had a greater chance for glory. The world to be won and nothing to be lost. It is thrilling to think—to know that for any act of mine, I shall get twice as much praise or twice as much blame. It is quite exciting to hold the center of the national stage, with the spectators not knowing whether to laugh or to weep.

The position of my white neighbor is much more difficult. No brown specter 8 pulls up a chair beside me when I sit down to eat. No dark ghost thrusts its leg against mine in bed. The game of keeping what one has is never so exciting as the game of getting.

I do not always feel colored. Even now I often achieve the unconscious Zora of 9 Eatonville before the Hegira.[5] I feel most colored when I am thrown against a sharp white background.

Writing as a college student, Hurston keeps returning to the vantage point (p. 131) of childhood.

For instance at Barnard. "Beside the waters of the Hudson"[6] I feel my 10 race. Among the thousand white persons, I am a dark rock surged upon, and overswept, but through it all, I remain myself. When covered by the waters, I am; and the ebb but reveals me again.

Sometimes it is the other way around. A white person is set down in our midst, 11 but the contrast is just as sharp for me. For instance, when I sit in the drafty basement that is The New World Cabaret with a white person, my color comes. We enter chatting about any little nothing that we have in common and are seated by the jazz waiters. In the abrupt way that jazz orchestras have, this one plunges into a number. It loses no time in circumlocutions, but gets right down to business. It constricts the thorax and splits the heart with its tempo and narcotic harmonies. This orchestra grows rambunctious, rears on its hind legs and attacks the tonal veil with primitive fury, rending it, clawing it until it breaks through to the jungle beyond. I follow those heathen—follow them exultingly. I dance wildly inside myself; I yell within, I whoop; I shake my assegai[7] above my head, I hurl it true to the mark *yeeeeooww!* I am in the jungle and living in the jungle way. My face is painted red and yellow and my body is painted blue. My pulse is throbbing like a war drum. I want to slaughter something—give pain, give death to what, I do not know. But the piece ends. The men of the orchestra wipe their lips and rest their fingers. I creep back slowly to the veneer we call civilization with the last tone and find the white friend sitting motionless in his seat, smoking calmly.

5. *Hegira:* Great escape; literally, Muhammad's flight from Mecca in A.D. 622.
6. *"Beside the waters of the Hudson":* In Psalm 137, the Jewish people, exiled from Jerusalem, long for their homeland as they mourn "by the rivers of Babylon." Barnard is located near the Hudson River.
7. *Assegai:* African hunting spear.

"Good music they have here," he remarks, drumming the table with his   12
fingertips.

Music. The great blobs of purple and red emotion have not touched him. He has   13
only heard what I felt. He is far away and I see him but dimly across the ocean and
the continent that have fallen between us. He is so pale with his whiteness then
and I am so colored.

At certain times I have no race, I am *me*. When I set my hat at a certain angle and   14
saunter down Seventh Avenue, Harlem City, feeling as snooty as the lions in front
of the Forty-Second Street Library, for instance. So far as my feelings are con-

Zora Neale Hurston in the 1950s.

cerned, Peggy Hopkins Joyce on the Boule Mich[8] with her gorgeous raiment, stately carriage, knees knocking together in a most aristocratic manner, has nothing on me. The cosmic Zora emerges. I belong to no race nor time. I am the eternal feminine with its string of beads.

I have no separate feeling about being an American citizen and colored. I am merely a fragment of the Great Soul that surges within the boundaries. My country, right or wrong.   15

Sometimes, I feel discriminated against, but it does not make me angry. It merely astonishes me. How *can* any deny themselves the pleasure of my company? It's beyond me.   16

But in the main, I feel like a brown bag of miscellany propped against a wall. Against a wall in company with other bags, white, red and yellow. Pour out the contents, and there is discovered a jumble of small things priceless and worthless. A first-water diamond, an empty spool, bits of broken glass, lengths of string, a key to a door long since crumbled away, a rusty knife-blade, old shoes saved for a road that never was and never will be, a nail bent under the weight of things too heavy for any nail, a dried flower or two still a little fragrant. In your hand is the brown bag. On the ground before you is the jumble it held—so much like the jumble in the bags, could they be emptied, that all might be dumped in a single heap and the bags refilled without altering the content of any greatly. A bit of colored glass more or less would not matter. Perhaps that is how the Great Stuffer of Bags filled them in the first place—who knows?   17

8. *Peggy Hopkins Joyce on the Boule Mich:* Joyce was an American actress and celebrity in the 1920s known for her extravagant style. Boulevard Saint-Michel is a street in Paris once famous for the intellectuals and artists who dominated its shops and cafes.

✳ ⟍⋯⋯

READING CLOSELY

1. Which is more important in Zora Neale Hurston's view: race or personal identity? Explain.

2. Before young Zora "became colored" (2), what was the main difference in her mind between white folks and colored folks?

3. What happened to change Hurston's sense of race and color? What effects did this experience have upon her life?

4. When and why does Hurston "feel" her race most sharply?

5. Why does Hurston describe the position of her white neighbor as "much more difficult" (8)?

Strategies and Structures

1. Hurston begins her description of how she feels by denying that she is the grand-daughter of an Indian chief. What point is she making about her identity?

2. In the next three paragraphs, Hurston describes her childhood self. What are some of the main characteristics and qualities of "Zora of Orange County" (5)? What DOMINANT IMPRESSION of her childhood does Hurston convey here?

3. What qualities does Hurston assign to her adult self when she feels surrounded by a sea of whiteness—as, for example, when she is in college?

4. Hurston's essay originally appeared in a magazine intended for a liberal Christian readership. In what ways is her message addressed to such an audience?

5. *Other Methods.* Hurston ends by COMPARING the contents of various mixed bags of odds and ends (17). What is the point of this comparison?

Thinking about Language

1. Notice the PUN in Hurston's title. How would the meaning change if she had said "colored *like* me"?

2. Hurston refers to her front porch in Eatonville as a "gallery" and to the passers-by as "actors" (3). Where else does she use METAPHORS from the theater to describe her experience of race in America?

3. "The operation was successful," says Hurston (7). What operation is she talking about? Why the surgical metaphor?

4. A trained anthropologist, Hurston claims to return to the jungle in paragraph 11. How does her language in this paragraph—"circumlocutions," "tonal veil," "primitive fury," "the veneer we call civilization"—bear upon that claim?

For Writing

1. You have just entered a favorite nightspot, real or imagined. The music is playing. You are not alone. Describe the scene in a paragraph or two.

2. Write an essay describing your own first experience with racial, economic, or gender differences.

E. B. WHITE

Once More to the Lake

Elwyn Brooks White (1899–1985) was born in Mount Vernon, New York. He graduated from Cornell University in 1921 and worked as a journalist and advertising copywriter before joining the staff of the New Yorker *in 1926. From 1938 to 1943, he also wrote a regular column for Harper's Magazine. White's numerous books include the children's classic* Charlotte's Web *(1952) and his updating of William Strunk's 1918* Elements of Style *(1959), a guide to writing.*

Written in August 1941 on the eve of World War II, "Once More to the Lake" originally appeared in Harper's and helped to establish White's reputation as a leading essayist of his day. The lake described here is Great Pond in south-central Maine. As White returns to this familiar scene, it seems unchanged—at first.

ONE SUMMER, along about 1904, my father rented a camp on a lake in Maine and took us all there for the month of August. We all got ringworm from some kittens and had to rub Pond's Extract on our arms and legs night and morning, and my father rolled over in a canoe with all his clothes on; but outside of that the vacation was a success and from then on none of us ever thought there was any place in the world like that lake in Maine. We returned summer after summer—always on August 1 for one month. I have since become a salt-water man, but sometimes in summer there are days when the restlessness of the tides and the fearful cold of the sea water and the incessant wind that blows across the afternoon and into the evening make me wish for the placidity of a lake in the woods. A few weeks ago this feeling got so strong I bought myself a couple of bass hooks and a spinner and returned to the lake where we used to go, for a week's fishing and to revisit old haunts.

I took along my son, who had never had any fresh water up his nose and who had seen lily pads only from train windows. On the journey over to the lake I began to wonder what it would be like. I wondered how the time would have marred this unique, this holy spot—the coves and streams, the hills that the sun set behind, the camps and the paths behind the camps. I was sure that the tarred road would have found it out, and I wondered in what other ways it would be desolated. It is strange how much you can remember about places like that once you allow your mind to

SUGGESTED MLA CITATION: White, E.B. "Once More to the Lake." 1941. *Back to the Lake*. 1941. Ed. Thomas Cooley. 2nd ed. New York: Norton, 2012. 163–68. Print.

return into the grooves that lead back. You remember one thing, and that suddenly reminds you of another thing. I guess I remembered clearest of all the early mornings, when the lake was cool and motionless, remembered how the bedroom smelled of the lumber it was made of and of the wet woods whose scent entered through the screen. The partitions in the camp were thin and did not extend clear to the top of the rooms, and as I was always the first up I would dress softly so as not to wake the others, and sneak out into the sweet outdoors and start out in the canoe, keeping close along the shore in the long shadows of the pines. I remembered being very careful never to rub my paddle against the gunwale for fear of disturbing the stillness of the cathedral.

The lake had never been what you would call a wild lake. There were cottages 3 sprinkled around the shores, and it was in farming country although the shores of the lake were quite heavily wooded. Some of the cottages were owned by nearby farmers, and you would live at the shore and eat your meals at the farmhouse. That's what our family did. But although it wasn't wild, it was a fairly large and undisturbed lake and there were places in it that, to a child at least, seemed infinitely remote and primeval.

I was right about the tar: it led to within half a mile of the shore. But when I got 4 back there, with my boy, and we settled into a camp near a farmhouse and into the kind of summertime I had known, I could tell that it was going to be pretty much the same as it had been before—I knew it, lying in bed the first morning, smelling the bedroom and hearing the boy sneak quietly out and go off along the shore in a boat. I began to sustain the illusion that he was I, and therefore, by simple transposition, that I was my father. This sensation persisted, kept cropping up all the time we were there. It was not an entirely new feeling, but in this setting, it grew much stronger. I seemed to be living a dual existence. I would be in the middle of some simple act, I would be picking up a bait box or laying down a table fork, or I would be saying something, and suddenly it would be not I but my father who was saying the words or making the gesture. It gave me a creepy sensation.

We went fishing the first morning. I felt the same damp moss covering the 5 worms in the bait can, and saw the dragonfly alight on the tip of my rod as it hovered a few inches from the surface of the water. It was the arrival of this fly that convinced me beyond any doubt that everything was as it always had been, that the years were a mirage and that there had been no years. The small waves were the same, chucking the rowboat under the chin as we fished at anchor, and the boat was the same boat, the same color green and the ribs broken in the same places, and under the floorboards the same freshwater leavings and débris—the dead helgramite, the wisps of moss, the rusty discarded fishhook, the dried blood from yesterday's catch. We stared silently at the tips of our rods, at the dragonflies that came and went. I lowered the tip of mine into the water, tentatively, pensively dislodging the fly, which darted two feet away, poised, darted two feet back, and came to rest again a little farther up the rod. There had been no years between the ducking of this dragonfly and the other one—the one that was part of memory. I looked at the boy, who was silently watching his fly, and it was my hands that held his rod, my eyes watching. I felt dizzy and didn't know which rod I was at the end of.

We caught two bass, hauling them in briskly as though they were mackerel, pulling them over the side of the boat in a businesslike manner without any landing net, and stunning them with a blow on the back of the head. When we got back for a swim before lunch, the lake was exactly where we had left it, the same number of inches from the dock, and there was only the merest suggestion of a breeze. This seemed an utterly enchanted sea, this lake you could leave to its own devices for a few hours and come back to, and find that it had not stirred, this constant and trustworthy body of water. In the shallows, the dark, water-soaked sticks and twigs, smooth and old, were undulating in clusters on the bottom against the clean ribbed sand, and the track of the mussel was plain. A school of minnows swam by, each minnow with its small individual shadow, doubling the attendance, so clear and sharp in the sunlight. Some of the other campers were in swimming, along the shore, one of them with a cake of soap, and the water felt thin and clear and unsubstantial. Over the years there had been this person with the cake of soap, this cultist, and here he was. There had been no years.

Up to the farmhouse to dinner through the teeming, dusty field, the road under our sneakers was only a two-track road. The middle track was missing, the one with the marks of the hooves and the splotches of dried, flaky manure. There had always been three tracks to choose from in choosing which track to walk in; now the choice was narrowed down to two. For a moment I missed terribly the middle alternative. But the way led past the tennis court, and something about the way it lay there in the sun reassured me; the tape had loosened along the backline, the alleys were green with plantains and other weeds, and the net (installed in June and removed in September) sagged in the dry noon, and the whole place steamed with midday heat and hunger and emptiness. There was a choice of pie for dessert, and one was blueberry and one was apple, and the waitresses were the same country girls, there having been no passage of time, only the illusion of it as in a dropped curtain—the waitresses were still fifteen; their hair had been washed, that was the only difference—they had been to the movies and seen the pretty girls with the clean hair.

Summertime, oh, summertime, pattern of life indelible, the fade-proof lake, the woods unshatterable, the pasture with the sweetfern and the juniper forever and ever, summer without end; this was the background, and the life along the shore was the design, the cottages with their innocent and tranquil design, their tiny docks with the flagpole and the American flag floating against the white clouds in the blue sky, the little paths over the roots of the trees leading from camp to camp and the paths leading back to the outhouses and the can of lime for sprinkling, and at the souvenir counters at the store the miniature birch-bark canoes and the post-cards that showed things looking a little better than they looked. This was the American family at play, escaping the city heat, wondering whether the newcomers in the camp at the head of the cove were "common" or "nice," wondering whether it was true that the people who drove up for Sunday dinner at the farm-house were turned away because there wasn't enough chicken.

Don't forget to tell the reader *why* (p. 127) you're describing "all this."

It seemed to me, as I kept remembering all this, that those times and those summers had been infinitely precious and worth saving. There had been jollity and peace and goodness. The arriving (at the beginning of August) had been so big a business in itself, at the railway station the farm wagon drawn up, the first smell of the pine-laden air, the first glimpse of the smiling farmer, and the great importance of the trunks and your father's enormous authority in such matters, and the feel of the wagon under you for the long ten-mile haul, and at the top of the last long hill catching the first view of the lake after eleven months of not seeing this cherished body of water. The shouts and cries of the other campers when they saw you, and the trunks to be unpacked, to give up their rich burden. (Arriving was less exciting nowadays, when you sneaked up in your car and parked it under a tree near the camp and took out the bags and in five minutes it was all over, no fuss, no loud wonderful fuss about trunks.) 9

Peace and goodness and jollity. The only thing that was wrong now, really, was the sound of the place, an unfamiliar nervous sound of the outboard motors. This was the note that jarred, the one thing that would sometimes break the illusion and set the years moving. In those other summertimes all motors were inboard; and when they were at a little distance, the noise they made was a sedative, an ingredient of summer sleep. They were one-cylinder and two-cylinder engines, and some were make-and-break and some were jump-spark, but they all made a sleepy sound across the lake. The one-lungers throbbed and fluttered, and the twin-cylinder ones purred, and purred, and that was a quiet sound, too. But now the campers all had outboards. In the daytime, in the hot mornings, these motors made a petulant, irritable sound; at night, in the still evening when the afterglow lit the water, they whined about one's ears like mosquitoes. My boy loved our rented outboard, and his great desire was to achieve single-handed mastery over it, and authority, and he soon learned the trick of choking it a little (but not too much), and the adjustment of the needle valve. Watching him I would remember the things you could do with the old one-cylinder engine with the heavy flywheel, how you could have it eating out of your hand if you got really close to it spiritually. Motorboats in those days didn't have clutches, and you would make a landing by shutting off the motor at the proper time and coasting in with a dead rudder. But there was a way of reversing them, if you learned the trick, by cutting the switch and putting it on again 10 exactly on the final dying revolution of the flywheel, so that it would kick back against compression and begin reversing. Approaching a dock in a strong following breeze, it was difficult to slow up sufficiently by the ordinary coasting method, and if a boy felt he had complete mastery over his motor, he was tempted to keep it running beyond its time and then reverse it a few feet from the dock. It took a cool nerve, because if you threw the switch a twentieth of a second too soon you would catch the flywheel when it still had speed enough to go up past center, and the boat would leap ahead, charging bull-fashion at the dock.

We had a good week at the camp. The bass were biting well and the sun shone 11 endlessly, day after day. We would be tired at night and lie down in the accumulated heat of the little bedrooms after the long hot day and the breeze would stir almost imperceptibly outside and the smell of the swamp drift in through the rusty screens. Sleep would come easily and in the morning the red squirrel would be on the roof, tapping out his gay routine. I kept remembering everything, lying in bed in the mornings—the small steamboat that had a long rounded stern like the lip of a Ubangi, and how quietly she ran on the moonlight sails, when the older boys played their mandolins and the girls sang and we ate doughnuts dipped in sugar, and how sweet the music was on the water in the shining night, and what it had felt like to think about girls then. After breakfast, we would go up to the store and the things were in the same place—the minnows in a bottle, the plugs and spinners[1] disarranged and pawed over by the youngsters from the boys' camp, the Fig Newtons and the Beeman's gum. Outside, the road was tarred and cars stood in front of the store. Inside, all was just as it had always been, except there was more Coca-Cola and not so much Moxie and root beer and birch beer and sarsaparilla. We would walk out with the bottle of pop apiece and sometimes the pop would backfire up our noses and hurt. We explored the streams, quietly, where the turtles slid off logs and dug their way into the soft bottom; and we lay on the town wharf and fed worms to the tame bass. Everywhere we went I had trouble making out which was I, the one walking at my side, the one walking in my pants.

One afternoon while we were there at that lake a thunderstorm came up. It was 12 like the revival of an old melodrama that I had seen long ago with childish awe. The second-act climax of the drama of the electrical disturbance over a lake in America has not changed in any important respect. This was the big scene, still the big scene. The whole thing was so familiar, the first feeling of oppression and heat and a general air around camp of not wanting to go very far away. In midafternoon (it was all the same) a curious darkening of the sky, and a lull in everything that had made life tick; and then the way the boats suddenly swung the other way at their moorings with the coming of a breeze out of the new quarter, and the

---

1. *Plugs and spinners*: Types of fishing lures.

premonitory rumble. Then the kettle drum, then the snare, then the bass drum and cymbals, then crackling light against the dark, and the gods grinning and licking their chops in the hills. Afterward the calm, the rain steadily rustling in the calm lake, the return of light and hope and spirits, and the campers running out in joy and relief to go swimming in the rain, their bright cries perpetuating the deathless joke about how they were getting simply drenched, and the children screaming with delight at the new sensation of bathing in the rain, and the joke about getting drenched linking the generations in a strong indestructible chain. And the comedian who waded in carrying an umbrella.

When the others went swimming, my son said he was going in, too. He pulled his dripping trunks from the line where they had hung all through the shower and wrung them out. Languidly, and with no thought of going in, I watched him, his hard little body, skinny and bare, saw him wince slightly as he pulled up around his vitals the small, soggy, icy garment. As he buckled the swollen belt, suddenly my groin felt the chill of death.   13

Reading Closely

1. When and with whom did E. B. White first visit the lake he describes so palpably? With whom—and in approximately what time period—does he return to the lake, as described in his essay?

2. What DOMINANT IMPRESSION of the lake and its surrounding do you take away from White's description? Explain.

3. In paragraph 2, is White describing the lake as it was in the past, or as it is in the present time of his essay? How about in paragraphs 4–6? And in paragraph 11? Explain.

4. In addition to his own adventures on the lake, White is also describing those of "the American family at play" (8). What sentiments and behaviors does he identify as particularly American?

5. Do American families still take summer vacations "at the lake"? How has the pattern of family play—on a lake or elsewhere—changed since White wrote his essay? How has it remained the same?

Strategies and Structures

1. In his description of the "primeval" lake, White stresses its qualities of calm and timelessness (3). What particular details contribute most effectively to this impression? What is his point in making it?

2. When he returned to the lake with his young son, the two of them went fishing, says White, "the first morning" (5). Point out other direct references to time in White's essay. How does he use CHRONOLOGY and the passing of time to organize his entire description?

3. One way in which the lake of his childhood has definitely changed, says White, is in its sounds. What new sounds does he describe? How does he incorporate this change into his description of the lake as a timeless place?

4. How would White's essay have been different without the last paragraph, in which he watches his young son get ready to go swimming?

5. *Other Methods.* As White describes the lake, he also tells a story about it. What's the plot of that story? How does White's NARRATIVE fit in with and support his description?

THINKING ABOUT LANGUAGE

1. What is the difference between an illusion and a "mirage" (5)? How and where do White's physical descriptions of the lake lead him to willful misinterpretations of the scene?

2. When he describes the lake as not only "constant" but "trustworthy" (6), White has PERSONIFIED the natural scene. When and where does it seem to take on a mind of its own in sharp contrast to his desires?

3. Why does White repeat the word *same* in paragraph 5?

4. When out in the boat alone as a boy, White did not want to disturb the "stillness of the cathedral" (2). What are the implications of this phrase? In what ways is White's son depicted as a chip off the old block?

5. The lake that White describes might be said to reside as much in memory as in the state of Maine. Why might fishing in a pond or lake provide an especially apt METAPHOR for probing memory—and writing about it?

FOR WRITING

1. Briefly describe a memorable family vacation or other outing. What do you remember most about it, and why? Try to recall the details that led you to this memory.

2. Recall a place that seemed "unique" or "holy" to you when you first visited it. Write an essay describing how it has changed since then, and how it has remained the same. In choosing details to include, think about what dominant impression you want to give.

3. Write an essay describing how a familiar sight, taste, or sound triggers your remembrance of things past. Try to tie what you find back in with the present.

RITA DOVE

American Smooth

Rita Dove (b. 1952) was the Poet Laureate of the United States from 1993 to 1995. A native of Akron, Ohio, where she played the cello from a young age, she attended Miami University in Oxford, Ohio, and the Writer's Workshop at the University of Iowa. Dove is currently Commonwealth Professor of English at the University of Virginia at Charlottesville. Her poetry collections include On the Bus with Rosa Parks *(1999),* American Smooth *(2004), and* Sonata Mulattica *(2009). Dove is married to the German writer Fred Viebahn, her partner in the ballroom dances described in* American Smooth.*

Her method in these poems, Dove told an interviewer, was "to provide a humble description of the dance technique—what each part of the body should be doing . . . in the hopes of finding the poem's true desire, to achieve flight of consciousness, a lifting of the spirit as well as of the human form." In the title poem of American Smooth, *however, the speaker focuses her description on the sensation (and appearance) of weightlessness, which she considers the "goal" of any dance.*

> We were dancing—it must have
> been a foxtrot or a waltz,
> something romantic but
> requiring restraint,
> rise and fall, precise   5
> execution as we moved
> into the next song without
> stopping, two chests heaving
> above a seven-league
> stride—such perfect agony   10
> one learns to smile through,
> ecstatic mimicry
> being the *sine qua non*
> of American Smooth.
> And because I was distracted   15
> by the effort of
> keeping my frame

SUGGESTED MLA CITATION: Dove, Rita. "American Smooth." 2004. *Back to the Lake*. Ed. Thomas Cooley. 2nd ed. New York: Norton, 2012. 170–71. Print.

(the leftward lean, head turned
just enough to gaze out   20
past your ear and always
smiling, smiling),
I didn't notice
how still you'd become until
we had done it   25
(for two measures?
four?)—achieved flight,
that swift and serene
magnificence,
before the earth   30
remembered who we were
and brought us down.

READING CLOSELY

1. In "American Smooth" is Rita Dove describing the particular moves of two people dancing, or how those moves felt to one of them at the time? Or both of
   these? Explain.

2. According to Dove, the essential ingredient or quality that DEFINES American
   Smooth is "ecstatic mimicry" (12). What do you think she means by this
   phrase?

3. Why is the speaker in Dove's poem always "smiling, smiling" (21)?

STRATEGIES AND STRUCTURES

1. From whose perspective does Dove describe the dancing couple in her poem?
   Why do you think she chooses this POINT OF VIEW?

2. Is the description of the dancers more SUBJECTIVE or OBJECTIVE? Where does
   the speaker in Dove's poem reach the heights, so to speak, of subjectivity?
   Where is he or she most objective in describing the physical scene?

3. What DOMINANT IMPRESSION of the dancers and the dance does Dove give the
   reader in "American Smooth"? Which particular details in her description do
   you think contribute most directly to this impression?

4. Dove renders her entire poem in two long, flowing sentences. Why do you think
   she choose this structure for her theme?

5. *Other Methods.* Dove describes a dance step that she and her partner executed so well that they seemed, for a moment, to be flying. What does the dance step EXEMPLIFY in American culture generally? What else is she describing?

Thinking about Language

1. In "Puss in Boots" and other folk and fairy tales, "seven-league boots" allow the wearer to cover great distances—a league is often defined as approximately three miles—in a single stride. Explain the ALLUSION to this magical footwear in line 9 of Dove's poem.

2. "Perfect agony" is a contradiction in terms (10). Is the OXYMORON justified here? Why or why not?

3. *Sine qua non* is Latin for "without which none" (13). How appropriate is the phrase as Dove uses it here? Explain.

4. What's so "American," according to Dove, about the smooth style of dancing (and more?) that she is describing?

For Writing

1. In a paragraph or two, explain how to execute a particular dance step—such as the dos-à-do, enchufla, gancho, grapevine, heel pull, or moonwalk—by describing what skilled dancers do when they execute that step.

2. Write an essay describing a time on the dance floor, or basketball or tennis court, or in the gym or swimming pool, or on a skateboard or bicycle when you felt as if you were achieving flight. Be sure to describe not only how you felt but the exact moves that made you feel that way.

CHAPTER 6

Example

Few things are harder to put up with than the annoyance of a good example.
—MARK TWAIN

An art dealer knows at a glance that a supposedly ancient statue is a fake. After five minutes in a new course, a student accurately predicts that the professor is going to be a brilliant teacher—or a bore. Listening to a husband and wife bicker in his office, a trained psychologist can tell, with 90 percent accuracy, whether the couple will still be together in fifteen years. These are all examples that journalist Malcolm Gladwell uses to illustrate "thin-slicing," the idea that human beings can make accurate judgments based on "the very thinnest slice" of information.

Examples help us to understand such concepts by giving us a slice of information that is typical of the whole pie. Because a single good example is often worth a dozen lengthy explanations, we use examples all the time to support or explain what we have to say. The use of examples—exemplification—is so basic to human communication, in fact, that it is hard to imagine writing without them.

Defining Exemplification:
Giving a "For Instance"

When you define something, such as thin-slicing or the law of supply and demand, you say what it is. When you exemplify something, you give an instance or illustration. To show us what he means by thin-slicing, Gladwell cites the example of an experienced police officer who knows from the look of fear on a gang member's face that he doesn't have to shoot, even though the youth is in the act of pulling a gun:

"He was fourteen, looked like he was nine. If he was an adult I think I probably would have shot him. I sure perceived the threat of that gun. . . . I think
the fact that I was an experienced officer had a lot to do with my decision. I
could see a lot of fear in his face, which I also perceived in other situations,
and that led me to believe that if I would just give him just a little bit more
time that he might give me an option to not shoot him."

—Malcolm Gladwell, *Blink*

This is, as Gladwell goes on to say, "a beautiful example" of the complicated psychological process he is explaining.

Examples are specific items or instances—a crispy taco with guacamole, "The
Raven," a fast-thinking cop who decides not to shoot a teenager—that can be taken
to represent a whole group: Tex-Mex food, the poems of Edgar Allan Poe, psychological thin-slicing.

In this chapter, we will see how to choose examples that truly represent—or
exemplify—your subject. We'll consider how many and what kinds of examples are
sufficient to make your point about that subject, and then discuss how to organize
an entire essay around those examples. Finally, we'll review critical points to watch
for as you read over an exemplification essay, as well as common errors to avoid
when you edit.

Why Do We Cite Examples?

For most of us, it is easier to digest a piece of pie than the whole pie at once. The
same goes for examples: They make general concepts easier to grasp (and swal-
low), and they give the flavor of the whole in a single bite. As writers, we cite
examples to explain ABSTRACT ideas or support general statements by making
them more CONCRETE and specific.

Suppose we were writing about a street bazaar and wanted to make the point that
it seemed to offer everything. This may sound like a straightforward statement, but
it could refer to almost anything—from livestock to homemade bread. To clarify
what we mean, we would need to give specific examples, as in the following:

Everything was for sale—flowers, bolts of cloth, candles, fruits and vegetables, shoes, coffee beans, toys, cheap jewelry, canned goods, religious articles, books, kerosene, candy, nylons, towels—all of it spilling onto the street
in colorful profusion.   —Frank Conroy, *Stop-Time*

Using examples like this helps us (and our readers) to narrow down the universe
from "everything" to something a little more specific. It shows just what corner of
the great bazaar we're talking about, and it gives the reader a more definite sense of

the bazaar's "colorful profusion." Even more important, by using concrete examples like bolts of cloth and kerosene, Conroy explains exactly what was for sale, making his statement clearer and more interesting.

Composing an Exemplification Essay

An exemplification essay consists of basically two parts: a statement about a general category of things or ideas ("everything was for sale") and specific items from that category that illustrate the statement ("bolts of cloth, candles, fruits and vegetables, shoes, coffee beans, toys, cheap jewelry," and so on). What if Conroy had illustrated his statement about the profusion of items on sale in the marketplace with the following examples instead: boxes and boxes of ladies' gloves, stall after stall of ladies' hats, piles and piles of ladies' shoes?

While these examples would illustrate the large numbers of items on offer in the marketplace, they lack variety and, consequently, don't fully support Conroy's statement that "everything" was on sale. When you compose an exemplification essay, consider which particular aspects of your subject you want to emphasize and look for examples that illustrate all of those qualities or characteristics.

As you come up with representative examples, you will also need to decide just how many examples to use and how best to organize them and present them to your readers. The exact number and kinds of examples you cite, however, will depend upon your AUDIENCE and PURPOSE, as well as the main point you're illustrating.

Thinking about Purpose and Audience

The purpose of "All Seven Deadly Sins Committed at Church Bake Sale," the satirical piece from the *Onion* included in this chapter, is to entertain readers who have some idea of what happens at church bake sales and who will be amused by an "exposé" of such a (normally) innocent event. For this purpose and audience, the writer chooses humorous, exaggerated examples of "sinful" behavior at the sale.

But suppose you wanted to write a straightforward, informative report about a bake sale for the church bulletin. In that case, you would focus on actual examples of the people staffing the booths and the kinds of baked goods sold. Or if you were writing about the bake sale in order to persuade others to participate next time, you might offer examples of the money earned at various booths, how much fun participants had, and what good causes the money will be used for. In each case, your purpose shapes the kinds of examples you use.

So does your audience. No matter what your subject, you need to take into account how much your audience already knows (or does not know) about your subject—the *Onion* piece is careful to define "deadly" sins for readers who might be in doubt—and how sympathetic they are likely to be to your position. Suppose you are writing a paper for a course in health and nutrition, and your purpose is to argue that the health of Americans in general has declined over the last decade. If you were writing for your teacher alone—or for an audience of doctors or nutritionists—a few key examples would probably suffice to make your point.

Your paper, however, is intended for a more general audience, such as your classmates. So you will need to give more background information and cite more (and more basic) examples than you would if you were addressing an audience of specialists. If your readers are unfamiliar with your subject or not likely to see it as you do, you are going to have to work even harder to come up with sufficient examples. For instance, you may have to give extra examples to remind the athletes in your audience that their physical condition is not necessarily representative of the general state of health among all Americans.

Generating Ideas:
Finding Good Examples

Techniques like LISTING, BRAINSTORMING, and CLUSTERING can help you come up with examples on almost any subject. As you select examples, look for ones that display as many of the typical characteristics of your subject as possible.

Suppose you were writing an essay about the seven deadly sins, and you decided to focus on the sin of gluttony. One characteristic of gluttony is overeating. As you looked around for good examples of this characteristic, you might be tempted to choose someone like the international speed-eating champion Sonya Thomas, who holds world records for devouring chicken wings (183 in twelve minutes), tacos (40 in ten minutes), and oysters (444 in eight minutes). She would seem to be a prime example of gluttony. Thomas, however, weighs only about a hundred pounds; and though she eats a lot, Thomas has many other characteristics, such as discipline and endurance, that we typically associate with great athletes. Perhaps she isn't such a good example of a glutton after all.

So as you look for examples, search for ones that exemplify *all* the essential traits of the subject you're examining. Gluttons, for instance, not only eat a lot; they are often lazy. To exemplify the concept of gluttony more accurately and completely, therefore, we need to look for something or someone who exhibits both of these essential traits. How about Jabba the Hutt, the obese alien of *Star Wars* fame? Would he, perhaps, make a better example of gluttony than Sonya Thomas?

Jabba eats a lot—that's why he is so grossly overweight. Also, when not eating, he is forever tugging at his water pipe, another sign of overindulgence. What about lethargy, a prime characteristic of the glutton? Jabba can hardly rise from his cushions, much less dart around the galaxy participating in eating contests. And when he does attempt to move, he waddles heavily from side to side. Since Jabba embodies most of the chief characteristics of a glutton—he is both fat *and* lazy—he would make a better example of gluttony than the trim and energetic Thomas.

Organizing and Drafting an Exemplification Essay

Once you have a number of examples that exhibit the chief characteristics of your subject, you're ready to organize them and put them in a draft. The simplest way to organize an exemplification essay is to state your THESIS at the beginning and then give your best examples to support it. You could also present your examples in order of increasing importance or interest, perhaps saving the best for last. Or, if you plan to use a large number of examples, you might organize them into categories.

However you organize your essay, you'll need to state your point clearly, provide sufficient and representative examples, and use transitions to help readers follow your text. The templates on page 178 can help you with your draft.

STATING YOUR POINT

Usually, in an exemplification essay, you will state your point directly in a thesis statement in your introduction. For example:

College teams depend more on teamwork than on star athletes for success.

In general, the health of Americans has declined over the last ten years.

Hillary Clinton's 2008 presidential campaign made a number of tactical errors.

From a close reading of almost any major scene in *The Great Gatsby*, we can conclude that Fitzgerald's narrator, Nick Carraway, is not to be trusted.

As observed on the popular websites devoted to harmful campus gossip, online anonymity poses serious ethical problems.

Each of these thesis statements cries out for specific examples to support it. How many specific examples would you need to do the job sufficiently—and what kinds?

PROVIDING SUFFICIENT EXAMPLES

Sufficiency isn't strictly a matter of numbers. Ultimately, whether or not your examples are sufficient to prove your point will depend on your audience. If your readers are inclined to agree with you, one or two well-chosen examples may suffice, which is what sufficiency implies: enough to do the job and no more. So consider your intended audience, and choose examples you think they will find interesting and convincing.

TEMPLATES FOR DRAFTING

When you begin to draft an essay based on examples, you need to identify the subject, say what its main characteristics are, and indicate specific examples that exhibit those characteristics—moves fundamental to exemplification. See how David Barboza makes such moves in the beginning of his essay in this chapter:

> Marketing experts call it extending the heritage brand . . . stocking the shelves with new twists on old, familiar names. Snickers, for instance, flavor Edy's ice cream. Nestlé candies are sprinkled on Chips Ahoy cookies. —DAVID BARBOZA, "Piling on the Cookies"

Barboza identifies his subject (the marketing practice of "extending the heritage brand"), says what the main characteristic of that practice is ("stocking the shelves with new twists on old, familiar names"), and indicates specific examples that exhibit that characteristic (Snickers in Edy's ice cream; Nestlé candies on Chips Ahoy cookies). Here is one more example taken from this chapter:

> Since commencement speakers traditionally offer advice to the young in June, here, in no particular order, are a dozen of the quotations that one reader calls to mind in moments of confusion, stress, and sorrow. —MICHAEL DIRDA, "Commencement Advice"

The following templates can help you make some of these basic moves in your own writing. But don't take these as formulas where you just fill in the blanks. There are no shortcuts to good writing, but these templates can serve as starting points.

▶ About X, it can generally be said that _____; a good example would be _____.

▶ The main characteristics of X are _____ and _____, as exemplified by _____, _____ and _____.

▶ For the best example(s) of X, we can turn to _____.

▶ _____ is a particularly representative example of X because _____.

▶ Additional examples of X include _____, _____, and _____.

▶ From these examples of X, we can conclude that _____.

Also, consider how broad or narrow your subject is. As you select examples to support a thesis, you have basically two choices: you can use multiple brief examples or one or two extended examples.

Multiple examples work well when you are dealing with different aspects of a large subject (a presidential campaign strategy) or exemplifying trends involving large numbers of people (Americans whose health has declined, college athletes). Extended examples, on the other hand, work better when you are talking about the implications of a particular case (a single scene in a novel; a particular website).

> To illustrate a marketing strategy, David Barboza uses multiple examples of Oreos (p. 194).

Take the proposition that the health of Americans, on average, has declined over the last ten years. To support a sweeping general statement like this, which applies to millions of people, you would probably need to use multiple examples rather than one or two extended ones.

On its website, the Institute of Medicine of the National Academies, lists eighteen indicators of the nation's health. If you were drawing on this data to make your point about the decline in health among Americans in recent years, you would not likely focus on only one or two of these indicators, since health is a broad topic that encompasses many factors. Instead, you would want to cite multiple examples—low birth weights in infants, tobacco use, obesity, reduced access to health insurance, shorter average life expectancies, and decreased spending on health care—of the many different factors that contribute to the general decline you are illustrating.

Now let's consider how a newspaper columnist uses a single, extended example to support his thesis about the problem of anonymity on the Internet:

> One site, called JuicyCampus.com, which maintains message boards on 59 university campuses, has been attracting special attention. As a recent article in *Radar Magazine* put it, JuicyCampus.com is "a virtual bathroom wall upon which college students across the country scrawl slurs, smears, and secrets, true or otherwise, about their classmates." In one feature, to take one modest example, . . . there were 47 postings in response, several of which gave names, apparently real ones.
> —RICHARD BERNSTEIN, "The Growing Cowardice of Online Anonymity"

Bernstein's thesis—that Internet anonymity raises serious ethical problems—addresses a large issue; but here is a case where a single example might be sufficient to make the point because it refers to many similar incidents (59 campuses, 47 postings) and because many readers could easily imagine themselves as victims of the practice that Bernstein describes. However, if your audience is likely to be divided on an issue, such as a political one, you would need to give more examples.

> Procter & Gamble uses an extended example to sell men's body wash (p. 207).

USING A RANGE OF REPRESENTATIVE EXAMPLES

Michael Dirda cites many examples from literature to illustrate the value of reading (p. 199).

Be sure that your examples fairly and accurately support the point you're making. For instance, if you were trying to convince readers that a particular political candidate failed to get elected because of errors in campaign tactics, you would need to cite a number of mistakes from different points in the campaign. Or if you were writing about how the best college athletic teams depend on teamwork for success, you would want to choose examples from several different teams.

Those examples should be as representative as possible. If you are writing, say, about the health benefits of swimming every day, Michael Phelps is probably not a good example. Even though Phelps is a great swimmer, he is not representative (or typical) of swimmers in general, the subject you're exemplifying.

USING TRANSITIONS BETWEEN EXAMPLES

To make a point with exemplification, you need to do more than state your claim and then give examples, no matter how effective they may be. You need to relate those examples to each other and to the point you're making by using clear TRANSITIONS and other connecting words and phrases.

"Piling on the Cookies" introduces new examples by asking, "Is Kraft . . . running out of ideas?" (p. 196, ¶16).

You can always use the phrases "for example" and "for instance": "The sloth, for example, is one of many animals that survive because of their protective coloration. Other animals—for instance, wolves and wild dogs—do so by going around in packs." But consider using other transitions and connecting phrases as well, such as: *more specifically, exactly, precisely, thus, namely, indeed, that is, in other words, in fact, in particular.* ("The sloth, in particular, survives by blending in with its surroundings.") Or try using a RHETORICAL QUESTION, which you then go on to answer: "So what strategy of survival does the sloth exemplify?"

USING OTHER METHODS

See how an historian makes her point by telling the life stories of several women (p. 211).

The purpose of examples is to give concrete and specific illustrations of a general topic. Consequently, the examples themselves should be presented in ways that are as concrete and specific as you can make them. Let's say you're writing on the topic of common survival strategies among mammals. As an example, you've chosen the three-toed sloth, a tree-inhabiting eater of insects and plants from Central and South America. You can present such an example in a number of ways.

For instance, you can DESCRIBE it in some detail: "covered with unkempt fur that looks like the trunk of the tree it hides in." Or you can NARRATE what it does: "nothing at all, even when approached by the most dangerous of predators." Or you can analyze the CAUSES AND EFFECTS of its distinctive behavior: "such passivity fools predators into looking elsewhere for live food." And so on.

Reading an Exemplification Essay with a Critical Eye

Once you've drafted your exemplification essay, ask someone else to read it and tell you which examples they find especially effective and which ones, if any, they think should be replaced or developed more sharply. Here are questions to keep in mind when checking an exemplification essay.

PURPOSE AND AUDIENCE. What is the overall purpose of the essay—to inform? entertain? persuade? How well does the text achieve that purpose? How familiar is the intended audience likely to be with the subject of the essay? What additional information might they find useful? What terms might they need to have defined or further explained?

THE POINT. What is the main point of the essay? Is it stated in a thesis? If not, should it be? How and how well do the examples support the thesis?

ORGANIZATION. Does the essay use multiple shorter examples, a few extended examples, or a combination of the two? Is this arrangement appropriate to the thesis of the essay—using multiple examples, for instance, to support a generalization that applies in many instances and extended examples to illustrate particular cases?

SUFFICIENT EXAMPLES. Are the examples presented in the essay sufficient to illustrate its key point or points? If not, how could the examples be made more persuasive? Would more examples be more convincing? Or do some examples need to be developed more fully? Which ones?

CONCRETE AND SPECIFIC EXAMPLES. Do the examples explain the topic in ways that are concrete (perceptible to the senses) and specific (narrowed down)? If not, how might they be sharpened and clarified?

REPRESENTATIVE EXAMPLES. Do the examples fairly and accurately represent the group they claim to represent? If the essay is based on one or two extended examples, do they represent *all* the important characteristics of the subject?

TRANSITIONS. Check all the transition words and phrases in the essay. How effectively do they introduce and link the examples? Do they explicitly connect the examples to the ideas they are illustrating? Where might transitions be added or strengthened?

OTHER METHODS. Does the essay incorporate any other methods of development? Would it be improved by including some DESCRIPTION or NARRATION, for example?

Editing for Common Errors in Examples

Exemplification invites certain kinds of errors, particularly with lists or a series of examples. The following tips will help you check your writing for errors that often turn up in exemplification.

If you list a series of examples, be sure they are parallel in structure

▶ Animals avoid predators in many ways. They travel in groups, move fast, blend~~ing~~ in with their surroundings, and look~~ing~~ threatening.

Edit out *etc.*, *and so forth*, or *and so on* when they don't add materially to your sentence

▶ Animals typically avoid predators by traveling in groups, moving fast, <u>and</u> blending in with their surroundings~~, etc~~.

Check your use of *i.e.* and *e.g.*

These abbreviations of Latin phrases are often used interchangeably to introduce examples, but they do not mean the same thing: *i.e.* means "that is" and *e.g.* means "for example." Since most of your readers do not likely speak Latin, it is a good idea to use the English equivalents.

▶ The chameleon is an animal that uses protective coloration—~~i.e.~~ <u>that is</u>, it changes color to blend in with its surroundings.

▶ Some animals change colors to blend in with their surroundings—~~e.g.~~ <u>for example</u>, the chameleon.

Student Example

Monica Wunderlich's "My Technologically Challenged Life" appeared in 2004 in *Delta Winds*, an anthology of student writing published each year by the English department of San Joaquin Delta College in Stockton, California. Wunderlich first wrote the essay as an assignment for an English course. It gives many humorous examples of the difficulties she has encountered with ordinary technology (or the lack of it) in her everyday life. At the nursing facility where the author worked while attending college, however, the lack of up-to-date equipment was no laughing matter—as Wunderlich's more disturbing examples make clear.

My Technologically Challenged Life

It probably seems easy for someone to use a computer to solve a task or call a friend on a cellular phone for the solution. I, however, do not have access to such luxuries. <u>My home, workplace, and automobile</u> are almost barren of anything electronic. It's not as if I don't want technology in my life, but I feel as if technology has taken on the role of a rabbit, and I am the fox with three legs that just can't seem to get it. And after many useless attempts at trying to figure it out, I have almost given up.

In my house, technology does not exist, at least not for my parents. In fact it was 1995 when my father finally had to part with his beloved rotary phone,[1] not because it was worn out, but because it would not work with the new automated menus that companies were using. Reaching an actual person was difficult the old way because of the physical impossibility of being able to *push* 1, 2, or 3 when a phone possesses no buttons. It was quite embarrassing, especially since I was fifteen and all of my friends had "normal" phones. My dad's biggest argument was that "It's a privacy issue. No one can tap into our phone calls and listen to our conversations." Well, the last time I had checked, none of us were trafficking dope.

I also had the privilege of not using a computer. It was hard going through high school without one, for I had many teachers who demanded many essays from me. Yet I had no way to type them. My sister was in the same boat, so we tried tag-teaming[2] my parents into getting us a computer. But to no avail. We kept getting things like "They're too expensive," or "We have no room for one," or "We'll get one later." Later! My parents should have just said NEVER! So my sister and I resorted to spending hours at our friends' houses, because their parents were nice to them and bought computers. The only problem was that our friends had lives and

1

Three-category organization promises multiple examples and indicates order in which they'll appear

2

Example: rotary phone

3

Example: no computer

---

1. *Rotary phone*: A dial-faced style of telephone in widespread use throughout much of the twentieth century.

2. *Tag-teaming*: A wrestling term referring to two people working as a team in alternate turns.

weren't always around at our disposal. So Plan B for essay completion was using a cheesy electronic word processor that my dad had borrowed from my *grandparents* to supposedly "help us out." This beast of a machine wasn't much help, though, because it was a pain in the neck to use. It had a teeny tiny little screen that wouldn't show the entire typed line, so by the time the line was printed, I'd find about ten uncorrected mistakes, and I'd have to start over. However, nothing is permanent and walls do come down, and so be it—the Wunderlichs buy their first computer! Two years after I graduate high school. As of yet, we still do not have the Internet.

My job is another place where technology is lacking. I work in a home for the elderly, and I take care of about eight to ten patients a night. I have to take some of these patients' vital signs, and I speak on behalf of anyone who has ever worked in the medical profession when I say that the most efficient way to take vital signs is electronically. However, my employers do not grant us the equipment for electronic vitals. We are still using glass thermometers, which are not only a waste of time (3 seconds vs. 3 minutes for an oral temp), but they are extremely dangerous. Residents are known to bite down on the thermometers, exposing themselves to harmful mercury. I can't even begin to count how many thermometers I have dropped and broken since I've worked there. One time I dropped a thermometer and didn't realize I had broken it. So I picked it up to shake it down, but instead I flung mercury everywhere. An electronic thermometer just makes more sense when trying to make the residents' environment as safe as possible.

We also have to use manual blood pressure cuffs. They're just the normal cuffs that are wrapped around the arm, pumped up, and read using the bouncing needle. The problem is that none of our blood pressure cuffs are calibrated correctly, and the needles are way out of kilter. This makes it impossible to get an accurate reading. An ingenious solution would be digital cuffs, but that is highly unlikely. Actually, the home did try to supply some digital cuffs, but they were

4

Example: glass thermometers

Example: manual blood pressure cuffs

5

stolen. One man's sticky fingers equals inconvenience for the rest of us, and the home no longer supplied us with such time-saving technology. Using manual equipment is hard not only for us but also for the nurses. The care home does not allow feeding machines in the facility, yet people who need to be fed by a stomach tube are still admitted. This means that the nurses have to allot a special time from their med pass to hook up a syringe to the patient's stomach tube and pour their "steak dinner in a can" down the tube little by little. This tedious process takes about twenty minutes, and nurses don't really have twenty minutes to throw around, so it really crowds their schedules. If we had feeding machines, the nurses would only have to change a bag when a machine beeps. Problem solved if things went my way.

Another part of my life that is technologically crippled is my car. As much as I like my car, I still think it could use a few more bells and whistles. I drive a 2002 Volkswagen Jetta, which would probably make the reader think, "Oh, a new car. There must be plenty of technology in that new car?" My answer to that is "No, there isn't." The only technology is the 5 billion standard airbags for when I do something really stupid. Other than that I have to shift it manually. If I want to roll down my window, I have to turn a crank. My car did not come with a CD player, so I shelled out $500 for one. I've had this stereo since last May, and I still can't figure out how to set the clock or preset stations. Volkswagen technology could not stop my car from exercising its "check engine light" once every three weeks. Even though the design techs included a cute warning light, my blood still boiled every time the light would come on proudly, and I made yet another pilgrimage to the dealership . . . on my day off. It would be nice if my car came equipped with one of those Global Positioning System things as well. I am really good at getting lost, and if I had one of these systems a year ago, I would not have found myself driving over both the Bay Bridge and the Golden Gate Bridge when I was supposed to be on the Richmond Bridge. (Ironically enough, I did this during the weekend that terrorists were supposed

6

Example: no feeding machines

RHETORICAL QUESTION indicates more examples to come

Examples presented in cluster: manual transmission and windows, after-market stereo, faulty engine light, no GPS

to be blowing up the Bay and Golden Gate Bridges.) And if I had had any passengers while tempting fate that day, I could have kept them distracted from the fact that we were lost (and possibly going to die) by letting them watch a movie on one of those in-car DVD players. But of course I don't have an in-car DVD player, so my hypothetical passengers would probably have been frantic.

No matter how much technology is out there, I seem to be getting through the day without most of it. It would seem hard to imagine someone else living without such modern conveniences, and, yes, at times I feel very primitive. However, I am slowly catching on to what's new out there even though incorporating every modern convenience into my day is out of the question. I am learning even though it is at a snail's pace. Hopefully I'll have it all figured out by the time cars fly, or else I will be walking.

7

Final example: flying cars

Analyzing a Student Exemplification Essay

In "My Technologically Challenged Life," Monica Wunderlich draws upon rhetorical strategies and techniques that good writers use all the time when they exemplify a subject. The following questions, in addition to focusing on particular aspects of Wunderlich's text, will help you to identify those common strategies and techniques so you can adapt them to your own writing. These questions will also help to prepare you for the analytical questions—on content, structure, and language—that you'll find after all the other selections in this chapter, along with suggestions for writing on related topics.

READING CLOSELY

1. What role do Monica Wunderlich's parents play in limiting her access to technology? How do they explain their behavior? Does their reasoning sound familiar to you? How so?

2. At times, Wunderlich blames herself for her technological difficulties. Who or what else is at fault, especially at the health-care facility? How serious are such technological problems at her workplace?

3. Why does Wunderlich refer to the weekend when terrorists were "supposed to be blowing up" two of San Francisco's main bridges (6)? What does this observation have to do with technology?

STRATEGIES AND STRUCTURES

1. Since Wunderlich's essay was written as an assignment for an English class, her main PURPOSE was to amuse her teacher and classmates and to inform them about the technological "challenges" she faces every day. How well do you think she achieves this purpose? Explain.

2. Wunderlich's title tells the reader that her life is "technologically challenged," a point she supports with examples throughout her essay. Should she have made this main point more explicitly in a THESIS statement? Why or why not?

3. Wunderlich organizes her examples by grouping them according to each "part of my life" (6). How, and how well, does this scheme help her to structure her essay?

4. What is IRONIC about the example of Wunderlich's car?

5. *Other Methods.* When she writes about the lack of technology in the facility where she works, Wunderlich is also presenting an ARGUMENT about working conditions and the quality of patient care. To whom is this argument addressed? Are her examples sufficient to support it? Why or why not?

THINKING ABOUT LANGUAGE

1. Look up the term *Luddite.* What does the name mean, and where does it come from? Who might Wunderlich consider a Luddite?

2. Wunderlich compares herself to a three-legged fox chasing a rabbit (1). How effective do you find this ANALOGY?

3. What does Wunderlich's METAPHOR of "tag-teaming" imply about the extent of her and her sister's persistence (3)?

4. "Hopefully," says Wunderlich about her attempt to catch up with technology, "I'll have it all figured out by the time cars fly" (7). Where else in her essay, and for what purposes, does Wunderlich use HYPERBOLE like this?

FOR WRITING

1. Is your personal life or work "challenged" in some way, technologically or otherwise? Using examples, write a paragraph or two about a particular challenge and how you deal with it (or fail to do so).

2. If you could have the latest technology in every field, what specific devices, gadgets, and gear would you go for? Write an essay giving examples of the choices you would make and why.

Car Talk T-Shirt

The Magliozzi brothers, Tom and Ray, use their *Car Talk* broadcasts and columns to dispense mechanical and safety advice. They also sell T-shirts, coffee mugs, and other paraphernalia. The target of the messages on this T-shirt is drivers who use cell phones while they're behind the wheel. Tom and Ray could sell two T-shirts if they put each message on a separate shirt. One would offer a platitude: "It's hard to concentrate on two things at the same time." The other would offer statistics: "You're four times more likely to have an accident when you're on a cell phone." Neither of these statements is likely to inspire drivers to turn off their phones. The first statement is both general and abstract. The second is slightly more specific because it cites particular numbers and devices. But it's still pretty abstract because it refers to concepts (percentages, accidents) rather than an actual event or sensation. The purpose of using examples is to make generalizations more specific and abstractions more concrete. Never at a loss for words, Tom and Ray know this—so they wove the two statements into a smashing example of their point about not driving and talking on a cell phone (or doing anything else distracting) at the same time. If you find the message fitting, Tom and Ray want you to buy and wear their shirt. It should be read, however, only while sitting or walking.

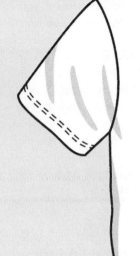

You're four times
It's hard to
more likely to
concentrate on
have an accident
two things
when you're on
at the same time.
a cell phone.

THE ONION

All Seven Deadly Sins Committed at Church Bake Sale

The Onion *is a satirical weekly newspaper that was founded in 1988 by two juniors at the University of Wisconsin, Tim Keck and Christopher Johnson, who distributed a handful of copies to their friends around the Madison area. Today the* Onion *boasts more than three million regular readers nationwide and attributes its success to "fearless reporting and scathing commentary." Consider, for instance, these* Onion *headlines: "Cases of Glitter Lung on the Rise among Elementary-School Art Teachers," "Study Reveals Pittsburgh Unprepared for Full-Scale Zombie Attack," "Supreme Court Mistakenly Used Belgium's Constitution for Last 3 Rulings." Such satire has won the* Onion *a Thurber Prize for American Humor and a handful of Webby Awards. Several collections of its articles have made the* New York Times *best-seller list, including* Ad Nauseam *(2003) and* Our Dumb World *(2007).*

The Onion's *brand of satire is marked by its pitch-perfect mimicry of the reporting styles that many papers routinely use to inflate the banal into the newsworthy. In the following article, an* Onion *investigative reporter sniffs out numerous concrete and specific examples of the "deadly sins" committed at a church bake sale.*

GADSDEN, AL—The seven deadly sins—avarice, sloth, envy, lust, gluttony, pride, and wrath—were all committed Sunday during the twice-annual bake sale at St. Mary's of the Immaculate Conception Church. 1

See p. 177 for what makes a "sufficient" number of examples. You don't have to cite all 347.

In total, 347 individual acts of sin were committed at the bake sale, with nearly every attendee committing at least one of the seven deadly sins as outlined by Gregory the Great in the fifth century. 2

"My cookies, cakes, and brownies are always the highlight of our church bake sales, and everyone says so," said parishioner Connie Barrett, 49, openly committing the sin of pride. "Sometimes, even I'm amazed by how well my goodies turn out." 3

Fellow parishioner Betty Wicks agreed. 4

"Every time I go past Connie's table, I just have to buy something," said the 245-pound Wicks, who commits the sin of gluttony at every St. Mary's bake sale, as well as most Friday nights at Old Country Buffet. "I simply can't help myself—it's all so delicious." 5

The popularity of Barrett's mouth-watering wares elicited the sin of envy in many of her fellow vendors. 6

SUGGESTED MLA CITATION: *The Onion*. "All Seven Deadly Sins Committed at Church Bake Sale." 2007. *Back to the Lake*. Ed. Thomas Cooley. 2nd ed. New York: Norton, 2012. 190–92. Print.

"Connie has this fantastic book of recipes her grandmother gave her, and she won't share them with anyone," church organist Georgia Brandt said. "This year, I made white-chocolate blondies and thought they'd be a big hit. But most people just went straight to Connie's table, got what they wanted, and left. All the while, Connie just stood there with this look of smug satisfaction on her face. It took every ounce of strength in my body to keep from going over there and really telling her off." 7

While the sins of wrath and avarice were each committed dozens of times at the event, Barrett and longtime bake-sale rival Penny Cox brought them together in full force. 8

"Penny said she wanted to make a bet over whose table would make the most money," said Barrett, exhibiting avarice. "Whoever lost would have to sit in the dunk tank at the St. Mary's Summer Fun Festival. I figured it's for such a good cause, a little wager couldn't hurt. Besides, I always bring the church more money anyway, so I couldn't possibly lose." 9

Moments after agreeing to the wager, Cox became wrathful when Barrett, the bake sale's co-chair, grabbed the best table location under the pretense of having to keep the coffee machine full. Cox attempted to exact revenge by reporting an alleged Barrett misdeed to the church's priest. 10

Patti George (far right) commits the sin of envy as she eyes fellow parishioner Mary Hoechst's superior strawberry pie.

"I mentioned to Father Mark [O'Connor] that I've seen candles at Connie's 11
house that I wouldn't be surprised one bit if she stole from the church's storage
closet," said Cox, who also committed the sin of sloth by forcing her daughter to
set up and man her booth while she gossiped with friends. "Perhaps if he investigates this, by this time next year, Connie won't be co-chair of the bake sale and in
her place we'll have someone who's willing to rotate the choice table spots."

The sin of lust also reared its ugly head at the bake sale, largely due to the pres- 12
ence of Melissa Wyckoff, a shapely 20-year-old redhead whose family recently
joined the church. While male attendees ogled Wyckoff, the primary object of lust
for females was the personable, boyish Father Mark.

Though attendees' feelings of lust for Wyckoff and O'Connor were never acted 13
on, they did not go unnoticed.

"There's something not right about that Melissa Wyckoff," said envious and 14
wrathful bake-sale participant Jilly Brandon, after her husband Craig offered Wyckoff one of her Rice Krispie treats to "welcome her to the parish." "She might have
just moved here from California, but that red dress of hers should get her kicked
out of the church."

According to St. Mary's treasurer Beth Ellen Coyle, informal church-sponsored 15
events are a notorious breeding ground for the seven deadly sins.

"Bake sales, haunted houses, pancake breakfasts . . . such church events are rife 16
with potential for sin," Coyle said. "This year, we had to eliminate the 'Guess Your
Weight' booth from the annual church carnival because the envy and pride had
gotten so out of hand. Church events are about glorifying God, not violating His
word. If you want to do that, you're no better than that cheap strumpet Melissa
Wyckoff."

READING CLOSELY

1. Who established the names and number of the seven deadly sins as we know
   them today?

2. How "deadly" do you find the sins reported here? That is, how well do the
   reporter's examples represent the general concept he says he is exemplifying?

3. The *Onion* reporter records "347 individual acts of sin" at the church bake sale
   (2). Is anything suspicious about these statistics? How do you suppose the
   reporter came up with this number?

4. Which sins does parishioner Connie Barrett commit? How does her bake-sale success encourage the sins of others?

5. Which single sin among the seven do the patrons of the bake sale only contemplate, rather than act upon? Who inspires it?

STRATEGIES AND STRUCTURES

1. A spoof is a gentle PARODY or mildly satirical imitation. What general PURPOSE does a spoof or parody usually serve? What is the writer's specific purpose here, and who is the intended AUDIENCE?

2. Pride, avarice, and the other "deadly sins" are ABSTRACT concepts. How do the reporter's examples make them more CONCRETE and specific? Are the examples sufficient, or should there be more? Explain.

3. The reporter gives numerous examples of what people say at the church bake sale. Why? What purpose do these verbal examples serve?

4. *Other Methods.* To bolster the examples, the reporter uses elements of NARRATIVE. What are some of them?

THINKING ABOUT LANGUAGE

1. What, exactly, is a "strumpet," and why do you think the reporter uses this rather than a stronger word to describe Melissa Wyckoff (16)?

2. Deadly (or mortal) sins can be distinguished from venial sins. According to your dictionary, what is the difference between the two kinds? Give examples.

3. Give a SYNONYM for each of the following words: "avarice," "sloth," "gluttony," and "wrath" (1).

4. Another word for "pride" is *hubris.* What is the difference between the two, according to your dictionary?

FOR WRITING

1. Write a paragraph about one sin you would add to the traditional list.

2. Write an exemplification essay illustrating how the seven deadly sins are routinely committed in the library, in your classes, or in some other place at your school.

DAVID BARBOZA

Piling on the Cookies

David Barboza was still an undergraduate at Boston University when he became a part-time correspondent for the New York Times. *Seven years after graduation, in 1997, the newspaper hired him as a staff writer for the business section.*

Over the course of his career, Barboza has made a specialty of spotting trends—as in "Piling on the Cookies." This article makes clear that sometimes the best way to tell a story is by detailing a well-chosen example. Here, Barboza uses the Oreo cookie as an extended example of a significant trend in modern marketing: what industry insiders call "line extension." The article first appeared in the New York Times *in 2003.*

FINDING OLD-FASHIONED Oreo sandwich cookies on supermarket shelves is no easy task these days. 1

The toothsome snack's progeny, like the flashier Fudge Mint Covered Oreo, the heftier Oreo Double Stuf and the bite-sized Mini Oreo, now crowd the cookie aisle, leaving the 91-year-old original wedged into the tiniest of corners. 2

P. 177 explains how to state the point you're exemplifying right off the bat like this.

Marketing experts call it extending the heritage brand. Rather than spending millions to develop and market new brands, food marketers are stocking the shelves with new twists on old, familiar names. Snickers, for instance, flavor Edy's ice cream. Nestlé candies are sprinkled on Chips Ahoy cookies. Trix cereal has migrated into Yoplait yogurt. And Reese's Pieces have become a cereal called Reese's Puffs. 3

But few foods are as ubiquitous as the humble charcoal-colored Oreo, which has a basketful of spinoffs, from candy bars to ice cream to pie crusts. Such versatility has helped to more than double the sale of all things Oreo over the last decade—close to $1 billion. Not bad for a brand that is older than the automobile assembly line. 4

There are, for instance, Oreo O's breakfast cereal, Oreo ice cream, Oreo Jell-O, Oreo pudding crust, cake mix, frosting, brownies, granola bars, and, just in time for Halloween, Oreos with pumpkin-colored cream fillings. 5

Marketing experts say Oreo is not just a cookie anymore, it's practically a flavor. But, they warn, there are dangers in tinkering with valuable brands. Chiefly, they worry about saturating the market, and there are some signs from Kraft Foods Inc. that cookie sales are slowing. 6

SUGGESTED MLA CITATION: Barboza, David. "Piling on the Cookies." 2003. *Back to the Lake*. Ed. Thomas Cooley. 2nd ed. New York: Norton, 2012. 194–97. Print.

**DOUBLE DELIGHT
MINT 'N CREME**
Introduced in 2003

**DOUBLE DELIGHT
PEANUT BUTTER &
CHOCOLATE**
2003

**DOUBLE DELIGHT
COFFEE 'N CREME**
2003

UH OH OREO
(Vanilla cookie, chocolate filling)
2003

CHOCOLATE CREME OREO
2001

FOOTBALL OREO
(Football design on biscuit)
Seasonal

DOUBLE STUFF
1974

ORIGINAL
1912

Piling on the Cookies
In the Oreo's first eight decades,
Nabisco tried only a handful of variations on the original. But in recent
years, it has stretched the line to
more than two dozen by varying the
size, the filling, the biscuit recipe—
nearly everything but the brand
name. Here are some examples now
on store shelves.

Still, they marvel at how Kraft and Nabisco have found so many new ways to use 7
Oreos and to get people to buy them. Nabisco, the creator of Oreos, merged with
Kraft in 2000 and Kraft was spun off from Philip Morris a year later.

"The industry term for this phenomena is line extension," says Alan Brew, a 8
marketing expert at Addison, a corporate branding consultant in San Francisco.
"This widens the franchise. And it's defensive. To stop a micro-product from coming in, you attack yourself, all the time, before someone else attacks you."

Yet close comparisons are hard to come by. Coke evolved into Diet Coke, Cherry   9
Coke, Diet Cherry Coke, and even Vanilla Coke. But that was nothing like the
hyper-evolving, perpetually repackaged, category-migrating Oreo.

There is the Double Delight Oreo, the Uh-Oh Oreo (vanilla cookie with choco-   10
late filling), Oreo Cookie Barz, Football Oreos, Oreos Cookies & Creme Pie, Oreos
in Kraft Lunchables, for kids, and Oreo cookies with a variety of cream fillings
(mint, chocolate, coffee) and sizes (6-pack, 12-pack, snack pack and more).

According to the latest Oreo promotions, there is even an Oreo cookie that,   11
when liberally dunked in a glass of milk, will turn the milk blue and win some
lucky Oreo dunker a $1 million prize.

"Every year we talk to consumers and Oreo lovers," says Daryl Brewster, Kraft's   12
president of the biscuits, snacks and confections. "And what we found is tremendous amounts of desire for the next Oreo experience."

These days, food companies like to talk of eating "experiences." Ketchup isn't   13
just ketchup, it's jazzed up with green food coloring and made into a kind of finger
paint for finger food—for children to play with and squirt on mashed potatoes.

Kraft approaches the Oreo in the same way. Eating an Oreo isn't just eating an   14
Oreo, they say, it's the experience of dunking it in milk, twisting it apart and licking it clean.

Believing as they do in the Oreo experience, the issue for Kraft executives boils   15
down to this: Why introduce a new cookie brand when you can just keep reinvent-
ing the Oreo?

"It's much more economical to extend a brand rather than create a new one,"   16
says Judy Hopelain, a brand strategist at Prophet, a consulting firm in San Francisco. "It's also probably a lot easier to get shelf space for a well-known brand."

The strategy seems to have worked, analysts said.   17

"Between 1998 and 2001, the Oreo had annual compound growth of 13 per-   18
cent," says John McMillin, a longtime food analyst at Prudential Securities. "These
days, few things in the food industry even grow 3 percent."

But Kraft's most recent profit report suggests the Oreo gravy train may be slow-   19
ing. The company said that cookie sales overall have weakened, but some of that
weakness was offset by a strong introduction this year [2003] of the Uh-Oh Oreo.

Some Wall Street analysts are now warning of trouble ahead because cookie   20
sales generally are forecast to continue to fall. Kraft officials declined to say whether
Oreo sales were declining, or whether the drop was in other brands, like Chips
Ahoy or Ritz crackers.

"The Oreo line extensions have been successful," said William Leach, a con-   21
sumer analyst at Neuberger Berman, an investment firm based in New York, "but
the whole line is getting soft."

There are other problems, as well. The Oreo, like most mass-produced cookies, 22 gets some of its texture from trans fatty acids, which raise the level of fat and cholesterol in the blood, and may lower the level of high density lipoproteins, often called good cholesterol. Last year the National Academy of Sciences said the level of trans fats in the diet should be as low as possible.

Kraft and Nabisco have responded to the controversy in a familiar way, by intro- 23 ducing yet another kind of Oreo, a reduced-fat variety to join the double-filled and the fudge-covered.

Kraft executives say that for the last few years, focus groups and market research 24 shows that consumers want more and more varieties of the Oreo, which was created in 1912 by the National Biscuit Company, later known as Nabisco.

But there is a concern that too much tinkering could tarnish the brand. The les- 25 son of New Coke—introduced and then withdrawn by the Coca-Cola Company after complaints from faithful customers—has not been lost on Kraft.

That is not to say that Oreo fans will not test the limits on their own. Just ask 26 those people who delight in making deep-fried Oreos by soaking them in pancake batter before frying them in cooking oil.

Is Kraft, which has already blanketed the world with its billion-dollar cookie, 27 running out of ideas?

Nope. 28

"There are some places we won't go," Mr. Brewster, at Kraft, says. "But there 29 are still a lot of places. As long as we continue to listen to consumers, we'll be O.K."

READING CLOSELY

1. According to David Barboza, why are "old-fashioned" Oreos hard to find on grocery shelves these days (1)?

2. What is Barboza's main point, and how does his example of the hard-to-find "original" cookie illustrate that point (2)?

3. Why, according to marketing experts, do companies extend old brands instead of introducing entirely new product lines?

4. Although Kraft Foods has been successful in extending the Oreo brand, what are some problems in the food industry in general?

Strategies and Structures

1. Barboza begins his article by explaining the concept of "line extension." What CONCRETE and specific examples does he use to illustrate that general concept?

2. What is Barboza's PURPOSE in writing about marketing strategies? Who is his intended AUDIENCE? How can you tell?

3. Barboza explains how the executives at Kraft Foods have extended the Oreo line in particular. What specific examples does he give? Are they sufficient to make his point? Why or why not?

4. Barboza often makes a general statement and then immediately gives a concrete example to back it up. Point out several instances, and explain how (and how well) these examples actually represent his ideas.

5. Throughout his article, Barboza uses TRANSITIONS and connectors like *for instance* and *still*. What other transitions does Barboza use, and how do they help him remind readers of his main point?

6. *Other Methods.* Oreo, says Barboza, is no longer just a cookie but "practically a flavor" (6), and consuming an Oreo is not just an act of eating but "an experience" (13, 14). How does he use examples to illustrate these new DEFINITIONS?

Thinking about Language

1. In paragraph 2, why do you think Barboza uses the word "progeny" instead of *descendants* or *offspring* (2)?

2. What is a "spinoff," and how does Barboza apply the word to companies as well as products (4, 7)?

3. How do the hyphenated words in paragraph 9 help to illustrate what Barboza is saying about the evolution of the humble Oreo?

4. What makes a vanilla cookie filled with chocolate an "Uh-Oh Oreo" (10)?

5. Explain the PUN on "gravy train" in paragraph 19.

For Writing

1. Write a paragraph exemplifying an eating "experience" you have had (13–14).

2. Many companies extend their products and brands, as, for example, Nike and Adidas have done with their athletic shoes, or auto manufacturers do with frequent changes in models and styling and with add-ons, such as mud flaps and magnesium wheels. Using a product, brand, or service you are familiar with, write an exemplification essay illustrating line extension.

MICHAEL DIRDA

Commencement Advice

Michael Dirda (b. 1948) is a book critic for the Washington Post. *He grew up in Lorain, Ohio, where his father complained that "all that kid wants to do is stick his nose in a book." Dirda attended Oberlin College and earned a PhD in comparative literature from Cornell University. In 1993, he won a Pulitzer Prize for literary journalism. Dirda has taught writing on the college level and is the author of* Bound to Please: An Extraordinary One-Volume Literary Education *(2004) and* Classics for Pleasure *(2007).*

"Commencement Advice," first published in the Book World section of the Washington Post *in 1999, takes literature to be a form of instruction as well as a source of aesthetic pleasure. It offers copious examples of life lessons from the author's reading and personal experience.*

Aɴʏᴏɴᴇ ᴡʜᴏ's ᴇᴠᴇʀ ɢᴏɴᴇ ᴛᴏ sᴄʜᴏᴏʟ is likely to feel a certain jauntiness 1 come the end of June. Summer is here. No more classes, no more books, no more teacher's dirty looks.[1] Swimming pools and parks beckon; trips to the mountains, beaches, or grandparents loom. The world, once more, seems, as Matthew Arnold said, "a land of dreams, so various, so beautiful, so new."[2]

For a 17- or 18-year-old graduate, that elation is multiplied a hundredfold. School 2 is not only out for the summer; it's over with for good. Oh, for many there's college in the offing, but that's somehow different: an Eden of parties and romance, broken hearts that rapidly heal, kegs of foaming beer, lazy Saturday afternoons at the stadium watching football, and—after four years of mind-numbing, dizzying bliss—a degree, rapidly followed by a high-paying job, a Porsche 911, and that first million. So goes the pastoral daydream. Alas, our barefoot boy or girl will discover soon enough that the world is actually, as Arnold also reminded us, a "darkling plain / Swept with confused alarms of struggle and flight, / Where ignorant armies clash by night."

1. *No more [pencils], no more books, no more teacher's dirty looks*: a chant sung gleefully by U.S. children on the last day of school.

2. *Matthew Arnold (1822–1888)*: a major poet and literary critic of Victorian Britain. This quotation and the one in the next paragraph are from his poetic meditation on the uncertainty of love and life, "Dover Beach" (1867).

SUGGESTED MLA CITATION: Dirda, Michael. "Commencement Advice." 1999. *Back to the Lake.* Ed. Thomas Cooley. 2nd ed. New York: Norton, 2012. 199–204. Print.

Literature offers various aesthetic pleasures, but it has also traditionally pro- 3
vided instruction and counsel on how to live, confront adversity, and find solace.
The moral essay—from Marcus Aurelius to Montaigne to Matthew Arnold—has a
long tradition, and one that still lingers on in bestselling manuals about the lessons
we learn from kindergarten and the soul's need for chicken soup.[3] Over the years I
have been an occasional skimmer of such guides but have found that most of my
own ground rules for better living—or at least for getting through life—derive from
For advice on the usual order in which to present examples, see p. 177. some of the less obvious byways of my reading. Since commencement
speakers traditionally offer advice to the young in June, here, in no par-
ticular order, are a dozen of the quotations that one reader calls to mind
in moments of confusion, stress, and sorrow.

1. "Life is trouble." So proclaims the hero of Nikos Kazantzakis's novel *Zorba* 4
the Greek.[4] Struggle, conflict, tension, disappointment, failure—these are all
signs that one is alive. If you try new things, some of them simply aren't going to
work out. But one ought to shine in use, and the all too common desire for a
Lotos-land existence of endless summer is really an unacknowledged death wish.[5]
Expect the worst, says Carl Sandburg in his forgotten poem. "The People, Yes,"[6]
and you won't be disappointed. Life is trouble. Only death is no trouble at all.

2. Keep an "interior citadel." The philosopher-emperor Marcus Aurelius 5
passed much of his reign on battlefields. But even on the fraying edges of the
Roman Empire he always strove to maintain a stoic's inner tranquility, amount-
ing almost to indifference to the world outside. He accomplished this by retreat-
ing regularly to an "interior citadel," a place in the mind where he could fortify
himself against what Hamlet, that failed Danish stoic, called the "slings and

---

3. *Lessons . . . chicken soup*: References to Robert Fulghum's *All I Really Need to Know I Learned in Kindergarten* (1986) and the *Chicken Soup for the Soul* series (first book published in 1993). Both offer inspirational stories and folk wisdom. *Michel Eyquem de Montaigne* (1533–1592): French moralist who published his *Essays* in 1580. *Marcus Aurelius* (121–180 C.E.): Roman emperor who wrote his *Meditations* while on a military campaign during the last decade of his life.

4. *Zorba the Greek*: Best-known work by the Greek novelist, poet, and philosopher. Kazantzakis (1883–1957) published *Zorba* in English translation in 1946.

5. *Lotos-land*: A dual literary reference. In Homer's *Odyssey*, Odysseus and his crew are shipwrecked on an island where the men eat a flower that causes forgetfulness and lassitude. Alfred, Lord Tenny-son's 1843 poem "The Lotos-Eaters" describes the same land as a place where it is always afternoon. The flowers they wrote about were the Egyptian blue lotus, also known as the blue waterlily, which is reputed to produce narcotic effects in those who eat it.

6. *"The People, Yes"*: Sandburg (1878–1967) published this epic poem of the American language and people in 1936. He is best remembered for his *Chicago Poems* (1916) and for his biography of Lincoln.

arrows of outrageous fortune."[7] From there, atop the crenelated ramparts, one can metaphorically look down on troubles from a great height, serene and detached. As Satan once observed, the mind is its own place, and in itself can make a Heaven of Hell, a Hell of Heaven.[8]

3. **"Constant work is the law of art as it is of life."** Balzac followed every word of this sentence to the letter, burning many candles at both ends so that he could write all night the magnificent, melodramatic novels of *La Comédie humaine*.[9] If you hope to accomplish something worthwhile during your time on earth, you will have to work. As a young man or woman, your goal should be to find the kind of job, craft, profession, or useful activity that you are willing to marry, till death do you part. After all, to miss out on one's proper work may be the greatest mistake of a lifetime. If you are born to be an artist, don't settle for being a mere lawyer or stockbroker. Compared to satisfying work, even pleasure pales to insignificance.

4. **"Do what you are doing."** This, I believe, is both a Jesuit motto and a Zen imperative. That is, if you are making dinner or playing soccer or writing a memo, really focus your whole being on just that. Do it well. Thereby, you invest even the most trivial activities with significance, turning the mundane into the spiritual, perhaps even the ecstatic. A monk tending a garden at dawn is praying. By concerted acts of attention, you can make everything you do a kind of poetry.

5. **"The most effective weapon of any man is to have reduced his share of histrionics to a minimum."** This was the watchword of André Malraux,[10] the larger-than-life novelist, adventurer, art historian, politician. Malraux believed in maturity, in being a grown-up. Our natural tendency is to exaggerate our sorrows, anger, and desires. But deep within we know that we are overreacting, indeed overacting. We get caught up in the situation, carried away by our own pleasure in personal melodrama. So we perform for the audience, sometimes an audience of only one. Instead of such staginess, we should remind ourselves that

7. *"Slings . . . fortune"*: The line is from Hamlet's "to be, or not to be" soliloquy in Act III of Shakespeare's play.

8. *The mind . . . Heaven*: allusion to the words of Satan in *Paradise Lost* (1667; Book 1, line 255) by the British poet John Milton (1608–1674).

9. *La Comédie humaine: The Human Comedy* is the collective name of the works of the French novelist Honoré de Balzac (1799–1850). The quotation is from *Cousin Bette* (1848).

10. *André Malraux* (1901–1976): French writer and statesman who spoke of the need to act like a grown-up in his autobiography, *Anti-Memoirs* (1968).

clarity is as much a mental and emotional virtue as it is a stylistic one. Do we really feel this riot of emotion? Is there any point to all this brouhaha? Should a grown-up behave like this?

6. "Cover your tracks." Bertolt Brecht[11] made this the refrain to one of his political poems. When you go into the big city, he says, know that you are never safe; people will be watching every move you make. Your only hope of getting out alive is to "cover your tracks." "Whatever you say, don't say it twice. / If you find your ideas in anyone else, disown them. / The man who hasn't signed anything, who has left no picture / Who was not there, who said nothing: / How can they catch him? / Cover your tracks." For me, this phrase stands as the rough equivalent to the more famous "Trust no one" formula of *The X-Files*.[12] In fact, one should trust everyone but give away nothing that really matters—except to those who love you. "Cover your tracks" means to be careful, destroy your rough drafts, and never let them see you sweat. ^{9}

7. "A thing is only worth so much time." Parents tend to specialize in certain slogans, and this was my father's favorite. It is a doctrine that needs to be applied with caution, because some things—painting a picture, writing a poem—require that we spend whatever time is needed to do them right. But many activities can needlessly absorb immense chunks of our lives. You can spend every Saturday afternoon for a year test-driving new cars before you pick the wrong one anyway. You can agonize for weeks whether to go for a physical or not. You can work fourteen-hour days downtown. But should you? Aren't there more important matters to attend to? "The cost of a thing," wrote Thoreau, "is the amount of what I will call life which is required to be exchanged for it immediately or in the long run."[13] This leads on to the following, associated motto: ^{10}

8. "Get on with your work." At moments of emotional crisis, people sometimes just want to plop down and cry. You can do this for a minute or two, and probably should, but also remember that, as Disraeli[14] said, "Grief is the agony of an instant: the indulgence of grief the blunder of a life." When I grow melancholy— ^{11}

11. *Bertolt Brecht* (1898–1956): German dramatist and poet. This advice is from "Handbook for City Dwellers" (1926).

12. *The X-Files*: TV show that ran from 1993 to 2002, in which FBI agents Dana Scully and Fox Mulder investigated paranormal phenomena and ran afoul of government conspiracies—hence the advice to "trust no one."

13. *"The cost . . . long run"*: Henry David Thoreau (1817–1862) offers this definition in the "Economy" chapter of *Walden* (1854).

14. *Benjamin Disraeli* (1804–1881) was twice prime minister of Britain.

the occupational disease of writers—I start doing household chores: I wash dishes and clothes, dust and vacuum, reorganize my bureau, box up books. While performing such activities, I'm allowed to be as depressed as I want, provided I keep on working. That's the key. Usually, within a few hours I feel better. At the very least I end up with a clean house.

9. **"We must laugh before we are happy, for fear of dying without having laughed at all."** A corollary to this insightful observation from La Bruyere is William James's dictum that if you act as though you were happy, even when you're not, your mind will eventually trick itself into a cheerier mood.[15] What better gift, though, could the gods bestow than a sense of humor? "One can pretend to be serious," said the French playwright Sacha Guitry,[16] "but one can't pretend to be witty." If you don't naturally possess a lighthearted spirit, at least try to acquire a sense of irony and compassion, and learn to smile at your own foolishness—and the world's. As a dear friend used to remind me, self-pity is most unattractive.

10. **"Live all you can. It's a mistake not to,"** announces Lambert Strether in a climactic moment of Henry James's late masterpiece *The Ambassadors*. As the years roll by, it is tempting to settle for a half-life of routine, order, and accommodation. But all of us ought to strive to be overreachers, ever restless, ever adventurous. T. S. Eliot said, "Old men should be explorers,"[17] but so should young men and women and 50-year-olds. Henry James also provides excellent advice for cultivating one's spirit: "Be one on whom nothing is lost." That is, pay attention, observe, learn, be as sensitive and responsive as your nature permits.

11. **Choose some heroes and imitate them.** To me, Montaigne, Samuel Johnson, Stendhal, Jane Austen, Chekhov, and Colette[18] are not merely great writers; they are also wonderfully humane and sympathetic human beings. Shrewd, self-aware, free of cant, urbane, kindly—they are my secular saints. Once you have

15. *If you act . . . cheerier mood:* Dirda is paraphrasing the pragmatic philosophy of the American psychologist William James (1843–1916). *Jean de La Bruyere (1645–1696):* French moralist and essayist; his *Characters* appeared in 1688.

16. *Sacha Guitry* (1885–1957) was also an actor.

17. *"Old man . . . explorers":* A line from *Four Quartets*, which Eliot (1888–1965) published in book form in 1943.

18. *Colette* (1873–1954): Pen-name of the French novelist Sidonie-Gabrielle Colette. *Anton Pavlovich Chekhov* (1860–1904): Russian master of the short story who was also a playwright. *Jane Austen* (1775–1817): Known for her novels of polite British society. *Stendhal* (1783–1842): Pen-name of the French novelist Marie-Henri Beyle. *Dr. Samuel Johnson* (1709–1784): British lexicographer, essayist, and literary critic.

imbibed the personalities of such master spirits, you can turn to them as guides through life's moral thickets and ethical swamps. What would Samuel Johnson say in this situation? What counsel would Colette give? How would Stendhal react?

12. "Memento mori." We must all die, and doubtless it will be on a sunny day 15 when the whole world seems young and fresh. No one likes to think about that last bad quarter-hour, but it will come round eventually. Theologians in earlier centuries insisted that we meditate on death, so that we might review our lives, amending them where needed. That same practice can help even the most profane among us. If I were to die now, would I be wracked with regrets? Are there matters I should have attended to? Be prepared. In one of Tolstoy's[19] parables, a peasant is plowing a field. The narrator asks the old man what he would do if he knew that Death was coming to take him away within the hour. The peasant answers, "Keep plowing." How many of us could offer a comparably serene reply?

So there's my advice to this year's graduates. Easy enough to give, I realize, and 16 hard to follow—as I know, too. But let me conclude with one strongly personal plea, making a baker's dozen: Read the classics. The world is awash in bestsellers and frivolous nonfiction, but just as our bodies need physical exercise, so our brains need demanding books. Set aside some part of the day for real reading. Work your way through Plato; be touched by Cather's *A Lost Lady* and shocked by Rousseau's *Confessions*; feel the burning fever of *Death in Venice*; listen in on Samuel Johnson's repartee, and marvel before *One Hundred Years of Solitude*.[20] Books, like great art and music and love, make us feel passionately alive. And isn't that what we all want?

19. *Lev Nikolayevich Tolstoy* (1828–1910): Russian novelist and philosopher; his parables are collected in *Master and Man and Other Parables and Tales* (1895).

20. *One Hundred Years of Solitude* (1967): A book by Colombian novelist Gabriel García Márquez (b. 1928), who is known for his use of magical realism. *Death in Venice* (1912): the work of German novelist Thomas Mann (1875–1955). *Jean-Jacques Rousseau* (1712–1778): French writer and political theorist whose *Confessions* appeared in 1782. *Willa Cather* (1873–1947): American novelist who published *A Lost Lady* in 1923. *Plato* (427–347 B.C.E.): Greek philosopher who was a student of Socrates and the teacher of Aristotle.

READING CLOSELY

1. Michael Dirda's essay consists mainly of three paragraphs of introduction followed by a list of examples. What, exactly, is he exemplifying? What is Dirda's main point?

2. What mistaken idea is Dirda exemplifying in paragraph 2 by referring, among other delights, to "lazy Saturday afternoons at the stadium watching football . . . followed by a high-paying job, a Porsche 911, and that first million"? Why do you think he introduces this false notion?

3. According to Dirda, why should we maintain an "interior citadel" (5)?

4. In Dirda's view, how important is a person's job or profession? To what extent do you agree (or disagree) with Dirda about "satisfying work" (6)? Explain.

5. Dirda bases his essay (and the advice it gives) on a particular view of the role of literature and reading. What is that view, and where does he state it most directly? Do you agree? Why or why not?

STRATEGIES AND STRUCTURES

1. How and where does Dirda identify his AUDIENCE and state his PURPOSE? Why do you think Dirda immediately restates that purpose?

2. Given his purpose and audience, why do you think Dirda builds his essay around multiple brief examples rather one or two extended examples?

3. In addition to using numerous examples from literature, Dirda incorporates CONCRETE, specific examples from his own experience and from everyday life. Which of Dirda's examples do you find especially interesting or appropriate? How and how well do they illustrate his point, in your opinion?

4. Dirda presents his articles of advice "in no particular order" (3). Why doesn't he arrange them in order of importance?

5. Each of Dirda's paragraphs is a mini-essay that states its point with a quotation, gives a number of specific examples, and then states its point again with some variation. Is this an effective strategy? Why or why not?

6. Within paragraphs, Dirda's ideas are clearly connected to one another. Should he have included more transitions and other connecting words *between* paragraphs to link the parts of his essay together as a whole? Why or why not?

7. *Other Methods.* Besides exemplifying his subject, Dirda is also analyzing a PROCESS. What is he explaining how to do, and what is the intended result of the process?

Thinking about Language

1. Since graduation occurs at the *end* of high school or college, why is Dirda giving *commencement* advice?

2. One meaning of *moral* is "pertaining to right and wrong"; another is "teaching a lesson." In which sense is Dirda using the word when he refers to the tradition of "the moral essay" (3)?

3. Usually, a "pastoral" poem or tale is set in the country and deals with the simple life (2). Explain the IRONY in Dirda's allusion to this tradition.

4. What is a "baker's dozen," and where does the term come from (16)? Why does Dirda give us just that many articles of advice?

5. What does Dirda mean by "destroy your rough drafts" (9)? Explain the ANALOGY he is using here.

6. What is a maxim and how might the word be applied to Dirda's essay?

For Writing

1. Choose one of Dirda's sayings and write a paragraph illustrating it with specific examples of your own.

2. Write an exemplification essay giving commencement advice to the new graduates of your high school or college.

3. Write an essay exemplifying how reading good literature provides (or does not provide) instruction on how to live.

JOANNA WEISS

Happy Meals and Old Spice Guy

> *Joanna Weiss (b. 1972) is a reporter and columnist for the* Boston Globe. *She majored in history and literature at Harvard, graduating in 1994. Studying "Hist & Lit" is a "great foundation for a journalism career," says Weiss, because it teaches you "to hone your arguments and think on your feet. . . . And you'll get practice for the days when you routinely have to sum up your worldview in 700 words." A contributor to* Slate, *Weiss writes mostly about gender and pop culture. She is now at work on a novel satirizing "breastfeeding, politics, and female competition."*
>
> *In this* Globe *column from 2010, Weiss focuses on two examples—McDonald's Happy Meals and Proctor and Gamble's "Old Spice Guy"—of the advertising and marketing strategies of large corporations as they learn to deal with social media such as YouTube and Twitter. Are the new techniques working with consumers? "It's too early to know," says Weiss, "if we're buying or not."*

IN THE LAUDABLE QUEST to fight childhood obesity, it's hard to get kids to exercise, control their portions, and hold the salt. It's easy to blame the Happy Meal toy. This spring, officials in Santa Clara, California, banned toy giveaways with kids' fast food meals. Last month, the Center for Science in the Public Interest threatened to sue McDonald's, saying the toys are a deceptive marketing practice.

Of course, there has been backlash, and not just from kids who fear they might miss out on "Last Airbender" figurines. A group of competing Save-The-Happy-Meal-Toys Facebook pages has sprung up, each with a fan base of nostalgic hipsters. The Happy Meal, it turns out, isn't just a bundle of adorably-packaged calories. It's a bundle of adorably-packaged calories that represents childhood.

There's something to be said for the power of marketing, the ways it can influence us even when we think we're too smart and too cool. Notre Dame University marketing professor Carol Phillips says that when her students brag that they aren't susceptible to advertising, she points to their shoes, their hats, and their computers.

See p. 175 for tips on choosing examples to fit your audience.

And she tells them that marketing isn't limited to ads; it's packaging, store placement, associations. And entertainment, too, as in last weekend's brilliant Old Spice social media campaign, in which the suave and shirtless "Old Spice Guy" posted YouTube responses to questions asked through Twitter. He offered image advice to

SUGGESTED MLA CITATION: Weiss, Joanna. "Happy Meals and Old Spice Guy." 2010. *Back to the Lake.* Ed. Thomas Cooley. 2nd ed. New York: Norton, 2012. 207–09. Print.

SMELL LIKE A MAN, MAN.
Old Spice

The manly man on a white horse in this ad from Procter & Gamble's 2010 Old Spice campaign is a good example of advertising informed by marketing research, which shows that men's body wash is usually purchased by wives and girlfriends.

President Obama. He helped a guy propose to his girlfriend. He might be the most beloved man in America, even though we know he's trying to sell us body wash.

It's too early to know if we're buying or not, though some old-school marketing   5
gurus have noted that sales of Old Spice are down. For all of its power, advertising has its limits—and ads are a reflection of the marketplace as much as they're an influence. Ad agencies do assiduous research into what people already want; "Old Spice Guy" came about because Procter & Gamble understood that women buy most of their husbands' body wash, and presumably want it to smell manly.

McDonald's is buffeted by market forces, too, which is why the fast food giant   6
has taken some baby steps into the wholesome-food game. One way the chain turned sluggish sales around in the early 2000s, Phillips notes, is by putting a few salads on the menu.

Campaigns against obesity have affected the Happy Meal, too: In 2006, the *Los*   7
Angeles Times reported that Disney executives were balking over Happy Meal tie-ins,

in part because they feared an association with fatty food. Today, the main Happy Meals web page mentions fries and soft drinks, but only shows pictures of lowfat milk and apples.

Is it bait-and-switch advertising? Sure. And McDonald's could be far more 8 aggressive in pushing apples over fries in actual stores. But at this point, are parents really unaware that french fries aren't a health food?

The anti–Happy Meal types prefer to paint parents as wimps, powerless against 9 a corporate marketing campaign. One anti–Ronald McDonald polemic, issued by a group called Corporate Accountability International, says McDonald's "undermines parental values" and creates "a fundamental restructuring of the family dynamic." The evidence: "Every time a parent has to say no to a child, it's another let down, another way that a parent has to feel bad about not making that child happy."

Well, my kids don't like it when I tell them they can't play with knives, but I 10 don't let it get to me. I also understand that the secret to survival in an ad-heavy world isn't avoiding marketing, but understanding it. Kids can be taught that what's on an ad isn't necessarily what they need. And the power of ads can be harnessed for good. If a YouTube video can make us talk about Old Spice, the right viral campaign could boost the market power of the nectarine.

A healthy lifestyle, after all, has clear appeal, which a clever marketer could 11 surely harness. Today, kids are lured by the Happy Meal in all of its weight-adding splendor. But after a few years, isn't it likely they'll want to look like Old Spice Guy, instead?

✗ ⋯⋰

READING CLOSELY

1. Joanna Weiss focuses on two main examples—McDonald's Happy Meals and Procter & Gamble's bare-chested Old Spice Guy. What do they exemplify about the buying habits of modern consumers?

2. The marketing of fast food, body wash, and other consumer products, says Weiss, is not limited to advertising. What else does she think it entails, according to the marketing experts she cites?

3. Retail giants like Procter & Gamble are always looking for new ways to sell their products. What are some of them, as exemplified by the Old Spice marketing campaign?

4. What does Weiss mean when she says that "the secret to survival in an ad-heavy world isn't avoiding marketing, but understanding it" (10). Do you agree? Why or why not?

STRATEGIES AND STRUCTURES

1. Procter & Gamble uses the Old Spice Guy to suggest who might need their body wash. Weiss uses him as an example of "a healthy lifestyle" (11). For what AUDIENCES and PURPOSES, respectively?

2. What point is Weiss making with her don't-play-with-knives example (10)? With the example of the "nectarine" (11)?

3. Weiss says it's "too early" to tell what EFFECT the Procter & Gamble campaign will have on the sale of Old Spice products (5). Where and how does she explain what CAUSED the company to launch this particular campaign?

4. According to Weiss, the Old Spice campaign exemplifies the "limits" of advertising (5). How and how well does she use this example to make her point?

5. *Other Methods.* Weiss uses a number of specific examples to show "the power of marketing," including its power to deceive (3). How and where does she also construct an ARGUMENT about harnessing that power to do "good" (10)?

THINKING ABOUT LANGUAGE

1. Why does Weiss ask if parents are "really unaware that french fries aren't a health food" (8)? Where else does she use RHETORICAL QUESTIONS in her essay? For what purpose?

2. What is "bait-and-switch advertising" (8)? Why is it called that?

3. Why does Weiss use terms like "wimps" and "ad-heavy" when referring to attitudes toward consumer products (9, 10)?

FOR WRITING

1. Choose an advertisement for a product aimed at children and write a paragraph or two explaining how you would use that ad as an example to show young consumers "that what's on an ad isn't necessarily what they need" (10).

2. Write an exemplification essay showing typical marketing strategies and techniques that companies use to successfully (or unsuccessfully) sell their products. Choose your examples from ad campaigns that you find especially effective (or misdirected).

LAUREL THATCHER ULRICH

Well-Behaved Women Seldom Make History

Laurel Thatcher Ulrich (b. 1938) is a professor of history and women's studies at Harvard University. She is the author of books and articles on the women of colonial America, including Good Wives *(1982) and* A Midwife's Tale *(1990), a biography of Martha Ballad that won a Pulitzer Prize for history in 1991. Ulrich grew up in Utah and attended the University of Utah, Simmons College, and the University of New Hampshire.*

In 1976, Ulrich wrote a scholarly article that included the following phrase in the opening paragraph: "Well-behaved women seldom make history." Not long after her article was published, this line, often slightly altered, began appearing on bumper stickers and T-shirts across the country. In the following selection, which comprises the introductory chapter to her latest book, Ulrich uses her now-famous phrase as an example not only of the fragility of fame and popular culture, but of how history itself gets made—and written.

Some time ago a former student e-mailed me from California: "You'll be delighted to know that you are quoted frequently on bumpers in Berkeley." Through a strange stroke of fate I've gotten used to seeing my name on bumpers. And on T-shirts, tote bags, coffee mugs, magnets, buttons, greeting cards, and websites. 1

> When you cite examples in a series, try to use the same grammatical form (p. 182).

I owe this curious fame to a single line from a scholarly article I published in 1976. In the opening paragraph, I wrote: "Well-behaved women seldom make history." That sentence, slightly altered, escaped into popular culture in 1995, when journalist Kay Mills used it as an epigraph for her informal history of American women, *From Pocahontas to Power Suits*. Perhaps by accident, she changed the word *seldom* to *rarely*. Little matter. According to my dictionary, *seldom* and *rarely* mean the same thing: "Well-behaved women *infrequently*, or on *few occasions*, make history." This may be one of those occasions. My original article was a study of the well-behaved women celebrated in Puritan funeral sermons. 2

In 1996, a young woman named Jill Portugal found the "rarely" version of the quote in her roommate's copy of *The New Beacon Book of Quotations by Women*. She wrote me from Oregon asking permission to print it on T-shirts. I was amused by her request and told her to go ahead; all I asked was that she send me a T-shirt. The 3

SUGGESTED MLA CITATION: Ulrich, Laurel Thatcher. "Well-Behaved Women Seldom Make History." 2007. *Back to the Lake*. Ed. Thomas Cooley. 2nd ed. New York: Norton, 2012. 211–19. Print.

success of her enterprise surprised both of us. A plain white shirt with the words "Well-behaved women rarely make history" printed in black roman type became a best-selling item. Portugal calls her company "one angry girl designs." Committed to "taking over the world, one shirt at a time," she fights sexual harassment, rape, pornography, and what she calls "fascist beauty standards."

Her success inspired imitators, only a few of whom bothered to ask permission. 4 My runaway sentence now keeps company with anarchists, hedonists, would-be witches, political activists of many descriptions, and quite a few well-behaved women. It has been featured in *CosmoGirl*, the *Christian Science Monitor*, and *Creative Keepsake Scrapbooking Magazine*. According to news reports, it was a favorite of the pioneering computer scientist Anita Borg. The Sweet Potato Queens of Jackson, Mississippi, have adopted it as an "official maxim," selling their own pink-and-green T-shirt alongside another that reads "Never Wear Panties to a Party."

See p. 180 to make sure you choose a range of examples that fit the situation.

My accidental fame has given me a new perspective on American popular cul- 5 ture. While some women contemplate the demise of feminism, others seem to have only just discovered it. A clerk in the Amtrak ticket office in D.C.'s Union Station told a fellow historian that all the women in her office wore the button. "I couldn't resist telling her that I was acquainted with you, and she just lit right up, and made me promise to tell you that the women at the Amtrak office thank you for all your 'words of wisdom.'"

. . .

The "well-behaved women" quote works because it plays into longstanding stereo- 6 types about the invisibility and the innate decorum of the female sex. Many people think women are less visible in history than men because their bodies impel them to nurture. Their job is to bind the wounds, stir the soup, and bear the children of those whose mission it is to fight wars, rule nations, and define the cosmos. Not all those who make this argument consider women unimportant—on the contrary, they often revere the contributions of women as wives, mothers, and caregivers—or at least they say so. But they also assume that domestic roles haven't changed much over the centuries, and that women who perform them have no history. A New Hampshire pastor captured this notion when he wrote in his commonplace book in 1650, "Woman's the center & lines are men." If women occupy the fixed center of life, and if history is seen as a linear progression of public events, a changing panorama of wars and kingdoms, then only those who through outrageous behavior, divine intervention, or sheer genius step into the stream of public consequence have a history.

The problem with this argument is not only that it limits women. It also limits 7 history. Good historians are concerned not only with famous people and public events but with broad transformations in human behavior, things like falling death rates or transatlantic migration. Here seemingly small actions by large numbers of people can bring about profound change. But this approach runs up against another imperative of history—its reliance on written sources. Until recent times most women (and a great many men) were illiterate. As a consequence their activities were recorded, if at all, in other people's writing. People who caused trouble might show up in court records, newspapers, or their masters' diaries. Those who quietly went about their lives were either forgotten, seen at a distance, or idealized into anonymity. Even today, publicity favors those who make—or break—laws.

But the difficulty is bigger than that. History is an account of the past based on surviving sources, but it is also a way of making sense out of the present. In the heat and confusion of events, people on all sides of an issue mine old stories for inspiration, enlightenment, or confirmation. Their efforts add to the layers of understanding attached to the original events, shaping what later generations know and care about. Scholars sometimes call these popular reconstructions of the past "memory" to distinguish them from formal history. But serious history is also forged in the tumult of change. History is not just what happened in the past. It is what later generations choose to remember. 8

. . .

Historians don't own history. But we do have a lot of experience sifting through competing evidence. Historical research is a bit like detective work. We re-create past events from fragments of information, trying hard to distinguish credible accounts from wishful thinking. One of our jobs is to explore the things that get left out when a person becomes an icon. Recent scholarship on the Sweet Potato Queens' heroine, Mae West, is a good example. There is no question about West's reputation for misbehavior. She said it herself: "When I'm bad, I'm better." Beginning her stage career at the age of six, she moved from playing the saintly Little Eva in *Uncle Tom's Cabin* to shimmying her way to fame. In uptight Boston, theater owners cut off the lights "with West's first ripple." But in New York she was the darling of urban sophisticates who wanted to explore the scamy side of life without leaving their theater seats. When she moved to Hollywood in the 1930s, censors tried to clean up her scripts, but she knew how to fill even the blandest lines with sexual innuendo. *Variety* complained that "Mae couldn't sing a lullaby without making it sexy." 9

That is how Mae West made history. But what sort of history did she make? Some recent studies focus on her debts to the male homosexuals whose outrageous impersonations defined *camp* in the 1920s. Others claim that her largest debt was to African American entertainers. West's shimmy, for example, ultimately derived from West African traditions adapted in rural dance halls, or "jooks." Her ballad "Honey let yo' drawers hang down low" (which may have inspired the Sweet Potato Queens' "Never Wear Panties to a Party") was a favorite in southern jooks. In the 10

Mae West, photographed in the 1930s.

early twentieth century, West, the sexually active, streetwise girl from Brooklyn, gave middle-class audiences a glimpse of worlds that both fascinated and repelled. Like the legendary Godiva,[1] she allowed people to imagine the unimaginable. Because she was also a savvy businesswoman, she was able to live off other people's fantasies.

A first-year student at a California university told me that to make history, people need to do the unexpected. She offered the example of civil rights activist Rosa Parks, "who would not leave her seat." I like her emphasis on the unexpected. It not only captures the sense of history as the study of how things change, it offers a somewhat more complex way of understanding the contribution of a woman like Parks. ¹¹

Was Parks a well-behaved woman? The Montgomery, Alabama, bus company did not think so. As the student from California recognized, Parks made history precisely because she dared to challenge both social norms and the law. Her refusal to obey the statute that required her to give up her seat to a white passenger ¹²

1. *Godiva:* Lady Godiva, an eleventh-century Anglo-Saxon noblewoman who reportedly rode naked through the streets of Coventry to protest taxes imposed by her husband.

sparked the 361-day-long boycott that thrust Martin Luther King into the public eye and led to a historic Supreme Court decision outlawing segregation on public transportation. Yet Parks became an icon for the civil rights movement not only for her courage but because the media identified her as a hard-working seamstress who simply got tired of moving to the back of the bus. Few people outside Montgomery knew her as the politically conscious secretary of the local NAACP, nor understood how many years she and her husband had been working for social justice before that fateful day on the bus. In 1954 and 1955, Parks had attended workshops on desegregation sponsored by the radical Highlander Folk School in Tennessee, a public education project that Mississippi's Senator James Eastland excoriated as a "front for a conspiracy to overthrow this country."

Nor has popular history recorded the names of other Montgomery women— 13 teenagers—whose arrests that year for refusing to give up their seats failed to ignite a movement. Years later, E. D. Nixon, president of the Montgomery NAACP, explained why he hadn't chosen any of these other women to make a historic stand against segregation. "OK, the case of Louise Smith. I found her daddy in front of his shack, barefoot, drunk. Always drunk. Couldn't use her. In that year's second case, the girl, very brilliant but she'd had an illegitimate baby. Couldn't use her. The last case before Rosa was the daughter of a preacher who headed a reform school for years. My interview of her convinced me that she wouldn't stand up to pressure. She were even afraid of me. When Rosa Parks was arrested, I thought, 'This is it!' 'Cause she's morally clean, she's reliable, nobody had nothing on her, she had the courage of her convictions." Parks's publicly acknowledged good behavior helped to justify her rebellion and win support for her cause. As one friend recalled, she "was too sweet to even say 'damn' in anger."

After Parks's death in the fall of 2005, the airways were filled with tributes cele- 14 brating the life of the "humble seamstress," the "simple woman" who sparked a revolution because her feet were tired. Reviewing these eulogies, syndicated columnist Ellen Goodman asked, "Is it possible we prefer our heroes to be humble? Or is it just our heroines?" She wondered if it wasn't time Americans got over the notion that women are "accidental heroines," unassuming creatures thrust into the public eye by circumstances beyond their control. Goodman noted that Parks and her compatriots spent years preparing for just such an opportunity. She concluded: "Rosa Parks was 'unassuming'—except that she rejected all the assumptions about her place in the world. Rosa Parks was a 'simple woman'—except for a mind made up and fed up. She was 'quiet'—except, of course, for one thing. Her willingness to say 'no' changed the world."

The California student said that in contrast to Parks a "well-behaved woman" is 15 "a quiet, subservient, polite, indoors, cooking, cleaning type of girl who would never risk shame by voicing her own opinion." There is a delicious irony in this

Rosa Parks' mug shot, taken shortly after her arrest on December 1, 1955, for refusing to obey a bus driver's order to give up her seat to a white passenger.

part of her definition. Notice that it associates a particular kind of work—cooking and cleaning—with subservience and passivity. Yet the boycott that made Parks famous was sustained by hundreds of African American domestic servants—cooks and maids—who walked to work rather than ride segregated buses. They too did the unexpected.*

Serious history talks back to slogans. But in the contest for public attention, slogans usually win. Consider my simple sentence. It sat quietly for years in the folds of a scholarly journal. Now it honks its ambiguous wisdom from coffee mugs and tailgates. 16

. . .

In my scholarly work, my form of misbehavior has been to care about things that other people find predictable or boring. My second book is a case in point. At a distance, the life of Martha Moore Ballard was the stuff from which funeral sermons were made. She was a "good wife" in every sense of the word, indistinguishable from all the self-sacrificing and pious women celebrated in Puritan eulogies. In conventional terms, she did not make history. She cherished social order, respected authority, and abhorred violence. As a midwife and healer, she relied on home-grown medicines little different from those found in English herbals a century before her birth. Her religious sentiments were conventional; her reading was limited to the Bible, edifying pamphlets, and newspapers. Although she lived through the American Revolution, she had little interest in politics. She was a caregiver and a sustainer rather than a mover and shaker. 17

Ballard made history by performing a methodical and seemingly ordinary act— writing a few words in her diary every day. Through the diary we know her as a pious herbalist whose curiosity about the human body led her to observe and record autopsies as well as nurse the sick, whose integrity allowed her to testify in a sensational rape trial against a local judge who was her husband's employer, and whose sense of duty took her out of bed at night not only to deliver babies but to care for the bodies of a wife and children murdered by their own husband and father. The power of the diary is not only in its sensational stories, however, but 18

* Awele Makeba's powerful one-woman show, "Rage Is Not a 1-Day Thing," dramatizes the lives of sixteen little-known participants, male and female, black and white. For details see her website, http://www.awele.com/programs.htm. For a list of resources prepared for the fiftieth anniversary of the boycott in 2005, see http://www.teachingforchange.org/busboycott/busboycott.htm. Additional documents can be found in Stewart Burns, ed., *Daybreak of Freedom: The Montgomery Bus Boycott* (Chapel Hill and London: University of North Carolina Press, 1997). Herbert Kohl, *She Would Not Be Moved: How We Tell the Story of Rosa Parks and the Montgomery Bus Boycott* (New York and London: The New Press, 2005), urges teachers to move from the theme "Rosa Was Tired" to the more historically accurate concept "Rosa Was Ready." [Author's note]

in its patient, daily recording of seemingly inconsequential events, struggles with fatigue and discouragement, conflicts with her son, and little things—like the smell of a room where a dead body lay. In Ballard's case, the drama really was in the humdrum. The steadiness of the diary provided the frame for everything else that happened.

. . .

Although I have received mail addressed to Martha Ballard and have been identi- 19
fied on at least one college campus as a midwife, I am only a little bit like my eighteenth-century subject. Like her, I was raised to be an industrious housewife and a self-sacrificing and charitable neighbor, but sometime in my thirties I discovered that writing about women's work was a lot more fun than doing it. I remember thinking one winter day how ironic it was that I was wrapped in a bathrobe with the heat of a wood stove rising toward my loft as I wrote about a courageous woman who braved snowstorms and crossed a frozen river on a cake of ice to care for mothers in labor. I felt selfish, pampered, and decadent. But I did not stop what I was doing. I did not know why I needed to write Martha's story, and I could not imagine that anybody else would ever want to follow me through my meandering glosses on her diary. I was astonished at the reception of the book. Even more important than the prizes was the discovery of how important this long-dead midwife's story was to nurses, midwives, and anonymous caregivers dealing with quite different circumstances today. These readers helped me to see that history is more than an engaging enterprise. It is a primary way of creating meaning. The meaning I found in Martha Ballard's life had something to do with my own life experience, but perhaps a lot more to do with the collective experiences of a generation of Americans coping with dramatic changes in their own lives.

When I wrote that "well-behaved women seldom make history," I was making a 20
commitment to help recover the lives of otherwise obscure women. I had no idea that thirty years later, my own words would come back to me transformed. While I like some of the uses of the slogan more than others, I wouldn't call it back even if I could. I applaud the fact that so many people—students, teachers, quilters, nurses, newspaper columnists, old ladies in nursing homes, and mayors of western towns—think they have the right to make history.

Some history-making is intentional; much of it is accidental. People make his- 21
tory when they scale a mountain, ignite a bomb, or refuse to move to the back of the bus. But they also make history by keeping diaries, writing letters, or embroidering initials on linen sheets. History is a conversation and sometimes a shouting match between present and past, though often the voices we most want to hear are barely audible. People make history by passing on gossip, saving old records, and

by naming rivers, mountains, and children. Some people leave only their bones, though bones too make history when someone notices.

Historian Gerda Lerner has written: "All human beings are practicing historians. . . . We live our lives; we tell our stories. It is as natural as breathing." But if no one cares about these stories, they do not survive. People do not only make history by living their lives, but by creating records and by turning other people's lives into books or slogans.   22

READING CLOSELY

1. According to Laurel Thatcher Ulrich, what accounts for the near-viral popularity of her slogan about well-behaved women and history? Do you think this is a good explanation? Why or why not?

2. Throughout history, says Ulrich, "well-behaved" women have rarely left their mark on the public record. Why not?

3. Historically, according to Ulrich, how has "good behavior" in women been DEFINED? By whom and for what purpose or purposes?

4. In her essay, Ulrich gives numerous examples of women who have made history. How "well-behaved" were they? Explain by referring to several of the particular instances she cites.

STRATEGIES AND STRUCTURES

1. Ulrich's essay was written as an introduction to a book in which she explores the circumstances under which women have made history. How, and how well, do you think her essay serves such a PURPOSE? Does it make you want to read her book? Why or why not?

2. A professional historian, Ulrich is not writing strictly for other scholars here. Who *is* her AUDIENCE? Why do you think so? Point to specific clues in her text.

3. Ulrich begins her essay by giving the history of her slogan about women who make history. How, and how well, does this account exemplify what Ulrich goes on to say about what history is and how it gets made?

4. Among the many examples in Ulrich's essay of women who did make history, which ones do you find particularly compelling? Why?

5. Where and how does Ulrich use herself and her own career as examples? Are they fitting examples? Explain.

6. *Other Methods.* "The problem with this argument," writes Ulrich, "is not only that it limits women. It also limits history" (7). What limited DEFINITION of history is Ulrich referring to here? How does she define history? What ARGUMENT is *she* making?

THINKING ABOUT LANGUAGE

1. Ulrich says that her original slogan was probably altered "by accident" (2). Was the accidental change also an editorial improvement? Why or why not?

2. Why is Ulrich so careful to point out that *seldom* and *rarely* "mean the same thing" (2)?

3. Some phrases are inherently ambiguous. Is "well-behaved" a good example, especially when applied to women (or men or children) in general? Why or why not?

4. What "delicious irony" is Ulrich referring to in paragraph 15? Why does she find this particular example of IRONY to be so "delicious"?

FOR WRITING

1. Make a list of slogans you have seen—on car bumpers, T-shirts, or wherever—that you think are particularly good (or bad) examples of the argument they are intended to support. Choose one, and write a paragraph or two using that slogan to make a point.

2. Write an essay about a relatively obscure person—whether well- or ill-behaved—whom you think should be better known than she or he is. Be sure to explain how you came to know or know about this person, why you think she or he should be more famous, and why this person failed to make history—or why history failed to take this person sufficiently into account.

Ritual Acts vi

Adrienne Rich (b. 1929) has been a major voice in American poetry for more than half a century. A 1951 graduate of Radcliffe College, she won the Yale Series of Younger Poets Competition that year for her first book, A Change of World. *Rich's early work revealed her quiet mastery of traditional poetic themes and approaches, but she moved decisively away from such formalism with her third book,* Snapshots of a Daughter-in-Law *(1963). During this period, she also became an increasingly outspoken political activist, advocating racial and sexual equality and opposing the Vietnam War. In 1973 she won the National Book Award for her collection* Diving into the Wreck. *She has published more than twenty-five books of poetry and prose.*

The following excerpt is the concluding section of the poem "Ritual Acts," from The School among the Ruins, *Rich's 2004 collection. Here, as earlier in the poem, Rich is exemplifying a "ruined" world in which poetry is "a kind of teaching."*

A goat devouring a flowering plant   1
A child squeezing through a fence to school
A woman slicing an onion
A bare foot sticking out
A wash line tied to a torn-up tree   5
A dog's leg lifted at a standpipe[1]
An old man kneeling to drink there
A hand on the remote

We would like to show but to not be obvious
except to the oblivious   10
We want to show ordinary life
We are dying to show it

---

1. *Standpipe*: a vertical pipe connected to a central water supply. Refers here to the only source of water in poor third-world villages.

SUGGESTED MLA CITATION: Rich, Adrienne. "Ritual Acts vi." 2004. *Back to the Lake*. Ed. Thomas Cooley. 2nd ed. New York: Norton, 2012. 221. Print.

Reading Closely

1. What is Adrienne Rich exemplifying in this poem? How do you know?

2. Assuming that "we" refers to the poet, or to poets in general, what main point is Rich making about the writing of poetry?

Strategies and Structures

1. Rich begins with specific examples and then tells us explicitly what she is illustrating. Why do you think she follows this order, instead of stating her thesis first and *then* giving her examples?

2. What is Rich's PURPOSE in writing this poem? Who are "the oblivious," and why might the poet make an exception of them (9)?

3. Rich's examples consist mainly of CONCRETE, specific "acts." Why does she represent her particular subject with people (and animals) doing things?

4. *Other Methods.* Actions are the soul of NARRATIVE writing. Do Rich's examples present us with a coherent story? Why or why not?

Thinking about Language

1. "Ritual" acts are repeated actions that form part of a rite or ceremony. Why might Rich refer to the events of everyday life as a ceremony?

2. How does Rich use parallel grammatical structures in this poem?

3. Why do you think a poet would use the word "show," rather than *tell* or *explain*, to describe her craft (9, 11, 12)?

4. Is Rich using the word "dying" in a strictly literal sense (11)? Or is she speaking figuratively, too? Explain.

For Writing

1. List the acts you would choose to exemplify the rituals of ordinary life.

2. Write an ANALYSIS of Rich's use of concrete examples in this or another poem.

CHAPTER 7

Process Analysis

Writing is a multistage process. . . . The stages are interactive and frequently occur simultaneously. The writing process consists of prewriting, drafting, revising, editing, and publishing.

—Nora M. Kneebone, West Iron County Middle School

How to undecorate the tree is my business. There's no one around to give advice, so I do it my way. I take the end of a rope of gold tinsel and give it a jerk. The tree spins around, and I clean the whole thing off in eight seconds.
                                                                    —Erma Bombeck

What does taking down a Christmas tree have in common with replacing an empty roll of toilet tissue, painting baseboards, or removing a splinter with a needle? According to the household humorist Erma Bombeck, these are all lonely jobs; when it comes time to do them, the rest of the family has disappeared, so no one is around to help. These activities have something else in common, too. Like the business of writing about them, each one constitutes a process that can be understood and explained through process analysis.

Defining Process Analysis:
Telling How or How To

A process is a series of actions that produces an end result, such as getting rid of last year's Christmas tree. When you analyze a process, you separate those actions into a number of steps: unplug the lights on the tree, remove the ornaments and store them away till next year, unwind the lights and tinsel, gently lower the tree onto an old sheet, and so on.

There are two basic kinds of process analysis, directive and explanatory. A directive process analysis tells the reader how to do something, such as take down a Christmas tree, throw a boomerang, administer CPR, or avoid being eaten by an alligator. An explanatory process analysis tells the reader how something works or is made—the U.S. Senate, cloning, a key lime pie.

In this chapter, we will explore how to analyze a process, including how to break it into a sequence of steps, how to select the specific details that best suit your purpose and audience, and how to organize and present those details effectively. We will also review the critical points to watch for as you read over and revise a process analysis, as well as common errors to avoid when you edit.

Why Do We Analyze Processes?

The human mind is naturally analytical, inclined to take things apart to see how the pieces fit together. There are many reasons for analyzing a process. Sometimes we simply want to understand how something works, as when we analyze how wind flowing over a curved wing creates a difference in pressure that lifts an airplane. Other times we want to know how to do something, such as fly a plane. If the process produces an undesirable result, as with the spread of a disease, our purpose in analyzing it may be to prevent it from occurring again.

Or we may need to know how to save a skunk in distress, as Robert Connors did (p. 256).

Composing a Process Analysis

When you compose a process analysis, your first task is to break down the process into its main steps. If you are analyzing how to take down a Christmas tree using the Bombeck method, the process is simple and the steps are few: grab a rope of tinsel by one end, give it a jerk, and catch the ornaments as they spin off. Even in this simple case, you'll notice, the steps of the process must be presented to the reader in a particular order, usually CHRONOLOGICAL. With a multistage process—such as writing an essay or playing a video game—figuring out that order can be challenging, especially if the process has more than one possible outcome.

Removing the decorations from a Christmas tree is a process that *could* be accomplished in a single step. (All you really have to do is shake the tree.) Let's take a more challenging example, such as that of a complicated natural process, one we can analyze but not necessarily control—the spread of the bubonic plague.

The spread of the plague is an excellent example of a natural process we'd like to eradicate. A carrier, usually a flea, bites an infected animal, usually a rat. The flea picks up infected blood and transfers the bacilli that cause the plague to the human victim, again by biting. Having entered the bloodstream, the bacilli travel to the lymph nodes, where they begin to replicate. Eventually the lymph nodes swell, creating what Wendy Orent describes in *Plague* as "the huge, boggy, exqui-sitely painful mass we know as a bubo." The order is always the same—up to a point. The buboes never appear before the victim is infected. And the victim is never infected before the flea bites. What happens after the buboes appear, however—whether the victim lives or dies—is not fixed.

The order of events in natural disasters can also be difficult to determine with certainty. In an earthquake or hurricane, for example, it is true that the ground trembles or the wind blows first; but then many things start to happen all at once. In other words, the actions and events of many processes are, as Nora Kneebone observed, "interactive and frequently occur simultaneously." When you write about a process, however, you must present events in an orderly sequence. Whatever it turns out to be, the sequence in which you choose to relate those events will pro-vide the main principle for organizing your written analysis.

Thinking about Purpose and Audience

One purpose for writing a process anlaysis is to tell your readers how to do something. For this purpose, a basic set of instructions or directions will usually do the job, as when you give someone the recipe for your Aunt Mary's famous pound cake.

Debra Houchins gives such a set of instructions on p. 235.

When, however, you want your audience to understand, not duplicate, a com-plicated process—such as the spread of a disease, the cloning of a sheep, or the chemistry that makes a cake rise—your analysis should be more explanatory than directive. So instead of giving instructions ("add the sugar to the butter"), you would go over the inner workings of the process in some detail, telling readers, for example, *what happens* when they add baking powder to the cake mixture.

Here's a chef's analysis of the baking process:

The first step in making a pound cake is to take a fat, such as butter or short-ening, or a combination of the two, and beat it with an electric mixer. This incorporates air bubbles. Then, sugar is sprinkled slowly into the butter. As the sharp sugar crystals cut into the butter, tiny pockets are formed and fill with air as the mixer blades pull more butter over the top of the hole to close it. This makes the butter double in volume and become creamy in texture, which is why this procedure is called "creaming." . . . Then, the eggs are usually added, which adds more volume and allows the mixture to hold even more air. The dry ingredients, including the baking soda or powder, are then added, usually alternating with liquid. When the baking soda or powder comes into contact with liquid, carbon dioxide is released. As the batter heats up, bubbles form and the batter rises.

—RICK McDANIEL, "Chemistry 101 for Pound Cakes"

This is much more information than your readers will need if you are just giving them a recipe for pound cake. However, if you are writing for a food magazine and you want readers to understand why their cakes may fall if they open the oven door during the baking process—it's because the bubbles collapse before the batter sets up—then such explanatory details are appropriate.

The nature of your audience, too, will affect the information you include in your analysis. How much does your intended reader already know about the process you're analyzing? Why might he or she want to know more, or less? If you are giving a set of instructions, will the reader require any special tools or equipment? What problems or glitches is the reader likely to encounter? Will you need to indicate where he or she can look for more information on your topic? Ask questions like these, and select the steps and details you present accordingly.

Generating Ideas:
Asking How Something Works

BRAINSTORMING, LISTING, and other methods of discovery can help you generate ideas for your process analysis. When you analyze a process, the essential question to ask yourself is *how*. How does a cake rise? How do I make chicken salad? How does an engine work? How do I back out of the garage?

When you're thinking about writing a process analysis, ask yourself a *how* question about your topic, research the answer, and write down all of the steps involved. These will form the foundation of your process analysis. For instance, "How do I back out of the garage?" might result in a list like this:

> step on the gas
> turn the key in the ignition
> put the car in reverse
> cut the steering wheel to the right
> back out of the garage

This list includes all the essential steps for backing a car out of a garage, but you wouldn't want your reader to try to follow them in this order. Once you have a list of all the steps in your process, you need to begin thinking about how to present them to your reader.

Organizing and Drafting a Process Analysis

First you'll need to put the steps in a certain order with appropriate transitions between them. Then choose pronouns and verb forms that fit the type of analysis you're writing, whether directive or explanatory. Think about the main point you want your analysis to make and state it clearly. Finally, consider whether you should demonstrate the process visually. The templates on page 228 can help you get started.

PUTTING THE STEPS IN ORDER

Many processes, especially those linked by CAUSE AND EFFECT, follow a prescribed order. For example, before the bacillus that causes bubonic plague can enter a victim's bloodstream, a flea must first bite an infected rat, then bite the human. The process of infection won't work if the steps that make up the process unfold in any other order.

But sometimes the steps that make up a process can take place in almost any order. Consider the following tongue-in-cheek analysis of manly behavior:

> The Wild Man process involves five basic phases: Sweating, Yelling, Crying, Drum-Beating, and Ripping Your Shirt Off Even If It's Expensive.
> —JOE BOB BRIGGS, "Get in Touch with Your Ancient Spear"

A man in the process of reverting to his "wild" self would not necessarily go through the phases of the process in the exact order indicated here. For example, he might tear his shirt off first, before sweating or yelling. (Yelling first might even help to induce the sweating phase.)

When you write about the wild man (or any other) process, however, you must organize and present the main steps of the process in *some* order. If the process is a linear one, such as driving to a particular address in Dallas, you simply start at the earliest point in time and move forward, step by step, to the end result. If the process is cyclical, such as what's happening in your car engine as you drive, you will have to pick a logical point in the process and then proceed through the rest of the cycle. If, however, the process you are analyzing does not naturally follow chronology, try arranging the steps of your analysis from most important to least important, or the other way around.

> Dave Barry presents survival steps in the order he learned them in "fright school" (p. 246).

USING TRANSITIONS

As you recount the main steps in the process one by one, let the reader know when you are moving from one step to another by including clear TRANSITIONS, such as *next, from there, after five minutes, then.* The actions and events that make up a process are repeatable—unlike those in a narrative, which happen only *once* upon a time. So you will frequently use such expressions as *usually, normally, in most cases, whenever.* But also note any deviations from the normal order that might occur by using transitions like *sometimes, rarely, in one instance.*

TEMPLATES FOR DRAFTING

When you begin to draft a process analysis, you need to say what process you're analyzing and to identify some of the most important steps in the process—moves fundamental to any process analysis. See how nature writer Diane Ackerman makes such moves in the following example:

> But how do the colored leaves fall? As a leaf ages, the growth hormone, auxin, fades, and cells at the base of the petiole divide. Two or three rows of small cells, lying at right angles to the axis of the petiole, react with water, then come apart, leaving the petioles hanging on by only a few threads of xylem. A light breeze, and the leaves are airborne.
> —DIANE ACKERMAN, "Why Leaves Turn Color in the Fall"

Ackerman identifies the process she's analyzing (the falling of leaves) and indicates some important steps in the process (leaf ages; growth hormone fades; stem cells divide, react with water, and come apart; leaf drops). Here is an example on how to avoid hostile situations, taken from this chapter:

> The most sensible way to avoid these threats, according to the instructor, is to remain alert, use common sense, be inconspicuous, and avoid dangerous areas, such as the planet Earth.
> —DAVE BARRY, "I Will Survive . . . Or at Least I'll Be Delayed"

The following templates can help you make some of these basic moves in your own writing. But don't take these as formulas where you just fill in the blanks. There are no shortcuts to good writing, but these templates can serve as starting points.

▶ In order to understand how process X works, we can divide it into the following steps: _____, _____, _____, and _____.

▶ The various steps that make up X can be grouped into the following stages: _____, _____, and _____.

▶ The end result of X is _____.

▶ In order to repeat X, you must first _____; then _____ and _____; and finally _____.

▶ The tools and materials you will need to replicate X include _____, _____, and _____.

▶ The most important reasons for understanding / repeating X are _____, _____, and _____.

USING APPROPRIATE PRONOUNS

In an explanatory process analysis, you need to focus on the things (fleas and rats, engines, oranges) and activities (infection, compression and combustion, culling and scrubbing) that make up the process. Thus you will write about the process most of the time in the THIRD PERSON (*he, she, it,* and *they*):

> Moving up a conveyer belt, oranges are scrubbed with detergent before they roll on into the juicing machines. —JOHN McPHEE, *Oranges*

In a directive process analysis, by contrast, you are telling the reader directly how to do something. So you should typically use the second person (*you*): "When making orange juice, first you need to cut the oranges in half."

The *you* may be implied, as in "Find Another Brother" (p. 253).

USING APPROPRIATE VERB FORMS

In an explanatory process analysis, you indicate how something works or is made, so your verbs should be in the indicative mood:

> As the rotor <u>moves</u> around the chamber, each of the three volumes of gas alternately <u>expands</u> and <u>contracts</u>. It is this expansion and contraction that <u>draws</u> air and fuel into the engine, <u>compresses</u> it, and <u>makes</u> useful power. —KARIM NICE, "How Rotary Engines Work"

In a directive process analysis, on the other hand, you are telling the reader how to do something, so your verbs should be in the imperative mood, as in these instructions for reviewing for exams:

> <u>Start</u> preparing for your exams the first day of class. . . . <u>Plan</u> reviews as part of your regular weekly study schedule. . . . <u>Read</u> over your lecture notes and <u>ask</u> yourself questions on the material you don't know well. . . . <u>Review</u> for several short periods rather than one long period. —*University of Minnesota Duluth Student Handbook*

Notice that the verbs in these two examples are both in the present tense. That is because they express habitual actions. Instructions are always written in the present tense because they tell how something is (or should be) habitually done: "As you place the oranges on the conveyor belt, keep hair and fingers clear of the rollers."

Explanations, on the other hand, are written in the present tense when they tell how a process is habitually performed:

> At low tide, researchers collect the algae by the handful and place it in plastic baggies. Back at the lab, they separate out the different strains and examine each type under a microscope.

But explanations are written in the *past* tense when they explain how a process was performed on a particular occasion, even though the process itself is repeatable:

> At low tide, researchers collected the algae by the handful and placed it in plastic baggies. Back at the lab, they separated out the different strains and examined each type under a microscope.

Be careful not to switch between past tense and present tense in your analysis, unless you're intentionally switching from explaining how a process is usually performed (present) to how it was performed on a particular occasion (past).

STATING YOUR POINT

A good process analysis should have a point to make—a THESIS. That point should be clearly expressed in a thesis statement so the reader will know why you're analyzing the process and what to expect. In addition, your thesis statement should in some way identify the process and indicate its end result. For example:

> You cannot understand how the Florida citrus industry works without understanding how fresh orange juice gets processed into "concentrate."
>
> —JOHN MCPHEE, *Oranges*

This thesis statement clearly tells the reader what process the writer is analyzing (making concentrate from fresh orange juice), why he's analyzing it (as a foundation for understanding the Florida citrus industry), and what the end result of the process is (orange juice concentrate). As you draft a process analysis, make sure your thesis statement includes all of this information, so that your reader knows just what to expect from your analysis.

EXPLAINING A PROCESS VISUALLY

Sometimes a process is best explained by *showing* how it works. (Just try writing a paragraph telling readers how to tie their shoes, for example.) If that's the case with some part of the process you're analyzing, you may want to include a diagram or drawing, such as the one on the next page.

Notice that words accompany each step in this visual explanation. When you use a visual, make sure it is clearly labeled for the reader, whether that means describing what the visual shows and indicating the sequence of events, as here, or labeling parts of a diagram (for instance, the parts of an engine).

1. Place the necktie around your collar and arrange the tie so that the wider end (A) is longer than the narrow end (B), then cross A over B.

2. Twist A around and behind B.

3. Bring A up.

4. Pull A down through the loop.

5. Bring A around front, crossing over B from left to right.

6. Again thread A up and through the loop.

7. Pull A down through the front of the knot.

8. Tighten the knot: hold B with one hand and pull the knot up toward the collar with the other hand.

CONCLUDING A PROCESS ANALYSIS

A process is not complete until it yields a final result. Likewise, a process analysis is not complete until it explains how the process ends—and what this result means for the reader.

As Michael Munger observes (p. 264), the end of the writing process "is often more editing."

The process of turning orange juice into concentrate, for example, does not end when the juice is extracted from the fruit. The extracted juice must be further refined and then shipped to the consumer, as John McPhee explains in the conclusion of his analysis: "From the extractor the orange concentrate flows into holding tanks from which it is later tapped, packaged, frozen, and shipped to grocery stores all over the country." And that, he might have added, is how you get your "fresh" o.j. in the morning.

Even this is not the end of the story, however. If you were writing a directive analysis of the process of making orange juice from concentrate, your conclusion would need to remind readers to add cold water to the concentrate before serving.

USING OTHER METHODS

Analyzing the likely outcomes of a process and the steps leading to it may not always tell your readers everything they want or need to know. To explain a complicated process fully and completely, you may need to draw on other methods besides process analysis. Take, for instance, the process by which teenagers become addicted to tobacco. A teenager, let's call her Courtney, crosses the threshold from casual smoking to addiction. (Already we are expanding our analysis by giving an EXAMPLE.) Courtney now smokes half a dozen cigarettes every day. The process goes on—and on.

Over the next five years, Courtney gradually increases her intake of nicotine, a few cigarettes at a time, until one day she is a confirmed pack-a-day-plus smoker. Why? Why does Courtney become addicted while her sister, Brittany, never goes beyond a few cigarettes a day? Merely knowing *how* the process of addiction occurs—that it takes place in phases, from nonsmoking to experimentation to addiction—isn't necessarily going to tell us *why* it occurs, though that's an important question to consider.

For the answer—and to make our analysis more meaningful—we could draw on the other methods discussed in this book. For example, we could CLASSIFY and DIVIDE teenage smokers into types: quitters (those who experiment with smoking but soon give it up); chippers (those who continue to smoke but never get addicted to tobacco); and addicts (those who regularly smoke six or more cigarettes a day).

Analyzing what categories teenage smokers fall into still doesn't tell us why some chippers become addicts while others never do. To learn why individual smokers cross the line, we also need to analyze the CAUSES of nicotine addiction.

It turns out that as long as Courtney smokes about five cigarettes a day and no more, she can go on for years without becoming addicted. Once she starts smoking more than that, however, the residual level of nicotine in her body reaches what Malcolm Gladwell calls a "tipping point," and Courtney slowly sides into addiction. Having analyzed the causes of Courtney's addiction, we might then ARGUE that she and her peers should never start smoking in the first place.

Reading a Process Analysis with a Critical Eye

One complex process that doesn't proceed in linear fashion is writing. Although the phases of the writing process are sequential—that is, you have to organize and draft an essay before you can revise and edit it—they are also repeatable, unlike the steps in most strictly linear processes. (You wouldn't want to bake a cake, for example, and then take it out of the oven and stir it again.) So once you've "completed" your draft, go back, check it over thoroughly, and revise what you've written. Repeat as necessary.

Since the heart of your analysis is the process itself, you need to make sure, first of all, that your reader will be able to follow every step. So ask a friend or classmate to review your draft and tell you whether he or she has any questions about how the process works—or any suggestions for making it clearer. Here are some questions to keep in mind when checking a process analysis.

PURPOSE AND AUDIENCE. Is the purpose of the analysis to tell the audience how to do something, or is it to explain how something works or is made? How likely is the intended audience to want or need this information? What additional information, if any, should the analysis provide? For example, is there any special equipment that readers might need to know about? Any terms that need to be defined?

ORGANIZATION. Are all of the important steps of the process included? Are they arranged chronologically, or in some other order that makes sense—such as from most important to least important?

TRANSITIONS. Are there clear transitions between each step? Are the transitions overly predictable (*first, second, third*)? If so, consider changing them for variety.

PRONOUNS. Is the analysis primarily directive or explanatory? If it's directing the reader to do something, is it written mostly in the second person, referring to the reader as *you*? If the analysis is primarily explanatory, is it written mostly in the third person (*he, she, it,* and *they*)?

VERBS. If the analysis is directive, are the verbs in the imperative (or commanding) mood? If it's explanatory, are they in the indicative (or stating) mood? Is there any needless switching between the two moods? With verbs in the imperative mood, remember, the pronoun *you* is often understood rather than explicitly stated: "(You) Check over every aspect of your draft carefully."

THE POINT. What is the point of the analysis? Is there a thesis statement at the beginning that tells the reader why this particular process is being analyzed and what to look for in the rest of the essay? Is the significance or end result of the process clearly indicated?

VISUALS. Are charts, drawings, or other illustrations included to help explain the process? If not, should there be? Are the visuals labeled and anchored appropriately in the text?

CONCLUSION. Does the analysis end with a clear indication of the outcome of the process? If there are several possible outcomes, does it indicate what they are and which results are most likely?

OTHER METHODS. Does the analysis include other methods of development? For instance, does it give EXAMPLES of the process? Does it analyze what CAUSED key actions or events in the process and what EFFECTS they might have? Does it CLASSIFY or DIVIDE part of the process? Does it offer an ARGUMENT about the process?

Editing for Common Errors in a Process Analysis

Process analysis invites certain types of errors, particularly in the choice of pronouns and verb forms. The following tips will help you check your writing for these two common problems.

Check your pronouns

Remember to use third-person pronouns (*he, she, it, they*) when you're explaining how something works or is done—and to use the second-person pronoun (*you*) when you're telling someone how to do something.

▸ When trees are harvested, ~~you have to~~ they are cut down ~~each one~~ by hand.

The reader is not actually harvesting the trees.

▸ To harvest trees properly, ~~they~~ you must ~~be~~ cut them down by hand.

Here the reader is the one harvesting the trees.

Check your verbs to make sure you haven't switched needlessly between the indicative and the imperative

▶ According to the recipe, we should stir in the nuts. ~~Then~~ and then sprinkle cinnamon on top.

Or

▶ ~~According to the recipe, we should stir~~ Stir in the nuts. ~~Then~~ and then sprinkle cinnamon on top.

Student Example

Debra Houchins is a features editor of the *Collegiate Times*, the student-run newspaper at Virginia Tech University in Blacksburg. An English and psychology major from Danville, Virginia, Houchins is the author of "Vampire in the Attic," a short story about schizophrenia that appeared in the 2010 edition of the undergraduate research journal *Philogia*.

"Nesquik and Nilla Wafers" appeared in the *Collegiate Times* in 2010. It deals with one of Houchins' favorite topics—food. In addition to explaining how to make tiramisu without expensive ladyfingers and liqueur, her essay provides a recipe for living frugally, so as to enjoy the occasional luxury even on a student budget.

Nesquik and Nilla Wafers:
How to Make Tiramisu on a Student Budget

As a college student, one of my biggest concerns—outside of my actual studies—is balancing my obsession with extravagance and my student poverty. I save obsessively and am more frugal than most people I know (my friends would probably use the term "cheap" to describe me). But my cushy savings allows me to sort out disasters like my recent laptop meltdown and plan out budgeted world travels. I might be "cheap" for 11 and a half months out of the year, but for two weeks I'm queen of the world.

I have a problem, though, and that problem is food.

1

Explains the PURPOSE for making an inexpensive version of a luxury dessert

EXAMPLES bolster Houchins' ARGUMENT in favor of frugality

2

I love good food. I try to spend only $30 a week on it, and I   3
rejoice anytime I manage to stay under budget. I can't help myself; I
need fresh fruits and veggies and all the materials to make dinners
from scratch every night. And of course, my homemade sweets.

To save money, I look up recipes and modify them to work with   4
what I already have in my kitchen or what money-saving substitutes
I can buy instead.

This week, I got an intense craving for some tiramisu, and   5
honestly, my meager $30 food budget wasn't going to cover
ladyfingers, unsweetened cocoa powder, and coffee liquor. So I
found a decent-looking recipe online and searched my kitchen, then
hit up the grocery store. I ended up spending about $10 extra outside
of my regular spending, but it was well worth it.

I ended up changing several things in the original recipe, but   6
when I served the dish to friends, no one said, "Hey, did you switch
the cocoa powder for your boyfriend's Nesquik?" or "Why didn't you
use vanilla sugar? It has a much more subtle taste than just regular
granulated sugar and vanilla extract!" In fact, no one said much
because they were too busy gorging themselves on cake.

The substitutions I ended up making were vanilla wafers for   7
ladyfingers, regular coffee for coffee liquor, Nesquik instead of cocoa
powder, and vanilla extract and sugar instead of vanilla sugar. In the
end, I only had to buy the cheese (which was the most pricey
expenditure at $3.50 for each container) and the wafers.

As for the Nesquik, it's going to be something you'll probably use   8
a lot more than cocoa powder, so even if you don't have any on hand
think about how often you'll drink yummy chocolate milk versus
how often you're going to be doing extensive baking before you go
shopping. Also, one of your friends is bound to have some kind of
chocolate milk powder mix anyway.

I grabbed an 8-by-8 inch circular baking pan to make it in, but a   9
pie tin works fine too.

So here's all you need to do to treat yourself and your friends,   10
while not spending a fortune:

Actions not directly part of the recipe are in the past tense

Analysis uses the FIRST PERSON when it is explanatory

What You'll Need
   6 egg yolks
   1/2 cup of table sugar
   4 teaspoons vanilla extract
   1 box of vanilla wafers (I use the reduced-fat generic kind)
   2 cups of coffee
   Nesquik
   2 8-ounce containers of mascarpone cheese

<u>First</u>, I separated the eggs, making sure to save the egg whites in a Tupperware container. After such a sugary treat, a super healthy breakfast of egg whites is just as useful to your health as it is delicious. Immediately place the egg whites in the fridge.

Pour the egg yolks in a large mixing bowl (it's going to need to be a pretty good size) and <u>then</u> add the sugar and the vanilla. Mix these together thoroughly with either a wooden spoon or a whisk. If you just prefer to use an electric mixer, make sure it's set on low. (It might be easier if you have an electric mixer, but let's take a second to remember that I'm a person who'd rather save three bucks than just buy cocoa powder. There's no way I'd dish out $20 for something I can do by hand.)

The directions of the original recipe say to fold the mascarpone cheese (which is like cream cheese but with a smoother texture and no flavor) into the yolk and sugar mixture, but I gave up on folding after five minutes and just carefully stirred it in.

Now for the fun part:

Pour the coffee <u>you</u> made (<u>you</u> can even use instant coffee, but java is the one thing I don't skimp on) into a mug or glass bowl. <u>You</u> can choose whether or not <u>you</u> want to try to quickly dip the vanilla wafers into the coffee and place on the tin before they disintegrate, or go ahead and arrange the wafers into the pan and then sprinkle it on. I chose the latter because I lack the necessary coordination and timing to pull off the former.

Just try to cover the bottom with wafers. You can stack a little if you like, but don't overdo it or the tiramisu will be too heavy and rich.

11 **TRANSITIONS** show the steps in **CHRONOLOGICAL** order

12

13

Clear division between preparation and assembly

14

15 **Analysis uses the second person when it is directive**

16

Once your wafers have all had their coffee, layer on half of the 17
cheese mixture. Smooth it out before making another layer of coffee-
soaked wafer.

Once you've finished, cover with some plastic wrap and chill in 18
the fridge for at least an hour.

**Last step
explains what
the Nesquik
is for** ⋯⋯•

Before serving, sprinkle the Nesquik on top, giving it that pretty, 19
dusted look tiramisu is famous for.

The finished dessert, topped with Nesquik.

Analyzing a Student Process Analysis

In "Nesquik and Nilla Wafers," Debra Houchins draws upon rhetorical strategies
and techniques that good writers use all the time when they analyze a process. The
following questions, in addition to focusing on particular aspects of Houchins' text,
will help you to identify those common strategies and techniques so you can adapt
them to your own writing. These questions will also help to prepare you for the
analytical questions—on content, structure, and language—that you'll find after all
the other selections in this chapter, along with suggestions for writing on related
topics.

READING CLOSELY

1. Most of the time, how does Debra Houchins indulge her taste for "extravagance" and yet live on a student budget (1)?

2. According to Houchins, food is always a "problem" for her (2). Why?

3. How, and how well, does she solve this perennial problem?

STRATEGIES AND STRUCTURES

1. Houchins assumes that her readers are living on a Nesquik-and-vanilla-wafers budget. What does she assume about that AUDIENCE's tastes, and how does this assumption give her something to write about?

2. How, and how well, does Houchins' recipe adaptation serve as an EXAMPLE of the frugal lifestyle she advocates?

3. Houchins tells what happened to the tiramisu before she explains how to make it. Why? What part of the process does this outcome help to explain?

4. Is Houchins giving directions for making something here, or explaining how she did it? Or both? Explain.

5. *Other Methods.* In addition to providing a recipe, Houchins DESCRIBES her student budget lifestyle. How do these NARRATIVE elements contribute to her analysis of making an inexpensive dessert?

THINKING ABOUT LANGUAGE

1. Houchins says her friends would probably call her "cheap"; why might she herself prefer the term "frugal" (1)?

2. Houchins describes her savings as "cushy" (1). What does this word suggest about the PURPOSE of having savings, in her view?

3. Houchins says she makes her dinner every night "from scratch" (3). What does this phrase mean, and what is its likely origin?

FOR WRITING

1. Make a list of the ingredients for your favorite dessert or other dish. In a paragraph or two, explain how and where to obtain those ingredients.

2. Write an essay explaining how to make tiramisu or some other luxurious dish to readers who are not on a budget. (How, by the way, would you have to change your explanation if you were writing to a different, less affluent audience?)

How to Dance Like Fred and Ginger

A process analysis tells how to do something by breaking it down into steps. Recipes are common examples, as is the set of instructions on a gasoline pump or ATM machine. In these illustrated instructions for learning to dance like Fred Astaire and Ginger Rogers, the various steps in the process are identified in the drawings beneath each photograph of the master dancers in action. When you write a process analysis, you may want to include illustrations along with your text; the visuals should actually help to explain the process, however, and not merely serve as decoration. With the text itself, you simply start at the beginning of the process: "One of the most popular ballroom dances is the foxtrot. Begin in the classic ballroom position with the man facing the woman, hands clasped and held to one side." And you walk the reader through the process step by step: "A simplified version of the foxtrot can be broken into five main moves: step forward, step back, left rock turn, forward advance, and promenade. In the first step, the man moves forward with the left foot as if walking...." And so on through all the steps. Don't stop until you reach the end result of the process you're analyzing—the completed cake, nuclear reaction, or "feather finish" of the foxtrot.

CROSS STEP & TOE BEAT   CIRCULAR ROCK (Fox-trot Step)   HEEL & TOE CLICK

First you do a Fox Trot step . . . then you whirl gracefully into the heel and toe slide, tap first the heel and then the toe, tapping leg swinging rhythmically to the right and left; bring the rear foot forward a few inches at each tap. Then you roll into it . . . swing from the partial side-to-side position into the full side, take three Fox Trots forward and three backward, gentleman leaning forward as the lady backs, lady leaning forward as the gentleman backs.

241

JOSHUA PIVEN, DAVID BORGENICHT, AND JENNIFER WORICK

How to Pull an All-Nighter

*Joshua Piven (b. 1971) and David Borgenicht have made an industry out of teaching people how to deal with unlikely situations. In 1998, while watching a movie in which a man without piloting experience was forced to land a plane, Borgenicht concluded that life is filled with "worst-case scenarios" for which the average person is utterly unprepared. He recruited Piven, a fellow University of Pennsylvania graduate, to help him research and write a manual for such situations—*The Worst-Case Scenario Survival Handbook *(1999). Addressing situations that range from the merely improbable (delivering a baby in a taxicab) to the barely imaginable (a sword fight), the book was so popular that there are now* Worst-Case Scenario *handbooks for everything from holidays and golfing to weddings and dating.*

The Worst-Case Scenario Survival Handbook: College *(2004), co-authored by Jennifer Worick, brings the Worst-Case outlook to college life. "How to Pull an All-Nighter" is from that collection and deals with a process that some students might actually engage in—staying up all night to study. As with the authors' instructions for surviving a stadium riot or shark attack, however, readers of this point-by-point analysis might be better advised to avoid the situation in the first place.*

Eat a light dinner. Do not skip a meal, but do not eat to the point of drowsiness or sluggishness. Select foods with protein, like chicken breast, and complex carbohydrates, such as whole-wheat bread, brown rice, or beans, to provide you with energy and stamina for a long night. Later, when you feel your energy ebb, eat an energy bar. 1

Consume peppermint. Peppermint is a stimulant; even a whiff of it will make you more alert and awake. Eat peppermint candy, chew peppermint gum, or drink peppermint-flavored herbal tea. Rub peppermint oil on your temples or wrists. 2

Turn on the radio or television. A bit of white noise in the background will engage your senses. Select a classical or jazz station on the radio. If you turn on the television, turn to an infomercial or shopping channel. Keep the volume low. Do not select a rerun of your favorite situation comedy or anything you might otherwise be interested in. 3

SUGGESTED MLA CITATION: Piven, Joshua, David Borgenicht, and Jennifer Worick. "How to Pull an All-Nighter." 2004. *Back to the Lake.* Ed. Thomas Cooley. 2nd ed. New York: Norton, 2012. 242–44. Print.

Turn on a strong overhead light. A bright light will help you see what you are 4
reading as well as prevent you from falling into a deep sleep. Close the curtains
and put clocks out of sight; your body will become confused as to what time of
night it is.

Turn down the thermostat. The cold temperature will help keep you awake. 5
Make sure the temperature does not dip below 50°F, at which you are susceptible to hypothermia, especially if you have wet hair or skin. A high temperature
slows your pulse and makes you drowsy.

Do not lie down. Pinch yourself or wear tight shoes and constricting under- 6
wear. Physical discomfort will keep you distracted and awake.

Consume caffeine. Drink caffeinated beverages or eat a few caffeinated mints, 7
but proceed with caution: Too much caffeine can leave you distracted and wired.
Three hundred milligrams is considered a safe daily amount of caffeine for
adults, which translates into a six-pack of soda or three to four cups of brewed
coffee.

Breathe deeply. Go to an open window or step outside for a few minutes. Stand 8
up straight, close your eyes, and inhale deeply through your nose. Hold the
breath for as long as you can. Exhale slowly through your nose or mouth. Repeat
several times. Deep breathing will clear your mind and give you a shot of
energy.

Stretch. Stretch your limbs by taking a walk or doing a few yoga poses. This will 9
work out any tension you are holding in your muscles.

- Lift your arms over your head and reach for the sky, alternating arms.
- Lean over to each side and then lean forward from the waist, bringing your
  arms out in front of you and down to the ground.
- Let your arms dangle; swing them from side to side.

Do a headstand. Increase your circulation by standing on your head. 10

- Find an area of clear floor space next to a wall.
- Kneel on the floor, facing the wall.
- Place your head on the floor a few inches from the wall.
- Place your forearms on the floor on either side of your head.
- Raise your body and legs slowly up the wall. Keep your body weight
  on your arms, not your head. Lean against the wall as needed.

Give the steps in
the right order
if you want your
reader to repli-
cate a process
(p. 227).

Standing on your head will increase circulation.

Raise your heart rate. If you find yourself nodding off, do a few calisthenics to   11
raise your heart rate. Do 25 jumping jacks, or skip rope or jog in place for
5 minutes.

Get a study partner. Even if he is not cramming for the same exam, you and   12
your partner can quiz each other and talk as you start to get drowsy. Do not stay
up with someone you know will distract you with either idle chatter or sexual
tension.

Be Aware

Even if you don't plan on going to sleep, set your alarm clock. To make sure that   13
you are awake when you need to be, set every alarm you can find—watches,
computers, cell phones, and hand-held electronic devices often have built-in
alarms. Arrange for a friend or your roommate to back up the alarms with a
wake-up call.

READING CLOSELY

1. What are the main steps into which Joshua Piven, David Borgenicht, and Jennifer Worick divide the process of pulling an all-nighter?

2. Which steps do you think would be most effective? Least effective? Why?

3. What steps would you add to (or remove from) this process analysis?

STRATEGIES AND STRUCTURES

1. Who might care about the process that the authors of this selection are explaining? What particular AUDIENCE do they have in mind? How can you tell?

2. The authors of this selection do not say why they are explaining how to pull an all-nighter. What might their PURPOSE be, and should they state it more directly? Why or why not?

3. The instructions in this selection could be followed in almost any order. Why? On the other hand, why do individual directives—such as those for breathing deeply, stretching, and doing a headstand—actually require the reader to follow a particular sequence?

4. An essay has an introduction, a body, and a conclusion. What parts of the essay form are missing from "How to Pull an All-Nighter"? If this selection is not really an essay, what it is? Explain.

5. How and how well does the illustration in this selection take the place of verbal explanations?

6. *Other Methods.* As Piven, Borgenicht, and Worick analyze the process of staying awake all night, they give a number of specific EXAMPLES. Which ones do you think contribute most to the analysis? Why?

THINKING ABOUT LANGUAGE

1. The verbs in the headings that introduce each section of this text are all in the imperative mood. Why?

2. What pronoun is understood in each heading? What grammatical "person" is it in? Why?

3. In what sense are the authors of the selection using the word "translates" (7)?

FOR WRITING

1. Write a paragraph or two telling someone how to pull an all-nighter.

2. Write an essay explaining how to study so as to avoid all-nighters and other educational pitfalls.

DAVE BARRY

I Will Survive . . . Or at Least I'll Be Delayed

Dave Barry (b. 1947) is the author of more than thirty books of humor. A graduate of Haverford College, Barry taught writing for a consulting firm before joining the Miami Herald *as a humor columnist in 1983. (When you write a business letter, Barry advised his students, do not say things like, "Enclosed, please find the enclosed enclosures.") Barry's columns—collected in such volumes as* Dave Barry Is Not Making This Up *(1995) and* Dave Barry: Boogers Are My Beat *(2003)—earned him a Pulitzer Prize for commentary in 1988 and appeared weekly until 2005. His latest book,* I'll Mature When I'm Dead *(2010), covers various aspects of adulthood—surprising many people, including his publisher, who claims that Barry "struggled hard against growing up his entire life."*

"I Will Survive . . . Or at Least I'll Be Delayed" is a garbled review of the lessons that Barry learned in Hostile Environment Training—and a parody of how-to writing. First published in the Miami Herald *in 2004, these mangled directives make fun of overly simplified instructions for dealing with impossible situations "involving dangerous elements such as terrorists, kidnappers, robbers, rioters, or fans of the Oakland Raiders football team."*

WHEN I GOT INTO JOURNALISM, I expected to do many things. None of them involved standing on a colleague's groin.

But recently I learned that I might be called upon to do exactly that. I learned this in Fright School, which is known formally as Hostile Environment Training. This is a course, taught by corporate security consultants, that teaches you what to do if you find yourself in a situation involving dangerous elements such as terrorists, kidnappers, robbers, rioters, or fans of the Oakland Raiders.

I didn't think I needed this training, because I've lived for the past 20 years in a hostile environment, namely, Miami, where virtually everybody, including nuns, is packing heat.[1] But along with many other journalists, I was ordered by my company to attend Fright School because this summer I'm going to the Olympics and both political conventions. I'm writing this column before leaving for those events, and I sincerely hope that, by the time summer's over, we'll all be heaving large

---

1. *Packing heat:* Carrying a gun.

SUGGESTED MLA CITATION: Barry, Dave. "I Will Survive . . . Or at Least I'll Be Delayed." 2004. *Back to the Lake.* Ed. Thomas Cooley. 2nd ed. New York: Norton, 2012. 246–48. Print.

sighs of relief from knowing that nothing bad happened, and nobody had to actually stand on anybody's groin.

But just in case you ever find yourself in a hostile situation or, God forbid, a   4
Raiders home game, today I'm going to pass along the lessons I learned in Fright
School, as recorded in my notes.

My first note says "cargo pants," because that's what the instructor was wearing.   5
He was a muscular, military-looking British guy who was quite cheerful, considering that he ended roughly every fourth sentence with: "And if THAT happens, you're going to die."

The instructor began by reviewing the various kinds of hostile situations we, as   6
journalists, might encounter. The three main points I got from that were:

1. A lot of things can happen.
2. All of these things can kill you.
3. So DON'T PANIC.

Among the specific threats we discussed were "dirty bombs," germ warfare,   7
mines, and booby traps. Because we took only the truncated one-day version of
the course, the instructor couldn't go deeply into these threats, other than to
note that they are all fatal. (He also pointed out that his company had the
world's foremost authority on booby traps, and "he does a presentation that's
quite entertaining.")

The most sensible way to avoid these threats, according to the instructor, is to   8
remain alert, use common sense, be inconspicuous, and avoid dangerous areas,
such as the planet Earth. He also recommended that we carry the following items
at all times: water, food, protective eyewear, protective headgear, an
"escape hood" for gas attacks, a whistle, a personal alarm and a first-aid
kit. He didn't say how you could look inconspicuous while carrying all
these items: Maybe you could put them in your cargo pants and just
pretend to have enormous thighs.

> As explained on p. 226, be sure to tell the reader when a process requires special equipment.

Here are a couple of other survival tips from the instructor that I wrote down: 9

"If you're going to use an escape rope, try to get some knots in it."   10

"Try to anticipate any strikes or blows."   11

Also, if you're going to get shot, the farther you are from the shooter, the better.   12
I learned that valuable tip during the first-aid section of our training. The instructor began this section by noting that some people are reluctant to attempt first aid.
"But," he said, "if your colleague is dying, and you don't do anything, he's going to
die, isn't he? And he's not going to thank you, is he?"

To which sports columnist Tom Powers replied: "He's not going to complain,   13
either."

In first-aid training, we learned about the Trimodal Death Distribution, with   14
the three Modes of Death being: Instant, Late and Delayed. The instructor said:
"We're interested in the delayed diers."

I missed a lot of what he said next, because he was showing graphic color slides   15
of injuries, and one of them, entitled "Impaled Object," required me to put my
head between my knees for several minutes. But I definitely recall hearing the
instructor say, several times, that if your colleague is bleeding profusely from the
femoral artery, you should stop it by standing on his groin. This may be solid
advice, but before I follow it, I intend to confer with the colleague.

> ME: Do you mind if I stand on your groin?
> COLLEAGUE: Thanks, but I'd rather bleed to death.
> ME (relieved): OK, then!

But we're talking worst-case scenarios, here. As I said, I'm hoping that nobody   16
needs any of this training, and that we all have a peaceful, hostility-free, and fun
summer. Maybe I'll even see you at the conventions or Olympics! Assuming there
are eye holes in my escape hood.

READING CLOSELY

1. Do you think Dave Barry's "Fright School" instructor actually included planet
   Earth in his list of "dangerous areas" to be avoided (8)? Where else in this column does Barry seem to be exaggerating? Where does he seem to be reporting
   what really happened or was said?

2. Barry gives a number of survival "tips" in paragraphs 9–16. What do they all
   have in common, and why do you think he chose them for an essay on such a
   serious subject?

3. Why was Barry's instructor unable to go more deeply into some of the specific
   threats, such as germ warfare, that Barry and his fellow journalists might face?

STRATEGIES AND STRUCTURES

1. What is Barry's PURPOSE in writing this column? Is it to explain what he learned,
   to highlight the inadequacy of his training, to entertain readers and make them
   laugh? Some combination of these? How can you tell?

2. What process is Barry analyzing here? Is his analysis primarily explanatory or
   directive? Explain.

3. Where does Barry give the main steps of the process he is analyzing? How helpful are they? Where else in his essay does Barry include additional steps or directions?

4. Barry sometimes writes in the third person, as when he says of his instructor, "He was a muscular, military-looking British guy" (5). Which personal pronoun (or pronouns) does Barry use more frequently, however? Why?

5. A solid process analysis presents the steps of the process in some orderly fashion with clear TRANSITIONS between each step. How well does Barry's analysis measure up to this standard? Explain.

6. *Other Methods.* Barry ends his column with a little DIALOGUE between himself and a fictional injured colleague. How does he prepare the way for this ending? Where else (and for what purposes) does Barry use other elements of NARRATIVE to support his analysis?

THINKING ABOUT LANGUAGE

1. A PARODY is a humorous imitation of a particular form of writing or behavior. What is Barry parodying here and why?

2. Barry's essay is about several "worst-case scenarios" (16). What is a *scenario* exactly, and why can these scenarios be analyzed as different *cases*?

3. What are the implications of Barry's nickname for the course in hostile environment training?

FOR WRITING

1. Write a paragraph or two analyzing one of the threats that Barry mentions in paragraph 7.

2. Write a parody of a process analysis in which you explain something you "learned" in a chemistry, math, writing, or some other class.

3. Citing Barry's column and other sources, write a set of instructions, either tongue-in-cheek or serious, explaining how to survive in a hostile environment.

ALEX HORTON

On Getting By: Advice for College-Bound Vets

Alex Horton (b. 1985) is a U.S. Army veteran of the war in Iraq. A native of Texas, Horton now lives in Washington, D.C., where he writes for VAntage Point, *a website hosted by the Department of Veterans Affairs to help vets navigate the federal bureaucracy and obtain their benefits. In 2006, Horton started a blog,* Army of Dude, *from his barracks simply to keep in touch with his family and to tell them about Army life. He had disliked writing in high school; but in the military, he says, "writing became my only creative outlet, a way to relay thoughts and experiences that I would never dare speak out loud. . . . This blog was a closely guarded secret."*

"On Getting By" is a post from January 2010, written after Horton was back in school under the GI Bill. It outlines a behavioral system based on Horton's firsthand analysis of adapting to the "unfamiliar, unpredictable and strange environment on campus." In the original version, Horton linked to other posts, both within and outside his blog; these links have been replaced here with footnotes.

IN MY PREVIOUS POST, I outlined some basic principles* needed to successfully navigate the murky waters of education under the GI Bill. The challenges in dealing with the VA for education benefits are considerable, yet veterans new to college face an unfamiliar, unpredictable and strange environment on campus. If taken all at once, these hurdles can quickly overwhelm a student veteran and distract from the overall goal: to finish a degree on time with benefits to spare. Next week I will be in class for my fifth semester of higher education, and in my time I have tinkered with a system of how to bring up my veteran status, discussing Iraq and Afghanistan in the classroom and dealing with the myriad reactions fellow students have had. The system cannot be expected to work for everyone, but as veterans file into classrooms for the first time this spring, these tips could help in the development of a coping system better tailored for you. These should simply help to get you started. | 1

Modesty Is the Best Policy

There are only two kinds of veterans in school: those who prattle on about their time in the military and overseas, and those who do not. The former will find any opportunity to bring up their time in Afghanistan or Iraq, even if it is not rele- | 2

---

* "Here To There: Tips and Tricks for the Student Veteran," December 29, 2009. [Author's link]

SUGGESTED MLA CITATION: Horton, Alex. "On Getting By: Advice for College-Bound Vets." 2010. *Back to the Lake.* Ed. Thomas Cooley. 2nd ed. New York: Norton, 2012. 250–54. Print.

vant to class discussion. They forget one of the tenets of military experience—the role of the consummate professional. Joining the military and serving in a time of war are sacred acts and carry a certain degree of respect and modesty. We owe it to our injured buddies and fallen friends not to brag about our exploits overseas. We have done our fair share of things that set us apart from others in the classroom, and that is exactly why it is best to retain an understated presence among others.

This is a difficult situation as it applies to reintegration, as the chasm between 3 veterans and civilians has never been wider. From World War II to Vietnam, it would have been a difficult task to know someone that neither served overseas nor had a family member or friend who did. Now there are whole classrooms filled with those people. As Matthew McConaughey spoke prophetically in *Dazed and Confused*, "I get older, they stay the same age." An 18-year-old in college this year would have been nine years old during the invasion of Afghanistan and eleven years old during the invasion of Iraq. They have grown up with war to the point of it becoming a mind numbingly prosaic concept. It would be a frustrating battle to try and close the rift with those who don't see a rift at all. The best thing to do is use your judgment when bringing up your veteran status in the classroom. I've done it just a few times and felt uncomfortable enough to think twice about the next time. Now I tend to mention it in private conversation, not when I have the floor in public, and even then it is a casual touch on the subject. When you are ready to talk . . .

. . . Prepare for a Question Salvo

No matter how much you try to keep it stashed away from students and coworkers, 4 your military experience will come out sooner or later. There are things you simply cannot hide forever, like going to prison or reading *Twilight*.[1] Once you begin to move past casual conversation, it's only a matter of time before that period of your life is visited. It usually begins with a discussion of age. When I tell people I'm 24, the follow-up questions are almost always, "What have you done since high school?" or, "Why did you wait so long to go to school?" People tend to catch on if you mention extended vacations in the Middle East or recite monologues, so at that point it is best to come clean. However, be prepared for the questions they are more than willing to hurl your way. They might not know anyone who has deployed, but our hyperviolent culture has removed any restraint left in the world and enables them to ask any question that comes to mind. Here is what you can expect, in order of the most frequently asked:

1. *Twilight*: Published in 2005, the first book in a quartet of vampire romance novels for young adults by Stephenie Meyer.

1. What's it like?
2. Was it really hot?
3. Did you kill anyone?
4. How hot was it? Like, really hot?
5. Do you regret it?
6. Did you see any camel spiders?
7. Were you in Iran?

It's hard to get upset at some of those questions, as I find it difficult to think of 5
what I'd ask if the roles were switched. #3 can be blamed on ignorance and apathy,
but #5 is the most troubling I've heard. It suggests that there is something shame-
ful about service, duty and sacrifice. Both questions trivialize an important part of
our lives. The best answer to #3 I've heard comes from the The Kitchen Dispatch*
comment section: "I will forgive you for asking that question if you forgive me for
not answering it." Something that personal should never be asked, only told.

The flip side to some of those cavalier probes are questions that handle the topic 6
with kid gloves. Once a coworker found out I was in the Army, she asked, "Did you
go to . . . one of those places they send people?" It was uncomfortable for her just to
utter those dirty "I" and "A" words, like we were speaking about some subversive
topic. The kind of questions you will get will be all over the map, spanning from a
place of genuine interest to the depths of sheer morbidity. Be prepared to answer
anything, or politely let them know the subject isn't appropriate for casual banter.

Let the Right Ones In

Popular culture is replete with images of the maladjusted veteran, from Rambo to 7
Travis Bickle to Red Forman. These characters are ingrained in our national conscious and typically become placeholders in the event someone doesn't personally
know a veteran. When these sources are taken at face value, war veterans are invariably crazy, depressive, easily startled, quick to anger and alcoholics. We come from
broken homes, trying to escape jail time and were too dumb or poor to go to college
after high school. The best way to combat these silly notions is to let people get to
know you, the person, before you, the veteran. Those stereotypes aren't going anywhere soon, so the best idea is to take the concept of guarding your veteran status in
the classroom and carry it over to blossoming relationships. That way your service
and overseas experience complement your personality and don't define it. Revealing
too much at one time can damage a friendship before it takes off. Just like in the
classroom, take it slow. If they are worth keeping around, they'll understand why.
We have met our lifelong friends already; we can afford to be picky.

* Kanani Fong, "Seven Things Never to Say to a Veteran," January 3, 2010. [Author's link]

Try to Keep a Straight Face

There's a huge disparity between what you have been asked to do in the service and 8
what you will be asked to do in school. At the very basic level you were asked to
maintain a clean weapon and uniform. Many of you were tasked with watching the
back of your fellow soldiers while in imminent danger or operating complex
machinery and vehicles. At school, you'll be held responsible for showing up and
turning in work before deadlines. That's it. Like I mentioned in the earlier post,
college seems like an insurmountable gauntlet of crushed dreams when you're in
the military. Once you transition to civilian life and take a few classes, you'll be
astounded at the lack of discipline and drive in some of your classmates. It's a big
joke, but try to maintain composure. I'm not saying it's easy the whole way through,
but I guarantee you've done something harder than a five-page essay. As they say,
the rest is downhill.

Find Another Brother

If you were in active duty, the friends you met along the way are now scattered 9
across the country. Perhaps I've always been an introvert, but I don't make friends
as easy as some people. I've met just two people in fourteen classes that I consider
friends, and one of them is an Afghanistan veteran. It's easy to understand why we
get along. Do your best to find other veterans in your class and say hello. Talking to
them will come easier than the 18 year old hipster next to you, with his passion for
ironic hats.[2] Find out if there is a veteran's organization on campus, but be wary of
their motives. While some will join to find support and befriend fellow veterans,
others will use it for recognition. . . .

Enjoy the Ride

Besides getting a degree or learning new skills, people go to college to meet new 10
people and to experience a different life. If you've served since September 12, 2001,
you've already had a bit of each. But don't let that stop you from enjoying everything school has to offer. It's the last time very little will be expected of you, unless
you get another government job. Then you're golden.

If you are recently out of the military and on your way to college, these tenets, 11
coupled with the GI Bill pointers, should help you get started in academia. Like
most things, your experience may vary, and I would hope you don't safeguard your
veteran status like it's a dark secret or the true location of Jimmy Hoffa's body. It's

---

2. *Ironic hats:* Hats and caps displaying humorous or ironic messages (such as "Ironic Hat") or
indicating a trade or profession that the wearer clearly does not belong to.

something to be proud of, but not flaunted. It's something to share with your friends who genuinely want to know about the world you lived in, but not with the people who have twisted notions of what you have done overseas. The last thing you want people to know you as is the guy who went to Iraq. You want them to say "Hey, that's Alex, he's good people," and not "I wonder how many ear necklaces he has. I'm betting two." Hopefully these tips will help even just a tiny bit in that regard.

One of the last steps in analyzing a process is to say what the end result should be (p. 232).

✠

Reading Closely

1. What process is Alex Horton analyzing? Do you think his "system" is likely to serve its intended purpose (1)? Why or why not?

2. Horton thinks veterans should not "hide" their military service from their classmates (4). How does he think they should deal with the subject? Do you think this is good advice? Why or why not?

3. How appropriate do you consider Horton's proposed answer to the question, "Did you kill anyone?" (5). Explain.

4. According to Horton, how are military veterans usually DEFINED in "popular culture" (7)? How accurate is his assessment? How and where should it be changed?

Strategies and Structures

1. Who is the intended AUDIENCE for Horton's blog post? Who else might find his "tips" to be useful? For what PURPOSE?

2. Horton divides veterans into two categories. What are they, and how does this CLASSIFICATION system help to explain how student veterans can best adapt to their new circumstances?

3. How (and how well) does the first step in Horton's analysis prepare the way for the later steps?

4. When Horton presents his list of questions in step two, he wonders what questions he would ask "if the roles were switched" (5). What does asking himself this suggest about his character and credibility as a writer?

5. What point is Horton making when he uses the EXAMPLE of "the five-page essay" (8)? Is it a good example? Why or why not?

6. *Other Methods*. Where else does Horton COMPARE AND CONTRAST being in the military with being in school? How (and how well) does the comparison support his analysis of how veterans can get by in their new circumstances?

THINKING ABOUT LANGUAGE

1. What is Horton's (humorous) point in putting "going to prison" in the same phrase with "reading *Twilight*" (4)?

2. Horton describes the culture he and other veterans are returning to as "hyper-violent" (4). Any IRONY here? Explain.

3. Horton uses the word *conscious* when what he means is *consciousness* (7). Are such verbal slips more acceptable in a blog than in more formal academic writing? Why or why not?

4. In a blog, how appropriate are such slang terms as "come clean" and "you're golden" (4, 10)? Explain.

FOR WRITING

1. Write a paragraph or two telling veterans what questions you think they will need to be ready to answer—and why—when they enter college.

2. What advice would you give high-school students to help them "get started in academia" (11)? Write an analysis of the process based on your experience.

ROBERT CONNORS

How in the World Do You Get a Skunk Out of a Bottle?

Robert Connors (1951–2000) was a writing teacher at the University of New Hampshire. As a scholar, he focused on the history of writing and writing instruction. The author of Composition-Rhetoric: Backgrounds, Theory, and Pedagogy *(1997), Connors published many influential journal articles on topics ranging from the comments teachers make on student papers to the history of citation systems. In 1981, Connors received the Braddock Award for his article on the modes of discourse—a study of the very methods taught in this book. When his life was abruptly ended by a motorcycle accident in 2000, the University of New Hampshire named its writing center for him—a center Connors himself had established there a decade earlier.*

"How in the World Do You Get a Skunk Out of a Bottle?" first appeared in Yankee *magazine in 1991; it is not about writing but about the author's zest for life and nature. A personal narrative of his encounter with a trapped animal, it includes a detailed analysis of the delicate procedure by which he set the creature free.*

THE SANDY DIRT of Canterbury Road is just right as I pant my way past Johnson's hayfield. The air cool enough for delight but not cold enough for long johns and stocking cap, the early sun slanting low. No sound but my labored breathing and the chunking noise of sneakers on dirt. Just another morning. Or so I think. 1

Then I see him, off to my right. Twenty-five feet or so from the road in a cutover hayfield. A skunk. One of the kind that are mostly white, with the black mainly on their sides. From the corner of my eye I watch him turn, move. I detour to the other side of the road. 2

But something seems wrong, in the way that he moves or the way that he looks. Some glint of strangeness. I slow my pace, looking over my right shoulder. The skunk moves through the stubble toward the road. I stop and shade my eyes against the low sunlight. The skunk comes closer. And then I see it. 3

A glass jar. About 4 1/2 inches long, about three inches in diameter, with a pinched-in neck—a large baby-food jar, perhaps. It is jammed over the skunk's head, completely covering it past the ears. Unable to hear or smell, the skunk raises his head in a clumsy, unnatural way. His dim eyes catch sight of my bright purple warm-up jacket. He begins, slowly but unmistakably, to come toward me. 4

SUGGESTED MLA CITATION: Connors, Robert. "How in the World Do You Get a Skunk Out of a Bottle?" 1991. *Back to the Lake.* Ed. Thomas Cooley. 2nd ed. New York: Norton, 2012. 256–59. Print.

For tips on when to use *you* in a process analysis, see p. 229.

As you probably know, this is not what skunks or any wild animals typi- 5
cally do. But as I stand on the bright, hard-packed road, this skunk is clearly
coming toward me. More, I can't help but feel that he is coming *to* me.

I begin to talk to him. Only later does it occur to me that he is probably unable 6
to hear anything with the jar on his head, but the talk is more for my sake anyway.

"Oh, boy," I say, as the skunk trundles closer, "if you aren't a textbook case in 7
conservation ethics, I've never seen one." I back away a step. What if he's rabid?
He lifts his head, feebly, to the right, to the left. I can see the long white silky hairs
of his back, the fogged translucence of the glass jar.

I have a sudden desire to turn, go, keep running, get home. 8

By this time the skunk has reached the high grass at the edge of the road. And 9
there he stops. His sides heave; the tight neck of the jar can hardly admit any air,
and each breath is a struggle of seven or eight seconds' duration. The skunk is shivering as well, slight tremors running through his whole body as he crouches,
watching me. Clearly, the skunk is going to die and not of starvation. He is suffo-
cating as I watch.

"What do you want me to do?" I say. "You've got to come to me. I can't come to 10
you. Who knows what mental state you're in?" The skunk looks at me. "Look, I'd
love to help you. But the covered end of you isn't the end I'm worried about." The
skunk wags his head slightly, tries to breathe. "What were you looking for in there
anyway, you dumb-head? That jar's been out here empty for years."

By now I realize that this skunk is my responsibility. The police would probably 11
kill him in order to save him. Getting someone from Fish and Game would take
hours. I am the one here, now.

Maybe I can throw a big rock and break the jar. Not get close enough to be 12
sprayed, but break the glass. Let the skunk breathe.

No. Any rock heavy enough to break the glass from a distance couldn't be thrown 13
accurately. It might hit the skunk and injure him. Even if the glass broke, the edges
might slash the skunk's face or get into his eyes. And with that kind of jar, the neck
might not break with the bottle part, leaving the skunk with a jagged necklace of
razor-edged glass that would sooner or later kill him. No, the rock idea is out.

Perhaps I can find something to throw over him—a coat or a blanket so he can't 14
spray me—and grab the jar. But all I have is this warm-up jacket—too small to
cover him and too light to keep him from turning.

"I don't know, old skunkoid," I say, moving slightly closer to where he sits, 15
motionless except for the shivering. "There's no way that I'm just going to go over
to you and pull that jar off." One step closer. I have no idea what I *am* going to do.
Hunkering down, I keep on talking. "You understand my position. I have to go
teach college today. If you spray me, you will seriously undercut my efficiency." He
is still not moving. Stand up, move one step closer. Squat down again.

"I'm not going to hurt you. I present no threat. I'm scared to death of you, and 16
you probably are of me." Stand up, one step closer, squat down.

I can see the bloody scratches along the skunk's neck where he tried with claws 17
to free himself from the jar. I keep on talking, just to make noise, piling nonsense
on nonsense.

Stand, step, squat, and I am three feet from the skunk. He regards me. Deep 18
breath. Then, very slowly, I reach out with my right hand. "Don't worry now, bubba.
I'm not here to hurt you. This jar is the problem." Slowly, slowly, reaching, the
skunk still quiet, then *got it!* My hand clamps down on the warm rigidity of the jar.

Suddenly the skunk, until now motionless, is galvanized. He pulls back in panic, 19
his paws scrabbling at the grass; at my hand. I pull hard on the jar. Now it will
come off and he will run away. One way or another, this is it.

But this is not it. Pulling hard, I find I am dragging the skunk, who pushes fran- 20
tically backward, onto the dirt road. His head is *impacted* into the jar. It will not
come out.

Discarded food containers can be traps for unsuspecting animals. To free a stuck skunk,
animal handlers recommend the following process: (1) approach skunk from front; (2) drop
clear plastic bin over skunk; (3) slip cloth soaked in chloroform under bin; (4) wait until
skunk is drowsy; (5) lift bin and pull jar loose; (6) stand back while freed skunk wakes up
and wanders off. To prevent recurrence: cap jars, crush cans, and discard all used containers where animals cannot get to them.

"Oh, boy, come *on*." The skunk is now completely in the road, struggling furi- 21
ously to get away, twisting and turning as I hold the jar tight. The one good thing
at this point is that he is so completely wedged that he can't turn and fire,
although there is little doubt that he regrets this keenly. As long as I have his
head, I'm safe. I pull again and am only able to drag the skunk farther. "Oh,
great. Now I get to take you home." He grunts audibly, pulls again, scrabbling up
packed dirt.

There's nothing for it. I have to grab him with one hand and try to pull the jar 22
off with the other. With my left hand, I grasp him around the shoulder blades. His
hair is soft. He would be nice to stroke. "Come on come on come on. . . ." I twist
the jar hard to the left, and his head inside assumes a crazy angle, but he stops
struggling. I pull hard on the jar. It does not move. "Come on, you. . . ." The jar
is *really* socked onto his neck, which has swollen in some way. Grabbing hard at his
shoulder blades, I twist and pull harder.

I am exerting all my strength now. And I see the threads of the jar turn, slowly, 23
then more quickly. "OK, something moving, heads up," then more movement, an
upward sliding, and then with an audible *pop* the jar is off.

Without any thought except *escape*, I jump up, whirl, run. Unscathed. Un- 24
sprayed. At a safe distance, I stop and look back. The skunk stands in the middle of
the road. He breathes deeply, several times, shakes himself from stem to stern,
takes a few tottering steps across the road.

On the other side, he halts, then turns to look at me. I look back. For perhaps 25
30 seconds, we regard each other with great benignity. Then I hold up my index
finger in a tutorial fashion.

"Next time you see me," I say, "don't spray me." He watches me gravely a 26
moment more, then turns and plods off into a cemetery across the road.

There is something in my hand. An empty jar. Starting to run up the long hill to 27
Main Street, I pitch it as hard as I can, sidearm, way out into a swamp. I hear it
splash as I run on up the hill into a sunny morning whose colors are joy, joy, joy.

$$\star\mathrel{....\cdot\cdot}$$

READING CLOSELY

1. Naturally enough, Robert Connors has "a sudden desire to turn, go, keep running, get home" when he sees the skunk coming toward him (8). Why does he
   stick around instead of following this instinct?

2. Do you think Connors is correct to assume that the skunk has benign feelings
   toward him? Why or why not?

3. Connors is explaining how to do something most of his readers will never need to do. Why? What is his PURPOSE in analyzing how to get a skunk out of a bottle?

Strategies and Structures

1. Why do you think Connors casts his title in the form of a question? What is his purpose in answering it?

2. Once Connors decides that the skunk is his "responsibility," he begins the process of extracting it from the bottle (11). That process ends in paragraph 23 when the jar finally pops off. What are the main steps that Connors takes in between to achieve this end result?

3. Connors analyzes the process of freeing the skunk in chronological order. What TRANSITIONS does he use to organize and connect the various steps of the process?

4. How would Connors' analysis be different if he were giving instructions for freeing a trapped animal?

5. *Other Methods.* Connors begins his essay with a DESCRIPTION of the morning air and light. Where else does he describe the scene, and how do these descriptive elements contribute to his analysis of the process of meeting and dealing with an animal in trouble?

Thinking about Language

1. Why does Connors change "toward" to "to" in paragraph 5?

2. What does Connors mean by the phrase "conservation ethics" (7)? How does his essay address this idea?

3. Why does Connors hold up his finger in "tutorial fashion" when he bids goodbye to the skunk (25)?

4. We don't normally think of joy as a "color" (27). What has happened to Connors' senses on this crisp, cool morning as a result of his encounter with the skunk?

For Writing

1. Write a paragraph or two explaining the process you would have told Connors to go through if he had asked you how to remove the jar from the skunk's head without sedating it?

2. One answer to the question raised by Connors' title might be, "Very carefully." Going beyond this obvious first step, write an essay analyzing how to deal with a difficult situation the reader might encounter in the woods, at work, in an airport, or while traveling in an unfamiliar city or country.

MICHAEL C. MUNGER

Ten Tips on Making Writing Work

Michael C. Munger (b. 1958) is the chairman
Duke University. A native of Florida, he earned de
lege and Washington University in St. Louis. In 2008,
governor of North Carolina. Besides studying the ideolo
south, he is an expert in public policy, focusing on how
financed. He is the author of, among other books, Policy An

In this selection (originally titled "10 Tips on How to Write Le
issue of the Chronicle of Higher Education, *Munger turns his analytic*
ing process rather than the political process. Although his "tips" are aimea
at readers of the nation's leading trade newspaper for university academicians—this essay
was one of the Chronicle's *regular "Do Your Job Better" columns—Munger's analysis*
and advice will be of use to anyone who wants to write better. Or at least "less badly."

Most academics, including administrators, spend much of our time writing. [1]
But we aren't as good at it as we should be. I have never understood why our trade
values, but rarely teaches, nonfiction writing.

In my nearly 30 years at universities, I have seen a lot of very talented people fail [2]
because they couldn't, or didn't, write. And some much less talented people (I see
one in the mirror every morning) have done OK because they learned how to write.

It starts in graduate school. There is a real transformation, approaching an [3]
inversion, as people switch from taking courses to writing. Many of the graduate
students who were stars in the classroom during the first two years—the people
everyone admired and looked up to—suddenly aren't so stellar anymore. And a few
of the marginal students—the ones who didn't care that much about pleasing the
professors by reading every page of every assignment—are suddenly sending their
own papers off to journals, getting published, and transforming themselves into
professional scholars.

The difference is not complicated. It's writing. [4]

. . . [O]ther writers on these pages have talked about how hard it is to write well, [5]
and of course that's true. Fortunately, the standards of writing in most disciplines
are so low that you don't need to write well. What I have tried to produce below are
10 tips on scholarly nonfiction writing that might help people write less badly.

SUGGESTED MLA CITATION: Munger, Michael C. "Ten Tips on How to Write Less Badly." 2c
Back to the Lake. Ed. Thomas Cooley. 2nd ed. New York: Norton, 2012. 261–64. Print.

ercise. You get better and faster with practice. If you were 6
athon a year from now, would you wait for months and then
? No, you would build up slowly, running most days. You might
s and work up to more demanding and difficult terrain. To become
te. Don't wait for that book manuscript or that monster external-
ort to work on your writing.

goals based on output, not input. "I will work for three hours" is a 7
sion; "I will type three double-spaced pages" is a goal. After you write three
ges, do something else. Prepare for class, teach, go to meetings, whatever. If
ter in the day you feel like writing some more, great. But if you don't, then at
east you wrote something.

3. Find a voice; don't just "get published." James Buchanan won a Nobel in 8
economics in 1986. One of the questions he asks job candidates is: "What are you
writing that will be read 10 years from now? What about 100 years from now?"
Someone once asked me that question, and it is pretty intimidating. And embarrassing, because most of us don't think that way. We focus on "getting published"
as if it had nothing to do with writing about ideas or arguments. Paradoxically, if
all you are trying to do is "get published," you may not publish very much. It's
easier to write when you're interested in what you're writing about.

4. Give yourself time. Many smart people tell themselves pathetic lies like, "I do 9
my best work at the last minute." Look: It's not true. No one works better under
pressure. Sure, you are a smart person. But if you are writing about a profound
problem, why would you think that you can make an important contribution off
the top of your head in the middle of the night just before the conference?

Writers sit at their desks for hours, wrestling with ideas. They ask questions, 10
talk with other smart people over drinks or dinner, go on long walks. And then
write a whole bunch more. Don't worry that what you write is not very good and
isn't immediately usable. You get ideas *when* you write; you don't just write down
ideas.

The articles and books that will be read decades from now were written by men 11
and women sitting at a desk and forcing themselves to translate profound ideas
into words and then to let those words lead them to even more ideas. Writing can
be magic, if you give yourself time, because you can produce in the mind of some
other person, distant from you in space or even time, an image of the ideas that
ist in only your mind at this one instant.

5. Everyone's unwritten work Making... more brilliant it is. We have all met... faculty members. They are at their most... a cigarette in the other, in some bar or at a... They can tell you just what they will write...

So use the present tense to express habitual action in a process analysis (p. 229).

Years pass, and they still have... "What are you working on?" It reve... ally working on anything, except tha...

You, on the other hand, actually... keeps evolving. You don't like the section... are not sure what will happen next. When someone asks, "W... ing on?," you stumble, because it is hard to explain. The smug guy with the beer and the cigarette? He's a poseur and never actually writes anything. He can practice his pat little answer endlessly, through hundreds of beers and thousands of cigarettes. Don't be fooled: You are the winner here. When you are actually writing, and working as hard as you should be if you want to succeed, you will feel inadequate, stupid, and tired. If you don't feel like that, then you aren't working hard enough.

6. Pick a puzzle. Portray, or even conceive, of your work as an answer to a puzzle. There are many interesting types of puzzles:

> "X and Y start with same assumptions but reach opposing conclusions. How?"
>
> "Here are three problems that all seem different. Surprisingly, all are the same problem, in disguise. I'll tell you why."
>
> "Theory predicts [something]. But we observe [something else]. Is the theory wrong, or is there some other factor we have left out?"

Don't stick too closely to those formulas, but they are helpful in presenting your work to an audience, whether that audience is composed of listeners at a lecture or readers of an article.

7. Write, then squeeze the other things in. Put your writing ahead of your other work. I happen to be a "morning person," so I write early in the day. Then I spend the rest of my day teaching, having meetings, or doing paperwork. You may be a "night person" or something in between. Just make sure you get in the habit of reserving your most productive time for writing. Don't do it as an afterthought or tell yourself you will write when you get a big block of time. Squeeze the other things in; the writing comes first.

...e get frustrated because 17
...estions that interest them.
...houghts are profou... wonderful thing is that you may
... analytical purchase ...p a mountain, just by keeping your
...n't write at all. So sta... ahead of the other for a long time. It is
...you have traveled quit... your terms precisely, or know just how your
...own and putting one ... actually written it all down.
...d to refine your questio...
...gument will work unti... ...houghts are **often wrong.** Or, at least, they are not 18

9. Your most prof... ...cision in asking your question, or posing your puzzle, will
completely corr... ...e question is hard.
not come easi... ...gh to myself when new graduate students think they know what 19
I alwa... ...t to work on and what they will write about for their dissertations. Nearly
they w... all o...the best scholars are profoundly changed by their experiences in doing
research and writing about it. They learn by doing, and sometimes what they learn
is that they were wrong.

10. Edit your work, over and over. Have other people look at it. One of the 20
great advantages of academe is that we are mostly all in this together, and we all
know the terrors of that blinking cursor on a blank background. Exchange papers
with peers or a mentor, and when you are sick of your own writing, reciprocate
by reading their work. You need to get over a fear of criticism or rejection.
Nobody's first drafts are good. The difference between a successful scholar and a
failure need not be better writing. It is often more editing.

If you have trouble writing, then you just haven't written enough. Writing lots 21
of pages has always been pretty easy for me. I could never get a job being only a
writer, though, because I still don't write well. But by thinking about these tips,
and trying to follow them myself, I have gotten to the point where I can make writing work for me and my career.

READING CLOSELY

1. Michael Munger's tips for writing "less badly" are tailored in particular to
   "scholarly nonfiction" (5). What kind of writing is this, and why does Munger
   think that improving it wouldn't be too hard to do?

MICHAEL C. MUNGER

Ten Tips on Making Writing Work for You

Michael C. Munger (b. 1958) is the chairman of the political science department at Duke University. A native of Florida, he earned degrees in economics at Davidson College and Washington University in St. Louis. In 2008, Munger ran (unsuccessfully) for governor of North Carolina. Besides studying the ideology of racism in the antebellum south, he is an expert in public policy, focusing on how elections are conducted and financed. He is the author of, among other books, Policy Analysis *(2000).*

In this selection (originally titled "10 Tips on How to Write Less Badly") from a 2010 issue of the Chronicle of Higher Education, *Munger turns his analytic skills to the writing process rather than the political process. Although his "tips" are aimed directly at readers of the nation's leading trade newspaper for university academicians—this essay was one of the* Chronicle's *regular "Do Your Job Better" columns—Munger's analysis and advice will be of use to anyone who wants to write better. Or at least "less badly."*

Most academics, including administrators, spend much of our time writing. But we aren't as good at it as we should be. I have never understood why our trade values, but rarely teaches, nonfiction writing.

In my nearly 30 years at universities, I have seen a lot of very talented people fail because they couldn't, or didn't, write. And some much less talented people (I see one in the mirror every morning) have done OK because they learned how to write.

It starts in graduate school. There is a real transformation, approaching an inversion, as people switch from taking courses to writing. Many of the graduate students who were stars in the classroom during the first two years—the people everyone admired and looked up to—suddenly aren't so stellar anymore. And a few of the marginal students—the ones who didn't care that much about pleasing the professors by reading every page of every assignment—are suddenly sending their own papers off to journals, getting published, and transforming themselves into professional scholars.

The difference is not complicated. It's writing.

. . . [O]ther writers on these pages have talked about how hard it is to write well, and of course that's true. Fortunately, the standards of writing in most disciplines are so low that you don't need to write well. What I have tried to produce below are 10 tips on scholarly nonfiction writing that might help people write less badly.

SUGGESTED MLA CITATION: Munger, Michael C. "Ten Tips on How to Write Less Badly." 2010. *Back to the Lake.* Ed. Thomas Cooley. 2nd ed. New York: Norton, 2012. 261–64. Print.

1. Writing is an exercise. You get better and faster with practice. If you were going to run a marathon a year from now, would you wait for months and then run 26 miles cold? No, you would build up slowly, running most days. You might start on the flats and work up to more demanding and difficult terrain. To become a writer, write. Don't wait for that book manuscript or that monster external-review report to work on your writing. ⁶

2. Set goals based on output, not input. "I will work for three hours" is a delusion; "I will type three double-spaced pages" is a goal. After you write three pages, do something else. Prepare for class, teach, go to meetings, whatever. If later in the day you feel like writing some more, great. But if you don't, then at least you wrote something. ⁷

3. Find a voice; don't just "get published." James Buchanan won a Nobel in economics in 1986. One of the questions he asks job candidates is: "What are you writing that will be read 10 years from now? What about 100 years from now?" Someone once asked me that question, and it is pretty intimidating. And embarrassing, because most of us don't think that way. We focus on "getting published" as if it had nothing to do with writing about ideas or arguments. Paradoxically, if all you are trying to do is "get published," you may not publish very much. It's easier to write when you're interested in what you're writing about. ⁸

4. Give yourself time. Many smart people tell themselves pathetic lies like, "I do my best work at the last minute." Look: It's not true. No one works better under pressure. Sure, you are a smart person. But if you are writing about a profound problem, why would you think that you can make an important contribution off the top of your head in the middle of the night just before the conference? ⁹

Writers sit at their desks for hours, wrestling with ideas. They ask questions, talk with other smart people over drinks or dinner, go on long walks. And then write a whole bunch more. Don't worry that what you write is not very good and isn't immediately usable. You get ideas *when* you write; you don't just write down ideas. ¹⁰

The articles and books that will be read decades from now were written by men and women sitting at a desk and forcing themselves to translate profound ideas into words and then to let those words lead them to even more ideas. Writing can be magic, if you give yourself time, because you can produce in the mind of some other person, distant from you in space or even time, an image of the ideas that exist in only your mind at this one instant. ¹¹

5. Everyone's unwritten work is brilliant. And the more unwritten it is, the 12 more brilliant it is. We have all met those glib, intimidating graduate students or faculty members. They are at their most dangerous holding a beer in one hand and a cigarette in the other, in some bar or at an office party. They have all the answers. They can tell you just what they will write about, and how great it will be.

So use the present tense to express habitual action in a process analysis (p. 229).

Years pass, and they still have the same pat, 200-word answer to 13 "What are you working on?" It never changes, because they are not actually working on anything, except that one little act.

You, on the other hand, actually are working on something, and it 14 keeps evolving. You don't like the section you just finished, and you are not sure what will happen next. When someone asks, "What are you working on?," you stumble, because it is hard to explain. The smug guy with the beer and the cigarette? He's a poseur and never actually writes anything. So he can practice his pat little answer endlessly, through hundreds of beers and thousands of cigarettes. Don't be fooled: You are the winner here. When you are actually writing, and working as hard as you should be if you want to succeed, you will feel inadequate, stupid, and tired. If you don't feel like that, then you aren't working hard enough.

6. Pick a puzzle. Portray, or even conceive, of your work as an answer to a 15 puzzle. There are many interesting types of puzzles:

> "X and Y start with same assumptions but reach opposing conclusions. How?"
> "Here are three problems that all seem different. Surprisingly, all are the same problem, in disguise. I'll tell you why."
> "Theory predicts [something]. But we observe [something else]. Is the theory wrong, or is there some other factor we have left out?"

Don't stick too closely to those formulas, but they are helpful in presenting your work to an audience, whether that audience is composed of listeners at a lecture or readers of an article.

7. Write, then squeeze the other things in. Put your writing ahead of your 16 other work. I happen to be a "morning person," so I write early in the day. Then I spend the rest of my day teaching, having meetings, or doing paperwork. You may be a "night person" or something in between. Just make sure you get in the habit of reserving your most productive time for writing. Don't do it as an afterthought or tell yourself you will write when you get a big block of time. Squeeze the other things in; the writing comes first.

8. Not all of your thoughts are profound. Many people get frustrated because they can't get an analytical purchase on the big questions that interest them. Then they don't write at all. So start small. The wonderful thing is that you may find that you have traveled quite a long way up a mountain, just by keeping your head down and putting one writing foot ahead of the other for a long time. It is hard to refine your questions, define your terms precisely, or know just how your argument will work until you have actually written it all down.   17

9. Your most profound thoughts are often wrong. Or, at least, they are not completely correct. Precision in asking your question, or posing your puzzle, will not come easily if the question is hard.   18

I always laugh to myself when new graduate students think they know what they want to work on and what they will write about for their dissertations. Nearly all of the best scholars are profoundly changed by their experiences in doing research and writing about it. They learn by doing, and sometimes what they learn is that they were wrong.   19

10. Edit your work, over and over. Have other people look at it. One of the great advantages of academe is that we are mostly all in this together, and we all know the terrors of that blinking cursor on a blank background. Exchange papers with peers or a mentor, and when you are sick of your own writing, reciprocate by reading their work. You need to get over a fear of criticism or rejection. Nobody's first drafts are good. The difference between a successful scholar and a failure need not be better writing. It is often more editing.   20

If you have trouble writing, then you just haven't written enough. Writing lots of pages has always been pretty easy for me. I could never get a job being only a writer, though, because I still don't write well. But by thinking about these tips, and trying to follow them myself, I have gotten to the point where I can make writing work for me and my career.   21

READING CLOSELY

1. Michael Munger's tips for writing "less badly" are tailored in particular to "scholarly nonfiction" (5). What kind of writing is this, and why does Munger think that improving it wouldn't be too hard to do?

2. Munger's advice is aimed most directly at professional scholars and university teachers and administrators. Is it limited to that AUDIENCE, or do you think his analysis applies to the work of other writers as well? Which ones?

3. According to Munger, what's so "magic" about writing in general (11)? Do you agree with his assessment? Why or why not?

4. If you don't feel "inadequate, stupid, and tired" after writing all day, says Munger, what's the matter with you (14)?

5. Which of Munger's tips do you think might help you most with your own academic writing? Why?

STRATEGIES AND STRUCTURES

1. Munger admits that he doesn't write well (21). How does this admission affect his credibility as someone giving advice about how to write? Explain.

2. "You get ideas *when* you write; you don't just write down ideas" (10). How, and how well, might these words serve to describe the writing process as a whole?

3. In which stage of the writing process, according to Munger, does an academic writer most directly determine whether his or her work as a scholar is "successful" or a "failure" (20)? Why is this part of the process so important?

4. Munger speaks of "puzzles" and "formulas" for writing (15). Do such templates degrade the writing process, or are they useful devices for getting started with new ideas? Explain.

5. In paragraph 17, Munger recommends using a number of different methods of development when writing an academic paper. Which ones does he emphasize?

6. *Other Methods.* Point out places in Munger's analysis where he introduces elements of NARRATIVE—about his own writing experience. How (and how well) does telling about his own struggle with writing help Munger to analyze the process of writing "less badly"?

THINKING ABOUT LANGUAGE

1. What is the point of Munger's ANALOGY between writing and running a marathon (6)? Between writing and climbing a mountain (17)? Are the COMPARISONS appropriate?

2. According to Munger, what's the difference between a "delusion" and a "goal" in academic writing (7)? Are his DEFINITIONS accurate? Why or why not?

3. A person who constantly talks about writing brilliantly but doesn't actually write, says Munger, is a "poseur" (14). Check this word in your dictionary. Is Munger using it accurately? Why might he choose this term instead of, for example, *liar*?

4. Why do you think Munger chose to characterize his advice to academic writers as tips for writing "less badly" rather than writing "better" or writing "well"? Why "tips" instead of "rules" or "guidelines"?

For Writing

1. Choose one of Munger's tips, and write a few paragraphs explaining in more detail how it might be used to help someone improve his or her writing.

2. Using Munger's analysis of the writing process as a guide, write an essay about how you write and how you might learn to write better—or about how other writers might improve (or damage) their writing by following (or avoiding) your example.

EMILY DICKINSON

The Way I read a Letter's—this—

Emily Dickinson (1830–1886) led an intensely private life that has become the stuff of literary legend. Born to a well-to-do family in Amherst, Massachusetts, Dickinson grew up among books and lively conversation, and—except for less than a year at the Mount Holyoke Female Seminary—she resided in the family home near Amherst College all her life. Over time, Dickinson become more and more reclusive, dressing mainly in white, seeing few visitors outside the family, and working on her poems—nearly eighteen hundred in all, only a handful of which were published during her lifetime. After Dickinson's death, her sister discovered among the poet's papers forty booklets of poems bound with string and unbound copies of almost four hundred poems.

"The Way I read a Letter's—this—" explains how the poet typically opened and read a letter from a correspondent with whom she was spiritually, but probably not physically, intimate. Dickinson scholars disagree on the identity of that correspondent, but the person with whom she exchanged the largest number of highly personal letters was her sister-in-law Susan Gilbert Dickinson. The "You" to whom Dickinson refers is probably the reader of the poem, as opposed to the author of the letter.

The Way I read a Letter's—this—   1
'Tis first—I lock the Door—
And push it with my fingers—next—
For transport it be sure—

And then I go the furthest off   5
To counteract a knock—
Then draw my little Letter forth
And slowly pick the lock—

Then—glancing narrow, at the Wall—
And narrow at the floor   10
For firm Conviction of a Mouse
Not exorcised before—

SUGGESTED MLA CITATION: Dickinson, Emily. "The Way I read a Letter's—this—." 1891. *Back to the Lake*. Ed. Thomas Cooley. 2nd ed. New York: Norton, 2012. 267–68. Print.

Peruse how infinite I am
To no one that You—know—
And sigh for lack of Heaven—but not   15
The Heaven God bestow—

✦ ⟋

READING CLOSELY

1. Emily Dickinson is explaining how to read an intimate letter. How can you tell?

2. Why does the author of the letter comment on "how infinite" the recipient is (13)?

3. To what "Heaven" is Dickinson referring if not to the one that "God bestow" (16)? Explain.

STRATEGIES AND STRUCTURES

1. Dickinson breaks the process of reading her letter into six steps. What are they?

2. Why does the speaker in Dickinson's poem go through the first five steps before she actually "peruses" the contents of the letter (13)?

3. For whom is Dickinson analyzing this process, and what is the effect of her using the personal pronoun "You" to address her audience (14)?

4. *Other Methods.* In addition to explaining how she reads a letter, Dickinson also shows the emotional effect of the process. What is this EFFECT, and what is its CAUSE?

THINKING ABOUT LANGUAGE

1. What "lock" is Dickinson picking in line 8? Why does she use this METAPHOR, and how does the first step in her analysis prepare the way for it?

2. "Exorcised" (12) is a word usually reserved for demons and evil spirits. Why does Dickinson use it here?

3. What are the CONNOTATIONS of "peruse" (13), and why does Dickinson use this term instead of the more common *read*?

FOR WRITING

1. Write a paragraph analyzing how *you* read a letter.

2. Write an essay explaining the process you go through when you read a poem.

CHAPTER 8

Comparison and Contrast

> When you compare apples to apples, our repair center represents the
> pick of the crop.
> —FRANK'S AUTO BODY

When you take a shower, assuming you live in the Western hemisphere and it's a weekday, you probably want to get clean as quickly and efficiently as you can. If you bathe in a tub, you may soak a little longer; but chances are you will still be the first (and last) to use the bathwater. Not so in Japan.

By comparison with the Western way of bathing, the Japanese way is drawn out and ritualistic. Preferring the tub to the shower, the Japanese like to bathe slowly and deliberately, even when they are in a hurry. Often whole families soak in the same warm water, with the male head-of-household going first. This togetherness is more a means of establishing family and social unity than of conserving water, however. Getting clean is just as important to the Japanese as to their Western counterparts. So before stepping into the communal tub, each Japanese bather washes thoroughly from a bucket provided for that purpose.

Japanese and Western cultures have something else in common, besides a deep respect for cleanliness. No matter how we draw our baths, we draw comparisons when we think—and write—about the similarities and differences between two or more subjects.

Defining Comparison:
Finding Similarities and Differences

When we compare or contrast anything—two people, two ways of bathing, two cultures—we look at both the similarities (comparison) and the differences (contrast) between them. Which of these we emphasize in an essay depends, in part, on what we are comparing. In the case of the Japanese bath as compared to the Western version, for example, the differences are more numerous and striking than the similarities.

Consider this passage from a book on the subject:

> In the West, a bath is a place where one goes to cleanse the body; in Japan, it is where one goes to cleanse the soul. . . . When one bathes in Japan, it is about much more than cleanliness, though cleanliness is important. It is about family and community, the washing of each other's backs before bathing; about time to be alone and contemplative—time to watch the moon rise above the garden. . . . Unlike in America, where speed and efficiency are valued, . . . the Japanese make bathing a ritual—a prescribed order of rinsing, washing, and soaking that is passed down from one generation to the next, becoming an integral part of the society at large.
> —BRUCE SMITH AND YOSHIKO YAMAMOTO, *The Japanese Bath*

This passage is mostly contrast; that is, it stresses the differences between the two activities being compared. They *are* still being compared, however: comparisons are about relationships, whether of sameness or difference. In this chapter, therefore, we will use the word *comparison* both for drawing similarities between two related subjects *and* for pointing out their differences. (The word *contrast* will be reserved for discussing differences only.) We will also look more deeply into when and why we compare things, how to make effective comparisons, and how to organize an entire essay around common strategies of comparison and contrast that good writers use all the time. Finally, we'll review the critical points to watch for as you read over and revise your essay, as well as common errors to avoid when you edit.

Why Do We Compare?

Whether you live in America or Japan, one form of comparison is almost as familiar to you as bathing—comparison shopping. The reason you compare before you buy, of course, is so you can select the best product for your needs at the best price. For this purpose you may consult a buying guide, such as *Consumer Reports* magazine.

In a recent issue, the professional comparers at *Consumer Reports* compared similar makes, models, and brands of tablet computers, dishwashing soap, online florists, stain remover, barbecue sauce, 3D TVs, and food processors—all so consumers can be aware of the differences among them.

One of the main reasons we compare things—and not just consumer products— is to discover differences between two subjects that we would otherwise expect to be similar. For example, on a botany exam you might compare the leaf structure of two related species of ferns. Or, in literature, you might compare two Shakespearean sonnets.

> Bruce Catton does this with two very different Civil War generals on p. 307.

We also make comparisons in order to find similarities between subjects that we might otherwise consider to be entirely different, as in this opening paragraph from a book on what happens to the human body after death:

> The way I see it, being dead is not terribly far off from being on a cruise ship. Most of your time is spent lying on your back. The brain has shut down. The flesh begins to soften. Nothing much new happens, and nothing is expected of you. —MARY ROACH, *Stiff*

We don't normally think of being dead and taking a cruise as being very much alike. By pointing out similarities between the two that we may not have noticed, however, Roach enables us to see both of these subjects—particularly the grimmer one—in a new light. This particular kind of comparison between two seemingly unrelated subjects is called an ANALOGY: it explains a less-familiar subject by comparing it to something we are likely to know more about.

Composing an Essay That Compares and Contrasts

The root meaning of the word *compare* is "to put with equals," and so the first thing you need to do when composing a comparison essay is to choose subjects that are truly comparable—apples to apples, oranges to oranges.

If two subjects are different in every way, there is little point in comparing them. The same is true if they are entirely alike. Your subjects should have enough in common to provide a solid basis of comparison. A train and a jetliner, for instance, are very different machines; but both are modes of transportation, and that shared characteristic can become the basis for comparing them.

When you look for shared characteristics in your subjects, don't stretch your comparison too far, however. You don't want to make the logical blunder that the Duchess commits in Lewis Carroll's *Alice in Wonderland*:

> "Very true," said the Duchess: "flamingos and mustard both bite. And the moral of that is—'Birds of a feather flock together.'"
>
> "Only mustard isn't a bird," Alice remarked.
>
> "Right as usual," said the Duchess: "what a clear way you have of putting things."

Flamingos and mustard both bite, but not in ways that are similar enough to make them truly comparable. So beware what you compare. Before you bring two subjects together as equals in an essay, make sure they are "birds of a feather" by looking carefully at the characteristics that make them different from others but similar to one another. Those characteristics should be significant enough to form a solid basis of comparison. In Wonderland, you might compare turtles and tanks, for example, on the grounds that both move relatively slowly and have hard outer coverings. In the real world, however, don't bring two subjects together when the differences between them are far more significant than the similarities. Better to compare mustard and ketchup, or flamingos and roseate spoonbills—unless, of course, you plan to show just how much two apparently dissimilar subjects (being dead and going on a cruise, skyscrapers and airplanes) actually have in common.

Thinking about Purpose and Audience

Suppose that you are comparing running shoes for the simple purpose of buying a new pair to replace your old ones. In this case, you are comparing them in order to evaluate them—to decide which shoe fits your needs best, so you can choose the right one at the right price. However, if you were writing a comparison of several kinds of running shoes for *Consumer Reports*, you would be comparing your subjects in order to inform readers about them. Instead of evaluating the shoes and choosing a pair to fit your needs, your purpose would be to give readers the information they need to choose for themselves.

With comparisons, as with shoes, one size does not fit all. Whether you're writing a comparison to inform, evaluate, or for some other purpose, always keep the specific needs of your audience in mind. How much do your readers already know about your topic? Why should they want or need to know more? What distinctions can you make that they haven't already thought of?

If you are comparing running shoes for a runner's magazine or a shoe catalogue, for example, your readers are probably running enthusiasts who already know a good bit about your subject; so you should distinguish carefully among the different brands or models you're discussing. Thus you might point out that New Balance models 901 and 816 are both durable, lightweight training shoes. The 901, however, is meant for the runner who is (in the words of the manufacturer) "looking for greater stability from heel to toe," while the 816 offers "a deeper toe box for runners needing more space in the forefoot."

A comparison like this is geared toward readers who are experienced runners and have highly specialized needs. Such fine distinctions would be lost on readers who are simply looking for the cheapest running shoe available, or the highest quality one, or the most stylish. So before you compare, size up your readers, and tailor your comparison to fit their specific needs.

Generating Ideas:
Asking How Two Things Are Alike or Different

BRAINSTORMING and LISTING can help as you think about your comparison. Once you have a clear basis for comparing two subjects—flamingos and roseate spoonbills are both large pink birds; trains and jetliners are modes of mass transportation; NB 901s and 816s are medium-priced running shoes—the next step is to look for specific points of comparison between them. So ask yourself the key questions that any comparison raises: How, specifically, are your two subjects alike? How do they differ?

As you probe for similarities and differences between your subjects, make a point-by-point list like the following:

DIFFERENCES

American bath	Japanese bath
fast and efficient	slow and contemplative
usually solitary	often communal, even public
bather scrubs own back	family members scrub one another's backs
about getting clean	about family and community
mundane	ritualistic
stare at ceramic tile	watch the moon rise
concerned with the body	concerned with the soul

SIMILARITIES

American bath	Japanese bath
cleanliness is important	cleanliness is important

Listing the main ways in which two subjects are alike or different will help you to determine whether they're actually worth comparing—and will also help you to get the similarities and differences straight in your own mind before attempting to explain them to an audience.

Notice that in the lists above, each point on the American side matches the point on the Japanese side. If the point on the American side is "stare at ceramic tile," the point on the Japanese side is also about what you look at while bathing: "watch the moon rise." When you draw up your list, make sure you look at the same elements in both subjects. If you talk about the communal aspect of the Japanese bath, you need to mention whether American baths are communal or solitary—or your comparison will be incomplete.

Organizing and Drafting a Comparison

So when comparing marriages (p. 288), pay particular attention to how long they last.

Once you have a list of the specific ways in which your two subjects are alike or different, you're ready to organize, and then to begin drafting, your comparison. Make sure, however, that your main points of comparison deal with significant characteristics of your two subjects and that you draw a sufficient number of them. The templates on page 277 can help you get started.

CHOOSING A METHOD OF ORGANIZATION

There are fundamentally two ways of organizing a comparison essay: you can go point by point or subject by subject. Let's look at the POINT-BY-POINT method at work in a comparison of the career patterns of two ambitious women:

> Both Cleo and Alice are hard-driving workers; both are achievers; both spend so much time working that they have very little left for traditional leisure pursuits. The fundamental difference between Alice and Cleo is that they define work differently. Cleo is working *for* her company. Alice works *through* her company while working for herself. Cleo is a stabilizer. Alice is a scrambler. Most of us fall into one of these two camps. To make the most of your own career and psych out the people around you, it's essential to be able to tell them apart.
>
> —ELWOOD CHAPMAN, *Working Woman*

With a point-by-point organization like this, you discuss each point of comparison (or contrast) between your two subjects before going on to the next point. Here's an informal outline of Chapman's point-by-point comparison:

1. Kind of workers

   Cleo is hard-driving, an achiever
   Alice is hard-driving, an achiever

2. Time spent working

   Cleo spends all her time working
   Alice spends all her time working

3. How they define work

   Cleo works for her company
   Alice works for herself

4. How they affect their coworkers

   Cleo is a stabilizer
   Alice is a scrambler

After using the point-by-point method to compare the two workers in the first paragraph of his essay, Chapman switches to the SUBJECT-BY-SUBJECT method in the next two paragraphs:

Cleo is a classic workaholic. She works from dawn till dusk (more than five days a week as necessary) with a major utility. She earns a good salary, is highly esteemed by her bosses for her loyalty and reliability, and enjoys extraordinary job security (it probably would cost her employer at least 20 percent more than she earns to replace her).

Alice, a mid-management person in a financial institution, also works overtime, though she rarely spends more than 35 to 40 hours a week on actual work assignments. The rest of her time is given over to company information-gathering, checking out opportunities with competing firms, image building and similar activities.

This method discusses each subject individually, making a number of points about one subject and then covering more or less the same points about the other subject. Here is another informal outline of Chapman's subject-by-subject comparison:

Roger Cohen uses this method to compare two rhesus monkeys (p. 291).

1. Cleo

    workaholic
    earns a good salary
    respected for her loyalty and reliability
    enjoys extraordinary job security

2. Alice

    workaholic
    rarely spends all her time on work assignments
    rest of time spent on career building

Which method of organization should you use? Any method that presents your points of comparison and contrast clearly and simply to the reader is a good method of organization. However, you will probably find that the point-by-point method works best for beginning and ending an essay, while the subject-by-subject method serves you well for longer stretches in the main body of your essay.

One reason for using the subject-by-subject method to organize most of your essay is that the point-by-point method, when relentlessly applied, can make the reader a little seasick: stabilizers give time, scramblers steal time; stabilizers avoid stress, scramblers seek it; stabilizers hate change, scramblers use it; stabilizers want job security, scramblers switch jobs with every opportunity; stabilizers are humble, scramblers trust themselves to the brink of disaster. And so on.

With the point-by-point method, you make more or less the same number of points for both subjects. With the subject-by-subject method, on the other hand, you can make as many points as you like on each subject. You do not have to give equal weight to both. The subject-by-subject method is, thus, indispensable for treating a subject in depth, whereas the point-by-point method is an efficient way of presenting a balanced comparison. Because it touches on both subjects more or less equally, the point-by-point method can also help you convince readers that two subjects are, indeed, fundamentally alike (or dissimilar).

The point-by-point method, in other words, is particularly useful for establishing a basis of comparison at the beginning of an essay, for reminding readers along the way why two subjects are being compared, and for summing up. Thus, after treating Cleo and Alice separately throughout most of his article, Chapman comes back to the point-by-point method in the final paragraph:

> As used by David Sedaris (p. 296), this method is also great for purposes of humor.

> Alice is already ahead of Cleo in income and career status. Alice also receives a very genuine if different sort of esteem—the sort of wary respect the fox gets from the rabbit. And although Alice does not have the traditional job security that Cleo clings to, she has a different and far more valuable kind: she knows that whatever may happen in her current job, she can find another easily.

Like the fox and the rabbit, says Chapman, scramblers usually get ahead in their careers, while stabilizers tend to lag a little behind. Chapman is not recommending Alice over Cleo as a career model, however. He's simply highlighting the differences between them because his main point in comparing the two women is to argue that most workers fall into the two camps they represent.

STATING YOUR POINT

Your main point in drawing a comparison will determine whether you emphasize the similarities or the differences between your subjects. If you are comparing coaches you had in high school, for instance, you might focus on their differences in order to show the reader what constitutes a good (or bad) coach. If you're comparing two good blind dates to explain what makes for a successful one, however, you would focus on the similarities.

Whatever the main point of your comparison might be, make it clear right away in the form of an explicit THESIS statement, and tell the reader which you are going to emphasize—the similarities or the differences between your subjects. Then, in the body of your essay, draw a sufficient number of specific points of comparison to prove your main point.

PROVIDING SUFFICIENT POINTS OF COMPARISON

How many points of comparison are enough to do the job? Sufficiency isn't strictly a matter of numbers. It depends, in part, on just how inclined your audience is to accept (or reject) the main point your comparison is intended to make.

TEMPLATES FOR DRAFTING

When you begin to draft a comparison, you need to identify your subjects, state the basis on which you're comparing them, and indicate whether you plan to emphasize their similarities or their differences—moves fundamental to any comparison. See how Gitangeli Sapra makes such moves near the beginning of her essay in this chapter:

> Even if Western middle-class men are growing more faithful, as some experts suggest, 40% of "marriages made for love" still end in divorce. By contrast, the rate of break-ups of arranged marriages in the Asian community is far lower.
>
> —GITANGELI SAPRA, "I'm Happy with an Arranged Marriage"

Sapra identifies her two subjects ("marriages made for love," arranged marriages), states the basis on which she's comparing them ("rate of break-ups"), and indicates that she is planning to emphasize the differences (40 percent in divorce, "far lower"). Here is one more example from this chapter:

> They were two strong men, these oddly different generals, and they represented the strengths of two conflicting currents that, through them, had come into final collision.
>
> —BRUCE CATTON, "Grant and Lee: A Study in Contrasts"

The following templates can help you make some of these basic moves in your own writing. But don't take these as formulas where you just fill in the blanks. There are no shortcuts to good writing, but these templates can serve as starting points.

- ▶ X and Y can be compared on the grounds that both are _____.
- ▶ Like X, Y is also _____, _____, and _____.
- ▶ Although X and Y are both _____, the differences between them far outweigh the similarities. For example, X is _____, _____, and _____, while Y is _____, _____, and _____.
- ▶ Unlike X, Y is _____.
- ▶ Despite their obvious differences, X and Y are basically alike in that _____.
- ▶ At first glance, X and Y seem _____; however, a closer look reveals _____.
- ▶ In comparing X and Y, we can clearly see that _____.

If you are comparing subjects that your readers are not familiar with, you may have to give more reasons for drawing the parallel than you would if your readers already know a lot about your subjects. In comparing dying to going on a cruise, for example, Mary Roach compares the two on the humorous basis that they are both forms of leisure, and she draws five points of comparison between them: (1) much of the time is spent lying on your back; (2) the brain shuts down; (3) the flesh begins to soften; (4) nothing new happens; (5) not much is expected of you. Roach might have gone on to make additional points of comparison, such as (6) you don't go anywhere in particular and (7) there's not much room in the cabin. Five points, however, are probably enough to persuade the reader that the two subjects are worth comparing, and any more than that would be going overboard.

To determine how many points of comparison you need to make, follow Roach's example: give a sufficient number to get your larger point across, but not so many that you run the comparison into the ground. In other words, whether your points of comparison are sufficient to support your thesis is not determined so much by how many you give as by how persuasive they seem to the reader. So consider your intended readers, and choose points of comparison you think they will find useful, interesting, or otherwise convincing.

> Nicholas Kristof cites just one local farmer who "names all his cows" (p. 304, ¶10).

USING OTHER METHODS

Comparison deals with subjects that have something significant in common, so CLASSIFICATION and DEFINITION can be useful in writing that compares. The following paragraph, for example, uses both methods to establish a firm basis for comparing writing to other ways of using language:

> Traditionally, the four language processes of listening, talking, reading, and writing are paired in either of two ways. The more informative seems to be the division many linguists make between first-order and second-order processes with talking and listening characterized as first-order processes; reading and writing, as second-order.
>
> —JANET EMIG, "Writing as a Mode of Learning"

The author of this passage from a formal academic paper in linguistics and language acquisition is comparing writing to other "language processes," particularly talking. Her main point in making the comparison is to argue that, among all the ways in which humans learn to use language, writing is unique.

To support this point and develop her comparison, Emig uses a number of other methods besides comparison and contrast. First, she classifies writing as a "second-order" use of language, and the more natural process of talking as a "first-order" use. Then, elsewhere in her introduction, Emig defines these two basic kinds of language activities: first-order language skills, such as talking, are learned *without* formal instruction, whereas second-order language skills, such as writing, are learned only *with* formal instruction.

Not every linguist would agree that writing is unique among human language activities. But it would be difficult to contest Emig's point that learning to write well takes a special, perhaps unique, form of language instruction by knowledgeable teachers who are dedicated to a difficult task. How else, but through highly specialized training, could we learn to draw formal written comparisons and contrasts in such academic disciplines as history, geography, sociology—and linguistics?

Reading a Comparison Essay with a Critical Eye

Once you've drafted a comparison essay, ask someone else to look over your draft and tell you how effective he or she finds your basic comparison—and why. Then read it over yourself, too, with a critical eye. Here are some questions to keep in mind when checking a comparison.

SUBJECTS OF COMPARISON. What specific subjects does this essay compare? Are those subjects similar enough to justify the comparison? On what basis are they compared? Does the text emphasize the similarities or the differences between them? Or does it give equal weight to both?

PURPOSE AND AUDIENCE. Who are the intended readers, and what is the general purpose of the comparison—to inform? to evaluate? some other purpose? Does the comparison achieve this purpose? If not, what changes might help? What background information is included, and is it sufficient for the intended readers to fully understand the text? Are there any key terms that readers might need to have defined?

THE POINT. What is the main point of the essay? Has it been made clear to the reader? Is there an explicit thesis statement? If not, should there be?

ORGANIZATION. How is the essay organized? Where does it use the point-by-point method of organization? The subject-by-subject method? When comparing subjects point by point, does the essay give more or less equal weight to each subject? When treating first one subject and then the other, does the essay follow more or less the same order in laying out the points of comparison for each subject?

POINTS OF COMPARISON. What are the specific points of comparison in the essay? Are they sufficient to convince the reader that the comparison is valid? Do they cover the same elements in both subjects? Have any important points been omitted—and if so, what are they?

OTHER METHODS. What other methods are used besides comparison and contrast? Does the essay CLASSIFY subjects? DEFINE them? Make an ARGUMENT about them? What other methods might support the comparison?

Editing for Common Errors in Comparisons

As with other kinds of writing, comparisons use distinctive patterns of language and punctuation—and thus invite some common mistakes. The following tips will help you check your writing for errors that often crop up in comparisons.

Check that all comparisons are complete

Remember that all comparisons examine at least two items; check to see that both are mentioned. Readers need to understand what is being compared.

▶ When you take a bath, it is always better to relax than to hurry.

▶ Most hot tubs are not as hot as typical Japanese baths.

Be sure that all comparisons are grammatically consistent

Check to see that the items you're comparing are parallel in grammatical form. The original version of this sentence unintentionally compares a bath with a place.

▶ U.S. baths tend to be much less ritualistic than those in Japan.

Clarify comparisons that can be taken more than one way

▶ Fumio taught me more than Sam did.

Or

▶ Fumio taught me more than he taught Sam.

Check for common usage errors

GOOD, WELL, BETTER

Good is an adjective; *well* is the adverb form. *Better* is both adjective and adverb.

▶ Hilary is a *good* musician; she plays the violin as *well* as Tom does and *better* than I do.

BETWEEN, AMONG

Use *between* when you're comparing two items; use *among* when you're comparing three or more.

▶ *Between* Britain and France, France has the better health care system.

▶ *Among* all the countries of Europe, France has the best health care system.

Student Example

Jamie Gullen is a native of New York City. While an undergraduate at Cornell University, she spent several months in Copenhagen as a participant in the Danish Institute for Study Abroad (DIS). At first, Gullen expected her host country to be "culturally similar" to the one she had left behind. Comparing the two cultures during her months abroad, however, Gullen soon realized how much she had to learn—about herself as well as her hosts. The following essay is the result of that comparative process. It won a prize in the DIS student essay contest in the spring of 2006 under its original title, "Self-Discovery and the Danish Way of Life."

The Danish Way of Life

As my final weeks in Copenhagen began drawing to a close, I was surprised to find myself waiting patiently at a red light even though there were no cars or bikes in the near vicinity. As a New York City native, this observation was cause for a significant pause and some serious self-reflection. My thoughts settled on my first month in Copenhagen when I was having a discussion with a fellow DIS student. She was saying she had expected to feel some significant change in who she was from being abroad, but so far she felt like the same person she had always been. This got me thinking about whether or not I had experienced a significant change of self from being abroad in a culture totally different from the one in which I grew up. At that time, I did not have a good response to that question, but as I stood waiting for the green light on a spring night in Copenhagen, I found I had stumbled upon some important insights.

The answer I came to is that the very core of who I am and the things that matter most to me have remained very much the same. But rather than viewing this in a negative light as some kind of stagnation or lack of personal growth, I realized it was exactly the opposite. Study abroad doesn't change who you are; it helps you discover who you are. By removing the immediate cultural

Gullen uses NARRATION to set up her comparison

The essay will emphasize differences between the two cultures

environment in which I was immersed from the day I was born,
I was able to discern which values and habits were really central
to who I am as a person and which were merely the results of the
influences of my family, friends, school, city, country, and cultural
surroundings.

Before I came to Denmark, I expected it to be fairly culturally
similar to the United States. It is a democratic Western country
where English is widely spoken and where American culture pervades
television and movies, and the Danish government is very closely
aligned with the American government. I was shocked to find out
that the Danish way of life couldn't be more different from what
I was expecting. The biggest difference I experienced originates
with the Danish word *hygge*. This word has no direct translation
into English, and when I asked a Danish person to define it for me,
it took her five minutes just to begin to touch upon what the word
signifies. That is because it is much more than a word; it is a way
of life. What she told me was that *hygge* is most closely translated as
the English word *cozy* and that it is experienced socially. It is a closeness and intimacy between friends, enjoyment of food and wine; it is
dinner that lasts for four hours because of good conversation; and it
is décor with dim lighting and candles everywhere. While I have
experienced *hygge* during my stay in Denmark both with Danes and
my fellow DIS students, it took some time for me to process the true
significance of the word.

The turning point, in my understanding of both *hygge* and myself,
was on my program's short study tour in western Denmark. As I discussed everything from Danish politics to local Danish soccer teams
with some natives in the small town of Kolding, the conversation
casually turned to differences between the Danish and the American
way of life. I was noting that many Danish people I have met view
their careers as a way to provide for themselves financially and to
engage in fields that interest them intellectually, but their conception of self-worth is not tied up in the prestige of their jobs or the

Gullen's PURPOSE in making the comparison is self-evaluation

Shared characteristics establish a basis for the comparison

DEFINING a key term captures the differences between the two countries

Turning point allows for a comparison of her mindset before and after the trip

Subject-by-subject method; Danish characteristics first, then American ones

number of hours worked each week or the amount of the paycheck they bring home in comparison to their peers. It was through this observation that I realized the true importance of *hygge*; it recognizes the humanness of life and the individuality of the person. It is an appreciation of what really matters: friends, family, love, intimacy, and happiness.

Growing up, I lived in a fast-paced city, attended a rigorous high   5
school and college, was surrounded by career-driven highly motivated peers, and was encouraged by my parents to put academics first. Coming to Denmark and experiencing *hygge* and the Danish way of life and learning served as a jolt to the immediate cultural world that had shaped me. I was forced to consider life from another angle. What I found is that deep down I have always held the *hygge* values to be of importance, and I have always wanted to be engaged in helping other people find a happy and peaceful way of life. It is just easier now to see how my external cultural evironment has impacted and shaped these values and my sense of DIS, Danish, and my international self.

When I arrive home in New York City, it will no doubt take very   6
little time for me to join in with the throngs of jaywalkers marching
defiantly across Madison Avenue, but what I have learned from
being abroad in Denmark about who I am and what matters most to
me will be knowledge that stays with me forever.

> Conclusion returns to opening narrative

Analyzing a Student Comparison

In "The Danish Way of Life," Jamie Gullen draws upon rhetorical strategies and techniques that good writers use all the time when they make a comparison. The following questions, in addition to focusing on particular aspects of Gullen's text, will help you to identify those common strategies and techniques so you can adapt them to your own writing. These questions will also help to prepare you for the analytical questions—on content, structure, and language—that you'll find after all the other selections in this chapter, along with suggestions for writing on related topics.

READING CLOSELY

1. What was the biggest difference between Danish and American culture that Jamie Gullen experienced while studying abroad in Denmark?

2. According to Gullen, how do the Danes approach their jobs and careers as compared with their American counterparts?

3. Gullen says that "study abroad doesn't change who you are" (2). What does it do, in her view? How?

4. What important lesson did Gullen learn from her period of study abroad?

STRATEGIES AND STRUCTURES

1. How does Gullen use the NARRATIVE device of waiting for a traffic light to help structure her entire essay?

2. In her introduction, Gullen says she "stumbled upon some important insights" as an American studying in Denmark (1). Gullen does not specify what those insights are, however, until after she compares the two countries in the main body of her essay. Should she have done so earlier? Why or why not?

3. How did the act of making comparisons lead Gullen to a "turning point" in her understanding of both her host country and herself (4)? Does her comparison emphasize the similarities between the two cultures, or their differences, or both? Explain.

4. Gullen sums up what she learned from her Danish experience in paragraph 5. Why doesn't she end there? What does paragraph 6 add to her comparison?

5. *Other Methods.* The "biggest difference" between Denmark and America that she encountered during her study abroad, says Gullen, can be summed up in the Danish word *hygge* (3). How does Gullen use an extended DEFINITION of this term to support her comparison of the two countries?

THINKING ABOUT LANGUAGE

1. The Danes, says Gullen, usually translate *hygge* as the English word *cozy* (3). Judging from Gullen's definition of the term, how would you translate it?

2. What are the CONNOTATIONS of "stumbled" and "natives" (1, 4)?

3. A "turning point" implies an irreversible change (4). What, if anything, is irreversible about Gullen's experience as a student in Denmark?

FOR WRITING

1. Write a paragraph contrasting what you see as a key difference between the culture of mainstream America with that of some other country or group.

2. Think of another country you would like to visit (or have already visited). Write an essay that compares that culture and your own. What do you expect (or what did you find) to be the main similarities and differences between them?

A Souvenir Coffee Mug

In the inscription on this coffee mug, purchased in a bookstore on the Kenyon campus in Gambier, Ohio, the novelist E. L Doctorow compares two institutions of higher learning. One is his alma mater, a private college known for its liberal arts program, particularly music. The other is a large state institution known for its . . . football team. When you make comparisons like this, choose two subjects (Kenyon, Ohio State) from the same general category (schools in Ohio) that are nevertheless different enough in some details (poetry, football) to make the comparison worthwhile. The details you choose will depend on your purpose for drawing the comparison. The Kenyon coffee mug, for instance, is intended to promote the liberal arts: "We grapple with metaphors," said one Kenyon administrator; "they clinch in the mud." Down the road at Ohio State, university officials would call this poetic license. To promote the range of academic programs offered by a large public university, their competing coffee mugs might read: "The way they do poetry at Kenyon, we do football at Ohio State—and medieval literature, law, medicine, business, and engineering."

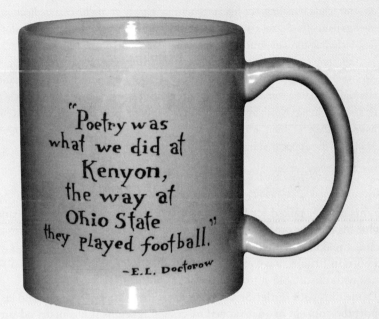

"Poetry was
what we did at
Kenyon,
the way at
Ohio State
they played football."

—E.L. Doctorow

GITANGELI SAPRA

I'm Happy with an Arranged Marriage

Gitangeli Sapra (b. 1979) studied journalism at London's Harrow College while work-ing as a reporter at the Watford Observer. *She later took a day job as a marketing director while pursuing her freelance writing career at night. This dedication to writ-ing has paid off—Sapra's work has appeared in some of Britain's most prestigious dai-lies, including the* Telegraph *and the* Times.

The compare-and-contrast approach that Sapra uses in "I'm Happy with an Arranged Marriage" is one that she comes by naturally. Growing up in Britain, Sapra has had to balance contemporary European social norms with the traditions of her fam-ily's native India. Nowhere is the contrast between these different cultures more pro-nounced than in their attitudes toward marriage. "I'm Happy with an Arranged Marriage" first appeared in the Sunday Times *of London in May 2003.*

NUMBER SEVEN was preceded by his breath. Number three did not open his mouth, his mother talked for him. I never actually saw prospective husband num-ber eight: his mother preferred that I keep my gaze averted, Bollywood style.[1]

Such is the dance of modern-day arranged marriage, at least as I, a 24-year-old Hindu born in Britain, have experienced it. Although so far it has been a series of meetings with unsuitable suitors, I am not at all dismayed.

As Dame Elizabeth Butler-Sloss, president of the Family Division, said last week: "I support the concept of an arranged marriage. It seems it has many advantages."

> When you emphasize dif-ferences, your comparison is a contrast (p. 269).

Even if Western middle-class men are growing more faithful, as some experts suggest, 40% of "marriages made for love" still end in divorce. By contrast, the rate of break-ups of arranged marriages in the Asian com-munity is far lower.

This may be because arranged unions are based on mutual interests and similar levels of education rather than physical attraction. The involvement of both fami-lies is also a deterrent to affairs—who would want to risk the wrath of their mother, mother-in-law, brother and grandfather, as well as their wife, for a few hours of fun?

1. *Bollywood*: A blending of "Bombay" (the city now called Mumbai) and "Hollywood." In India there is a thriving movie industry that makes hundreds of mostly Hindi-language films each year. The industry, the place, and the films themselves are often referred to as Bollywood.

SUGGESTED MLA CITATION: Sapra, Gitangeli. "I'm Happy with an Arranged Marriage." 2003. *Back to the Lake*. Ed. Thomas Cooley. 2nd ed. New York: Norton, 2012. 288–89. Print.

Nor is the system as draconian as many might imagine. Arranged marriages 6 are simply introductions—the element of choice remains. True, initial meetings between would-be brides and grooms take place in front of their families, but subsequent "dates" are usually unchaperoned. And you are not expected to make any decisions until at least the sixth meeting.

A wild rush? I know of couples who agreed to marry after only the second meeting. 7 Several children later, the initial attraction has developed into an abiding love and respect. One friend even said yes on the first meeting, despite her intended turning up with his mother, aunt, uncle, three brothers and the dog. Eight years and two children later, she has no regrets.

Some marriages that are forced do still take place—perhaps 1,000 a year among 8 Pakistanis born in Britain. But the distinction is clear. As Butler-Sloss said: "Forced marriage is as unacceptable in the Indian subcontinent among those who understand the sharia (law) as in the Western world."

Nor is it just young Asians who see the benefits of arranged unions. Steven 9 Brown, chief executive of the Jewish Marriage Council, which runs its own matchmaking service, said: "The latest thing is shidduch dating, where a matchmaker introduces couples who go out unchaperoned to a Jewish restaurant four or five times to see if they have anything in common.

"Among the orthodox, arranged marriages are very much the done thing. The 10 degree of people remaining married after meeting like this is higher than in other cases."

Even Western women, post–Bridget Jones[2] and single, are keen on exploring 11 the idea. After all, the union of the Prince of Wales and Diana Spencer was as orchestrated as any Delhi marriage.

Claire Oswald, 38, a writer who is white, Western, and single, recently lamented 12 in the Asian women's magazine *Memsahib* that no system of arranged marriage was available to her.

"I would love to have an arranged marriage," she wrote. "It's great that there is 13 so much family involvement and that the people who care about you help you to find a husband."

I am soon to meet number 12—a doctor, as my mother keeps telling everyone. 14 There is no pressure. But as I hurtle towards 25—middle-aged for an arranged marriage—I hope this one works out.

2. *Bridget Jones*: The heroine of best-selling novels by Helen Fielding about the trials of dating in London.

READING CLOSELY

1. Gitangeli Sapra is comparing arranged marriages with those "made for love" (4). What main advantages and disadvantages does she find in each type?

2. Are you convinced by Sapra's ARGUMENT that arranged marriages are superior to ones based on "physical attraction" (5)? Why or why not?

3. Sapra does not approve of all arranged marriages. What kind does she still find unacceptable? Why? What do you think?

STRATEGIES AND STRUCTURES

1. Sapra is a British citizen of Indian ancestry. Is she writing for readers with her own ethnic background, or for someone else? How do you know?

2. Are Sapra's points of comparison between the two types of marriage sufficient to support her claim that one is superior to the other? Why or why not?

3. How convincing do you find Sapra's EXAMPLES? Are there any that do her case more harm than good? If so, which ones?

4. *Other Methods.* According to Sapra, what is the main CAUSE of the lower percentage of divorces among arranged marriages as compared to "love" marriages? How convincing do you find this analysis?

THINKING ABOUT LANGUAGE

1. In Hebrew, a *shidduch* is a "match" (9). Why does Sapra use this term to DESCRIBE the kind of marriage she advocates?

2. Is "made for love" (4) an adequate label of the kind of marriage that Sapra is contrasting with arranged marriages? Why or why not? What term would you suggest?

FOR WRITING

1. Write a paragraph outlining the advantages of "marriage for love."

2. Write an essay comparing dates you set up on your own with dates arranged for you, at least in part, by somebody else. Be sure to comment on the advantages and disadvantages of each.

ROGER COHEN

The Meaning of Life

Roger Cohen (b. 1955) is a journalist and regular columnist for the New York Times *and the* International Herald Tribune. *He grew up in London and studied history and French at Oxford University, where he received a master's degree in 1977. He is the coauthor of* In the Eye of the Storm *(1991), a biography of General Norman Schwarzkopf, and the author of two other books on war and warfare:* Hearts Grown Brutal *(1998), about the destruction of the former Yugoslavia, and* Soldiers and Slaves *(2005), an account of American POWs in World War II.*

In "The Meaning of Life," an Op-Ed column from the Times *(July 16, 2009), Cohen compares and contrasts two rhesus monkeys, Canto and Owen, subjects of experiments in aging at the University of Wisconsin. Cohen's comparison, which leads him to speculate on much larger matters, is based on the photos of Canto and Owen reproduced on page 292.*

WHAT'S LIFE FOR? That question stirred as I contemplated two rhesus monkeys, Canto, aged 27, and Owen, aged 29, whose photographs appeared last week in *The New York Times.*

The monkeys are part of a protracted experiment in aging being conducted by a University of Wisconsin team. Canto gets a restricted diet with 30 percent fewer calories than usual while Owen gets to eat whatever the heck he pleases.

Preliminary conclusions, published in *Science* two decades after the experiment began, "demonstrate that caloric restriction slows aging in a primate species," the scientists leading the experiment wrote. While just 13 percent of the dieting group has died in ways judged due to old age, 37 percent of the feasting monkeys are already dead.

These conclusions have been contested by other scientists for various reasons I won't bore you with—boredom definitely shortens life spans.

Meanwhile, before everyone holds the French fries, the issue arises of how these primates—whose average life span in the wild is 27 (with a maximum of 40)—are feeling and whether these feelings impact their desire to live.

Monkeys' emotions were part of my childhood. My father, a doctor, worked with them all his life. His thesis at the University of Witwatersrand in Johannesburg, South Africa, was on the menstrual cycle of baboons.

No matter what you're comparing, be sure to explain how it supports your thesis (p. 276).

SUGGESTED MLA CITATION: Cohen, Roger. "The Meaning of Life." 2009. *Back to the Lake.* Ed. Thomas Cooley. 2nd ed. New York: Norton, 2012. 291–93. Print.

Canto and Owen, two rhesus monkeys who are the subjects of experiments in aging at the University of Wisconsin.

When he settled in Britain in the 1950s, he had some of his baboons (average life span 30) shipped over, ultimately donating a couple to the London Zoo.

Upon visiting the zoo much later, he got a full-throated greeting from the baboons, who rushed to the front of their cage to tell him they'd missed him. Moral of story: Don't underestimate monkeys' feelings.   7

Which brings me to low-cal Canto and high-cal Owen: Canto looks drawn, weary, ashen and miserable in his thinness, mouth slightly agape, features pinched, eyes blank, his expression screaming, "Please, no, not another plateful of seeds!"   8

Well-fed Owen, by contrast, is a happy camper with a wry smile, every inch the laid-back simian, plump, eyes twinkling, full mouth relaxed, skin glowing, exuding wisdom as if he's just read Kierkegaard[1] and concluded that "Life must be lived forward, but can only be understood backward."   9

It's the difference between the guy who got the marbleized rib-eye and the guy who got the oh-so-lean filet. Or between the guy who got a Château Grand Pontet St. Emilion with his brie and the guy who got water. As Edgar notes in *King Lear*, "Ripeness is all."[2] You don't get to ripeness by eating apple peel for breakfast.   10

1. *Søren Kierkegaard (1813–1855)*: Danish philosopher and theologian.
2. *"Ripeness is all"*: From Act 5, Scene 2 of Shakespeare's *King Lear* (1608).

Speaking of St. Emilion, scientists, aware that most human beings don't have 11 the discipline to slash their calorie intake by almost a third, have been looking for substances that might mimic the effects of caloric restriction. They have found one candidate, resveratrol, in red wine.

The thing is there's not enough resveratrol in wine to do the trick, so scientists 12 are trying to concentrate it, or produce a chemical like it in order to offer people the gain (in life expectancy) without the pain (of dieting).

I don't buy this gain-without-pain notion. Duality resides, indissoluble, at life's 13 core—Faust's two souls within his breast, Anna Karenina's[3] shifting essence. Life without death would be miserable. Its beauty is bound to its fragility. Dawn is unimaginable without the dusk.

When life extension supplants life quality as a goal, you get the desolation of 14 Canto the monkey. Living to 120 holds zero appeal for me. Canto looks like he's itching to be put out of his misery.

There's an alternative to resveratrol. Something is secreted in the love-sick that 15 causes rapid loss of appetite—caloric restriction—yet scientists have been unable to reproduce this miracle substance, for if they did they would be decoding love. Because love is too close to the divine, life's essence, it seems to defy such breakdown.

My mother died of cancer at 69. Her father lived to 98, her mother to 104. I said 16 my mother died of cancer. But that's not true. She was bipolar and depression devastated her. What took her life was misery.

We don't understand what the mind secretes. The process of aging remains full 17 of enigma. But I'd bet on jovial Owen outliving wretched Canto. I suspect those dissenting scientists I didn't bore you with are right.

My 98-year-old grandfather had a party trick, making crisscross incisions into a 18 watermelon, before allowing it to fall open in a giant red blossom. It was as beautiful as a lily opening—and, still vivid, close to what life is for.

When my father went to pick up his baboons at Heathrow airport, he stopped at 19 a grocery store to buy them a treat. "Two pounds of bananas, please," he said. But there were none. "O.K.," he said, "Then I'll take two pounds of carrots." The shopkeeper gave him a very strange look before hurriedly handing over the carrots.

I can hear my 88-year-old father's laughter as he tells this story. Laughter 20 extends life. There's little of it in the low-cal world and little doubt pudgy Owen will have the last laugh.

3. *Anna Karenina:* An 1878 novel by Russian writer Leo Tolstoy. *Faust:* A figure in German legend who serves as the basis for many literary works; an ambitious scholar, Faust gives his soul to the devil in exchange for unlimited knowledge and magical powers.

Reading Closely

1. What's Roger Cohen's answer to the profound question that begins his essay (1), and how adequate is it?

2. What does Cohen mean when he says (quoting the Danish philosopher Søren Kierkegaard) that "life must be lived forward, but can only be understood backward" (9)?

3. Cohen notes that "boredom definitely shortens life spans" (4). Do you agree? Why or why not?

4. "Duality," says Cohen, "resides . . . at life's core" (13). What is the nature of that duality as he DEFINES it?

Strategies and Structures

1. Cohen bases his conclusions about the meaning of life on a comparison of two rhesus monkeys. Do they provide sufficient evidence for his claims? Why or why not?

2. Point to specific details in Cohen's DESCRIPTION of the two primates that contribute especially well to the comparison he is drawing between them. Why do you find these details in particular to be effective?

3. Visual elements in an essay should be more than mere decoration. How relevant is the photograph of Canto and Owen to the comparison Cohen is making? Explain.

4. How and how well does the "moral" of the story that Cohen tells about his father at the London Zoo apply to the rest of his essay (7)?

5. *Other Methods.* What is the moral of the little NARRATIVE about Cohen's grandfather and the watermelon (18)? About his father and the carrots? About his mother's early death? How do these and the other ANECDOTES in Cohen's essay contribute to the comparison he is making and to the conclusions he draws from it?

Thinking about Language

1. What are the implications of "stirred" (1)? Why does Cohen use this word instead of saying, for instance, that some questions came to mind or popped up?

2. The enigmatic phrase from Shakespeare's *King Lear*—"Ripeness is all"—has been variously interpreted. How does Cohen interpret it? Is this interpretation justified?

3. What is the purpose of the ALLUSIONS to *Faust* and *Anna Karenina* in Cohen's musings on the "duality" of life (13)?

FOR WRITING

1. Write a paragraph each describing Canto and Owen as pictured in the photograph that accompanies Cohen's essay. Concentrate on the visible physical characteristics of the two monkeys.

2. Using their physical characteristics as a basis, write a comparison of Canto and Owen that makes an interesting point about the scientists' claim that such primate studies "demonstrate that caloric restriction slows aging" (3). Be sure to speculate on the significance of this claim.

DAVID SEDARIS

Remembering My Childhood on the Continent of Africa

David Sedaris (b. 1956) made a name for himself as an elf in "Santaland," the story about working with the Santas at Macy's he told on National Public Radio's Morning Edition *in 1992. His hilarious autobiographical tales have been an NPR staple ever since, and his numerous book-length collections, from* Barrel Fever *(1994) to* When You Are Engulfed in Flames *(2008), have all been best sellers. In 2001 Sedaris won the Thurber Prize for American Humor and was named "Humorist of the Year" by* Time *magazine. His latest collection is* Squirrel Seeks Chipmunk *(2010).*

Lopsided comparisons have always been a rich source of comedy. In "Remembering My Childhood on the Continent of Africa," taken from his collection Me Talk Pretty One Day *(2000), Sedaris juxtaposes his own "unspeakably dull" childhood in Raleigh, North Carolina, with that of his partner, Hugh Hamrick, a diplomat's son who grew up in Africa.*

WHEN HUGH WAS IN THE FIFTH GRADE, his class took a field trip to an Ethiopian slaughterhouse. He was living in Addis Ababa at the time, and the slaughterhouse was chosen because, he says, "it was convenient."

This was a school system in which the matter of proximity outweighed such petty concerns as what may or may not be appropriate for a busload of eleven-year-olds. "What?" I asked. "Were there no autopsies scheduled at the local morgue? Was the federal prison just a bit too far out of the way?"

Hugh defends his former school, saying, "Well, isn't that the whole point of a field trip? To see something new?"

"Technically yes, but . . ."

"All right then," he says. "So we saw some new things."

One of his field trips was literally a trip to a field where the class watched a wrinkled man fill his mouth with rotten goat meat and feed it to a pack of waiting hyenas. On another occasion they were taken to examine the bloodied bedroom curtains hanging in the palace of the former dictator. There were tamer trips, to textile factories and sugar refineries, but my favorite is always the slaughterhouse. It wasn't a big company, just a small rural enterprise run by a couple of brothers operating out of a low-ceilinged

To compare two subjects in depth like this, use the subject-by-subject method (p. 274).

SUGGESTED MLA CITATION: Sedaris, David. "Remembering My Childhood on the Continent of Africa." 2000. *Back to the Lake.* Ed. Thomas Cooley. 2nd ed. New York: Norton, 2012. 296–301. Print.

concrete building. Following a brief lecture on the importance of proper sanitation, a small white piglet was herded into the room, its dainty hooves clicking against the concrete floor. The class gathered in a circle to get a better look at the animal, who seemed delighted with the attention he was getting. He turned from face to face and was looking up at Hugh when one of the brothers drew a pistol from his back pocket, held it against the animal's temple, and shot the piglet, execution-style. Blood spattered, frightened children wept, and the man with the gun offered the teacher and bus driver some meat from a freshly slaughtered goat.

When I'm told such stories, it's all I can do to hold back my feelings of jealousy. 7 An Ethiopian slaughterhouse. Some people have all the luck. When I was in elementary school, the best we ever got was a trip to Old Salem or Colonial Williamsburg, one of those preserved brick villages where time supposedly stands still and someone earns his living as a town crier. There was always a blacksmith, a group of wandering patriots, and a collection of bonneted women hawking corn bread or gingersnaps made "the ol'-fashioned way." Every now and then you might come across a doer of bad deeds serving time in the stocks, but that was generally as exciting as it got.

Certain events are parallel, but compared with Hugh's, my childhood was 8 unspeakably dull. When I was seven years old, my family moved to North Carolina. When he was seven years old, Hugh's family moved to the Congo. We had a collie and a house cat. They had a monkey and two horses named Charlie Brown and Satan. I threw stones at stop signs. Hugh threw stones at crocodiles. The verbs are the same, but he definitely wins the prize when it comes to nouns and objects. An eventful day for my mother might have involved a trip to the dry cleaner or a conversation with the potato-chip deliveryman. Asked one ordinary Congo afternoon what she'd done with her day, Hugh's mother answered that she and a fellow member of the Ladies' Club had visited a leper colony on the outskirts of Kinshasa. No reason was given for the expedition, though chances are she was staking it out for a future field trip.

Due to his upbringing, Hugh sits through inane movies never realizing that 9 they're often based on inane television shows. There were no poker-faced sitcom martians in his part of Africa, no oil-rich hillbillies or aproned brides trying to wean themselves from the practice of witchcraft.[1] From time to time a movie would arrive packed in a dented canister, the film scratched and faded from its slow trip around the world. The theater consisted of a few dozen folding chairs arranged before a bedsheet or the blank wall of a vacant hangar out near the airstrip.

---

1. *Martians . . . practice of witchcraft*: References to *My Favorite Martian, The Beverly Hillbillies*, and *Bewitched*, popular U.S. TV shows in the 1960s.

Occasionally a man would sell warm soft drinks out of a cardboard box, but that was it in terms of concessions.

When I was young, I went to the theater at the nearby shopping center and watched a movie about a talking Volkswagen. I believe the little car had a taste for mischief but I can't be certain, as both the movie and the afternoon proved unremarkable and have faded from my memory. Hugh saw the same movie a few years after it was released. His family had left the Congo by this time and were living in Ethiopia. Like me, Hugh saw the movie by himself on a weekend afternoon. Unlike me, he left the theater two hours later, to find a dead man hanging from a telephone pole at the far end of the unpaved parking lot. None of the people who'd seen the movie seemed to care about the dead man. They stared at him for a moment or two and then headed home, saying they'd never seen anything as crazy as that talking Volkswagen. His father was late picking him up, so Hugh just stood there for an hour, watching the dead man dangle and turn in the breeze. The death was not reported in the newspaper, and when Hugh related the story to his friends, they said, "You saw the movie about the talking car?"

I could have done without the flies and the primitive theaters, but I wouldn't have minded growing up with a houseful of servants. In North Carolina it wasn't unusual to have a once-a-week maid, but Hugh's family had houseboys, a word that never fails to charge my imagination. They had cooks and drivers, and guards who occupied a gatehouse, armed with machetes. Seeing as I had regularly petitioned my parents for an electric fence, the business with the guards strikes me as the last word in quiet sophistication. Having protection suggests that you are important. Having that protection paid for by the government is even better, as it suggests your safety is of interest to someone other than yourself.

Hugh's father was a career officer with the U.S. State Department, and every morning a black sedan carried him off to the embassy. I'm told it's not as glamorous as it sounds, but in terms of fun for the entire family, I'm fairly confident that it beats the sack race at the annual IBM picnic. By the age of three, Hugh was already carrying a diplomatic passport. The rules that applied to others did not apply to him. No tickets, no arrests, no luggage search: he was officially licensed to act like a brat. Being an American, it was expected of him, and who was he to deny the world an occasional tantrum?

They weren't rich, but what Hugh's family lacked financially they more than made up for with the sort of exoticism that works wonders at cocktail parties, leading always to the remark "That sounds fascinating." It's a compliment one rarely receives when describing an adolescence spent drinking Icees at the North Hills Mall. No fifteen-foot python ever wandered onto my school's basketball court. I begged, I prayed nightly, but it just never happened. Neither did I get to witness a military coup in which forces sympathetic to the colonel arrived late at night to assassinate my next-door neighbor. Hugh had been at the Addis Ababa teen club when the electricity was cut off and soldiers arrived to evacuate the building. He and his friends had to hide in the back of a jeep and cover themselves with blankets during the ride home. It's something that sticks in his mind for one reason or another.

Among my personal highlights is the memory of having my picture taken with 14 Uncle Paul, the legally blind host of a Raleigh children's television show. Among Hugh's is the memory of having his picture taken with Buzz Aldrin on the last leg of the astronaut's world tour. The man who had walked on the moon placed his hand on Hugh's shoulder and offered to sign his autograph book. The man who led Wake County schoolchildren in afternoon song turned at the sound of my voice and asked, "So what's your name, princess?"

When I was fourteen years old, I was sent to spend ten days with my maternal 15 grandmother in western New York State. She was a small and private woman named Billie, and though she never came right out and asked, I had the distinct impression she had no idea who I was. It was the way she looked at me, squinting through her glasses while chewing on her lower lip. That, coupled with the fact that she never once called me by name. "Oh," she'd say, "are you still here?" She was just beginning her long struggle with Alzheimer's disease, and each time I entered the room, I felt the need to reintroduce myself and set her at ease. "Hi, it's me. Sharon's boy, David. I was just in the kitchen admiring your collection of ceramic toads." Aside from a few trips to summer camp, this was the longest I'd ever been away from home, and I like to think I was toughened by the experience.

About the same time I was frightening my grandmother, Hugh and his family 16 were packing their belongings for a move to Somalia. There were no English-speaking schools in Mogadishu, so, after a few months spent lying around the family compound with his pet monkey, Hugh was sent back to Ethiopia to live with a beer enthusiast his father had met at a cocktail party. Mr. Hoyt installed security systems in foreign embassies. He and his family gave Hugh a room. They invited him to join them at the table, but that was as far as they extended themselves. No one ever asked him when his birthday was, so when the day came, he kept it to himself. There was no telephone service between Ethiopia and Somalia, and letters to his parents were sent to Washington and then forwarded on to Mogadishu, meaning that his news was more than a month old by the time they got it. I suppose it wasn't much different than living as a foreign-exchange student. Young people do it all the time, but to me it sounds awful. The Hoyts had two sons about Hugh's age who were always saying things like "Hey that's *our* sofa you're sitting on" and "Hands off that ornamental stein. It doesn't belong to you."

He'd been living with these people for a year when he overheard Mr. Hoyt tell a 17 friend that he and his family would soon be moving to Munich, Germany, the beer capital of the world.

"And that worried me," Hugh said, "because it meant I'd have to find some
other place to live."   18

Where I come from, finding shelter is a problem the average teenager might   19
confidently leave to his parents. It was just something that came with having a
mom and a dad. Worried that he might be sent to live with his grandparents in
Kentucky, Hugh turned to the school's guidance counselor, who knew of a family
whose son had recently left for college. And so he spent another year living with
strangers and not mentioning his birthday. While I wouldn't have wanted to do it
myself, I can't help but envy the sense of fortitude he gained from the experience.
After graduating from college, he moved to France knowing only the phrase "Do
you speak French?"—a question guaranteed to get you nowhere unless you also
speak the language.

While living in Africa, Hugh and his family took frequent vacations, often in the   20
company of their monkey. The Nairobi Hilton, some suite of high-ceilinged rooms
in Cairo or Khartoum: these are the places his people recall when gathered at a
common table. "Was that the summer we spent in Beirut or, no, I'm thinking of
the time we sailed from Cyprus and took the *Orient Express* to Istanbul."

Theirs was the life I dreamt about during my vacations in eastern North Caro-   21
lina. Hugh's family was hobnobbing with chiefs and sultans while I ate hush puppies at the Sanitary Fish Market in Morehead City, a beach towel wrapped like a
hijab around my head.[2] Someone unknown to me was very likely standing in a
muddy ditch and dreaming of an evening spent sitting in a clean family restaurant,
drinking iced tea and working his way through an extra-large seaman's platter, but
that did not concern me, as it meant I should have been happy with what I had.
Rather than surrender to my bitterness, I have learned to take satisfaction in the
life that Hugh has led. His stories have, over time, become my own. I say this with
no trace of a kumbaya.[3] There is no spiritual symbiosis; I'm just a petty thief who
lifts his memories the same way I'll take a handful of change left on his dresser.
When my own experiences fall short of the mark, I just go out and spend some of
his. It is with pleasure that I sometimes recall the dead man's purpled face or the
report of the handgun ringing in my ears as I studied the blood pooling beneath the
dead white piglet. On the way back from the slaughterhouse, we stopped for Cokes
in the village of Mojo, where the gas-station owner had arranged a few tables and
chairs beneath a dying canopy of vines. It was late afternoon by the time we

2. *Hijab*: A veil worn by Muslim women. *Hush puppies*: Small, deep-fried balls of dough.

3. *Kumbaya*: The title and refrain of an African American folk song that originated as a slave spiritual. The song was a popular hit in the 1960s and is sung by many youth organizations; the word has
come to be associated with unity and closeness.

returned to school, where a second bus carried me to the foot of Coffeeboard Road. Once there, I walked through a grove of eucalyptus trees and alongside a bald pasture of starving cattle, past the guard napping in his gatehouse, and into the waiting arms of my monkey.

READING CLOSELY

1. As children in school, both David Sedaris and Hugh Hamrick took occasional field trips. What is Sedaris' point in comparing their experiences? Broadly speaking, how do they compare?

2. Why did Sedaris find the movie about a talking Volkswagen to be "unremarkable" (10)? How did Hugh react to it, and why was his experience so different?

3. Instead of surrendering to his "bitterness," Sedaris has learned "to take satisfaction" from Hugh's account of his childhood (21). Why does Sedaris claim to be bitter, and how seriously are we supposed to take his claim?

4. Besides satisfaction and loose change, what else has Sedaris learned to "take" from Hugh's life?

5. Whose childhood would you prefer to remember having lived, Sedaris' or Hugh's? Why?

STRATEGIES AND STRUCTURES

1. In comparing the early lives of himself and his partner, Sedaris emphasizes the differences. On what basis does he compare their experiences nevertheless? What did their childhoods have in common?

2. In paragraph 8, Sedaris uses the point-by-point method to organize his comparison. What would have been the result if he had kept on alternating like this between his two subjects throughout the rest of the essay? Explain.

3. How sufficient do you find Sedaris' main points of comparison for explaining his jealousy of Hugh's childhood (7)? How and how well do they prepare us for the ending, in which Sedaris takes over his friend's memories?

4. *Other Methods.* Sedaris' comparison includes many elements of personal NARRATIVE. What are some of them? (Cite specific examples from the text.) How would the essay be different without any narrative?

THINKING ABOUT LANGUAGE

1. His life and Hugh's shared the same verbs, says Sedaris, but different nouns and objects (8). What does Sedaris mean by this, and why is he comparing the lives of two boys to grammatical parts of speech?

2. Among the "personal highlights" of his childhood, says Sedaris, is "the memory of having my picture taken with Uncle Paul, the legally blind host of a Raleigh children's television show" (14). How is Sedaris using IRONY here?

3. A "hijab" is a veil (21). What sort of hijab does Sedaris wear in the Sanitary Fish Market in Morehead City?

4. Sedaris describes himself as a "petty thief" (21). What is he stealing in this essay, and what has caused him to sink to this level?

FOR WRITING

1. Ask a friend or family member to write down his or her recollections of an important event that you have both experienced. You do the same. Then, in a paragraph or so, compare and contrast the two versions.

2. In an essay, compare your childhood with that of someone whose early experience was very different from your own. Your counterpart can be someone you know personally or someone you don't know, as long as you're familiar with details of his or her childhood.

NICHOLAS D. KRISTOF

Food for the Soul

Nicholas D. Kristof (b. 1959) is a journalist who writes about such global issues as poverty, health, and human trafficking. Born in Chicago, he grew up on a livestock and cherry farm in Oregon. After graduating from Harvard, he studied law as a Rhodes Scholar at Oxford University. In 1990, Kristof and his wife, Sheryl WuDunn, won a Pulitzer Prize for their coverage of the fight for democracy in China's Tiananmen Square. Together they have written books on China and other parts of Asia as rising powers, including Thunder from the East *(2000). In* Half the Sky *(2009), the couple focused on the worldwide oppression of women and their opportunities for improvement. Kristof's newspaper columns won him a second Pulitzer in 2006 for his commentary on genocide in Darfur.*

In "Food for the Soul," an August 2009 Op-Ed piece from the New York Times, *Kristof draws on his memories of growing up on a family farm. "That kind of diverse, chaotic family farm is now disappearing," he writes. It is being supplanted by another kind—the "factory farm"—and the contrast between the two, as Kristof presents them here, could not be more stark.*

O N A SUMMER VISIT back to the farm here where I grew up, I think I figured out 1 the central problem with modern industrial agriculture. It's not just that it produces unhealthy food, mishandles waste and overuses antibiotics in ways that harm us all.

More fundamentally, it has no soul. 2

The family farm traditionally was the most soulful place imaginable, and that 3 was the case with our own farm on the edge of the Willamette Valley. I can't say we were efficient: for a time we thought about calling ourselves "Wandering Livestock Ranch," after our Angus cattle escaped in one direction and our Duroc hogs in another.

When coyotes threatened our sheep operation, we spent $300 on a Kuvasz, a 4 breed of guard dog that is said to excel in protecting sheep. Alas, our fancy-pants new sheep dog began her duties by dining on lamb.

It's always said that if a dog kills one lamb, it will never stop, and so the local 5 rule was that if your dog killed one sheep you had to shoot it. Instead we engaged

SUGGESTED MLA CITATION: Kristof, Nicholas D. "Food for the Soul." 2009. *Back to the Lake*. Ed. Thomas Cooley. 2nd ed. New York: Norton, 2012. 303–05. Print.

in a successful cover-up. It worked, for the dog never touched a lamb again and for the rest of her long life fended off coyotes heroically.

That kind of diverse, chaotic family farm is now disappearing, replaced by insipid food assembly lines. 6

The result is food that also lacks soul—but may contain pathogens. In the last two months, there have been two major recalls of ground beef because of possible contamination with drug-resistant salmonella. When factory farms routinely fill animals with antibiotics, the result is superbugs that resist antibiotics. 7

Michael Pollan, the food writer, notes that monocultures in the field result in monocultures in our diets. Two-thirds of our calories, he says, now come from just four crops: rice, soy, wheat and corn. Fast-food culture and obesity are linked, he argues, to the transformation from family farms to industrial farming. 8

In fairness, industrial farming is extraordinarily efficient, and smaller diverse family farms would mean more expensive food. So is this all inevitable? Is my nostalgia like the blacksmith's grief over Henry Ford's assembly lines superseding a more primitive technology? Perhaps, but I'm reassured by one of my old high school buddies here in Yamhill, [Oregon,] Bob Bansen. He runs a family dairy of 225 Jersey cows so efficiently that it can still compete with giant factory dairies of 20,000 cows. 9

Bob names all his cows, and can tell them apart in an instant. He can tell you each cow's quirks and parentage. They are family friends as well as economic assets. 10

"With these big dairies, a cow means nothing to them," Bob said. "When I lose a cow, it bothers me. I kick myself." That might seem like sentimentality, but it's also good business and preserves his assets. 11

American agriculture policy and subsidies have favored industrialization and consolidation, but there are signs that the Obama administration Agriculture Department under Secretary Tom Vilsack is becoming more friendly to small producers. I hope that's right. 12

Is one enough? See p. 276 for tips on how many points of comparison you need to draw.

One of my childhood memories is of placing a chicken egg in a goose nest when I was about 10 (my young scientist phase). That mother goose was thrilled when her eggs hatched, and maternal love is such that she never seemed to notice that one of her babies was a neckless midget. 13

As for the chick, she never doubted her goosiness. At night, our chickens would roost high up in the barn, while the geese would sleep on the floor, with their heads tucked under their wings. This chick slept with the goslings, and she tried mightily to stretch her neck under her wing. No doubt she had a permanent crick in her neck. 14

Then the fateful day came when the mother goose took her brood to the water for the first time. She jumped in, and the goslings leaped in after her. The chick stood on the bank, aghast. 15

For the next few days, mother and daughter tried to reason it out, each deeply   16
upset by the other's intransigence. After several days of barnyard trauma, the chick
underwent an identity crisis, nature triumphed over nurture, and she redefined
herself as a hen.

She moved across the barn to hang out with the chickens. At first she still slept   17
goose-like, and visited her "mother" and fellow goslings each day, but within two
months she no longer even acknowledged her stepmother and stepsiblings and
behaved just like other chickens.

Recollections like that make me wistful for a healthy rural America composed   18
of diverse family farms, which also offer decent and varied lives for the animals
themselves (at least when farm boys aren't conducting "scientific" experiments).
In contrast, a modern industrialized operation is a different world: more than
100,000 hens in cages, their beaks removed, without a rooster, without geese or
other animals, spewing out pollution and ending up as so-called food—a calorie
factory, without any soul.

READING CLOSELY

1. What main differences does Nicholas Kristof point to when comparing old-
   fashioned family farms with modern "food assembly lines" (6)? Are the differences significant? Why or why not?

2. Is Kristof fair in his characterization of "modern industrial agriculture" as soulless (1)? Why or why not?

3. Kristof concedes that industrialized farms are much more efficient than family
   farms (9). Instead of emphasizing their negative qualities, should he have tried
   to find other positive attributes to assign to big farms? Why or why not?

4. Kristof asks if his "nostalgia" for the old family farm is "like the blacksmith's
   grief over Henry Ford's assembly line" (9). Is it? Explain.

STRATEGIES AND STRUCTURES

1. What is Kristof's point in citing the EXAMPLE of Bob Bansen and his farm? Is it
   a good example? Why or why not?

2. How scientific is Kristof's comparison? Does it matter that he mostly tells anecdotes instead of citing Farm Bureau statistics? Why or why not?

3. According to Kristof (and the experts he cites), how is obesity CAUSED by "the
   transformation from family farms to industrial farming" (8). What other
   EFFECTS of the transformation does he refer to?

4. *Other Methods.* Why does Kristof end his essay with the story of the chick who thought it was a goose? How and how well does this little NARRATIVE support what he has to say about the value of the family farm?

THINKING ABOUT LANGUAGE

1. Why does Kristof tell the ANECDOTE of the sheep dog that dined on lamb?

2. What's the difference in meaning (if any) between *food for the soul* and *soul food*? How is Kristof playing on this verbal association?

3. What are the implications of "spewing" (18)? How does this verb tie in with the idea of a "calorie factory" (18)?

FOR WRITING

1. Write a paragraph or two describing a farm, large or small, that you have visited or lived on. Be sure to include details that capture the farm's physical characteristics, as well as your feelings toward it.

2. Write an essay comparing some aspect of modern agribusiness with more old-fashioned methods of food production. In addition to the disadvantages, if any, of the new methods, be sure to say what some of their advantages are.

BRUCE CATTON

Grant and Lee: A Study in Contrasts

Bruce Catton (1899–1978), grew up in Benzonia, Michigan, listening to the stories told by Union army veterans and reenacting the battles of the Civil War. After serving briefly in the U.S. Navy during World War I, Catton worked as a reporter until the outbreak of World War II, during which he served as director of information for the War Production Board. A founding editor of American Heritage magazine, he wrote many volumes about the Civil War, including A Stillness at Appomattox (1954), which won a Pulitzer Prize and a National Book Award. In 1976 Catton was honored with a Presidential Medal of Freedom as America's foremost historian of the Civil War.

"Grant and Lee: A Study in Contrasts" was first published in The American Story (1955), a collection of essays by leading historians. Catton compares the U.S. Civil War generals Ulysses S. Grant, who led the Union army, and Robert E. Lee, who led the forces of the Confederacy.

WHEN ULYSSES S. GRANT and Robert E. Lee met in the parlor of a modest house at Appomattox Court House, Virginia, on April 9, 1865, to work out the terms for the surrender of Lee's Army of Northern Virginia, a great chapter in American life came to a close, and a great new chapter began.

These men were bringing the Civil War[1] to its virtual finish. To be sure, other armies had yet to surrender, and for a few days the fugitive Confederate government would struggle desperately and vainly, trying to find some way to go on living now that its chief support was gone. But in effect it was all over when Grant and Lee signed the papers. And the little room where they wrote out the terms was the scene of one of the poignant, dramatic contrasts in American history.

They were two strong men, these oddly different generals, and they represented the strengths of two conflicting currents that, through them, had come into final collision.

---

1. *Civil War* (1861–1865): The war fought between those states and territories of the United States that remained loyal to the federal government in Washington under President Abraham Lincoln ("the Union") and the slave-holding Southern states that formed a separate government led by Jefferson Davis ("the Confederacy").

SUGGESTED MLA CITATION: Catton, Bruce. "Grant and Lee: A Study in Contrasts." 1955. *Back to the Lake.* Ed. Thomas Cooley. 2nd ed. New York: Norton, 2012. 307–11. Print.

Lee's surrender to Grant at Appomattox Court House, Virginia, on April 7, 1865, as depicted in a Currier and Ives lithograph.

Back of Robert E. Lee was the notion that the old aristocratic concept might   4
somehow survive and be dominant in American life.

Lee was tidewater Virginia,[2] and in his background were family, culture, and   5
tradition . . . the age of chivalry transplanted to a New World which was making
its own legends and its own myths. He embodied a way of life that had come down
through the age of knighthood and the English country squire. America was a land
that was beginning all over again, dedicated to nothing much more complicated
than the rather hazy belief that all men had equal rights and should have an equal
chance in the world. In such a land Lee stood for the feeling that it was somehow
of advantage to human society to have a pronounced inequality in the social structure. There should be a leisure class, backed by ownership of land; in turn, society
itself should be keyed to the land as the chief source of wealth and influence. It
would bring forth (according to this ideal) a class of men with a strong sense of
obligation to the community; men who lived not to gain advantage for themselves,
but to meet the solemn obligations which had been laid on them by the very fact that
they were privileged. From them the country would get its leadership; to them it
could look for the higher values—of thought, of conduct, of personal deportment—
to give it strength and virtue.

Lee embodied the noblest elements of this aristocratic ideal. Through him, the   6
landed nobility justified itself. For four years, the Southern states had fought a desperate war to uphold the ideals for which Lee stood. In the end, it almost seemed
as if the Confederacy fought for Lee; as if he himself was the Confederacy . . . the
best thing that the way of life for which the Confederacy stood could ever have to
offer. He had passed into legend before Appomattox. Thousands of tired, underfed,
poorly clothed Confederate soldiers, long since past the simple enthusiasm of the
early days of the struggle, somehow considered Lee the symbol of everything for
which they had been willing to die. But they could not quite put this feeling into
words. If the Lost Cause, sanctified by so much heroism and so many deaths, had a
living justification, its justification was General Lee.

Grant, the son of a tanner on the Western frontier, was everything Lee was not.   7
He had come up the hard way and embodied nothing in particular except the eternal toughness and sinewy fiber of the men who grew up beyond the mountains. He
was one of a body of men who owed reverence and obeisance to no one, who were
self-reliant to a fault, who cared hardly anything for the past but who had a sharp
eye for the future.

---

2. *Tidewater Virginia*: The coastal plain region of eastern Virginia where rivers flow inland from the
Chesapeake Bay, here synonymous with aristocracy and old families. The first English colony in North
America, Jamestown, settled in 1607, is in the Tidewater area.

These frontier men were the precise opposites of the tidewater aristocrats. Back   8
of them, in the great surge that had taken people over the Alleghenies[3] and into the
opening Western country, there was a deep, implicit dissatisfaction with a past
that had settled into grooves. They stood for democracy, not from any reasoned
conclusion about the proper ordering of human society, but simply because they
had grown up in the middle of democracy and knew how it worked. Their society
might have privileges, but they would be privileges each man had won for himself.
Forms and patterns meant nothing. No man was born to anything, except perhaps
to a chance to show how far he could rise. Life was competition.

Yet along with this feeling had come a deep sense of belonging to a national   9
community. The Westerner who developed a farm, opened a shop, or set up in
business as a trader, could hope to prosper only as his own community prospered—
and his community ran from the Atlantic to the Pacific and from Canada down to
Mexico. If the land was settled, with towns and highways and accessible markets,
he could better himself. He saw his fate in terms of the nation's own destiny. As its
horizons expanded, so did his. He had, in other words, an acute dollars-and-cents
stake in the continued growth and development of his country.

And that, perhaps, is where the contrast between Grant and Lee becomes most   10
striking. The Virginia aristocrat, inevitably, saw himself in relation to his own
region. He lived in a static society which could endure almost anything except
change. Instinctively, his first loyalty would go to the locality in which that society
existed. He would fight to the limit of endurance to defend it, because in defending
it he was defending everything that gave his own life its deepest meaning.

The Westerner, on the other hand, would fight with an equal tenacity for the   11
broader concept of society. He fought so because everything he lived by was tied to
growth, expansion, and a constantly widening horizon. What he lived by would
survive or fall with the nation itself. He could not possibly stand by unmoved in
the face of an attempt to destroy the Union. He would combat it with everything
he had, because he could only see it as an effort to cut the ground out from under
his feet.

So Grant and Lee were in complete contrast, representing two diametrically   12
opposed elements in American life. Grant was the modern man emerging; beyond
him, ready to come on the stage, was the great age of steel and machinery, of
crowded cities and a restless burgeoning vitality. Lee might have ridden down from
the old age of chivalry, lance in hand, silken banner fluttering over his head. Each
man was the perfect champion of his cause, drawing both his strengths and his
weaknesses from the people he led.

3. *Alleghenies*: The Allegheny Mountains, which run from northern Pennsylvania to southwestern
Virginia.

Yet it was not all contrast, after all. Different as they were—in background, in 13
personality, in underlying aspiration—these two great soldiers had much in common. Under everything else, they were marvelous fighters. Furthermore, their
fighting qualities were really very much alike.

Each man had, to begin with, the great virtue of utter tenacity and fidelity. 14
Grant fought his way down the Mississippi Valley in spite of acute personal discouragement and profound military handicaps. Lee hung on in
the trenches at Petersburg after hope itself had died. In each man there
was an indomitable quality . . . the born fighter's refusal to give up as
long as he can still remain on his feet and lift his two fists.

> For winding up a comparison, the point-by-point method (p. 274) can be especially useful.

Daring and resourcefulness they had, too; the ability to think faster and move 15
faster than the enemy. These were the qualities which gave Lee the dazzling campaigns of Second Manassas and Chancellorsville and won Vicksburg for Grant.

Lastly, and perhaps greatest of all, there was the ability, at the end, to turn 16
quickly from war to peace once the fighting was over. Out of the way these two
men behaved at Appomattox came the possibility of a peace of reconciliation. It
was a possibility not wholly realized, in the years to come, but which did, in the
end, help the two sections to become one nation again . . . after a war whose bitterness might have seemed to make such a reunion wholly impossible. No part of
either man's life became him more than the part he played in this brief meeting in
the McLean house at Appomattox. Their behavior there put all succeeding generations of Americans in their debt. Two great Americans, Grant and Lee—very different, yet under everything very much alike. Their encounter at Appomattox was
one of the great moments of American history.

✳ ⟋

READING CLOSELY

1. According to Bruce Catton, Grant and Lee represented two distinct "currents"
   in American life and history (3). What were those currents, and what contrasting qualities and ideals does Catton associate with each man?

2. Even though they were "in complete contrast," says Catton, Grant and Lee also
   "had much in common" (12, 13). In what ways were the two men alike?

3. Although Grant and Lee were both "great Americans," as Catton says, they were
   deadly enemies. Why did each man take the side he did?

4. Why, according to Catton, are all future generations of Americans "in their
   debt" (16)? Do you agree? Why or why not?

STRATEGIES AND STRUCTURES

1. On what basis is Catton comparing his two subjects? Where does he tell the reader what that basis of comparison is?

2. Why does Catton emphasize the differences between the two men he is comparing? For what audience and purpose is he drawing such a strong contrast?

3. Catton uses the subject-by-subject method through most of his essay. When and why does he switch to the point-by-point method?

4. *Other Methods.* Besides comparing and contrasting the two generals, Catton's study also analyzes the CAUSES AND EFFECTS of the American Civil War. How does this analysis support and clarify his comparison?

THINKING ABOUT LANGUAGE

1. What view of history—and Grant's and Lee's roles in it—is suggested by Catton's use of METAPHORS from the theater in paragraphs 2 and 16?

2. Why do you think Catton capitalizes "Lost Cause" in paragraph 6?

3. "Obeisance" (7) means homage of the sort paid to a king. Why might Catton choose this term instead of *obedience* when describing General Grant?

4. What are the CONNOTATIONS of "sinewy fiber" (7), and how does Catton's general DESCRIPTION of Grant justify the use of this phrase?

FOR WRITING

1. Make an outline of the key points you would make in a comparison and contrast of two famous generals, great athletes, favorite aunts, or other people.

2. Write an essay comparing and contrasting two present-day public figures—for example, two U.S. presidents—whose actions, you feel, will put all succeeding generations of Americans in their debt.

WILLIAM SHAKESPEARE

Sonnet 130

William Shakespeare (1554–1616) is not only English literature's greatest dramatist but also one of its greatest poets. Plays performed on the Elizabethan stage were rich with poetry for both practical reasons (there were few elaborate sets or special effects, so a play's setting had to be conjured almost entirely through words) and reasons of convention (audiences expected poetry, not realistic dialogue). Shakespeare's reputation as a great poet would be assured even if he had written nothing but dramas.

In 1592, however, an outbreak of plague led authorities to close the theaters for two years, and the playwright turned to the composition of verse narratives. In 1609 the first edition of Shakespeare's sonnets was published. These sonnets were immediately recognized—and have been regarded ever since—as supreme expressions of the sonnet form. Sonnet 130 is about two ways of drawing comparisons.

My mistress' eyes are nothing like the sun;　　　　　　　　　　1
Coral is far more red, than her lips red:
If snow be white, why then her breasts are dun;
If hairs be wires, black wires grow on her head.
I have seen roses damasked, red and white,　　　　　　　　　　5
But no such roses see I in her cheeks;
And in some perfumes is there more delight
Than in the breath that from my mistress reeks.
I love to hear her speak, yet well I know
That music hath a far more pleasing sound:　　　　　　　　　　10
I grant I never saw a goddess go,
My mistress, when she walks, treads on the ground:
And yet by heaven, I think my love as rare,
As any she belied with false compare.

SUGGESTED MLA CITATION: Shakespeare, William. "Sonnet 130." 1609. *Back to the Lake.* Ed. Thomas Cooley. 2nd ed. New York: Norton, 2012. 313. Print.

Reading Closely

1. The speaker of Shakespeare's poem can find no similarities between the bright-
   ness of his lady's eyes and that of the sun, or the color of her cheeks and the
   pink (damask), white, or red of the rose. Why not?

2. What kind of lover *would* make such comparisons?

3. What is Shakespeare's speaker assuming about the character of his "mistress"
   and what will please her (1)? Explain.

Strategies and Structures

1. Who, do you suppose, is the intended AUDIENCE for Shakespeare's love poem: a
   particular lady, ladies in general, or readers of traditional love poetry, whether
   male or female? Some combination of these? Why do you think so?

2. Shakespeare's poem emphasizes the differences between the lady and the lovely
   things to which he compares her. What is his purpose in avoiding the extravagant praise found in so many love poems of the period?

3. The English (or Shakespearean) sonnet consists of three quatrains followed by a
   couplet. Each group of four lines presents a different aspect of a subject, and the
   final two lines tie the whole together in some way. If the first four lines of Sonnet 130 deal with various sights, what is compared in lines 5–8? Lines 9–12?

4. How (and how well) do the final two lines of Shakespeare's poem resolve the
   tension generated by the rest of the comparison? Explain.

5. *Other Methods.* The woman in Sonnet 130 appears in many other Shakespearean
   sonnets, where she is known as "the dark lady." How does the DESCRIPTION of
   her in this poem fit this general characterization?

Thinking about Language

1. Besides signifying general drabness, "dun" (3) is a mousey brown color. Is
   Shakespeare saying that the lady's skin is this color, or is he countering one
   HYPERBOLE with another? Explain.

2. To the reader of Shakespeare's day, "wires" (4) would have called to mind fine
   threads of beaten gold used in jewelry or embroidery. What is supposed to be
   shocking here is the color of the lady's hair. Why?

3. The meaning of "reeks" has changed since Shakespeare's time (8). Originally,
   the word meant "to emit smoke" rather than "to stink." How does this meaning
   fit in with Shakespeare's description, especially in line 12, of the lady as a down-
   to-earth creature?

FOR WRITING

1. In line 14, "any she" may mean "any woman." With this in mind, translate the last two lines of Shakespeare's poem into modern English.

2. Write a paragraph summarizing the main points of comparison that Shakespeare makes in Sonnet 130.

CHAPTER 9

Classification

You can divide your whole life into two basic categories. You're either staying in or going out. —JERRY SEINFELD, *Seinlanguage*

Let's say you live near the coast of Florida or Louisiana or the Carolinas, and you have just survived a hurricane. The power is back on; so is the water. The roof, however, is not. What kind of roof did you have? Which kinds held up well in the storm? What kind should you put back on your house? These are all questions of classification.

Defining Classification:
Breaking a Subject into Categories

When you DESCRIBE something, you say what its characteristics are: "My old roof was a tasteful gray with green ridge caps." Classification is concerned with characteristics, too: "This is not my roof in your front yard. This is a metal roof, the kind they have across the lake. My roof was tile." When you classify something (a roof, an aquatic mammal, someone's personality), however, you say what category it belongs to—metal, asphalt, tile; dolphin, manatee, whale; introverted, extroverted—based on the characteristics of each category. There are basically two ways to classify.

When we classify individuals, we sort them into groups: this dog is a hound, that one is a terrier. When we classify groups—dogs, bicycles—we divide them into subgroups—hounds, terriers, retrievers; street bikes, mountain bikes, racing bikes. In this chapter, we will learn what constitutes a category (or significant group), how to devise a valid classification system, and how to use that system to construct an essay. We'll also review the critical points to watch for as you read over and revise your essay, as well as common errors to avoid as you edit. We will use the term *classification* to refer to both sorting and dividing, since, in either case, we are always going to be organizing a subject into categories.

Why Do We Classify?

We classify things in order to choose the kinds that best meet our needs. The hurricane was a direct hit, and neither tile nor asphalt roofs stood up well. What other kinds are there, and which kind is most likely to survive the next high wind?

Choosing among similar kinds of objects or ideas is only one reason for using classification in our thinking and writing, however. We classify people and things for many purposes: to evaluate (good dog, bad dog); to determine causes (mechanical failure, weather, or pilot error?); to conduct experiments (test group, control group), and to measure results (winners, losers, and runners-up).

We also classify in order to make sense of the world, grouping individuals according to the common traits that tell us the most about them. Consider the duckbill platypus. Even though it has a bill and lays eggs, biologists classify the platypus as a mammal with birdlike characteristics rather than a bird with mammalian ones. Why?

It's not simply that the platypus has mostly mammalian traits, such as hair, milk glands, and a neocortex region in the brain. Among all living mammals, only the platypus and the spiny anteater retain a few of the birdlike characteristics once common to many mammals. That these creatures are in a class by themselves tells us that, far from being a bird, the platypus simply branched off early from the family tree, before other mammals lost those traits in the course of evolution.

So if you're ever inclined to think of classification systems as mere catalogues, remember the platypus. By accurately classifying this strange mammal and other apparent anomalies, we can discover not only where each one belongs in the scheme of things, we can learn more about the basis of the natural order itself.

Composing a Classification Essay

Classification is a way of ordering the world—and of organizing a piece of writing, from a shopping list to an essay or even a whole book. In this chapter we will focus on how to use classification to organize an essay.

Whether you are writing about animals, people, machines, movies, or political movements, the first step in composing a classification essay is to divide your subject into appropriate categories. Those categories will be determined by the various attributes of your subject, of course; but they will also depend on your PRINCIPLE OF CLASSIFICATION—the basis on which you are classifying your subject. Dogs, for example, are usually classified on the basis of breed or size. If you're classifying dogs by size, your categories might be standard, miniature, and toy. But if breed is your principle of classification, then your categories would be golden retriever, greyhound, poodle, Irish setter, and so on.

Thinking about Purpose and Audience

In order to classify anything accurately, you have to examine all its important attributes. The specific traits you focus on and the categories you divide your subject into, however, will be determined largely by your purpose and audience. Consider the example of the roof that blew off in a hurricane. If your purpose is to determine—and write an article for your neighborhood newsletter explaining—what kind of roof will stay on best in the next hurricane, you're going to look closely at such traits as weight and wind resistance. And you are going to pay less attention to other traits, such as color or energy efficiency or even cost, that you might consider more closely if you had a different purpose in mind.

Once you've determined which kind of roof has the highest wind rating, you probably are not going to have a hard time convincing these readers (many of whom also lost their roofs) that this is the kind to buy. They may expect you to prove that the kind you are recommending does in fact have the characteristics you claim for it (superior resistance to wind), but they are not likely to question the importance of those characteristics or the validity of focusing on them in your article. However, since your audience of homeowners may not be experts in roofing materials, you'll want to make sure you define any technical terms and use language they'll be familiar with. You won't always be able to assume that your readers will appreciate the way you choose to classify a subject, however. So be prepared to explain why your audience should accept the criteria you use to classify your subject and the weight you place on particular attributes.

Amy Tan (p. 345) found this out, she says, when her reader was her mother.

Generating Ideas: Considering What Kinds There Are

Classifying can be intellectually demanding work, as it was for the man who was hired by the hour to sort a bushel of apples into green, ripe, and rotten. After an hour and a half went by and the man had only two puny piles to show for his labor, his employer asked why he was so slow. The man shook his head and replied, "It's the decisions."

There are many techniques you can use—CLUSTERING, LOOPING, LISTING, and more—to help you decide what subject you want to classify and why. Once you have a subject in mind and a reason for classifying it—you're in an apple orchard and you're hungry—the next decision you need to consider is what kinds there are. Then you can choose the ones that best suit your PURPOSE and AUDIENCE.

Why tell a bald-faced lie when there are so many other kinds to choose from (p. 336)?

Let's say your subject is movies. Movies can be classified by genre—drama, comedy, romance, horror, thriller, musical. This might be a good classification system to use if you are analyzing movies for a film course. For the purpose of reviewing movies for a campus audience, however, a different set of categories would be more appropriate.

If you are reviewing movies in the school newspaper, your principle of classification would be their quality, and you would divide them into, say, five categories: "must see," "excellent," "good," "mediocre," and "to be avoided at all costs." If you were reviewing some of those same movies for a parenting magazine, however, you might use different categories: "good for all ages," "preschool," "six and up," and "not suitable for children."

When you're coming up with categories for a classification essay, again make sure your categories are appropriate to your purpose and audience.

Organizing and Drafting a Classification Essay

The backbone of a classification essay is the system you create by dividing your subject into categories that interest your readers and that are directly relevant to the point you're making. Those categories should deal with significant aspects of your subject and should be inclusive without overlapping. Also think about including visuals, and about other methods of development you might want to use in addition to classification. The templates on page 320 can help you get started.

ORGANIZING A CLASSIFICATION ESSAY

In the opening paragraphs of your essay, tell the reader what you're classifying and why, and explain your classification system, because the rest of your essay will be organized around that system. If you were writing an essay classifying bicycles, for example, something like this might make a good introduction:

> If you are buying or renting a bicycle, you need to know which features to look for in order to meet your needs. Bikes can best be divided into the following categories: mountain bikes, racing bikes, messenger bikes, touring bikes, and stunt bikes. If you understand these six basic types and the differences among them, you can make an informed decision, whether you're choosing a bicycle for a lifetime or just for the afternoon.

TEMPLATES FOR DRAFTING

When you begin to draft a classification essay, you need to identify your subject and explain the basis on which you're classifying it—moves fundamental to any classification. See how Deborah Tannen makes such moves in the beginning of her essay in this chapter:

> Unfortunately, men and women often have different ideas about what's appropriate, different ways of speaking. . . . Here [are] the biggest areas of miscommunication.
> —DEBORAH TANNEN, "But What Do You Mean?"

Tannen identifies her subject ("areas of miscommunication") and explains the basis on which she's classifying them (differences between men and women). Here is one more example from this chapter:

> Language is the tool of my trade. And I use them all—all the Englishes I grew up with. —AMY TAN, "Mother Tongue"

The following templates can help you make some of these basic moves in your own writing. But don't take these as formulas where you just fill in the blanks. There are no shortcuts to good writing, but these templates can serve as starting points.

▶ X can be classified on the basis of _____.

▶ Classified on the basis of _____, some of the most common types of X are _____, _____, and _____.

▶ X can be divided into two basic types, _____ or _____.

▶ Experts in the field typically divide X into _____, _____, and _____.

▶ Some other, less common types of X are _____, _____, and _____.

▶ This particular X clearly belongs in the _____ categeory, since it is _____, _____, and _____.

▶ _____, _____, and _____ are examples of this type of X.

▶ By classifying X in this way, we can see _____.

Not only does an introduction like this tell the reader what you're classifying and why, it provides a solid outline for organizing the rest of your essay.

Typically, the body of a classification essay is devoted to a point-by-point discussion of each of the categories that make up your classification system. Thus if you are classifying bicycles into mountain bikes, racing bikes, messenger bikes, touring bikes, and stunt bikes, you would spend a paragraph, or at least several sentences, explaining the most important characteristics of each type. Depending upon the complexity of your subject, there will be more or fewer categories to explain; but remember that you must have at least two categories—vertebrates and invertebrates, good movies and bad movies—if you are to have a viable classification system.

Once you've laid out, in some detail, the categories that make up your classification system, remind the reader what your principle of classification is, and what point you are making by classifying your subject this way. The point of classifying bicycles by function, for example, is to inform the reader what categories of bicycles exist and which type is best suited to the reader's needs—climbing mountains, racing, delivering packages, doing tricks, or just cruising around.

> Erin McKean classifies words by function (p. 359) to show how easily they can be "verbed."

STATING YOUR POINT

Classification isn't an end in itself, but a way of relating objects and ideas to each other within an orderly framework. So when you compose a classification essay, ask yourself not only what categories your subject can be divided into, but also what you can learn about that subject by classifying it in that way. Then tell the reader in a THESIS statement what your main point is and why you're dividing up your subject as you do. Usually, you'll want to state your main point in the introduction of your essay as you explain your classification system. Occasionally, your thesis statement may not come until the end, after you've thoroughly explained how your classification system works.

Let's look at a classification essay in which the point of the classification is not obvious. Here is the main introductory paragraph:

> I have moved more often than I care to remember. However, one thing always stays the same no matter where I have been. There is always a house next door, and that house contains neighbors. Over time, I have begun putting my neighbors into one of four categories: too friendly, unsociable, irritable, and just right.   —JONATHAN R. GOULD JR., "The People Next Door"

Having introduced his subject and outlined his four-part classification system at the beginning of his essay, Gould devotes a paragraph to each of the four categories, taking them in order and looking at particular neighbors who fit each one—the "overly friendly" neighbor who had to be told that his house was on fire "in an attempt to make him leave," the "unsociable" neighbor who looked at the fresh-baked apple pie offered by Gould's wife "as if she intended to poison them," and so on. But what is Gould's point in classifying his neighbors according to this scheme?

In addition to making us smile, Gould's point is to make an observation about human nature. Here's the last paragraph of his essay:

> I have always felt it was important to identify the types of neighbors that were around me. Then I am better able to maintain a clear perspective on our relationship and understand their needs. After all, people do not really change; we just learn how to live with both the good and the bad aspects of their behavior.

Gould could have explained his point at the beginning of his essay, but he chose to build up to it instead. In a humorous essay, this can be an effective strategy—part of the fun is wondering where the game is headed and how it's going to end. When you have a more serious purpose in mind, however, you're better off making your main point clear in the beginning of your essay and then, in the conclusion, saying how what you've just written proves that point.

"We don't really care about diversity," says David Brooks in his first paragraph (p.352).

CHOOSING SIGNIFICANT CHARACTERISTICS

Whatever your purpose is, base your categories on the most significant characteristics of your subject—ones that explain something important about it. All neighbors, for example, have at least one thing in common: they are people who live nearby. This trait, however, doesn't tell us much about them. Proximity may be an essential trait in DEFINING neighbors, but it is not a very useful characteristic for classifying them. For the same reason, you probably would not discuss such attributes as color or decoration when classifying bicycles. Whether a bicycle is blue with red racing stripes or red with blue stripes may be important aesthetically, but these attributes do not tell the reader what kind it is, since all different kinds of bicycles come in all different colors. Color, in other words, while important for classifying wine and laundry, isn't significant when it comes to bicycles. So as you choose your categories, make sure they're based on significant characteristics that actually help the reader to distinguish one type from another.

With bicycles, these would be such attributes as weight, strength, configuration of the handlebars, and thickness of the tires. Thick, knobby tires, heavy frames, and strong cross-braced handlebars that protect the rider from sudden jolts are significant characteristics of mountain bikes. Thin, smooth tires, lightweight frames, and dropped handlebars that put the rider in a more streamlined position are typical of racing bikes. Wide but relatively smooth tires, raised (but not cross-braced) handlebars, and sturdy, medium-weight frames—not to mention large padded seats—indicate touring bikes. And so on.

Citing significant characteristics is even more essential when you have a two-part classification system, also called a binary system. A binary system has the advantage of being very inclusive. All people can be divided into the living and the dead, for instance. Binary classification systems, however, potentially sacrifice depth for breadth. That is, you can use a binary system to classify a lot of people or things, but it may not necessarily tell the reader much about them. Pointing out that Shakespeare, for example, belongs in the "dead" category doesn't tell readers nearly as much about him as explaining that he was a playwright, a poet, and an actor.

> Deborah Tannen (p. 363) uses a binary system: male and female.

CHOOSING CATEGORIES THAT ARE INCLUSIVE AND DON'T OVERLAP

Not only must you divide your subject into categories that are truly distinctive, those categories must be inclusive enough to cover most cases. And they must not overlap.

Classifying ice cream into chocolate and vanilla alone isn't very useful because this system leaves out several other important kinds, such as strawberry, pistachio, and rum raisin. The categories in a good classification system include all kinds: for instance, no-fat, low-fat, and full-fat ice cream. And they should not overlap. Thus, chocolate, vanilla, homemade, and Ben and Jerry's do not make a good classification system because the same scoop of ice cream could fit into more than one category.

BREAKING CATEGORIES INTO SUBCATEGORIES

The categories in a classification essay should be broadly inclusive; but if your categories start to become too broad to be useful, try dividing them into narrower subcategories. Suppose you were drafting an essay on the Great Depression of the 1930s for a history class, and you were focusing on "tramps," the itinerant men (and occasionally women) who took to the road—especially the railroads—in search of food and work. In the lingo of the day, those tramps who begged, you would point out, were classified as "dings," and those who worked for a living were called "working stiffs." A third kind, who neither begged nor worked, were called "nose divers."

"Nose divers" designated a relatively narrow category of tramp—those who attended church and worshipped or prayed ("nose dived") in order to partake of meals and beds provided by the church. "Working stiffs," on the other hand, could get their living by almost any means; and to classify them accurately, you would need to divide this broad, general kind into subtypes—harvest tramp, tramp miner, fruit tramp, construction tramp, and sea tramp. Your essay would then go on to specify the chief characteristics of each of these narrower categories.

USING VISUALS

If you are dealing with multiple categories, consider including illustrations in your essay. Statistical graphics, such as bar graphs, allow readers to grasp complex classification systems at a glance. The one below, based on data from the Bureau of Labor Statistics, classifies ten different occupations according to their projected rates of growth over a ten-year period. Which occupations will grow the fastest between 2008 and 2018? By what percentages will their numbers increase? Which occupations will grow at a lesser rate? How much will a particular occupation—physician assistants, for example—grow in relation to other occupations? Sometimes, questions like these are best answered by presenting your data visually.

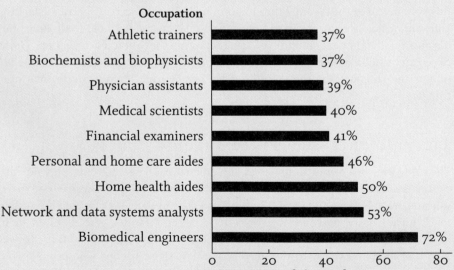

FASTEST-GROWING OCCUPATIONS (PROJECTED), 2008–2018

Data from Bureau of Labor Statistics, U.S. Department of Labor, 2009.

USING OTHER METHODS

DEFINITION can be especially useful when you classify something because you will need to define your categories (and any subcategories) according to their distinguishing characteristics. You will also need to DESCRIBE those characteristics. Sometimes you may have reason to analyze the CAUSES of certain characteristics, or what EFFECTS they may have. The author of the following passage uses all three methods (and more) to classify the ailments of horses confined to their stalls:

> In his natural state the horse is a range animal. If he cannot roam a reasonable territory, he may express his frustration by developing some unpleasant or even health-threatening habits. Chewing on fences or stall boards may be followed by cribbing and wind-sucking, vices in which the horse bites down on a hard surface and swallows air at the same time, to the accompaniment of little grunts. (Some will argue that cribbing is a genetically acquired habit, but it is rarely seen in a horse at liberty.)
>
> Further, a continually stabled horse may become a weaver, swaying from side to side in a restless, compulsive pattern. To me, this is as sad a scenario as watching a caged tiger pace back and forth behind bars. Cribbers and weavers, for obvious reasons, frequently develop digestive problems. The message is clear, then: as much turnout for as many hours as possible.   —MAXINE KUMIN, *Women, Animals, and Vegetables*

In this passage, Kumin classifies overly confined horses as cribbers and weavers. Defining the behaviors of both kinds as "unpleasant or even health-threatening habits," she then describes the characteristics that distinguish each kind: the cribber "bites down on a hard surface and swallows air at the same time," whereas the weaver sways "from side to side in a restless, compulsive pattern."

Kumin is so concerned about the welfare of overly confined horses, however, that she does more than simply classify, define, and describe their ailments. She analyzes the cause of those ailments and ARGUES for a particular remedy. Cribbing and weaving are not genetic conditions, says Kumin; they are acquired behaviors caused by the confinement itself. Her point, therefore, is clear: horse owners should let their animals range more freely, instead of confining them to the stable.

Reading a Classification Essay with a Critical Eye

The most important part of any classification essay is the classification system itself. Does yours have one? How many categories does it include? What are they? Once you've drafted your essay, ask someone else to read your draft and tell you how well your classification system supports your point—and how it might be improved. Should any categories be redefined or omitted? Should any new ones be added? Here are some questions to keep in mind when checking a classification.

PURPOSE AND AUDIENCE. Is there a good reason for classifying this particular subject this way? Who is the intended audience of the essay? Does the essay give sufficient background information for the audience to understand (and accept) the proposed classification? Are key terms defined, especially ones that might be unfamiliar to some readers?

THE POINT. Is the main point of the essay clearly laid out in a THESIS statement? How and how well does the classification itself support the main point?

THE CLASSIFICATION SYSTEM AND THE CATEGORIES. Is the classification system appropriate for the subject and purpose of the essay? What is the PRINCIPLE OF CLASSIFICATION? Should that principle be revised in any way? If so, how? Do the categories suit the essay's purpose and audience?

SIGNIFICANT CHARACTERISTICS. Do the characteristics that make up the categories tell the reader something important about the subject? Does the essay demonstrate that the things being classified actually have these characteristics?

INCLUSIVE CATEGORIES. Do the categories include most cases? If not, what new categories need to be added in order to make the classification system complete?

OVERLAPPING CATEGORIES. Can any individual item fit into more than one of the categories that make up the classification system? If so, how might the principle of classification be revised so they don't overlap?

SUBCATEGORIES. Would any of the basic categories that make up the classification system be clearer or easier to explain if they were divided into subgroups?

VISUALS. Would a graph, diagram, or other illustration make the categories easier to understand?

OTHER METHODS. Does the essay use other methods of development? For instance, does it clearly DEFINE all the basic categories and subcategories? Does it fully DESCRIBE the distinctive attributes of each category? Does it analyze what CAUSED those attributes, or what EFFECTS they might have? Does it make an ARGUMENT?

Editing for Common Errors in a Classification Essay

Classification invites problems with listing groups or attributes. Here are some tips for checking your writing for these errors—and editing any that you find.

If you've listed categories in a single sentence, make sure they are parallel in form

▸ A horse can be nervous, aggressive, or calm~~ly accept a saddle~~.

▸ Some say work can be divided into two categories. We're either working too hard or ~~it's a waste of~~ <u>wasting</u> time.

Check that adjectives are in the following order: size, age, color

Adjectives identify characteristics, so you'll probably use at least some adjectives when you write a classification essay.

▸ <u>big,</u> old brown ~~big~~ boots

Student Example

Michelle Watson was a student at Roane State Community College in eastern Tennessee when she wrote this classification essay for an English class. "Shades of Character" is based on Watson's research in child psychology and education, particularly her study of typical childhood personalities. Watson's instructor, Jennifer Jordan-Henley, chose the essay for publication on the website of the college's Online Writing Lab.

Citing the work of several experts, Watson classifies children's personalities according to commonly recognized types. This classification system provides a framework for organizing the entire essay, which discusses each type in turn, paying close attention to the significant attributes that distinguish one "shade" of behavior from another. Watson documents her sources using the MLA style.

Shades of Character

Anyone who has spent time around children will notice that each [1] one has a special personality all his or her own. Children, like adults, have different traits that make up their personalities. Experts have researched these traits in detail, and they classify children into different categories. Some experts have named more than three categories, but Dr. Peter L. Mangione[1] has chosen three that most experts agree with. These categories are "flexible," "fearful," and "feisty." Children generally may have similar interests, but the way they interact and deal with these interests displays their personality types.

The flexible personality is the most common of the three types. [2] About "forty percent of all children fall into the flexible or easy group" (Mangione). These children usually handle feelings of anger and disappointment by becoming only mildly upset. This does not mean that they do not feel mad or disappointed, they just choose to react mildly. These actions mean the flexible child is easy to take care of and be around. According to Mangione, such children usually "adapt to new situations and activities quickly, are toilet-trained easily, and are generally cheerful." Flexible children are subtle in their need for attention. Instead of yelling and demanding it, they will slowly and politely let their caregivers know about the need. If they do not get the attention right away, they "seldom make a fuss." They patiently wait, but they still make it known that they need the attention. These children also are easygoing, so routines like feeding and napping are regular (Mangione).

Flexible children may be referred to as "good as gold" because of [3] their cheerful attitudes. Since these are well-behaved children, the

---

Classification system is made up of three personality types determined by experts

Explains the PRINCIPLE OF CLASSIFICATION for the categories

Watson devotes two paragraphs to each category; ¶2 & 3 explain the significant characteristics of "flexible" children

Suggests the PURPOSE for classifying children (to aid in their care)

---

1. *Dr. Peter L. Mangione*: A child psychologist and codirector of the Center for Child and Family Studies in Sausalito, California. He is the content developer and writer of the video *Flexible, Fearful, or Feisty: The Different Temperaments of Infants and Toddlers* (1990), produced by the California Department of Education. All quotations from Dr. Mangione are from this video.

caregiver needs to make sure the child is getting the attention he or she needs. The caregiver should "check in with the flexible child from time to time" (Mangione). By checking in with the child regularly, the caregiver will be more knowledgeable about when the child needs attention and when he or she does not.

The next temperament is the fearful type. These are the more quiet and shy children. This kind makes up about 15 percent of all children, according to Mangione. They adapt slowly to new environments and take longer than flexible children when warming up to things. When presented with a new environment, fearful children often cling to something or someone familiar, whether it be the main caregiver or a material object such as a blanket. The fearful child will cling until he or she feels comfortable with the new situation. This can result in a deep attachment of the child to a particular caregiver or object. Fearful children may also withdraw when pushed into a new situation too quickly (Mangione). They may also withdraw when other children are jumping into a new project or situation they are not comfortable with. These children may tend to play alone rather than with a group.

In dealing with fearful children, caregivers find they need more attention than flexible children. A good technique for helping these children is having "a sequence of being with, talking to, stepping back, remaining available, and moving on" (Mangione). The caregiver can also help fearful children by giving them "extra soothing combined with an inch-by-inch fostering of independence and assertiveness" (Viorst 174). One of the most effective techniques is just taking everything slowly and helping the child to become more comfortable with his or her surroundings.

The third temperament type is called feisty. About "ten percent" of children fit into this category (Mangione). Feisty children express their opinions in a very intense way. Whether they are happy or mad, everyone around them will know how they feel. These children remain active most of the time, and this causes them to be very

4

Significant characteristics of "fearful" children explained in ¶4 & 5

5

6

By including percentages, Watson shows how little her categories overlap and how inclusive they are, since the categories cover in total about 65% of the population

aggressive. Feisty children often have a tendency toward "negative persistence" and will go "on and on nagging, whining and negotiating" if there is something they particularly want ("Facts About Temperament"). Unlike flexible children, feisty children are irregular in their napping and feeding times, but they do not adapt well to changes in their routines. They get "used to things and won't give them up" ("Facts About Temperament"). Anything out of the ordinary can send them into a fit. If these children are not warned of a change, they may react very negatively (Mangione). Feisty children also tend to be very sensitive to their surrounding environment. As a result, they may have strong reactions to their surroundings.

Significant characteristics of "feisty" children explained in ¶6 & 7

When dealing with feisty children, the caregiver should know   7
strategies that receive positive results when different situations arise. Mangione supports the "redirection technique" to calm feisty children. This method helps when the child is reacting very negatively to a situation. According to Mangione, to properly implement the redirection technique, the caregiver should

> begin by recognizing and empathizing with the feelings of the feisty child and placing firm limits on any unacceptable behavior. This response lets the child know that both his or her desire for the toy and feelings of anger when denied the toy are acceptable to the caregiver. At the same time, the caregiver should clearly communicate to the child that expressing anger through hurtful or disruptive behavior is not acceptable. The child will probably need time to experience his or her emotions and settle down. Then offer an alternative toy or activity that may interest the child, who is then given time to consider the new choice and to accept or reject it.

Caregivers should consider that these children generally do not have regular feeding and napping times. The caregiver should be flexible when working with these children and should try to conform more to the desires of the child (Mangione). If there is going to be a change in a child's routine, the caregiver has an easier time when the child has been warned of the change.

Generally speaking, children can be divided into three groups, but caregivers must not forget that each child is an individual. Children may have the traits of all three of the personality groups, but they are categorized into the one they are most like. Whatever their temperament, children need to be treated according to their individual needs. When these needs are met appropriately the child will be happier, and those around the child will feel better also. Knowing the general personality types and how to react to them will help to make the caregiver's job much easier and aid in the relief of unnecessary stress.

8   Conclusion reiterates the categories and ends with a THESIS statement explaining why it's helpful to classify children this way

Works Cited

"Facts About Temperament." *Australian Temperament Project*. Australian Temperament Project, n.d. Web. 25 Oct. 2000.

Mangione, Peter L., cont. dev./writ. *Flexible, Fearful, or Feisty: The Different Temperaments of Infants and Toddlers*. Prod. J. Ronald Lally. Cont. dev. S. Signer and J. Ronald Lally. Dir. Janet Poole. Media Services Unit, California Dept. of Education, 1990. Videocassette.

Viorst, Judith. "Is Your Child's Personality Set at Birth?" *Redbook* Nov. 1995: 174+. *Academic OneFile*. Web. 23 Oct. 2000.

Analyzing a Student Classification

In "Shades of Character," Michele Watson draws upon rhetorical strategies and techniques that good writers use all the time when they classify things. The following questions, in addition to focusing on particular aspects of Watson's text, will help you to identify those common strategies and techniques so you can adapt them to your own writing. These questions will also help to prepare you for the analytical questions—on content, structure, and language—that you'll find after all the other selections in this chapter, along with suggestions for writing on related topics.

READING CLOSELY

1. According to Michelle Watson, experts in child psychology agree on at least three basic types when classifying the personalities of young children: "flexible," "fearful," and "feisty" (1). What are the main characteristics of each type?

2. If every child has "a special personality all his or her own," how is it that Watson and the experts she cites can group them into personality types (1)? Explain.

3. "Feisty children," says Watson, "express their opinions in a very intense way" (6). What specific techniques does she offer for dealing with such children?

STRATEGIES AND STRUCTURES

1. Watson not only identifies "the general personality types" of young children; she explains "how to react to them" (8). Why? Who is her intended audience, and what is her main point in classifying infants and toddlers as she does?

2. Watson lays out her classification system in the opening paragraph of her essay. What is her principle of classification? Why does she use this principle instead of classifying by sex, height, weight, or some other physical characteristic?

3. In what order does Watson present the personality types in her classification system? Is this arrangement logical? Why or why not?

4. How significant are the characteristics that Watson uses to define her three personality types? Does she always describe the same kind of behavior, such as how a child reacts to objects, when defining each type? Should she? Explain.

5. *Other Methods.* In the conclusion of her essay, Watson reminds the reader that "children can be divided into three groups" (8). What ARGUMENT is she also making here? How and how well does her classification of children support that argument?

THINKING ABOUT LANGUAGE

1. What are the CONNOTATIONS of "feisty" (1)? What other terms might experts have chosen for this personality type, and why do you think they settled on this one?

2. Watson speaks of *caregivers* throughout her essay. Why do you think she uses this term instead of *parents* or *family members*?

3. How would you DEFINE "negative persistence" (6)?

FOR WRITING

1. Which of Watson's three personality types were you as a child? Write a paragraph using your early behavior as an EXAMPLE of the type.

2. Using the three-part system that Watson discusses, write an essay classifying you and your siblings, or several other children you have known, into each of the various types. Be sure to explain your purpose in classifying them this way.

A Classic Movie Poster

When we classify something, we divide it into different categories based on the distinguishing features of each category. Italian pasta, for example, can be divided into different types—spaghetti, fettuccine, lasagna, and so on—based on its thickness, shape, and other characteristics. Or take movies. Movies can be classified according to setting, characters, costumes, and type of action. Westerns, for example, are generally set in the American West, the characters represent clear-cut moral values (often indicated by the color of their hats), and the action consists mainly of shootouts. These categories and distinguishing characteristics are particularly clear-cut when the western is a *spaghetti western*—a subcategory of film popular in Italy and typically made by Italian directors using a multinational cast. Sergio Leone's *The Good, the Bad, and the Ugly* (English title) is a classic example. As indicated on this poster, Leone divides his hombres and their deeds into three categories. Clint Eastwood, of course, is in the good category (Il Buono). Lee Van Cleef is in the bad category (Il Brutto)—where he belongs. From the standpoint of an accurate classification system, however, there is a problem with the third category. Is Eli Wallach (Il Cattivo) really any uglier than the other two? Moreover couldn't an hombre who is good (or bad) also be ugly? Or not? In real life, categories that overlap like this aren't good for classifying man and/or beast. But, of course, this classification system was not really designed to classify people but to draw viewers in various languages. And for that purpose it's practically perfect, if not exactly beautiful.

STEPHANIE ERICSSON

The Ways We Lie

Stephanie Ericsson (b. 1953) was two months pregnant with her first child when her husband suddenly died. Already an author of screenplays and two books about addiction, Ericsson poured her grief into her journals, which were excerpted in the Utne Reader *and then collected in a volume of essays,* Companion Through the Darkness: Inner Dialogues on Grief *(1993). The book struck a chord with both critics and readers.*

"There are many ways to lie," writes Ericsson in this essay from the Utne Reader. *Beginning with a broad definition of lie, "The Ways We Lie" identifies some of the most common kinds, including the falsehoods we tell ourselves as well as those we inflict upon other people.*

THE BANK CALLED TODAY and I told them my deposit was in the mail, even though I hadn't written a check yet. It'd been a rough day. The baby I'm pregnant with decided to do aerobics on my lungs for two hours, our three-year-old daughter painted the living-room couch with lipstick, the IRS put me on hold for an hour, and I was late to a business meeting because I was tired. 1

I told my client the traffic had been bad. When my partner came home, his haggard face told me his day hadn't gone any better than mine, so when he asked, "How was your day?" I said, "Oh, fine," knowing that one more straw might break his back. A friend called and wanted to take me to lunch. I said I was busy. Four lies in the course of a day, none of which I felt the least bit guilty about. 2

We lie. We all do. We exaggerate, we minimize, we avoid confrontation, we spare people's feelings, we conveniently forget, we keep secrets, we justify lying to the big-guy institutions. Like most people, I indulge in small falsehoods and still think of myself as an honest person. Sure I lie, but it doesn't hurt anything. Or does it? 3

I once tried going a whole week without telling a lie, and it was paralyzing. I discovered that telling the truth all the time is nearly impossible. It means living with some serious consequences: The bank charges me $60 in overdraft fees, my partner keels over when I tell him about my travails, my client fires me for telling her I didn't feel like being on time, and my friend takes it personally when I say I'm not hungry. There must be some merit to lying. 4

SUGGESTED MLA CITATION: Ericsson, Stephanie. "The Ways We Lie." 1993. *Back to the Lake.* Ed. Thomas Cooley. 2nd ed. New York: Norton, 2012. 336–43. Print.

But if I justify lying, what makes me any different from slick politicians or the   5
corporate robbers who raided the S&L industry?[1] Saying it's okay to lie one way
and not another is hedging. I cannot seem to escape the voice deep inside me that
tells me: When someone lies, someone loses.

See p. 325 for
more about
using definition
along with
classification.

What far-reaching consequences will I, or others, pay as a result of my   6
lie? Will someone's trust be destroyed? Will someone else pay *my* penance
because I ducked out? We must consider the *meaning of our actions.* Decep-
tion, lies, capital crimes, and misdemeanors all carry meanings. *Webster's*
definition of *lie* is specific:

1. a false statement or action especially made with the intent to deceive;
2. anything that gives or is meant to give a false impression.

A definition like this implies that there are many, many ways to tell a lie. Here are
just a few.

The White Lie

A man who won't lie to a woman has very little consideration for her feelings.

—BERGEN EVANS

The white lie assumes that the truth will cause more damage than a simple, harmless   7
untruth. Telling a friend he looks great when he looks like hell can be based on a decision that the friend needs a compliment more than a frank opinion. But, in effect, it
is the liar deciding what is best for the lied to. Ultimately, it is a vote of no confidence.
It is an act of subtle arrogance for anyone to decide what is best for someone else.

Yet not all circumstances are quite so cut-and-dried. Take, for instance, the ser-   8
geant in Vietnam who knew one of his men was killed in action but listed him as
missing so that the man's family would receive indefinite compensation instead of
the lump-sum pittance the military gives widows and children. His intent was hon-
orable. Yet for twenty years this family kept their hopes alive, unable to move on to
a new life.

Facades

Et tu, Brute?   —CAESAR

We all put up facades to one degree or another. When I put on a suit to go to see a   9
client, I feel as though I am putting on another face, obeying the expectation that

---

1. *S&L industry:* Savings and loan (S&L) associations accept savings deposits from consumers and
issue home mortgage loans. In the S&L crisis of the 1980s, more than a thousand independent savings
and loan institutions in America collapsed, costing the U.S. government an estimated $125 billion and
probably contributing to the economic recession of the early 1990s.

serious businesspeople wear suits rather than sweatpants. But I'm a writer. Normally, I get up, get the kid off to school, and sit at my computer in my pajamas until four in the afternoon. When I answer the phone, the caller thinks I'm wearing a suit (though the UPS man knows better).

But facades can be destructive because they are used to seduce others into an 10 illusion. For instance, I recently realized that a former friend was a liar. He presented himself with all the right looks and the right words and offered lots of new consciousness theories, fabulous books to read, and fascinating insights. Then I did some business with him, and the time came for him to pay me. He turned out to be all talk and no walk. I heard a plethora of reasonable excuses, including in-depth descriptions of the big break around the corner. In six months of work, I saw less than a hundred bucks. When I confronted him, he raised both eyebrows and tried to convince me that I'd heard him wrong, that he'd made no commitment to me. A simple investigation into his past revealed a crowded graveyard of disenchanted former friends.

Ignoring the Plain Facts

Well, you must understand that Father Porter is only human. . . .

—A Massachusetts priest

In the '60s, the Catholic Church in Massachusetts began hearing complaints that 11 Father James Porter was sexually molesting children. Rather than relieving him of his duties, the ecclesiastical authorities simply moved him from one parish to another between 1960 and 1967, actually providing him with a fresh supply of unsuspecting families and innocent children to abuse. After treatment in 1967 for pedophilia, he went back to work, this time in Minnesota. The new diocese was aware of Father Porter's obsession with children, but they needed priests and recklessly believed treatment had cured him. More children were abused until he was relieved of his duties a year later. By his own admission, Porter may have abused as many as a hundred children.

Ignoring the facts may not in and of itself be a form of lying, but consider the 12 context of this situation. If a lie is *a false action done with the intent to deceive*, then the Catholic Church's conscious covering for Porter created irreparable consequences. The church became a co-perpetrator with Porter.

Deflecting

When you have no basis for an argument, abuse the plaintiff.   —Cicero

I've discovered that I can keep anyone from seeing the true me by being selectively 13 blatant. I set a precedent of being up-front about intimate issues, but I never bring up the things I truly want to hide; I just let people assume I'm revealing everything. It's an effective way of hiding.

Any good liar knows that the way to perpetuate an untruth is to deflect attention from it. When Clarence Thomas[2] exploded with accusations that the Senate hearings were a "high-tech lynching," he simply switched the focus from a highly charged subject to a radioactive subject. Rather than defending himself, he took the offensive and accused the country of racism. It was a brilliant maneuver. Racism is now politically incorrect in official circles—unlike sexual harassment, which still rewards those who can get away with it.

Some of the most skillful deflectors are passive-aggressive people who, when accused of inappropriate behavior, refuse to respond to the accusations. This you-don't-exist stance infuriates the accuser, who, understandably, screams something obscene out of frustration. The trap is sprung and the act of deflection successful, because now the passive-aggressive person can indignantly say, "Who can talk to someone as unreasonable as you?" The real issue is forgotten and the sins of the original victim become the focus. Feeling guilty of name-calling, the victim is fully tamed and crawls into a hole, ashamed. I have watched this fighting technique work thousands of times in disputes between men and women, and what I've learned is that the real culprit is not necessarily the one who swears the loudest.

Omission

The cruelest lies are often told in silence.　　　　—R. L. STEVENSON

Omission involves telling most of the truth minus one or two key facts whose absence changes the story completely. You break a pair of glasses that are guaranteed under normal use and get a new pair, without mentioning that the first pair broke during a rowdy game of basketball. Who hasn't tried something like that? But what about omission of information that could make a difference in how a person lives his or her life?

For instance, one day I found out that rabbinical legends tell of another woman in the Garden of Eden before Eve. I was stunned. The omission of the Sumerian goddess Lilith from Genesis—as well as her demonization by ancient misogynists as an embodiment of female evil—felt like spiritual robbery. I felt like I'd just found out my mother was really my stepmother. To take seriously the tradition that Adam was created out of the same mud as his equal counterpart, Lilith, redefines all of Judeo-Christian history.

---

2. *Clarence Thomas*: U.S. Supreme Court justice who was accused of sexual harassment during his 1991 Senate confirmation hearings.

Some renegade Catholic feminists introduced me to a view of Lilith that had 18
been suppressed during the many centuries when this strong goddess was seen
only as a spirit of evil. Lilith was a proud goddess who defied Adam's need to control her, attempted negotiations, and when this failed, said adios and left the Garden of Eden.

This omission of Lilith from the Bible was a patriarchal strategy to keep women 19
weak. Omitting the strong-woman archetype of Lilith from Western religions and
starting the story with Eve the Rib has helped keep Christian and Jewish women
believing they were the lesser sex for thousands of years.

Stereotypes and Clichés

> Where opinion does not exist, the status quo becomes stereotyped and all
> originality is discouraged.   —BERTRAND RUSSELL

Stereotype and cliché serve a purpose as a form of shorthand. Our need for vast 20
amounts of information in nanoseconds has made the stereotype vital to modern
communication. Unfortunately, it often shuts down original thinking, giving those
hungry for the truth a candy bar of misinformation instead of a balanced meal. The
stereotype explains a situation with just enough truth to seem unquestionable.

All the "isms"—racism, sexism, ageism, et al.—are founded on and fueled by 21
the stereotype and the cliché, which are lies of exaggeration, omission, and ignorance. They are always dangerous. They take a single tree and make it a landscape.
They destroy curiosity. They close minds and separate people. The single mother
on welfare is assumed to be cheating. Any black male could tell you how much of
his identity is obliterated daily by stereotypes. Fat people, ugly people, beautiful
people, old people, large-breasted women, short men, the mentally ill, and the
homeless all could tell you how much more they are like us than we want to think.
I once admitted to a group of people that I had a mouth like a truck driver. Much
to my surprise, a man stood up and said, "I'm a truck driver, and I never cuss."
Needless to say, I was humbled.

Groupthink

> Who is more foolish, the child afraid of the dark, or the man afraid of the
> light?   —MAURICE FREEHILL

Irving Janis, in *Victims of GroupThink*, defines this sort of lie as a psychological 22
phenomenon within decision-making groups in which loyalty to the group has
become more important than any other value, with the result that dissent and the
appraisal of alternatives are suppressed. If you've ever worked on a committee or
in a corporation, you've encountered groupthink. It requires a combination of

other forms of lying—ignoring facts, selective memory, omission, and denial, to name a few.

The textbook example of groupthink came on December 7, 1941. From as early 23 as the fall of 1941, the warnings came in, one after another, that Japan was preparing for a massive military operation. The Navy command in Hawaii assumed Pearl Harbor was invulnerable—the Japanese weren't stupid enough to attack the United States' most important base. On the other hand, racist stereotypes said the Japanese weren't smart enough to invent a torpedo effective in less than 60 feet of water (the fleet was docked in 30 feet); after all, U.S. technology hadn't been able to do it.

On Friday, December 5, normal weekend leave was granted to all the command- 24 ers at Pearl Harbor, even though the Japanese consulate in Hawaii was busy burning papers. Within the tight, good-ole-boy cohesiveness of the U.S. command in Hawaii, the myth of invulnerability stayed well entrenched. No one in the group considered the alternatives. The rest is history.

Out-and-Out Lies

The only form of lying that is beyond reproach is lying for its own sake.
—OSCAR WILDE

Of all the ways to lie, I like this one the best, probably because I get tired of trying 25 to figure out the real meanings behind things. At least I can trust the bald-faced lie. I once asked my five-year-old nephew, "Who broke the fence?" (I had seen him do it.) He answered, "The murderers." Who could argue?

At least when this sort of lie is told it can be easily confronted. As the person 26 who is lied to, I know where I stand. The bald-faced lie doesn't toy with my perceptions—it argues with them. It doesn't try to refashion reality, it tries to refute it. *Read my lips.*[3] . . . No sleight of hand. No guessing. If this were the only form of lying, there would be no such thing as floating anxiety or the adult-children-of-alcoholics movement.

Dismissal

Pay no attention to that man behind the curtain! I am the Great Oz!
—THE WIZARD OF OZ

Dismissal is perhaps the slipperiest of all lies. Dismissing feelings, perceptions, or 27 even the raw facts of a situation ranks as a kind of lie that can do as much damage to a person as any other kind of lie.

---

3. *Read my lips*: A phrase made especially famous during President George H. W. Bush's 1988 election campaign. He emphatically said, "Read my lips: no new taxes." Once in office, he did raise taxes.

The roots of many mental disorders can be traced back to the dismissal of real- 28
ity. Imagine that a person is told from the time she is a tot that her perceptions are
inaccurate. *"Mommy, I'm scared."* "No, you're not, darling." *"I don't like that man
next door, he makes me feel icky."* "Johnny, that's a terrible thing to say, of course
you like him. You go over there right now and be nice to him."

I've often mused over the idea that madness is actually a sane reaction to an 29
insane world. Psychologist R. D. Laing supports this hypothesis in *Sanity, Madness &
the Family*, an account of his investigations into families of schizophrenics. The
common thread that ran through all of the families he studied was a deliberate,
staunch dismissal of the patient's perceptions from a very early age. Each of the
patients started out with an accurate grasp of reality, which, through meticulous
and methodical dismissal, was demolished until the only reality the patient could
trust was catatonia.

Dismissal runs the gamut. Mild dismissal can be quite handy for forgiving the 30
foibles of others in our day-to-day lives. Toddlers who have just learned to manipulate their parents' attention sometimes are dismissed out of necessity. Absolute
attention from the parents would require so much energy that no one would get
to eat dinner. But we must be careful and attentive about how far we take our
"necessary" dismissals. Dismissal is a dangerous tool, because it's nothing less
than a lie.

Delusion

> We lie loudest when we lie to ourselves.   —ERIC HOFFER

I could write the book on this one. Delusion, a cousin of dismissal, is the ten- 31
dency to see excuses as facts. It's a powerful lying tool because it filters out information that contradicts what we want to believe. Alcoholics who believe that the
problems in their lives are legitimate reasons for drinking rather than results of
the drinking offer the classic example of deluded thinking. Delusion uses the
mind's ability to see things in myriad ways to support what it wants to be the
truth.

But delusion is also a survival mechanism we all use. If we were to fully contem- 32
plate the consequences of our stockpiles of nuclear weapons or global warming, we
could hardly function on a day-to-day level. We don't want to incorporate that
much reality into our lives because to do so would be paralyzing.

Delusion acts as an adhesive to keep the status quo intact. It shamelessly employs 33
dismissal, omission, and amnesia, among other sorts of lies. Its most cunning
defense is that it cannot see itself.

The liar's punishment . . . is that he cannot believe anyone else.

—George Bernard Shaw

These are only a few of the ways we lie. Or are lied to. As I said earlier, it's not 34 easy to entirely eliminate lies from our lives. No matter how pious we may try to be, we will still embellish, hedge, and omit to lubricate the daily machinery of living. But there is a world of difference between telling functional lies and living a lie. Martin Buber once said, "The lie is the spirit committing treason against itself." Our acceptance of lies becomes a cultural cancer that eventually shrouds and reorders reality until moral garbage becomes as invisible to us as water is to a fish.

How much do we tolerate before we become sick and tired of being sick and 35 tired? When will we stand up and declare our *right* to trust? When do we stop accepting that the real truth is in the fine print? Whose lips do we read this year when we vote for president? When will we stop being so reticent about making judgments? When do we stop turning over our personal power and responsibility to liars?

Maybe if I don't tell the bank the check's in the mail I'll be less tolerant of the 36 lies told me every day. A country song I once heard said it all for me: "You've got to stand for something or you'll fall for anything."

Reading Closely

1. According to Ericsson, what basic characteristics do all lies have in common? How, and how well, do the kinds of lies she lists fit this basic DEFINITION?

2. Ericsson classifies lies into ten different categories. Which kinds of lies does she herself admit to committing? Who does she say commits the other kinds?

3. Some kinds of lies, says Ericsson, are more serious than others. Which kinds does she find least harmful? Which kinds do the most damage? How?

4. Why doesn't Ericsson get more worked up about "out-and-out" (or "bald-faced") lies (25–26)?

5. "We lie," says Ericsson. "We all do" (3). Do you agree? Why or why not?

6. "We must consider the *meaning of our actions*," says Ericsson (6). Why? What reasons does she give for taking responsibility for our lies? Do you agree with Ericsson's ARGUMENT, especially with what she says about "trust" (25, 35)? Why or why not?

STRATEGIES AND STRUCTURES

1. Throughout her essay, Ericsson admits that she tells lies. Why do you think she adopts this confessional strategy? How effective do you find it? Why?

2. Why is Ericsson classifying lies in this essay? Where does she state her main point in doing so most directly?

3. Ericsson identifies the main characteristics, as she sees them, of each category of lie that she discusses. How significant do you find these characteristics?

4. Ericsson says that some kinds of lies, such as "groupthink," are made up of "a combination of other forms of lying" (22). Does this sort of overlapping invalidate her system? Why or why not?

5. Ericsson warns against stereotyping in paragraphs 20–21. On what basis does she object to stereotypes? Can she be accused of engaging in this practice at any point in her essay? Explain your answer by referring to specific kinds of lies and their characteristics.

6. *Other Methods.* Ericsson gives EXAMPLES of each of the different categories of lies. Which examples do you find most effective? Least effective? Explain.

THINKING ABOUT LANGUAGE

1. What are the differences between a white lie and an out-and-out lie? What are the CONNOTATIONS of each expression?

2. How can lying be committed in silence?

3. Ericsson writes that "our acceptance of lies becomes a cultural cancer" (34). Why do you think she uses the expression "cultural cancer"?

FOR WRITING

1. Have you ever lied in one or more of the ways that Ericsson cites? Write a paragraph or two on each kind of lie you've told giving examples from your own experience but classifying them according to Ericsson's categories.

2. Write a classification essay on the ways people do one of the following: tell the truth, avoid work, make friends, break with friends, find a job, quit a job, or delude themselves.

AMY TAN

Mother Tongue

Amy Tan (b. 1952), a daughter of Chinese immigrants, was born in Oakland, Califor-
nia. She earned an MA in linguistics from San Jose State University and worked on
programs for disabled children before becoming a freelance business writer. In 1987
she visited China for the first time. On returning to the United States, she set to work
on a collection of interconnected stories about Chinese American mothers and daugh-
ters. The Joy Luck Club *(1989) was an international success, and was translated into*
seventeen languages (including Chinese). Since then Tan has published several novels,
including The Kitchen God's Wife *(1991),* The Bonesetter's Daughter *(2001), and*
*Saving Fish from Drowning *(2005)—in addition to two children's books and a book*
of nonfiction, The Opposite of Fate: A Book of Musings *(2003), which explores*
lucky accidents, choice, and memory.

In her essay "Mother Tongue," which first appeared in the Threepenny Review, *a*
literary magazine, in 1990, Tan classifies various forms of the English language, from
her mother's "broken English" (a term she dislikes) to the complex prose of academia.
"And I use them all," she writes "all the Englishes I grew up with."

I AM NOT A SCHOLAR OF ENGLISH or literature. I cannot give you much more than 1
personal opinions on the English language and its variations in this country or
others.

I am a writer. And by that definition, I am someone who has always loved lan- 2
guage. I am fascinated by language in daily life. I spend a great deal of my time
thinking about the power of language—the way it can evoke an emotion, a visual
image, a complex idea, or a simple truth. Language is the tool of my trade. And I
use them all—all the Englishes I grew up with.

Recently, I was made keenly aware of the different Englishes I do use. I was giv- 3
ing a talk to a large group of people, the same talk I had already given to half a
dozen other groups. The nature of the talk was about my writing, my life, and my
book, *The Joy Luck Club*. The talk was going along well enough, until I remembered
one major difference that made the whole talk sound wrong. My mother was in the
room. And it was perhaps the first time she had heard me give a lengthy speech,
using the kind of English I have never used with her. I was saying things like, "The
intersection of memory upon imagination" and "There is an aspect of my fiction

SUGGESTED MLA CITATION: Tan, Amy. "Mother Tongue." 1990. *Back to the Lake.* Ed. Thomas
Cooley. 2nd ed. New York: Norton, 2012. 345–50. Print.

that relates to thus-and-thus"—a speech filled with carefully wrought grammatical phrases, burdened, it suddenly seemed to me, with nominalized forms, past perfect tenses, conditional phrases, all the forms of standard English that I had learned in school and through books, the forms of English I did not use at home with my mother.

Just last week, I was walking down the street with my mother, and I again found 4 myself conscious of the English I was using, the English I do use with her. We were talking about the price of new and used furniture and I heard myself saying this: "Not waste money that way." My husband was with us as well, and he didn't notice any switch in my English. And then I realized why. It's because over the twenty years we've been together I've often used the same kind of English with him, and sometimes he even uses it with me. It has become our language of intimacy, a different sort of English that relates to family talk, the language I grew up with.

So you'll have some idea of what this family talk I heard sounds like, I'll quote 5 what my mother said during a recent conversation which I videotaped and then transcribed. During this conversation, my mother was talking about a political gangster in Shanghai who had the same last name as her family's, Du, and how the gangster in his early years wanted to be adopted by her family, which was rich by comparison. Later, the gangster became more powerful, far richer than my mother's family, and one day showed up at my mother's wedding to pay his respects. Here's what she said in part:

"Du Yusong having business like fruit stand. Like off the street kind. He is Du 6 like Du Zong—but not Tsung-ming Island people. The local people call putong, the river east side, he belong to that side local people. That man want to ask Du Zong father take him in like become own family. Du Zong father wasn't look down on him, but didn't take seriously, until that man big like become a mafia. Now important person, very hard to inviting him. Chinese way, came only to show respect, don't stay for dinner. Respect for making big celebration, he shows up. Mean gives lots of respect. Chinese custom. Chinese social life that way. If too important won't have to stay too long. He come to my wedding. I didn't see, I heard it. I gone to boy's side, they have YMCA dinner. Chinese age I was nineteen."

You should know that my mother's expressive command of English belies how 7 much she actually understands. She reads the *Forbes*[1] report, listens to *Wall Street Week*, converses daily with her stockbroker, reads all of Shirley MacLaine's books with ease—all kinds of things I can't begin to understand. Yet some of my friends tell me they understand 50 percent of what my mother says. Some say they understand 80 to 90 percent. Some say they understand none of it, as if she were speak-

---

1. *Forbes*: A business-oriented periodical that focuses on stocks, bonds, business trends, and other items of interest to investors.

ing pure Chinese. But to me, my mother's English is perfectly clear, perfectly natural. It's my mother tongue. Her language, as I hear it, is vivid, direct, full of observation and imagery. That was the language that helped shape the way I saw things, expressed things, made sense of the world.

Lately, I've been giving more thought to the kind of English my mother speaks. 8 Like others, I have described it to people as "broken" or "fractured" English. But I wince when I say that. It has always bothered me that I can think of no way to describe it other than "broken," as if it were damaged and needed to be fixed, as if it lacked a certain wholeness and soundness. I've heard other terms used, "limited English," for example. But they seem just as bad, as if everything is limited, including people's perceptions of the limited English speaker.

I know this for a fact, because when I was growing up, my mother's "limited" 9 English limited *my* perception of her. I was ashamed of her English. I believed that her English reflected the quality of what she had to say. That is, because she expressed them imperfectly her thoughts were imperfect. And I had plenty of empirical evidence to support me: the fact that people in department stores, at banks, and at restaurants did not take her seriously, did not give her good service, pretended not to understand her, or even acted as if they did not hear her.

My mother has long realized the limitations of her English as well. When I was 10 fifteen, she used to have me call people on the phone to pretend I was she. In this guise, I was forced to ask for information or even to complain and yell at people who had been rude to her. One time it was a call to her stockbroker in New York. She had cashed out her small portfolio and it just so happened we were going to go to New York the next week, our very first trip outside California. I had to get on the phone and say in an adolescent voice that was not very convincing, "This is Mrs. Tan."

And my mother was standing in the back whispering loudly, "Why he don't send 11 me check, already two weeks late. So mad he lie to me, losing me money."

And then I said in perfect English, "Yes, I'm getting rather concerned. You had 12 agreed to send the check two weeks ago, but it hasn't arrived."

Then she began to talk more loudly. "What he want, I come to New York tell 13 him front of his boss, you cheating me?" And I was trying to calm her down, make her be quiet, while telling the stockbroker, "I can't tolerate any more excuses. If I don't receive the check immediately, I am going to have to speak to your manager when I'm in New York next week." And sure enough, the following week there we were in front of this astonished stockbroker, and I was sitting there red-faced and quiet, and my mother, the real Mrs. Tan, was shouting at his boss in her impeccable broken English.

We used a similar routine just five days ago, for a situation that was far less 14 humorous. My mother had gone to the hospital for an appointment, to find out about a benign brain tumor a CAT scan had revealed a month ago. She said she had spoken very good English, her best English, no mistakes. Still, she said, the hospital did not apologize when they said they had lost the CAT scan and she had come for nothing. She said they did not seem to have any sympathy when she told them she was anxious to know the exact diagnosis, since her husband and son had both died of brain tumors. She said they would not give her any more information until the next time and she would have to make another appointment for that. So she said she would not leave until the doctor called her daughter. She wouldn't budge. And when the doctor finally called her daughter, me, who spoke in perfect English—lo and behold—we had assurances the CAT scan would be found, promises that a conference call on Monday would be held, and apologies for any suffering my mother had gone through for a most regrettable mistake.

I think my mother's English almost had an effect on limiting my possibilities in life as well. Sociologists and linguists probably will tell you that a person's developing language skills are more influenced by peers. But I do think that the language spoken in the family, especially in immigrant families which are more insular, plays a large role in shaping the language of the child. And I believe that it affected my results on achievement tests, IQ tests, and the SAT. While my English skills were never judged as poor, compared to math, English could not be considered my strong suit. In grade school I did moderately well, getting perhaps B's, sometimes B-pluses, in English and scoring perhaps in the sixtieth or seventieth percentile on achievement tests. But those scores were not good enough to override the opinion that my true abilities lay in math and science, because in those areas I achieved A's and scored in the ninetieth percentile or higher. 15

This was understandable. Math is precise; there is only one correct answer. Whereas, for me at least, the answers on English tests were always a judgment call, a matter of opinion and personal experience. Those tests were constructed around items like fill-in-the-blank sentence completion, such as, "Even though Tom was _____, Mary thought he was _____." And the correct answer always seemed to be the most bland combinations of thoughts, for example, "Even though Tom was shy, Mary thought he was charming," with the grammatical structure "even though" limiting the correct answer to some sort of semantic opposites, so you wouldn't get answers like, "Even though Tom was foolish, Mary thought he was ridiculous." Well, according to my mother, there were very few limitations as to what Tom could have been and what Mary might have thought of him. So I never did well on tests like that. 16

The same was true with word analogies, pairs of words in which you were supposed to find some sort of logical, semantic relationship—for example, "*Sunset* is to *nightfall* as _____ is to _____." And here you would be presented with a list of four possible pairs, one of which showed the same kind of relationship: *red* is to 17 *stoplight, bus* is to *arrival, chills* is to *fever, yawn* is to *boring*. Well, I could never think that way. I knew what the tests were asking, but I could not block out of my mind the images already created by the first pair, *"sunset* is to *nightfall"*—and I would see a burst of colors against a darkening sky, the moon rising, the lowering of a curtain of stars. And all the other pairs of words—red, bus, stoplight, boring— just threw up a mass of confusing images, making it impossible for me to sort out something as logical as saying: "A sunset precedes nightfall" is the same as "a chill precedes a fever." The only way I would have gotten that answer right would have been to imagine an associative situation, for example, my being disobedient and staying out past sunset, catching a chill at night, which turns into feverish pneu- monia as punishment, which indeed did happen to me.

I have been thinking about all this lately, about my mother's English, about achieve- 18 ment tests. Because lately I've been asked, as a writer, why there are not more Asian Americans represented in American literature. Why are there few Asian Americans enrolled in creative writing programs? Why do so many Chi- nese students go into engineering? Well, these are broad sociological questions I can't begin to answer. But I have noticed in surveys—in fact, just last week—that Asian students, as a whole, always do significantly better on math achievement tests than in English. And this makes me think that there are other Asian-American students whose English spoken in the home might also be described as "broken" or "limited." And perhaps they also have teachers who are steering them away from writing and into math and science, which is what happened to me.

For pointers on using classifica- tion to serve a larger purpose, see p. 317.

Fortunately, I happen to be rebellious in nature and enjoy the challenge of dis- 19 proving assumptions made about me. I became an English major my first year in college, after being enrolled as pre-med. I started writing nonfiction as a freelancer the week after I was told by my former boss that writing was my worst skill and I should hone my talents toward account management.

But it wasn't until 1985 that I finally began to write fiction. And at first I wrote 20 using what I thought to be wittily crafted sentences, sentences that would finally prove I had mastery over the English language. Here's an example from the first draft of a story that later made its way into *The Joy Luck Club*, but without this line: "That was my mental quandary in its nascent state." A terrible line, which I can barely pronounce.

Fortunately, for reasons I won't get into today, I later decided I should envision 21 a reader for the stories I would write. And the reader I decided upon was my mother, because these were stories about mothers. So with this reader in mind— and in fact she did read my early drafts—I began to write stories using all the Englishes I grew up with: the English I spoke to my mother, which for lack of a better term might be described as "simple"; the English she used with me, which for lack of a better term might be described as "broken"; my translation of her Chinese, which could certainly be described as "watered down"; and what I imagined to be her translation of her Chinese if she could speak in perfect English, her internal language, and for that I sought to preserve the essence, but neither an English nor a Chinese structure. I wanted to capture what language ability tests can never reveal: her intent, her passion, her imagery, the rhythms of her speech and the nature of her thoughts.

Apart from what any critic had to say about my writing, I knew I had succeeded where it counted when my mother finished reading my book and gave me her verdict: "So easy to read." 22

Reading Closely

1. Amy Tan classifies the various "Englishes" that she uses into two basic categories. What are they, and what are the main characteristics of each kind?

2. How many different types of English did Tan learn from talking with her mother, a native speaker of Chinese? What are the different attributes of each type?

3. According to Tan, what are the essential attributes of "standard" English (3)? How did she learn to use this kind of English?

4. Which kinds of English does Tan use most often as a writer? Why?

Strategies and Structures

1. "So you'll have some idea of what this family talk I heard sounds like, I'll quote what my mother said during a recent conversation" (5). Here and elsewhere in her essay Tan addresses the reader directly as "you." Why do you think she does this?

2. Why is Tan classifying the different kinds of English she knows and uses? Is she, for example, conveying information, arguing a point, telling an entertaining story—some other purpose? Explain.

3. Should Tan have laid out her classification system more fully at the beginning of her essay instead of waiting until the end? Why or why not?

4. In paragraphs 15–18, Tan advances an ARGUMENT about IQ and achievement tests. What's her point here, and how does she use classification to support it?

5. *Other Methods.* Tan classifies "all the Englishes" she grew up with in para-

graph 21, near the end of her essay. How well does this classification system fit the specific EXAMPLES she has cited earlier? Explain.

THINKING ABOUT LANGUAGE

1. Explain the PUN in Tan's title. How does it prepare us for the rest of her essay?

2. Tan does not want to use "broken" or "fractured" as names for the kind of English her mother speaks (8). Why not?

3. Tan never gives a name to the kind of English she uses to represent her mother's "internal language" (21). What would you call it? Why?

FOR WRITING

1. In a paragraph or two, give several examples of "standard" (or "nonstandard") English, and explain why they belong in this category.

2. How many different kinds of English, or other languages, do you use at home, at school, or among friends? Write an essay classifying them, and explaining how and when you use each type.

DAVID BROOKS

People Like Us

David Brooks (b. 1961) was born in Toronto and grew up in New York City. Soon after graduating from the University of Chicago with a degree in history, he began his journalism career as a police reporter for a newspaper wire service. Brooks next spent nine years at the Wall Street Journal, *first as a book-review editor and then as a foreign correspondent. In 1995 he joined the staff of the* Weekly Standard, *a publication of the emerging neoconservative movement; he appears regularly as a political analyst on PBS television and National Public Radio, and contributes a regular column to the Op-Ed page of the* New York Times. *Brooks has authored three books of social commentary,* Bobos in Paradise: The New Upper Class and How They Got There *(2000),* On Paradise Drive: How We Live Now (And Always Have) in the Future Tense *(2004), and* The Social Animal: The Hidden Sources of Love, Character and Achievement *(2011).*

"People Like Us" first appeared in 2003 in the Atlantic, *a magazine devoted to politics, business, and entertainment. Although the essay focuses on the various principles of classification by which people sort themselves according to a simple binary system—them and us—Brooks also contemplates a number of alternate "groupings." Classification is thus a method of development in the essay as well as its main subject.*

MAYBE IT'S TIME to admit the obvious. We don't really care about diversity all 1
that much in America, even though we talk about it a great deal. Maybe somewhere in this country there is a truly diverse neighborhood in which a black Pentecostal minister lives next to a white anti-globalization activist, who lives next to an Asian short-order cook, who lives next to a professional golfer, who lives next to a postmodern-literature professor and a cardiovascular surgeon. But I have never been to or heard of that neighborhood. Instead, what I have seen all around the country is people making strenuous efforts to group themselves with people who are basically like themselves.

Human beings are capable of drawing amazingly subtle social distinctions and 2
then shaping their lives around them. In the Washington, D.C., area Democratic lawyers tend to live in suburban Maryland, and Republican lawyers tend to live in suburban Virginia. If you asked a Democratic lawyer to move from her $750,000 house in Bethesda, Maryland, to a $750,000 house in Great Falls, Virginia, she'd

SUGGESTED MLA CITATION: Brooks, David. "People Like Us." 2003. *Back to the Lake.* Ed. Thomas Cooley. 2nd ed. New York: Norton, 2012. 352–56. Print.

look at you as if you had just asked her to buy a pickup truck with a gun rack and to shove chewing tobacco in her kid's mouth. In Manhattan the owner of a $3 million SoHo loft would feel out of place moving into a $3 million Fifth Avenue apartment. A West Hollywood interior decorator would feel dislocated if you asked him to move to Orange County. In Georgia a barista from Athens would probably not fit in serving coffee in Americus.

It is a common complaint that every place is starting to look the same. But in 3 the information age, the late writer James Chapin once told me, every place becomes more like itself. People are less often tied down to factories and mills, and they can search for places to live on the basis of cultural affinity. Once they find a town in which people share their values, they flock there, and reinforce whatever was distinctive about the town in the first place. Once Boulder, Colorado, became known as congenial to politically progressive mountain bikers, half the politically progressive mountain bikers in the country (it seems) moved there; they made the place so culturally pure that it has become practically a parody of itself.

But people love it. Make no mistake—we are increasing our happiness by seg- 4 menting off so rigorously. We are finding places where we are comfortable and where we feel we can flourish. But the choices we make toward that end lead to the very opposite of diversity. The United States might be a diverse nation when considered as a whole, but block by block and institution by institution it is a relatively homogeneous nation.

When we use the word "diversity" today we usually mean racial integration. But 5 even here our good intentions seem to have run into the brick wall of human nature. Over the past generation reformers have tried heroically, and in many cases successfully, to end housing discrimination. But recent patterns aren't encouraging: according to an analysis of the 2000 census data, the 1990s saw only a slight increase in the racial integration of neighborhoods in the United States. The number of middle-class and upper-middle-class African-American families is rising, but for whatever reasons—racism, psychological comfort—these families tend to congregate in predominantly black neighborhoods.

In fact, evidence suggests that some neighborhoods become more segregated 6 over time. New suburbs in Arizona and Nevada, for example, start out reasonably well integrated. These neighborhoods don't yet have reputations, so people choose their houses for other, mostly economic reasons. But as neighborhoods age, they develop personalities (that's where the Asians live, and that's where the Hispanics live), and segmentation occurs. It could be that in a few years the new suburbs in the Southwest will be nearly as segregated as the established ones in the Northeast and the Midwest.

Even though race and ethnicity run deep in American society, we should in 7 theory be able to find areas that are at least culturally diverse. But here, too, people show few signs of being truly interested in building diverse communities: If you run a retail company and you're thinking of opening new stores, you can choose among dozens of consulting firms that are quite effective at locating your potential customers. They can do this because people with similar tastes and preferences tend to congregate by ZIP code.

The most famous of these precision marketing firms is Claritas, which breaks 8 down the U.S. population into sixty-two psycho-demographic clusters, based on such factors as how much money people make, what they like to read and watch, and what products they have bought in the past. For example, the "suburban sprawl" cluster is composed of young families making about $41,000 a year and living in fast-growing places such as Burnsville, Minnesota, and Bensalem, Pennsylvania. These people are almost twice as likely as other Americans to have three-way calling. They are two and a half times as likely to buy Light n' Lively Kid Yogurt. Members of the "towns & gowns" cluster are recent college graduates in places such as Berkeley, California, and Gainesville, Florida. They are big consumers of Dove Bars and *Saturday Night Live*. They tend to drive small foreign cars and to read *Rolling Stone* and *Scientific American*.

Looking through the market research, one can sometimes be amazed by how 9 efficiently people cluster—and by how predictable we all are. If you wanted to sell imported wine, obviously you would have to find places where rich people live. But did you know that the sixteen counties with the greatest proportion of imported-wine drinkers are all in the same three metropolitan areas (New York, San Francisco, and Washington, D.C.)? If you tried to open a motor-home dealership in Montgomery County, Pennsylvania, you'd probably go broke, because people in this ring of the Philadelphia suburbs think RVs are kind of uncool. But if you traveled just a short way north, to Monroe County, Pennsylvania, you would find yourself in the fifth motor-home-friendliest county in America.

P. 318 explains how to choose different principles of classification.
Geography is not the only way we find ourselves divided from people 10 unlike us. Some of us watch Fox News, while others listen to NPR. Some like David Letterman, and others—typically in less urban neighborhoods—like Jay Leno. Some go to charismatic churches; some go to mainstream churches. Americans tend more and more often to marry people with education levels similar to their own, and to befriend people with backgrounds similar to their own.

My favorite illustration of this latter pattern comes from the first, noncontro- 11 versial chapter of *The Bell Curve*.[1] Think of your twelve closest friends, Richard J. Herrnstein and Charles Murray write. If you had chosen them randomly from the

---

1. *The Bell Curve* (1994): A book about the role of intelligence in social and economic success that controversially connected race and intelligence.

American population, the odds that half of your twelve closest friends would be college graduates would be six in a thousand. The odds that half of the twelve would have advanced degrees would be less than one in a million. Have any of your twelve closest friends graduated from Harvard, Stanford, Yale, Princeton, Caltech, MIT, Duke, Dartmouth, Cornell, Columbia, Chicago, or Brown? If you chose your friends randomly from the American population, the odds against your having four or more friends from those schools would be more than a billion to one.

Many of us live in absurdly unlikely groupings, because we have organized our lives that way.

It's striking that the institutions that talk the most about diversity often practice it the least. For example, no group of people sings the diversity anthem more frequently and fervently than administrators at just such elite universities. But elite universities are amazingly undiverse in their values, politics, and mores. Professors in particular are drawn from a rather narrow segment of the population. If faculties reflected the general population, 32 percent of professors would be registered Democrats and 31 percent would be registered Republicans. Forty percent would be evangelical Christians. But a recent study of several universities by the conservative Center for the Study of Popular Culture and the American Enterprise Institute found that roughly 90 percent of those professors in the arts and sciences who had registered with a political party had registered Democratic. Fifty-seven professors at Brown were found on the voter-registration rolls. Of those, fifty-four were Democrats. Of the forty-two professors in the English, history, sociology, and political-science departments, all were Democrats. The results at Harvard, Penn State, Maryland, and the University of California at Santa Barbara were similar to the results at Brown.

What we are looking at here is human nature. People want to be around others who are roughly like themselves. That's called community. It probably would be psychologically difficult for most Brown professors to share an office with someone who was pro-life, a member of the National Rifle Association, or an evangelical Christian. It's likely that hiring committees would subtly—even unconsciously— screen out any such people they encountered. Republicans and evangelical Christians have sensed that they are not welcome at places like Brown, so they don't even consider working there. In fact, any registered Republican who contemplates a career in academia these days is both a hero and a fool. So, in a semi-self-selective pattern, brainy people with generally liberal social mores flow to academia, and brainy people with generally conservative mores flow elsewhere.

The dream of diversity is like the dream of equality. Both are based on ideals we celebrate even as we undermine them daily. (How many times have you seen someone renounce a high-paying job or pull his child from an elite college on the grounds that these things are bad for equality?) On the one hand, the situation is appalling. It is appalling that Americans know so little about one another. It is appalling that many of us are so narrow-minded that we can't tolerate a few people with ideas significantly different from our own. It's appalling that evangelical Christians are practically absent from entire professions, such as academia, the media, and filmmaking. It's appalling that people should be content to cut themselves off from everyone unlike themselves.

The segmentation of society means that often we don't even have arguments ₁₆ across the political divide. Within their little validating communities, liberals and conservatives circulate half-truths about the supposed awfulness of the other side. These distortions are believed because it feels good to believe them.

On the other hand, there are limits to how diverse any community can or should ₁₇ be. I've come to think that it is not useful to try to hammer diversity into every neighborhood and institution in the United States. Sure, Augusta National[2] should probably admit women, and university sociology departments should probably hire a conservative or two. It would be nice if all neighborhoods had a good mixture of ethnicities. But human nature being what it is, most places and institutions are going to remain culturally homogeneous.

It's probably better to think about diverse lives, not diverse institutions. Human ₁₈ beings, if they are to live well, will have to move through a series of institutions and environments, which may be individually homogeneous but, taken together, will offer diverse experiences. It might also be a good idea to make national service a rite of passage for young people in this country: it would take them out of their narrow neighborhood segment and thrust them in with people unlike themselves. Finally, it's probably important for adults to get out of their own familiar circles. If you live in a coastal, socially liberal neighborhood, maybe you should take out a subscription to *The Door*, the evangelical humor magazine; or maybe you should visit Branson, Missouri. Maybe you should stop in at a megachurch. Sure, it would be superficial familiarity, but it beats the iron curtains that now separate the nation's various cultural zones.

Look around at your daily life. Are you really in touch with the broad diversity ₁₉ of American life? Do you care?

2. *Augusta National:* A prestigious golf club in Augusta, Georgia, that is the site of a major professional golf event, the Masters' Tournament. Augusta National excludes women from becoming members. Because the club is home to a sporting event with widespread public interest and attention, there has been public debate on the issue in recent years and pressure on the club to change its policy.

Reading Closely

1. What prevents Americans from achieving true diversity, according to Brooks? In his view, what main criterion do we all use for dividing ourselves into groups?

2. What principle of classification do marketing firms such as Claritas use to classify people (8)? What is the purpose of their classifications?

3. How useful is economic data for classifying people in social and political ways? That is, how much does what people buy tell us about who they are? Explain.

4. According to Brooks, how likely is it that Americans will reshuffle themselves into a more diverse population? What has CAUSED our homogeneous society, in his view, and what does he think can be done to correct it?

5. What does Brooks mean when he says, "It's probably better to think about diverse lives, not diverse institutions" (18)? Do you agree? Why or why not?

Strategies and Structures

1. "Look around at your daily life," Brooks admonishes (19). To what AUDIENCE is he speaking here? What kinds of readers might be most likely to resist Brooks' claim that the lack of diversity in American society is "obvious" (1)?

2. What is the main PRINCIPLE OF CLASSIFICATION in the first half of Brooks' essay? How and how well does Brooks use it to support his point about the lack of diversity in America?

3. What principle of classification is Brooks illustrating when he refers to *The Bell Curve* (11)? When he refers to several "elite universities" (13)?

4. Most of the ways in which Americans group themselves, says Brooks, are "absurdly unlikely" (12). Which of his many EXAMPLES do you find particularly strong—or weak? Why?

5. Throughout his essay, Brooks proposes a number of alternative ways to group people. What are some of them? On what principle of classification are they based? How do they support what Brooks says about diversity?

6. *Other Methods.* Brooks is using classification to support an ARGUMENT about classification. How so? Is this an effective strategy? Why or why not?

Thinking about Language

1. Brooks uses a number of synonyms for *segregate* and *segregation*. What are some of them? Why doesn't he simply adopt the more familiar term instead?

2. The word "diversity" comes up throughout Brooks's essay. How and where does he DEFINE it?

3. In reasoning why people prefer to be around their peers, Brooks states: "That's called community" (14). Is he being IRONIC here? Explain.

4. "Iron curtains" (18) is a phrase from the days of America's cold war with the former Soviet Union. Why do you think Brooks uses it in an essay about cultural divisions at home?

FOR WRITING

1. Write a paragraph enumerating the types of people you would expect to find in an ideally diverse neighborhood.

2. Write a classification essay in which you respond to the statement that "we don't really care about diversity all that much in America" (1). You can agree or disagree, but prove your point by dividing Americans into a number of categories that show their similarities or differences.

ERIN McKEAN

Verbed!
Not Every Noun Wants to Stay That Way

Erin McKean (b. 1971) is a lexicographer and founder of Wordnik, a website described on its home page as offering "the most comprehensive dictionary in the known universe." McKean studied linguistics at the University of Chicago, graduating in 1993. Formerly editor-in-chief of the New Oxford American Dictionary, *she now edits the language quarterly* Verbatim. *Her books include,* Totally Weird and Wonderful Words *(2006),* That's Amore! The Language of Love for Lovers of Language *(2006), and* The Secret Lives of Dresses *(2011).*

As a language enthusiast, McKean is well aware that words traditionally belong to certain classes, or parts of speech. Those that name people or things, for instance, can be classified as nouns, whereas those that denote action are verbs—and so on. In the following 2010 article from the Boston Globe, *however, McKean demonstrates that individual words have a way of morphing from one type to another. Certain nouns, for instance, are bent on becoming verbs, and there is little that the language police can do to stop it.*

WHAT DO THESE WORDS and phrases have in common? *Friend, Google, TiVo, log in, contact, barbecue, unlike, concept, text, Photoshop, leverage, party, Xerox, reference, architect, parent, improv, transition, diligence, host, chair, gift, heart, impact?* 1

They've all been declared—by someone, somewhere, whether a usage expert or just a self-appointed language cop—"not verbs." It doesn't matter whether they're useful, interesting, or entertaining as verbs; to many people, if a word began its life as a noun, then "verbing" it (like I did there) is *just wrong.* 2

This visceral reaction is the motivating force behind the recently popular *login-isnotaverb.com,* one man's impassioned plea against this kind of verbing. The site's elaborate (and funny) arguments against *login*'s verb status really boil down to a simple denial. "I will repeat the important part for clarity: 'login' is not a verb. It's simply not," he writes. 3

The history of English, however, suggests that the language is remarkably flexible in terms of what can be verbed. Almost any word can be drafted to serve as a verb, even words we think of as eternal and unchanging, stuck in their more 4

SUGGESTED MLA CITATION: McKean, Erin. "Verbed! Not Every Noun Wants to Stay That Way." 2010. *Back to the Lake.* Ed. Thomas Cooley. 2nd ed. New York: Norton, 2012. 359–61. Print.

traditional roles. It's easy to think of scenarios where "She *me'd* him too much and they broke up" and "My boss *tomorrowed* the meeting again" make sense.

See p. 325 for guidance in using description along with classification.

(Linguists discussing this process sometimes avoid the nonstandard word verbing by using the technical terms *denominal derivation* or *conversion* instead. Rhetoricians are even less likely to use the word verbing and use the general term *antimeria* to describe any use of a word in a different part of speech.) 5

Objections to verbification in English tend to be motivated by personal taste, not clarity. Verbed words are usually easily understood. When a word like *friend* is declared not a verb, the problem isn't that it's confusing; it's that the protester finds it deeply annoying. 6

Some of the outrage might be connected to verbing's popularity as a feature of business jargon: *Liase, incentivize, leverage,* and *status* are often cited as horrible bizspeak to be shunned at all costs. (Why are businesses supposed to be super-efficient in everything but their use of language? "He didn't have a chance to status us before he left" is four words shorter than "He didn't have a chance to give us a status update before he left.") 7

Some not-a-verb declarations are made for reasons that are more financial than linguistic: Google, TiVo, Adobe, and Xerox want to defend their trademarks, and one way to do that is to announce loudly, and at every opportunity, that *Google, TiVo, Photoshop,* and *Xerox* are not, repeat NOT, verbs. Xerox occasionally runs ads in major magazines (most recently in the *Hollywood Reporter* this past May) reminding people that Xerox is still a trademark, and asking writers not to use Xerox the trademark as a verb. 8

Given the outrage, why do people verb? Often, it's a shortcut: There comes a point where *text* is just a shorter way to say "send a text message." And there's a kind of cultural currency to verbing, which might be a reason that it's a staple of television writing. (There's an episode of *Seinfeld* where Kramer says "Let's bagel!"; and *Buffy the Vampire Slayer* used proper names as verbs on multiple occasions, including *Keyser Soze, Clark Kent,* and *Scully.*) 9

But something deeper is going on, too: When done well, verbing delights our brains. Philip Davis, a professor at the School of English at the University of Liverpool, devised a study in 2006 that tested just what happens when people read sentences with verbed nouns in them—and not just any verbed nouns, nouns verbed by Shakespeare. (Shakespeare was an inveterate noun-verber; he verbed *ghost,* in "Julius Caesar, / Who at Phillipi the good Brutus ghosted"; *dog,* in "Destruction straight shall dog them at the heels"; and even *uncle,* in "Grace me no grace, nor uncle me no uncle.") 10

So what did happen? When people were confronted with verbed nouns (in sentences such as "I was not supposed to go there alone: You said you would companion me.") EEGs measured their brains recognizing a syntactic anomaly, but not a semantic one. In other words, the subjects understood—in a time measured in 11 milliseconds—that something cool and new was happening. And they immediately got what it meant. Their double-take was measurably different from the one caused by hearing nouns or verbs unrelated to the context of the entire sentence ("you said you would charcoal me" "you said you would incubate me").

Granted, it was just one study, and using Shakespearean language to boot. But if there's even a slight chance that verbing attentions people, wouldn't it be a shame not to take advantage of it? 12

READING CLOSELY

1. How does Erin McKean DEFINE "verbing" (2)?

2. Why are some people opposed to verbing as a language act? Is their indignation justified? Why or why not?

3. According to McKean, the history of the English language shows "that the language is remarkably flexible in terms of what can be verbed" (4). What does this characteristic of a particular part of speech also show about the English language in general? Explain.

4. When people verb, says McKean, they're not just taking language shortcuts. What else are they doing?

STRATEGIES AND STRUCTURES

1. According to traditional grammar, every word in the English language can be classified according to only eight parts of speech—nouns, pronouns, verbs, adverbs, adjectives, prepositions, conjunctions, and interjections. How and where does McKean use this classification system in her essay?

2. What is the basis for this traditional system of classifying words? Is it some inherent quality in the word, or is the system based on how words are used in a phrase or sentence? Explain.

3. McKean's essay deals mostly with one type of *antimeria*—that of turning nouns into verbs (5). What other types might there be? Can you point out examples in her essay?

4. What is McKean's purpose in citing the Liverpool study (10)? How, and how well, does this research support the point she is making?

5. *Other Methods.* As in her opening paragraph—which is basically a list of EXAMPLES—McKean uses examples liberally throughout her essay. Is this a good strategy, especially when dealing with peculiarities of words and language? Why or why not?

THINKING ABOUT LANGUAGE

1. According to traditional grammar, *like* is a preposition (*a woman like her*), and as is a conjunction (*dress as she does*). So is McKean *"just wrong"* when she refers to turning a noun into a verb "like I did there" (2)? Why or why not?

2. What does McKean mean by a "language cop" (2)? What might be some SYNONYMS for this term?

3. Look up *syntactic* and *semantic* in your dictionary (11). To which different aspects of any language do these terms refer?

4. *Friend* is used extensively as a verb on Facebook (1), but the English language has a perfectly good verb, *befriend*, meaning "to make a friend of." Why doesn't Facebook just use that?

FOR WRITING

1. Write a paragraph or two explaining why it is okay (or "just wrong") to make verbs out of nouns.

2. Many dictionaries tag individual words with usage labels, such as *slang, informal*, or *obsolete*. Check the front of your dictionary for the system it uses—or look online for one—and write a classification essay explaining that system and giving several examples of each type. Be sure to indicate how well you think the system serves its purpose.

DEBORAH TANNEN

But What Do You Mean?

Deborah Tannen (b. 1945) is a professor of linguistics at Georgetown University. Best known for her studies of how men and women communicate, she is the author of twenty books and more than 100 articles, including You Just Don't Understand: Men and Women in Conversation *(1990) and* You're Wearing *That?* Understanding Mothers and Daughters in Conversation *(2006).*

"But What Do You Mean?" first appeared in Redbook *magazine in 1994 and summarizes much of Tannen's best-selling book* Talking from 9 to 5: Women and Men at Work *(1994). In this essay, Tannen classifies the most common ways in which men and women miscommunicate in the workplace.*

CONVERSATION IS A RITUAL. We say things that seem obviously the thing to say, 1 without thinking of the literal meaning of our words, any more than we expect the question "How are you?" to call forth a detailed account of aches and pains.

Unfortunately, women and men often have different ideas about what's appro- 2 priate, different ways of speaking. Many of the conversational rituals common among women are designed to take the other person's feelings into account, while many of the conversational rituals common among men are designed to maintain the one-up position, or at least avoid appearing one-down. As a result, when men and women interact—especially at work— it's often women who are at the disadvantage. Because women are not trying to avoid the one-down position, that is unfortunately where they may end up.

> The areas you divide any subject into should be inclusive but not overlap (p. 323).

Here, the biggest areas of miscommunication. 3

1. Apologies

Women are often told they apologize too much. The reason they're told to stop 4 doing it is that, to many men, apologizing seems synonymous with putting oneself down. But there are many times when "I'm sorry" isn't self-deprecating, or even an apology; it's an automatic way of keeping both speakers on an equal footing. For example, a well-known columnist once interviewed me and gave me her phone number in case I needed to call her back. I misplaced the number and had to go through the newspaper's main switchboard. When our conversation was winding

SUGGESTED MLA CITATION: Tannen, Deborah. "But What Do You Mean?" 1994. *Back to the Lake.* Ed. Thomas Cooley. 2nd ed. New York: Norton, 2012. 363–68. Print.

down and we'd both made ending-type remarks, I added, "Oh, I almost forgot—I lost your direct number, can I get it again?" "Oh, I'm sorry," she came back instantly, even though she had done nothing wrong and *I* was the one who'd lost the number. But I understood she wasn't really apologizing; she was just automatically reassuring me she had no intention of denying me her number.

Even when "I'm sorry" *is* an apology, women often assume it will be the first   5 step in a two-step ritual: I say "I'm sorry" and take half the blame, then you take the other half. At work, it might go something like this:

> A: When you typed this letter, you missed this phrase I inserted.
> B: Oh, I'm sorry. I'll fix it.
> A: Well, I wrote it so small it was easy to miss.

When both parties share blame, it's a mutual face-saving device. But if one per-   6 son, usually the woman, utters frequent apologies and the other doesn't, she ends up looking as if she's taking the blame for mishaps that aren't her fault. When she's only partially to blame, she looks entirely in the wrong.

I recently sat in on a meeting at an insurance company where the sole woman,   7 Helen, said "I'm sorry" or "I apologize" repeatedly. At one point she said, "I'm thinking out loud. I apologize." Yet the meeting was intended to be an informal brainstorming session, and *everyone* was thinking out loud.

The reason Helen's apologies stood out was that she was the only person in the   8 room making so many. And the reason I was concerned was that Helen felt the annual bonus she had received was unfair. When I interviewed the colleagues, they said that Helen was one of the best and most productive workers—yet she got one of the smallest bonuses. Although the problem might have been outright sexism, I suspect her speech style, which differs from that of her male colleagues, masks her competence.

Unfortunately, not apologizing can have its price too. Since so many women use   9 ritual apologies, those who don't may be seen as hard-edged. What's important is to be aware of how often you say you're sorry (and why), and to monitor your speech based on the reaction you get.

2. Criticism

A woman who cowrote a report with a male colleague was hurt when she read a   10 rough draft to him and he leapt into a critical response—"Oh, that's too dry! You have to make it snappier!" She herself would have been more likely to say, "That's a really good start. Of course, you'll want to make it a little snappier when you revise."

Whether criticism is given straight or softened is often a matter of convention.   11 In general, women use more softeners. I noticed this difference when talking to an editor about an essay I'd written. While going over changes she wanted to make, she said, "There's one more thing. I know you may not agree with me. The reason I noticed the problem is that your other points are so lucid and elegant." She went on hedging for several more sentences until I put her out of her misery: "Do you want to cut that part?" I asked—and of course she did. But I appreciated her tentativeness. In contrast, another editor (a man) I once called summarily rejected my idea for an article by barking, "Call me when you have something new to say."

Those who are used to ways of talking that soften the impact of criticism may 12 find it hard to deal with the right-between-the-eyes style. It has its own logic, however, and neither style is intrinsically better. People who prefer criticism given straight are operating on an assumption that feelings aren't involved: "Here's the dope. I know you're good; you can take it."

3. Thank-Yous

A woman manager I know starts meetings by thanking everyone for coming, even 13 though it's clearly their job to do so. Her "thank-you" is simply a ritual.

A novelist received a fax from an assistant in her publisher's office; it contained 14 suggested catalog copy for her book. She immediately faxed him her suggested changes and said, "Thanks for running this by me," even though her contract gave her the right to approve all copy. When she thanked the assistant, she fully expected him to reciprocate: "Thanks for giving me such a quick response." Instead, he said, "You're welcome." Suddenly, rather than an equal exchange of pleasantries, she found herself positioned as the recipient of a favor. This made her feel like responding, "Thanks for nothing!"

Many women use "thanks" as an automatic conversation starter and closer; 15 there's nothing literally to say thank you for. Like many rituals typical of women's conversation, it depends on the goodwill of the other to restore the balance. When the other speaker doesn't reciprocate, a woman may feel like someone on a seesaw whose partner abandoned his end. Instead of balancing in the air, she has plopped to the ground, wondering how she got there.

4. Fighting

Many men expect the discussion of ideas to be a ritual fight—explored through 16 verbal opposition. They state their ideas in the strongest possible terms, thinking that if there are weaknesses someone will point them out, and by trying to argue against those objections, they will see how well their ideas hold up.

Those who expect their own ideas to be challenged will respond to another's 17 ideas by trying to poke holes and find weak links—as a way of *helping*. The logic is that when you are challenged you will rise to the occasion: Adrenaline makes your mind sharper; you get ideas and insights you would not have thought of without the spur of battle.

But many women take this approach as a personal attack. Worse, they find it impossible to do their best work in such a contentious environment. If you're not used to ritual fighting, you begin to hear criticism of your ideas as soon as they are formed. Rather than making you think more clearly, it makes you doubt what you know. When you state your ideas, you hedge in order to fend off potential attacks. Ironically, this is more likely to *invite* attack because it makes you look weak. 18

Although you may never enjoy verbal sparring, some women find it helpful to learn how to do it. An engineer who was the only woman among four men in a small company found that as soon as she learned to argue she was accepted and taken seriously. A doctor attending a hospital staff meeting made a similar discovery. She was becoming more and more angry with a male colleague who'd loudly disagreed with a point she'd made. Her better judgment told her to hold her tongue, to avoid making an enemy of this powerful senior colleague. But finally she couldn't hold it in any longer, and she rose to her feet and delivered an impassioned attack on his position. She sat down in a panic, certain she had permanently damaged her relationship with him. To her amazement, he came up to her afterward and said, "That was a great rebuttal. I'm really impressed. Let's go out for a beer after work and hash out our approaches to this problem." 19

5. Praise

A manager I'll call Lester had been on his new job six months when he heard that the women reporting to him were deeply dissatisfied. When he talked to them about it, their feelings erupted; two said they were on the verge of quitting because he didn't appreciate their work, and they didn't want to wait to be fired. Lester was dumbfounded: He believed they were doing a fine job. Surely, he thought, he had said nothing to give them the impression he didn't like their work. And indeed he hadn't. That was the problem. He had said *nothing*—and the women assumed he was following the adage "If you can't say something nice, don't say anything." He thought he was showing confidence in them by leaving them alone. 20

Men and women have different habits in regard to giving praise. For example, Deirdre and her colleague William both gave presentations at a conference. Afterward, Deirdre told William, "That was a great talk!" He thanked her. Then she asked, "What did you think of mine?" and he gave her a lengthy and detailed critique. She found it uncomfortable to listen to his comments. But she assured herself that he meant well, and that his honesty was a signal that she, too, should be honest when he asked for a critique of his performance. As a matter of fact, she had noticed quite a few ways in which he could have improved his presentation. But she never got a chance to tell him because he never asked—and she felt put 21 down. The worst part was that it seemed she had only herself to blame, since she *had* asked what he thought of her talk.

But had she really asked for his critique? The truth is, when she asked for his opinion, she was expecting a compliment, which she felt was more or less required following anyone's talk. When he responded with criticism, she figured, "Oh, he's playing 'Let's critique each other'"—not a game she'd initiated, but one which she was willing to play. Had she realized he was going to criticize her and not ask her to reciprocate, she would never have asked in the first place.

It would be easy to assume that Deirdre was insecure, whether she was fishing for a compliment or soliciting a critique. But she was simply talking automatically, performing one of the many conversational rituals that allow us to get through the day. William may have sincerely misunderstood Deirdre's intention—or may have been unable to pass up a chance to one-up her when given the opportunity.

6. Complaints

"Troubles talk" can be a way to establish rapport with a colleague. You complain about a problem (which shows that you are just folks) and the other person responds with a similar problem (which puts you on equal footing). But while such commiserating is common among women, men are likely to hear it as a request to *solve* the problem.

One woman told me she would frequently initiate what she thought would be pleasant complaint-airing sessions at work. She'd talk about situations that bothered her just to talk about them, maybe to understand them better. But her male office mate would quickly tell her how she could improve the situation. This left her feeling condescended to and frustrated. She was delighted to see this very impasse in a section in my book *You Just Don't Understand*, and showed it to him. "Oh," he said, "I see the problem. How can we solve it?" Then they both laughed, because it had happened again: He short-circuited the detailed discussion she'd hoped for and cut to the chase of finding a solution.

Sometimes the consequences of complaining are more serious: A man might take a woman's lighthearted griping literally, and she can get a reputation as a chronic malcontent. Furthermore, she may be seen as not up to solving the problems that arise on the job.

7. Jokes

I heard a man call in to a talk show and say, "I've worked for two women and neither one had a sense of humor. You know, when you work with men, there's a lot of joking and teasing." The show's host and guest (both women) took his comment at face value and assumed the women this man worked for were humorless. The guest said, "Isn't it sad that women don't feel comfortable enough with authority to see the humor?" The host said, "Maybe when more women are in authority roles, they'll be more comfortable with power." But although the women this man worked for *may* have taken themselves too seriously, it's just as likely that they each had a terrific sense of humor, but maybe the humor wasn't the type he was used to. They may have been like the woman who wrote to me: "When I'm with men, my wit or cleverness seems inappropriate (or lost!) so I don't bother. When I'm with my women friends, however, there's no hold on puns or cracks and my humor is fully appreciated."

The types of humor women and men tend to prefer differ. Research has shown 28 that the most common form of humor among men is razzing, teasing, and mock-hostile attacks, while among women it's self-mocking. Women often mistake men's teasing as genuinely hostile. Men often mistake women's mock self-deprecation as truly putting themselves down.

Women have told me they were taken more seriously when they learned to joke 29 the way the guys did. For example, a teacher who went to a national conference with seven other teachers (mostly women) and a group of administrators (mostly men) was annoyed that the administrators always found reasons to leave boring seminars, while the teachers felt they had to stay and take notes. One evening, when the group met at a bar in the hotel, the principal asked her how one such seminar had turned out. She reported, "As soon as you left, it got much better." He laughed out loud at her response. The playful insult appealed to the men—but there was a trade-off. The women seemed to back off from her after this. (Perhaps they were put off by her using joking to align herself with the bosses.)

There is no "right" way to talk. When problems arise, the culprit may be style 30 differences—and *all* styles will at times fail with others who don't share or understand them, just as English won't do you much good if you try to speak to someone who knows only French. If you want to get your message across, it's not a question of being "right"; it's a question of using language that's shared—or at least understood.

✦⸺⸳⸳⸳⸳⸴

READING CLOSELY

1. In this essay, what principle of classification is Deborah Tannen using to classify "different ways of speaking" (2)?

2. In what fundamental way do the "conversational rituals" of men and women differ, according to Tannen (2)? Do you think she's right? Why or why not?

3. Tannen says she is classifying the "different ways" in which men and women speak (2). What else is she classifying?

4. Women, says Tannen, tend to apologize more often than men do. Why? She also finds that women often say "thank-you" when they don't really mean it (13). What *do* they often mean by "thank-you"?

5. In Tannen's view, when women complain, they are often trying to "establish rapport" (24). How does she say most men respond to this technique?

6. Women, says Tannen, often see "verbal opposition" as a direct attack (16). How does she say that men see it?

STRATEGIES AND STRUCTURES

1. "Although you may never enjoy verbal sparring, some women find it helpful to learn how to do it" (19). To whom is Tannen speaking here? Can you find other evidence that indicates the identity of her intended AUDIENCE?

2. What is Tannen's underlying purpose in classifying the verbal behavior of men and women in terms of the workplace? How can you tell?

3. Tannen divides her subject into seven main "arcas" (3). Are these categories based on significant characteristics? Are they mutually exclusive? Do they cover all kinds of communication? Explain.

4. Tannen breaks "jokes" into the "the types of humor women and men tend to prefer" (28). Why does she use subcategories here and not elsewhere in her classification?

5. How and how well does Tannen use classification to structure her ARGUMENT about women in the workplace?

6. *Other Methods.* Much of Tannen's evidence is ANECDOTAL—that is, she tells brief stories to make her points. How effective do you find these NARRATIVE elements of her essay? Explain.

THINKING ABOUT LANGUAGE

1. "Conversation," says Tannen, "is a ritual" (1). What is ritual behavior, and why do you think Tannen uses this term?

2. What are the CONNOTATIONS of "hard-edged" when it's applied to women (9)? What are its connotations when applied to men?

3. What is "right-between-the-eyes style" (12)? What two things are being compared in this METAPHOR?

4. Tannen accuses a man of "barking" (11) and several women of allowing their emotions to "erupt" (20). How do these choices of words confirm or contradict her assertions about the way men and women communicate?

FOR WRITING

1. Can you think of any "areas of miscommunication" (3) between men and women that Tannen has overlooked? Write a paragraph on each kind, providing specific examples.

2. Write an essay about the different ways in which one of the following groups of people communicate (or miscommunicate) with each other: siblings, children and parents, students and teachers, engineers and liberal arts majors, old people and young people, or some other group or groups.

ANNE SEXTON

Her Kind

Anne Sexton (1928–1974) was a poet, playwright, model, and author of children's books. Born in Newton, Massachusetts, she began writing poetry in high school. Sexton did not focus on her writing until 1957, however, when she enrolled in a poetry workshop at the Boston Center for Adult Education. Ten years later she won a Pulitzer Prize in poetry for her collection Live or Die *(1966). For most of her adult life, Sexton suffered from depression and mental illness. Writing helped Sexton to maintain her sanity, apparently; but on her birthday in 1974, she committed suicide by carbon monoxide poisoning. (Of Sexton's untimely death, her fellow poet, Denise Levetov, wrote that "we who are alive must make clear, as she could not, the distinction between creativity and self-destruction.")*

"Her Kind" is the keynote poem in Sexton's first book of poems, To Bedlam and Part Way Back *(1960). At one point during its composition, Sexton called the poem "Witch" but changed the title when, after much revision, she introduced a second, more detached point of view in the last two lines of each stanza. It is this "I" who classifies the woman she is observing in each stanza and who then affirms that she belongs (or has belonged) to the same "kind."*

> I have gone out, a possessed witch,
> haunting the black air, braver at night;
> dreaming evil, I have done my hitch
> over the plain houses, light by light:
> lonely thing, twelve-fingered, out of mind.   5
> A woman like that is not a woman, quite.
> I have been her kind.
>
> I have found the warm caves in the woods,
> filled them with skillets, carvings, shelves,
> closets, silks, innumerable goods;   10
> fixed the suppers for the worms and the elves:
> whining, rearranging the disaligned.
> A woman like that is misunderstood.
> I have been her kind.

SUGGESTED MLA CITATION: Sexton, Anne. "Her Kind." 1960. *Back to the Lake.* Ed. Thomas Cooley. 2nd ed. New York: Norton, 2012. 371–72. Print.

I have ridden in your cart, driver,   15
waved my nude arms at villages going by,
learning the last bright routes, survivor
where your flames still bite my thigh
and my ribs crack where your wheels wind.
A woman like that is not ashamed to die.   20
I have been her kind.

READING CLOSELY

1. According to Anne Sexton's biographer, Diane Wood Middlebrook, "Her Kind" depicts a different woman in each stanza. In the first is "the witch"; then "the housewife"; and, finally, "the adulteress." Does the poem support this reading? Why or why not?

2. Whether Sexton is writing about three different women or the same woman at different moments in her life, how do they (or she) typically behave? Why? What might be some of the CAUSES?

3. How does the "I" in the first line of each stanza COMPARE AND CONTRAST with the "I" in the last line? Explain.

4. In the last stanza, the woman is riding in a cart. Where is she going?

STRATEGIES AND STRUCTURES

1. Sexton identifies three distinguishing characteristics—one in each stanza—of the "kind" of woman she is writing about. What are they?

2. On what basis—age, social status, psychological condition, and so forth—is Sexton constructing her classification system? What other types might there be?

3. Sexton's speaker claims to have been the kind of woman she is imagining. How, and how well, do her DESCRIPTIONS of particular specimens support this claim?

4. *Other Methods.* Each stanza of "Her Kind" tells a story. How, and how well, does Sexton use these NARRATIVES to explain what kind of woman she is writing about?

THINKING ABOUT LANGUAGE

1. The "I" in Sexton's first stanza says she has done her "hitch" (line 3). Beside rhyming with "witch," this word suggests a tour of duty, as in the military. Why would Sexton use such a term here?

2. Sexton uses the present perfect tense when her speaker says, "I have been her kind" (lines 7, 14, 21). Why doesn't she use the present tense (*am*)?

3. What does "her kind" often mean in common speech? What alternative "kind" does it assume? How does Sexton build on such assumptions in her poem?

4. The woman in the cart says she is not "ashamed" to die (line 20). Why is this assertion more startling than if she had simply said she was not "afraid" to die?

FOR WRITING

1. Sexton's poem consists of three seven-line stanzas, each beginning and ending with "I have." If you had to add a stanza to her poem that began and ended this way, what would happen in those seven lines? Make a list of the actions that would occur.

2. "A woman like that is misunderstood" (line 13). Choose several of Sexton's poems—or those of some other poet whose work interests you—and write an essay about the kind of woman (or man) the poet presents to the reader as particularly misunderstood. How does the poet help the reader to understand such figures, or block the way to understanding them?

CHAPTER 10

Definition

A guy with a twelve-inch arm can have much more noticeable muscles than a guy with an eighteen-inch arm because he has better definition.

—PETE SISCO, *Train Smart*

You know what getting ripped off is. How about getting ripped? According to bodybuilder Pete Sisco, *getting ripped* refers to muscle definition: You build up your muscles so they stick out and are easier to see. Likewise, when you define something—from bodybuilding to high-definition electronics—you make its fundamental nature sharp and clear.

In her essay "So, You Want to Be a Writer," novelist Allegra Goodman defines a writer as someone who is truly at home with "peace and quiet," qualities which she then goes on to define as follows: *Quiet*, says Goodman—using the technique of defining something by telling what it is not—is simply the absence of noise. *Peace*, however, she notes, is more difficult to grasp. "Peace is not the same as quiet," Goodman writes. "Peace means you avoid checking your email every ten seconds. Peace means you are willing to work offline, screen calls, and forget your to-do list for an hour."

In a broader definition, *peace* might be defined as the absence of war, or as a state of contentment and inner serenity. Goodman, however, is defining her subject from the perspective of the frazzled writer who is striving to avoid distractions and concentrate on her own thoughts and words. For her intended readers (those who want to be writers), Goodman chooses a relatively narrow definition of her subject, one that suits both her audience and purpose.

Defining Definition:
Telling What Something Is

A definition explains what something is—and is not—by identifying the characteristics that set it apart from all others like it. An accomplished writer, for example,
is a person who habitually deals with words and ideas, often in electronic form.
The same is true of any chronic browser of the Internet. Unlike the chronic Internet user, however, the writer—at least in Allegra Goodman's definition—must be
willing and able to disconnect from the Web (and any other source of distraction)
when it threatens to destroy his or her concentration.

Or take athletes. Bodybuilders, runners, and swimmers can all be defined as
athletes who need to keep their body fat under control and to build up muscle
strength. Consequently, their muscles are often sharply defined. Among these
three types of athletes, however, only bodybuilders train primarily for muscle definition and bulk. In other words, training for muscle definition and bulk is a characteristic that *defines* bodybuilders alone. Runners and swimmers may want and
need strong muscles, too, but what *defines* them is their speed on the track and in
the pool, not the size or look of their muscles on the beach. Definitions set up
boundaries; they say, in effect: "This is the territory occupied by my subject, and
everything outside these boundaries is something else." Definition can also be a
method of developing a subject in writing, and in this chapter we will see how to
organize an entire essay around a definition.

Basic dictionary definitions have two parts: the general class to which the term
belongs, and the specific characteristics that distinguish the term from other terms
in that class. This is the pattern that definitions have followed since Dr. Samuel
Johnson compiled the *Dictionary of the English Language* more than 250 years ago.
For example, Johnson's famous definition of a "lexicographer," or dictionary maker,
as "a harmless drudge" fits this pattern: *drudge* is the general class, and *harmless* is
a characteristic that distinguishes the lexicographer from other kinds of drudges.

Here are a few more current examples of basic definitions:

TERM BEING DEFINED	GENERAL CLASS	DISTINGUISHING CHARACTERISTIC(S)
writer	user of words	requires peace and quiet
muscle	body tissue	fibrous, capable of contracting
osprey	hawk	fish-eating

Because basic definitions like these help to explain the fundamental nature of a subject, they can be useful for beginning almost any kind of essay. When you want to define a subject in depth, however, you will need an *extended definition*. An extended definition includes all the parts of a basic definition—the term you're defining, its general class, and its essential distinguishing characteristics. Unlike a basic definition, however, an extended definition doesn't stop there. It goes on to discuss other important distinguishing characteristics of the subject as well. For instance, if the basic definition of a bodybuilder is "an athlete who trains for muscle definition and bulk," an extended definition of a bodybuilder might look at a bodybuilder's focus and motivation, training regimen, bodybuilding competitions, and so on. Extended definitions also use many of the other methods of development discussed in this book, such as NARRATION, DESCRIPTION, and EXAMPLE.

In this chapter, we will not only see how to write basic definitions that are sharp and clear, we will learn how to construct an extended definition and make it the backbone of a complete essay. We will consider how to use SYNONYMS and ETYMOLOGIES in a definition, and how to use other methods of development. We'll also review the critical points to watch for as you read over and revise your essay, as well as common errors to avoid when you edit.

Why Do We Define?

Being naturally curious, human beings define in order to understand the fundamental nature of things. For example, if you were defining *abolitionism* for an exam in U.S. history, you might first give a brief dictionary definition—"advocacy of the abolishment of slavery in the United States"—but you would move on to discuss the abolition movement before the Civil War and the legal abolishment of slavery by President Lincoln's Emancipation Proclamation. Writing about this term would thus help you make sense of history, in this case the history of an important social and political movement in American culture.

Sometimes, however, understanding a definition can be personally enlightening. The great antislavery orator Frederick Douglass escaped from slavery as a young man. In 1845, he wrote about how he came to learn the meaning of *abolition*:

> If a slave ran away and succeeded in getting clear . . . or did anything very wrong in the mind of a slaveholder, it was spoken of as the fruit of *abolition*. Hearing the word in this connection very often, I set about learning what it meant. The dictionary afforded me little or no help. I found it was "the act of abolishing"; but then I did not know what was to be abolished. Here I was perplexed. I did not dare to ask anyone about the meaning, for I was satisfied

that it was something they wanted me to know very little about. After a patient waiting, I got one of our city papers, containing an account . . . of the slave trade between the States. From this time I understood the words *abolition* and *abolitionist*, and always drew near when that word was spoken, expecting to hear something of importance to myself and fellow-slaves. The light broke in upon me by degrees. —FREDERICK DOUGLASS, *Narrative*

Such is the power and purpose of definitions: without them, we're in the dark about many things of importance to us. Before he could write so powerfully about the concept of *abolition*, young Douglass first had to learn what it meant in common usage. Defining, then, is ultimately a process of exploration. We extend our definitions in order to extend our horizons—and those of our readers.

For a killer example, see "How to Know If You're Dead" (p. 402).

Composing a Definition Essay

When you compose a definition essay, your first challenge is to find a topic worth defining. That topic may be complex, like relativity or Marxism or capitalism. Or, sometimes, you may devote an entire essay to a definition because you are arguing that a word or concept means something that others might not have thought of, or might disagree with. For example, if you were defining *intelligent design* in an essay you might want to say, at some length, not only what intelligent design is but why the reader should (or should not) believe in it. Definitions that require a whole essay often deal with terms that are open to debate or controversy. For example: What constitutes *racism* or *sexual harassment*? When does a *fetus* becomes a viable human being? What characterizes *friendship*?

Dictionary definitions will help you begin to think about such questions, but to write an essay that defines something fully—especially if it's something complicated or controversial—you will need to construct an extended definition and probably to call upon other methods of development. That is, you may need to DESCRIBE the subject, give EXAMPLES of it, analyze what CAUSED it or how it works, or COMPARE it with others. Take the concept of *longitude*, for example. Longitude can be defined as "distance measured east and west on the earth's surface." This basic definition doesn't fully define the subject, however. To extend such a definition, you might describe the place from which longitude is measured (the Royal Observatory in Greenwich, England, just outside of London on a steep hill), analyze how it's measured (in minutes and degrees from the prime meridian), and compare it with *latitude* (distance on the earth's surface as measured north and south of the equator).

To define the word *harem*, Fatema Mernissi narrates her childhood in Morocco (p. 410).

Thinking about Purpose and Audience

When you define something, your general purpose is to say what it is, but you may have any number of specific reasons for doing this. You may be conveying useful information to someone, demonstrating that you understand the meaning of an important term or concept, arguing for a particular definition, or just entertaining the reader. In her essay in this chapter, "How to Know If You're Dead." Mary Roach, for example, defines her subject for most of these reasons combined. "When I tried to explain beating-heart cadavers to my stepdaughter Phoebe yesterday," she writes, "it didn't make sense to her. But if their heart is beating, aren't they still a person? she wanted to know. In the end she decided they were 'a kind of person you could play tricks on but they wouldn't know.'" This, says Roach, "is a pretty good way of summing up" the meaning of a difficult and sometimes controversial term.

Whatever your specific purpose (or purposes) for constructing a definition, you need to consider why your audience might want (or be reluctant) to know more about it and what it means. Also think about how the reader might already define the term. What information can you supply to make it easier for the reader to understand your definition, or be more receptive to it?

To take another example, if you were defining longitude in a manual for would-be sailors, you would compare it with latitude and explain how each measures different directions on the globe. You would also point out that determining longitude requires an accurate timepiece—if not a Global Positioning System—whereas latitude can be estimated just by eyeballing the angle of the sun or stars above the horizon. Since you're defining longitude for navigational purposes, you won't need to point out that, in the days before accurate clocks, measuring (or mismeasuring) longitude posed a grave danger to sailors on the high seas. However, such historical information—though irrelevant in a sailing manual—might be of vital interest if you were constructing a broad definition of longitude for a general audience, as in this passage from an entire book on the subject:

> Here lies the real, hard-core difference between latitude and longitude. . . .
> The zero-degree parallel of latitude [the equator] is fixed by the laws of
> nature, while the zero-degree meridian of longitude shifts like the sands of
> time. This difference makes finding latitude child's play, and turns the deter-
> mination of longitude, especially at sea, into an adult dilemma—one that
> stumped the wisest minds of the world for the better part of human history.
> —Dava Sobel, Longitude

In Longitude, Sobel defines her subject as a scientific, political, and philosophical concept. In an essay, rather than a book, you can't define longitude or any other subject on such a global scale, but you can focus on those aspects of your subject that best suit your purpose and that your audience is most likely to find interesting and useful.

Jack Horner gives his own spatial definition of *dyslexia* on p. 418.

Generating Ideas:
Asking What Something Is—and Is Not

LISTING, CLUSTERING, BRAINSTORMING, and other techniques of discovery can help you generate ideas for a definition. In order to define your subject, you will need to consider what its distinguishing characteristics are—what makes it different from other things in the same general class. How do you know which characteristics are essential to your definition? Start by thinking about the characteristics that tell us the most about it. For instance, suppose we wanted to define what an *engineer* is. We know that engineers often use tools and have specialized knowledge about how things are built. But these characteristics also apply to carpenters and burglars. What characteristics tell us the most about engineers?

According to one expert, these characteristics are all *essential* to engineers:

- They are fascinated with the physical world.
- They value utility over beauty or knowledge.
- They have a thorough understanding of mathematics and science.
- They are trained to apply that knowledge to physical objects and systems.
- Their purpose in doing so is to remake the world by shaping it to practical use. —MICHAEL DAVIS, "Defining 'Engineer'"

As you come up with a list of essential distinguishing characteristics for your subject, you should also ask what your subject is *not*. Here is how Davis answers that question when defining engineers:

- Engineers are not pure scientists. They may generate knowledge, but that knowledge is not an end in itself, as it can be for a mathematician or physicist.
- Though they may produce beautiful structures, such as bridges or towers, engineers are not artists (in the way that architects are).
- Engineers are not primarily interested in rules (lawyers) or money (accountants) or people (managers).
- Engineers must write reports that are both clear and accurate, but they are not primarily writers either.

The essential distinguishing characteristics that you list—the traits that tell what your subject is and is not—will form the foundation of your definition essay.

Organizing and Drafting a Definition Essay

When you have a clear idea of your purpose and audience—and a solid list of distinguishing characteristics for your subject—you are ready to start organizing and drafting your essay. First you will need to construct a basic definition of your subject—and then to extend that definition. There are a number of techniques for doing this that can help, including the other methods of development discussed in this book. The templates on the next page can also help you get started.

STATING YOUR POINT

By itself, an extended definition does not constitute a well-organized essay; you need to explain the point your definition is intended to make. A THESIS statement—usually made in the introduction and perhaps repeated with variations at the end—is a good way to do this. Here is a thesis statement for an extended definition of a *farmer*, written by Craig Schafer, an Ohio State student who grew up on a farm in the Midwest: "By definition, a farmer is someone who tills the soil for a living, but I define a true farmer according to his or her attitudes toward the land." This is a good thesis statement because it gives a clear basic definition of its subject—and then promises to extend it in interesting ways that the reader may or may not agree with at first.

SPECIFYING ADDITIONAL DISTINGUISHING CHARACTERISTICS

Bobbie Ann Mason goes into the many characteristics of "being country" on p. 422.
Of all the ways you can extend a basic definition, perhaps the most effective is simply to specify additional characteristics that set your subject apart. Thus, to support his definition of a farmer as a person with certain attitudes toward the land, Schafer goes on to specify what those attitudes are, devoting a paragraph to each:

• A farmer is a born optimist. He plants his crops with no assurance that nature will cooperate or that markets will be favorable.

• A farmer is devoted to the soil. He enjoys letting it sift through his fingers or just sniffing the fresh clean aroma of a newly plowed field.

• A farmer is self-denying. His barn is often better planned and sometimes more modern than his house.

• A farmer is independent. Unions have found it impossible to organize him.

By ascribing interesting, even controversial, characteristics like these to your subject, you can take it well beyond the narrow confines of ordinary dictionary definitions. Everybody knows what a farmer is. But a farmer with attitude—or rather, attitudes—is a different story.

TEMPLATES FOR DRAFTING

When you begin to draft a definition, you need to identify your subject, assign it to a general class, and specify particular characteristics that distinguish it from others in that same class. These moves are fundamental to any definition. See how Fatema Mernissi makes such moves in her essay in this chapter:

> Harem was the place where a man sheltered his family, his wife or wives, and children and relatives. It could be a house or a tent, and it referred both to the space and to the people who lived within it.
> —FATEMA MERNISSI, "The Harem Within"

Mernissi identifies her subject ("harem"), assigns it to a general class (places), and specifies the particular characteristic ("where a man sheltered his family") that distinguishes it from others in that class. Here is one more example from this chapter:

> H. is unique in that she is both a dead person *and* a patient on the way to surgery. She is what's known as a "beating-heart cadaver," alive and well everywhere but her brain.
> —MARY ROACH, "How to Know If You're Dead"

The following templates can help you make some of these basic moves in your own writing. But don't take these as formulas where you just fill in the blanks. There are no shortcuts to good writing, but these templates can serve as starting points.

▶ In general, X can be defined as a kind of _____.

▶ What specifically distinguishes X from others in this category is _____.

▶ X is usually a _____; but it can also be a _____, or even a _____.

▶ X is often used to mean _____, but a better synonym would be _____ or _____.

▶ One way to define X is as the opposite of _____, the distinguishing features of which are _____, _____, and _____.

▶ If we define X as _____, we can then define Y as _____.

▶ By defining X in this way, we can see that _____.

USING SYNONYMS

Another way to extend a definition is by offering SYNONYMS. If you can substitute a more familiar word for the term you are defining, the reader may be more likely to understand and accept your definition. For example, if you were defining a *blog* for readers unfamiliar with the Internet, you might say that it is an electronic journal or diary. You could then go on to say which particular characteristics of journals apply to blogs and which ones don't. Both blogs and journals, you might point out, record the personal thoughts of their authors; but blogs, unlike journals, typically include links to other sites and blogs, and invite response.

Geoffrey Nunberg does this with *terror* and *terrorism* on p. 432.

USING ETYMOLOGIES

Often you can usefully extend the definition of a term by tracing its history, or etymology. This is what an engineer at the University of Houston did when he asked, "Who are we who have been calling ourselves *engineers* since the early nineteenth century?" Here's part of his answer:

> The word *engineering* probably derives from the Latin word *ingeniatorum*. In 1325 a contriver of siege towers was called by the Norman word *engynours*. By 1420 the English were calling a trickster an *yngynore*. By 1592 we find the word *enginer* being given to a designer of phrases—a wordsmith. The *Oxford English Dictionary* gets to the first use of the modern word engineer in 1635, but you might not be crazy about its use. Someone is quoted as calling the devil—"that great engineer, Satan."
>
> —JOHN H. LIENHARD, "The Polytechnic Legacy"

Although few people today would use the word *engineer* to describe Satan, knowing the history of the word and its earlier variations can help us define what an engineer is, namely one who devises things with cleverness and ingenuity, whether it's a siege tower or a carefully crafted piece of writing. You can find the etymology of a word in most dictionaries, alongside the definition.

USING OTHER METHODS

As you draft a definition essay, draw on the other methods in this book to round out your definition and support your thesis. Let's say you are defining *cowboy*. You could note that the cowboy is a vital part of the cattle industry and an iconic figure in American culture who is usually thought to be "the rugged silent type." You could ARGUE that this is a misconception, founded

For more on using argument, see the box on p. 384.

on equating him too often with the likes of the Marlboro Man. Then you could go on to describe the attitudes and daily work of the cowboy as you define him.

This is what Gretel Ehrlich, a writer who lives on a ranch in Wyoming, does in her extended definition of the American cowboy. Ehrlich's thesis is that "in our hellbent earnestness to romanticize the cowboy we've ironically disesteemed his true character." What is that true character? Ehrlich is going to define it for us, beginning with this basic definition: "A cowboy is someone who loves his work."

Ehrlich might have started with the standard dictionary definition of a cowboy as "a man, usually on horseback, who herds and tends cattle on a ranch, especially in the western U.S." By choosing "loves his work" from among all the other characteristics that might be said to define a cowboy, however, she introduces a distinguishing characteristic of her subject that the reader may not have considered. She then goes on to extend her definition by using a number of other methods of development, as shown in the examples below from her book, *The Solace of Open Spaces*. First she DESCRIBES the work that is the key distinguishing characteristic of her subject.

> A cowboy is someone who loves his work. Since the hours are long—ten to fifteen hours a day—and the pay is $30 he has to. What's required of him is an odd mixture of physical vigor and maternalism. His part of the beef-raising industry is to birth and nurture calves and take care of their mothers. For the most part his work is done on horseback and in a lifetime he sees and comes to know more animals than people.

Next, Ehrlich ANALYZES THE PROCESS of how a cowboy does some of his work:

> If a cow is stuck in a boghole he throws a loop around her neck, takes his dally (a half hitch around the saddle horn), and pulls her out with horsepower. If a calf is born sick, he may take her home, warm her in front of the kitchen fire, and massage her legs until dawn.

Then Ehrlich introduces a little NARRATIVE of a particular cowboy saving a horse:

> One friend, whose favorite horse was trying to swim a lake with hobbles on, dove under water and cut her legs loose with a knife, then swam her to shore, his arm around her neck lifeguard-style, and saved her from drowning.

Because Ehrlich is using her definition to make an argument about the "true character" of the cowboy, an important part of her definition is devoted to COMPARING AND CONTRASTING her idea of a cowboy with that of the cowboy as he is typically (or stereotypically) defined.

USING DEFINITION TO FRAME AN ARGUMENT

"In this world," said Benjamin Franklin, "nothing is certain but death and taxes." No matter what you think of taxes, they won't kill you—literally. By putting taxes and death in the same framework, however, Franklin humorously asserts that the two terms belong in the same general class with the same distinguishing characteristic (both are "certain"). This sort of framing is a clever way of implying that two terms have other characteristics in common as well, in this case negative ones.

Suppose you were the mayor of a small town and you wanted to build a recreation center. How might you convince the citizens of your town that a tax increase (to pay for the new recreation center) was a good thing?

The linguist George Lakoff has pondered such questions. If you consider taxes, for instance, to be a necessary evil, Lakoff suggests, you might present them as "dues." Then you would be defining them as what you pay to live in a civilized society where there are services that have been paid for by previous taxpayers. Defined this way, Lakoff argues, paying taxes becomes an act of patriotism.

Defining a term (*taxes*) by associating it with other terms (*dues*) that carry CONNOTATIONS (patriotism) you want to "rub off" on your key term is a strategy of ARGUMENT that Lakoff and others call "framing." In the following passage, for example, Gretel Ehrlich defines (or redefines) what it means to be a cowboy—normally framed in masculine terms—by framing her subject in feminine terms:

> Cowboys are perhaps the most misunderstood group of workers anywhere. Romanticized in the movies and on billboards as handsome, macho loners always heading off into the sunset, they are more likely to be homebodies or social misfits too shy to work with people. Their work has more to do with mothering and nurturing than with exhibitions of virility. A cowboy can bottle-feed a calf around the clock, forecast weather, use a sewing machine, make anything out of canvas or leather, and serve as midwife to any animal.

Marlboro Man or midwife? The frame of reference in which you define a subject can predispose your readers to accept not only your definition but the larger point your definition is intended to make.

Instead of the macho, trigger-happy man our culture has perversely wanted him to be, the cowboy is more apt to be convivial, quirky, and soft-hearted.

Ehrlich also analyzes the actual CAUSES AND EFFECTS of the cowboy's behavior as she sees them—all in the service of defining what a true cowboy is to her.

If he's "strong and silent" it's because there is probably no one to talk to. If he "rides away into the sunset" it's because he's been on horseback since four in the morning moving cattle and he's trying, fifteen hours later, to get home to his family. If he's "a rugged individualist" he's also part of a team: ranch work is teamwork and even the glorified open range cowboys of the 1880s rode up and down the Chisholm Trail in the company of twenty or thirty other riders.

This definition does two things: it takes a fresh look at the characteristics usually attributed to the cowboy, and it introduces the author's own, more expansive characteristics. When you construct a new definition or rework an accepted one as Ehrlich does, the new characteristics that you introduce do not have to outlaw the old ones. They just need to open up enough space for the reader to come over to your side of the fence. Thus, the cowboy can still be defined as "strong and silent" when he has to be—like a hero from a Western. But if the American cowboy is to be conceived as more than a cardboard figure, he can also be regarded as "convivial, quirky, and soft-hearted" at times.

Reading a Definition Essay with a Critical Eye

Once you have a draft of your definition essay, ask a friendly critic to read it and tell you what's working and what isn't. Then read it over yourself with an eye for what can be improved. Here are some questions to keep in mind when checking a definition essay.

PURPOSE AND AUDIENCE. For whom is this definition written? What is its purpose—To define something the reader probably doesn't know much about? To demonstrate your knowledge to an already knowledgeable reader? How is the reader likely to define the subject? Does the definition confirm a standard definition, or challenge or expand it in some way? How?

THE BASIC DEFINITION. Does the definition identify the general class to which the subject of the essay belongs, plus the distinguishing characteristics that separate that subject from others in the same class? If not, how might the definition be improved?

THE POINT. What is the main point of the definition? Is it stated as a thesis, preferably in the introduction of the essay? How might the main point be made even clearer to the reader?

DISTINGUISHING CHARACTERISTICS. How does the essay extend the basic definition? Does it introduce essential distinguishing characteristics of the subject? Are the characteristics sufficient to define the subject? Have any essential characteristics been left out? Which characteristics are most informative? Do any need to be sharpened or omitted? Does the definition say what the subject is not? Should it?

SYNONYMS AND ETYMOLOGIES. Are words with similar meanings or word histories used to help define key terms? If not, would either of these devices improve the definition?

OTHER METHODS. What other basic methods of development are used: DESCRIPTION? COMPARISON AND CONTRAST? Something else? If they are not used, how might such methods be incorporated into the definition?

Editing for Common Errors in Definitions

The following tips will help you check your writing for errors that often appear in definitions.

Check that any word referred to *as a word* is in italics

▶ The term *cowboy* is easy to define, but the life of a cowboy is not so easy to characterize.

▶ Generally referred to as *abolitionism*, the movement to abolish slavery changed the course of U.S. history.

▶ Abolitionism was especially strong in the Northern states, but many Southerners were abolitionists, too.

Where *cowboy* and *abolitionism* are italicized in these sentences, they are being referred to as words. When they are not italicized, they are referring to concepts.

Check each basic definition to make sure it includes the class to which the term belongs

▶ Engineering <u>is a professional field that</u> applies science for practical purposes.

▸ A Labrador retriever <u>is a breed of dog that</u> has a friendly disposition and
  is patient with children.

Without *professional field* and *breed of dog*, the preceding sentences are statements
about their subjects rather than definitions of them.

Check for common usage errors

IS WHERE, IS WHEN

Where and *when* should not be used to introduce definitions.

▸ Engineering is ~~where you put~~ <u>the practice of putting</u> science to use.
▸ A recession is ~~when~~ <u>the economic condition in which</u> prices go up and
  sales go down.

COMPRISE, COMPOSE

Comprise means "to consist of." *Compose* means "to make up." The whole *comprises*
the parts; the parts *compose* the whole.

▸ The United States ~~composes~~ <u>comprises</u> fifty states.
▸ Fifty states ~~comprise~~ <u>compose</u> the United States.

Student Example

Gail Babilonia was an undergraduate at Rutgers when she wrote "The Celebrity
Chef" as a research paper for an English course. It was one of twelve student essays
selected for publication in the 2004 issue of *Dialogues@RU: A Journal of Undergraduate Research*.

"The Celebrity Chef" is a study in communications theory that does more than
define a new kind of cook. Using various communications models, this essay also
defines a new brand of celebrity whose audience, in turn, can be understood as
participants, spectators, or targets.

The Celebrity Chef

Begins with an ETYMOLOGY explaining the recent history of *chef*

When we hear <u>the word *chef*</u>, we imagine a nameless Frenchman dressed in an all-white apron and a tall white hat with ownership rights to a fancy, upscale restaurant. However, today the chef at a well-known restaurant may no longer be hidden in the kitchen; well-known chefs can be seen every day on television. The celebrity chef is a recent addition to both the culinary and media worlds. Not too long ago, there were only a few: Julia Child was the most famous, and remains an icon today. Now, however, there are many more chefs to watch on the Food Network. Emeril Lagasse is the most popular, and demonstrates the role that celebrity chefs currently play in our lives. <u>Although a recent addition, celebrity chefs have had a great influence on our culture: they have changed our ideas about celebrity and about the social status of the chef; they have redefined the kind of food ordinary people can have, and transformed the way men feel about cooking</u>. However, the impact of the celebrity chef is one that most of us barely recognize.

THESIS statement explains main point in defining a new kind of chef, followed by aspects of the topic Babilonia plans to explore

COMPARES the life and goals of a student chef as distinct from those of the celebrity chef

Few students in a culinary institute expect to use their certification to become a "celebrity chef" or a Food Network television personality. There is far too much hard work involved in becoming a trained chef to have time to think about being a famous one. Tania Ralli, a student currently enrolled at the French Culinary Institute in New York City, explains: "[W]e were cooking five hours a night, three nights a week, after full days at our regular jobs. The cost, $28,000 in tuition and fees, signaled the depth of our commitment" (Ralli F4). Because tuition and fees are so high, many students must work full time and attend school in addition to their jobs. In their classes, the students cook recipes over and over in preparation for a final exam in which they cook two recipes randomly selected from among the hundreds that they have learned. However, Ralli claims, "cooking school was more than learning about technique. From developing heat-resistant hands to managing temperamental personalities, we developed the stamina necessary in a professional kitchen" (F4). The students are critiqued based on their efficiency and speed, and on the taste and presentation of their food; they are not trained to be charismatic, friendly, or photogenic. Students focus on surviving in professional kitchens, not on cooking under studio lights. Becoming famous is not a priority for most would-be chefs: students enter the culinary world in hopes of having more practical things like job security, benefits, and decent pay. By and large, they are too sensible to daydream about becoming the next Emeril, which is fortunate because becoming a celebrity chef is beyond their control: becoming a famous chef really depends on the media and the audience.

What makes a chef a "celebrity chef"? According to David Giles, an author who explored the psychology of fame and celebrity, "the defining characteristic of a celebrity is that there is essentially a media production" (2) on television, radio, or in the movies through which a personality is exposed to the public. Actors are celebrities because their media productions are the movies and television shows that they appear in. The celebrity chef receives wide exposure through the media and is well known because of the media; the celebrity chef's own show, and frequent appearances on popular daytime talk shows are his media productions. Without media attention and publicity, a celebrity chef loses the defining characteristic that distinguishes him from a restaurant chef. In connection with celebrity, Giles discusses the differences between two groups of accomplished people, athletes and academics, one exposed to the public more than the other:

3   Defines the celebrity aspect of the term *celebrity chef*

Defines celebrity by COMPARING distinguishing features of athletes vs. academics

> The priorities of the media or the dominant culture determines which spheres of activity are most likely to yield fame to the people within them. In Britain . . . there are huge numbers of footballers [soccer players] who are famous to the general public regardless of our interest in football. . . . Generally speaking, academics are not likely to be as famous as sports people; unless we appear regularly on television, our activities simply aren't visible enough, important enough, or as photogenic as the activities of people working in other fields. (6)

The celebrity chef, of course, corresponds to the famous athlete   4
who is recognized even by people who may not follow sports, and
the chef hidden away in a restaurant corresponds to the invisible and
unphotogenic academic who receives little public recognition.
Celebrity chefs have status because they are exposed to the general
public, and are "visible enough" to keep the public's attention
directed toward them (Giles 6). Both a chef in a restaurant and a
celebrity chef have had proper training in fine culinary schools
and have worked for years alongside great chefs as their mentors.

> Main distin-
> guishing feature
> of the celebrity
> chef is media
> exposure

However, a celebrity chef is exposed to the public through the
media, especially through television, constantly appearing outside
the restaurant kitchen as a guest on popular talk shows and on
packages of his own line of kitchenware. The public is continuously
exposed to what celebrity chefs have to offer, but we are exposed
to the great restaurant chefs only when we are actually at their
restaurant, or read about them (if we follow the culinary world)
in publications like *Gourmet* and *Food and Wine*. The point is that
celebrity chefs are exposed through mass media—we know of them
because we have no control over when we will stumble upon them
on our favorite morning talk show or at the kitchenware section of
department stores.

The epitome of the celebrity chef is Emeril Lagasse. No other   5
chefs on the Food Network have shows or audiences like he has, and
his show is a true media production. First of all, the set of *Emeril
Live* breaks away from traditional instructive cooking shows: instead
of having Emeril demonstrating and speaking into the camera,
the show has a talk-show format with a live audience and music
provided by Doc Gibbs and the *Emeril Live* Band. The band defines
Emeril as "essentially (part of) a media production" (Giles 2). On no
other cooking show is the chef accompanied by a live band, which
connects *Emeril Live* to entertainment shows like *The Tonight Show*[1]

1. *The Tonight Show/Jay Leno: The Tonight Show*, a television institution, is a one-
hour program that is broadcast on the NBC network after the late news. Jay Leno
hosted the show from 1992 to the end of May 2009, then resumed hosting duties in
January 2010. Bandleader Kevin Eubanks left the show in May 2010.

rather than to other cooking shows (Emeril even has conversations with his bandleader Doc Gibbs just as Jay Leno does with his band leader, Kevin Eubanks). Moreover, Emeril's show is unique in that it both serves to teach people how to cook and to entertain them, which is what makes him different from any other chef and what makes him a true celebrity.

Aside from the elements of Emeril's show that are a product of set designers, producers, and other creative television production executives, the <u>response of the audience</u> sets Emeril apart. Denis McQuail, a professor emeritus of communication at the University of Amsterdam, Netherlands, describes what he calls an "audience-sender relationship" which can be broken down into three categories: the audience as a target, the audience as participants, and the audience as spectators (40). These categories can help us to understand the rapport that Emeril has with his audience, which makes him a celebrity. Emeril enters from the back of the set, shakes everyone's hands, and makes small-talk with some of the audience members before reaching his place behind the studio's stove. From his entrance, we see how Emeril establishes a relationship with the audience; he could simply start his show by entering from backstage without greeting the audience members, but in doing so, he makes the audience what McQuail calls "participants":

> Communication is defined in terms of sharing and participation, increasing the commonality between sender and receiver, rather than in changing "receivers" in line with the purpose of the "sender"; . . . communication is not instrumental or utilitarian, and the attitude of the audience is likely to be playful or personally . . . committed in one way or another. Audience members are essentially participants. (41)

When he makes contact with the audience, Emeril receives a response that is both "playful" and "personally committed"; he receives this type of feedback because he takes a relaxed and laid-back approach to instructive cooking, constantly including his audience so that they do not feel intimidated by the complicated dishes that

6

Another distinguishing characteristic of the celebrity chef is audience response

7

he prepares. Furthermore, he gives the audience the opportunity to participate by echoing his notorious sound effect "BAM!" and by being able to taste the food that he has cooked before them. In the way he approaches the audience, he "increases the commonality between the sender [himself] and the receiver [the audience]." He makes himself approachable and down to earth, which makes the audience feel comfortable with him. In addition to being participants, the audience of *Emeril Live* also functions as what McQuail calls the "audience as spectators" (41). Since Emeril has already established the audience as participants, this affects how his audience responds as spectators, which in turn affects Emeril's status as a celebrity:

> The [audience as spectator] arises in a model of communication in which the source . . . simply capture[s] the attention of the audience, regardless of communicative effect. Audience attention is what is measured by ratings and thus cashable in the form of subscriptions, box office receipts, and payments from advertisers. It is also cashable in terms of status and influence within the media and in society generally. Fame and celebrity are more likely to result from sheer amount of public exposure than from measured "effects" or from measures of audience "appreciation." (41–42)

This model can be seen in the way that Emeril "captures" the attention of the audience by entertaining them with funny sound effects and facial expressions while he cooks. Because Emeril has already engaged his audience into his show as participants, he receives this loyalty of his audience as spectators as measured, by his ratings, and by the attendance at his sold-out *Emeril Live* personal appearances. Through these appearances, moreover, Emeril increases his "cashable" status of fame and celebrity through frequent "public exposure."

We have to keep in mind that Emeril's character is a production of the media that is aimed toward a particular audience. McQuail's model of the "audience as a target" explains that "the communication

8

9

Uses communications theory to define the audience as "spectator"

Uses communications theory to define the audience as "target"

process is considered primarily as the sending of signals or messages over time for the purposes of control or influence. The receiver, and thus the audience, is perceived as a *destination* or *target* for the purposeful transfer or meaning" (41). Emeril's production executives target a specific audience, and control his popularity by giving *Emeril Live* primetime spots on the Food Network, daily at 8 P.M. and 11 P.M., and Emeril's other show *The Essence of Emeril*, at 4 P.M., giving him constant visibility in terms of a specific audience. Emeril's "destination" or "target" seems to be working-class Americans, since the shows air at times when working Americans would be arriving home or settling down to watch television after dinner or at bedtime. This scheduling ensures that Emeril is able to gain the audience's loyalty by making his "media production" available at the times when most of his target audience is watching, and "control" the audience's attention by strategically choosing the most advantageous times to air his shows, which in turn increases his celebrity.

McQuail's audience-response models suggest that Emeril has a   10
great responsibility to his audience in order to maintain his image as a celebrity chef. Although Emeril gains his audience by being charismatic, friendly, and approachable, at the same time, he is creating an illusion by having the audience believe that there is only one way in which he can behave. Richard Dyer, a lecturer in film at the University of Warwick, writing about stars <u>(we can use the terms "stars" and "celebrities" interchangeably since both refer to public figures)</u>, claims that

> Uses *star* as a SYNONYM for celebrity

> the roles and/or performance of a star in a film were taken as revealing the personality of the star. . . . What was only sometimes glimpsed and seldom brought out by Hollywood or the stars was that personality was itself a construction known and expressed only through films, stories, publicity. (22–23)

The public sometimes has a difficult time separating the actor's true character from the character he plays, but is aware of the difference. However, with Emeril there is a different situation because Emeril is part of a media production: there is a constructed public persona that Emeril projects to the audience, and Emeril's funny character is designed to create an illusion that there is only one Emeril. His fans forget that as they watch this chef demonstrate how to prepare food, they are also watching him "cook up" an appealing character, because the audience is unable to differentiate Emeril's persona on television from his identity off camera. Since there is a media production and Emeril is the celebrity-product, the producers have to make sure that Emeril maintains his persona. Convincing the audience that Emeril has only one personality changes the traditional idea of celebrity, since with movie stars, for example, people identify with the characters who are being played rather than with the actors themselves. The audience does not see Emeril "acting" while he is cooking on his television show, and since Emeril projects only one persona, people feel that they are able to identify with him.

As a teacher, Emeril also changes the traditional idea of celebrity. 11 Usually, celebrities are admired for being photogenic or skillful; however, these qualities are not something that people can learn or apply to their own lives. Observing the audience at the show, we see the audience waiting attentively, ready to learn, as if they are waiting for a miracle to happen before their eyes. But that's the thing. Emeril emphasizes how "EASY" it is to prepare these dishes. He constantly uses phrases such as "it's as simple as that" and "it's not rocket science" to encourage the audience to try to cook the dishes themselves. By introducing a recipe as "easy to make," Emeril instills the desire to cook, and the confidence to cook, the kind of food that is usually only served in expensive and intimidating restaurants. Consequently, Emeril's instruction helps to democratize fine food. People may not be able to dine in upscale restaurants because they lack the time or the money, but Emeril changes the idea that fine food is only available at expensive restaurants. By making great food available, Emeril reaches out to those who ordinarily would not experience exquisitely prepared food, and emphasizes

Introduces particular characteristics that distinguish Lagasse from other celebrities

that it is not hard for people to cook well themselves. <u>This shows us the difference</u> between a "celebrity" and a "celebrity chef": where celebrities are usually simply entertainers, celebrity chefs are inspirations, teachers, and leaders. The audience is able to connect with the celebrity chef because each show has a lesson that the audience can take home and use. The audiences of movies and television can only watch and admire what the actors do; they can not take home instructions on how to act; however, the celebrity chef can give the audience the knowledge necessary to cook an elaborate meal at home, which ultimately has a greater impact than a movie has on a person's life.

The celebrity chef also challenges our gender stereotypes. For many years, food in the home has been associated with the women of the household. Traditionally, women have cooked for the family and taken charge of the food served at every meal. Ironically, however, men dominate the culinary world—professional cooking and *haute cuisine* are mostly associated with male chefs and restaurateurs, and industrial kitchens are filled with male chefs. Susan Gregory, a researcher in the sociology of food and the sociology of the family attributes women's dominance of the kitchens at home and the household in general to the nurture factor (Bowlby, Gregory, and McKie 62): cooking at home is part of care and nurturing, and therefore associated with women. That Emeril changes this idea is evident in the people who attend the tapings of *Emeril Live*. Emeril's show attracts men to his audience because in many ways he makes cooking both masculine and possible for them. Recently, when he taped an episode of *Emeril Live* at an Air Force base, the audience was predominately male, and this is, in turn, seen by his television audience. Whenever he sprinkles a spice or garnishes a dish, he utters his notorious sound effect, "BAM!" which seems to appeal to the noisy little boy in the men in his audience. The fact that Emeril is a *male* celebrity chef is what gives him the power to redefine the cooking boundaries in the American household. Emeril is a celebrity, accomplished and qualified, but above all, he helps men feel more

12

Distinguishes between celebrities and celebrity chefs

Introduces the key distinguishing feature of the celebrity chef as a cultural figure comfortable with cooking because he presents himself as someone that guys can relate to, and makes men "participants" in the show.

With the growing popularity of food in the media, celebrity chefs 13 have had an enormous impact on food in our lives. However, not everyone feels that chefs deserve all this media attention. Stephen Bayley, a British media journalist, concludes that it is

> Time, I think, to bury the celebrity chef in all his annoying forms . . . Chefs are artisans who should be confined to their workplace: what they should have in their hands is a spatula and a skillet, not a media schedule. They should be sweating brutally over hot stoves, not perspiring elegantly under the television lights. . . . There he goes, preening and strutting, discommoding the credulous gluttons who pay his salary. (82)

Bayley sums up certain class-based objections to celebrity chefs— that chefs are artisans, not stars, and should stay in the kitchen and serve us, not perform for us. However, as a celebrity chef, Emeril Lagasse has used his status as a chef and a celebrity to encourage his audiences to cook food that is usually reserved for the famous and wealthy, and by instilling in them the confidence to go home and cook his dishes themselves. Most important, Emeril is able to reach out to ordinary men and reassure them that his kind of cooking is not just for the women of the household, or the chefs of the wealthy. By providing entertainment with cooking, Emeril gives the men of his audience the confidence to approach cooking with a different perspective. Moreover, he has changed the culinary and media worlds by fusing them together and adding "BAM!"

Conclusion
defines Emeril's
distinct
contribution

Works Cited

Bayley, Stephen. "The Celebrity Chef." *New Statesman* 17 Dec. 2001: 82. Print.

Bowlby, Sophia, Susan Gregory, and Linda McKie. *Gender, Power and the Household*. New York: St. Martin's Press, 1999. Print.

Dyer, Richard. *Stars*. London: British Film Institute, 1979. Print.

Emeril Live. Perf. Emeril Lagasse. Food Network. 8 Nov. 2003. Television.

Emeril Live. Perf. Emeril Lagasse. Food Network. 23 Nov. 2003. Television.

The Essence of Emeril. Perf. Emeril Lagasse. Food Network. 21 Aug. 2004. Television.

Giles, David. *Illusions of Immortality*. New York: St. Martin's Press, 2000. Print.

Lewis, Robert C. "Restaurant Advertising Appeals and Consumers' Intentions." *Journal of Advertising Research* 21.5 (1981): 69–74. Print.

McQuail, Denis. *Audience Analysis*. Thousand Oaks, CA: Sage Publications, 1997. Print.

Ralli, Tania. "Learning to Sauté in a Melting Pot." *New York Times* 23 Sept. 2003: F-1. Print.

Analyzing a Student Definition Essay

In "The Celebrity Chef," Gail Babilonia draws upon rhetorical strategies and techniques that good writers use all the time when they define things. The following questions, in addition to focusing on particular aspects of Babilonia's text, will help you to identify those common strategies and techniques so you can adapt them to your own writing. These questions will also help to prepare you for the analytical questions—on content, structure, and language—that you'll find after all the other selections in this chapter, along with suggestions for writing on related topics.

READING CLOSELY

1. How does Gail Babilonia define a "celebrity chef" (1)?

2. According to Babilonia, what makes Emeril Lagasse a perfect EXAMPLE of a celebrity chef?

3. How has Lagasse made cooking an "acceptable" activity for men (12)?

4. How do chefs like Lagasse use their celebrity status to change our ideas and attitudes about food?

5. What is Babilonia's main point in defining a celebrity chef rather than some other kind of celebrity?

STRATEGIES AND STRUCTURES

1. Babilonia's entire essay is built on a single extended example, that of Emeril Lagasse. Is this one case, as she develops it, sufficient to define her subject? Why or why not?

2. What is the purpose of Babilonia's frequent references to the work of David Giles, a professor who has written about the psychology of celebrity (3)? How effective do you find this and Babilonia's other references to experts?

3. Babilonia is defining a celebrity chef. To what extent is she also defining what makes a celebrity? Explain.

4. *Other Methods.* Not only does Babilonia explain how chefs are trained, she analyzes how celebrities are made and how Lagasse, in particular, goes about being a celebrity. How and how well do these forays into PROCESS ANALYSIS serve to support her definition? Point to passages that you find particularly instructive.

THINKING ABOUT LANGUAGE

1. How does Babilonia use the stereotype of the "nameless Frenchman dressed in an all-white apron" to advance her definition of a celebrity chef (1)?

2. Why do you think cooking schools refer to themselves as "culinary institutes" rather than as "cooking schools" (2)?

3. What is the purpose of Babilonia's ANALOGY between a chef hidden away in the kitchen and an "unphotogenic academic" (4)?

4. Stephen Bayley, a British journalist, thinks its time to "bury" the celebrity chef (13). Why has he chosen such a harsh term?

5. What is "BAM" and how did Lagasse "add" it to both cooking and his show (13)? What's his recipe for success?

FOR WRITING

1. "A celebrity is a person who is famous for being famous." Write a paragraph defining celebrity that *contradicts* this famous definition, attributed to, among others, the artist Andy Warhol and the American historian Daniel J. Boorstin. (Boorstin actually said a celebrity is "a person who is known for his well-knowness," while Warhol spoke of everyone's "fifteen minutes of fame").

2. Write a paragraph defining one of the following: heroism, fame, notoriety, repute, infamy.

3. Write an essay defining what a chef traditionally is and does. Be sure to explain how chefs get to be chefs.

An Epitaph

When we define something (or someone), we say what its distinguishing characteristics are. In this cartoon by Roz Chast, a frequent contributor to the *New Yorker*, the deceased's entire life is defined by his verbal and math scores on a standardized test. Chast's purpose in penning the cartoon is to amuse the reader, but she is also making fun of overly narrow definitions. Test scores do not adequately define life—or death. For some people and institutions (such as college admissions offices), narrow definitions can run deep—too deep if they lose sight of the complexities of the person or thing they are defining. Like Mr. Jones' epitaph, good definitions require precision. But when you construct a definition, keep your (and the reader's) eye on the distinguishing features that actually give (or gave) life to your subject.

MARY ROACH

How to Know If You're Dead

Mary Roach is a San Francisco–based journalist whose first book, Stiff: The Curious Lives of Human Cadavers *(2003), propelled her to the forefront of popular science writers; one reviewer called her "the funniest science writer in the country." When asked how she came to write a best-seller about a subject most readers would regard as morbid, Roach replied, "Good question. It's possible that I'm a little strange." In fact, a glance at a few of the articles she's written gives one a sense of Roach's wide-ranging, quirky sensibilities: "Don't Jump!" ("Exactly what happens when a person leaps off the Golden Gate Bridge?"); "Turning Orange" ("Raw carrot abuse is nothing to laugh at"); "How to Feel Better about Falling Apart" ("Here's how I cope with my disgusting, sagging middle-aged body"). Roach's book* Spook: Science Tackles the Afterlife *(2005) takes up where* Stiff *leaves off, and her most recent book,* Packing for Mars: The Curious Science of Life in the Void *(2011), explores life in the cosmos.*

In "How to Know If You're Dead," which first appeared in Stiff, *Roach explores the meaning of* dead *and finds, surprisingly, that the definition is a subject of disagreement among doctors, lawyers, and would-be spiritualists. Despite the jaunty tone of her prose, Roach is meticulous in her scientific reporting; the meaning of death, she finds, casts more than a little light on the meaning of life.*

A PATIENT ON THE WAY TO SURGERY travels at twice the speed of a patient on the way to the morgue. Gurneys that ferry the living through hospital corridors move forward in an aura of purpose and push, flanked by caregivers with long strides and set faces, steadying IVs, pumping ambu bags, barreling into double doors. A gurney with a cadaver commands no urgency. It is wheeled by a single person, calmly and with little notice like a shopping cart.

For this reason, I thought I would be able to tell when the dead woman was wheeled past. I have been standing around at the nurses' station on one of the surgery floors of the University of California at San Francisco Medical Center, watching gurneys go by and waiting for Von Peterson, public affairs manager of the California Transplant Donor Network, and a cadaver I will call H. "There's your patient," says the charge nurse. A commotion of turquoise legs passes with unexpected forward-leaning urgency.

SUGGESTED MLA CITATION: Roach, Mary. "How to Know If You're Dead." 2003. *Back to the Lake.* Ed. Thomas Cooley. 2nd ed. New York: Norton, 2012. 402–08. Print.

H is unique in that she is both a dead person *and* a patient on the way to sur- 3
gery. She is what's known as a "beating-heart cadaver," alive and well everywhere
but her brain. Up until artificial respiration was developed, there was no such
entity; without a functioning brain, a body will not breathe on its own. But hook it
up to a respirator and its heart will beat, and the rest of its organs will, for a matter
of days, continue to thrive.

H doesn't look or smell or feel dead. If you leaned in close over the gurney, you 4
could see her pulse beating in the arteries of her neck. If you touched her arm, you
would find it warm and resilient, like your own. This is perhaps why the nurses
and doctors refer to H as a patient, and why she makes her entrance to the OR at
the customary presurgery clip.

Since brain death is the legal definition of death in this country, H the person is 5
certifiably dead. But H the organs and tissues is very much alive. These two seemingly contradictory facts afford her an opportunity most corpses do not   How you frame
have: that of extending the lives of two or three dying strangers. Over the   a term (p. 384)
next four hours, H will surrender her liver, kidneys, and heart. One at a   can influence
how the reader
time, surgeons will come and go, taking an organ and returning in haste   sees it.
to their stricken patients. Until recently, the process was known among transplant
professionals as an "organ harvest," which had a joyous, celebratory ring to it, perhaps a little too joyous, as it has been of late replaced by the more businesslike
"organ recovery."

In H's case, one surgeon will be traveling from Utah to recover her heart, and 6
another, the one recovering both the liver and the kidneys, will be taking them two
floors down. UCSF is a major transplant center, and organs removed here often
remain in house. More typically, a transplant patient's surgeon will travel from
UCSF to a small town somewhere to retrieve the organ—often from an accident
victim, someone young with strong, healthy organs, whose brain took an unexpected hit. The doctor does this because typically there is no doctor in that small
town with experience in organ recovery. Contrary to rumors about surgically
trained thugs cutting people open in hotel rooms and stealing their kidneys,[1] organ
recovery is tricky work. If you want to be sure it's done right, you get on a plane
and go do it yourself.

Today's abdominal recovery surgeon is named Andy Posselt. He is holding an 7
electric cauterizing wand, which looks like a cheap bank pen on a cord but functions like a scalpel. The wand both cuts and burns, so that as the incision is made,

---

1. *Rumors . . . stealing their kidneys:* Reference to a persistent urban legend about people getting
drunk at parties, passing out, and waking up in a hotel-room bathtub surrounded in ice and finding that one or both of their kidneys has been removed. These stories are always presented as true
and as coming from a reputable but distant source ("it happened to my neighbor's cousin's wife's
coworker's son").

any vessels that are severed are simultaneously melted shut. The result is that there is a good deal less bleeding and a good deal more smoke and smell. It's not a bad smell, but simply a seared-meat sort of smell. I want to ask Dr. Posselt whether he likes it, but I can't bring myself to, so instead I ask whether he thinks it's bad that I like the smell, which I don't really, or maybe just a little. He replies that it is neither bad nor good, just morbid.

I have never before seen major surgery, only its scars. From the length of them, I had imagined surgeons doing their business, taking things out and putting them in, through an opening maybe eight or nine inches long, like a woman poking around for her glasses at the bottom of her purse. Dr. Posselt begins just above H's pubic hair and proceeds a good two feet north, to the base of her neck. He's unzipping her like a parka. Her sternum is sawed lengthwise so that her rib cage can be parted, and a large retractor is installed to pull the two sides of the incision apart so that it is now as wide as it is long. To see her this way, held open like a Gladstone bag,[2] forces a view of the human torso for what it basically is: a large, sturdy container for guts. 8

On the inside, H looks very much alive. You can see the pulse of her heartbeat in her liver and all the way down her aorta. She bleeds where she is cut and her organs are plump and slippery-looking. The electronic beat of the heart monitor reinforces the impression that this is a living, breathing, thriving person. It is strange, almost impossible, really, to think of her as a corpse. When I tried to explain beating-heart cadavers to my stepdaughter Phoebe yesterday, it didn't make sense to her. But if their heart is beating, aren't they still a person? she wanted to know. In the end she decided they were "a kind of person you could play tricks on but they wouldn't know." Which, I think, is a pretty good way of summing up most donated cadavers. The things that happen to the dead in labs and ORs are like gossip passed behind one's back. They are not felt or known and so they cause no pain. 9

The contradictions and counterintuitions of the beating-heart cadaver can exact an emotional toll on the intensive care unit (ICU) staff, who must, in the days preceding the harvest, not only think of patients like H as living beings, but treat and care for them that way as well. The cadaver must be monitored around the clock and "life-saving" interventions undertaken on its behalf. Since the brain can no longer regulate blood pressure or the levels of hormones and their release into the bloodstream, these things must be done by ICU staff, in order to keep the organs from degrading. Observed a group of Case Western Reserve University School of Medicine physicians in a *New England Journal of Medicine* article entitled "Psychosocial and Ethical Implications of Organ Retrieval": "Intensive care unit personnel 10

2. *Gladstone bag*: An early suitcase, hinged to open in the middle and lie flat.

may feel confused about having to perform cardiopulmonary resuscitation on a patient who has been declared dead, whereas a 'do not resuscitate' order has been written for a living patient in the next bed."

. . .

The modern medical community is on the whole quite unequivocal about the brain 11 being the seat of the soul, the chief commander of life and death. It is similarly unequivocal about the fact that people like H are, despite the hoochy-koochy going on behind their sternums, dead. We now know that the heart keeps beating on its own not because the soul is in there, but because it contains its own bioelectric power source, independent of the brain. As soon as H's heart is installed in someone else's chest and that person's blood begins to run through it, it will start beating anew—with no signals from the recipient's brain.

The legal community took a little longer than the physicians to come around to 12 the concept of brain death. It was 1968 when the *Journal of the American Medical Association* published a paper by the Ad Hoc Committee of the Harvard Medical School to Examine the Definition of Brain Death advocating that irreversible coma be the new criterion for death, and clearing the ethical footpath for organ transplantation. It wasn't until 1974 that the law began to catch up. What forced the issue was a bizarre murder trial in Oakland, California.

The killer, Andrew Lyons, shot a man in the head in September 1973 and left 13 him brain-dead. When Lyons's attorneys found out that the victim's family had donated his heart for transplantation, they tried to use this in Lyons's defense: If the heart was still beating at the time of surgery, they maintained, then how could it be that Lyons had killed him the day before? They tried to convince the jury that, technically speaking, Andrew Lyons hadn't murdered the man, the organ recovery surgeon had. According to Stanford University heart transplant pioneer Norman Shumway, who testified in the case, the judge would have none of it. He informed the jury that the accepted criteria for death were those set forth by the Harvard committee, and that that should inform their decision. (Photographs of the victim's brains "oozing from his skull," to quote the *San Francisco Chronicle,* probably didn't help Lyons's case.) In the end, Lyons was convicted of murder. Based on the outcome of the case, California passed legislation making brain death the legal definition of death. Other states quickly followed suit.

Andrew Lyons's defense attorney wasn't the first person to cry murder when a 14 transplant surgeon removed a heart from a brain-dead patient. In the earliest days of heart transplants, Shumway, the first U.S. surgeon to carry out the procedure, was continually harangued by the coroner in Santa Clara County, where he practiced. The coroner didn't accept the brain-death concept of death and threatened that if Shumway went ahead with his plans to remove a beating heart from a brain-dead person and use it to save another person's life, he would initiate murder charges. Though the coroner had no legal ground to stand on and Shumway went ahead anyway, the press gave it a vigorous chew. New York heart transplant surgeon Mehmet Oz recalls the Brooklyn district attorney around that time making the same threat. "He said he'd indict and arrest any heart transplant surgeon who went into his borough and harvested an organ."

The worry, explained Oz, was that someday someone who wasn't actually brain-dead was going to have his heart cut out. There exist certain rare medical conditions that can look, to the untrained or negligent eye, a lot like brain death, and the legal types didn't trust the medical types to get it right. To a very, very small degree, they had reason to worry. Take, for example, the condition known as "locked-in state." In one form of the disease, the nerves, from eyeballs to toes, suddenly and rather swiftly drop out of commission, with the result that the body is completely paralyzed, while the mind remains normal. The patient can hear what's being said but has no way of communicating that he's still in there, and that no, it's definitely not okay to give his organs away for transplant. In severe cases, even the muscles that contract to change the size of the pupils no longer function. This is bad news, for a common test of brain death is to shine a light in the patient's eyes to check for the reflexive contraction of the pupils. Typically, victims of locked-in state recover fully, provided no one has mistakenly wheeled them off to the OR to take out their heart.   15

Like the specter of live burial that plagued the French and German citizenry in the 1800s, the fear of live organ harvesting is almost completely without foundation. A simple EEG will prevent misdiagnosis of the locked-in state and conditions like it.   16

On a rational level, most people are comfortable with the concept of brain death and organ donation. But on an emotional level, they may have a harder time accepting it, particularly when they are being asked to accept it by a transplant counselor who would like them to okay the removal of a family member's beating heart. Fifty-four percent of families asked refuse consent. "They can't deal with the fear, however irrational, that the true end of their loved one will come when the heart is removed," says Oz. That they, in effect, will have killed him.   17

Even heart transplant surgeons sometimes have trouble accepting the notion that the heart is nothing more than a pump. When I asked Oz where he thought the soul resided, he said, "I'll confide in you that I don't think it's all in the brain. I have to believe that in many ways the core of our existence is in our heart." Does that mean he thinks the brain-dead patient isn't dead? "There's no question that the heart without a brain is of no value. But life and death is not a binary system." It's a continuum. It makes sense, for many reasons, to draw the legal   18 line at brain death, but that doesn't mean it's really a line. "In between life and death is a state of near-death, or pseudo-life. And most people don't want what's in between."

. . .

The harvesting of H is winding down. The last organs to be taken, the kidneys, are 19 being brought up and separated from the depths of her open torso. Her thorax and abdomen are filled with crushed ice, turned red from blood. "Cherry Sno-Kone," I write in my notepad. It's been almost four hours now, and H has begun to look more like a conventional cadaver, her skin dried and dulled at the edges of the incision.

The kidneys are placed in a blue plastic bowl with ice and perfusion fluid. A 20 relief surgeon arrives for the final step of the recovery, cutting off pieces of veins and arteries to be included, like spare sweater buttons, along with the organs, in case the ones attached to them are too short to work with. A half hour later, the relief surgeon steps aside and the resident comes over to sew H up.

As he talks to Dr. Posselt about the stitching, the resident strokes the bank of fat 21 along H's incision with his gloved hand, then pats it twice, as though comforting her. When he turns back to his work, I ask him if it feels different to be working on a dead patient.

"Oh, yes," he answers. "I mean, I would never use this kind of stitch." He has 22 begun stitching more widely spaced, comparatively crude loops, rather than the tight, hidden stitches used on the living.

I rephrase the question: Does it feel odd to perform surgery on someone who 23 isn't alive?

His answer is surprising. "The patient *was* alive." I suppose surgeons are used to 24 thinking about patients—particularly ones they've never met—as no more than what they see of them: open plots of organs. And as far as that goes, I guess you could say H *was* alive. Because of the cloths covering all but her opened torso, the young man never saw her face, didn't know if she was male or female.

While the resident sews, a nurse picks stray danglies of skin and fat off the 25 operating table with a pair of tongs and drops them inside the body cavity, as though H were a handy wastebasket. The nurse explains that this is done intentionally: "Anything not donated stays with her." The jigsaw puzzle put back in its box.

The incision is complete, and a nurse washes H off and covers her with a blanket 26 for the trip to the morgue. Out of habit or respect, he chooses a fresh one. The transplant coordinator, Von, and the nurse lift H onto a gurney. Von wheels H into an elevator and down a hallway to the morgue. The workers are behind a set of swinging doors, in a back room. "Can we leave this here?" Von shouts. H has become a "this." We are instructed to wheel the gurney into the cooler, where it joins five others. H appears no different from the corpses already here.*

But H *is* different. She has made three sick people well. She has brought them 27 extra time on earth. To be able, as a dead person, to make a gift of this magnitude is phenomenal. Most people don't manage this sort of thing while they're alive. Cadavers like H are the dead's heros.

It is astounding to me, and achingly sad, that with eighty thousand people on 28 the waiting list for donated hearts and livers and kidneys, with sixteen a day dying there on that list, that more than half of the people in the position H's family was in will say no, will choose to burn those organs or let them rot. We abide the surgeon's scalpel to save our own lives, our loved ones' lives, but not to save a stranger's life. H has no heart, but heartless is the last thing you'd call her.

---

* Unless H's family is planning a naked open-casket service, no one at her funeral will be able to tell she's had organs removed. Only with tissue harvesting, which often includes leg and arm bones, does the body take on a slightly altered profile, and in this case PVC piping or dowels are inserted to normalize the form and make life easier for mortuary staff and others who need to move the otherwise somewhat noodle-ized body. [Author's note.]

✦⋯⋯

Reading Closely

1. A "beating-heart cadaver," says Mary Roach, is "both a dead person *and* a patient on the way to surgery" (3). How is this possible? What are some of the "contradictions and counterintuitions" posed by a beating-heart cadaver (10)?

2. What is the legal definition of death in the United States, according to Roach? What was the role of the Andrew Lyons case in establishing this definition (13)?

3. Define the condition known as "locked-in state" (15). Why do such medical conditions worry some people in regard to organ transplants?

4. How is the legal and medical definition of death complicated by Roach's conversation with Dr. Oz in paragraph 18?

Strategies and Structures

1. What ARGUMENT is Roach making on the basis of her extended definition? What is her main point? Where does she state it?

2. Fifty-four percent of the families whom doctors ask for permission to retrieve the organs of brain-dead patients, says Roach, refuse permission (17). As she

notes later, that's "more than half" (28). Do you think such statistics bolster Roach's argument? In what way?

3. Roach uses a number of direct quotations from physicians, nurses, and others. Is this an effective strategy? Support your answer with several examples from the selection.

4. *Other Methods.* How does the EXAMPLE of patient H contribute to Roach's definition of death? How does it contribute to her ARGUMENT?

THINKING ABOUT LANGUAGE

1. Why, according to Roach, did the medical community change its terminology from "harvesting" organs to "recovering" them (5)? What do you think of the change?

2. Roach uses many nonmedical terms and SIMILES in her essay, such as "like a shopping cart" (1), "hoochy-koochy" (11), and "Cherry Sno-Kone" (19). Point out other examples. Given the seriousness of her subject, do you find such informal language appropriate or inappropriate? Explain your reaction.

3. What cleared "the ethical footpath for organ transplantation," says Roach, was a report published in 1968 in the *Journal of the American Medical Association* (12). What are the implications of this "footpath" METAPHOR?

4. In paragraph 14, while talking about the press coverage of the case, Roach uses the CONCRETE image "vigorous chew" rather than an ABSTRACT phrase such as "good coverage." Which do you prefer, and why?

5. Is Von, the transplant coordinator, right to refer to patient H as "this" (26)? Why or why not?

FOR WRITING

1. Write a paragraph giving the legal definition of death as doctors and lawyers have come to define it since 1968.

2. Write a paragraph defining death according to some criterion other than "irreversible coma" (12).

3. In paragraph 18, Roach asks Dr. Oz where he thinks the soul resides. Write a definition essay addressing this question. Be sure to deal with the implications of the physician's observation that death isn't "really a line" (18).

FATEMA MERNISSI

The Harem Within

Fatema Mernissi (b. 1940) was born and raised in a traditional Moroccan household—a harem. Mernissi's female relatives, however, insisted that she receive the education that they had been denied. Her interest in political science eventually led her to the Sorbonne in Paris; Brandeis University in Boston, where she earned her doctorate; and the University of Mohammed V in Morocco, where she taught sociology. Above all, Mernissi has devoted her career to examining—and challenging—the strictures placed upon women in traditional Islamic societies. Her publications include The Veil and the Male Elite: A Feminist Interpretation of Women's Rights in Islam *(1988);* Doing Daily Battle: Interviews with Moroccan Women *(1991); and* Islam and Democracy: Fear of the Modern World *(1992).*

"The Harem Within" first appeared as a chapter in Mernissi's memoir Dreams of Trespass: Tales of a Harem Girlhood *(1995).*

OUR HAREM IN FEZ was surrounded by high walls and, with the exception of the little square chunk of sky that you could see from the courtyard below, nature did not exist. Of course, if you rushed like an arrow up to the terrace, you could see that the sky was larger than the house, larger than everything, but from the courtyard, nature seemed irrelevant. It had been replaced by geometric and floral designs reproduced on tiles, woodwork, and stucco. The only strikingly beautiful flowers we had in the house were those of the colorful brocades which covered the sofas and those of the embroidered silk drapes that sheltered the doors and windows. You could not, for example, open a shutter to look outside when you wanted to escape. All the windows opened onto the courtyard. There were none facing the street.

Once a year, during springtime, we went on a *nzaha*, or picnic, at my uncle's farm in Oued Fez, ten kilometers from the city. The important adults rode in cars, while the children, divorced aunts, and other relatives were put into two big trucks rented for the occasion. Aunt Habiba and Chama always carried tambourines, and they would make such a hell of a noise along the way that the truck driver would go crazy. "If you ladies don't stop this," he would shout, "I'm going to drive off the road and throw everyone into the valley." But his threats always came to nothing, because his voice would be drowned out by the tambourines and hand clapping.

SUGGESTED MLA CITATION: Mernissi, Fatima. "The Harem Within." 1995. *Back to the Lake.* Ed. Thomas Cooley. 2nd ed. New York: Norton, 2012. 410–15. Print.

"Our harem in Fez was surrounded by high walls and, with the exception of the little square chunk of sky that you could see from the courtyard below, nature did not exist."

On picnic day, everyone woke up at dawn and buzzed around the courtyard as if it were a religious festival day with groups of people organizing food here, drinks there, and putting drapes and carpets into bundles everywhere. Chama and Mother took care of the swings. "How can you have a picnic without swings?" they would argue whenever Father suggested they forget about them for once, because it took so much time to hang them from the trees. "Besides," he would add, just to provoke Mother, "swings are fine for children, but when heavy grownups are involved, the poor trees might suffer." While Father talked and waited for Mother to get angry, she would just keep on packing up the swings and the ropes to tie them with, without a single glance in his direction. Chama would sing aloud, "If men can't tie the swings / women will do it / Lallallalla," imitating the high-pitched melody of our national anthem "Maghribuna watanuna" (Our Morocco, Our Homeland). Meanwhile, Samir and I would be feverishly looking for our espadrilles,[1] for there was no help to be had from our mothers, so involved were

1. *Espadrille:* Lightweight women's shoes made of canvas and hemp rope. The shoes and their name have their origin in France; their use by Mernissi and her family may reflect Morocco's history as a French colony.

they in their own projects, and Lalla Mani would be counting the number of glasses and plates "just to evaluate the damage, and see how many will be broken by the end of the day." She could do without the picnic, she often said, especially since as far as tradition was concerned, its origin was dubious. "There's no record of it in the Hadith,"[2] she said, "It might even be counted as a sin on Judgment Day."

We would arrive on the farm in mid-morning, equipped with dozens of carpets   4 and light sofas and *khanouns*.[3] Once the carpets had been unfolded, the light sofas would be spread out, the charcoal fires lit, and the shish kebabs grilled. The tea-kettles would sing along with the birds. Then, after lunch, some of the women would scatter into the woods and fields, searching for flowers, herbs, and other kinds of plants to use in their beauty treatments. Others would take turns on the swings. Only after sunset would we make the journey back to the house, and the gate would be closed behind us. And for days after that, Mother would feel miserable. "When you spend a whole day among trees," she would say, "waking up with walls as horizons becomes unbearable."

You could not get into our house, except by passing through the main gate con-   5 trolled by Ahmed the doorkeeper. But you could get out a second way, by using the roof-level terrace. You could jump from our terrace to the neighbors' next door, and then go out to the street through their door. Officially, our terrace key was kept in Lalla Mani's possession, with Ahmed turning off the lights to the stairs after sunset. But because the terrace was constantly being used for all kinds of domestic activities throughout the day, from retrieving olives that were stored in big jars up there, to washing and drying clothes, the key was often left with Aunt Habiba, who lived in the room right next to the terrace.

The terrace exit route was seldom watched, for the simple reason that getting   6 from it to the street was a difficult undertaking. You needed to be quite good at three skills: climbing, jumping, and agile landing. Most of the women could climb up and jump fairly well, but not many could land gracefully. So, from time to time, someone would come in with a bandaged ankle, and everyone would know just what she'd been up to. The first time I came down from the terrace with bleeding knees, Mother explained to me that a woman's chief problem in life was figuring out how to land. "Whenever you are about to embark on an adventure," she said, "you have to think about the landing. Not about the takeoff. So whenever you feel like flying, think about how and where you'll end up."

But there was also another, more solemn reason why women like Chama and   7 Mother did not consider escaping from the terrace to be a viable alternative to

---

2. *Hadith*: A written collection of the sayings and traditions associated with Muhammad and his companions.

3. *Khanouns*: Portable metal or pottery fire containers used for grilling food over charcoal.

using the front gate. The terrace route had a clandestine, covert dimension to it, which was repulsive to those who were fighting for the principle of a woman's right to free movement. Confronting Ahmed at the gate was a heroic act. Escaping from the terrace was not, and did not carry with it that inspiring, subversive flame of liberation.

None of this intrigue applied, of course, to Yasmina's farm. The gate had hardly   8 any meaning, because there were no walls. And to be in a harem, I thought, you needed a barrier, a frontier. That summer, when I visited Yasmina, I told her what Chama had said about how harems got started. When I saw that she was listening, I decided to show off all my historical knowledge, and started talking about the Romans and their harems, and how the Arabs became the sultans of the planet thanks to Caliph Harun al-Rashid's one thousand women, and how the Christians tricked the Arabs by changing the rules on them while they were asleep. Yasmina laughed a lot when she heard the story, and said that she was too illiterate to evaluate the historical facts, but that it all sounded very funny and logical too. I then asked her if what Chama had said was true or false, and Yasmina said that I needed to relax about this right-and-wrong business. She said that there were things which could be both, and things which could be neither. "Words are like onions," she said. "The more skins you peel off, the more meanings you encounter. And when you start discovering multiplicities of meanings, then right and wrong becomes irrelevant. All these questions about harems that you and Samir have been asking are all fine and good, but there will always be more to be discovered." And then she added, "I am going to peel one more skin for you now. But remember, it is only one among others."

The word "harem," she said, was a slight variation of the word *haram*, the forbid-   9 den, the proscribed. It was the opposite of *halal*, the permissible. Harem was the place where a man sheltered his family, his wife or wives, and children and relatives. It could be a house or a tent, and it referred both to the See p. 382 for using etymologies to extend a definition. space and to the people who lived within it. One said "Sidi So-and-So's harem," referring both to his family members and to his physical home. One thing that helped me see this more clearly was when Yasmina explained that Mecca, the holy city, was also called Haram. Mecca was a space where behavior was strictly codified. The moment you stepped inside, you were bound by many laws and regulations. People who entered Mecca had to be pure: they had to perform purification rituals, and refrain from lying, cheating, and doing harmful deeds. The city belonged to Allah and you had to obey his *shari'a*, or sacred law, if you entered his territory. The same thing applied to a harem when it was a house belonging to a man. No other men could enter it without the owner's permission, and when they did, they had to obey his rules. A harem was about private space and the rules regulating it. In addition, Yasmina said, it did not need walls. Once you knew what was forbidden, you carried the harem within. You had it in your head, "inscribed under your forehead and under your skin." That idea of an invisible harem, a law tattooed in the mind, was frightfully unsettling to me. I did not like it at all, and I wanted her to explain more.

The farm, said Yasmina, was a harem, although it did not have walls. "You only need walls, if you have streets!" But if you decided, like Grandfather, to live in the countryside, then you didn't need gates, because you were in the middle of the fields and there were no passersby. Women could go freely out into the fields, because there were no strange men hovering around, peeping at them. Women could walk or ride for hours without seeing a soul. But if by chance they did meet a male peasant along the way, and he saw that they were unveiled, he would cover his head with the hood of his own *djellaba*[4] to show that he was not looking. So in this case, Yasmina said, the harem was in the peasant's head, inscribed somewhere under his forehead. He knew that the women on the farm belonged to Grandfather Tazi, and that he had no right to look at them.

This business of going around with a frontier inside the head disturbed me, and discreetly I put my hand to my forehead to make sure it was smooth, just to see if by any chance I might be harem-free. But then, Yasmina's explanation got even more alarming, because the next thing she said was that any space you entered had its own invisible rules, and you needed to figure them out. "And when I say space," she continued, "It can be any space—a courtyard, a terrace, or a room, or even the street for that matter. Wherever there are human beings, there is a *qa'ida*, or invisible rule. If you stick to the *qa'ida*, nothing bad can happen to you." In Arabic, she reminded me, *qa'ida* meant many different things, all of which shared the same basic premise. A mathematical law or a legal system was a *qa'ida*, and so was the foundation of a building. *Qa'ida* was also a custom, or a behavioral code. *Qa'ida* was everywhere. Then she added something which really scared me: "Unfortunately, most of the time, the *qa'ida* is against women."

"Why?" I asked. "That's not fair, is it?" And I crept closer so as not to miss a word of her answer. The world, Yasmina said, was not concerned about being fair to women. Rules were made in such a manner as to deprive them in some way or another. For example, she said, both men and women worked from dawn until very late at night. But men made money and women did not. That was one of the invisible rules. And when a woman worked hard, and was not making money, she was stuck in a harem, even though she could not see its walls. "Maybe the rules are ruthless because they are not made by women," was Yasmina's final comment. "But why aren't they made by women?" I asked. "The moment women get smart and start asking that very question," she replied, "instead of dutifully cooking and washing dishes all the time, they will find a way to change the rules and turn the

10

11

12

4. *Djellaba*: A traditional Moroccan robe.

whole planet upside down." "How long will that take?" I asked, and Yasmina said, "A long time."

I asked her next if she could tell me how to figure out the invisible rule or *qa'ida*, whenever I stepped into a new space. Were there signals, or something tangible that I could look for? No, she said, unfortunately not, there were no clues, except for the violence after the fact. Because the moment I disobeyed an invisible rule, I would get hurt. However, she noted that many of the things people enjoyed doing most in life, like walking around, discovering the world, singing, dancing, and expressing an opinion, often turned up in the strictly forbidden category. In fact, the *qa'ida*, the invisible rule, often was much worse than walls and gates. With walls and gates, you at least knew what was expected from you.

At those words, I almost wished that all rules would suddenly materialize into frontiers and visible walls right before my very eyes. But then I had another uncomfortable thought. If Yasmina's farm was a harem, in spite of the fact that there were no walls to be seen, then what did *hurriya*, or freedom, mean? I shared this thought with her, and she seemed a little worried, and said that she wished I would play like other kids, and stop worrying about walls, rules, constraints, and the meaning of *hurriya*. "You'll miss out on happiness if you think too much about walls and rules, my dear child," she said. "The ultimate goal of a woman's life is happiness. So don't spend your time looking for walls to bang your head on." To make me laugh, Yasmina would spring up, run to the wall, and pretend to pound her head against it, screaming, "*Aie, aie!* The wall hurts! The wall is my enemy!" I exploded with laughter, relieved to learn that bliss was still within reach, in spite of it all. She looked at me and put her finger to her temple, "You understand what I mean?"

Of course I understood what you meant, Yasmina, and happiness did seem absolutely possible, in spite of harems, both visible and invisible. I would run to hug her, and whisper in her ear as she held me and let me play with her pink pearls. "I love you Yasmina. I really do. Do you think I will be a happy woman?"

"Of course you will be happy!" she would exclaim. "You will be a modern, educated lady. You will realize the nationalists' dream. You will learn foreign languages, have a passport, devour books, and speak like a religious authority. At the very least, you will certainly be better off than your mother. Remember that even I, as illiterate and bound by tradition as I am, have managed to squeeze some happiness out of this damned life. That is why I don't want you to focus on the frontiers and the barriers all the time. I want you to concentrate on fun and laughter and happiness. That is a good project for an ambitious young lady."

READING CLOSELY

1. How does the house in which Fatema Mernissi grew up differ from a typical American or other Western home? Consider the physical characteristics of the house as well as the spiritual ones.

2. Why does Mernissi pay so much attention to the two possible exits from the house—the main one through the front gate and a "clandestine" one through the terrace (7)?

3. Why do you think Mernissi mentions her father only briefly when she is DESCRIBING the preparations for the annual family picnic? What is the role of Ahmed the doorkeeper in the family harem?

4. In paragraphs 2–4, Mernissi describes the family's annual picnic, or *nzaha*, in some detail. How is the *nzaha* like a *harem*, and how is it different?

5. Why do you think Mernissi is so interested in the definition of a harem? What advice does her aunt give about her preoccupation with this term? Does this advice seem to be the main point of the selection? Why or why not?

STRATEGIES AND STRUCTURES

1. According to Mernissi, a harem is a kind of "private space" (9). What additional characteristics do she and Aunt Yasmina introduce in order to extend and refine this basic definition?

2. How and where does Aunt Yasmina use ETYMOLOGIES and ANTONYMS to help explain what a harem is?

3. Aunt Yasmina introduces an "alarming" synonym for *harem* in paragraph 11. What is it, and how does her use of the term help young Mernissi to understand what is being explained to her?

4. How effective, finally, do you find "illiterate" Aunt Yasmina as an interpreter of meanings and definer of words (8)? What is Mernissi's main point in quoting so many of her aunt's definitions? Is there anything subversive about Yasmina's role? Explain.

5. *Other Methods.* How do the events of Mernissi's NARRATIVE—such as the conflict with the bus driver, Chama's singing about the swings, and the conversation with Yasmina—help to support her definition of "the harem within" and other key terms?

Thinking about Language

1. Why does Mernissi use the word "escape" when describing her family home (1)? How does her description of the place fit in with what she says about nature?

2. The dictionary definition of *harem* is "the section of a house reserved for women in a Muslim household." What are the CONNOTATIONS of *harem* as Mernissi uses the term?

3. Mernissi's mother tells her that a woman's main problem in life is "figuring out how to land" (6). What does she mean by this METAPHOR?

4. Defining words, says Aunt Yasmina, is like peeling onions (8). Why does she use this ANALOGY? Is the comparison accurate? Why or why not?

5. A harem is not only a physical place, says Mernissi, but an idea "inscribed under your forehead," "a law tattooed in the mind" (9). What are the implications of *inscribed* and *tattooed* in this definition?

For Writing

1. In a paragraph or two, define what you thought a harem was before you read Mernissi's essay, and explain how you would define the term now.

2. Write a definition essay about an idea or place that significantly affected your childhood in a positive or negative way. Include a COMPARISON of your perspective on that idea or place today with your perspective back then.

3. Write a narrative about some unwritten rules that you have encountered. Include an interpreter, like Aunt Yasmina, who defines the rules for you, or at least makes you aware of them.

JACK HORNER

The Extraordinary Characteristics of Dyslexia

Jack Horner (b. 1946) grew up in Shelby, Montana, and studied geology and zoology at the University of Montana. He is Regents Professor of Paleontology at the Montana State University and curator of paleontology at the Museum of the Rockies, which has the largest dinosaur collection in the United States. A technical advisor for the Jurassic Park *movies, Horner was the first person to discover dinosaur eggs in the Western Hemisphere. He is now doing research on the evolution and ecology of dinosaurs and is particularly interested in their growth and behavior.*

Although he holds multiple honorary degrees, Horner did not graduate from college because of a common developmental reading disorder often called dyslexia. As children, people with dyslexia often have difficulty learning to recognize written words and, thus, the meaning of sentences; and they may have related problems with writing and math. Dyslexia does not indicate a lack of intelligence, however; it is caused by differences in the way the human brain processes symbolic information. In "The Extraordinary Characteristics of Dyslexia" (published in 2008 by the International Dyslexia Association in Perspectives on Language and Literacy*), Horner bypasses the usual symptoms and defines it as a way of understanding the world that, in some respects, may be superior to more "normal" ways.*

EACH OF US can narrate an early experience of failure in schools. Because of 1 it, most of us have known some form of peer persecution. But what most non-dyslexics don't know about us, besides the fact that we simply process information differently, is that our early failures often give us an important edge as we grow older. It is not uncommon that we "dyslexics" go on to succeed at the highest of levels.

P. 379 explains how to define a term by saying what it is not.
I don't care much for the word *dyslexia*. I generally think of "us" as 2 spatial thinkers and non-dyslexics as linear thinkers, or people who could be most often described as being *dys-spatios*. For spatial thinkers, reading is clearly necessary but over-rated. Most of us would rather write about our own adventures than read about someone else's. Most spatial thinkers are extremely visual, highly imaginative, and work in three dimensions, none of which have anything to do with time. Linear thinkers (*dys-spatics*) generally operate in a two-dimensional world where time is of the utmost importance. We spatial thinkers

SUGGESTED MLA CITATION: Horner, Jack. "The Extraordinary Characteristics of Dyslexia." 2008. *Back to the Lake.* Ed. Thomas Cooley. 2nd ed. New York: Norton, 2012. 418–20. Print.

fail tests given by linear thinkers because we don't think in terms of time or in terms of written text. Instead, our perception is multidimensional, and we do best when we can touch, observe, and analyze. If we were to give spatial tests to linear thinkers, they would have just as much trouble with our tests as we do with theirs. It is unfortunate that we are the minority and have to deal with the linear-thinkers' exams in order to enter the marketplace to find jobs. Even though we often fail or do miserably on these linear-thinker tests, we often end up in life achieving exceptional accomplishments. From the perspective of the linear thinkers, we spatial thinkers seem to "think outside the box," and this accounts for our accomplishments. However, we think outside the box precisely because we have never been in one. Our minds are not clogged up by preconceived ideas acquired through excessive reading. We are, therefore, free to have original thoughts enhanced by personal observations.

In 1993, I was inducted into the American Academy of Achievement, an organization started in 1964, that annually brings together the highest achievers in America with the brightest American high-school students. The achievers included United States presidents, Nobel Laureates, movie stars, sports figures, and other famous people. The high school students were winners of the best scholarships like the Rhodes, the Westinghouse, the Truman, and so on. In other words, it was supposed to be a meeting of the best of the best according to the linear thinkers who "judge" such things. The idea was that the achievers would somehow, over the course of a three-day meeting, influence the students, and push them on to extraordinary achievement. Interestingly, however, most of us "achievers" admitted that we would never have qualified to be in such a student group. The largest percentage of the achievers were actually people who had difficulties in school and didn't get scholarships, or awards, or other accolades. Most of the achievers were spatial thinkers, while most of the students were linear thinkers. From 1964 until 2000, less than half a dozen students broke the barrier to be inducted at the American Academy of Achievement's annual get-together. How could it be that so many promising students, judged by the linear thinkers themselves, failed to reach the highest levels of achievement? 3

I think the answer is simple. Linear thinkers are burdened by high expectations from everyone, including themselves. They go out and get good jobs, but they seldom follow their dreams because dream-following is risk-taking, and risk-taking carries the possible burden of failure. 4

We spatial thinkers have known failure our entire lives and have grown up without expectations, not from our teachers, often not from our parents, and sometimes, not even from ourselves. We don't meet the expectations of linear thinkers and are free to take risks. We are the people who most often follow our dreams, who think differently, spatially, inquisitively. 5

Personally, I think dyslexia and the consequences of dyslexia—learning to deal   6
with failure—explains my own success. From my failures, I've learned where I
need help, such as reading and math. But I've also learned from my accomplishments what I'm better at than the linear thinkers. When I'm teaching linear thinkers here at Montana State University, I know to be patient, as they have just as
hard a time with spatial problems as I have with linear ones. We both have learning talents and learning challenges, but I would never think of trading my spatial
way of thinking for their linear way of thinking. I think dyslexia is an extraordinary
characteristic, and it is certainly not something that needs to be fixed, or cured, or
suppressed! Maybe it's time for a revolution! Take us out of classes for special ed,
and put us in classes for spatial ed, taught of course, by spatial thinkers!

READING CLOSELY

1. Jack Horner says that "non-dyslexics" are "linear thinkers" (2). What does he
    mean by this definition? Do you think it's accurate? Why or why not?

2. On the other hand, says Horner, people who arc called *dyslexic* are actually "spa-
    tial thinkers" (2). Again, what does he mean, and how accurate is *this* definition?

3. Why does Horner think that his spatial perspective has helped him to succeed
    in his life and career?

4. Why does he think linear thinkers, including "many promising students," even
    when judged by other linear thinkers, "failed to reach the highest levels of
    achievement" (3)?

STRATEGIES AND STRUCTURES

1. What is Horner's PURPOSE in defining dyslexia in positive terms as having
    "extraordinary characteristics"?

2. In addition to spatial thinkers, what other AUDIENCE might Horner and the
    International Dyslexia Association be interested in reaching? Explain.

3. Nowhere in his essay does Horner cite a standard textbook definition of *dys-
    lexia*. In addition to the extraordinary characteristics, should he have included
    the ordinary ones in his definition as well? Why or why not?

4. Beside being "spatial thinkers," people with dyslexia have other distinguishing
    characteristics, according to Horner. What are some of them? Which ones seem
    particularly effective for extending his basic definition?

5. Horner uses his own life and career as an EXAMPLE. How and how well does that example help to explain what it means, in his view, to be dyslexic?

6. *Other Methods.* Horner sees a CAUSE-AND-EFFECT relationship between having (or not having) dyslexia and succeeding (or failing) to reach "the highest levels of achievement" (3). What evidence does he offer in support of this analysis? How sufficient is that evidence to prove causality? Explain.

THINKING ABOUT LANGUAGE

1. New words are often coined by ANALOGY with words that already exist (for example, *workaholic* and *alcoholic*). How does Horner derive the word "dys-spatics" (2)?

2. Thinking "outside the box" is a CLICHÉ (2). Should Horner have avoided the phrase? Why or why not?

3. What are the implications of *burdened* (4)? Is Horner being IRONIC here?

4. Explain the PUN in "spatial ed" (6).

FOR WRITING

1. Write a paragraph or two explaining how "an early experience of failure in schools" or "peer persecution" has "given you an important edge" now (1).

2. Write a definition essay explaining what dyslexia is, what its causes are thought to be, and how it's usually treated. Be sure to cite your sources—and, if appropriate, an interesting case or two, whether "extraordinary" or typical.

BOBBIE ANN MASON

Being Country

Bobbie Ann Mason (b. 1940) is a writer-in-residence at the University of Kentucky in Lexington. A novelist, essayist, and short story writer, she is also the author of a biography, Elvis Presley (2002). Mason grew up in western Kentucky on a farm near Mayfield. After graduating from the University of Kentucky in 1962, she received advanced degrees from the State University of New York at Binghamton and the University of Connecticut. Mason writes mostly about the lives of working people in rural Kentucky. Her novels and short story collections include In Country (1985), Zigzagging Down a Wild Trail (2002), An Atomic Romance (2005), Nancy Culpepper (2006), and The Girl in the Blue Beret (2011).

"Being Country" is a chapter from Mason's Clear Springs: A Family Story (2000). In this autobiographical narrative, Mason uses the history and daily life of her extended family to define what it means to be country, showing, in rich detail, how she embraced a way of life that, as a teenager, she also dreamed of leaving behind.

FOOD WAS THE CENTER of our lives. Everything we did and thought revolved around it. We planted it, grew it, harvested it, peeled it, cooked it, served it, consumed it—endlessly, day after day, season after season. This was life on a farm—as it had been time out of mind.

The area around Clear Springs, on Panther Creek, was one of the first white settlements in the Jackson Purchase. In the spring of 1820, Peyton Washam, his fifteen-year-old son Peter, and a third man whose name has been forgotten came to Panther Creek from Virginia with a plan to build a cabin and plant some corn. Mrs. Washam and the seven other children, whom they had left in a settlement about a hundred miles away, would come along later. Before the men could begin building, they had to slash a clearing from the wilderness. It was tougher than they expected. They had plenty of water, for the place abounded with springs, but they soon ran out of food and supplies. They sent for more, but before these arrived they were reduced to boiling and eating their small treasure (half a bushel) of seed corn—the dried corn that would have let them get out a crop. Then Peyton Washam came down with a fever. He sent for his wife to come quickly. She arrived late at night and got lost in the canebrake—a thicket of canes growing up to thirty feet high. Frightened in the noisy darkness, she waited, upright and sleepless, beneath

SUGGESTED MLA CITATION: Mason, Bobbie Ann. "Being Country." 1999. *Back to the Lake.* Ed. Thomas Cooley. 2nd ed. New York: Norton, 2012. 422–30. Print.

an old tree till daylight, according to the accounts. She hurried on then, propelled by worry, but when she reached her husband's camp, she was too late. He had died during the night. Afterwards, she lived out his dream, settling in the vicinity with her children. The area her husband had chosen eventually grew into the community where a dozen branches of my family took root.

This story vexes me. What a bold but pathetic beginning! What careless, untrained pioneers. How could Peyton Washam and his cohorts have run out of food so soon? If they arrived in the spring, they should have planted that seed corn before long (between mid-April and mid-May). Why, in a mild Kentucky spring, did they not get a garden out right away? How could they have run out of supplies before they got their corn in the ground? Of course they had to clear some canebrake, which wasn't easy. But it wasn't as hard as clearing trees. You can even eat cane like a vegetable. In May, there would have been a carpet of wild strawberries. If Peyton Washam was too sick to forage, why didn't the kid and the other guy go pick something? What kind of pioneer eats his seed corn? Why didn't they shoot a squirrel?

Mrs. Washam is the hero of the tale. She survived and her children joined her. She probably could handle a gun. I'm sure she knew how to get out a garden. I picture her coming alone with a basket of cornbread and fried pies, looking for her sick, hungry husband, trying to follow directions scribbled on a piece of paper. Turn left *before* the canebrake. Follow the creek to the large old tree. Or maybe Peyton Washam's handwriting was bad—maybe he meant an *oak* tree.

This was the rough and foolhardy beginning of Clear Springs. The expedition was a man's notion, with a woman coming to the rescue. The men were starving without her. It makes perfect sense to me, in light of everything I know about the rural life that came down to me from that community. When I think of Clear Springs, I think first of the women cooking. Every Christmas we went out to the Mason homeplace for a grand celebration dinner that included at least a dozen cakes. And in the summer we went to big homecoming feasts—called dinner-on-the-ground—at nearby McKendree Methodist Church, which was on Mason land.

One day Mama and Granny were shelling beans and talking about the proper method of drying apples. I was nearly eleven and still entirely absorbed with the March girls in *Little Women.*[1] Drying apples was not in my dreams. Beth's death was weighing darkly on me at that moment, and I threw a little tantrum—what Mama called a hissy fit.

---

1. *Little Women:* Louisa May Alcott's novel about a family of four sisters, published in 1868–1869. The death of Beth, the second-youngest sister, is an especially poignant part of the book that often reduces readers to tears.

"Can't y'all talk about anything but food?" I screamed. 7

There was a shocked silence. "Well, what else is there?" Granny 8
asked.

You can always define something by identifying its most important characteristic, p. 379.

Granny didn't question a woman's duties, but I did. I didn't want to be 9
hulling beans in a hot kitchen when I was fifty years old. I wanted to *be*
somebody, maybe an airline stewardess. Also, I had been listening to the
radio. I had notions.

Our lives were haunted by the fear of crop failure. We ate as if we didn't know 10
where our next meal might come from. All my life I have had a recurrent food
dream: I face a buffet or cafeteria line, laden with beautiful foods. I spend the
entire dream choosing the foods I want. My anticipation is deliciously agonizing. I
always wake up just as I've made my selections but before I get to eat.

Working with food was fraught with anxiety and desperation. In truth, no one 11
in memory had missed a meal—except Peyton Washam on the banks of Panther
Creek wistfully regarding his seed corn. But the rumble of poor Peyton's belly must
have survived to trouble our dreams. We were at the mercy of nature, and it wasn't
to be trusted. My mother watched the skies at evening for a portent of the morrow.
A cloud that went over and then turned around and came back was an especially
bad sign. Our livelihood—even our lives—depended on forces outside our control.

I think this dependence on nature was at the core of my rebellion. I hated the 12
constant sense of helplessness before vast forces, the continuous threat of failure.
Farmers didn't take initiative, I began to see; they reacted to whatever presented
itself. I especially hated women's part in the dependence.

My mother allowed me to get spoiled. She never even tried to teach me to cook. 13
"You didn't want to learn," she says now. "You were a lady of leisure, and you
didn't want to help. You had your nose in a book."

I believed progress meant freedom from the field and the range. That meant 14
moving to town, I thought.

Because we lived on the edge of Mayfield, I was acutely conscious of being 15
country. I felt inferior to people in town because we grew our food and made our
clothes, while they bought whatever they needed. Although we were self-sufficient
and resourceful and held clear title to our land, we lived in a state of psychological
poverty. As I grew older, this acute sense of separation from town affected me
more deeply. I began to sense that the fine life in town—celebrated in magazines,
on radio, in movies—was denied us. Of course we weren't poor at all. Poor people
had too many kids, and they weren't landowners; they rented decrepit little houses
with plank floors and trash in the yard. "Poor people are wormy and eat wild
onions," Mama said. We weren't poor, but we were country.

We had three wardrobes—everyday clothes, school clothes, and Sunday clothes. 16
We didn't wear our school clothes at home, but we could wear them to town. When

"All the ingredients except the flour, sugar, and salt came from our farm—the chickens, the hogs, the milk and butter, the Irish potatoes, the beans, peas, corn, cabbage, apples, peaches."

we got home from church, we had to change back into everyday clothes before we ate Mama's big Sunday dinner.

"Don't eat in your good clothes!" Mama always cried. "You'll spill something on them." 17

Mama always preferred outdoor life, but she was a natural cook. At harvest time, after she'd come in from the garden and put out a wash, she would whip out a noon-time dinner for the men in the field—my father and grandfather and maybe some neighbors and a couple of hired hands: fried chicken with milk gravy, ham, mashed potatoes, lima beans, field peas, corn, slaw, sliced tomatoes, fried apples, biscuits, and peach pie. This was not considered a banquet, only plain hearty food, fuel for work. All the ingredients except the flour, sugar, and salt came from our farm—the chickens, the hogs, the milk and butter, the Irish potatoes, the beans, peas, corn, cabbage, apples, peaches. Nothing was processed, except by Mama. She was always butchering and plucking and planting and hoeing and shredding and slicing and creaming (scraping cobs for the creamed corn) and pressure-cooking and canning and freezing and thawing and mixing and shaping and baking and frying. 18

We would eat our pie right on the same plate as our turnip greens so as not to   19
mess up another dish. The peach cobbler oozed all over the turnip-green juice and
the pork grease. "It all goes to the same place," Mama said. It was boarding-house
reach, no "Pass the peas, please." Conversation detracted from the sensuous pleasure of filling yourself. A meal required meat and vegetables and dessert. The beverages were milk and iced tea ("ice-tea"). We never used napkins or ate tossed
salad. Our salads were Jell-O and slaw. We ate "poke salet" and wilted lettuce.
Mama picked tender, young pokeweed in the woods in the spring, before it turned
poison, and cooked it a good long time to get the bitterness out. We liked it with
vinegar and minced boiled eggs. Wilted lettuce was tender new lettuce, shredded,
with sliced radishes and green onions, and blasted with hot bacon grease to blanch
the rawness. "Too many fresh vegetables in summer gives people the scours,"
Daddy said.

Food was better in town, we thought. It wasn't plain and everyday. The centers   20
of pleasure were there—the hamburger and barbecue places, the movie shows, all
the places to buy things. Woolworth's, with the pneumatic tubes overhead rushing

South side of Mayfield courthouse square, 1957.

money along a metallic mole tunnel up to a balcony; Lochridge & Ridgway, with an engraved sign on the third-story cornice: STOVES, APPLIANCES, PLOWS. On the mezzanine at that store, I bought my first phonograph records, brittle 78s of big-band music—Woody Herman and Glenn Miller, and Glen Gray and his Casa Loma Orchestra playing "No Name Jive." A circuit of the courthouse square took you past the grand furniture stores, the two dime stores, the shoe stores, the men's stores, the ladies' stores, the banks, the drugstores. You'd walk past the poolroom and an exhaust fan would blow the intoxicating smell of hamburgers in your face. Before she bought a freezer, Mama stored meat in a rented food locker in town, near the ice company. She stored the butchered calf there, and she fetched hunks of him each week to fry. But hamburgers in town were better. They were greasier, and they came in waxed-paper packages.

At the corner drugstore, on the square, Mama and Janice and I sat at filigreed 21 wrought-iron tables on a black-and-white mosaic tile floor, eating peppermint ice cream. It was very cold in there, under the ceiling fans. The ice cream was served elegantly, in paper cones sunk into black plastic holders. We were uptown.

The A&P grocery, a block away, reeked of the rich aroma of ground coffee. 22 Daddy couldn't stand the smell of coffee, but Mama loved it. Daddy retched and scoffed in his exaggerated fashion. "I can't stand that smell!" Granny perked coffee, and Granddaddy told me it would turn a child black. I hated coffee. I wouldn't touch it till I was thirty. We savored store-bought food—coconuts, pineapples, and Vienna sausages and potted meat in little cans that opened with keys. We rarely went to the uptown A&P. We usually traded at a small mom-and-pop grocery, where the proprietors slapped the hands of black children who touched the candy case. I wondered if they were black from coffee.

In the summer of 1954, when I was about to enter high school, my mother got a 23 chance to run a nearby restaurant on the highway across the train track. My parents knew the owner, and one day he stopped by and asked Mama if she'd like to manage the place. She wasn't working at the Merit[2] at that time, and she jumped at the opportunity.

"Why, anybody could cook hamburgers and French fries for the public," Mama 24 said confidently. "That would be easy."

I went with her to inspect the restaurant—a square cinder-block building with a 25 picture-window view of the highway. There were no trees around, just a graveled parking area. It was an informal sort of place, with a simple kitchen, a deep fryer, a grill, some pots and pans. There were five or six tables and a counter with stools. Mama saw potential.

2. *Merit:* Kentucky's civil service system.

"Catfish platters," she said. "Fish. Hush puppies. Slaw. French fries." 26

I was so excited I couldn't sleep. Running our own little restaurant could mean 27 we wouldn't have to work in the garden. I wanted nothing more to do with okra and beans. Besides, the restaurant had an apartment above it. I wanted to live there, on the highway. Marlene was still running her frozen-custard stand nearby, and now I too would get to meet strangers traveling through. Mama and I inspected the apartment: a living room, a kitchen, and two bedrooms. It was all new and fresh. I loved it.

"Oh, please, let's move here," I begged, wishing desperately for novelty, deliver- 28 ance, and an endless supply of Co'-Colas.

Mama's eyes lit up. "We'll see," she said. 29

A restaurant would be ideal for her. "It's a chance to make big money," she 30 told me. She told the owner she would try it for a while, to see how she liked it. If she became the manager, then she would rent it for a hundred dollars a month.

"If it works out, maybe I could make a hundred dollars a *week*," she said. 31

I tagged along with her when she worked at the restaurant. I felt important 32 waiting on customers—strangers driving along the highway and stopping for a bite to eat right where I was. I wanted to meet somebody from New York. When I drew glasses of foamy Coca-Cola from the fountain, the Coke fizzed over crushed ice. I made grilled-cheese sandwiches in the grilled-cheese machine. I experimented with milk shakes. I was flying.

Most of all, I loved the jukebox. The jukebox man came by to change records 33 and insert new red-rimmed paper strips of titles: Doris Day and Johnnie Ray duets, "Teardrops from My Eyes" by Ruth Brown, and "P.S. I Love You" by a Kentucky vocal group called the Hilltoppers. I listened avidly to everything. I was fourteen and deeply concerned about my suntan, and I was saving pocket money to buy records.

The restaurant had a television set, which sat in a corner with something called 34 a television light on top—a prism of soft colors which supposedly kept people from ruining their eyes on TV rays. I had hardly ever watched television, and I was cap- tivated by Sid Caesar's variety show and *I Love Lucy*. When the evening crowd came in, Mama trotted back and forth from the kitchen with her hamburger platters and catfish platters. She would stop and laugh at something Lucy and Ethel were doing on the screen.

Mama had to give up the restaurant even before the trial period ended. She didn't 35 do it voluntarily. Granddaddy stepped in and told her she had to.

"We need you here at home," he said. "Running a eating place out on the high- 36 way ain't fitten work."

Daddy didn't stand up for her. "How would you make anything?" he asked her. 37 "By the time you pay out that hundred dollars a month and all the expenses, you won't have nothing left. First thing you know, you'll get behind and then you'll be owing *him*."

Granny said, "And who's going to do your cooking here?"   38

That was that. Afterwards, Mama cooked her hamburger platters at home, but   39
they weren't the same without the fountain Cokes and the jukebox and the television. I thought I saw a little fire go out of her then. Much later, her fire would almost die. But my own flame was burning brighter. I had had a glimpse of life outside the farm, and I wanted it.

I can still see Mama emerging from that restaurant kitchen, carrying two ham-   40
burger platters and gabbing with her customers as if they were old friends who had dropped in to visit and sit a spell. In the glass of the picture window, reflections from the TV set flicker like candles at the church Christmas service.

And then the blackberries were ripe. We spent every July and August in the berry   41
patch. The tame berries had spread along the fencerows and creek banks. When they ripened, Mama would exclaim in wonder, "There are *worlds* of berries down there!" She always "engaged" the berries to customers. By June, she would say, "I've already got forty gallons of berries engaged."

We strode out at dawn, in the dew, and picked until the mid-morning sun bore   42
down on our heads. To protect her hands from the briars, Mama made gloves from old bluejeans. Following the berries down the creek bank, we perched on ledges and tiptoed on unsure footing through thickets. We tunneled. When Mama saw an especially large berry just out of reach, she would manage to get it somehow, even if she had to lean her body against the bush and let it support her while she plucked the prize. We picked in quart baskets, then poured the berries into red-and-white Krey lard buckets. The berries settled quickly, and Mama picked an extra quart to top off the full buckets. By nine o'clock the sun was high, and I struggled to the house with my four gallons, eager to wash the chiggers off and eat some cereal.

From picking blackberries, I learned about money. I wouldn't eat the berries,   43
even on my cereal: I wanted the money. One summer I picked eighty gallons and earned eighty dollars—much more than Mama made in a week when she worked at the Merit. Granny said food was everything, but I was hungry for something else—a kind of food that didn't grow in the ground. Yet I couldn't deny that we were always feasting. We ate sumptuous meals, never missing dessert. Once in a while, Daddy brought home exotic treats—fried oysters in little goldfish cartons or hot tamales wrapped in corn shucks. At Christmas, the dairy he drove for produced jugs of boiled custard, and we slurped gallons of it even though it was not really as good as Granny's, which was naturally yellow from fresh country eggs. Granny complained that store-bought eggs were pale. When the cows needed feed, Daddy took a load of corn from the corncrib to the feed mill and had it ground and mixed

with molasses and wheat and oats. He brought it home and filled the feed bin, a big box with a hinged lid, like a giant coffin. I would chew a mouthful now and then for the sweetening.

One spring I rode the corn planter behind Daddy on the tractor. He had plowed and disked and harrowed the ground. Sitting in a concave metal seat with holes in it, I rode the planter, which drilled furrows to receive the seed. At the end of each row I closed the hoppers so they wouldn't release seed while he turned the tractor in a wide loop. When he nosed down the next row, I opened the hoppers at his signal, so that the seed would trickle out again, evenly spaced, behind the drill. The planter covered the seed behind us. We didn't talk much in our awkward caravan. As we rode the long hot rows, rich floods of remembered music accompanied me as vividly as if I had been wearing a Walkman. Top Ten numbers like "Ruby," "The Song from Moulin Rouge," and "Rags to Riches" rolled through my head with the promise that I would not have to plant corn when I grew up. 44

As I look back, the men recede into the furrows, into the waves of the ocean, and the women stand erect, churning and frying. 45

Reading Closely

1. According to Bobbie Ann Mason, what it means to be "country" can be defined by what one characteristic in particular? How did this distinguishing feature come to be so important?

2. Mason says her family wasn't poor—they owned their own land, and they always had plenty to eat. So what does she mean when she says "we lived in a state of psychological poverty" (15)?

3. "I was hungry," says Mason, "for something else—a kind of food that didn't grow in the ground" (43). What kind of food is she talking about here?

4. When Mason's mother had to give up running her own restaurant, her daughter thought she "saw a little fire go out of her" (39). What fire? Why did it diminish?

5. As a girl, Mason liked picking blackberries. Why? Why didn't she like riding behind the tractor and planting corn with her father? Why did she dislike farming in general?

6. Mason refers several times to specific songs, musicians, and TV shows. What do these references tell us about her as a teenager growing up in rural America?

STRATEGIES AND STRUCTURES

1. In addition to giving a little family background, what is Mason's PURPOSE in beginning her chapter with the NARRATIVE of the settlement of the area in Kentucky where her family's farm was located? Where and why does "seed corn" come up again in her essay (2, 3)?

2. If Mrs. Washam is "the hero" of that opening tale, who is the hero of the rest of the tale Mason is telling (4)? What do the two have in common? Explain.

3. What other characteristics and qualities of "being country"—besides those having to do with producing, preparing, and eating food—does Mason introduce? Where? How do these characteristics help to broaden her basic definition?

4. Mason defines life in the country in part by COMPARING it with life in town. Where does she develop this comparison, and what does it contribute to her definition?

5. *Other Methods.* Mason frequently uses DESCRIPTION to extend her definition and help explain what she means by her key terms. Point out descriptive details in her essay that you find particularly effective for this purpose.

THINKING ABOUT LANGUAGE

1. Why does Mason refer to herself as "being country" instead of, for example, "being from the country" (15)?

2. Mason says the old settlement story about the family land "vexes" her (3). What are the implications of this word? How does she show her vexation?

3. Why does Mason explain that her family pronounced *iced tea* as "ice-tea" (19)?

4. "I was flying," says Mason of her time as a helper in her mother's restaurant (32). How does this HYPERBOLE tie in with her earlier dreams of becoming an airline stewardess (9)?

5. When describing her memories of her mother at the restaurant, Mason compares the flicker of the TV to the flicker of candles in a church (40). Why? What's the purpose of this ANALOGY?

6. Mason remembers the feed bin on the family farm as looking "like a giant coffin" (43). How does this SIMILE fit in with her other corny memories—or rather memories of corn?

FOR WRITING

1. In a few paragraphs, describe a group of people doing some kind of particular work that defines who and what they are.

2. Write an essay about growing up that shows how you and your family defined yourselves. Be sure to indicate where and how you didn't fit the mold—or the mold didn't fit you.

GEOFFREY NUNBERG

The War of Words: "Terror" and "Terrorism"

Geoffrey Nunberg (b. 1945), a professor at the University of California at Berkeley and chair of the usage panel of the American Heritage Dictionary, *has devoted his career to examining the words we use and what they reveal. "There has never been an age as wary as ours," he writes, "of the tricks words can play, obscuring distinctions and smoothing over the corrugations of the actual world." Nunberg has examined those tricks not only in scholarly works but also in countless articles for the general reader. He writes a regular feature on words for the* New York Times, *and his voice is familiar to listeners of the National Public Radio program* Fresh Air. *Many of Nunberg's commentaries on language, culture, and politics have been collected in* The Way We Talk Now *(2001),* Going Nucular *(2004), and* Talking Right *(2007).*

In "The War of Words: 'Terror' and 'Terrorism,'" Nunberg illustrates how the definitions of words have become one more weapon in our political battles, helping to shape perceptions and influence policy. This article first appeared in the New York Times *in 2004.*

"T HE LONG-TERM DEFEAT OF TERROR will happen when freedom takes hold in 1 the broader Middle East," President George W. Bush said on June 28, as he announced the early transfer of sovereignty to the Iraqis.

The "defeat of terror"—the wording suggests that much has changed since 2 September 11, 2001. In his speech on that day, Bush said, "We stand together to win the war against terrorism," and over the next year the White House described the enemy as terrorism twice as often as terror. But in White House speeches over the past year, those proportions have been reversed. And the shift from "terrorism" to "terror" has been equally dramatic in major newspapers, according to a search of several databases.

Broad linguistic shifts such as these usually owe less to conscious decisions by 3 editors or speechwriters than to often-unnoticed changes in the way people perceive their world. Terrorism may itself be a vague term, as critics have argued. But terror is still more amorphous and elastic, and alters the understanding not just of the enemy but of the war against it.

True, phrases like "terror plots" or "terror threat level" can make terror seem 4 merely a headline writer's shortening of the word terrorism. But even there, "ter-

SUGGESTED MLA CITATION: Nunberg, Geoffrey. "The War of Words: 'Terror' and 'Terrorism.'" 2004. *Back to the Lake.* Ed. Thomas Cooley. 2nd ed. New York: Norton, 2012. 432–34. Print.

ror" draws on a more complex set of meanings. It evokes both the actions of terrorists and the fear they are trying to engender.

"Do we cower in the face of terror?" Bush asked on Irish television a few days 5
before the handover in Iraq, with "terror" doing double work.

And unlike "terrorism," "terror" can be applied to states as well as to 6
insurgents, as in the president's frequent references to Saddam Hussein's
"terror regime." Even if Saddam can't actually be linked to the attacks of
September 11, "terror" seems to connect them etymologically.

> Word histories (p. 382) are most effective when they're tied to history in general.

The modern senses of "terror" and "terrorism" go back to a single histori- 7
cal moment: "la Terreur," Robespierre's Reign of Terror[1] in 1793 and 1794.
"Terror," Robespierre said, "is nothing other than justice, prompt, severe, inflexible; it is therefore an emanation of virtue."

It was the ruthless severity of that emanation that moved Edmund Burke[2] to 8
decry "those hell-hounds called terrorists," in one of the first recorded uses of "terrorist" in English.

For Robespierre and his contemporaries, "terror" conveyed the exalted emotion 9
people may feel when face to face with the absolute. That was what led Albert
Camus[3] to describe terror as the urge that draws people to the violent certainties of
totalitarianism, where rebellion hardens into ideology.

With time, though, the word's aura of sublimity faded. By 1880, "holy terror" 10
was only a jocular name for an obstreperous child and "terrible" no longer suggested the sense of awe it had in "terrible swift sword." By the Jazz Age,[4] "terrific"
was just a wan superlative. Terror was still a name for intense fear, but it no longer
connoted a social force.

"Terrorism," too, has drifted since its origin. By modern times, the word could 11
refer only to the use of violence against a government, not on its behalf—though
some still claimed the "terrorist" designation proudly.

It wasn't until the beginning of the post-colonial period[5] that all groups rejected 12
the terrorist label in favor of names such as freedom fighters or mujahadeen. By

---

1. *Reign of Terror*: Period from September 1793 to July 1794 during which the government established by the French Revolution executed tens of thousands of its critics. *Maximilien Robespierre* (1758–1794): an attorney who became one of the most powerful and bloodthirsty leaders of the French Revolution.

2. *Edmund Burke* (1729–1797): British statesman and orator who supported the American Revolution but opposed the revolution in France because of its violence.

3. *Albert Camus* (1913–1960): French writer and philosopher known for blending Christianity and existentialism.

4. *Jazz Age*: The 1920s. *"Terrible swift sword"*: A line from Julia Ward Howe's lyrics to the patriotic song "Battle Hymn of the Republic" (1861) that refers to the wrath of God.

5. *Post-colonial period*: The decades immediately after World War II in which many African and other countries gained independence from their nineteenth-century colonial rulers. In general, *post-colonialism* refers to the many issues, such as creating a national identity, that countries face after their former colonizers have withdrawn.

then, "terrorism" was no longer a genuine -ism, but the name for a reprehensible strategy, often extended as a term of abuse for anyone whose methods seemed ruthless.

But the recent uses of "terror" seem to draw its disparate, superseded senses   13 back together in a way that Burke might have found familiar. Today, it is again a name that encompasses both the dark forces that threaten "civilization" and the fears they arouse.

The new senses of the noun are signaled in another linguistic shift in the press   14 and in White House speeches. Just as "terrorism" has been replaced by "terror," so "war" is much more likely now to be followed by "on" rather than "against."

That "war on" pattern dates from the turn of the 20th century, when people   15 adapted epidemiological metaphors to describe campaigns against social evils such as alcohol, crime and poverty—endemic conditions that could be mitigated but not eradicated.

"The war on terror," too, suggests a campaign aimed not at human adversaries   16 but at a pervasive social plague. At its most abstract, terror comes to seem as persistent and inexplicable as evil itself, without raising any inconvenient theological qualms. And in fact, the White House's use of "evil" has declined by 80 percent over the same period that its use of "terror" has been increasing.

Like wars on ignorance and crime, a "war on terror" suggests an enduring state   17 of struggle—a "never-ending fight against terror and its relentless onslaughts," as Albert Camus put it in *The Plague*, his 1947 allegory of the rise and fall of Fascism.

It is as if the language is girding itself for the long haul.   18

Reading Closely

1. The word *terror*, says Geoffrey Nunberg, "draws on a more complex set of meanings" than the word *terrorism* (4). What are some of those differences in meaning between the two terms as Nunberg defines them?

2. During the French Revolution, according to Nunberg, how did the traditional definition of *terror* change? What important element did the Revolution introduce into the modern meaning of the term?

3. According to Nunberg, how has the meaning of *terrorism* changed (11)?

4. Why is Nunberg concerned with changes in how words are defined? What is his THESIS about such changes?

STRATEGIES AND STRUCTURES

1. Nunberg begins with a specific EXAMPLE (of "broad linguistic shifts") before he explains what he is defining (3). How effective do you find this strategy? Why?

2. "Even if Saddam can't actually be linked to the attacks of September 11, 'terror' seems to connect them etymologically" (6). What issue is Nunberg raising here? Does he ARGUE a position on that issue, or does he remain more or less objective? Explain.

3. How does Nunberg himself use ETYMOLOGIES to make connections in his essay? Is this an effective strategy? Why or why not?

4. *Other Methods.* In the body of his essay, Nunberg is COMPARING AND CONTRASTING the definitions, old and new, of *terror* and *terrorism*. Explain how he extends these comparisons in the last quarter of his essay.

THINKING ABOUT LANGUAGE

1. What is the purpose of Nunberg's ALLUSION to Albert Camus' ideas in paragraphs 9 and 17?

2. What does Nunberg mean when he says that "war on" is an "epidemiological" metaphor (15)?

3. Why, according to Nunberg, has the use of the word *evil* in American political discourse declined by 80 percent in recent years (16)?

4. "Girding" (as in "girding one's loins") is what a warrior typically does in preparation for battle (18). Why do you think Nunberg ends his essay with this METAPHOR? Who or what is embattled?

FOR WRITING

1. Write a paragraph or two defining "long haul" (18) by explaining its history as a transportation term.

2. What significant changes   in politics, priorities, and preoccupations   do you think have affected the meanings of basic English words, especially since 9/11? Citing Nunberg's examples and any others you want to draw on, write an essay explaining and defining some of those new meanings.

A Good Man Is Hard to Find

Mary Flannery O'Connor (1925–1964) was born in Savannah, Georgia, studied at the Georgia State College for Women, and earned an MFA at the Writer's Workshop of the University of Iowa. Soon afterward, she was diagnosed with lupus, a painful auto-immune disorder that would trouble her for the rest of her brief life. Eight years after she died of the disease, her posthumously collected Complete Stories *won the 1972 National Book Award. She wrote two novels,* Wise Blood *(1952) and* The Violent Bear It Away *(1960), but she's best known for her witty, sharply observed, darkly ironic, and sometimes shockingly violent short stories—the epitome of what is known as "Southern Gothic."*

Above all, O'Connor's fiction is marked by her obsessions with morality and mortality, as well as her unwillingness to accept simplistic explanations for life's mysteries. "A Good Man Is Hard to Find," the title story in her 1955 collection, culminates in a kind of debate over the definition of "goodness"—is it a quality deep inside every human heart, something that can be awakened at any time, in the Christian sense of "redemption"? Or are there some people in whom no goodness resides, people who are simply irredeemable? O'Connor provides no easy answer.

THE GRANDMOTHER didn't want to go to Florida. She wanted to visit some of her connections in east Tennessee and she was seizing at every chance to change Bailey's mind. Bailey was the son she lived with, her only boy. He was sitting on the edge of his chair at the table, bent over the orange sports section of the *Journal.* "Now look here, Bailey," she said, "see here, read this," and she stood with one hand on her thin hip and the other rattling the newspaper at his bald head. "Here this fellow that calls himself The Misfit is aloose from the Federal Pen and headed toward Florida and you read here what it says he did to these people. Just you read it. I wouldn't take my children in any direction with a criminal like that aloose in it. I couldn't answer to my conscience if I did." 1

Bailey didn't look up from his reading so she wheeled around then and faced the children's mother, a young woman in slacks, whose face was as broad and innocent as a cabbage and was tied around with a green head-kerchief that had two points on the top like rabbit's ears. She was sitting on the sofa, feeding the baby his apricots out of a jar. "The children have been to Florida before," the old lady said. "You 2

SUGGESTED MLA CITATION: O'Connor, Flannery. "A Good Man Is Hard to Find." 1955. *Back to the Lake.* Ed. Thomas Cooley. 2nd ed. New York: Norton, 2012. 436–49. Print.

all ought to take them somewhere else for a change so they would see different parts of the world and be broad. They never have been to east Tennessee."

The children's mother didn't seem to hear her but the eight-year-old boy, John Wesley, a stocky child with glasses, said, "If you don't want to go to Florida, why dontcha stay at home?" He and the little girl, June Star, were reading the funny papers on the floor.   3

"She wouldn't stay at home to be queen for a day," June Star said without raising her yellow head.   4

"Yes and what would you do if this fellow, The Misfit, caught you?" the grandmother asked.   5

"I'd smack his face," John Wesley said.   6

"She wouldn't stay at home for a million bucks," June Star said. "Afraid she'd miss something. She has to go everywhere we go."   7

"All right, Miss," the grandmother said. "Just remember that the next time you want me to curl your hair."   8

June Star said her hair was naturally curly.   9

The next morning the grandmother was the first one in the car, ready to go. She had her big black valise that looked like the head of a hippopotamus in one corner, and underneath it she was hiding a basket with Pitty Sing, the cat, in it. She didn't intend for the cat to be left alone in the house for three days because he would miss her too much and she was afraid he might brush against one of the gas burners and accidentally asphyxiate himself. Her son, Bailey, didn't like to arrive at a motel with a cat.   10

She sat in the middle of the back seat with John Wesley and June Star on either side of her. Bailey and the children's mother and the baby sat in front and they left Atlanta at eight forty-five with the mileage on the car at 55890. The grandmother wrote this down because she thought it would be interesting to say how many miles they had been when they got back. It took them twenty minutes to reach the outskirts of the city.   11

The old lady settled herself comfortably, removing her white cotton gloves and putting them up with her purse on the shelf in front of the back window. The children's mother still had on slacks and still had her head tied up in a green kerchief, but the grandmother had on a navy blue straw sailor hat with a bunch of white violets on the brim and a navy blue dress with a small white dot in the print. Her collars and cuffs were white organdy trimmed with lace and at her neckline she had pinned a purple spray of cloth violets containing a sachet. In case of an accident, anyone seeing her dead on the highway would know at once that she was a lady.   12

She said she thought it was going to be a good day for driving, neither too hot nor too cold, and she cautioned Bailey that the speed limit was fifty-five miles an   13 hour and that the patrolmen hid themselves behind billboards and small clumps of trees and sped out after you before you had a chance to slow down. She pointed out interesting details of the scenery: Stone Mountain; the blue granite that in some places came up to both sides of the highway; the brilliant red clay banks slightly streaked with purple; and the various crops that made rows of green lace-work on the ground. The trees were full of silver-white sunlight and the meanest of them sparkled. The children were reading comic magazines and their mother had gone back to sleep.

"Let's go through Georgia fast so we won't have to look at it much," John Wesley said.   14

"If I were a little boy," said the grandmother, "I wouldn't talk about my native state that way. Tennessee has the mountains and Georgia has the hills."   15

"Tennessee is just a hillbilly dumping ground," John Wesley said, "and Georgia is a lousy state too."   16

"You said it," June Star said.   17

"In my time," said the grandmother, folding her thin veined fingers, "children were more respectful of their native states and their parents and everything else. People did right then. Oh look at the cute little pickaninny!" she said and pointed to a Negro child standing in the door of a shack. "Wouldn't that make a picture, now?" she asked and they all turned and looked at the little Negro out of the back window. He waved.   18

"He didn't have any britches on," June Star said.   19

"He probably didn't have any," the grandmother explained. "Little niggers in the country don't have things like we do. If I could paint, I'd paint that picture," she said.   20

The children exchanged comic books.   21

The grandmother offered to hold the baby and the children's mother passed him over the front seat to her. She set him on her knee and bounced him and told him about the things they were passing. She rolled her eyes and screwed up her mouth and stuck her leathery thin face into his smooth bland one. Occasionally he gave her a faraway smile. They passed a large cotton field with five or six graves fenced in the middle of it, like a small island. "Look at the graveyard!" the grandmother said, pointing it out. "That was the old family burying ground. That belonged to the plantation."   22

"Where's the plantation?" John Wesley asked.   23

"Gone With the Wind," said the grandmother. "Ha. Ha."   24

When the children finished all the comic books they had brought, they opened the lunch and ate it. The grandmother ate a peanut butter sandwich and an olive and would not let the children throw the box and the paper napkins out the window. When there was nothing else to do they played a game by choosing a cloud   25 and making the other two guess what shape it suggested. John Wesley took one the shape of a cow and June Star guessed a cow and John Wesley said, no, an automobile, and June Star said he didn't play fair, and they began to slap each other over the grandmother.

The grandmother said she would tell them a story if they would keep quiet. 26
When she told a story, she rolled her eyes and waved her head and was very dramatic. She said once when she was a maiden lady she had been courted by a Mr. Edgar Atkins Teagarden from Jasper, Georgia. She said he was a very good-looking man and a gentleman and that he brought her a watermelon every Saturday afternoon with his initials cut in it, E. A. T. Well, one Saturday, she said, Mr. Teagarden brought the watermelon and there was nobody at home and he left it on the front porch and returned in his buggy to Jasper, but she never got the watermelon, she said, because a nigger boy ate it when he saw the initials, E. A. T.! This story tickled John Wesley's funny bone and he giggled and giggled but June Star didn't think it was any good. She said she wouldn't marry a man that just brought her a watermelon on Saturday. The grandmother said she would have done well to marry Mr. Teagarden because he was a gentleman and had bought Coca-Cola stock when it first came out and that he had died only a few years ago, a very wealthy man.

They stopped at The Tower for barbecued sandwiches. The Tower was a part 27
stucco and part wood filling station and dance hall set in a clearing outside of Timothy. A fat man named Red Sammy Butts ran it and there were signs stuck here and there on the building and for miles up and down the highway saying, TRY RED SAMMY'S FAMOUS BARBECUE. NONE LIKE FAMOUS RED SAMMY'S! RED SAM! THE FAT BOY WITH THE HAPPY LAUGH. A VETERAN! RED SAMMY'S YOUR MAN!

Red Sammy was lying on the bare ground outside The Tower with his head 28
under a truck while a gray monkey about a foot high, chained to a small chinaberry tree, chattered nearby. The monkey sprang back into the tree and got on the highest limb as soon as he saw the children jump out of the car and run toward him.

Inside, The Tower was a long dark room with a counter at one end and tables at 29
the other and dancing space in the middle. They all sat down at a board table next to the nickelodeon and Red Sam's wife, a tall burnt-brown woman with hair and eyes lighter than her skin, came and took their order. The children's mother put a dime in the machine and played "The Tennessee Waltz," and the grandmother said that tune always made her want to dance. She asked Bailey if he would like to dance but he only glared at her. He didn't have a naturally sunny disposition like she did and trips made him nervous. The grandmother's brown eyes were very bright. She swayed her head from side to side and pretended she was dancing in her chair. June Star said play something she could tap to so the children's mother

put in another dime and played a fast number and June Star stepped out onto the dance floor and did her tap routine.

"Ain't she cute?" Red Sam's wife said, leaning over the counter. "Would you like to come be my little girl?" 30

"No I certainly wouldn't," June Star said. "I wouldn't live in a broken-down place like this for a million bucks!" and she ran back to the table. 31

"Ain't she cute?" the woman repeated, stretching her mouth politely. 32

"Arn't you ashamed?" hissed the grandmother. 33

Red Sam came in and told his wife to quit lounging on the counter and hurry up with these people's order. His khaki trousers reached just to his hip bones and his stomach hung over them like a sack of meal swaying under his shirt. He came over and sat down at a table nearby and let out a combination sigh and yodel. "You can't win," he said. "You can't win," and he wiped his sweating red face off with a gray handkerchief. "These days you don't know who to trust," he said. "Ain't that the truth?" 34

"People are certainly not nice like they used to be," said the grandmother. 35

"Two fellers come in here last week," Red Sammy said, "driving a Chrysler. It was a old beat-up car but it was a good one and these boys looked all right to me. Said they worked at the mill and you know I let them fellers charge the gas they bought? Now why did I do that?" 36

"Because you're a good man!" the grandmother said at once. 37

"Yes'm,[1] I suppose so," Red Sam said as if he were struck with this answer. 38

His wife brought the orders, carrying the five plates all at once without a tray, two in each hand and one balanced on her arm. "It isn't a soul in this green world of God's that you can trust," she said. "And I don't count nobody out of that, not nobody," she repeated, looking at Red Sammy. 39

"Did you read about that criminal, The Misfit, that's escaped?" asked the grandmother. 40

"I wouldn't be a bit surprised if he didn't attact this place right here," said the woman. "If he hears about it being here, I wouldn't be none surprised to see him. If he hears it's two cent in the cash register, I wouldn't be a tall surprised if he . . ." 41

"That'll do," Red Sam said. "Go bring these people their Co'-Colas," and the woman went off to get the rest of the order. 42

"A good man is hard to find," Red Sammy said. "Everything is getting terrible. I remember the day you could go off and leave your screen door unlatched. Not no more." 43

1. *Yes'm/Nome*: O'Connor's way of representing the southern pronunciation of "yes, ma'am" and "no, ma'am."

He and the grandmother discussed better times. The old lady said that in her 44 opinion Europe was entirely to blame for the way things were now. She said the way Europe acted you would think we were made of money and Red Sam said it was no use talking about it, she was exactly right. The children ran outside into the white sunlight and looked at the monkey in the lacy chinaberry tree. He was busy catching fleas on himself and biting each one carefully between his teeth as if it were a delicacy.

They drove off again into the hot afternoon. The grandmother took cat naps and 45 woke up every few minutes with her own snoring. Outside of Toombsboro she woke up and recalled an old plantation that she had visited in this neighborhood once when she was a young lady. She said the house had six white columns across the front and that there was an avenue of oaks leading up to it and two little wooden trellis arbors on either side in front where you sat down with your suitor after a stroll in the garden. She recalled exactly which road to turn off to get to it. She knew that Bailey would not be willing to lose any time looking at an old house, but the more she talked about it, the more she wanted to see it once again and find out if the little twin arbors were still standing. "There was a secret panel in this house," she said craftily, not telling the truth but wishing that she were, "and the story went that all the family silver was hidden in it when Sherman came through but it was never found . . ."

"Hey!" John Wesley said. "Let's go see it! We'll find it! We'll poke all the wood- 46 work and find it! Who lives there? Where do you turn off at? Hey Pop, can't we turn off there?"

"We never have seen a house with a secret panel!" June Star shrieked. "Let's go 47 to the house with the secret panel! Hey Pop, can't we go see the house with the secret panel!"

"It's not far from here, I know," the grandmother said. "It wouldn't take over 48 twenty minutes."

Bailey was looking straight ahead. His jaw was as rigid as a horseshoe. "No," he 49 said.

The children began to yell and scream that they wanted to see the house with 50 the secret panel. John Wesley kicked the back of the front seat and June Star hung over her mother's shoulder and whined desperately into her ear that they never had any fun even on their vacation, that they could never do what THEY wanted to do. The baby began to scream and John Wesley kicked the back of the seat so hard that his father could feel the blows in his kidney.

"All right!" he shouted and drew the car to a stop at the side of the road. "Will 51 you all shut up? Will you all just shut up for one second? If you don't shut up, we won't go anywhere."

"It would be very educational for them," the grandmother murmured. 52

"All right," Bailey said, "but get this: this is the only time we're going to stop for anything like this. This is the one and only time." 53

"The dirt road that you have to turn down is about a mile back," the grandmother directed. "I marked it when we passed." 54

"A dirt road," Bailey groaned. 55

After they had turned around and were headed toward the dirt road, the grandmother recalled other points about the house, the beautiful glass over the front doorway and the candle-lamp in the hall. John Wesley said that the secret panel was probably in the fireplace. 56

"You can't go inside this house," Bailey said. "You don't know who lives there." 57

"While you all talk to the people in front, I'll run around behind and get in a window," John Wesley suggested. 58

"We'll all stay in the car," his mother said. 59

They turned onto the dirt road and the car raced roughly along in a swirl of pink dust. The grandmother recalled the times when there were no paved roads and thirty miles was a day's journey. The dirt road was hilly and there were sudden washes in it and sharp curves on dangerous embankments. All at once they would be on a hill, looking down over the blue tops of trees for miles around, then the next minute, they would be in a red depression with the dust-coated trees looking down on them. 60

"This place had better turn up in a minute," Bailey said, "or I'm going to turn around." 61

The road looked as if no one had traveled on it in months. 62

"It's not much farther," the grandmother said and just as she said it, a horrible thought came to her. The thought was so embarrassing that she turned red in the face and her eyes dilated and her feet jumped up, upsetting her valise in the corner. The instant the valise moved, the newspaper top she had over the basket under it rose with a snarl and Pitty Sing, the cat, sprang onto Bailey's shoulder. 63

The children were thrown to the floor and their mother, clutching the baby, was thrown out the door onto the ground; the old lady was thrown into the front seat. The car turned over once and landed right-side-up in a gulch off the side of the road. Bailey remained in the driver's seat with the cat—gray-striped with a broad white face and an orange nose—clinging to his neck like a caterpillar. 64

As soon as the children saw they could move their arms and legs, they scrambled out of the car, shouting, "We've had an ACCIDENT!" The grandmother was curled up under the dashboard, hoping she was injured so that Bailey's wrath would not come down on her all at once. The horrible thought she had had before the accident was that the house she had remembered so vividly was not in Georgia but in Tennessee. 65

Bailey removed the cat from his neck with both hands and flung it out the window against the side of a pine tree. Then he got out of the car and started looking for the children's mother. She was sitting against the side of the red gutted ditch, holding the screaming baby, but she only had a cut down her face and a broken shoulder. "We've had an ACCIDENT!" the children screamed in a frenzy of delight. 66

"But nobody's killed," June Star said with disappointment as the grandmother limped out of the car, her hat still pinned to her head but the broken front brim standing up at a jaunty angle and the violet spray hanging off the side. They all sat down in the ditch, except the children, to recover from the shock. They were all shaking. 67

"Maybe a car will come along," said the children's mother hoarsely 68

"I believe I have injured an organ," said the grandmother, pressing her side, but no one answered her. Bailey's teeth were clattering. He had on a yellow sport shirt with bright blue parrots designed in it and his face was as yellow as the shirt. The grandmother decided that she would not mention that the house was in Tennessee. 69

The road was about ten feet above and they could see only the tops of the trees on the other side of it. Behind the ditch they were sitting in there were more woods, tall and dark and deep. In a few minutes they saw a car some distance away on top of a hill, coming slowly as if the occupants were watching them. The grandmother stood up and waved both arms dramatically to attract their attention. The car continued to come on slowly, disappeared around a bend and appeared again, moving even slower, on top of the hill they had gone over. It was a big black battered hearse-like automobile. There were three men in it. 70

It came to a stop just over them and for some minutes, the driver looked down with a steady expressionless gaze to where they were sitting, and didn't speak. Then he turned his head and muttered something to the other two and they got out. One was a fat boy in black trousers and a red sweat shirt with a silver stallion embossed on the front of it. He moved around on the right side of them and stood staring, his mouth partly open in a kind of loose grin. The other had on khaki pants and a blue striped coat and a gray hat pulled down very low, hiding most of his face. He came around slowly on the left side. Neither spoke. 71

The driver got out of the car and stood by the side of it, looking down at them. He was an older man than the other two. His hair was just beginning to gray and he wore silver-rimmed spectacles that gave him a scholarly look. He had a long creased face and didn't have on any shirt or undershirt. He had on blue jeans that were too tight for him and was holding a black hat and a gun. The two boys also had guns. 72

"We've had an ACCIDENT!" the children screamed. 73

The grandmother had the peculiar feeling that the bespectacled man was some- 74
one she knew. His face was as familiar to her as if she had known him all her life
but she could not recall who he was. He moved away from the car and began to
come down the embankment, placing his feet carefully so that he wouldn't slip. He
had on tan and white shoes and no socks, and his ankles were red and thin. "Good
afternoon," he said. "I see you all had you a little spill."

"We turned over twice!" said the grandmother. 75

"Oncet," he corrected. "We seen it happen. Try their car and see will it run, 76
Hiram," he said quietly to the boy with the gray hat.

"What you got that gun for?" John Wesley asked. "Whatcha gonna do with that 77
gun?"

"Lady," the man said to the children's mother, "would you mind calling them 78
children to sit down by you? Children make me nervous. I want all you all to sit
down right together there where you're at."

"What are you telling US what to do for?" June Star asked. 79

Behind them the line of woods gaped like a dark open mouth. "Come here," said 80
their mother.

"Look here now," Bailey began suddenly, "we're in a predicament! We're in . . ." 81

The grandmother shrieked. She scrambled to her feet and stood staring. "You're 82
The Misfit!" she said. "I recognized you at once!"

"Yes'm," the man said, smiling slightly as if he were pleased in spite of himself 83
to be known, "but it would have been better for all of you, lady, if you hadn't of
reckernized me."

Bailey turned his head sharply and said something to his mother that shocked 84
even the children. The old lady began to cry and The Misfit reddened.

"Lady," he said, "don't you get upset. Sometimes a man says things he don't 85
mean. I don't reckon he meant to talk to you thataway."

"You wouldn't shoot a lady, would you?" the grandmother said and removed a 86
clean handkerchief from her cuff and began to slap at her eyes with it.

The Misfit pointed the toe of his shoe into the ground and made a little hole and 87
then covered it up again. "I would hate to have to," he said.

"Listen," the grandmother almost screamed, "I know you're a good man. You 88
don't look a bit like you have common blood. I know you must come from nice
people!"

"Yes mam," he said, "finest people in the world." When he smiled he showed a 89
row of strong white teeth. "God never made a finer woman than my mother and
my daddy's heart was pure gold," he said. The boy with the red sweat shirt had
come around behind them and was standing with his gun at his hip. The Misfit
squatted down on the ground. "Watch them children, Bobby Lee," he said. "You
know they make me nervous." He looked at the six of them huddled together in

front of him and he seemed to be embarrassed as if he couldn't think of anything to say. "Ain't a cloud in the sky," he remarked, looking up at it. "Don't see no sun but don't see no cloud neither."

"Yes, it's a beautiful day," said the grandmother. "Listen," she said, "you shouldn't call yourself The Misfit because I know you're a good man at heart. I can just look at you and tell." 90

"Hush!" Bailey yelled. "Hush! Everybody shut up and let me handle this!" He was squatting in the position of a runner about to sprint forward but he didn't move. 91

"I pre-chate that, lady," The Misfit said and drew a little circle in the ground with the butt of his gun. 92

"It'll take a half a hour to fix this here car," Hiram called, looking over the raised hood of it. 93

"Well, first you and Bobby Lee get him and that little boy to step over yonder with you," The Misfit said, pointing to Bailey and John Wesley. "The boys want to ast you something," he said to Bailey. "Would you mind stepping back in them woods there with them?" 94

"Listen," Bailey began, "we're in a terrible predicament! Nobody realizes what this is," and his voice cracked. His eyes were as blue and intense as the parrots in his shirt and he remained perfectly still. 95

The grandmother reached up to adjust her hat brim as if she were going to the woods with him but it came off in her hand. She stood staring at it and after a second she let it fall on the ground. Hiram pulled Bailey up by the arm as if he were assisting an old man. John Wesley caught hold of his father's hand and Bobby Lee followed. They went off toward the woods and just as they reached the dark edge, Bailey turned and supporting himself against a gray naked pine trunk, he shouted, "I'll be back in a minute, Mamma, wait on me!" 96

"Come back this instant!" his mother shrilled but they all disappeared into the woods. 97

"Bailey Boy!" the grandmother called in a tragic voice but she found she was looking at The Misfit squatting on the ground in front of her. "I just know you're a good man," she said desperately. "You're not a bit common!" 98

"Nome, I ain't a good man," The Misfit said after a second as if he had considered her statement carefully, "but I ain't the worst in the world neither. My daddy said I was a different breed of dog from my brothers and sisters. 'You know,' Daddy said, 'it's some that can live their whole life out without asking about it and it's others has to know why it is, and this boy is one of the latters. He's going to be into everything!'" He put on his black hat and looked up suddenly and then away deep into the woods as if he were embarrassed again. "I'm sorry I don't have on a shirt before you ladies," he said, hunching his shoulders slightly. "We buried our clothes 99 that we had on when we escaped and we're just making do until we can get better. We borrowed these from some folks we met," he explained.

"That's perfectly all right," the grandmother said. "Maybe Bailey has an extra shirt in his suitcase." 100

"I'll look and see terrectly," The Misfit said. 101

"Where are they taking him?" the children's mother screamed. 102

"Daddy was a card himself," The Misfit said. "You couldn't put anything over on him. He never got in trouble with the Authorities though. Just had the knack of handling them." 103

"You could be honest too if you'd only try," said the grandmother. "Think how wonderful it would be to settle down and live a comfortable life and not have to think about somebody chasing you all the time." 104

The Misfit kept scratching in the ground with the butt of his gun as if he were thinking about it. "Yes'm, somebody is always after you," he murmured. 105

The grandmother noticed how thin his shoulder blades were just behind his hat because she was standing up looking down on him. "Do you ever pray?" she asked. 106

He shook his head. All she saw was the black hat wiggle between his shoulder blades. "Nome," he said. 107

There was a pistol shot from the woods, followed closely by another. Then silence. The old lady's head jerked around. She could hear the wind move through the tree tops like a long satisfied insuck of breath. "Bailey Boy!" she called. 108

"I was a gospel singer for a while," The Misfit said. "I been most everything. Been in the arm service, both land and sea, at home and abroad, been twict married, been an undertaker, been with the railroads, plowed Mother Earth, been in a tornado, seen a man burnt alive oncet," and he looked up at the children's mother and the little girl who were sitting close together, their faces white and their eyes glassy; "I even seen a woman flogged," he said. 109

"Pray, pray," the grandmother began, "pray, pray . . ." 110

"I never was a bad boy that I remember of," The Misfit said in an almost dreamy voice, "but somewheres along the line I done something wrong and got sent to the penitentiary. I was buried alive," and he looked up and held her attention to him by a steady stare. 111

"That's when you should have started to pray," she said. "What did you do to get sent to the penitentiary that first time?" 112

"Turn to the right, it was a wall," The Misfit said, looking up again at the cloudless sky. "Turn to the left, it was a wall. Look up it was a ceiling, look down it was a floor. I forget what I done, lady. I set there and set there, trying to remember what it was I done and I ain't recalled it to this day. Oncet in a while, I would think it was coming to me, but it never come." 113

"Maybe they put you in by mistake." the old lady said vaguely.   114

"Nome," he said. "It wasn't no mistake. They had the papers on me."   115

"You must have stolen something," she said.   116

The Misfit sneered slightly. "Nobody had nothing I wanted," he said. "It was a   117
head-doctor at the penitentiary said what I had done was kill my daddy but I known
that for a lie. My daddy died in nineteen ought nineteen of the epidemic flu and I
never had a thing to do with it. He was buried in the Mount Hopewell Baptist
churchyard and you can go there and see for yourself."

"If you would pray," the old lady said, "Jesus would help you."   118

"That's right," The Misfit said.   119

"Well then, why don't you pray?" she asked trembling with delight suddenly.   120

"I don't want no hep," he said. "I'm doing all right by myself."   121

Bobby Lee and Hiram came ambling back from the woods. Bobby Lee was drag-   122
ging a yellow shirt with bright blue parrots in it.

"Thow me that shirt, Bobby Lee," The Misfit said. The shirt came flying at him   123
and landed on his shoulder and he put it on. The grandmother couldn't name what
the shirt reminded her of. "No, lady," The Misfit said while he was buttoning it up,
"I found out the crime don't matter. You can do one thing or you can do another,
kill a man or take a tire off his car, because sooner or later you're going to forget
what it was you done and just be punished for it."

The children's mother had begun to make heaving noises as if she couldn't get   124
her breath. "Lady," he asked, "would you and that little girl like to step off yonder
with Bobby Lee and Hiram and join your husband?"

"Yes, thank you," the mother said faintly. Her left arm dangled helplessly and   125
she was holding the baby, who had gone to sleep, in the other. "Hep that lady up,
Hiram," The Misfit said as she struggled to climb out of the ditch, "and Bobby Lee,
you hold onto that little girl's hand."

"I don't want to hold hands with him," June Star said. "He reminds me of a pig."   126

The fat boy blushed and laughed and caught her by the arm and pulled her off   127
into the woods after Hiram and her mother.

Alone with The Misfit, the grandmother found that she had lost her voice. There   128
was not a cloud in the sky nor any sun. There was nothing around her but woods.
She wanted to tell him that he must pray. She opened and closed her mouth several times before anything came out. Finally she found herself saying, "Jesus.
Jesus," meaning, Jesus will help you, but the way she was saying it, it sounded as if
she might be cursing.

"Yes'm," The Misfit said as if he agreed. "Jesus thown everything off balance. It   129
was the same case with Him as with me except He hadn't committed any crime
and they could prove I had committed one because they had the papers on me. Of
course," he said, "they never shown me my papers. That's why I sign myself now. I

said long ago, you get you a signature and sign everything you do and keep a copy of it. Then you'll know what you done and you can hold up the crime to the punishment and see do they match and in the end you'll have something to prove you ain't been treated right. I call myself The Misfit," he said, "because I can't make what all I done wrong fit what all I gone through in punishment."

There was a piercing scream from the woods, followed closely by a pistol report. 130 "Does it seem right to you, lady, that one is punished a heap and another ain't punished at all?"

"Jesus!" the old lady cried. "You've got good blood! I know you wouldn't shoot a 131 lady! I know you come from nice people! Pray! Jesus, you ought not to shoot a lady. I'll give you all the money I've got!"

"Lady," The Misfit said, looking beyond her far into the woods, "there never was 132 a body that give the undertaker a tip."

There were two more pistol reports and the grandmother raised her head like a 133 parched old turkey hen crying for water and called, "Bailey Boy, Bailey Boy!" as if her heart would break.

"Jesus was the only One that ever raised the dead," The Misfit continued, "and 134 He shouldn't have done it. He thown everything off balance. If He did what He said, then it's nothing for you to do but thow away everything and follow Him, and if He didn't, then it's nothing for you to do but enjoy the few minutes you got left the best way you can—by killing somebody or burning down his house or doing some other meanness to him. No pleasure but meanness," he said and his voice had become almost a snarl.

"Maybe He didn't raise the dead," the old lady mumbled, not knowing what she 135 was saying and feeling so dizzy that she sank down in the ditch with her legs twisted under her.

"I wasn't there so I can't say He didn't," The Misfit said. "I wisht I had of been 136 there," he said, hitting the ground with his fist. "It ain't right I wasn't there because if I had of been there I would of known. Listen lady," he said in a high voice, "if I had of been there I would of known and I wouldn't be like I am now." His voice seemed about to crack and the grandmother's head cleared for an instant. She saw the man's face twisted close to her own as if he were going to cry and she murmured, "Why you're one of my babies. You're one of my own children!" She reached out and touched him on the shoulder. The Misfit sprang back as if a snake had bitten him and shot her three times through the chest. Then he put his gun down on the ground and took off his glasses and began to clean them.

Hiram and Bobby Lee returned from the woods and stood over the ditch, look- 137 ing down at the grandmother who half sat and half lay in a puddle of blood with her legs crossed under her like a child's and her face smiling up at the cloudless sky.

Without his glasses, The Misfit's eyes were red-rimmed and pale and defense- 138
less-looking. "Take her off and thow her where you thown the others," he said,
picking up the cat that was rubbing itself against his leg.

"She was a talker, wasn't she?" Bobby Lee said, sliding down the ditch with a 139
yodel.

"She would of been a good woman," The Misfit said, "if it had been somebody 140
there to shoot her every minute of her life."

"Some fun!" Bobby Lee said. 141

"Shut up, Bobby Lee," The Misfit said. "It's no real pleasure in life." 142

READING CLOSELY

1. How did The Misfit in Flannery O'Connor's story get his name?

2. Why does The Misfit think that Jesus "thrown everything off balance" by raising the dead (134)? Why is he concerned with matters of religious faith at all?

3. How religious is the grandmother in O'Connor's story? When she mentions Jesus, why does it sound "as if she might be cursing" (128)?

4. At the end of the story, when she *is* dead, the grandmother has "her legs crossed under her like a child's" (137). Where else in the story is the grandmother COM- PARED to a child? How does she compare in character and personality with June Star and John Wesley, the actual children in the story?

5. What is the grandmother doing when The Misfit shoots her? Why is he so upset at that particular moment?

STRATEGIES AND STRUCTURES

1. "A good man is hard to find," says Red Sammy Butts, proprietor of the Tower restaurant (43). Yet the grandmother has just called him a good man simply because he has allowed some travellers to charge their gas (37). How are the two of them defining goodness? What is O'Connor's point in introducing differ- ent definitions of goodness just before The Misfit appears in her narrative?

2. When, in an attempt to save herself, the grandmother calls The Misfit a good man, he replies, "I ain't a good man" (99). The Misfit is correct: he is, after all, a pathological killer who ruthlessly murders an entire family, including a baby. However, does The Misfit display any characteristics that might be defined as good if he weren't otherwise so evil?

3. "She would of been a good woman," The Misfit says to Bobby Lee, "if it had been somebody there to shoot her every minute of her life" (140). What does The Misfit mean by this? How has the grandmother (or *grand mother*) been truly good just before she is shot?

4. The grandmother dies with "her face smiling up at the cloudless sky," presumably toward heaven (137). Is there any sense in which The Misfit could be defined as her savior?

5. The Misfit defines *pleasure* as "meanness" (134). Yet at the end of the story he tells Bobby Lee, "It's no real pleasure in life" (142). Why not? Why can't the Misfit enjoy being murderously mean? What definition of the good life throws him off balance? Why does he take it to heart?

6. *Other Methods.* From whose perspective is this story NARRATED? Whose story is this? The Misfit's? The grandmother's? Explain.

THINKING ABOUT LANGUAGE

1. "A good man is hard to find" is the first line of the chorus in a popular song recorded by blues singer Bessie Smith in 1927. The next line in the original recording is, "You always get another kind." How well does this prediction fit O'Connor's story? Why would she name such a dark story after a popular song?

2. One reviewer of their first album says that the post-punk band Pitty Sing is named after "an evil cat in a Flannery O'Connor short story." It's not the cat's fault that someone lets it out of the bag. Who is the guilty party, and how does this PUN—"letting the cat out of the bag"—resonate throughout the story?

3. The cat Pitty Sing is named for a character in the *Mikado*, a comic opera by William S. Gilbert and Arthur Sullivan. "Pitty Sing" (10) is baby talk for "Pretty Thing." What does the cat's name tell you about the maturity level of some of the characters in the story?

4. Why does O'Connor describe The Misfit as reacting "as if a snake had bitten him" when the grandmother touches his shoulder (136)? What's the ALLUSION?

FOR WRITING

1. A psychiatrist would probably diagnose O'Connor's Misfit as a *psychopath*. Write a paragraph or two defining this neurosis as exemplified by O'Connor's villain.

2. Write an essay analyzing how conventional definitions of good and evil are called into question by O'Connor's classic story.

CHAPTER 11

Cause and Effect

For want of a nail the shoe was lost; for want of a shoe the horse was lost, and for want of a horse the rider was lost, being overtaken and slain by the enemy, all for want of care about a horse-shoe nail.

—BENJAMIN FRANKLIN, *The Way to Wealth*

Suppose you've made lasagna in a stainless-steel baking pan. Rather than transfer your leftovers to another container, you simply cover the pan with aluminum foil and store it in the refrigerator. When you come back a few days later to reheat the dish, you notice tiny holes in the aluminum. Why, you ask? Even more pressing: Can you safely eat your leftovers? What would be the effect on your body if you did? With these questions, you have just launched into an analysis of cause and effect.

Defining Cause and Effect:
Analyzing Why Things Happen—or Might Happen

When we analyze something, we take it apart to see how the pieces fit together. A common way in which things fit together, especially in the physical universe, is that one causes the other. In the case of your leftover lasagna, for example, the aluminum foil deteriorates because it is touching the tomato sauce as well as the stainless-steel pan. "When aluminum metal is in simultaneous contact with a different metal," writes the food critic Robert L. Wolke, who is also a professor of chemistry, the combination "constitutes an electric battery"—if there is also present "an electrical conductor such as tomato sauce."

When we analyze causes and effects, we not only explain why something happened (what caused the holes in the foil), we predict what might happen—for example, if you eat the lasagna anyway.

In this chapter, we will discuss how to analyze causes and effects; how to tell causation from coincidence; how to distinguish probable causes from merely possible ones; and how to organize a cause-and-effect essay by tracing events in chronological order from cause to effect—or backward in time from effect to cause. We'll also review the critical points to watch for as you read over your essay, as well as common errors to avoid when you edit.

Why Do We Analyze Causes and Effects?

According to the British philosopher David Hume in his *Enquiry Concerning Human Understanding*, much of the thinking that human beings do is "founded on the relation of cause and effect." Like Adam and Eve when they discovered fire (Hume's example), we analyze causes and effects in order to learn how things relate to each other in the physical world. Also, when we know what causes something, we can apply that knowledge to our future behavior and that of others: Don't put your hand in the fire because it will burn. Don't cover your leftover lasagna with aluminum foil because you'll get metal in your food if the foil touches the sauce.

Hume was not just speaking of the knowledge we gain from experience, however. By doing research and using our powers of reasoning in addition to those of direct observation, we can also analyze the causes and effects of things that we cannot experience directly, such as the causes of the Civil War, or the effects of AIDS on the social and political future of Africa, or what will happen to the U.S. economy if the health care system is (or is not) reformed. Thus the analysis of cause-and-effect relationships is just as important in the study of history, politics, economics, and many other fields as in the sciences.

Composing a Cause-and-Effect Analysis

When you analyze causes and effects, as Hume said, you exercise a fundamental power of human understanding. (Too bad Adam and Eve didn't do this *before* they ate the apple.) You also unleash a powerful means of organizing an entire essay as point by point you explain the results of your analysis to your reader. But keep in mind that even simple effects can have complex causes—as in our tomato sauce example. Technically speaking, the holes in the aluminum foil were caused by the transfer of electrons from the foil to the steel bowl *through* the tomato sauce. What caused the corrosive sauce to touch the foil in the first place? Clearly, yet another cause is in play here—human error, as indicated in the diagram on page 453.

If relatively simple effects—such as the holes in the aluminum foil—can have multiple causes like these, just think how many causes you will need to identify as

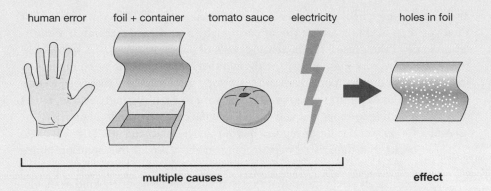

human error   foil + container   tomato sauce   electricity   holes in foil

multiple causes   **effect**

you analyze and explain more complex effects, such as the French Revolution, cancer, or why married men, on average, make more money than unmarried men.

Fortunately, as we shall see, even the most daunting array of causes can be reduced to a few basic ones. And thinking about the order in which they occur in time and their importance in producing a given effect, in turn, can provide you with a solid basis for organizing your essay.

Thinking about Purpose and Audience

As a professor of chemistry, Wolke fully understands the complexities of the chemical reaction he is analyzing, but the tomato sauce example here comes from *What Einstein Told His Cook*, a book he wrote to explain "kitchen science" to a general audience. So Wolke largely avoids the technical vocabulary of the laboratory and assumes no specialized knowledge on the part of the reader. Instead, he uses everyday language and offers practical applications for his scientific findings: store your leftovers in any kind of container you like, Wolke concludes, "just make sure that the foil isn't in contact with the sauce." When you write a cause-and-effect analysis, keep your readers in mind—use language appropriate for your audience and define any terms they may not know.

Wolke's purpose is to instruct his readers, and his topic is one that is easy to explain, at least for a chemist. Often, however, you will find yourself analyzing causes or effects that cannot be explained easily, and then you will actually need to ARGUE for possible causes or effects—to persuade your readers that a cause is plausible or an effect is likely.

Let's say you are taking Chemistry 101, and when you go to the campus bookstore to buy your textbook, you find that it costs $139. Your first thought is to write an article for the school newspaper accusing the bookstore of highway robbery, but then you stop to think: *why* is the price so high? You do some research and discover some of the causes: the increasing costs of paper, printing, and transportation; the costs of running a bookstore; the fact that authors need to be compensated for their work, and that publishers and bookstores are businesses that need to produce some kind of profit. Perhaps you'll still want to write an angry article, but at least you'll be able to show that you've *analyzed the causes* of the problem.

For an in-depth analysis, see "Why Are Textbooks So Expensive?" (p. 488).

And let's say you decide to suggest in your article that students buy only used books. But then you'd need to *consider the effects* of that solution. Since publishers and authors receive no payment for used books, buying them exclusively could mean that there would soon be no other kind available. That's an effect that would be attractive to an audience of used book dealers—but that might not be so appealing to students.

As with all kinds of writing, when you analyze causes or effects, you need to think about your larger purpose for writing and the audience you want to reach.

Generating Ideas:
Asking Why and What If

There are lots of ways to generate ideas for a cause-and-effect analysis—BRAINSTORMING, CLUSTERING, and more. The essential question to ask when you want to figure out what caused something, however, is *why*. Why does the foil covering your leftover lasagna have holes in it? Why did you fail the chemistry final? Why does a curve ball drop as it crosses home plate? Why was Napoleon defeated in his march on Russia in 1812?

If, on the other hand, you want to figure out what the effects of something are, then the basic question to ask is not *why* but *what*, or *what if*. What if you eat your leftover lasagna even though it might now contain invisible bits of aluminum?* What if you don't study for the chemistry exam? What are the results likely to be? What will happen if the curve ball fails to drop? What effect did the weather have on Napoleon's campaign?

As you pursue answers to the basic questions *why* and *what if*, keep in mind that a single effect may have multiple causes. If you were to ask why the U.S. financial system almost collapsed in the fall of 2008, for example, you would need to consider a number of possible causes, such as the following:

---

*Nothing much will happen, except that your lasagna may taste slightly metallic. You won't get sick from the metal because the hydrochloric acid in your stomach will dissolve the aluminum.

- greed and corruption on Wall Street
- vastly inflated real estate values
- subprime mortgage loans offered to unqualified borrowers
- massive defaults when those borrowers couldn't make their mortgage payments
- a widespread credit crunch and drying up of money for new loans.

As you probe more deeply into the causes of a major event like the financial crisis of 2008, you will discover that such effects not only have multiple causes; those causes are also interconnected. That is, they occur in chains—as in the proverb about a kingdom lost "all for want of care about a horse-shoe nail." When it comes time to organize your essay, you may find that following the chain of events in chronological order from cause to effect—or backward in time from effect to cause—is an excellent way to organize a cause-and-effect analysis.

Organizing and Drafting a Cause-and-Effect Analysis

Once you've asked yourself *why* and *what if* and you've identified a number of factors, you're ready to start organizing and drafting. You'll want to decide whether to emphasize causes or effects (or both); choose an appropriate method of organization; explain the point of your analysis; and distinguish immediate causes from remote causes and main causes from contributing causes. You'll also want to distinguish between true causes and mere coincidences. And think about using visuals and other methods of development, like NARRATIVE and PROCESS ANALYSIS in your analysis. The templates on page 456 can help you get started.

STATING YOUR POINT

As you draft a cause-and-effect analysis, you can start with effects and then examine their causes; or you can start with causes and go on to examine their effects. In either case, tell the reader right away which you are going to focus on and why—what your main point, or THESIS, is.

For a good example, see "Cancer's Oddest Effect" (p. 495).

For example, if you are analyzing the causes of the financial meltdown in the United States in 2008, you might signal the main point of your analysis in a statement like this one:

> The main cause of the financial meltdown in the United States in 2008 was the freezing of credit, which made it impossible for anyone to borrow money.

Once you've told the reader whether you're focusing on causes or effects and what your thesis is, you're ready to present your analysis.

TEMPLATES FOR DRAFTING

When you begin to draft a cause-and-effect analysis, you need to identify what you're analyzing and to indicate whether you plan to emphasize its causes or its effects—moves fundamental to any cause-and-effect analysis. See how Henry L. Roediger III makes these moves at the beginning of his essay in this chapter:

> What reasons are given for the high price of textbooks? . . . If I had to bet, the root cause is a feature of the marketplace that has changed greatly over the years and fundamentally reshaped the textbook market: sale of used books.
>
> —HENRY L. ROEDIGER III, "Why Are Textbook So Expensive?"

Roediger identifies what he's analyzing ("the high price of textbooks") and indicates that he is going to focus on the causes of this phenomenon ("the root cause is"). Here is one more example from this chapter:

> Nearly a third of black children in America are being born into poverty. The question is: Why?
> —HENRY LOUIS GATES JR.,
> "The Way to Reduce Black Poverty in America"

The following templates can help you make some of these basic moves in your own writing. But don't take these as formulas where you just fill in the blanks. There are no shortcuts to good writing, but these templates can serve as starting points.

- ▸ The main cause / effect of X is _____.

- ▸ X would also seem to have a number of contributing causes, including _____, _____, and _____.

- ▸ Some additional effects of X are _____, _____, and _____.

- ▸ Among the most important remote causes / effects of X are _____, _____, and _____.

- ▸ Although the causes of X are not known, we can speculate that a key factor is _____.

- ▸ X cannot be attributed to mere chance or coincidence because _____.

- ▸ Once we know what causes X, we are in a position to _____.

ORGANIZING A CAUSE-AND-EFFECT ANALYSIS

Causes always precede effects in time. Thus a natural way to present the effects of a given cause is by arranging them in CHRONOLOGICAL ORDER. If you were tracing the effects of the financial meltdown of 2008, for example, you would start with the crisis and then proceed chronologically, detailing its effects in the order in which they occurred, namely:

- banks and other financial institutions collapse as mortgage holders default
- the stock market plummets
- the federal government steps in with a massive bailout, providing a steady stream of much-needed credit to markets
- confidence is restored on Wall Street and Main Street

Reverse chronological order, in which you begin with a known effect and work backward through the possible causes, can also be effective for organizing a cause-and-effect analysis. In the case of the 2008 financial crisis, you would again begin with the crisis itself (the known effect): the financial engine stops because it has run out of credit. Then you would work backward in time through all the possible causes you could think of—presenting them in reverse chronological order:

- credit dries up because banks stop lending money to one another
- banks stopped lending because borrowers defaulted on existing loans
- borrowers defaulted because the values of their homes went down
- banks made risky loans on overvalued homes because Wall Street could easily sell those loans to investors
- Wall Street packaged bad loans and sold them to investors in order to increase profits and executive bonuses

You can also organize your analysis around the various types of causes, exploring the immediate cause before moving on to the remote causes (or vice versa) or exploring the contributing causes before the main cause (or vice versa).

DISTINGUISHING BETWEEN IMMEDIATE AND REMOTE CAUSES

As you look into the various causes of a particular effect, be sure to consider immediate and remote causes. This will require you to distinguish mechanical details in the causal chain from more theoretical causes.

An economist tackles this question in "Analyzing the Marriage Gap" (p. 500).

Benjamin Franklin, you'll notice, did not say that the main cause of the rider's death was the loss of a horseshoe nail. He said the main cause was a "want of care" about such nitty-gritty details.

The most nitty-gritty link in any causal chain—the one closest in time and most directly responsible for producing the effect—is the immediate cause. In the case of the financial meltdown of 2008, the immediate cause was the drying up of credit that made it almost impossible to get loans. Credit oils the wheels of commerce; when credit dries up, the wheels cease to turn and the financial engine stops.

Remote causes, by contrast with immediate ones, are less apparent to the observer and more distant in time from the observed effect. A remote cause of the financial meltdown of 2008 was the "subprime" lending to borrowers who, eventually, could not meet their mortgage payments. A more remote cause of the meltdown was the burst of the housing bubble: as the supply of available housing exceeded demand, housing values fell, and many borrowers found that their homes were worth less than the amount owed their mortgages.

Recklessness among homeowners on Main Street was not the most remote cause of the eventual meltdown, however. The most remote cause was greed on Wall Street. Subprime loans were risky—but they were very profitable. The lender took his profit and then, to trim his risks, packaged the bad loans with good ones and sold the package to unwary investors. When investors finally figured out what they had bought, fear trumped greed, and even banks were afraid to lend money to each other. Hence the drying up of credit—until the federal government intervened.

DISTINGUISHING BETWEEN THE MAIN CAUSE AND CONTRIBUTING CAUSES

To help your reader fully understand how a number of causes work together to produce a single effect, you will need to go beyond an explanation of the immediate cause or causes. Consider the partial collapse of terminal 2E at the Paris airport on the morning of May 23, 2004. The most immediate cause of the collapse, of course, was gravity; beyond that, it was the failure of the metal structure supporting the roof. (See diagram on the next page.) If we're really going to figure out why the building fell down, however, we're also going to have to look at the main cause and some of the contributing causes of the disaster.

The main cause is the one that has the greatest power to produce the effect. It must be both necessary to cause the effect and sufficient to do so. As it turns out, the main cause of the terminal collapse was faulty design. As Christian Horn writes

IMMEDIATE CAUSES OF THE COLLAPSE OF TERMINAL 2E

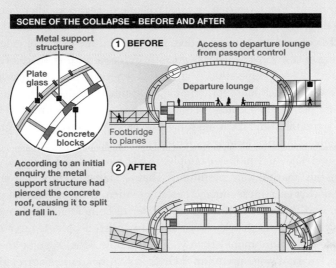

SCENE OF THE COLLAPSE - BEFORE AND AFTER

Metal support structure

Plate glass

Concrete blocks

① BEFORE

Access to departure lounge from passport control

Departure lounge

Footbridge to planes

According to an initial enquiry the metal support structure had pierced the concrete roof, causing it to split and fall in.

② AFTER

in *Architecture Week*, "The building was not designed to support the stress it was put under."

A contributing cause is a secondary cause, one that helps to produce the effect but not sufficient to do it alone. An important contributing cause to the collapse of terminal 2E was weak concrete. Another was the increased stress on the concrete roof shell due to the rapid expansion and contraction of the metal support structure. Still another was the wild fluctuation in temperature in the days leading up to the collapse, which contributed to the stress on the metal.

If terminal 2E had been properly designed, however, no combination of contributing causes would have been sufficient to bring it down. Contributing causes are necessary to produce an effect, but even taken together they are not sufficient to cause it.

DISTINGUISHING BETWEEN CAUSATION AND COINCIDENCE

It is well documented that married men as a group make more money—somewhere between 10 and 50 percent more—than unmarried men as a group. Does being married actually *cause* this wage difference, or is it merely a coincidence?

As you link together causes and effects, don't confuse causation with coincidence. Just because one event (getting married) happens *before* another (making more money), it does not necessarily follow that the first event actually caused the second.

To conclude that it always does is to commit the logical blunder of reasoning POST HOC, ERGO PROPTER HOC (Latin for "after this, therefore because of this"). Most superstitions are based on such *post hoc* reasoning. Mark Twain's Huck Finn, for example, commits this fallacy when he sees a spider burning in a candle: "I didn't need anybody to tell me that that was an awful bad sign and would fetch me some bad luck." Huck is going to encounter all sorts of troubles, but the burning spider isn't the cause.

> The villagers make this mistake in "The Lottery" (p. 504).

In our marriage and money example, being married is a necessary condition for earning the "marital wage premium." That is, statistics show that married men as a group *always* earn more money than single men. Is being married sufficient to make men wealthier? Or is it merely a matter of coincidence rather than causation? Most married people are older than unmarried people. Up to a point, most older people earn more money than younger people. Could age be the real cause behind the "marital wage premium"? Or is it simply another correlative? Before you assert that one event causes another, always consider whether the two could be merely coincidental.

USING VISUALS TO CLARIFY CAUSAL RELATIONSHIPS

Illustrations and images can help your reader to understand what caused a complicated effect—or the complicated causes behind a simple effect. Take, for instance, a famous map showing Napoleon's campaign in Russia in 1812 (see next page). This map shows "the successive losses in men" during the campaign. (Napoleon left France with over 400,000 soldiers; he returned with approximately 10,000!) The advance toward Moscow is shown by a light-colored line, while the retreat is represented by the darker line below it. The thickness of the lines represents the number of soldiers—the thicker the line, the more troops in the army. At the bottom of the map are temperatures for certain dates during the retreat. As the French army retreats from Moscow and the temperatures get colder, the line representing the number of troops gets thinner, graphically showing the loss of men.

The map conveys a mass of data that would take many words to write out: dates, temperatures, troop movements, numbers of troops, not to mention distances and the locations of rivers and cities. All this information is crucial in analyzing why so many of Napoleon's soldiers died or deserted in their retreat from Moscow in 1812. If you're analyzing why Napoleon lost so many soldiers in the Russian campaign, you might want to include a visual like this and then connect the dots for the reader: many factors contributed to the losses, but the man cause of the horrendous number of casualties suffered by the French army in the winter of 1812 was the freezing temperatures.

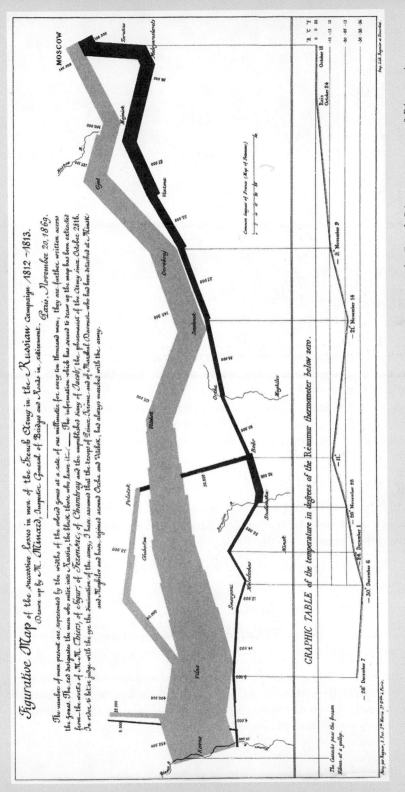

Since the map was made by the French engineer Charles Minard in 1861, the temperatures are in the French Réaumur system: −9° Réaumur is approximately 11.75° Fahrenheit; −26° Réaumur is approximately −26.5° Fahrenheit.

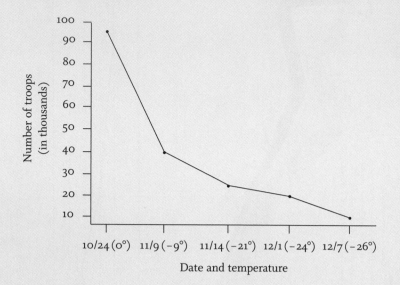

A graph showing the relationship between temperature and number of troops, such as the one that appears above, would also make the point that the cold winter caused the deaths or desertions of many soldiers.

If you decide to include visuals, be sure that they actually illuminate your analysis, and don't merely decorate it. Remember to label each part of a chart or graph, and position visuals as close as possible to your discussion of the topic they address.

USING OTHER METHODS

It is hard to explain *why* something happened without first explaining *what* happened and *how* it happened. So when you analyze causes and effects, consider using NARRATION to help explain the *what*:

> Recently, a young man by the name of Benny Paret was killed in the ring. The killing was seen by millions; it was on television.

And use PROCESS ANALYSIS to help explain the *how*:

> In the twelfth round, he was hit hard in the head several times, went down, was counted out, and never came out of the coma.

These are the words of Norman Cousins in a classic cause-and-effect analysis. Having set up his analysis by using other methods, Cousins then turns to the causes of Benny Paret's death. The immediate cause, obviously, was the fist that hit him. The main cause, Cousins explains, was something else:

The primary responsibility lies with the people who pay to see a man hurt. The referee who stops a fight too soon from the crowd's viewpoint can expect to be booed. The crowd wants the knockout; it wants to see a man stretched out on the canvas. This is the supreme moment in boxing.

—NORMAN COUSINS, "Who Killed Benny Paret?"

Cousins' essay was written in 1962. Yet another fighter was killed in the boxing ring as recently as 2007. The essay may not have achieved the effect Cousins hoped for—getting professional boxing thrown out of the ring of legitimate sport—but the impact of his words is still clear: "No one doubts that many people enjoy prize fighting and will miss it if it should be thrown out. And that is precisely the point." The point is also that good writers like Cousins often use cause-and-effect analysis to make a point when they are constructing ARGUMENTS, yet another method of development that goes hand-in-hand with cause-and-effect analysis.

Reading a Cause-and-Effect Analysis with a Critical Eye

Once you have written a draft (or two or three) of your essay, it's always wise to ask someone else to look over what you have written. Ask readers where they find your analysis clear and convincing, what specific evidence they find most effective, and where they think you need more (or less) explanation. Here are some questions to keep in mind when checking over a cause-and-effect analysis.

PURPOSE AND AUDIENCE. Why is the reader being asked to consider these particular causes or effects? Is the intended audience likely to find the analysis plausible as well as useful? What additional information might readers need?

ORGANIZATION. Does the essay emphasize causes or effects? Should it give more (or less) attention to either? Are causes and effects presented in a logical sequence?

CHRONOLOGICAL ORDER. Does the essay analyze causes and effects in chronological order where appropriate? Does it consistently link cause to effect, and effect to cause?

REVERSE CHRONOLOGICAL ORDER. Where effects are known but causes are uncertain, is it clear what chain of events most likely led to the effect(s) in question? Are those events presented in reverse chronological order? If not, how can the order of events be clarified?

THE POINT. What is the analysis intended to show? Is the point made clearly in a thesis statement? How and how well does the analysis support the point?

TYPES OF CAUSES. How well are the significant causes analyzed—the immediate cause, the most important remote causes, the main cause, and the most important contributing causes? What other causes (or effects) should be considered?

CAUSE OR COINCIDENCE? At any point, is a coincidence mistaken for a cause? Are all of the causes necessary to produce the indicated effects? Do they have the power to produce those effects?

VISUALS. Are charts, graphs, or diagrams included to clarify causal relationships? If not, would they be helpful? Are all visuals clearly and appropriately labeled?

USING OTHER METHODS. Does the essay use other methods of development besides cause-and-effect analysis? For instance, does it use narration to help explain what happened? Or does it use process analysis to show how—in addition to why—a particular effect came about? Does the analysis argue that one cause or effect is more likely than another?

Editing for Common Errors in a Cause-and-Effect Analysis

Writing about causes and effects generally calls for certain connecting words and verb forms—connecting words like *because* or *as a result*, verbs like *caused* or *will result in*. Here are some items to check for when you edit your analysis.

Check all connectors to be sure they're logical and precise

Words like *because* or *since* connect the "cause" part of a sentence to the "effect" part (or the reverse). Be sure the connectors you use make the causal link absolutely clear.

▸ ~~Since~~ Because the concrete deteriorated, the roof collapsed.

Since has two meanings, "for the reason that" and "after the time that," so it does not make clear whether the roof collapsed after the concrete deteriorated or because it deteriorated. *Because* is the more precise term.

▸ The concrete deteriorated, and ~~consequently~~ as a result the roof collapsed.

Consequently can mean "subsequently" or "as a result." The editing makes the causal link clear.

Check verbs to make sure they clearly express cause and effect

Some verbs directly express causation, whereas others only imply that one thing causes another.

VERBS THAT EXPRESS CAUSATION	VERBS THAT IMPLY CAUSATION
account for	follow
bring about	happen
cause	imply
effect	involve
make	implicate
result	take place

Using verbs that express causation makes your text more precise.

▶ The partial collapse of terminal 2E ~~involved~~ <u>was caused by</u> weak concrete.

Check for common usage errors

AFFECT, EFFECT

Affect is a verb meaning "influence." *Effect* is usually a noun meaning "result," but it can also be a verb meaning "bring about."

▶ Getting married did not affect his wages.

▶ Getting married did not have the effect of increasing his wages.

▶ Getting married did not effect a change in his wages.

REASON IS BECAUSE, REASON WHY

Avoid using these expressions; both are redundant. In the first case, use *that* instead of *because*. In the second, use *reason* alone.

▶ The reason the roof collapsed is ~~because~~ <u>that</u> the concrete deteriorated.

▶ Weakened concrete is the reason ~~why~~ the roof collapsed.

Student Example

Paula T. Kelso teaches at Lewis and Clark Community College in Godfrey, Illinois. Trained as a ballerina, Kelso has danced professionally in the Midwest, New York, North Carolina, and California. In the spring of 2002, as an undergraduate majoring in sociology at Southern Illinois University, Edwardsville, Kelso chose body obsession in ballet as the topic for her senior seminar. The resulting paper earned an A, and she presented it the following October at a meeting of the Illinois Sociology Association. In 2003, Kelso's study, which follows the documentation style of the American Psychological Association (APA), was published in *Edwardsville Journal of Sociology*.

"Behind the Curtain" is an insider's view of the destructive physical and psychological effects female dancers endure because of a professional culture of enforced starvation. Under the influence of legendary choreographer George Balanchine and his successors, Kelso argues, ballet in America adopted an impossible (and dangerous) ideal of female beauty.

Behind the Curtain:
The Body, Control, and Ballet

Many young girls and their parents are attracted to the ballet because of the applauding audiences, the lights, the sequins and feathers, the colorful, elaborate tutus, and satin pointe shoes. Where else can a young girl dream of becoming a princess, a swan, a dancing snowflake or flower, a sugarplum, or lilac fairy? Where else can she be a character right out of a fairy tale like Cinderella or Sleeping Beauty? Where else can she be rescued by and collapse into the arms of her handsome prince? Ballet is the magical world where these dreams can come true. Young girls and women can be all of these things, characters that symbolize femininity in a society that teaches young girls to be and want everything pink and pretty. However, in the shadows of the spotlight lurks an abusive world of eating disorders, verbal harassment, fierce competition, and injured, fatigued, and malnourished dancers. This world of fantasy is just that: fantasy and make-believe.

The Problem

Body image is defined as the way in which people see themselves in the mirror every day: the values, judgments, and ideas that they attach to their appearance. Benn and Walters (2001) argue that these judgments and ideas come from being socialized into particular ways of thinking, mainly from society's ideas of what beauty is, shown <u>especially in the current media and consumer culture</u> (p. 140). The average person is inundated with 3,000 advertisements daily (Kilbourne, 2002). In these advertisements, women are shown in little clothing and in stereotypical roles.

Margin notes:

Why ballet appeals to young girls and their parents: immediate cause, wish fulfillment; remote cause, social pressure

In addition to causes, Kelso plans to analyze effects, particularly negative ones

Kelso examines advertising and the media as immediate causes of how a culture defines physical beauty

These women are not real (Kilbourne, 2002). They have been altered by computer airbrushing, retouching, and enhancing, and in many cases, several women are used to portray the same model (Kilbourne, 2002). The cultural idea of what is beautiful has changed over the years. In the 1950s, Marilyn Monroe, who wore a size 16 at one point in her career, was considered the epitome of sexiness and beauty (Jhally, 1995). Contrast this with more recent examples such as Courtney Cox and Jennifer Aniston from the television show *Friends*, who are considered beautiful. They wear a size 2 (Jhally, 1995). While models and celebrities have become thinner, the average woman is heavier today. This makes an even larger difference between the real and the ideal.

Like the rest of society, dancers' appearances have also changed over the years. In the 1930s and 1940s, ballerinas were considered thin at the time but, as can be seen in photographs (see Figure 1), looked very healthy (Gordon, 1983). Since dancers have generally been slimmer than ideal, these dancers' becoming even thinner for today's ideal is a problem (see Figure 2). As one renowned ballet teacher said it: "It is a reflection of society, everything has become more streamlined" (Benn & Walters, 2001, p. 146).

In order to understand the pressures that dancers face to be thin, it is necessary to explore the ideas behind the practice of ballet. Women who become dancers are not exempt from cultural expectations that tell them in order to be successful and beautiful, they must also be very thin. They live with the same pressures as the rest of society, however, they also have to deal with the risk of unemployment if they gain any amount of weight or their bodies do not look a certain way (Gordon, 1983). In a career where education is discouraged because of the time it would take away from a dancer's most successful years, many professional dancers are not attending college and in some cases are even dropping out of high school (Gordon, 1983). These dancers are putting all of their resources into their body and its appearance. If a dancer does gain weight, develops an eating disorder, or becomes injured, she is

3 · · · · · Gives historical perspective: as ideals of female beauty changed over the years, so did the physical appearance of ballerinas

4 · · · · · Examines specific practices of modern ballet that encourage dancers to be thin

Figure 1. Then: Female dancers in 1930 had thicker legs and rounder bodies.

left out of work with relatively few choices for the future. Most professional companies have "appearance clauses" in their contracts, which usually state that if the dancer gains any noticeable amount of weight, she is eligible to lose her position in the company (Gordon, 1983; Saint Louis Ballet, 1993). These clauses also state that tattoos, piercings, and changing hair color are not permitted (Gordon, 1983). Haircuts are discouraged, and usually only allowed with the permission of the director.

ARGUES that the main cause of the anorexic look among ballerinas is a particular choreographer

Almost everyone credits George Balanchine, the renowned dancer, teacher, and choreographer, with the current aesthetic of ballet in the West, referred to by most as the "Balanchine body," or the "anorexic look" (Gordon, 1983). He has promoted the skeletal look by his costume requirements and his hiring practices, as well as the treatment of his dancers (Gordon, 1983). The ballet aesthetic currently consists of long limbs, and a skeletal frame, which accentuates the collarbones and length of the neck, as well as absence of breasts and hips (Benn & Walters, 2001; Gordon, 1983;

5

Figure 2. Now: Ballerinas typically have thinner legs and flatter bodies.

Kirkland, 1986). Balanchine was known to throw out comments to his dancers, such as: "eat nothing" and "must see the bones" (Kirkland, 1986, p. 56).

If Balanchine has created this aesthetic, other choreographers have followed and adopted it as the norm. Mikhail Baryshnikov, star dancer and former director of American Ballet Theatre, did not tolerate any body type but the Balanchine one (Gordon, 1983). During rehearsal and without any warning, he fired a corps de ballet member because she was too "fat" in his opinion (Gordon, 1983, p. 150). He said that he "couldn't stand to see her onstage anymore" (Gordon, 1983, p. 150). Fortunately, management intervened and the dancer was rehired. However, Baryshnikov and the rest of his management were known to have had meetings with their dancers in order to emphasize the importance of weight loss (Gordon, 1983). Obviously, dancers need to be fit and trim in order to be successful in their occupation, and no one should argue that staying fit is not helpful in order to see a dancer's body line;

6

Argues that other choreographers and directors are contributing causes however, it is the extreme skeletal goal that is cause for so much concern.

It is not uncommon for a dancer to walk into what she thinks will 7 be her daily ballet class and find a scale set up in the center of the dance studio instead (Gordon, 1983). These weigh-ins are arranged ahead of time and kept secret from the dancers. A director from American Ballet Theatre explained that warning the dancers would defeat the purpose. As one former dancer put it: "A forewarned dancer is a forestarved dancer"[1] (Gordon, 1983, p. 43). Not only are the dancers' weights recorded but many times are read aloud to the entire class. Even the youngest dancers, at one pre-professional academy, at age eleven "gasped in horror" as the teacher read their weights aloud at 50 to 60 pounds (Gordon, 1983, p. 43). Public humiliation is not uncommon in the ballet world (Benn & Walters, 2001; Hamilton, 1998). Directors and teachers are known to make hateful comments and even resort to name-calling in some cases (Gordon, 1983). One director told one of his dancers to "drop the weight in three weeks. I don't care how you do it" (Benn & Walters, 2001, p. 145). When she did in fact drop the weight by basically not eating, she was rewarded with a role in the performance that the company was rehearsing. Dancers learn at an early age that rewards and punishments are based upon weight. If a dancer loses weight, she is praised and rewarded with a role in a ballet. If she does not, she is punished by not being cast at all (Gordon, 1983). It seems that directors and teachers perceive how thin a dancer becomes as a sign of dedication to the art and is often times rewarded (Benn & Walters, 2001). Suzanne Gordon (1983) accompanied several members of an elite advanced pre-professional academy to a professional audition. She witnessed hundreds of dancers asked to walk across the floor of the studio, where many of them were then asked to leave. After fifteen or more years of professional training, these dancers were not allowed to even audition. Apparently, they

Analyzes how losing weight leads immediately to desirable roles and more remotely to the perception that a dancer is dedicated to her art

---

1. *Forewarned/forestarved*: A word play on the English proverb "forewarned is forearmed."

did not have the right "look." This practice is used by most professional companies across the United States (Gordon, 1983).

Directors and company managers are not the only ones who put pressure on dancers to stay thin. <u>Ballet critics often refer to body sizes when writing reviews of a performance</u> (Benn & Walters, 2001). This can be a nightmare for a dancer, particularly if a negative body shape statement is printed next to her name for anyone to read in the morning paper. For example, two critics wrote reviews after seeing a company perform a Balanchine Ballet (a ballet in which the dancers wear nothing but tights and leotards). One said he witnessed, "an awful lot of wobbling bottoms on display" and the other claimed that this particular company had "rejected the starved-greyhound look in ballerinas—but now things have gone too far the other way. Bonnard legs and Ingres bottoms[2] are all very well, but not on stage, and particularly not in Balanchine" (Benn & Walters, 2001, p. 149). These reviews were taken to heart by the company directors, who threatened to fire members of the corps de ballet if they did not lose the weight fast. So they did, by not eating (Benn & Walters, 2001).

8   Identifies another contributing cause of the anorexic look

According to research conducted by Benn and Walters (2001), dancers studied <u>were found to only consume 700 to 900 calories per day</u>. Many of the subjects were consuming less than 700. Surveys conducted in the United States, China, Russia, and Western Europe by Hamilton (1998) found that female dancers' weights were 10 to 15 percent below the ideal weight for their height. According to the American Psychiatric Association's official criteria for anorexia nervosa, the number one factor for diagnosis is if the person's weight is more than 15 percent below the ideal weight for height. This is dangerously close to most dancers! Another factor for diagnosing anorexia nervosa is if the person has developed amenorrhea, that is, if they have missed three consecutive menstrual cycles (Hamilton,

9   Identifies the main effect of the preceding causes

2. *Bonnard/Ingres*: French painters of the nineteenth and eighteenth centuries, respectively. They each painted women more round and plump than dancers today are supposed to be.

1998). According to Suzanne Gordon's research (1983), many dancers have ceased menstruating or have many cycle irregularities. Once someone stops menstruating, she may lose 4 percent of her bone mass annually for the next three to four years (Hamilton, 1998). This causes another set of problems: injury and osteoporosis.

Discusses negative effects caused by an inadequate diet ······• If dancers are not consuming enough calories, many times they are nutritionally deficient, which Hamilton (1998) supports in her arguments. If dancers are malnourished and continue to heavily exert themselves through dance, stress fractures, a common injury among dancers, are unavoidable (Gordon, 1983; Hamilton, 1998). Also, osteoporosis is common. One dancer took a bone density test and at 21 years old found she had the bones of a 70 year old (Hamilton, 1998). Dancers are not receiving crucial health and nutrition information, and they may not realize the harm they are inflicting on their bodies until it is too late. Benn and Walters (2001) found that only 18% of current dancers had received proper nutritional education.

Disproves a common misperception about cause and effect: ballerinas must be thin for male dancers to lift them ······• Many people believe the myth that female dancers must be skeletal because of the male dancers who have to partner and lift them. This is simply not true. Gordon (1983) interviewed several professional male dancers, who said that they preferred to partner heavier dancers rather than dancers who fit the "anorexic look." Patrick Bissell, a well-renowned dancer, says that "it's not easy to partner very thin dancers . . . they scream out all of a sudden because you pick them up . . . it makes you very tentative about how you touch them" (Gordon, 1983, p. 151). Another famous dancer, Jeff Gribler, agrees. He says that "It's easy to bruise a woman when you partner anyway, and if she seems too frail, you don't want to grip too hard. It can be really painful for her to be partnered" (Gordon, 1983, p. 152). Vane Vest, another dancer, says "these anorexic ballerinas—I can't bear to touch them . . . you partner a woman and lift her at the waist and you want to touch something. These skinny ballerinas, it's awful . . . how can you do a *pas de deux* with one of those girls?" (Gordon, 1983, p. 152). Gordon found in her research that ballerinas in Europe and elsewhere weigh more

10

than North American ballerinas, yet male dancers do not seem to have a problem partnering them (Gordon, 1983).

Another myth is that this unhealthy "Balanchine body" is the only body capable of the technical feats that ballet requires. People also believe that if dancers were not this thin, audiences would not come to the ballet. However some of the most famous and successful companies are located in Europe and elsewhere. European companies, even with dancers who are not emaciated, are very successful. Gordon (1983) found that in European companies, particularly the Royal Swedish Ballet, dancers look somewhat different. She noticed older dancers in their late thirties and forties, and also that dancers were not nearly as thin as American dancers (Gordon, 1983). These dancers were definitely thin, but they looked healthy. They had breasts, hips, and curves, and actually looked womanly. During a gala perfor-mance for American Ballet Theatre, Gordon sat next to a New York ballet critic. When guest artist Zhandra Rodriguez from Ballet de Caracas, Venezuela came on stage, Gordon immediately noticed that she had visible breasts. When she mentioned this to the critic, the critic retorted, "she can't be an American" (Gordon, 1983, p. 151).

11 | Attacks another common misperception: ballerinas must be thin to attract audiences

. . .

Analyses: Two Theories about the World of Ballet

Subculture Theory

Many wonder why dancers and their parents continue to take part in the ballet world after learning about some of its negative aspects. Subculture theory can explain why dancers continue to dance, even in the face of major internal and external obstacles and criticism. Subculture theory has mainly been used to explain deviance and crime in the past; however, it works well in analyzing ballet as a unique world of its own with different norms and values from the rest of society.

12 | Uses subculture theory to examine the effects of belonging to a particular group

A subculture can be defined as a group of people who share a common identity through a unique set of characteristics common to the entire group, yet not entirely distinct from the rest of the society

13

in which the group lives (Farley, 1998). The subculture is a part of the larger society, yet it has certain ideas, beliefs, behaviors, and values that set it apart in some way. Farley (1998) states that individuals with a common interest and occupation commonly form subcultures. Ballet is truly an entire world all to its own. It functions within society, but it is a distinct group that should be recognized as such. The world of ballet has its own ideas of what the body should look like that are more extreme than the rest of society; however, the current ballet aesthetic would not be popular if dancers lived in a culture that did not value extreme thinness. All ballet companies across the world value thinness; however, it seems that only North American companies, especially the United States, have this dangerous goal of skeletal thinness.

Dancers are raised in this subculture of ballet, many from as young as three years of age. They spend every night in this world among directors, teachers, and other students who help to normalize ballet's ideas and values, and they internalize these messages. Dancers rely on their teachers for support and guidance, but also for approval and selection of parts in ballets. This leads to a generalized fear instilled in the dancers. 14

. . .

Ideas of beauty and health are different in the ballet world than in the larger society. Many dancers believe themselves to be healthy because they form "their ideas of healthy and normal . . . according to the norms and values of the ballet world" (Benn & Walters, 2001, p. 142). Because dancers are surrounded by eating disorders, many believe themselves to be healthy because they do not deny themselves food completely and they do not binge and purge. Many dancers may look healthy enough, but in reality they are not. They would not be diagnosed as medically anorexic, but they are staying thin by means of "gentle starvation," meaning not consuming enough calories and being nutritionally deficient (Benn & Walters, 2001, p. 142). 15

Another aspect of the ballet world, which helps to define its 16
subculture, is the idea of control. There is an authoritarian power
culture in the ballet world that forces conformity to harmful
behaviors. Dancers have become accustomed to abusive treatment;
it becomes a normal part of life in the subculture. Dancers' acceptance
of such treatment has been referred to as "silent conformity" for the
"unquestioning, subservient way in which . . . [dancers accept]
abuse and unreasonable behavior" (Stinson, 1998; cited by Benn &
Walters, 2001, p. 140). This is one reason why ballet has been
compared to a cult in some of the literature (Benn & Walters, 2001;
Gordon, 1983; Smith, 1998). Directors and management have the
power, and they exert it over the dancers, who must obey certain
rules if they intend to continue dancing.

. . .

Paradox Theory

In *Women and the Knife: Cosmetic Surgery and the Colonization of* 17
Women's Bodies (1991), <u>Kathryn Morgan discusses four paradoxes
inherent in the choice to undergo cosmetic surgery</u>. The structure of
her argument works well with the paradoxes inherent in the ballet
world.

Paradox One: Art? Ballet is known as a performing *art*. Art implies 18
a creative process through which the artist can express her
innermost thoughts and feelings to an audience. Many dancers
dance because they learn to express themselves through movement.
However, all of ballet looks the same with cookie-cut out dancers
expressing themselves in the same ways to the same music. There is
no individual creativity to be explored here; only the creativity of the
director is seen. The director's feelings are then described to the
dancer and the dancer's job is to express that feeling to the audience.
Creativity tends to be quashed in the classroom by focusing only on
technique, which trains bodies to be a vehicle for someone else's
creativity. Gelsey Kirkland (1986), a world-renowned ballerina, says
in her autobiography that Balanchine had a "monopoly on taste and

> Uses paradox theory to examine four unintended effects of a dancer's devoting herself to modern ballet culture

creative control" at New York City Ballet (p. 49). She also says that the dancers relied on him for "ideas and psychological motivation" (cited by Benn & Walters, 2001, p. 148). Michelle Benash, another dancer, says that "you have to lose your personality; your movement, your style are dictated to you" (Gordon, 1983, p. 112). A former New York City Ballet dancer puts it this way: Balanchine believed "that women should provide the inspiration that triggers men's creativity" (Gordon, 1983, p. 173). <u>Dancers, then, merely become puppets for someone else's creativity and emotion.</u>

First unintended effect

Paradox Two: Control? All dancers must have control over their bodies in order to master the technique required to perform professionally. Dancers start training young so that their hips will form a certain way in order to have the required "turn out." They also must spend years training their leg, feet, and abdomen muscles in order to jump, balance, and dance on pointe properly. These skills require intense years of training and hard work in order to establish the right strength. <u>One would imagine that dancers would have plenty of control over their own bodies; however, management takes over this control by exerting power over the bodies' appearance.</u> Having the right technique and strength is not nearly enough to dance professionally, one must also exhibit the right "look." This look, as discussed previously, is unhealthy and almost impossible to achieve.

Second unintended effect

Paradox Three: The Wonders of the Human Form. Ballet is supposed to showcase what the human body is capable of physically accomplishing. Audiences come to see ballet because of the feats that they will likely see at the performance. Amazing jumps, turns, and tricks are fan favorites. However, <u>ballet is not showcasing what the human form can accomplish, it is merely showcasing what one, almost impossible, body type may be capable of executing.</u> Dancers are supposed to make these feats look effortless, but it is doubtful that anyone leaving the theatre feels as if they could mimic these steps without the required body.

Third unintended effect

Paradox Four: The Look. Dancers are usually referred to as beautiful and graceful creatures, capable of accomplishing

19

20

21

extraordinary feats on stage. Off stage, these dancers resemble broken young children. They oftentimes look emaciated and injured, collapsing offstage after performances or limping to their dressing rooms. Dancers are artists, but they are also athletes who train their bodies every day. Athletes are usually considered to be the epitome of the human form and very physically fit. One look backstage and these are not the thoughts that would come to mind of the dance world. <u>Most dancers are very unhealthy physically and oftentimes emotionally as well.</u>

Fourth unintended effect

Conclusion

The dangerous aesthetic of the ballet world is an area that needs   22
much more attention and further research. Artistic directors of companies do not like to discuss or acknowledge problems with the current ballet aesthetic, which can be seen in their reluctance to talk about these issues and the lack of available research on the topic. . . . Aside from a few current journal articles that discuss eating habits, no one has really attempted to see if the abusive world Gordon exposed in her book has changed at all since her research in the 1980s. *Off Balance: The Real World of Ballet* alerted us to the fact that ballet was not so lovely and magical backstage. . . . I can attest to experiencing all of the aspects of ballet, in my pre-professional training and in my professional dancing, that Gordon showed. I also know from fellow dancers in the Midwest, New York, North Carolina, and San Francisco that their experiences are and have been very similar to what Gordon portrays in her book. There have . . . been recent examples in the media, which suggest that not much has changed since the 1980s. For example, the Boston Ballet ballerina who died at 22 due to complications from an eating disorder (Segal, 2002). Management had told the dancer that she was "chunky" and that she needed to lose weight before she developed anorexia (Segal, 2002). Another example occurred in San Francisco, where nine-year-old Fredrika Keefer was denied admission to San Francisco Ballet School because she was considered too short and chunky by administration. . . . A fictitious example can be seen in the [2000]

movie *Center Stage*, where dancers at a highly competitive pre-professional school deal with eating disorders, weight issues, and competition. This film also addressed a director's control of his company, albeit briefly and sentimentalized. . . . Further research is important to assess the current situation in the dance world and to see if the aesthetic and treatment of dancers has improved at all since the dance community and the public have been made aware of the dangers.

Conclusion sums up Kelso's main point in analyzing the negative effects of the ultrathin aesthetic in modern ballet .... The health and sanity of dancers are being sacrificed for this art 23 form. Until dancers, audiences, and management accept a new, healthier paradigm, dancers will continue to suffer. Segal (2001) articulates it best when he writes:

> What we accept as the "tradition" of extreme thinness is arguably just a mid-to-late 20th century whim of the white ballet establishment. And it needs to stop, for the health of the art form and the women dedicated to it, before ballet training becomes a symbol, like Chinese foot binding, of a society's cruel subjugation of women to a crippling, inhuman illusion. (p. 2)

References

Benn, T., & Walters, D. (2001). Between Scylla and Charybdis. Nutritional education versus body culture and the ballet aesthetic: The effects on the lives of female dancers. *Research in Dance Education, 2*(2), 139–154.

Farley, J. (1998). *Sociology* (4th ed.). Upper Saddle River, NJ: Prentice-Hall.

Gordon, S. (1983). *Off balance: The real world of ballet.* New York, NY: Pantheon.

Hamilton, L. (1998). *Advice for dancers: Emotional counsel and practical strategies.* San Francisco, CA: Jossey-Bass.

Jhally, S. (Producer). (1995). *Slim hopes: Advertising and the obsession with thinness* [Motion picture].

Kilbourne, J. (2002, February). *The naked truth: Advertising's image of women.* Presentation to Principia College, Elsah, IL.

Kirkland, G. (1986). *Dancing on my grave.* Garden City, NY: Doubleday.

Morgan, K. P. (1991). Women and the knife: Cosmetic surgery and the colonization of women's bodies. In L. Richardson, V. Taylor, & N. Whittier (Eds.), *Feminist frontiers* (pp. 116–127). New York, NY: McGraw-Hill.

Saint Louis Ballet. (1993). Employment contract. St. Louis, MO: Saint Louis Ballet.

Segal, L. (2001, April 1). The shape of things to come. *Los Angeles Times.* Retrieved from http://www.latimes.com

Smith, C. (1998). On authoritarianism in the dance classroom. In S. B. Shapiro (Ed.), *Dance, power, and difference* (pp. 123–146). Leeds, UK: Human Kinetics.

Stinson, S. W. (1998). Seeking a feminist pedagogy for children's dance. In S. B. Shapiro (Ed.), *Dance, power, and difference* (pp. 23–48). Leeds, UK: Human Kinetics.

Analyzing a Student Cause-and Effect Analysis

In "Behind the Curtain," Paula T. Kelso draws upon rhetorical strategies and techniques that good writers use all the time when they analyze causes and effects. The following questions, in addition to focusing on particular aspects of Kelso's text, will help you to identify those common strategies and techniques so you can adapt them to your own writing. These questions will also help to prepare you for the analytical questions—on content, structure, and language—that you'll find after all the other selections in this chapter, along with suggestions for writing on related topics.

READING CLOSELY

1. According to Paula Kelso, where and how does American society get its ideals of female beauty? What is "not real" about them (2)? Why are ballerinas particularly susceptible to those ideals?

2. In Kelso's view, what was the role of choreographer George Balanchine and his followers in promoting "the skeletal look" among American ballerinas (5)? How convincing do you find Kelso's evidence?

3. One reason, supposedly, that ballerinas need to be thin is so that male dancers can lift them. How and how well does Kelso address this "myth" (10)? What other myths does she explore?

4. From their directors, teachers, and fellow students, says Kelso, young girls who aspire to become ballerinas often pick up a "generalized fear" (14). Of what? How and why is this fear "instilled" in them (14)?

STRATEGIES AND STRUCTURES

1. Why does Kelso begin her essay with a brief DESCRIPTION of the "magical" aspects of ballet (1)? What CONTRAST is she setting up? How effective do you find this opening strategy?

2. The immediate cause of anorexia nervosa is not eating enough calories to sustain life and health. What are some of the remote causes, especially among ballerinas, according to Kelso?

3. Of all the possible causes Kelso cites, which would you say is the main cause of the problems that plague ballerinas? Explain.

4. To support her analysis, Kelso uses a variety of brief EXAMPLES from outside sources, including stratified data about health issues, opinions from experts,

and questions from ballerinas. Jot down five or six examples that you find particularly effective.

5. *Other Methods.* Kelso's analysis of causes and effects in the "abusive world" of professional ballet could be the basis of an ARGUMENT (1). What is her main PURPOSE in conducting the analysis, and how might she use the results to argue her point?

THINKING ABOUT LANGUAGE

1. What are the CONNOTATIONS of *lurks* and *shadows* (1)?

2. Explain the specialized meanings, in a sociology paper, of the following terms: *socialized* (2), *normalize* (14), and *internalize* (14).

3. How and how effectively does Kelso use the "broken young children" SIMILE to develop her analysis (21)?

4. A PARADOX is an apparent contradiction that may, nonetheless, be true or valid. What is paradoxical about the observations that Kelso makes in paragraphs 17–21? What do they show about the culture of ballet in America?

FOR WRITING

1. In a culture obsessed with thinness, why are so many Americans overweight? Draft the opening paragraph of the essay you might write if you were analyzing the causes of this phenomenon.

2. Write an essay that analyzes the causes and effects of a common eating disorder.

3. Swimmers have bodies distinctive to their sports. So do wrestlers, gymnasts, and cyclists. Write an analysis of a particular sport and the typical effects, psychological as well as physical, that it has upon the athlete. Don't forget to say how the culture of the sport contributes to these effects.

A Rube Goldberg Pencil Sharpener

This whimsical drawing by American cartoonist Rube Goldberg (1883–1970) illustrates how causes and effects typically operate—in chains of linked events, with the effect of one event becoming the cause of another. For example, the *immediate* cause is the one closest to the end result—in this case, the actions of the woodpecker. The previous events (flying the kite, burning the pants, smoking out the possum) are the *contributing* causes. Goldberg's designs for elaborate machines and systems to perform simple tasks have inspired many imitators. Each year, for example, engineering students at Purdue University sponsor a national Rube Goldberg contest, which celebrates "machines that combine creativity with inefficiency and complexity." Contestants are presented with a simple task—to replace batteries in a flashlight and turn it on, for example—and are challenged to perform that task in at least twenty steps within a two-minute timeframe. The 2011 winners, a team of (for the most part) business and education majors from the University of Wisconsin–Stout, broke down the process of watering a plant into 135 steps.

EVERYDAY CAUSE AND EFFECT

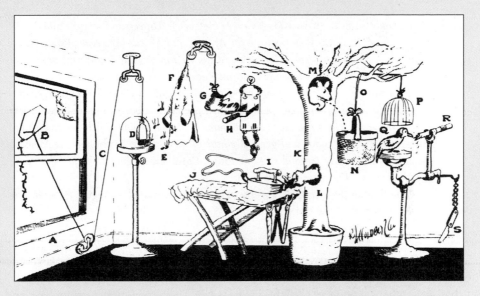

The Professor gets his think-tank working and evolves the simplified pencil sharpener.

Open window (**A**), and fly kite (**B**). String (**C**) lifts small door (**D**), allowing moths (**E**) to escape and eat red flannel shirt (**F**). As weight of shirt becomes less, shoe (**G**) steps on switch (**H**), which heats electric iron (**I**) and burns hole in pants (**J**). Smoke (**K**) enters hole in tree (**L**), smoking out opossum (**M**), which jumps into basket (**N**), pulling rope (**O**) and lifting cage (**P**), allowing woodpecker (**Q**) to chew wood from pencil (**R**), exposing lead. Emergency knife (**S**) is always handy in case opossum or the woodpecker gets sick and can't work.

HENRY LOUIS GATES JR.

The Way to Reduce Black Poverty in America

Henry Louis Gates Jr. (b. 1950) is Alphonse Fletcher Jr. University Professor and director of the W. E. B. Du Bois Institute for African and African American Research at Harvard. A graduate of Yale, Gates earned his PhD in English literature from Cambridge University. Gates' memoir, Colored People *(1994), won the Heartland Prize for nonfiction. His best-known scholarly work,* The Signifying Monkey *(1987), examines various forms of language play by which people in a position of weakness trick people in power. He is coeditor (with Kwame Anthony Appiah) of the encyclopedia* Encarta Africana *(1999) and general editor of the* Norton Anthology of African American Literature *(second edition, 2003). Gates hosted the PBS miniseries* African American Lives *in 2006 and 2008.*

"The Way to Reduce Black Poverty in America" appeared in August 2004 on the Op-Ed page of the New York Times.

G O INTO ANY INNER-CITY NEIGHBORHOOD, Barack Obama said in his keynote address to the [2004] Democratic National Convention, "and folks will tell you that government alone can't teach kids to learn. They know that parents have to parent, that children can't achieve unless we raise their expectations and eradicate the slander that says a black youth with a book is acting white." In a speech filled with rousing applause lines, it was a line that many black Democratic delegates found especially galvanizing. Not just because they agreed, but because it was a home truth they'd seldom heard a politician say out loud.

Why has it been so difficult for American black leaders to say such things in public, without being pilloried for "blaming the victim"? Why the huge flap over Bill Cosby's[1] insistence that black teenagers do their homework, stay in school, master standard English and stop having babies? Any black person who frequents a barbershop or beauty parlor in the inner city knows that Cosby was only echoing sentiments widely shared in the black community.

---

1. *Bill Cosby*: An African American stand-up comic and actor (b. 1937). He's perhaps best known for his program the *Cosby Show*, which ran from 1984 to 1992 and portrayed an affluent, highly educated African American family in everyday situations.

SUGGESTED MLA CITATION: Gates, Henry Louis, Jr. "The Way to Reduce Black Poverty in America." 2004. *Back to the Lake*. Ed. Thomas Cooley. 2nd ed. New York: Norton, 2012. 484–86. Print.

"If our people studied calculus like we studied basketball," my father, age 91, once remarked, "we'd be running MIT." When my brother and I were growing up in the 1950s, our parents convinced us that the "blackest" thing that we could be was a doctor or a lawyer.

Yet in too many black neighborhoods today, academic achievement has actually come to be stigmatized. "We are worse off than we were before *Brown v. Board*,"[2] says Dr. James Comer, a child psychiatrist at Yale. "And a large part of the reason for this is that we have abandoned our own black traditional core values, values that sustained us through slavery and Jim Crow segregation."[3]

Making it, as Obama told me, "requires diligent effort and deferred gratification. Everybody sitting around their kitchen table knows that."

"Americans suffer from anti-intellectualism, starting in the White House," Obama went on. "Our people can least afford to be anti-intellectual." Too many of our children have come to believe that it's easier to become a black professional athlete than a doctor or lawyer.

Reality check: According to the 2000 census, there were more than 31,000 black physicians and surgeons, 33,000 black lawyers and 5,000 black dentists. Guess how many black athletes are playing professional basketball, football and baseball combined. About 1,400.

"We talk about leaving no child behind," says Dena Wallerson, a sociologist at Connecticut College. "The reality is that we are allowing our own children to be left behind." Nearly a third of black children are born into poverty. The question is: why?

Scholars like my Harvard colleague William Julius Wilson say that the causes of black poverty are both structural and behavioral. Think of structural causes as "the devil made me do it," and behavioral causes as "the devil is in me." Structural causes are faceless systemic forces, like the disappearance of jobs. Behavioral causes are self-destructive life choices and personal habits. To break the conspiracy of silence, we have to address both of these factors.

Gates uses other methods, such as classification and definition, p. 462, to support his analysis.

It's important to talk about life chances—about the constricted set of opportunities that poverty brings. But to treat black people as if they're helpless rag dolls swept up and buffeted by vast social trends—as if they had no say in the shaping of their lives—is a supreme act of condescension. Only 50 percent of all black

2. *Brown v. Board*: In the landmark civil rights case *Brown v. Board of Education* (1954), the U.S. Supreme Court ruled that racial segregation in public schools denies students the equal protection under the law guaranteed by the Constitution. This decision overturned the doctrine of "separate but equal" facilities for black Americans established in *Plessy v. Ferguson*.

3. *Jim Crow segregation*: A reference to racist laws of the late nineteenth and early twentieth centuries that kept blacks and whites separated in public facilities.

Americans graduate from high school; an estimated 64 percent of black teenage girls will become pregnant.

Are white racists forcing black teenagers to drop out of school or to have babies? 11

Cosby got a lot of flak for complaining about children who couldn't speak stan- 12 dard English. Yet it isn't a derogation of the black vernacular—a marvelously rich and inventive tongue—to point out that there's a language of the marketplace, too, and learning to speak that language has generally been a precondition for economic success, whoever you are. When we let black youth become monolingual, we've limited their imaginative and economic possibilities.

These issues can be ticklish, no question, but they're badly served by silence or 13 squeamishness. We can't talk about the choices people have without talking about the choices people make.

READING CLOSELY

1. Poverty among black Americans is the main effect that Henry Louis Gates is analyzing. According to his analysis, what are the chief causes of that effect?

2. In paragraph 9, Gates speaks of a "conspiracy of silence." What conspiracy is he talking about?

3. What is Gates' main point about how to reduce black poverty in America? How effective do you find his solution? Explain.

4. In addition to income levels, what other social issues does Gates address? Give EXAMPLES, and explain their relationship to his main ARGUMENT.

STRATEGIES AND STRUCTURES

1. Gates begins his analysis by referring to Barack Obama and Bill Cosby. How do their public remarks EXEMPLIFY what he says about a "conspiracy of silence" (9)? Why would Gates, or any writer, refer to a (then) up-and-coming politician and a famous comedian when making a controversial point?

2. "The question is: why?" is a RHETORICAL QUESTION because Gates intends to answer it himself (8). Where does Gates ask other rhetorical questions, some of which require no answer at all? Try rewriting one of these questions as a statement. How does this change affect his argument?

3. Gates uses statistics in paragraphs 7 and 10. How do these facts and figures support his position?

4. Gates concludes his essay by linking speaking with doing: "We can't talk about the choices people have without talking about the choices people make" (13). Why do you think he ends this way? How else might he have concluded?

5. *Other Methods.* Gates CLASSIFIES "the causes of black poverty" into two types, "structural" and "behavioral" (9). How does he DEFINE each type?

THINKING ABOUT LANGUAGE

1. A "vernacular" is the informal spoken language of a group of people (12). Where does Gates himself use vernacular language in his essay? Why does he do so?

2. What is "standard English" (12)? What, according to Gates, is the role of standard English? Of vernacular English?

3. What are the implications of Gates's "rag doll" METAPHOR (10)?

FOR WRITING

1. Gates's article was written for the Op-Ed page of the *New York Times*, a page opposite the editorial page that's devoted to opinion pieces, usually on controversial issues of the day. Write a letter to the editor responding to Gates.

2. AIDS, sexually transmitted diseases, genocide, mental illness, the Holocaust, birth control, and divorce are taboo topics for various people and communities. Write an essay analyzing the effects that continued silence on one of these topics, or some other controversial subject, is likely to have on individuals and society.

3. "Anti-intellectualism," say Gates and Barack Obama, is not limited to a particular community; Americans in general "suffer" from it (6). Write an essay agreeing or disagreeing with this position.

HENRY L. ROEDIGER III

Why Are Textbooks So Expensive?

Henry L. Roediger III (b. 1947) is a professor of psychology at Washington University in St. Louis. Roediger is a specialist in memory and human learning, and the author or coauthor of many articles and psychology textbooks. What caused him to specialize in the psychology of memory? Roediger attributes his choice to an event in his childhood—the death of his mother when he was five years old. "That event changed my life drastically," says Roediger. "I was determined to hold on to my memories of her, to relive the past by remembering them. At a very early age, I spent a lot of time thinking about memory and how it works."

"Why Are Textbooks So Expensive?" appeared in 2005 in the Observer, *a journal published by the American Psychological Society, of which Roediger is a past president.*

NEWSLETTERS AND OTHER MISSIVES that I receive seem filled with stories about textbooks and textbook prices, with many wringing their hands over why textbooks are so expensive now relative to the more distant past (usually when the author of the article was in college). I suspect some articles arise from middle-aged parents who suddenly must pay for their own children's college textbooks and they recoil when they see a bill of $500 a semester or thereabouts.

What reasons are given for the high price of textbooks? Of course, there's general inflation, but evidence points to textbook prices outpacing inflation. Others point their fingers at the bright colors in many books (relative to older black and white models) and argue that production costs are needlessly pushed up by color. (A quick check of my own bookstore shows that many books without color are more expensive than those with color, probably due to the number of books in the print run.) Another suggested hypothesis is textbook publishers simply seek greater profit margins now than they did in the past. After all, the market used to be dominated by rather genteel textbook companies that really cared about scholarly texts and not so much about being wildly profitable. A comfortable, modest profit line was fine in the old days. Those days are now gone, because traditional textbook companies have been bought up by gigantic conglomerates that look only to the bottom line and seek huge profits. For these companies, so the theory goes, textbooks are just one more product line, no different from detergent or tires or toilet

SUGGESTED MLA CITATION: Roediger, Henry L., III. "Why Are Textbooks So Expensive?" 2005. *Back to the Lake.* Ed. Thomas Cooley. 2nd ed. New York: Norton, 2012. 488–93. Print.

paper, on which to make a profit. The fact that many formerly independent text-book companies are being bought up and merged under the same corporate umbrella could also be partly responsible, if this process reduces competition through having fewer companies. Another facet of the debate is the frequent revision schedule of basic textbooks. Most introductory psychology textbooks are revised every three years, some every two years. Doesn't this constant revision drive up the prices?

Although the reasons listed above may have some merit, I don't think any of them is fundamental to why textbook prices are so high. In fact, I suspect that most of the properties described above are effects and not causes. What is the cause? If I had to bet, the root cause is a feature of the marketplace that has changed greatly over the years and fundamentally reshaped the text-book market: sale of used books.   3

> The root cause is the *main* cause (p. 458).

The organized used book market represents the great change in the landscape of higher education publishing, but one that has gone relatively unnoticed.   4

Let us go back in time to what educational historians refer to as the later Paleolithic era in higher education, that is, the late 1960s, when I was in college. Here was how the used book market worked then. I was a psychology major and was about to take a course in history of psychology. A psychology major in my fraternity, Dave Redmond (now a big-time lawyer in Richmond, Virginia) was going on to law school and wanted to sell some of his psychology textbooks. He asked if I wanted to buy Edna Heidbreder's *Seven Psychologies*, for a dollar. I said OK. The book had cost him $2.95, which is still listed in my copy. . . .   5

. . . This was how the used book market worked in my day. One student sold books to another student on a hit or miss basis. Books didn't cost much. Oh, also, most students kept their books and started building a personal library. (This is another idea that seems to have faded with time. Personal library? Today's students assume everything they need to know is on the Internet.)   6

Let's fast forward to 1981. I was teaching at Purdue University and was considering (with Betty Capaldi and several others) writing an introductory psychology textbook, since textbook companies were wooing us to do so. However, neither Betty nor I had ever even taught introductory psychology, so we decided to teach independent sections one semester. We examined a lot of books and decided to use Phil Zimbardo's textbook, *Psychology and Life*. . . . Betty and I were each to teach a section of 475 students, so we ordered 950 books. Nine hundred fifty books was, and is, a big textbook order. Think of the profits to the company and the author!   7

A few days before classes were to begin, I happened by one of the three Purdue bookstores to buy something. I decided to go see the hundreds of copies of the book I had ordered, gleaming at me on the shelves. I found them, all right, but I was shocked at my discovery. Every single book on the shelf was a used copy! I   8 went through many of them, disbelieving, and saw that quite a few were in poor condition (marked up, spines damaged, etc.), yet the prices were still substantial. How could this be? Zimbardo's book had never been used at Purdue before recent times. Where did all these used copies come from? I decided to walk to the other two bookstores and discovered exactly the same situation; every book for sale was a used book in the other two stores. There wasn't a new book to be found.

The organized used book market represents the great change in the landscape of higher education publishing, but one that has gone relatively unnoticed by most academics (unless they are textbook authors). The implications are huge. Consider the situation in today's dollars (although I am estimating). A single author of a textbook might make a 15 percent royalty on the net price of the book (sometimes a bit more); the net price is the price the bookstore pays the textbook company for the book and the list price is the price set by the bookstore to sell to the student. The net price of an introductory psychology textbook today might be $65 (before the bookstore marks it up), so the author would make $9.75 per book. However, that is only if the book is bought from the company; if the student buys used books, the author makes nothing and neither does the company. If 950 used books are sold, the author would lose (be cheated out of?) $9,262, and the textbook company would perhaps lose a similar or larger amount. (Profit margins probably differ from company to company and book to book. They are a closely guarded secret.) Of course, at Purdue in 1981 the figures would have been smaller, but the principle the same. The fact of modern campus life is that used book companies buy up textbooks on one campus, warehouse them, and ship them to wherever the book is being adopted, and therefore prevent sales of new books.

Consider what this means. The textbook company that invested hundreds of thousands of dollars—maybe millions for introductory textbooks—to sign, develop, review, produce, market, and distribute a book over several years is denied its just profits. The author or authors who wrote the book over many years are denied their royalties. Meanwhile, huge profits are made by the used book companies who did nothing whatsoever to create the product. They are true parasites, deriving profits with no investment (and no value added to the product) while damaging their hosts. The issue here is similar to that in the movie and recording industries for pirated products that are sold very cheaply, denying the companies and the artists their profits. One major dissimilarity in these cases is that pirated movies and music are illegal whereas the used textbook market is legal. (There have been proposals to change this state of affairs. For example, one idea is that when used book companies resell texts they would pay the original textbook company and author a royalty.)

The high price of textbooks is the direct result of the used book market. A textbook is customarily used for one semester and (unlike the old days) students rarely keep their books now but sell them back to the bookstore (more on that anon). Therefore, the same text might be used by three to four students, but the textbook company and author profit the first time a book is sold and not thereafter. It stands to reason that textbooks must be priced aggressively, because the profits from the repeated sales will not go to the authors and companies that actually wrote and produced the books, but rather to the companies that specialize in buying and selling used books. Further, the reason textbooks are revised so frequently is to combat the used book market, which further drives up the company's costs. Frequent revisions also add wear and tear on the authors who must perpetually revise their books. (I've sometimes wanted to have two somewhat different versions of my textbooks and then alternate them.) Most fields of psychology hardly move at such a swift pace as to justify two- to three-year revision cycles of introductory textbooks. The famous textbooks of the 1950s and 1960s were revised every eight to 10 years or so, but after the used textbook market gained steam, revisions became frequent. Moreover, because of the used book market, profitability of many companies was hurt and they became ripe for takeovers, which further consolidated the market. That is why I said in the third paragraph that many factors used to "explain" the high prices of books are probably effects, with the cause being the organized used book companies that prey parasitically on the host publishing companies and threaten to destroy them.

Other changes have also affected the market. College and university bookstores 12 used to be owned by the school and operated as a service to the students and the faculty, but those days are past on most campuses. Now the bookstores are operated by large companies (Follett's, Barnes and Noble, and others), often the same ones who operate used book operations. Most "bookstores" have turned into carnivals where emphasis is placed on selling sweatshirts, trinkets, souvenirs and snacks and, oh, incidentally (used) books.

Another pernicious trend: After universities relinquished their hold on book- 13 stores, the bookstores aggressively raised the percentage markup on the net price paid to the publisher on new books. Thirty years ago a standard rate of markup was 20 percent and publishers provided list prices on their books (because markups were standard). I can recall the great hue and cry that arose when textbook stores started marking up books by 25 percent. However, a 25 percent markup for today's bookstores would look like chump change. Publishing companies now sell the bookstore the books based on a net price and the bookstore decides on the list price, often marking up the books 30 to 40 percent in the process. The profits go to the company owning the store and the company pays the college or university for the right to have a monopoly business on campus. However, many students have now learned that it is cheaper and (given the huge lines) sometimes easier to buy textbooks from other sources like Amazon.com.

Let me give you a concrete example. Last summer the eighth edition of my text- 14
book (with Barry Kantowitz and David Elmes), *Experimental Psychology: Understanding Psychological Research*, was published by Wadsworth Publishing Company.
The net price (the price the bookstore pays the company for a new book) the first
time the book is sold is $73.50. The authors receive 15 percent royalties on the
book, so we would split the $11 royalty three ways. However, at the Washington
University bookstore, the list price of the book is $99.75, a markup of $26.25 (or
35.7 percent)! Yes, that's right, the authors who wrote the book get $11.02 for their
years of hard work whereas the bookstore that ordered the books, let them sit on
the shelves for a couple of weeks, and sold them, gets $26.25 per book. (If books
are not sold, they are returned to the company for a full price refund. It's a no-risk
business.)

Yet the story gets even worse because of the used book problem. After the stu- 15
dent uses the book (and if it is in pretty good condition), the bookstore will buy it
back from the student at a greatly marked down price, somewhere between 25 and
50 percent. Let's assume that *Experimental Psychology* is bought back for 40 percent
of the list price (which is probably a generous assumption at most bookstores).
That would be $39.90. After buying it, the bookstore will mark it back up dramati-
cally and resell the book. Suppose the used book is sold for $75, which sounds like
a bargain relative to the new book price of $99.75, and it is. However, notice that
the profit markup for the bookstore on this used book would then be $35.10, which
is higher than the (still very large) profit made on the new book ($26.25). In fact,
the primary reason bookstores prefer selling used books to new books is the much
higher profit margins on used books. So, on the second (and third and fourth, etc.)
sales of the same book, the bookstore and used book company make huge cumula-
tive profits. The textbook company that invested large sums into developing the
book (and the authors who invested time and energy and research into writing it)
receive exactly zero on these resold books.

If this sounds bad, it actually gets worse. Another insidious influence in the 16
textbook industry is the problem of sales of complimentary copies. In order to market their wares to professors, it is customary for textbook companies to give out
free copies of their books. [Everyone] who teach[es] basic courses in the psychology curriculum receive[s] such books. This is just another price of doing business
for the book companies. However, many of these books find their way into the
used book market because some professors sell books to scavengers from the used
book companies who search through university campuses seeking to buy complimentary copies. Now these companies are soliciting professors to sell their complimentary copies by e-mail. I never sell my complimentary books, of course, because
I believe it unethical to sell for profit something I was given by a company in good
faith. However, apparently many professors do sell their books. Now the textbook

company gets hit by a double whammy: The book they produced to give to a professor for possible adoption enters the market and takes away a new book sale in the marketplace!

Is it any wonder that textbook prices are so high? The wonder is that they aren't higher. 17

. . .

The textbook companies themselves have few alternatives in dealing with this problem. They can and do raise the price of the books so that they try to recoup their investment on the first sale (hence the high price of textbooks). They can revise the book frequently, which renders the previous edition obsolete. They can try to bundle in or shrink-wrap some additional item (a workbook, a CD) with the new text, so that students will need to buy new books to get the free item. This strategy can work, but some bookstores will just unbundle the book from the study guide and sell both! (So, a study guide the bookstore received free can be sold for, say, $15.) Unless and until laws are changed to prevent the organized sale of used books, you can expect textbook prices to keep increasing. . . . 18

READING CLOSELY

1. Henry Roediger analyzes several of the usual reasons given for the steep rise in the prices of college textbooks (2), as well as what he says is the main or "root" cause (3). What are the usual reasons and what does he claim to be the main cause?

2. What is the point of the brief NARRATIVE that Roediger tells in paragraphs 5–6 about buying his undergraduate psychology book from a classmate? How about the narrative he tells in paragraphs 7–8? How do these stories relate to his main point? Where does he state it?

3. According to Roediger, what specific effects has the used-book market had on the authors and publishers of textbooks? On the consumers of those books?

4. How and why, according to Roediger, do college bookstores sell used copies of textbooks that have never been used on their campuses?

STRATEGIES AND STRUCTURES

1. Where and how does Roediger shift from analyzing causes to analyzing effects? Where does he switch back? How effective do you find this strategy? Why?

2. What is the purpose of the EXAMPLE that Roediger gives in paragraph 14? Why does he refer to it as a CONCRETE example? List some other concrete examples he uses. For what purposes does he use them?

3. As an author of textbooks himself, Roediger has a stake in his analysis that purchasers of textbooks do not have. Does that stake necessarily invalidate his claims? Why or why not?

4. *Other Methods.* Besides analyzing causes and effects, what ARGUMENT is Roediger making? What conclusions does he come to?

THINKING ABOUT LANGUAGE

1. In paragraphs 10 and 11, Roediger uses a biological ANALOGY. What is he comparing to what? How helpful do you find the comparison?

2. Roediger calls campus bookstores "carnivals" (12). Why?

3. How does Roediger DEFINE the "net price" of a newly published book (9)? How about the "profit margin" (9)?

4. Roediger uses HYPERBOLE when he calls the 1960s "the later Paleolithic era" (5). Why does he use hyperbole here? What does it contribute to the argument he is making?

FOR WRITING

1. Write a paragraph or two analyzing some effects of rising textbook costs from your own standpoint as a consumer.

2. Have you ever purchased a textbook that is labeled "free examination copy" or "not for resale"? If, as Roediger contends, the sale of such books contributes to the high cost of textbooks, what if anything do you think should be done about teachers and stores selling free copies they received from the publisher for review? Write an opinion piece for your campus newspaper (in other words, for an audience of students) arguing for or against this practice.

3. Some public school districts (and colleges) now purchase textbooks in electronic form. And, of course, *Amazon* now sells more ebooks than paper ones. Write an essay explaining what some of the effects of this trend might be.

DAN BARRY

Cancer's Oddest Effect

Dan Barry (b. 1958) is a reporter and columnist for the New York Times. *A native New Yorker, he studied journalism at St. Bonaventure and New York University. In 1994, Barry and his investigative team at the* Providence Journal-Bulletin *won a Pulitzer Prize for a series of articles exposing corruption in the Rhode Island court system. In 1995, Barry joined the staff of the* Times *and became a major contributor to the newspaper's award-winning coverage of 9/11 and Hurricane Katrina.*

The title of his autobiographical Pull Me Up *(2004) refers to the sense of drowning that Barry felt when he was first diagnosed with cancer at age 41. A few years later, as he indicates in "Cancer's Oddest Effect," which he wrote for the* Times *in 2009, Barry suffered "a profoundly unwelcome recurrence" of the disease. On both occasions, in addition to the usual side effects of the disease and the chemotherapy with which doctors treated it, Barry eventually returned to a strange state of confusion caused, in his analysis, by "a pre-existing human condition."*

WITHIN THE CHEMOTHERAPY alumni corps there exists a mutual respect not 1
unlike the bond shared by veterans of war. Sometimes that respect is silently conveyed; not everyone wants to talk about it. And sometimes it is shared in the shorthand of the battle-hardened.

Where? 2

Esophagus. 3

Who? 4

Sloan-Kettering.[1] 5

What kind? 6

Cisplatin, fluorouracil, Drano, Borax[2] . . . 7

Side effects? 8

The usual: nausea, vomiting, hair loss. And the toes are still numb. 9

Yeah. 10

1. *Sloan-Kettering*: Memorial Sloan-Kettering Cancer Center is the world's largest and oldest cancer research and treatment center.

2. *Cisplatin, . . . Borax*: Cisplatin and fluorouracil are drugs used in chemotherapy treatments. Drano and Borax are used to clean out clogged drains and kill roaches.

SUGGESTED MLA CITATION: Barry, Dan. "Cancer's Oddest Effect." 2009. *Back to the Lake*. Ed. Thomas Cooley. 2nd ed. New York: Norton, 2012. 495–98. Print.

At this point the two chemo alums may begin to sense a phantom metallic taste 11
at the back of their throat, a taste sometimes prompted by the intravenous infusion
of the corrosive chemicals intended to save their lives. A strong drink might be in
order; maybe two.

With that first, taste-altering sip, the two might begin to discuss another side 12
effect that has received attention lately, the one rudely called "chemo brain": the
cognitive fogginess that some patients experience after completing their regimen.
That fogginess does not always completely lift, and oncologists are now taking seriously what they might once have dismissed as a complaint rooted in advanced age
or cancer fatigue.

For me, reading about chemo brain has resurrected that faint taste of metal. I 13
underwent chemotherapy in 1999 and again in 2004, thanks to a profoundly
unwelcome recurrence. Depending on one's perspective, I was both unfortunate
and fortunate. Unfortunate in that I endured all the concomitant fears and indigni-
ties, twice. Fortunate in that I had the option of chemotherapy, twice. Not all can-
cers respond; not everyone is so lucky.

I experienced all the typical side effects. Nausea: for several days at a time, 14
though vomiting sometimes broke the monotony. Hair loss: I was balding anyway,
so chemo saved me from comb-over delusions. Neuropathy: even now, my toes feel
as if they were wrapped in cotton.

And, I now think, chemo brain—but a form that seems to be the common defi- 15
nition's opposite. My self-diagnosis is that I had a pre-existing case of fogginess
that lifted during and immediately after my chemotherapy regimen: I suddenly
experienced acute clarity. Then, as the effects and memory of chemotherapy faded,
my confusion returned. Twice.

See p. 457 for
tips on using
chronology to
organize causes
and effects.
In 1999, before the diagnosis of cancer and the prognosis of let's hope 16
for the best, I was enveloped in the haze of the everyday. Rather than
rejoicing in a loving wife, a daughter not yet 2, a job I enjoyed—in being,
simply, 41—I created felonies out of matters not worth a summons. Traffic
jams. Work conflicts. No Vienna Fingers[3] in the cupboard. Felonies all.

Cancer, as is often said, tends to focus the mind. But my diagnosis hovered in 17
the theoretical until the moment I began the first of six rounds of chemotherapy,
each one requiring a five-day hospital stay. The nurse hung bags of clear, innocent-
looking liquid from an IV pole, found a plump vein along my right arm—and the
fog slowly lifted.

Sickened by the mere smell of food, I suddenly saw the wonder in the most 18
common foods: an egg, a hard-boiled egg. Imprisoned and essentially chained to an

---

3. *Vienna Fingers:* Vanilla sandwich cookies made in an oblong "finger" shape.

IV pole, I would stare out my hospital room window at the people below, and feel a rush of the purest envy for their routine pursuits. Imagining the summer night air blowing cool through sweat-dampened shirts, I'd think how good a $3 ice cream would taste right about now, or a $5 beer, and how nice it would be to watch a baseball game of no consequence.

Men acting like boys, hitting, throwing, running on grass. I used to play baseball. 19

In the morning, after urinating away the remnants of poisons pumped into me, I 20 would roll my IV-pole partner back to the window and study again the people below, moving, hustling, ambling, to jobs, to appointments, to a diner, maybe, for one of the fried-egg sandwiches served countless times every morning in Manhattan.

Gradually, from midsummer to late fall, the chemotherapy transformed me into a 21 bald guy whose pallor was offset only by the hint of terror in his eyes. But the chemo also wiped away the muddle, revealing the world in all its mundane glory. I won't tell you that I wept at the sight of a puppy. But I did linger over my sleeping daughter to watch her tiny chest rise and fall. I did savor the complexities of a simple olive. I did notice fireflies, those dancing night sparks I had long ago stopped seeing.

After the chemotherapy, radiation and a few weeks to allow things to settle 22 down, as my doctor put it, I was declared "clean" in February 2000. Never again, I vowed, would I take these simple things for granted. I was blind, but now I see.

The fog, of course, returned as the effects and memory of chemo faded, no mat- 23 ter that my wife and I were now blessed with two daughters. How I hated traffic jams. And the Vienna Fingers! Who ate the last Vienna Finger?

Then, in the late spring of 2004, probably while I was railing about something 24 eminently unimportant, my cancer impolitely returned. Once again I felt the frigid breath of mortality at my neck. I also felt like a fool. What is the use of surviving cancer if you don't learn from it? Are not improved by it? Am I so thick that I need to receive the life-is-precious message twice?

I returned to Sloan-Kettering for more chemotherapy and more of the same 25 side effects—including my own manifestation of chemo brain. Fog lifted, world revealed.

After the chemotherapy came major surgery, which provided the exclamation 26 point to whatever chemo was trying to tell me. Once again I was declared clean. And this time, by God! This time!

I became a walking platitude, telling friends without a trace of irony to live 27 every day as though it were their last. Because, man, I've been there. And if I weren't so repressed I'd give you a hug.

Slowly, insidiously, the fog of the everyday has returned to enshroud me. It 28 came in wispy strips, a little more, then a little more, wrapping me like a mummy. Just the other day, in the car with my wife and my two daughters, I began railing about being stuck in a traffic jam.

Perspective, my wife said. Perspective.   29

I could not hear her. You see, I'm struggling with this pre-existing human 30
condition.

Reading Closely

1. For some cancer patients, says Dan Barry, a possible side effect of chemotherapy is "chemo brain" (12). What is the nature of this condition, as Barry DEFINES it?

2. In the past, doctors have diagnosed chemo brain as an effect of age or "cancer fatigue" (12). What does Barry think the cause is?

3. When he underwent chemotherapy, Barry himself suffered from a form of chemo brain "that seems to be the common definition's opposite" (15). How does Barry define the chemo brain he experienced?

4. In the last paragraph of his essay, Barry reports that he suffers from a "preexisting human condition" (30). What condition? What caused it?

Strategies and Structures

1. Barry's essay ascribes all the effects and side-effects that he deals with to two fundamental causes—chemotherapy and human nature. Throughout his essay, where and when does the second of these seem to kick in? Of the two, which seems the more incurable? Why?

2. What is the purpose of the DIALOGUE, at the beginning of Barry's essay, between himself and another cancer patient?

3. Barry's analysis focuses mainly on effects, which he presents in a particular order. What order? CHRONOLOGICAL? Least to most significant? Most to least? Other? Explain.

4. "What is the use of surviving cancer," Barry asks, "if you don't learn from it?" (24). This is a question about causes and effects, but it also introduces an ARGUMENT. How and where does Barry's analysis address this issue of learning from suffering? What conclusions does he come to?

5. *Other Methods.* In addition to analyzing their effects, Barry is telling the story of his two bouts of chemotherapy. How and where do the NARRATIVE elements of his essay contribute particularly well to his analysis? What's the role of Barry's wife in this narrative? Of the Vienna Fingers?

THINKING ABOUT LANGUAGE

1. When listing the drugs he was given, Barry includes Drano and Borax (7). How literally are we to take him here? What point is he making by associating these two brand names with the names of standard cancer drugs?

2. The "cognitive fogginess" that some patients experience after chemotherapy is known "rudely," says Barry, as "chemo brain" (12). What's rude about this name? Where else does Barry seem concerned with courtesy and politeness? Point out specific words and phrases.

3. Barry says that after he was declared cancer-free for the second time, he became "a walking platitude" (27). What is a platitude, and why does Barry use the word to describe himself?

4. What does Barry's wife mean when she says, "Perspective . . . . Perspective" (29)? To what extent does this word sum up what Barry learned from his bouts with cancer?

FOR WRITING

1. Write a brief dialogue between two "veterans" who have survived a battle, disease, trauma, or other rigorous experience (1). Try to use their speech as a sort of "shorthand" for analyzing the effects of the experience on each speaker (1).

2. Write an essay analyzing the typical side effects of some form of medical treatment. If some patients experience odd or unusual effects, feel free to discuss those, too.

HAL R. VARIAN

Analyzing the Marriage Gap

Hal R. Varian (b. 1947) is a professor of business and economics at the University of California at Berkeley, specializing in the economics of information technology. Co-author of Information Rules: A Strategic Guide to the Network Economy *(1998), Varian says in that book that movies, music, software, stock quotations, and other "information goods" have supplanted industrial goods "as the key drivers of world markets."*

In the labor market, say many economists, a key driver is marriage. "Analyzing the Marriage Gap" was first published in 2004 as one of Varian's regular business columns in the New York Times. *In it, Varian investigates the claim that married men make more money than unmarried men. There is no doubt that marriage has this effect, says Varian; "the question is why." As he analyzes the most likely causes for the wage gap between married and unmarried men, Varian also looks at the nature of causation in general.*

Mᴀʀʀɪᴇᴅ ᴍᴇɴ ᴍᴀᴋᴇ ᴍᴏʀᴇ ᴍᴏɴᴇʏ than single men—a lot more. Labor econo- 1
mists estimate that even when you control for age, education and other demo-
graphic effects, the "marriage wage premium" is 10 percent to 50 percent.

The question is why. 2

See p. 460 for correlation vs. causation. There are two broad classes of explanation. One view holds that marriage 3
causes men to receive higher wages. The other view is that higher wages are
simply correlated with, but not caused by, marital status.

There are a variety of reasons that marriage might cause higher wages. It might 4
be that employers prefer married men to single men because they are more productive. After all, they have spouses who share responsibility for household chores
and provide other sorts of support and assistance. Single men just have that empty
apartment.

On the other hand, it could be that employers have an irrational prejudice for 5
married men. Employers might view them as more productive, more reliable and
more committed, whether or not these things are true.

Whether there really is an employer preference for married men is irrelevant. 6
Marriage has a causal effect: single men who choose to marry will tend to receive
higher wages.

SUGGESTED MLA CITATION: Varian, Hal R. "Analyzing the Marriage Gap." 2004. *Back to the Lake.* Ed. Thomas Cooley. 2nd ed. New York: Norton, 2012. 500–02. Print.

The other class of theories holds that being married is simply correlated with higher wages. It may be that women are attracted to stable, hardworking men. Employers also find such men attractive, so they want to hire and promote them. If this is true, then we would see married men having higher wages. But it isn't that marriage caused those higher wages—rather, the same things that caused marriage caused the higher wages.

Such a correlation could also arise from irrelevant characteristics. Maybe women prefer good-looking guys, and employers also like handsome men, even when appearance has nothing to do with job productivity. In this case we would also observe that the same men who are more likely to be married are also more likely to be employed and have higher wages.

In the correlation explanations of the marriage premium, the same factors that caused the men to marry caused them to get higher wages—but there is no direct causal link between marriage and high wages. To drive this point home, suppose Hamlet is considering proposing to Ophelia,[1] but is consumed with doubts. "To be married or not to be married, that is the question."

If the causal theories are correct, then if Hamlet proposes and Ophelia accepts, his future wages would be higher on average than if he stayed single. If the correlation theories are correct, then choosing to marry would have no effect on Hamlet's future wages, and he may as well remain single.

Recently, two economists, Kate Antonovics of the University of California at San Diego and Robert Town of the University of Minnesota, have come up with a clever way to decide between the causal and the correlation theories. Their paper, "Are All the Good Men Married? Uncovering the Sources of the Marital Wage Premium," was published in the May 2004 issue of *The American Economic Review*.

Their approach is based on looking at monozygotic, or identical, twins. The authors argue that twins have the same genetic endowment and (usually) the same upbringing. Since twins have the same underlying physical and mental capabilities, they should have similar productivity. Even if employers are biased toward certain irrelevant characteristics, monozygotic twins should be affected by such biases equally.

Hence differences in wages between married and unmarried twins should be free of most of the effects that might cause a spurious correlation between marriages and wages. If a married twin has a higher wage than his single brother, the difference is probably caused by marriage, not just correlated with it.

The economists drew on a unique data set, the Minnesota Twins Registry, which tracked most twins born in Minnesota between 1936 and 1955. In the mid-1990's, the Registry sent the twins a questionnaire asking about their socio-economic

1. *Hamlet / Ophelia*: Lovers in Shakespeare's play *Hamlet*; Hamlet is well known for his indecision, and his "To be or not to be" soliloquy is one of Shakespeare's most famous.

status. Using this data, the researchers were able to construct a sample of 136 pairs of monozygotic twins, of whom 85 percent were married. In 23 percent of the cases, one twin was married, the other wasn't.

They extracted data from the survey on the hourly wages, weeks worked a year, age and educational attainment of the men in their sample and compared these with figures for all American males. The results implied that their sample was reasonably representative of the nation's population.   15

Consistent with other studies, they found a significant marriage premium. Controlling for education, age and other variables, the married men in their sample earned about 19 percent more than unmarried men. They then examined just the wage differences between twins, while still controlling for education. They found that married twins had 26 percent higher wages than their unmarried siblings. Hence, even among very similar men, those who are married earn substantially more.   16

The authors found essentially the same results if they factored in divorced or widowed status, or added variables like a spouse's work experience, number of children and wage history.   17

This result suggests that marriage really does have a causal impact on wages. Of course, it is not conclusive. After all, maybe the married twin really is different in some way from his brother, and that difference is important to both potential spouses and employers. Still, it is suggestive evidence.   18

So, here's the advice Hamlet would get from a labor economist: put your doubts aside and marry Ophelia. Stop moping around and go get a job. You may not be any happier, but at least you'll make more money.   19

Reading Closely

1. What possible causes for the marriage gap does Hal Varian cite? Which ones do you find most plausible? Why?

2. In addition to discussing specific causes of the marriage gap, what general questions does Varian raise about the nature of cause and effect?

3. The twins study, according to Varian, "should be free of most of the effects that might cause a spurious correlation between marriages and wages" (13). What are some of those effects? Why should a study based on identical twins be free of them?

4. What do you think is the main point of Varian's essay? How serious do you consider his advice to the Hamlets of the world to be—or not to be?

STRATEGIES AND STRUCTURES

1. How does Varian's EXAMPLE of the twins study by Antonovics and Town in paragraphs 11–18 support his analysis of the causes of the marriage gap?

2. The evidence of the twins study is "suggestive," says Varian, but "not conclusive" (18). Throughout his essay, how and how well does Varian distinguish between probable and possible causes? Explain.

3. *Other Methods.* Before he considers specific causes for the marriage gap, Varian COMPARES AND CONTRASTS "two broad classes of explanation" (3). What are they, and how do they differ from each other?

THINKING ABOUT LANGUAGE

1. Look up *spurious*, a word often applied to ARGUMENTS (13). Why does Varian use it in the context of a cause-and-effect analysis?

2. Explain Varian's ALLUSION to Shakespeare's *Hamlet*. What happens to Ophelia in the play? How appropriate is the allusion, in your opinion?

3. *Zygotes* are fertilized ova. So what would "monozygotic" twins be, and why would they be "identical" (12, 14)?

4. In a research experiment, what is meant by "control[ling] for" (1, 16)?

FOR WRITING

1. Do you think the marriage wage premium is caused by marriage? Write a hypothetical email to Varian questioning or agreeing with his evidence and analysis.

2. Women, in general, still earn less than men for the same work. Write an essay analyzing the causes of the gender pay gap.

3. "Irregular" workers—such as students, some military personnel, migrant laborers, and other immigrants—typically earn less than "regular" members of the civilian work force. Why? Analyze the causes in a particular case you know about, whether of an individual worker (including yourself) or a group.

SHIRLEY JACKSON

The Lottery

Shirley Jackson (1916–1965) was born in San Francisco, grew up mostly in Burlingame, California, and moved with her family to Rochester, New York, when she was 17. She studied first at the University of Rochester and later at Syracuse University, where she earned a degree in English in 1940. A disciplined and prolific writer, Jackson wrote over a hundred novels, short stories, books for children, and television scripts. Her best-known works include The Haunting of Hill House (1959) *and* We Have Always Lived in the Castle (1962). *She was married to the literary critic Stanley Edgar Hyman and lived with her family in Vermont. The Shirley Jackson Award is given annually for "outstanding achievement in the literature of psychological suspense, horror, and the dark fantastic."*

When "The Lottery" was first published in the New Yorker *in 1948, it caused a sensation. Irate readers canceled their subscriptions and flooded the author with hate mail for her unflattering portrayal of village life. Jackson responded by explaining that she had hoped "to shock the story's readers with a graphic dramatization of the pointless violence and general inhumanity in their own lives." It was to achieve this purpose that she chose to set "a particularly brutal ancient rite in the present and in my own village" (Bennington, Vermont). The harvest or vegetation ritual at the heart of Jackson's story is rooted in an ancient misunderstanding of cause and effect.*

T HE MORNING OF June 27th was clear and sunny, with the fresh warmth of a full-summer day; the flowers were blossoming profusely and the grass was richly green. The people of the village began to gather in the square, between the post office and the bank, around ten o'clock; in some towns there were so many people that the lottery took two days and had to be started on June 26th, but in this village, where there were only about three hundred people, the whole lottery took less than two hours, so it could begin at ten o'clock in the morning and still be through in time to allow the villagers to get home for noon dinner. 1

The children assembled first, of course. School was recently over for the summer, and the feeling of liberty sat uneasily on most of them; they tended to gather together quietly for a while before they broke into boisterous play, and their talk was still of the classroom and the teacher, of books and reprimands. Bobby Martin had already stuffed his pockets full of stones, and the other boys soon followed his 2

SUGGESTED MLA CITATION: Jackson, Shirley. "The Lottery." 1949. *Back to the Lake.* Ed. Thomas Cooley. 2nd ed. New York: Norton, 2012. 504–11. Print.

example, selecting the smoothest and roundest stones; Bobby and Harry Jones and Dickie Delacroix—the villagers pronounced this name "Dellacroy"—eventually made a great pile of stones in one corner of the square and guarded it against the raids of the other boys. The girls stood aside, talking among themselves, looking over their shoulders at the boys, and the very small children rolled in the dust or clung to the hands of their older brothers or sisters.

Soon the men began to gather, surveying their own children, speaking of plant-   3
ing and rain, tractors and taxes. They stood together, away from the pile of stones in the corner, and their jokes were quiet and they smiled rather than laughed. The women, wearing faded house dresses and sweaters, came shortly after their men-folk. They greeted one another and exchanged bits of gossip as they went to join their husbands. Soon the women, standing by their husbands, began to call to their children, and the children came reluctantly, having to be called four or five times. Bobby Martin ducked under his mother's grasping hand and ran, laughing, back to the pile of stones. His father spoke up sharply, and Bobby came quickly and took his place between his father and his oldest brother.

The lottery was conducted—as were the square dances, the teen-age club, the   4
Halloween program—by Mr. Summers, who had time and energy to devote to civic activities. He was a round-faced, jovial man and he ran the coal business, and peo-ple were sorry for him, because he had no children and his wife was a scold. When he arrived in the square, carrying the black wooden box, there was a murmur of conversation among the villagers, and he waved and called, "Little late today, folks." The postmaster, Mr. Graves, followed him, carrying a three-legged stool, and the stool was put in the center of the square and Mr. Summers set the black box down on it. The villagers kept their distance, leaving a space between them-selves and the stool, and when Mr. Summers said, "Some of you fellows want to give me a hand?" there was a hesitation before two men, Mr. Martin and his oldest son, Baxter, came forward to hold the box steady on the stool while Mr. Summers stirred up the papers inside it.

The original paraphernalia for the lottery had been lost long ago, and the black   5
box now resting on the stool had been put into use even before Old Man Warner, the oldest man in town, was born. Mr. Summers spoke frequently to the villagers about making a new box, but no one liked to upset even as much tradition as was represented by the black box. There was a story that the present box had been made with some pieces of the box that had preceded it, the one that had been constructed when the first people settled down to make a village here. Every year, after the lot-tery, Mr. Summers began talking again about a new box, but every year the subject was allowed to fade off without anything's being done. The black box grew shabbier each year; by now it was no longer completely black but splintered badly along one side to show the original wood color, and in some places faded or stained.

Mr. Martin and his oldest son, Baxter, held the black box securely on the stool 6 until Mr. Summers had stirred the papers thoroughly with his hand. Because so much of the ritual had been forgotten or discarded, Mr. Summers had been successful in having slips of paper substituted for the chips of wood that had been used for generations. Chips of wood, Mr. Summers had argued, had been all very well when the village was tiny, but now that the population was more than three hundred and likely to keep on growing, it was necessary to use something that would fit more easily into the black box. The night before the lottery, Mr. Summers and Mr. Graves made up the slips of paper and put them in the box, and it was then taken to the safe of Mr. Summers' coal company and locked up until Mr. Summers was ready to take it to the square next morning. The rest of the year, the box was put away, sometimes one place, sometimes another; it had spent one year in Mr. Graves's barn and another year underfoot in the post office, and sometimes it was set on a shelf in the Martin grocery and left there.

There was a great deal of fussing to be done before Mr. Summers declared the 7 lottery open. There were the lists to make up—of heads of families, heads of households in each family, members of each household in each family. There was the proper swearing-in of Mr. Summers by the postmaster, as the official of the lottery; at one time, some people remembered, there had been a recital of some sort, performed by the official of the lottery, a perfunctory, tuneless chant that had been rattled off duly each year; some people believed that the official of the lottery used to stand just so when he said or sang it, others believed that he was supposed to walk among the people, but years and years ago this part of the ritual had been allowed to lapse. There had been, also, a ritual salute, which the official of the lottery had had to use in addressing each person who came up to draw from the box, but this also had changed with time, until now it was felt necessary only for the official to speak to each person approaching. Mr. Summers was very good at all this; in his clean white shirt and blue jeans, with one hand resting carelessly on the black box, he seemed very proper and important as he talked interminably to Mr. Graves and the Martins.

Just as Mr. Summers finally left off talking and turned to the assembled villagers, 8 Mrs. Hutchinson came hurriedly along the path to the square, her sweater thrown over her shoulders, and slid into place in the back of the crowd. "Clean forgot what day it was," she said to Mrs. Delacroix, who stood next to her, and they both laughed softly. "Thought my old man was out back stacking wood," Mrs. Hutchinson went on, "and then I looked out the window and the kids was gone, and then I remembered it was the twenty-seventh and came a-running." She dried her hands on her apron, and Mrs. Delacroix said, "You're in time, though. They're still talking away up there."

Mrs. Hutchinson craned her neck to see through the crowd and found her hus- 9
band and children standing near the front. She tapped Mrs. Delacroix on the arm
as a farewell and began to make her way through the crowd. The people separated
good-humoredly to let her through; two or three people said, in voices just
loud enough to be heard across the crowd, "Here comes your Missus Hutchinson," and "Bill, she made it after all." Mrs. Hutchinson reached her husband, and
Mr. Summers, who had been waiting, said cheerfully, "Thought we were going to
have to get on without you, Tessie." Mrs. Hutchinson said, grinning, "Wouldn't
have me leave m'dishes in the sink, now, would you, Joe?," and soft laughter ran
through the crowd as the people stirred back into position after Mrs. Hutchinson's
arrival.

"Well, now," Mr. Summers said soberly, "guess we better get started, get this 10
over with, so's we can go back to work. Anybody ain't here?"

"Dunbar," several people said. "Dunbar, Dunbar." 11

Mr. Summers consulted his list. "Clyde Dunbar," he said. "That's right. He's 12
broke his leg, hasn't he? Who's drawing for him?"

"Me, I guess," a woman said, and Mr. Summers turned to look at her. "Wife 13
draws for her husband," Mr. Summers said. "Don't you have a grown boy to do it
for you, Janey?" Although Mr. Summers and everyone else in the village knew the
answer perfectly well, it was the business of the official of the lottery to ask such
questions formally. Mr. Summers waited with an expression of polite interest
while Mrs. Dunbar answered.

"Horace's not but sixteen yet," Mrs. Dunbar said regretfully. "Guess I gotta fill 14
in for the old man this year."

"Right," Mr. Summers said. He made a note on the list he was holding. Then he 15
asked, "Watson boy drawing this year?"

A tall boy in the crowd raised his hand. "Here," he said. "I'm drawing for 16
m'mother and me." He blinked his eyes nervously and ducked his head as several
voices in the crowd said things like "Good fellow, Jack," and "Glad to see your
mother's got a man to do it."

"Well," Mr. Summers said, "guess that's everyone. Old Man Warner make it?" 17

"Here," a voice said, and Mr. Summers nodded. 18

A sudden hush fell on the crowd as Mr. Summers cleared his throat and looked 19
at the list. "All ready?" he called. "Now, I'll read the names—heads of families
first—and the men come up and take a paper out of the box. Keep the paper folded
in your hand without looking at it until everyone has had a turn. Everything clear?"

The people had done it so many times that they only half listened to the direc- 20
tions; most of them were quiet, wetting their lips, not looking around. Then

Mr. Summers raised one hand high and said, "Adams." A man disengaged himself from the crowd and came forward. "Hi, Steve," Mr. Summers said, and Mr. Adams said, "Hi, Joe." They grinned at one another humorlessly and nervously. Then Mr. Adams reached into the black box and took out a folded paper. He held it firmly by one corner as he turned and went hastily back to his place in the crowd, where he stood a little apart from his family, not looking down at his hand.

"Allen," Mr. Summers said. "Anderson. . . . Bentham." 21

"Seems like there's no time at all between lotteries any more," Mrs. Delacroix 22 said to Mrs. Graves in the back row. "Seems like we got through with the last one only last week."

"Time sure goes fast," Mrs. Graves said. 23

"Clark. . . . Delacroix." 24

"There goes my old man," Mrs. Delacroix said. She held her breath while her 25 husband went forward.

"Dunbar," Mr. Summers said, and Mrs. Dunbar went steadily to the box while 26 one of the women said, "Go on, Janey," and another said, "There she goes."

"We're next," Mrs. Graves said. She watched while Mr. Graves came around 27 from the side of the box, greeted Mr. Summers gravely, and selected a slip of paper from the box. By now, all through the crowd there were men holding the small folded papers in their large hands, turning them over and over nervously. Mrs. Dunbar and her two sons stood together, Mrs. Dunbar holding the slip of paper.

"Harburt. . . . Hutchinson." 28

"Get up there, Bill," Mrs. Hutchinson said, and the people near her laughed. 29

"Jones." 30

"They do say," Mr. Adams said to Old Man Warner, who stood next to him, 31 "that over in the north village they're talking of giving up the lottery."

Why does Old Man Warner think the lottery is so important? See p. 460. Old Man Warner snorted. "Pack of crazy fools," he said. "Listening to the 32 young folks, nothing's good enough for *them*. Next thing you know, they'll be wanting to go back to living in caves, nobody work any more, live *that* way for a while. Used to be a saying about 'Lottery in June, corn be heavy soon.' First thing you know, we'd all be eating stewed chickweed and acorns. There's *always* been a lottery," he added petulantly. "Bad enough to see young Joe Summers up there joking with everybody."

"Some places have already quit lotteries," Mrs. Adams said. 33

"Nothing but trouble in *that*," Old Man Warner said stoutly. "Pack of young 34 fools."

"Martin." And Bobby Martin watched his father go forward. "Overdyke. . . . 35 Percy."

"I wish they'd hurry," Mrs. Dunbar said to her older son. "I wish they'd hurry." 36

"They're almost through," her son said. 37

"You get ready to run tell Dad," Mrs. Dunbar said.   38

Mr. Summers called his own name and then stepped forward precisely and   39
selected a slip from the box. Then he called, "Warner."

"Seventy-seventh year I been in the lottery," Old Man Warner said as he went   40
through the crowd. "Seventy-seventh time."

"Watson." The tall boy came awkwardly through the crowd. Someone said,   41
"Don't be nervous, Jack," and Mr. Summers said, "Take your time, son."

"Zanini."   42

After that, there was a long pause, a breathless pause, until Mr. Summers, holding   43
his slip of paper in the air, said, "All right, fellows." For a minute, no one moved,
and then all the slips of paper were opened. Suddenly, all the women began to
speak at once, saying, "Who is it?," "Who's got it?," "Is it the Dunbars?," "Is it the
Watsons?" Then the voices began to say, "It's Hutchinson. It's Bill," "Bill Hutchinson's got it."

"Go tell your father," Mrs. Dunbar said to her older son.   44

People began to look around to see the Hutchinsons. Bill Hutchinson was stand-   45
ing quiet, staring down at the paper in his hand. Suddenly, Tessie Hutchinson
shouted to Mr. Summers, "You didn't give him time enough to take any paper he
wanted. I saw you. It wasn't fair!"

"Be a good sport, Tessie," Mrs. Delacroix called, and Mrs. Graves said, "All of us   46
took the same chance."

"Shut up, Tessie," Bill Hutchinson said.   47

"Well, everyone," Mr. Summers said, "that was done pretty fast, and now we've   48
got to be hurrying a little more to get done in time." He consulted his next list.
"Bill," he said, "you draw for the Hutchinson family. You got any other households
in the Hutchinsons?"

"There's Don and Eva," Mrs. Hutchinson yelled. "Make *them* take their   49
chance!"

"Daughters draw with their husbands' families, Tessie," Mr. Summers said gen-   50
tly. "You know that as well as anyone else."

"It wasn't *fair*," Tessie said.   51

"I guess not, Joe," Bill Hutchinson said regretfully. "My daughter draws with   52
her husband's family, that's only fair. And I've got no other family except the
kids."

"Then, as far as drawing for families is concerned, it's you," Mr. Summers said   53
in explanation, "and as far as drawing for households is concerned, that's you, too.
Right?"

"Right," Bill Hutchinson said.   54

"How many kids, Bill?" Mr. Summers asked formally.   55

"Three," Bill Hutchinson said. "There's Bill, Jr., and Nancy, and little Dave. And   56
Tessie and me."

"All right, then," Mr. Summers said. "Harry, you got their tickets back?"   57

Mr. Graves nodded and held up the slips of paper. "Put them in the box, then,"   58
Mr. Summers directed. "Take Bill's and put it in."

"I think we ought to start over," Mrs. Hutchinson said, as quietly as she could.   59
"I tell you it wasn't *fair*. You didn't give him time enough to choose. *Every*body saw
that."

Mr. Graves had selected the five slips and put them in the box, and he dropped   60
all the papers but those onto the ground, where the breeze caught them and lifted
them off.

"Listen, everybody," Mrs. Hutchinson was saying to the people around her.   61

"Ready, Bill?" Mr. Summers asked, and Bill Hutchinson, with one quick glance   62
around at his wife and children, nodded.

"Remember," Mr. Summers said, "take the slips and keep them folded until   63
each person has taken one. Harry, you help little Dave." Mr. Graves took the hand
of the little boy, who came willingly with him up to the box. "Take a paper out of
the box, Davy," Mr. Summers said. Davy put his hand into the box and laughed.
"Take just *one* paper," Mr. Summers said. "Harry, you hold it for him." Mr. Graves
took the child's hand and removed the folded paper from the tight fist and held it
while little Dave stood next to him and looked up at him wonderingly.

"Nancy next," Mr. Summers said. Nancy was twelve, and her school friends   64
breathed heavily as she went forward, switching her skirt, and took a slip daintily
from the box. "Bill, Jr.," Mr. Summers said, and Billy, his face red and his feet over-
large, nearly knocked the box over as he got a paper out. "Tessie," Mr. Summers
said. She hesitated for a minute, looking around defiantly, and then set her lips and
went up to the box. She snatched a paper out and held it behind her.

"Bill," Mr. Summers said, and Bill Hutchinson reached into the box and felt   65
around, bringing his hand out at last with the slip of paper in it.

The crowd was quiet. A girl whispered, "I hope it's not Nancy," and the sound   66
of the whisper reached the edges of the crowd.

"It's not the way it used to be," Old Man Warner said clearly. "People ain't the   67
way they used to be."

"All right," Mr. Summers said. "Open the papers. Harry, you open little Dave's."   68

Mr. Graves opened the slip of paper and there was a general sigh through the   69
crowd as he held it up and everyone could see that it was blank. Nancy and Bill, Jr.,
opened theirs at the same time, and both beamed and laughed, turning around to
the crowd and holding their slips of paper above their heads.

"Tessie," Mr. Summers said. There was a pause, and then Mr. Summers looked   70
at Bill Hutchinson, and Bill unfolded his paper and showed it. It was blank.

"It's Tessie," Mr. Summers said, and his voice was hushed. "Show us her paper, Bill." 71

Bill Hutchinson went over to his wife and forced the slip of paper out of her hand. It had a black spot on it, the black spot Mr. Summers had made the night before with the heavy pencil in the coal-company office. Bill Hutchinson held it up, and there was a stir in the crowd. 72

"All right, folks," Mr. Summers said. "Let's finish quickly." 73

Although the villagers had forgotten the ritual and lost the original black box, they still remembered to use stones. The pile of stones the boys had made earlier was ready; there were stones on the ground with the blowing scraps of paper that had come out of the box. Mrs. Delacroix selected a stone so large she had to pick it up with both hands and turned to Mrs. Dunbar. "Come on," she said. "Hurry up." 74

Mrs. Dunbar had small stones in both hands, and she said, gasping for breath, "I can't run at all. You'll have to go ahead and I'll catch up with you." 75

The children had stones already, and someone gave little Davy Hutchinson a few pebbles. 76

Tessie Hutchinson was in the center of a cleared space by now, and she held her hands out desperately as the villagers moved in on her. "It isn't fair," she said. A stone hit her on the side of the head. 77

Old Man Warner was saying, "Come on, come on, everyone." Steve Adams was in the front of the crowd of villagers, with Mrs. Graves beside him. 78

"It isn't fair, it isn't right," Mrs. Hutchinson screamed, and then they were upon her. 79

READING CLOSELY

1. In Shirley Jackson's classic story, why do the villagers hold the lottery every year? What effect is it supposed to have?

2. What part of the country does "The Lottery" take place in? Why there and not, say, in southern California?

3. Why do the villagers use stones instead of knives or guns or some other means of killing the "winner" of the lottery?

4. Some of the younger people in the village want to do away with the ancient lottery. Who insists on keeping it? Why?

STRATEGIES AND STRUCTURES

1. Jackson does not assign a name or specific location to the village of her story. Why not? What is her PURPOSE in presenting her fictitious village as a generic place?

2. The people in "The Lottery" are typical folks. Point out specific aspects of their actions, speech, dress, roles in the community—even their names—that help Jackson to achieve this generalizing effect.

3. Suspense is the soul of the plot in Jackson's story. Suspense is usually achieved in a narrative by withholding information from the reader and then paying it out, either gradually or in larger bursts of revelation. Which method(s) does Jackson use here? Explain by pointing to specific passages in the story.

4. How does the SETTING of Jackson's narrative, including the weather and the time of the year, contribute to the PLOT of the story?

5. *Other Methods.* The villagers of Jackson's story assume that since the corn in their fields is "heavy" soon after the lottery, it must, therefore, grow and ripen *because of* the lottery (32). What's wrong with this kind of reasoning about cause and effect, and how does Jackson use it to undercut the ARGUMENT of the older villagers who say that established traditions must be maintained?

THINKING ABOUT LANGUAGE

1. What is a *scapegoat*? How and why does Mrs. Hutchinson play that role?

2. Mrs. Hutchinson dies by *lapidation*. Look up this word in your dictionary, and explain its etymology.

3. In the history of colonial America, who was Anne Hutchinson, and why might Jackson have chosen her last name for that of the doomed woman in her story?

4. Two of the principal figures in the affairs of the village are Mr. Summers, the owner of the coal company, and Mr. Graves, the postmaster. Explain the significance of their names.

5. The lottery itself, says Jackson, is steeped in "ritual" (6, 7, 74). Look up the definition of this word; how does it differ in meaning from *ceremony* or *celebration*?

FOR WRITING

1. In a paragraph like the first one in Jackson's story, write a brief NARRATIVE summing up the main activities of a group of people who are participating in a communal event, such as a parade, graduation, or funeral.

2. Write an essay analyzing how (and why) the spectators and participants typically behave at an athletic event, auction, concert, art show, or other gathering. Be sure to discuss the ritualistic or ceremonial aspects of the scene in your analysis.

CHAPTER 12

Argument

Come now, and let us reason together . . .   —ISAIAH 1:18

Well, do you want to have just one argument, or were you thinking of
taking a course?   —*Monty Python's Flying Circus*

For the sake of argument, let's assume that you are a parent, and you want your
children to grow up in a safe and healthy environment. Consequently, you
install a swimming pool in the backyard so they can learn to swim and get lots of
good exercise.

No sooner has the concrete dried on your new pool when your next-door neighbor comes over and says, "Nice pool."

"Yeah," you reply, "we want our children to be healthy and strong—swimming
is great exercise. Also, we want them to be safe; most of the earth's covered in
water, you know, and they should learn how to swim."

"Right," says your neighbor. "But a pool like that's not a good idea for little kids.
In fact, it's a safety hazard. Don't you know that far more children drown each year
than die from gunshot wounds? Your kids would be much safer if you tore out that
pool and bought a gun."

You disagree with your neighbor's belief that guns are safer than backyard swimming pools. Now you and your neighbor can *have* an argument—the kind that
might degenerate into a shouting match—or you can rationally question your
neighbor's claim and calmly state your own position on the matter. This second,
more rational sort of argument is the subject of this chapter.

Defining Argument:
Making and Supporting a Claim

When you construct an argument, you take a position on an issue and support that position with evidence. Suppose you believe that swimming pools are safe so long as they are properly fenced. This is your *claim*, and you can cite facts and figures, examples, expert testimony, or personal experience to support it.

In this chapter, we are going to examine how to make a claim and support it with evidence and logical reasoning. There are times, however, when logic isn't enough, so you will also learn how to appeal to your readers' emotions and how to establish your own credibility as a reliable person who deserves to be heard on ethical grounds. We'll also review the critical points to watch for as you read over and revise your essay, as well as common errors to avoid when you edit.

Why Do We Argue?

When we argue, we express our opinions and ideas in a way that gets others to take them seriously. Unlike statements of fact, opinions are not necessarily correct or incorrect. The ultimate purpose of a good argument is not to convince others that your claim is absolutely right or wrong. It is to demonstrate that it is plausible—

Barack Obama constructs this kind of argument, p. 560.

worth listening to, and maybe even acting upon. Many arguments, in fact, ask the reader to *explore* an issue, not just accept or reject a particular claim. Exploratory arguments are intended to open up discussion, to help us gain new knowledge, and even to lead to some kind of consensus.

Composing an Argument

Writing that *argues* a claim and asks readers to agree with it is sometimes distinguished from writing that seeks to *persuade* readers to take action. In this chapter, however, we will use the terms *argue* and *persuade* more or less interchangeably, because there's not much point in arguing that a claim is correct if you can't also persuade the reader that it's worth acting on.

Any claim worth making has more than one side, however; that is, rational people can disagree about it. We can all agree that backyard swimming pools can be dangerous under certain circumstances. We might reasonably disagree, however, on what those circumstances are and what to do about them.

When you make a claim, it should be arguable in this sense of being debatable. Some claims cannot reasonably be argued. For instance:

- *Matters of taste*: I hate broccoli.
- *Matters of faith*: And on the third day He arose.
- *Matters of fact*: In 1996, 742 children under age 10 drowned in the United States.

Matters of fact can be contested, of course. You might, for instance, know of a case of drowning that went unreported, and so you would point out that the figure ought to be 743 instead of 742. But a claim like this does not leave much room for debate. It can be established simply by checking the facts. An argument can collapse if its facts are wrong, but a good argument does not just state the facts. It argues something significant *about* the facts.

So when you compose a written argument, make sure your claim is arguable, or open to opinion—and that it's one you actually have a stake in. If you don't really care much about your topic, your reader probably won't either.

Thinking about Purpose and Audience

When you compose an argument, your purpose is to persuade other people to hear you out, to listen thoughtfully to what you have to say—even if they don't completely accept your views. Whatever your claim, your argument is more likely to appeal to your audience if it is tailored to their particular needs and interests.

For example, your next-door neighbor might be more inclined to accept a swimming pool in your backyard if, in addition to addressing the safety issue, you also argued that a nice pool would increase property values in the neighborhood. On the other hand, if you need to persuade the city planning department to issue you a permit so that you can build a pool, you'd be better off telling them that, because there is no public pool within a reasonable distance from your house, children in your neighborhood must now travel too far just to enjoy a swim during the summer.

So as you compose an argument, think about what your readers' views on the particular issue are likely to be. Of all the evidence you might present in support of your case, what kind would your intended readers most likely find reasonable and, thus, convincing?

Generating Ideas:
Finding Effective Evidence

You can start generating ideas for an argument by using the same techniques, like LISTING and BRAINSTORMING, that you use with other kinds of writing.

The most important question to ask as you think about your argument is *why*: Why should your audience accept your claim? What evidence—facts, figures, examples, and so on—can you provide to convince your readers that your claim is true? Let's look at some of the most effective types of evidence.

Suppose you want to argue that the SAT is unfair because it is biased in favor of certain socioeconomic groups. To support a claim like this effectively, you can use *facts, statistics, examples, expert testimony*, and *personal experience*.

Facts.   Because facts can be verified, they make good evidence for persuading readers to accept your point of view. In an essay arguing that the SAT favors the wealthy, for example, you might cite facts about the cost of tutors for the test:

> In New York City, a company called Advantage charges $500 for 50 minutes of coaching with their most experienced tutors and $165 for the same amount of time with their least experienced tutors.

Statistics.   A particularly useful form of evidence when you want to show a tendency or trend is statistics. This type of evidence is also verifiable and, thus, convincing to many readers. You could, for example, support your claim that the SAT favors the wealthy by citing statistics about income and test scores:

> On the 1992 SAT, test takers with family incomes over $70,000 scored an average of 1000 points out of a possible 1600. On the same SAT, test takers with family incomes of less than $10,000 scored an average of 767 points out of a possible 1600.

Examples.   Good examples make an argument more concrete and specific—and thus more likely to be understood and accepted by your audience. The following question, from an actual SAT exam, might be a good example of how the SAT favors wealthy students. The question asks the test taker to select a pair of words that matches the relationship expressed by the first pair:

RUNNER: MARATHON

(A) envoy: embassy

(B) martyr: massacre

(C) oarsman: regatta

(D) referee: tournament

(E) horse: stable

The correct answer is C: an oarsman competes in a regatta, an organized boat race, in much the same way as a runner competes in a marathon. But because regattas are, by and large, a pursuit of the wealthy, you could argue that the question favors the wealthy test taker—and so is a good example of socioeconomic bias in the SAT.

Expert testimony.   One of the most effective kinds of evidence is the direct testimony of experts in the field you are writing about. For example, to make a serious case against the SAT, you might quote a statement like this by Richard Atkinson, former president of the University of California: "Anyone involved in education should be concerned about how overemphasis on the SAT is distorting educational priorities and practices, how the test is perceived by many as unfair, and how it can have a devastating impact on the self-esteem and aspirations of young students. . . . There is widespread agreement that overemphasis on the SAT harms American education."

Personal experience.   Often you can effectively cite personal experience to support an argument, as with the following anecdote about how the SAT favors certain socioeconomic groups:

> No one in my family ever participated in a regatta—as a high school student, I didn't even know the meaning of the word. The only time I ever acted as an oarsman was in a leaky rowboat on Quarry Lake. So when I took the SAT a few years ago and encountered analogy questions that referred to regattas and other unfamiliar things, I barely broke 600 on the verbal aptitude section. Kenyon took me anyway, maybe because I play the violin. I graduated in the top ten percent of my class—with a combined major in music and English.

Many readers find personal testimony like this to be particularly moving, but be sure that any personal experience you cite as evidence is actually pertinent to the claim you're making.

No matter what type of evidence you present—whether facts and figures, examples, expert testimony, or personal experience—it must be pertinent to your argument and should be selected with an eye to convincing your audience that your claim is plausible and worth taking seriously.

> Sojourner Truth uses personal testimony to support her argument, p. 574.

Organizing and Drafting an Argument

Once you have a claim and evidence to support it, you're ready to start organizing and drafting your argument: to state your claim; appeal to your readers' needs and interests; and present yourself as trustworthy and reliable. You'll also need to anticipate and respond to likely objections. Finally, you'll want to think about which other methods of development, such as NARRATION and DEFINITION, might be useful in your argument. The templates on page 519 can help you get started.

ORGANIZING AN ARGUMENT

Claim and support. Any well-constructed argument is organized around these two basic elements. Let's consider an argument by an economist who teaches at the University of Chicago. In an editorial in the *Chicago Sun-Times* entitled "Pools More Dangerous Than Guns," Steven D. Levitt writes that "when it comes to children," a swimming pool in the backyard is more deadly than a gun in the house. This is Levitt's *claim.*

Levitt states this claim at the beginning of his argument, then gives evidence to support it in the next seven paragraphs of his essay. Most of his evidence is statistical: 742 drownings in one year, approximately 550 of those in residential pools; 6 million pools in the United States; 175 deaths as a result of guns; 200 million guns; one death per one million guns.

Levitt's evidence shows that approximately one child dies for every 11,000 pools in the United States, whereas one child dies for every one million guns. This is roughly a ratio of one hundred to one. Levitt concludes by connecting the dots for his readers when he says, "Thus, on average, the swimming pool is about 100 times more likely to kill a child than the gun is."

Levitt's argument follows a straightforward organization—claim, evidence, conclusion—that is effective for any argument:

1. State your claim clearly in your introduction.

2. In the main body of your argument, present evidence in support of your claim.

3. Develop the body of your argument until you have offered good reasons and sufficient evidence to support your claim.

4. In the conclusion, restate your claim and sum up how the evidence supports it.

STATING YOUR CLAIM

State your claim clearly and directly at the beginning of your argument—and take care not to claim more than you can possibly prove. As an arguable claim, "swimming pools are more dangerous than guns" is too broad. More dangerous for whom, we might ask? Under what circumstances?

We need to narrow this claim if we want to write an essay-length argument. We would do better to restate our claim as follows: "For young children who can't swim, swimming pools are more dangerous than guns." We have narrowed our claim to apply to a particular group, young children who do not yet know how to swim. Our claim could be still more restricted, however. In addition to narrowing it to a particular group, we could limit it to a particular kind of hazard. Thus we might write, "For young children who can't swim, *unprotected* swimming pools are more dangerous than guns." Because it is narrower, this is a more supportable claim than the one we started with.

TEMPLATES FOR DRAFTING

When you begin to draft an argument, you need to identify your subject and state the basic claim you plan to make about that subject—moves fundamental to any argument. See how Barack Obama makes these moves in his speech on "A More Perfect Union":

> [W]e cannot solve the challenges of our time unless we solve them together—unless we perfect our union by understanding that we may have different stories, but we hold common hopes; that we may not look the same and we may not have come from the same place, but we all want to move in the same direction—towards a better future for our children and our grandchildren.
>
> —BARACK OBAMA, "A More Perfect Union"

Obama identifies the subject of his argument ("the challenges of our time") and states his basic claim about that subject (that we must solve them together). Here is one more example from this chapter:

> Doping in sports isn't inherently wrong; it's wrong by the value system with which we judge sports.
>
> —JOE LINDSEY, "Why Legalizing Sports Doping Won't Work"

The following templates can help you make some of these basic moves in your own writing. But don't take these as formulas where you just fill in the blanks. There are no shortcuts to good writing, but these templates can serve as starting points.

▶ In this argument about X, the main point I want to make is _____.

▶ Others may say _____, but I would argue that _____.

▶ My contention about X is supported by the fact that _____.

▶ Additional facts that support this view of X are _____, _____, and _____.

▶ My own experience with X shows that _____.

▶ My view of X is supported by _____, who says that X is _____.

▶ What you should do about X is _____.

USING LOGICAL REASONING: INDUCTION AND DEDUCTION

When Steven Levitt writes "Thus, on average, the swimming pool is about 100 times more likely to kill a child than the gun is," he is using logical reasoning. For certain purposes—such as convincing a toddler to stay clear of an unguarded pool—logic is not very effective. In many writing situations, however, logical reasoning is indispensable for persuading others that your ideas and opinions are valid.

Thomas Jefferson uses both kinds effectively, p. 542.

There are two basic kinds of logical reasoning, *induction* and *deduction*. Induction is reasoning from particular evidence to a general conclusion. You reason inductively when you observe the cost of a gallon of gas at half-a-dozen service stations and conclude that the price of gas is uniformly high. Levitt uses induction in his argument about guns and swimming pools. He looks at the number of children who drowned in residential swimming pools in a particular year—550—and the number of children who died from gunshot wounds in the same year—175. Reasoning inductively from these particular cases, Levitt reaches his conclusion that pools are more dangerous than guns to young children.

Inductive reasoning is based on probability—it draws a conclusion from a limited number of specific cases. When you argue inductively, you are not claiming that a conclusion is certain but that it is likely. Even relatively few cases can provide you with the basis of a good inductive argument—if they are truly representative of a larger group. Exit polls of a few hundred people, for example, can often predict the outcome of an election involving thousands of voters. If it's truly representative, even a small sampling is sometimes enough. You would need only one or two cases of cholera on a high school swimming team, for instance, to infer that the pool in the gym is probably contaminated and that the whole school is in danger. Unless you take into account every possible individual case, though, inductive reasoning is never 100 percent certain: it usually requires an "inductive leap" at the end, as when you move from the individual cases of cholera on the team to the general inference that the school as a whole is threatened.

By contrast with induction, deduction moves from general principles to a particular conclusion. You reason deductively when your car stops running and—knowing that cars in general need fuel to run on and recalling that you started with half a tank and have been driving all day—you conclude that you are out of gas. Deductive arguments can be stated as SYLLOGISMS, which have a major premise, a minor premise, and a conclusion. For example:

Major premise: All unguarded swimming pools are dangerous.

Minor premise: This pool is unguarded.

Conclusion: This pool is dangerous.

This is a valid syllogism, meaning that the conclusion follows logically from the premises.

The great advantage of deduction over induction is that it deals with logical certainty rather than mere probability. As long as the premises you begin with are true and the syllogism is properly constructed, the conclusion must be true. You can run into trouble, however, when one or more of the premises are false, or when the syllogism isn't constructed properly.

In a properly constructed syllogism, the conclusion links the first part of the minor premise ("this pool") to the second part of the major premise ("dangerous"). One of the most common mistakes that people make in constructing syllogisms is simply repeating, in the minor premise, the trait named at the end of the major premise, as in the following example:

AN INVALID SYLLOGISM

Major premise: All planets are round.

Minor premise: My head is round.

Conclusion: My head is a planet.

Being round is a characteristic that "planets" and "my head" share, but many other things are round, too. A diagram can help us see why this syllogism doesn't work:

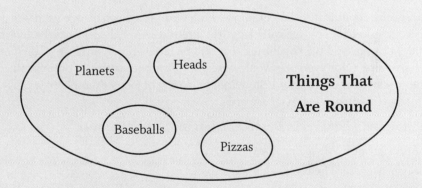

As this diagram illustrates, just being round doesn't mean that planets and heads have much else in common; in fact, they belong to entirely separate categories within the larger one of things that are round.

Advertisers use this kind of faulty reasoning all the time to try to convince you that you must buy their products if you want to be a cool person. Such reasoning is faulty because even if you accept the premise that, for example, all people who buy motorcycles are cool, there are lots of cool people who don't buy motorcycles—as indicated by the following diagram:

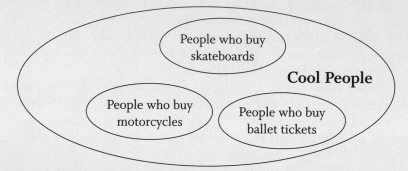

PROPERLY CONSTRUCTED SYLLOGISMS

Major premise: All planets are round.

Minor premise: Earth is a planet.

Conclusion: Earth is round.

Major premise: All people who buy motorcycles are cool.

Minor premise: Susan has bought a motorcycle.

Conclusion: Susan is cool.

Not so sure about this second example? Both of these syllogisms are valid—that is, the conclusion follows logically from the premises. A syllogism can be logically valid, however, and the conclusion may still be false—if one or more of the premises are false. (Not everyone would agree, for example, with the premise that all motorcycle owners are cool.) Study the following obvious example of a properly constructed syllogism with a false premise.

A PROPERLY CONSTRUCTED SYLLOGISM WITH A FALSE PREMISE

Major premise: All spiders have six legs.

Minor premise: The black widow is a spider.

Conclusion: The black widow has six legs.

The conclusion that black widows have six legs is logical, given the premises of this argument. However, since the major premise of the argument is wrong—spiders actually have eight legs—the conclusion of the argument is also wrong.

When you use deduction in your writing, your reader is less likely to question your reasoning if your argument follows the logic of a properly constructed syllogism or other model argument, such as one constructed by using the Toulmin method (see next page). Be prepared, however, to defend your premises if they are

THE TOULMIN METHOD

In a formal deductive argument, we begin with two general principles and draw a conclusion based on the logical relationship between them. In practical arguments, however, as the British philosopher Stephen Toulmin recognized, we often begin with a conclusion and look around for evidence to support it. Recognizing this less formal kind of deduction, Toulmin devised a system of argument that combines both logic and observation.

In Toulmin's system, an argument is made up of three basic parts: the *claim*, the *grounds*, and the *warrant*. For example:

Claim: Steven Spielberg is the greatest director in the history of film.
Grounds: His films have grossed more than those of any other director.
Warrant: The best measure of a film's quality is financial success.

The claim is the main point the argument is intended to prove. The grounds are the evidence on which that claim is based. And the warrant is the reason that the grounds justify the claim.

In a Toulmin argument, the grounds can be facts, statistics, examples, expert testimony, personal experience, or other kinds of evidence. It is an observable fact, for instance, that Spielberg has grossed approximately $8 billion at the box office—more than any other director in film history.

Though they constitute grounds for a claim, facts and other data are not alone sufficient, in Toulmin's view, to support that claim completely. It takes logic as well: a warrant is needed to explain how and why the grounds logically justify the claim. In this case, the warrant for accepting the claim about Spielberg as the world's greatest filmmaker is the assumption that films and directors are best judged by how much money they make.

Not everyone would agree with this assumption, of course. Most real-life arguments, in fact, are about the assumptions on which the argument is based. But breaking an argument down into Toulmin's three parts can be especially useful for spotting faulty or unstated assumptions—so you can strengthen them in your own arguments or question them in the arguments of others.

not as self-evident as "spiders have eight legs" or "all humans are mortal." If you are arguing, for example, that intelligent design should be taught in science classes, you might structure your basic argument like this:

Major premise: All scientific theories should be taught in science classes.

Minor premise: Intelligent design is scientific theory.

Conclusion: Intelligent design should be taught in science classes.

This is a well-constructed deductive argument. As long as your readers accept the premises—particularly the minor premise about the scientific nature of intelligent design—they will probably accept your conclusion. If you believe, however, that some readers may disagree with the premises of your argument—and you still hope to convince them—you should provide strong evidence to support those premises. Or, if necessary, you should consider how you might rework your premises altogether.

USING INDUCTION AND DEDUCTION IN VARIOUS ACADEMIC FIELDS

Because it draws upon observation and the analysis of particular data, induction is the method you are most likely to use when you construct an argument in the fields of engineering and the applied sciences. In the humanities and social sciences, induction is also particularly useful for analyzing specific written texts (the poems of Rita Dove, the letters of John Adams, a set of questionnaires) and for drawing general conclusions about them. You also use inductive reasoning when you cite personal experience as evidence, because you are arguing that something you observed or experienced personally has general significance for others.

Deductive reasoning, on the other hand, is particularly useful for constructing arguments in the fields of philosophy, ethics, theology, and the more theoretical sciences, such as mathematics and physics, where particular cases tend to be subject to universal principles (such as $E=MC^2$). For example, the argument that a large round object recently discovered in the night sky should be classified as a planet because it meets all the criteria that define planets in general would be a deductive argument.

AVOIDING LOGICAL FALLACIES

Logical fallacies are errors in logical reasoning. Though they can seem plausible and even persuasive, they lead to wrong-headed conclusions. Here are some of the most common logical fallacies to watch out for when you write (and read).

Post hoc, ergo propter hoc.   Latin for "after this, therefore because of this," this kind of faulty reasoning assumes that just because one event (such as rain) comes after another event (a rain dance), it occurs *because* of the first event. For example: "Soon after the country declared war, the divorce rate increased. War is harmful to marriages." Just because the country declared war before the divorce rate went up doesn't mean the declaration caused the increase.

Non sequitur.   Latin for "does not follow," a non sequitur is a statement that has little or no logical connection to the preceding statement: "The early Egyptians were masters of architecture and geometry. Thus they created a vast network of trade and commerce throughout the ancient world." Since mastering architecture and geometry has little to do with trade, this second statement is a non sequitur.

Begging the question.   An argument that takes for granted what it is supposed to prove: "Americans should be required to carry ID cards because Americans need to be prepared to prove their identity." This conclusion assumes that Americans need to prove their identities.

Appeal to doubtful authority.   This is the fallacy of citing as expert testimony the opinions of people who do not necessarily have special knowledge of the issue: "According to Madonna, the candidate who takes South Carolina will win the election." Madonna isn't an expert on politics, so citing her opinion on political matters to support an argument is an appeal to doubtful authority.

Ad hominem.   This fallacy attacks the person making an argument instead of addressing the actual issue: "She's the head of the union, and she's crazy. Don't pay any attention to her views on the economy." Saying she's the head of a union and calling her crazy focuses on her as a person rather than on her views of the issue.

Michael Lewis' little daughter employs an *ad hominem* attack on p. 578.

Either/or reasoning.   This fallacy, sometimes called a "false dilemma," treats a complicated issue as if it had only two sides: "Either you believe that God created the universe according to His plan, which is the view of religion; or you believe that the universe evolved randomly, which is the view of science." This statement doesn't allow for beliefs outside of these two options.

Hasty generalization.   This fallacy draws a conclusion based on far too little evidence: "In all four of the stories by Edgar Allan Poe that we read for English 201, the narrator is mentally ill. Poe himself must have been mad." There is not nearly enough evidence here to determine Poe's mental health.

False analogy.   This fallacy is committed when an argument is based on a faulty comparison: "Children are like dogs. A happy dog is a disciplined dog, and a happy child is one who knows the rules and is taught to obey them." Dogs and children aren't enough alike to assume that what is good for one is good for the other.

APPEALING TO YOUR READER'S EMOTIONS

Sound logical reasoning is hard to refute, but sometimes, in order to persuade readers to accept your claim, it will help to appeal to their emotions as well.

As an economist writing for a general audience, Steven Levitt knows that people often find numbers dry and unmoving. So after citing statistics to support his point that swimming pools are more dangerous than guns, he goes on to appeal to the emotions and feelings of his readers.

Levitt's purpose is not to promote guns; it is to alert parents to what he considers "an even greater threat to their children." Observing that a child can drown in only thirty seconds and that child drownings are "typically silent," Levitt warns parents not to let their guard down even for an instant, lest a pool (or even a bucket of water) "steal your child's life."

Steal is a carefully chosen word here. It implies evil intent—the pool lies in wait for the child, like a thief. We are well beyond logic and statistics now. Evil that is quick and silent demands an ever-watchful parent: "Simply stated, keeping your children safe around water is one of the single most important things a parent can do to protect a child."

For a classic appeal to emotion, see "I Have a Dream," p. 553.

Emotional? Of course. But this is emotionalism in a good cause, carefully applied to support a well-reasoned argument. And often, the best way to urge your readers to action is by tugging at their heartstrings. When you appeal to the reader's emotions, however, be careful to avoid sensationalism and alarmism—they can undermine your argument. So after sounding the alarm, Levitt calmly directs readers to the website of the U.S. Consumer Products Safety Commission, which "offers a publication detailing some simple steps for safeguarding pools."

ESTABLISHING YOUR OWN CREDIBILITY

When you construct an argument, you can demonstrate with irrefutable logic that what you have to say is valid and true. And you can appeal to the reader's emotions with genuine fervor. Your words may still fall on deaf ears, however, if your readers don't fully trust you. What makes Levitt's argument so credible in the end is that he himself has lost a child.

Levitt's first child, Andrew, did not drown. When the boy was just over a year old, he came down with meningitis and, within two days, died in the hospital. Levitt wrote his essay, in part, to channel a father's grief, which gives him an emotional and ethical authority that nothing else could. "As a father who has lost a son," Levitt writes, "I know first-hand the unbearable pain that comes with a child's death."

Levitt's loss is different in one crucial regard from that of the parent whose child dies in an unguarded swimming pool. "Amidst my grief," he says, "I am able to take some small solace in the fact that everything possible was done to fight the disease that took my son's life." Having said this, the grieving father closes with a final appeal to the reader, whom he addresses directly in the second person: "If my son had died in a backyard pool due to my own negligence, I would not even have that to cling to. . . . Parents who have lost children would do anything to get their babies back. . . . Safeguard your pool so you don't become one of us." You don't need to have children or a swimming pool to recognize the power of such an argument. Nor do you need such a close, personal tie to your subject in order to establish your own credibility.

There are many less dramatic ways to establish your credibility when you construct an argument. Readers are more likely to trust you, for example, if they feel you are presenting the issues objectively. So acknowledge opposing points of view, and treat them fairly and accurately. Then look for common ground where you and your reader can come together not just logically but psychologically. (For tips on how to do this, see the discussion of Rogerian logic on page 528.)

If you have experience or special expertise in your subject, let your readers know. For instance, if you're arguing that American ballet companies require their dancers to be too thin and you danced with a professional ballet company for three years, tell your readers that. Also, pay close attention to the tone of your argument. Whether you come across as calm and reasonable or full of righteous anger, your tone will say much about your own values and motives for writing—and about you as a person. Nothing does more to establish your credibility with your readers than to persuade them that they are listening to the words of a moral and ethical person who shares their values and understands their concerns.

Chief Seattle, p. 547, is the "good man speaking" of classical rhetoric.

ANTICIPATING OTHER ARGUMENTS

As you construct an argument, it's important to consider viewpoints other than your own, including objections that others might raise to your argument. Anticipating other arguments, in fact, is yet another way to establish your credibility and win the reader's confidence. Readers are more likely to see you as trustworthy if, instead of ignoring an opposing argument, you state it fairly and accurately and then refute it—by showing that the reasoning is faulty or that the evidence is insufficient or that the argument fails to consider some key aspect of the subject.

For instance, suppose you think that private ownership of firearms is a deterrent to crime and you oppose stricter gun-control laws. Some of your readers, however, may believe that private ownership of guns actually *increases* crime, and they may be prepared to cite studies showing that there are more homicides in places where there are more guns.

Anticipating this argument, you might refute it by saying, "Proponents of stricter gun-control legislation are right when they cite studies showing that more homicides occur in places where more people have guns. However, such studies refer, by and large, to 'loose' firearms. The situation is different where guns are protected—kept under lock and key where a child or intruder can't get to them. Responsible gun ownership actually reduces crime." Proponents of stricter gun controls still may not be entirely convinced, but they are far more likely to listen to your argument because you readily admit that guns can be dangerous and you address, head-on, a major point of opposition to your views.

Even when you do not have a ready response to an opposing argument, you'll still want to acknowledge it in order to show that you've thought carefully about all aspects of the issue.

USING ROGERIAN ARGUMENT

The psychologist Carl Rogers recognized that people are much more likely to listen to someone they feel is listening to them. If you want to persuade others to accept your views, Rogers reasoned, it is better to treat them as colleagues rather than adversaries. Instead of an "I'm right and you're wrong" approach, therefore, Rogers recommended using "win-win" strategies of argument that invite collaboration and consensus rather than confrontation and conflict. In other words, instead of having an argument, the Rogerian approach says, with Isaiah, "Come let us reason together."

To use Rogerian methods of argument in your own writing, you need to show your audience that you are well aware that the issue at hand can be viewed in different lights and that you have thoughtfully considered viewpoints other than your own. To do this, summarize opposing viewpoints carefully and accurately, and acknowledge their merit. Then introduce your views and look for common ground between them and the views of others. Explain how your views address these common concerns and what additional advantages they have, and give evidence in support of your point of view.

For example, suppose that you are in favor of greater gun-control legislation. Instead of lashing out at all gun owners, however, you decide to try a more conciliatory, Rogerian approach. You might begin by acknowledging that the U.S. Constitution guarantees certain rights to individuals, in particular the right to self-defense and to protect personal property. You might also acknowledge that many people, including hunters and target shooters, look on certain types of guns as gear or sporting goods. Others view them as collectibles and are interested in their history and manufacture.

Once you have shown your genuine concern and respect for the rights and enthusiasms of gun owners, you could look for ways in which gun-control legislation may actually serve their interests. For example, you might point out that strict licensing and training in the proper handling of firearms can help reduce injury and death among those who use guns for sport. In the event of theft, you might note, enforced registration of guns would also help collectors and other owners of valuable firearms to retrieve their stolen property. You might even concede that stricter gun-control legislation probably is not necessary in the case of people who already abide by existing gun-control laws, own guns legally, and use them responsibly. Having established as much common ground as you can among the parties in the gun-control debate, you are now ready to introduce and explain your position.

You favor stricter gun controls, even to the point of banishing firearms altogether. Why? You believe that guns are inherently dangerous and that they can fall into the hands of people who do not abide by the rules. Also, they can be *accidentally* misused. Wouldn't society as a whole be better off, you wonder, if guns were all but impossible to obtain—even if that meant curtailing the rights of some individuals? You realize that not everyone will agree with this position; but having made clear that you understand and sympathize with the views of the other side, you can reasonably expect that those who might otherwise dismiss your claims out of hand will be more inclined to listen to you. And you can even hope that readers who are not committed to either point of view will be more likely to adopt yours.

USING OTHER METHODS

Each method of writing discussed in chapters 4–11 can be useful when you construct an argument. If you are arguing for (or against) stricter gun-control laws, for example, you will need to DEFINE the present rules and what you mean by "stricter" ones. You may also need to use CAUSE-AND-EFFECT analysis to explain what good (or harm) new laws would do. Or you may want to COMPARE AND CONTRAST the old laws with the new ones; or draw on PROCESS ANALYSIS to explain how the new laws will be enforced.

Reading an Argument with a Critical Eye

Once you have a draft of your argument, ask someone to read it and tell you where your case seems particularly convincing and where it seems to break down. Then read the argument again critically yourself. Here are some questions to keep in mind when checking a written argument.

PURPOSE AND AUDIENCE. What is the basic purpose of the argument—To inform? To move the reader to action? Some other purpose? How well does the argument achieve its purpose? How might it be revised to do so better? Who is the intended audience? What will they already know about the topic, and will they need any additional background information? What are their views likely to be on the topic?

THE CLAIM. What is the claim? Is it stated clearly and directly in a THESIS statement? If not, should it be? Is it arguable—could reasonable people disagree about it? Is the claim limited enough to be covered well? If not, how could it be narrowed down further? Is it clear why this claim is significant, and why the reader should care about it?

EVIDENCE. What evidence is given to support the claim? Is it factually correct? If personal experience is cited as evidence, is it pertinent? Is the evidence sufficient to support the claim, or is additional evidence needed? What kind?

LOGICAL REASONING. How well do the parts of the essay hold together? What kind of reasoning connects the evidence with the claim—inductive? deductive? both? In general, how *convincing* is the argument? How could it be strengthened?

EMOTIONAL APPEALS. Does the argument appeal to readers' emotions? If so, to what end—to evoke readers' concerns, to move them to action? Is any emotional appeal sufficiently restrained? Is it convincing? If there's no emotional appeal, should there be?

CREDIBILITY. What kind of person does the author of this argument seem to be? Does he or she come across as an ethical person of good character who shares and respects readers' values? If not, what changes could convey that credibility? What special experience or knowledge, if any, does the author bring to this particular issue? In sum, does the author seem trustworthy?

ANTICIPATING OTHER ARGUMENTS. What other arguments might someone make about the topic? What objections might they raise to the claim? Are other arguments respectfully acknowledged and, where possible, refuted?

OTHER METHODS. What other methods of development does the argument use? For example, does it DEFINE the issues clearly? Does it analyze CAUSES AND EFFECTS? If other methods are not used, where might they be helpful?

Editing for Common Errors in Arguments

Certain errors in punctuation and usage are common in arguments. The following guidelines will help you check for such problems—and edit them as needed.

Check your punctuation with such connecting words as *if, therefore, thus, consequently, however, nevertheless,* and *because*

When the connecting word comes at the beginning of a sentence and links it to an earlier statement, the connecting word should be followed by a comma:

▶ Therefore‚ the minimum legal drinking age should not be lowered to age 18.

▶ Consequently‚ stronger immigration laws will be unnecessary.

When the connecting word comes at the beginning of a sentence and is part of an introductory clause—a group of words that includes a subject and verb—the entire clause should be followed by a comma:

▶ Because guest workers will be legally registered‚ stronger immigration laws will be unnecessary.

▶ If acting legally is just as easy as acting illegally‚ most people will choose the legal course of action.

When the connecting word indicates a logical relationship between two independent clauses—such as cause and effect, sequence, comparison, or contrast—the word is usually preceded by a semicolon and followed by a comma:

▶ Many of the best surgeons have the highest rates of malpractice‚ thus‚ the three-strikes-and-you're-out rule for taking away a doctor's license may do more harm than good.

When the connecting word comes in the middle of an independent clause, it should be set off by commas:

▶ A physician who removes the wrong leg‚ however‚ deserves a much harsher penalty than one who forgets to remove a sponge.

Check for common usage errors

HOWEVER, NEVERTHELESS

Use *however* when you acknowledge a different argument but want to minimize its consequence:

▶ The surgeon may have been negligent; ~~nevertheless,~~ <u>however,</u> he should not lose his license because the patient lied about the dosage he was taking.

Use *nevertheless* when you acknowledge a different argument but wish to argue for a harsher consequence anyway:

▶ The surgeon may not have been negligent; ~~however,~~ <u>nevertheless,</u> he should lose his license because the patient died.

IMPLY, INFER

Use *imply* when you mean "to state indirectly":

▸ The coach's speech ~~inferred~~ implied that he expected the team to lose the game.

Use *infer* when you mean "to draw a conclusion":

▸ From the coach's speech, the fans ~~implied~~ inferred that the team would lose the game.

Student Example

Matthew Douglas wrote "The Evil Empire?" in 2008 as an undergraduate in the School of Humanities and Sciences at Ithaca College in upstate New York. The essay about shopping at Walmart was his winning entry in a contest sponsored by the college's Department of Writing.

In 2011, according to the company's website, Walmart Stores, Inc., had "more than 9029 retail units under 60 different banners in 15 countries." What kind of empire has the giant established? "The Evil Empire?" takes a critical look at the discount ethic as practiced by one of America's largest retailers—and at the culture it mirrors.

> Douglas begins his argument with a brief NARRATIVE of the Walmart shopping experience

The Evil Empire?

"Hi, welcome to Walmart," says the greeter. You smile back politely in acknowledgement before you quickly enter the store. You have to shop. You have to find the best deals. You fill your cart with disposable razors, diapers for the baby, socks, batteries, dog biscuits, skim milk, chocolate candies, white bread, gum, mayonnaise, chunk cheese, your favorite magazine, and a few impulse buys with prices too good to pass up. It was just a quick visit today. You make your way to the register and the cashier rings up your items and tells you the total damage to your wallet. You smile to yourself knowing you saved a bundle of time and money. Walmart is your one stop shop. You leave the store with bags in hand, only to find a chanting mob outside the store: volunteers for the union. They yell out many of Walmart's faults: its discrimination toward women, its dismal health care benefits, and its barely livable wages. You wonder how much of this is true. You've heard these arguments before, but look at how much money Walmart saves you. Is it really as bad as the union says? Is Walmart some dark empire, or the chosen target for some of the many problems American consumerism has created? Has the company been singled out unfairly?

The key question to be addressed in Douglas' argument

Within fifty years Walmart has grown from a few stores in Arkansas to a multibillion-dollar corporation that spans the entire United States and many countries around the globe. Sam Walton opened the first Wal-Mart in 1962 to save the customer money, which is the Walmart motto. Expanding rapidly nationally and internationally, Walmart consists of more than 6,200 facilities and 1.6 million employees worldwide. Walmart affects millions of lives on a daily basis: over 138 million global customers visit the store each week ("Walmart Facts"). With numbers like these it's obvious how influential Walmart is both nationally and internationally. Walmart saves its shoppers money with every shopping experience. But many critics dislike the methods Walmart uses to save its consumers money.

Gives history and background information about Walmart

While so many vilify Walmart for its sins, few look at the big picture: if Walmart were to disappear off the face of the earth, other companies like it would still pay minimum wage to save you and me money. What about Target or Kmart? Walmart is not an evil, all-consuming empire but a product of its times. American culture made stores like Walmart possible; it is the consumerist culture that epitomizes America. It is the *need*, the *demand* for more stuff, and our desire for material wealth that fills our closets, our drawers, and our garages. As consumers we want the new, the flashy, and we want it now for a discount price. While I have oversimplified American consumerism and made it sound like the only factor, which it is not, consumerism is definitely a large contributor to big retail chains. Walmart, along with other big business stores like it, fulfills the desire for stuff and saves the consumer millions. In fact, Walmart saves its customers about $16 billion a year, writes Harvard business professor Pankaj Ghemawat and business consultant Ken

THESIS statement

2

3

Mark. But in order to pass on these savings to the consumer, Walmart associates receive what many believe to be sub-par healthcare coverage and salaries. Critics also charge that Walmart destroys local businesses and communities. In addition to unfairly targeting Walmart, many overlook the company's openness to criticism and willingness to change.

Introduces an important opposing viewpoint

According to freelance writer Liza Featherstone, Walmart is as bad 4 as the unions proclaim the corporation to be. Featherstone strongly criticizes Walmart in her 2005 article "Down and Out in Discount America." Walmart's obsession with saving the customer money, she argues, has a price. Its employees largely pay for that price in the form of low wages. According to Featherstone, the average Walmart worker makes just over $8 an hour (about $15,000 a year). She cites Al Zack, former vice president for strategic programs of United Food and Commercial Workers, who claims Walmart "needs to create more poverty to grow." Featherstone creates a comparison between Walmart and Henry Ford. Where Ford paid his employees plenty so they could buy Ford cars, Walmart does the opposite. Walmart's low wages help to keep poverty going, Featherstone reasons, thus allowing Walmart to grow. The low wages also keep them from being able to shop anywhere else but at Walmart. She claims Walmart uses welfare to supplement its low paycheck, citing that Walmart encourages its workers to apply for federal assistance. So it is the taxpayers' dollars that help Walmart associates get by (Featherstone). But, unfortunately, these are realities in retail. And Walmart is not alone. It is the price that some must pay so that American consumers can enjoy discount prices. Minimum wage helps to make these discount prices possible.

Today, the average American Walmart employee makes close to 5 $11 an hour (around $21,000 a year). This may not seem like much, but it is above the poverty line. Currently, Walmart's pay is four dollars higher than the federal minimum wage. Even when Featherstone's article was up to date in 2005, Walmart was still several dollars above the federal minimum wage ("Walmart Facts").

Cites Douglas' personal experience as EVIDENCE

I have held a part-time job at Price Chopper, a northeast grocery store chain, for five years, and I have yet to make $9 an hour. It is how the retail world works. To keep prices low for the customer, companies pay minimum wage, cut worker hours, and offer minimum healthcare. "The fact is," writes Robert Reich, former secretary of labor for President Bill Clinton, "today's economy offers us a Faustian bargain: it can give consumers deals largely because it hammers workers."

Besides Walmart's low pay, people criticize the company's healthcare. The plan is said to be too expensive for the average Walmart employee to afford. Thus, many reason, few Walmart associates have insurance. However, this is not the case. Walmart reported that as of this year, 92.7 percent of its employees had health insurance, a two percent increase from last year. In fact, the national average of uninsured workers nationwide is significantly higher than the number of Walmart employees that lack coverage. The U.S. Census Bureau recently announced 17.7 percent of Americans do not have healthcare, versus the 7.3 percent of Walmart's workers who lack coverage. Walmart's insurance includes medical and dental benefits but not eye care. But what it is short of, the company is trying to make up for. This year Walmart partnered with 1-800-CONTACTS in an effort to "help drive down healthcare costs." The long-term agreement will bring contact lenses to Walmart customers at lower costs. The two companies estimate this partnership could save consumers $400 million in the next three years. And because many of Walmart's employees are also Walmart customers, they will also be able to partake in this benefit (employees can even use their Walmart discount, which will help to save them even more money). Walmart also offers and continues to expand its $4 prescription plan. "Our $4 prescription program is proof that Wal-Mart is committed to meeting America's healthcare challenges," says Dr. John Agwunobi, senior vice president and president for Walmart's professional services division ("Walmart Facts").

6

> Refutes the position of unspecified naysayers

Walmart is also believed to be the sole cause for running small family businesses into the ground. Freelance writer Floyd McKay

7

reasons local downtowns become ghost towns when big-box retailers such as Walmart move in. He writes, "Wal-Mart is like a neutron bomb, sucking life out of small towns, leaving buildings without the essence of civic life." Critics like McKay state mom and pop stores cannot compete with Walmart's discount prices, forcing the small businesses to close for good.

Refutes McKay's argument ......•

However, business columnist Steve Maich counters that Walmart 8 actually boosts local economy rather than destroying it. Maich cites Carol Foote's experience with Walmart as an example of how the company helped her town. In 2000 Foote helped to organize bringing a Walmart to her hometown, Miramichi, New Brunswick. Critics warned Foote and other Walmart supporters that it would ruin local businesses. However, Foote suspected Walmart would invigorate local businesses just as it had done throughout the rest of Canada. She turned out to be right. In 2002, Ryerson University completed a major study of Walmart's impact on small retailers. What they found was the opening of big-box retailers like Walmart was an economic boon for the whole area: attracting other retailers and driving up sales at nearby stores. The study concluded, "It is difficult to make the case that a Walmart store actually puts other retailers out of business." Two years later, a survey conducted by Canadian Imperial Bank of Commerce found that of the 1,800 small businesses that participated in its study, the vast majority claimed Walmart had little or no impact on them. "And while critics portray [Walmart] as the work of a ravenous invading force," writes Maich, "the truth is most communities reached out to Wal-Mart and embraced it." Communities such as Miramichi. Foote says Walmart has created dozens of jobs for her hometown and "brought new life to the town's small commercial district" (qtd. in Maich).

Conclusion restates Douglas' thesis—with variations ......•

Like anything man-made, Walmart has its defects. I am not 9 saying Walmart is blameless. I am saying Walmart is not the only corporation at fault. Furthermore, the company knows it has flaws and is responding to them. Some of their responses include $4 prescriptions and the company's partnership with 1-800-CONTACTS.

Walmart is also committed to saving the environment. The company
has helped to permanently conserve 395,000 acres of land for critical
wildlife habitats. Walmart has also opened two experimental super-
centers built out of recycled materials; vegetable and motor oils heat
the stores. The two stores are dedicated to sustainability and will
lead the way in finding methods to apply environmental practices to
other Walmart facilities ("Walmart Facts"). Walmart is adapting and
in ways that other companies are not. It is this openness to change
that proves Walmart is concerned about more things than making a
quick buck. Many people often deem change too scary or too risky.
Yet Walmart takes such risks and creates good reforms that benefit
millions of lives each and every day. While Walmart is far from
perfect, it is not the evil empire many critics have made it out to be.

> Gives Douglas'
> final answer to
> the question
> raised in his
> title

Works Cited

Featherstone, Liza. "Down and Out in Discount America." *Nation*.
 Nation, 3 Jan. 2005. Web. 26 Mar. 2008.

Ghemawat, Pankaj, and Ken A. Mark. "The Price Is Right." *New York
 Times*. New York Times Company, 3 Aug. 2005. Web. 26 Mar.
 2008.

Maich, Steve. "Why Walmart Is Good." *Maclean's*. Rogers
 Publishing, 25 Jul. 2005. Web. 20 Mar. 2008.

McKay, Floyd J. "Walmart Nation: The Race to the Bottom." *Seattle
 Times*. Seattle Times Company, 18 Feb. 2004. Web. 21 Mar.
 2008.

Reich, Robert B. "Don't Blame Walmart." *New York Times*. New York
 Times Company, 28 Feb. 2005. Web. 13 Mar. 2008.

"Walmart Facts." *Walmart Corporate*. Walmart Stores, Inc., 2008.
 Web. 17 Mar. 2008.

Analyzing a Student Argument

In "The Evil Empire?" Matthew Douglas draws upon rhetorical strategies and techniques that good writers use all the time when they construct arguments. The following questions, in addition to focusing on particular aspects of Douglas' text, will help you to identify those common strategies and techniques so you can adapt them to your own writing. These questions will also help to prepare you for the analytical questions—on content, structure, and language—that you'll find after all the other selections in this chapter, along with suggestions for writing on related topics.

READING CLOSELY

1. If we look at "the big picture," says Matthew Douglas in answer to the question raised by his title, "Walmart is not an evil, all consuming empire" (3). If the retail giant is not "evil" in Douglas view, what *is* it? Do you agree? Why or why not?

2. "It is the price that some must pay so that American consumers can enjoy discount prices" (4). What "price" is Douglas referring to here? Is that price acceptable in your opinion? Why or why not?

3. According to Douglas, what are some of the steps that Walmart is taking to correct its perceived "flaws" (9)? Are these changes substantial, or are they aimed at better public relations. Or both? Explain.

STRATEGIES AND STRUCTURES

1. What is the purpose of the brief NARRATIVE, in Douglas' opening paragraph, about going to shop at Walmart and encountering a "chanting mob" upon leaving the store (1)? Why does Douglas tell this story in the second person (*you*) instead of the more common first person (*I*)? Is this an effective strategy? Why or why not?

2. Douglas first states the THESIS of his argument as follows: "Walmart is not an evil, all-consuming empire but a product of its times" (3). How and where does Douglas make adjustments to this thesis as his argument develops? Is this a legitimate strategy, or should an argument always conclude by rehearsing the exact CLAIM it started with? Explain.

3. Using freelance writers Liza Featherstone and Floyd McKay as naysayers, Douglas cites two main counterarguments to his claim about the benevolence of Walmart (4, 7). What are they? How and how well does he deal with each counter-claim? Point to specific EVIDENCE in his argument, and explain why you find it particularly convincing or otherwise.

4. "Like anything man-made, Walmart has its defects" (9). What assumptions does this statement make? Are they justified? Why or why not?

5. *Other Methods.* The main CAUSE of Walmart's retail practices, Douglas argues, is American "consumerism" (3). How does Douglas DEFINE this concept, and how successfully does he use that definition to explain and justify what he sees as the realities of the retail market?

THINKING ABOUT LANGUAGE

1. Where does the phrase "evil empire" come from, and how does Douglas use it to help make his case that the designation does not apply to Walmart?

2. Is "stuff" the right word to use in describing the desires and needs of American consumers, or should Douglas have chosen a more weighty term (3)? Explain.

3. The American consumer, says Douglas, citing an article by former secretary of labor Robert Reich, strikes a "Faustian bargain" by seeking low prices that are made possible by keeping the lid on labor and sales costs (5). Explain this ALLUSION to the scholar in German folklore who sold his soul to the devil in exchange for knowledge and other earthly benefits.

FOR WRITING

1. Visit *Walmartstores.com*'s Press Room page and write a paragraph or two reporting "Walmart Facts" that support (or contradict) your general impression of the chain.

2. Write an argument supporting the claim that Walmart, Target, McDonald's, or some other large-scale retailer is (or is not) exploiting its employees and customers. Cite plenty of evidence for your claim, and document your sources scrupulously.

Life Is Good

An argument makes a claim—in the example here, that "life is good"—and supports it with facts, figures, and other evidence, including the testimony of experts. In the case of the "Life is good" brand of clothing and accessories, the main evidence that the company offers to back up this sweeping claim is Jake, the broadly smiling stick-figure in a beret who appears on many of their products. In 1994, Bert and John Jacobs, the founders of the company, chose Jake as their spokesperson because he was "a symbol about what was right in the world." Since then, Jake has symbolized the good life on millions of T-shirts and coffee mugs—a projected $135 million worth in 2008 alone. Whether he's plinking his guitar, kicking back in a beach chair, or roasting marshmallows with his dog Rocket, Jake beams the message that happiness lies in the simple pleasures of life and is thus within the grasp of just about anyone. Such an argument appeals more to an audience's feelings and emotions, of course, than to its reason and logic. But so moving is the personal testimony of the cheerful Jake, apparently, that his smiling image has not only convinced consumers to accept his company's optimistic premise about life, but to wear it on their sleeves—and hats and dog collars.

THOMAS JEFFERSON

The Declaration of Independence

Thomas Jefferson (1743–1826) was born to a wealthy landowning family in colonial Virginia and studied mathematics and political philosophy at William and Mary College. He became a lawyer and was elected to the Virginia legislature in 1769, where he was a leading spokesman for the cause of American independence. During the Revolutionary War, he served as governor of Virginia; afterward, he became the nation's first secretary of state. He served as John Adams' vice-president and was elected president himself in 1800. Jefferson was also one of the leading architects of his day—and an inventor, naturalist, archeologist, violinist, horticulturist, and patron of the arts.

Jefferson stipulated that his epitaph would mention only three of his many achievements: author of Virginia's Statute of Religious Freedom, founder of the University of Virginia, and author of the Declaration of Independence. In its form and intent, the Declaration of Independence is primarily an argument—a point-by-point justification for American independence. Lawyerly in tone, it is essentially a legal brief addressed to both the British throne and the court of world opinion. Drafted largely by Jefferson, the Declaration lists the colonists' grievances against George III and concludes that Americans are left with no recourse but full independence. The document's ratification by the Continental Congress on July 4, 1776, marked the birth of the United States.

W HEN IN THE COURSE OF HUMAN EVENTS, it becomes necessary for one people 1
to dissolve the political bands which have connected them with another, and to assume among the powers of the earth, the separate and equal station to which the Laws of Nature and of Nature's God entitle them, a decent respect to the opinions of mankind requires that they should declare the causes which impel them to the separation.

We hold these truths to be self-evident, that all men are created equal, that they 2
are endowed by their Creator with certain unalienable Rights, that among these are Life, Liberty and the pursuit of Happiness. That to secure these rights, Governments are instituted among Men, deriving their just powers from the consent of the governed. That whenever any Form of Government becomes destructive of these ends, it is the Right of the People to alter or to abolish it, and to institute new Government, laying its foundation on such principles and organizing its powers in such form, as to them shall seem most likely to effect their Safety and Happiness.

SUGGESTED MLA CITATION: Jefferson, Thomas. "The Declaration of Independence." 1776. *Back to the Lake.* Ed. Thomas Cooley. 2nd ed. New York: Norton, 2012. 542–45. Print.

Prudence, indeed, will dictate that Governments long established should not be changed for light and transient causes; and accordingly all experience hath shewn, that mankind are more disposed to suffer, while evils are sufferable, than to right themselves by abolishing the forms to which they are accustomed. But when a long train of abuses and usurpations pursuing invariably the same Object evinces a design to reduce them under absolute Despotism, it is their right, it is their duty, to throw off such Government, and to provide new Guards for their future security. Such has been the patient sufferance of these Colonies; and such is now the necessity which constrains them to alter their former Systems of Government. The history of the present King of Great Britain is a history of repeated injuries and usurpations, all having in direct object the establishment of absolute Tyranny over these States. To prove this, let Facts be submitted to a candid world.

How to use inductive reasoning like this is discussed on p. 520.

He has refused his Assent to Laws, the most wholesome and necessary for the public good. 3

He has forbidden his Governors to pass Laws of immediate and pressing importance, unless suspended in their operation till his Assent should be obtained; and when so suspended, he has utterly neglected to attend to them. 4

He has refused to pass other Laws for the accommodation of large districts of people, unless those people would relinquish the right of Representation in the Legislature, a right inestimable to them and formidable to tyrants only. 5

He has called together legislative bodies at places unusual, uncomfortable, and distant from the depository of their public Records, for the sole purpose of fatiguing them into compliance with his measures. 6

He has dissolved Representative Houses repeatedly, for opposing with manly firmness his invasions on the rights of the people. 7

He has refused for a long time, after such dissolutions, to cause others to be elected; whereby the Legislative powers, incapable of Annihilation, have returned to the People at large for their exercise; the State remaining in the mean time exposed to all the dangers of invasion from without, and convulsions within. 8

He has endeavoured to prevent the population of these States; for that purpose obstructing the Laws of Naturalization of Foreigners; refusing to pass others to encourage their migration hither, and raising the conditions of new Appropriations of Lands. 9

He has obstructed the Administration of Justice, by refusing his Assent to Laws for establishing Judiciary powers. 10

He has made Judges dependent on his Will alone, for the tenure of their offices, and the amount and payment of their salaries. 11

He has erected a multitude of New Offices, and sent hither swarms of Officers to harass our people, and eat out their substance. 12

He has kept among us, in time of peace, Standing Armies without the Consent 13
of our legislatures.

He has affected to render the Military independent of and superior to the Civil 14
power.

He has combined with others to subject us to a jurisdiction foreign to our con- 15
stitution, and unacknowledged by our laws; giving his Assent to their acts of pretended Legislation:

For Quartering large bodies of armed troops among us: 16

For protecting them, by a mock Trial, from punishment for any Murders which 17
they should commit on the Inhabitants of these States:

For cutting off our Trade with all parts of the world: 18

For imposing Taxes on us without our Consent: 19

For depriving us in many cases, of the benefits of Trial by Jury: 20

For transporting us beyond the Seas to be tried for pretended offenses: 21

For abolishing the free System of English Laws in a neighbouring Province, 22
establishing therein an Arbitrary government, and enlarging its Boundaries so as to
render it at once an example and fit instrument for introducing the same absolute
rule into these Colonies:

For taking away our Charters, abolishing our most valuable Laws, and altering 23
fundamentally the Forms of our Governments:

For suspending our own Legislatures, and declaring themselves invested with 24
power to legislate for us in all cases whatsoever.

He has abdicated Government here, by declaring us out of his Protection and 25
waging War against us.

He has plundered our seas, ravaged our Coasts, burnt our towns and destroyed 26
the lives of our people.

He is at this time transporting large Armies of foreign Mercenaries to compleat 27
the works of death, desolation and tyranny, already begun with circumstances of
Cruelty & perfidy scarcely paralleled in the most barbarous ages, and totally unwor-
thy the Head of a civilized nation.

He has constrained our fellow Citizens taken Captive on the high Seas to bear 28
Arms against their Country, to become the executioners of their friends and Brethren, or to fall themselves by their Hands.

He has excited domestic insurrections amongst us, and has endeavoured to 29
bring on the inhabitants of our frontiers, the merciless Indian Savages, whose
known rule of warfare, is an undistinguished destruction of all ages, sexes and conditions.

In every stage of these Oppressions We have Petitioned for Redress in the most 30
humble terms: Our repeated Petitions have been answered only by repeated injury.
A Prince, whose character is thus marked by every act which may define a Tyrant,
is unfit to be the ruler of a free people.

Nor have We been wanting in attentions to our British brethren. We have warned 31 them from time to time of attempts by their legislature to extend an unwarrantable jurisdiction over us. We have reminded them of the circumstances of our emigration and settlement here. We have appealed to their native justice and magnanimity, and we have conjured them by the ties of our common kindred to disavow these usurpations, which would inevitably interrupt our connections and correspondence. They too have been deaf to the voice of justice and of consanguinity. We must, therefore acquiesce in the necessity, which denounces our Separation, and hold them, as we hold the rest of mankind, Enemies in War, in Peace Friends.

We, therefore, the Representatives of the United States of America, in General 32 Congress, Assembled, appealing to the Supreme Judge of the world for the rectitude of our intentions, do, in the Name, and by Authority of the good People of these Colonies, solemnly publish and declare, That these United Colonies are, and of Right ought to be Free and Independent States; that they are Absolved from all Allegiance to the British Crown, and that all political connection between them and the State of Great Britain, is and ought to be totally dissolved; and that as Free and Independent States, they have full Power to levy War, conclude Peace, contract Alliances, establish Commerce, and to do all other Acts and Things which Independent States may of right do. And for the support of this Declaration, with a firm reliance on the protection of divine Providence, we mutually pledge to each other our Lives, our Fortunes and our sacred Honor.

READING CLOSELY

1. According to Thomas Jefferson (and the fifty-five other signers of the Declaration of Independence) what is the purpose of government?

2. What claim is Jefferson making on the basis that King George's government has not fulfilled the purpose of government? What remedy is he calling for?

3. Of the many "injuries and usurpations" that Jefferson attributes to the British king, which seem most intolerable to you (2)? Why?

STRATEGIES AND STRUCTURES

1. "We hold these truths to be self-evident" (2). Another name for self-evident truths stated at the beginning of an argument is *premises*. On what specific premises is Jefferson's argument based? Which are the ones most critical to his case?

2. Is the underlying logic of the Declaration basically inductive or deductive? Or both? Explain.

3. Paragraph 31 seems to be a digression from Jefferson's main line of argument. Why do you think he includes it?

4. Jefferson and the other signers of the Declaration made their case for independence on logical grounds. Many of the issues they addressed, however, were highly emotional. Where and how does the Declaration appeal to the emotions of its audience as well as their sense of reason?

5. How does the Declaration present the authors as men of good character who want to do what is morally right? Refer to paragraph numbers in your response.

6. *Other Methods.* Jefferson says that King George has committed "every act which may define a Tyrant" (30). How does Jefferson use this DEFINITION to support his argument that the king is unfit to rule a free people?

Thinking about Language

1. In modern English, "unalienable" (2) should be *inalienable*. Why do you think a person of Jefferson's intelligence and education would make this error?

2. Why does Jefferson begin so many of his sentences with the personal pronoun *he*, referring to King George?

3. What is "consanguinity" (31)? How can it be said to have a "voice"?

4. According to your dictionary, do most of the following words derive from Latin or Anglo-Saxon? Why do you think the signers of the Declaration used such a vocabulary to address the king of England?

transient (2)	*usurpations* (2)	*evinces* (2)
despotism (2)	*constrains* (2)	*candid* (2)
abdicated (25)	*perfidy* (27)	*redress* (30)
magnanimity (31)	*acquiesce* (31)	*rectitude* (32)?

For Writing

1. You are King George, and you've just received the Declaration of Independence, a direct challenge to your authority over the American colonies. Compose a few paragraphs replying to Jefferson's charges and defending your actions and policies toward the colonies. Assume that the Declaration accurately describes those actions—don't base your argument on a denial.

2. Compose an essay arguing that "the pursuit of Happiness" (2) is unwise, that happiness cannot be guaranteed, and that the excessive pursuit of anything can lead to chaos in the life of the individual and in the state. Or, alternatively, defend Jefferson's claim that the pursuit of happiness is an inalienable right.

Reply to the U.S. Government

Chief Seattle (1786–1866) rose to leadership of the Suquamish and Duwamish Indian tribes through his prowess as a warrior, but he is remembered mainly as a man of peace. When his eldest son was killed in a fight with a rival tribe, he sought consolation from nearby Roman Catholic missionaries and was baptized in 1848. Though broken-hearted by the loss of the traditional Indian way of life, Seattle believed that the influx of white immigrants into his native Puget Sound region was unstoppable and that only by accommodating them could his people survive. The settlers reciprocated by naming their new city after him.

Seattle's reputation as an orator is legendary—literally so, because no authentic record exists of Seattle's words in his own language, Lushootseed. In 1854, the territorial governor of the Pacific Northwest, Isaac I. Stevens, presented Seattle with a formal U.S. government offer to buy over two million acres of Indian land around Puget Sound. Seattle responded with an impassioned speech—which was first published thirty-three years later in the Seattle Sunday Star, "translated" by Dr. Henry A. Smith, who indeed had been present at the speech but who spoke no Lushootseed. In any case, the text we have of Seattle's speech rings true as an eloquent assertion of the rights and dignity of his people.

YONDER SKY that has wept tears of compassion upon my people for centuries untold, and which to us appears changeless and eternal may change. Today is fair. Tomorrow may be overcast with clouds. My words are like the stars that never change. Whatever Seattle says the great chief at Washington can rely upon with as much certainty as he can upon the return of the sun or the seasons. The White Chief says that Big Chief at Washington sends us greetings of friendship and good-will. That is kind of him for we know he has little need of our friendship in return. His people are many. They are like the grass that covers vast prairies. My people are few. They resemble the scattering trees of a storm-swept plain. The great, and—I presume—good, White Chief sends us word that he wishes to buy our lands but is willing to allow us enough to live comfortably. This indeed appears just, even generous, for the Red Man no longer has rights that he need respect, and the offer may be wise also, as we are no longer in need of an extensive country. . . . I will not dwell on, nor mourn over, our untimely decay, nor reproach our paleface brothers with hastening it, as we too may have been somewhat to blame.

SUGGESTED MLA CITATION: Seattle. "Reply to the U.S. Government." 1854. *Back to the Lake*. Ed. Thomas Cooley. 2nd ed. New York: Norton, 2012. 547–51. Print.

660 – CHIEF SEATTLE.

Chief Seattle in 1864, from a photograph by L. B. Franklin.

Youth is impulsive. When our young men grow angry at some real or imaginary 2 wrong, and disfigure their faces with black paint, it denotes that their hearts are black, and then they are often cruel and relentless, and our old men and old women are unable to restrain them. Thus it has ever been. Thus it was when the white men first began to push our forefathers further westward. But let us hope that the hostilities between us may never return. We would have everything to lose and nothing to gain. Revenge by young men is considered gain, even at the cost of their own lives, but old men who stay at home in times of war, and mothers who have sons to lose, know better.

Our good father at Washington—for I presume he is now our father as well as 3 yours, since King George[1] has moved his boundaries further north—our great good father, I say, sends us word that if we do as he desires he will protect us. His brave warriors will be to us a bristling wall of strength, and his wonderful ships of war will fill our harbors so that our ancient enemies far to the northward—the Hydas and Tsimpsians[2]—will cease to frighten our women, children, and old men. Then in reality will he be our father and we his children. But can that ever be? Your God is not our God! Your God loves your people and hates mine. He folds his strong and protecting arms lovingly about the paleface and leads him by the hand as a father leads his infant son—but He has forsaken His red children—if they really are his. Our God, the Great Spirit, seems also to have forsaken us. Your God makes your people wax strong every day. Soon they will fill the land. Our people are ebbing away like a rapidly receding tide that will never return. The white man's God cannot love our people or He would protect them. They seem to be orphans who can look nowhere for help. How then can we be brothers? How can your God become our God and renew our prosperity and awaken in us dreams of returning greatness? If we have a common heavenly father He must be partial—for He came to his paleface children. We never saw Him. He gave you laws but He had no word for His red children whose teeming multitudes once filled this vast continent as stars fill the firmament. No; we are two distinct races with separate origins and separate destinies. There is little in common between us.

How to use deductive reasoning like this is discussed on p. 520.

To us the ashes of our ancestors are sacred and their resting place is hallowed 4 ground. You wander far from the graves of your ancestors and seemingly without regret. Your religion was written upon tablets of stone[3] by the iron finger of your God so that you could not forget. The Red Man could never comprehend nor

---

1. *King George*: George IV (1762–1830), king of England from 1820 to 1830. As the border with Canada (a British colony) moved north, more of Washington state became part of the United States.

2. *Hydas and Tsimpsians*: Native American tribes of British Columbia, Canada; "Hyda" is more commonly spelled "Haida."

3. *Written upon tables of stone*: A reference to the Ten Commandments. According to the Hebrew Bible, the Commandments were written by God and given to Moses on stone tablets.

remember it. Our religion is the traditions of our ancestors—the dreams of our old men, given them in solemn hours of night by the Great Spirit; and the visions of our sachems;[4] and it is written in the hearts of our people.

Your dead cease to love you and the land of their nativity as soon as they pass   5
the portals of the tomb and wander way beyond the stars. They are soon forgotten and never return. Our dead never forget the beautiful world that gave them being.

Day and night cannot dwell together. The Red man has ever fled the approach   6
of the White Man, as the morning mist flees before the morning sun. However, your proposition seems fair and I think that my people will accept it and will retire to the reservation you offer them. Then we will dwell apart in peace, for the words of the Great White Chief seem to be the words of nature speaking to my people out of dense darkness.

It matters little where we pass the remnant of our days. They will not be many.   7
A few more moons; a few more winters—and not one of the descendants of the mighty hosts that once moved over this broad land or lived in happy homes, pro-tected by the Great Spirit, will remain to mourn over the graves of a people once more powerful and hopeful than yours. But why should I mourn at the untimely fate of my people? Tribe follows tribe, and nation follows nation, like the waves of the sea. It is the order of nature, and regret is useless. Your time of decay may be distant, but it will surely come, for even the White Man whose God walked and talked with him as friend with friend, cannot be exempt from the common destiny. We may be brothers after all. We will see.

We will ponder your proposition, and when we decide we will let you know.   8
But should we accept it, I here and now make this condition that we will not be denied the privilege without molestation of visiting at any time the tombs of our ancestors, friends and children. Every part of this soil is sacred in the estimation of my people. Every hillside, every valley, every plain and grove, has been hallowed by some sad or happy event in days long vanished. . . . The very dust upon which you now stand responds more lovingly to their footsteps than to yours, because it is rich with the blood of our ancestors and our bare feet are conscious of the sympa-thetic touch. . . . Even the little children who lived here and rejoiced here for a brief season will love these somber solitudes and at eventide they greet shadowy returning spirits. And when the last Red Man shall have perished, and the memory of my tribe shall have become a myth among the White Men, these shores will swarm with the invisible dead of my tribe, and when your children's children think themselves alone in the field, the store, the shop, upon the highway, or in the silence of the pathless woods, they will not be alone. . . . At night when the streets

4. *Sachems*: High-level tribal leaders.

of your cities and villages are silent and you think them deserted, they will throng with the returning hosts that once filled and still love this beautiful land. The White Man will never be alone.

Let him be just and deal kindly with my people, for the dead are not powerless. 9 Dead, did I say? There is no death, only a change of worlds.

READING CLOSELY

1. According to Chief Seattle, why did the young men of his tribe go to war? What was their mood, and what was the significance of their painted faces?

2. The proposition that Seattle promises to think over at the end of his speech is the government's offer to buy over two million acres of Indian land. What condition does he place on accepting it?

3. Seattle doubts that the White Man and the Red Man will ever be brothers. Why? In what sense does he think they may be "brothers after all" (7)?

4. What does he say will happen "when the last Red Man shall have perished" (8)?

5. What does Seattle mean by "a change of worlds" (9)? How does this view of life after death differ from Christian ideas of heaven?

STRATEGIES AND STRUCTURES

1. What personal qualities would you attribute to Seattle after reading his speech? Point out specific statements and phrases that help to characterize him. How does paragraph 2 in particular show Seattle's character?

2. In general, do you think Seattle sounds trustworthy? Why or why not?

3. How and why does Seattle show his respect for the "Big Chief at Washington" (1)? How does the defeated chief show that he is not cowed by the Big Chief?

4. What reasons does Seattle give for why the Big Chief at Washington should grant his condition that the Duwamish people be allowed "without molestation" to visit their homeland (8)?

5. *Other Methods.* In the second half of his speech, Seattle COMPARES AND CONTRASTS "your dead" and "our dead" (5). What are some of the differences? How do those differences support his claim that "the dead are not powerless" (9)?

Thinking about Language

1. Seattle refers to the Big Chief at Washington as "our good father" (3). Why do you think he draws this ANALOGY between a head of state and the patriarch of a family?

2. The conquering whites, says Seattle, are like "the grass that covers vast prairies," and Native Americans are like "scattering trees" or a "receding tide," though they were once like the "stars" (1, 3). How do these nature METAPHORS fit in with Seattle's references to physical decay and the cycle of the seasons?

3. What does he mean when he says, "Day and night cannot dwell together" (6)?

4. In what sense is the translator using the word *sympathetic* when he reports Seattle as saying that "our bare feet are conscious of the sympathetic touch" (8)?

5. According to the translator of his speech, Seattle "arose with all the dignity of a senator" and spoke in "solemn and impressive tones." How does the language and style of this translation help to convey that dignity and solemnity? Include EXAMPLES in your response.

For Writing

1. You have been given the task of introducing Seattle before his speech. Write a paragraph or two for the occasion.

2. On behalf of the Big Chief at Washington, compose a reply to Seattle's speech in which you try to convince him to accept the proposal.

3. A class you want to take has reached its enrollment capacity, and the instructor asks you to explain in writing why she should let you in. Make the case for yourself as a valuable addition to the class.

MARTIN LUTHER KING JR.

I Have a Dream

> *Martin Luther King Jr. (1929–1968) was born in Atlanta, Georgia, at a time when racial discrimination was routine and institutionalized, especially in the South. King attended segregated schools and earned his BA in sociology from Morehouse College in 1948. Already an ordained Baptist minister, he then studied at Crozer Theological Seminary and at Boston University, where he received his PhD in systematic theology. In 1953, King became the pastor of Dexter Avenue Baptist Church in Montgomery, Alabama, just as the civil rights movement was beginning to crystallize. He won national recognition for leading a black boycott of Montgomery's segregated bus system and, in 1957, was elected president of a new organization, the Southern Christian Leadership Conference (SCLC), which combined King's Christian principles with a commitment to nonviolent protest. The SCLC's tireless campaign of marches, demonstrations, and civil disobedience gradually caught the public imagination. Inspired by King, President John F. Kennedy initiated the legislation that would become the Civil Rights Act of 1964. That same year, King was awarded the Nobel Peace Prize. Though he won the love and admiration of millions, he was also subjected to arrests, political harassment, and threats of violence. On April 4, 1968, he was assassinated as he stood on a hotel balcony in Memphis.*
>
> *One dramatic moment of King's career came on August 28, 1963, when he stood on the steps of the Lincoln Memorial to address a crowd of a quarter-million people who had heeded King's call for a March on Washington for Jobs and Freedom. King's "I Have a Dream" speech, steeped in the cadences of the Bible, the Declaration of Independence, and the Gettysburg Address, is a classic invocation of moral authority, a stirring call to "open the doors of opportunity to all of God's children."*

F IVE SCORE YEARS AGO, a great American, in whose symbolic shadow we stand,[1] signed the Emancipation Proclamation. This momentous decree came as a great beacon light of hope to millions of Negro slaves who had been seared in the flames of withering injustice. It came as a joyous daybreak to end the long night of captivity.

---

1. *In whose symbolic shadow we stand*: King's speech was delivered in front of the Lincoln Memorial. *A great American*: Reference to President Abraham Lincoln. *Five score years ago*: An echo of the opening line of Lincoln's 1863 Gettysburg Address, in which he dedicated a cemetery for fallen Civil War soldiers.

SUGGESTED MLA CITATION: King, Martin Luther, Jr. "I Have a Dream." 1963. *Back to the Lake*. Ed. Thomas Cooley. 2nd ed. New York: Norton, 2012. 553–57. Print.

But one hundred years later, we must face the tragic fact that the Negro is still 2
not free. One hundred years later, the life of the Negro is still sadly crippled by the
manacles of segregation and the chains of discrimination. One hundred years later,
the Negro lives on a lonely island of poverty in the midst of a vast ocean of material
prosperity. One hundred years later, the Negro is still languishing in the corners of
American society and finds himself an exile in his own land. So we have come here
today to dramatize an appalling condition.

In a sense we have come to our nation's capital to cash a check. When the archi- 3
tects of our republic wrote the magnificent words of the Constitution and the Declaration of Independence, they were signing a promissory note to which every
American was to fall heir. This note was a promise that all men would be guaranteed the inalienable rights of life, liberty, and the pursuit of happiness.

It is obvious today that America has defaulted on this promissory note insofar 4
as her citizens of color are concerned. Instead of honoring this sacred obligation,
America has given the Negro people a bad check which has come back marked
"insufficient funds." But we refuse to believe that the bank of justice is bankrupt.
We refuse to believe that there are insufficient funds in the great vaults of opportunity of this nation. So we have come to cash this check—a check that will give us
upon demand the riches of freedom and the security of justice. We have also come
to this hallowed spot to remind America of the fierce urgency of *now*. This is no
time to engage in the luxury of cooling off or to take the tranquilizing drug of
gradualism. *Now* is the time to rise from the dark and desolate valley of segregation
to the sunlit path of racial justice. *Now* is the time to open the doors of opportunity
to all of God's children. *Now* is the time to lift our nation from the quicksands of
racial injustice to the solid rock of brotherhood.

It would be fatal for the nation to overlook the urgency of the moment and to 5
underestimate the determination of the Negro. This sweltering summer of the
Negro's legitimate discontent will not pass until there is an invigorating autumn of
freedom and equality. Nineteen sixty-three is not an end, but a beginning. Those
who hope that the Negro needed to blow off steam and will now be content will
have a rude awakening if the nation returns to business as usual. There will be
neither rest nor tranquility in America until the Negro is granted his citizenship
rights. The whirlwinds of revolt will continue to shake the foundations of our
nation until the bright day of justice emerges.

But there is something that I must say to my people who stand on the warm 6
threshold which leads into the palace of justice. In the process of gaining our right-
ful place we must not be guilty of wrongful deeds. Let us not seek to satisfy our
thirst for freedom by drinking from the cup of bitterness and hatred.

See p. 527
for tips on
anticipating
objections.

We must forever conduct our struggle on the high plane of dignity and 7
discipline. We must not allow our creative protest to degenerate into physical

violence. Again and again we must rise to the majestic heights of meeting physical force with soul force. The marvelous new militancy which has engulfed the Negro community must not lead us to distrust of all white people, for many of our white brothers, as evidenced by their presence here today, have come to realize that their destiny is tied up with our destiny and their freedom is inextricably bound to our freedom. We cannot walk alone.

And as we walk, we must make the pledge that we shall march ahead. We can- 8
not turn back. There are those who are asking the devotees of civil rights, "When will you be satisfied?" We can never be satisfied as long as our bodies, heavy with the fatigue of travel, cannot gain lodging in the motels of the highways and the hotels of the cities. We cannot be satisfied as long as the Negro's basic mobility is from a smaller ghetto to a larger one. We can never be satisfied as long as a Negro in Mississippi cannot vote and a Negro in New York believes he has nothing for which to vote. No, no, we are not satisfied, and we will not be satisfied until justice rolls down like waters and righteousness like a mighty stream.

I am not unmindful that some of you have come here out of great trials and 9
tribulations. Some of you have come fresh from narrow cells. Some of you have come from areas where your quest for freedom left you battered by the storms of persecution and staggered by the winds of police brutality. You have been the veterans of creative suffering. Continue to work with the faith that unearned suffering is redemptive.

In his "I Have a Dream" speech, delivered in Washington, D.C., on August 28, 1963, Martin Luther King Jr. appealed to the emotions of his vast audience as well as their logic and sense of ethics.

Go back to Mississippi, go back to Alabama, go back to Georgia, go back to 10
Louisiana, go back to the slums and ghettos of our northern cities, knowing that
somehow this situation can and will be changed. Let us not wallow in the valley of
despair.

I say to you today, my friends, that in spite of the difficulties and frustrations of 11
the moment, I still have a dream. It is a dream deeply rooted in the American
dream.

I have a dream that one day this nation will rise up and live out the true mean- 12
ing of its creed: "We hold these truths to be self-evident: that all men are created
equal."

I have a dream that one day on the red hills of Georgia the sons of former slaves 13
and the sons of former slaveowners will be able to sit down together at a table of
brotherhood.

I have a dream that one day even the state of Mississippi, a desert state, swelter- 14
ing with the heat of injustice and oppression, will be transformed into an oasis of
freedom and justice.

I have a dream that my four children will one day live in a nation where they 15
will not be judged by the color of their skin but by the content of their character.

I have a dream today. 16

I have a dream that one day the state of Alabama, whose governor's lips are pres- 17
ently dripping with the words of interposition and nullification, will be transformed
into a situation where little black boys and black girls will be able to join hands
with little white boys and white girls and walk together as sisters and brothers.

I have a dream today. 18

I have a dream that one day every valley shall be exalted, and every hill and 19
mountain shall be made low, the rough places will be made plain, and the crooked
places will be made straight, and the glory of the Lord shall be revealed and all
flesh shall see it together.

This is our hope. This is the faith that I go back to the South with. With this 20
faith we will be able to hew out of the mountain of despair a stone of hope. With
this faith we will be able to transform the jangling discords of our nation into a
beautiful symphony of brotherhood. With this faith we will be able to work
together, to pray together, to struggle together, to go to jail together, to stand up
for freedom together, knowing that we will be free one day.

This will be the day, this will be the day when all of God's children will be able 21
to sing with new meaning:

My country 'tis of thee, sweet land of liberty, of thee I sing.
Land where my fathers died, land of the Pilgrim's pride,
from every mountainside, let freedom ring!

And if America is to be a great nation, this must become true. And so let free- 22
dom ring from the prodigious hilltops of New Hampshire. Let freedom ring from
the mighty mountains of New York! Let freedom ring from the heightening Alleghenies of Pennsylvania!

Let freedom ring from the snow-capped Rockies of Colorado!   23

Let freedom ring from the curvaceous slopes of California!   24

But not only that; let freedom ring from Stone Mountain of Georgia!   25

Let freedom ring from Lookout Mountain of Tennessee!   26

Let freedom ring from every hill and molehill of Mississippi.   27

From every mountainside, let freedom ring.   28

And when this happens, and when we allow freedom to ring—when we let it 29
ring from every village and every hamlet, from every state and every city, we will
be able to speed up that day when all of God's children—black men and white
men, Jews and Gentiles, Protestants and Catholics—will be able to join hands and
sing in the words of the old Negro spiritual:

Free at last! Free at last!
Thank God Almighty, we are free at last!

READING CLOSELY

1. The "great American" (1) to whom Martin Luther King Jr. refers in the first
   paragraph of his speech is, of course, Abraham Lincoln. Why does King begin
   by invoking Lincoln and the Emancipation Proclamation, which Lincoln signed
   in January 1863?

2. What is the "appalling condition" that King seeks "to dramatize" (2) to the
   quarter of a million civil rights activists who gathered around the Lincoln
   Memorial in Washington to hear his speech?

3. What does King admonish the multitude to do about the condition he is calling
   to their attention? Was he wise to insist that their actions not "degenerate into
   physical violence" (7)? Why or why not?

4. What is King's dream? When and how does he envision its becoming a reality?

STRATEGIES AND STRUCTURES

1. King takes it for granted that the condition of many African Americans in 1963
   is "appalling" (2). Is he committing the logical fallacy of begging the question?
   Explain.

2. In the third part of his speech (20–29), King says, "When we allow freedom to ring, . . . we will be able to speed up that day when all of God's children . . . will be able to join hands" (29). If we conceive of King's entire speech as a logical argument, how does this statement logically connect King's dream in paragraphs 11 to 19 to the reality he describes in paragraphs 1 to 10?

3. Though he uses logical reasoning, King's chief strategy in this speech, perhaps, is to appeal to his audience's sense of moral justice, beginning with the evocation of President Lincoln in the opening line. What other sources of authority does he refer to throughout the speech? How do these sources help King give the impression that he himself is a man of good character who deserves to be listened to and trusted?

4. Where and how does King appeal to his audience's emotions? Point out several examples that you find particularly persuasive.

5. What evidence can you find in the text of King's speech to indicate that it was written to be delivered orally instead of laid out on the printed page? Consider such elements as the length of his sentences, his choice of words, and the repetition of such phrases as, "I have a dream." How might King's experience as a minister have helped him to compose such a moving oration?

6. *Other Methods.* In the "I have a dream" section of his speech (11–19), King describes a future condition that is contrary to present fact. How does that condition COMPARE AND CONTRAST with the "appalling condition" he described earlier?

THINKING ABOUT LANGUAGE

1. King's speech is full of METAPHORS ("the flames of withering injustice"); SIMILES ("righteousness like a mighty stream"); and other figures of speech (1, 8). How does such figurative language help him, throughout his oration, to balance his call for action with his call for nonviolence?

2. Why does King begin his speech with the phrase "five score years ago" instead of simply saying "a hundred years ago"?

3. Explain the "bad check" metaphor in paragraphs 3–4 of King's speech.

4. Why does King speak of "the Negro" throughout his speech, instead of "African Americans" or "blacks"?

5. Why do you think King ends his speech with an ALLUSION to an "old Negro spiritual" (29)? How effective do you find this ending?

For Writing

1. King was not just speaking to the activists who joined him in Washington on that August day in 1963. He was mindful of a wider audience, including the press. Write a paragraph or two analyzing how King's speech anticipates the objections of those who might disagree with, or even be hostile to, his dream.

2. Write an essay describing and analyzing King's use of logical reasoning, his appeal to emotion, or the way he establishes his credibility. Whichever you choose, be sure to discuss how King's language supports it.

3. Write an essay in which you argue that nonviolent protest is the best way to achieve change—or that violence is sometimes necessary to change things. Refer to historical examples in your essay, like the civil rights movement or India's struggle for independence led by Mahatma Gandhi.

BARACK OBAMA

A More Perfect Union

Barack Obama (b. 1961), the son of a black father from Kenya and a white mother from Kansas, grew up mostly in Hawaii. A graduate of Columbia University and Harvard Law School, Obama served in the Illinois State Senate from 1997 to 2004, when he was elected to the U.S. Senate. In 2008 he became the first black president of the United States.

As the Democratic presidential nominee in the 2008 election, Obama sought to avoid making race a key issue in the campaign, preferring to run on his political platform, his record in the Senate, and his reputation for bringing together politicians of opposing parties and conflicting viewpoints. In March 2008, however, Obama faced a growing controversy triggered by the sermons of the Reverend Jeremiah Wright, his pastor for more than twenty years at Trinity United Church of Christ in Chicago. Wright, a former Marine, accused the U.S. government of fostering racism and claimed that it "lied about inventing the HIV virus as a means of genocide against people of color." "A More Perfect Union," a speech delivered at the National Convention Center in Philadelphia, Pennsylvania, on March 18, 2008, was Obama's response to the controversy. Condemning Wright's remarks but putting them in the historical context of the black experience in America, it soon became known as Obama's speech on race.

"W E THE PEOPLE, in order to form a more perfect union."[1]   1

Two hundred and twenty-one years ago, in a hall that still stands across the   2
street,[2] a group of men gathered and, with these simple words, launched America's improbable experiment in democracy. Farmers and scholars, statesmen and patriots who had traveled across an ocean to escape tyranny and persecution finally made real their declaration of independence at a Philadelphia convention that lasted through the spring of 1787.[3]

1. *We the people . . .* : The beginning of the preamble to the United States Constitution.

2. *Hall that still stands across the street*: A reference to Independence Hall in Philadelphia, site of the Constitutional Convention.

3. *Through the spring of 1787*: The Constitutional Convention of 1787 was convened to address problems with the Articles of Confederation, which united the American colonies under one government. At the convention, the founding fathers created a new document, the United States Constitution.

SUGGESTED MLA CITATION: Obama, Barack. "A More Perfect Union." 2008. *Back to the Lake.* Ed. Thomas Cooley. 2nd ed. New York: Norton, 2012. 560–71. Print.

The document they produced was eventually signed but ultimately unfinished. 3
It was stained by this nation's original sin of slavery, a question that divided the
colonies and brought the convention to a stalemate until the founders chose to
allow the slave trade to continue for at least twenty more years, and to leave any
final resolution to future generations.

Of course, the answer to the slavery question was already embedded within our 4
Constitution—a Constitution that had at its very core the ideal of equal citizenship
under the law; a Constitution that promised its people liberty, and justice, and a
union that could be and should be perfected over time.

And yet words on a parchment would not be enough to deliver slaves from 5
bondage, or provide men and women of every color and creed their full rights and
obligations as citizens of the United States. What would be needed were Americans in successive generations who were willing to do their part—through protests
and struggle, on the streets and in the courts, through a civil war and civil disobe-
dience and always at great risk—to narrow that gap between the promise of our
ideals and the reality of their time.

This was one of the tasks we set forth at the beginning of this campaign—to 6
continue the long march of those who came before us, a march for a more just,
more equal, more free, more caring and more prosperous America. I chose to run
for the presidency at this moment in history because I believe deeply that we cannot solve the challenges of our time unless we solve them together—unless we
perfect our union by understanding that we may have different stories, but we hold
common hopes; that we may not look the same and we may not have come from
the same place, but we all want to move in the same direction—towards a better
future for our children and our grandchildren.

This belief comes from my unyielding faith in the decency and generosity of the 7
American people. But it also comes from my own American story.

I am the son of a black man from Kenya and a white woman from Kansas. I was 8
raised with the help of a white grandfather who survived a Depression to serve in
Patton's army during World War II and a white grandmother who worked See p. 517 for
using personal
experience to
support an
argument.
on a bomber assembly line at Fort Leavenworth[4] while he was overseas.
I've gone to some of the best schools in America and lived in one of the
world's poorest nations. I am married to a black American who carries
within her the blood of slaves and slaveowners—an inheritance we pass on to our
two precious daughters. I have brothers, sisters, nieces, nephews, uncles, and cousins,

---

4. *Fort Leavenworth*: A U.S. Army fort in Kansas. *Patton's army*: A reference to General George S.
Patton (1885–1945), a leading American general during World War II. *Depression*: A severe economic
downturn that began in the United States after the stock market crashed in 1929 and ended around the
beginning of World War II in 1939.

of every race and every hue, scattered across three continents, and for as long as I live, I will never forget that in no other country on Earth is my story even possible.

It's a story that hasn't made me the most conventional candidate. But it is a story that has seared into my genetic makeup the idea that this nation is more than the sum of its parts—that out of many, we are truly one.　9

Throughout the first year of this campaign, against all predictions to the contrary, we saw how hungry the American people were for this message of unity. Despite the temptation to view my candidacy through a purely racial lens, we won commanding victories in states with some of the whitest populations in the country. In South Carolina, where the Confederate flag[5] still flies, we built a powerful coalition of African Americans and white Americans.　10

This is not to say that race has not been an issue in the campaign. At various stages in the campaign, some commentators have deemed me either "too black" or "not black enough." We saw racial tensions bubble to the surface during the week before the South Carolina primary. The press has scoured every exit poll for the latest evidence of racial polarization, not just in terms of white and black, but black and brown as well.　11

And yet, it has only been in the last couple of weeks that the discussion of race in this campaign has taken a particularly divisive turn.　12

On one end of the spectrum, we've heard the implication that my candidacy is somehow an exercise in affirmative action; that it's based solely on the desire of wide-eyed liberals to purchase racial reconciliation on the cheap. On the other end, we've heard my former pastor, Reverend Jeremiah Wright, use incendiary language to express views that have the potential not only to widen the racial divide, but views that denigrate both the greatness and the goodness of our nation; that rightly offend white and black alike.　13

I have already condemned, in unequivocal terms, the statements of Reverend Wright that have caused such controversy. For some, nagging questions remain. Did I know him to be an occasionally fierce critic of American domestic and foreign policy? Of course. Did I ever hear him make remarks that could be considered controversial while I sat in church? Yes. Did I strongly disagree with many of his political views? Absolutely—just as I'm sure many of you have heard remarks from your pastors, priests, or rabbis with which you strongly disagreed.　14

But the remarks that have caused this recent firestorm weren't simply controversial. They weren't simply a religious leader's effort to speak out against perceived injustice. Instead, they expressed a profoundly distorted view of this country—a　15

---

5. *Confederate flag*: The flag that represented the southern Confederate states that seceded during the Civil War. Because those states relied on slave labor and were opposed to ending slavery, today the flag is controversial—some see it as a symbol of racism, while others see it as a celebration of the South and southern culture.

view that sees white racism as endemic, and that elevates what is wrong with America above all that we know is right with America; a view that sees the conflicts in the Middle East as rooted primarily in the actions of stalwart allies like Israel, instead of emanating from the perverse and hateful ideologies of radical Islam.

As such, Reverend Wright's comments were not only wrong but divisive, divisive at a time when we need unity; racially charged at a time when we need to come together to solve a set of monumental problems—two wars, a terrorist threat, a falling economy, a chronic health care crisis and potentially devastating climate change; problems that are neither black or white or Latino or Asian, but rather problems that confront us all.

Given my background, my politics, and my professed values and ideals, there will no doubt be those for whom my statements of condemnation are not enough. Why associate myself with Reverend Wright in the first place, they may ask? Why not join another church? And I confess that if all that I knew of Reverend Wright were the snippets of those sermons that have run in an endless loop on the television and YouTube, or if Trinity United Church of Christ conformed to the caricatures being peddled by some commentators, there is no doubt that I would react in much the same way.

But the truth is, that isn't all that I know of the man. The man I met more than twenty years ago is a man who helped introduce me to my Christian faith, a man who spoke to me about our obligations to love one another; to care for the sick and lift up the poor. He is a man who served his country as a U.S. Marine; who has studied and lectured at some of the finest universities and seminaries in the country, and who for over thirty years led a church that serves the community by doing God's work here on Earth—by housing the homeless, ministering to the needy, providing day care services and scholarships and prison ministries, and reaching out to those suffering from HIV/AIDS.

In my first book, *Dreams from My Father*, I described the experience of my first service at Trinity:

> People began to shout, to rise from their seats and clap and cry out, a forceful wind carrying the reverend's voice up into the rafters. . . . And in that single note—hope—I heard something else; at the foot of that cross, inside the thousands of churches across the city, I imagined the stories of ordinary black people merging with the stories of David and Goliath, Moses and Pharaoh, the Christians in the lion's den, Ezekiel's field of dry bones.[6] Those

---

6. *David and Goliath . . . field of dry bones*: References to the Hebrew Bible. Ezekiel, a Hebrew prophet, had a vision of a field of dry bones that he made come together and grow flesh. "Christians in the lion's den" refers to the story of Daniel, who was thrown into a lions' den by King Darius for worshiping God instead of his king; God saved Daniel by shutting the lions' mouths. Moses defied the Pharaoh by leading the Israelites out of Egypt, where they were enslaved. David defeated the giant Goliath with a slingshot.

stories—of survival, and freedom, and hope—became our story, my story; the blood that had spilled was our blood, the tears our tears; until this black church, on this bright day, seemed once more a vessel carrying the story of a people into future generations and into a larger world. Our trials and triumphs became at once unique and universal, black and more than black; in chronicling our journey, the stories and songs gave us a means to reclaim memories that we didn't need to feel shame about . . . memories that all people might study and cherish—and with which we could start to rebuild.

That has been my experience at Trinity. Like other predominantly black churches 20 across the country, Trinity embodies the black community in its entirety—the doctor and the welfare mom, the model student and the former gang-banger. Like other black churches, Trinity's services are full of raucous laughter and sometimes bawdy humor. They are full of dancing, clapping, screaming and shouting that may seem jarring to the untrained ear. The church contains in full the kindness and cruelty, the fierce intelligence and the shocking ignorance, the struggles and successes, the love and, yes, the bitterness and bias that make up the black experience in America.

And this helps explain, perhaps, my relationship with Reverend Wright. As 21 imperfect as he may be, he has been like family to me. He strengthened my faith, officiated at my wedding, and baptized my children. Not once in my conversations with him have I heard him talk about any ethnic group in derogatory terms, or treat whites with whom he interacted with anything but courtesy and respect. He contains within him the contradictions—the good and the bad—of the community that he has served diligently for so many years.

I can no more disown him than I can disown the black community. I can no 22 more disown him than I can my white grandmother—a woman who helped raise me, a woman who sacrificed again and again for me, a woman who loves me as much as she loves anything in this world, but a woman who once confessed her fear of black men who passed by her on the street, and who on more than one occasion has uttered racial or ethnic stereotypes that made me cringe.

These people are a part of me. And they are a part of America, this country that 23 I love.

Some will see this as an attempt to justify or excuse comments that are simply 24 inexcusable. I can assure you it is not. I suppose the politically safe thing would be to move on from this episode and just hope that it fades into the woodwork. We can dismiss Reverend Wright as a crank or a demagogue, just as some have dismissed Geraldine Ferraro,[7] in the aftermath of her recent statements, as harboring some deep-seated racial bias.

But race is an issue that I believe this nation cannot afford to ignore right now. [25] We would be making the same mistake that Reverend Wright made in his offending sermons about America—to simplify and stereotype and amplify the negative to the point that it distorts reality.

The fact is that the comments that have been made and the issues that have [26] surfaced over the last few weeks reflect the complexities of race in this country that we've never really worked through—a part of our union that we have yet to perfect. And if we walk away now, if we simply retreat into our respective corners, we will never be able to come together and solve challenges like health care, or education, or the need to find good jobs for every American.

Understanding this reality requires a reminder of how we arrived at this point. [27] As William Faulkner once wrote, "The past isn't dead and buried. In fact, it isn't even past." We do not need to recite here the history of racial injustice in this country. But we do need to remind ourselves that so many of the disparities that exist in the African-American community today can be directly traced to inequalities passed on from an earlier generation that suffered under the brutal legacy of slavery and Jim Crow.[8]

Segregated schools were, and are, inferior schools; we still haven't fixed them, [28] fifty years after *Brown v. Board of Education*,[9] and the inferior education they provided, then and now, helps explain the pervasive achievement gap between today's black and white students.

Legalized discrimination—where blacks were prevented, often through violence, from owning property, or loans were not granted to African-American business owners, or black homeowners could not access FHA mortgages[10] or blacks [29]

7. *Geraldine Ferraro*: A member of the U.S. House of Representatives from 1978 to 1984, who ran for vice president alongside presidential candidate Walter Mondale in 1984. In March 2008, Ferraro, a supporter of Obama's Democratic opponent Hillary Clinton, told a Torrance, California, newspaper that "If Obama was a white man, he would not be in this position. And if he was a woman (of any color), he would not be in this position. He happens to be very lucky to be who he is. And the country is caught up in the concept."

8. *Jim Crow*: Laws that segregated blacks and whites in public facilities like schools, mass transportation, and restaurants.

9. *Brown v. Board of Education*: The 1954 Supreme Court case that ended legal racial segregation in public schools.

10. *FHA mortgages*: The Federal Housing Administration insures private mortgages, reducing the risk to lenders and allowing those who might not otherwise qualify for a mortgage to obtain one.

were excluded from unions, or the police force, or fire departments—meant that black families could not amass any meaningful wealth to bequeath to future generations. That history helps explain the wealth and income gap between black and white, and the concentrated pockets of poverty that persists in so many of today's urban and rural communities.

A lack of economic opportunity among black men, and the shame and frustration that came from not being able to provide for one's family, contributed to the erosion of black families—a problem that welfare policies for many years may have worsened. And the lack of basic services in so many urban black neighborhoods—parks for kids to play in, police walking the beat, regular garbage pick-up and building code enforcement—all helped create a cycle of violence, blight, and neglect that continues to haunt us. 30

This is the reality in which Reverend Wright and other African Americans of his generation grew up. They came of age in the late fifties and early sixties, a time when segregation was still the law of the land and opportunity was systematically constricted. What's remarkable is not how many failed in the face of discrimination, but rather how many men and women overcame the odds; how many were able to make a way out of no way for those like me who would come after them. 31

But for all those who scratched and clawed their way to get a piece of the American Dream, there were many who didn't make it—those who were ultimately defeated, in one way or another, by discrimination. That legacy of defeat was passed on to future generations—those young men and increasingly young women who we see standing on street corners or languishing in our prisons, without hope or prospects for the future. Even for those blacks who did make it, questions of race, and racism, continue to define their worldview in fundamental ways. For the men and women of Reverend Wright's generation, the memories of humiliation and doubt and fear have not gone away; nor has the anger and the bitterness of those years. That anger may not get expressed in public, in front of white co-workers or white friends. But it does find voice in the barbershop or around the kitchen table. At times, that anger is exploited by politicians, to gin up votes along racial lines, or to make up for a politician's own failings. 32

And occasionally it finds voice in the church on Sunday morning, in the pulpit and in the pews. The fact that so many people are surprised to hear that anger in some of Reverend Wright's sermons simply reminds us of the old truism that the most segregated hour in American life occurs on Sunday morning. That anger is not always productive; indeed, all too often it distracts attention from solving real problems; it keeps us from squarely facing our own complicity in our condition, and prevents the African-American community from forging the alliances it needs to bring about real change. But the anger is real; it is powerful; and to simply wish it away, to condemn it without understanding its roots, only serves to widen the chasm of misunderstanding that exists between the races. 33

In fact, a similar anger exists within segments of the white community. Most 34
working- and middle-class white Americans don't feel that they have been particularly privileged by their race. Their experience is the immigrant experience—as far
as they're concerned, no one's handed them anything, they've built it from scratch.
They've worked hard all their lives, many times only to see their jobs shipped overseas or their pension dumped after a lifetime of labor. They are anxious about their
futures, and feel their dreams slipping away; in an era of stagnant wages and global
competition, opportunity comes to be seen as a zero sum game,[11] in which your
dreams come at my expense. So when they are told to bus their children to a school
across town; when they hear that an African American is getting an advantage in
landing a good job or a spot in a good college because of an injustice that they
themselves never committed; when they're told that their fears about crime in
urban neighborhoods are somehow prejudiced, resentment builds over time.

Like the anger within the black community, these resentments aren't always 35
expressed in polite company. But they have helped shape the political landscape
for at least a generation. Anger over welfare and affirmative action helped forge the
Reagan Coalition.[12] Politicians routinely exploited fears of crime for their own
electoral ends. Talk show hosts and conservative commentators built entire careers
unmasking bogus claims of racism while dismissing legitimate discussions of racial
injustice and inequality as mere political correctness or reverse racism.

Just as black anger often proved counterproductive, so have these white resent- 36
ments distracted attention from the real culprits of the middle class squeeze—a
corporate culture rife with inside dealing,[13] questionable accounting practices, and
short-term greed; a Washington dominated by lobbyists and special interests; economic policies that favor the few over the many. And yet, to wish away the resentments of white Americans, to label them as misguided or even racist, without
recognizing they are grounded in legitimate concerns—this too widens the racial
divide, and blocks the path to understanding.

This is where we are right now. It's a racial stalemate we've been stuck in for 37
years. Contrary to the claims of some of my critics, black and white, I have never
been so naïve as to believe that we can get beyond our racial divisions in a single
election cycle, or with a single candidacy—particularly a candidacy as imperfect as
my own.

11. *Zero sum game*: A situation in which one party's loss is balanced by the other party's benefit; it
is impossible for both sides to win.

12. *Reagan Coalition*: The group of voters, both Republican and Democratic, who elected Ronald
Reagan president in 1980 and 1984. Though a Republican, Reagan attracted members of both major
political parties.

13. *Inside dealing*: Use of information not available to the general public to profit from purchase or
sale of stocks and bonds.

But I have asserted a firm conviction—a conviction rooted in my faith in God 38
and my faith in the American people—that working together we can move beyond
some of our old racial wounds, and that in fact we have no choice if we are to continue on the path of a more perfect union.

For the African-American community, that path means embracing the burdens 39
of our past without becoming victims of our past. It means continuing to insist on
a full measure of justice in every aspect of American life. But it also means binding
our particular grievances—for better health care, and better schools, and better
jobs—to the larger aspirations of all Americans—the white woman struggling to
break the glass ceiling, the white man who's been laid off, the immigrant trying to
feed his family. And it means taking full responsibility for own lives—by demanding more from our fathers, and spending more time with our children, and reading
to them, and teaching them that while they may face challenges and discrimination in their own lives, they must never succumb to despair or cynicism; they must
always believe that they can write their own destiny.

Ironically, this quintessentially American—and yes, conservative—notion of 40
self-help found frequent expression in Reverend Wright's sermons. But what my
former pastor too often failed to understand is that embarking on a program of
self-help also requires a belief that society can change.

The profound mistake of Reverend Wright's sermons is not that he spoke about 41
racism in our society. It's that he spoke as if our society was static; as if no progress
has been made; as if this country—a country that has made it possible for one of his
own members to run for the highest office in the land and build a coalition of white
and black, Latino and Asian, rich and poor, young and old—is still irrevocably
bound to a tragic past. But what we know—what we have seen—is that America
can change. That is true genius of this nation. What we have already achieved gives
us hope—the audacity to hope—for what we can and must achieve tomorrow.

In the white community, the path to a more perfect union means acknowledg- 42
ing that what ails the African-American community does not just exist in the minds
of black people; that the legacy of discrimination—and current incidents of discrimination, while less overt than in the past—are real and must be addressed. Not
just with words, but with deeds—by investing in our schools and our communities;
by enforcing our civil rights laws and ensuring fairness in our criminal justice system; by providing this generation with ladders of opportunity that were unavailable for previous generations. It requires all Americans to realize that your dreams
do not have to come at the expense of my dreams; that investing in the health,
welfare, and education of black and brown and white children will ultimately help
all of America prosper.

In the end, then, what is called for is nothing more, and nothing less, than what 43
all the world's great religions demand—that we do unto others as we would have

them do unto us. Let us be our brother's keeper,[14] Scripture tells us. Let us be our sister's keeper. Let us find that common stake we all have in one another, and let our politics reflect that spirit as well.

For we have a choice in this country. We can accept a politics that breeds divi- 44 sion, and conflict, and cynicism. We can tackle race only as spectacle—as we did in the O.J. trial—or in the wake of tragedy, as we did in the aftermath of Katrina[15]—or as fodder for the nightly news. We can play Reverend Wright's sermons on every channel, every day and talk about them from now until the election, and make the only question in this campaign whether or not the American people think that I somehow believe or sympathize with his most offensive words. We can pounce on some gaffe by a Hillary supporter as evidence that she's playing the race card,[16] or we can speculate on whether white men will all flock to John McCain in the general election regardless of his policies.

We can do that. 45

But if we do, I can tell you that in the next election, we'll be talking about some 46 other distraction. And then another one. And then another one. And nothing will change.

That is one option. Or, at this moment, in this election, we can come together 47 and say, "Not this time." This time we want to talk about the crumbling schools that are stealing the future of black children and white children and Asian children and Hispanic children and Native American children. This time we want to reject the cynicism that tells us that these kids can't learn; that those kids who don't look like us are somebody else's problem. The children of America are not those kids, they are our kids, and we will not let them fall behind in a twenty-first-century economy. Not this time.

This time we want to talk about how the lines in the Emergency Room are filled 48 with whites and blacks and Hispanics who do not have health care, who don't have the power on their own to overcome the special interests in Washington, but who can take them on if we do it together.

This time we want to talk about the shuttered mills that once provided a decent 49 life for men and women of every race, and the homes for sale that once belonged to Americans from every religion, every region, every walk of life. This time we want

14. *Let us be our brother's keeper*: A reference to the story of Cain and Abel in the Hebrew Bible. Cain killed his brother Abel out of jealousy; when God asked Cain where Abel was, Cain replied, "Am I my brother's keeper?"

15. *Katrina*: Hurricane Katrina, which devastated New Orleans in 2005. The city has a large black population, and some criticized the slow and inadequate federal response as being motivated by racial prejudice. *O.J. trial*: The 1994 trial of O.J. Simpson, a black football star accused of murdering his white ex-wife, Nicole Brown Simpson, and her friend, Ronald Goldman.

16. *Playing the race card*: Introducing the issue of race into an argument.

to talk about the fact that the real problem is not that someone who doesn't look like you might take your job; it's that the corporation you work for will ship it overseas for nothing more than a profit.

This time we want to talk about the men and women of every color and creed   50
who serve together, and fight together, and bleed together under the same proud flag. We want to talk about how to bring them home from a war that never should've been authorized and never should've been waged, and we want to talk about how we'll show our patriotism by caring for them, and their families, and giving them the benefits they have earned.

I would not be running for president if I didn't believe with all my heart that   51
this is what the vast majority of Americans want for this country. This union may never be perfect, but generation after generation has shown that it can always be perfected. And today, whenever I find myself feeling doubtful or cynical about this possibility, what gives me the most hope is the next generation—the young people whose attitudes and beliefs and openness to change have already made history in this election.

There is one story in particular that I'd like to leave you with today—a story I   52
told when I had the great honor of speaking on Dr. King's[17] birthday at his home church, Ebenezer Baptist, in Atlanta.

There is a young, twenty-three-year-old white woman named Ashley Baia who   53
organized for our campaign in Florence, South Carolina. She had been working to organize a mostly African-American community since the beginning of this campaign, and one day she was at a round-table discussion where everyone went around telling their story and why they were there.

And Ashley said that when she was nine years old, her mother got cancer. And   54
because she had to miss days of work, she was let go and lost her health care. They had to file for bankruptcy, and that's when Ashley decided that she had to do something to help her mom.

She knew that food was one of their most expensive costs, and so Ashley con-   55
vinced her mother that what she really liked and really wanted to eat more than anything else was mustard and relish sandwiches. Because that was the cheapest way to eat.

She did this for a year until her mom got better, and she told everyone at the   56
round-table that the reason she joined our campaign was so that she could help the millions of other children in the country who want and need to help their parents too.

Now Ashley might have made a different choice. Perhaps somebody told her   57
along the way that the source of her mother's problems were blacks who were on

---

17. *Dr. King*: Martin Luther King Jr. (1929–1968), the U.S. civil rights leader.

welfare and too lazy to work, or Hispanics who were coming into the country illegally. But she didn't. She sought out allies in her fight against injustice.

Anyway, Ashley finishes her story and then goes around the room and asks 58 everyone else why they're supporting the campaign. They all have different stories and reasons. Many bring up a specific issue. And finally they come to this elderly black man who's been sitting there quietly the entire time. And Ashley asks him why he's there. And he does not bring up a specific issue. He does not say health care or the economy. He does not say education or the war. He does not say that he was there because of Barack Obama. He simply says to everyone in the room, "I am here because of Ashley."

"I'm here because of Ashley." By itself, that single moment of recognition 59 between that young white girl and that old black man is not enough. It is not enough to give health care to the sick, or jobs to the jobless, or education to our children.

But it is where we start. It is where our union grows stronger. And as so many 60 generations have come to realize over the course of the two hundred and twenty-one years since a band of patriots signed that document in Philadelphia, that is where the perfection begins.

READING CLOSELY

1. Barack Obama sums up the message of his speech (and his campaign) in a single word. What is it? In which paragraphs does it appear?

2. In addition to racial tension, what other important issues, according to Obama, does America face today?

3. What does Obama see as the best way to deal with the country's problems? What does he see as the greatest threat to solving them?

4. Why does Obama refuse to "disown" Reverend Wright (22)?

5. Why does Obama nevertheless find Wright's remarks "inexcusable" (24)?

STRATEGIES AND STRUCTURES

1. First delivered in Philadelphia, across the street from Independence Hall, Obama's speech takes its title from the United States Constitution and begins with a direct reference to the men who composed that document (2). Why do you think Obama connects his words to those of the Founding Fathers? Why is this an effective strategy—or if it's not, why not?

2. Who is Obama's intended audience? What is his purpose in addressing them?

3. How does Obama anticipate objections to his speech, especially to how he characterizes his personal relationship with Reverend Wright? Refer to paragraph numbers in your response.

4. With regard to the issue of race, what is Obama's main CLAIM? What EVIDENCE does he use to support that claim? How convincing is that evidence?

5. How does Obama draw on personal experience? How pertinent is this evidence to his argument? Refer to paragraph numbers in your response.

6. How and how well does Obama establish his credibility as a person who understands the needs and values of "every race and every hue" (8)? Explain.

7. Why do you think Obama ends his speech with the story of Ashley and the "elderly black man" (58–59)? Is this an effective way to conclude? Why or why not?

8. *Other Methods*. Obama analyzes the CAUSES of "the anger and the bitterness" of Reverend Wright and his generation (32). What are some of them? What, according to Obama, are some of the potential EFFECTS of those feelings?

Thinking about Language

1. The word *perfect* is not normally used with *more* or *most*. The phrase "a more perfect union" is archaic and would be seen today as ungrammatical. How and where does Obama's speech play on this phrase?

2. A *story* is a NARRATIVE, an account of what happened to somebody in a particular time and place. The word can also mean the *material* for such a narrative—as in "that's the American story." Where and why does Obama use *story* in this second sense?

3. Obama refers to slavery as "this nation's original sin" (3). Theologians often use the phrase "original sin" to refer to the sin of Adam and Eve that caused them to be thrown out of the Garden of Eden and that was passed down to all later generations. Why do you think Obama uses it in a speech about a controversy involving his former pastor?

4. How does Obama use the personal pronoun *we* throughout his speech? Why do you think he uses it this way?

5. What are the CONNOTATIONS of the following words and phrases?

stained (3)	*seared into my genetic makeup* (9)
scoured (11)	*divisive* (12, 16)
on the cheap (13)	*firestorm* (15)
distorted (15)	*disown* (22)

FOR WRITING

1. Write a paragraph or two analyzing how Obama's speech appeals to his audience's emotions. Refer to paragraph numbers in your response.

2. Narrate a brief, true story about yourself or a relative or friend that could take place only in America, or that otherwise illustrates this "improbable experiment in democracy" (2).

3. Write an argument that supports or disagrees with the claim that "race is an issue that . . . this nation cannot afford to ignore right now" (25). Be sure to demonstrate your credibility by taking into account the needs and values of various racial and ethnic communities.

Ain't I a Woman?

Sojourner Truth (c. 1797–1883) is the name assumed by Isabella Baumfree, who was born into slavery in Hurley, New York. A tall and imposing figure with a deep voice whose first language was Dutch, Truth was legally freed in 1827. Though unable to read or write, she became a celebrated abolitionist and campaigner for women's rights.

"Ain't I a Woman?" is the title usually given to a brief extemporaneous speech that Truth delivered at the Women's Convention in Akron, Ohio, in 1851. The title phrase does not occur in the first recorded version of the speech—reported by editor Marius Robinson in the Salem, Ohio, Anti-Slavery Bugle, June 21, 1851—though Robinson records the speaker as asking, "[C]an any man do more than that?" The version reprinted here derives from the second published version, that of abolitionist writer and speaker Frances Dana Gage, in the National Anti-Slavery Standard on May 2, 1863. In addition to assigning a black Southern dialect to the speaker, Gage added the title phrase and more fire to Truth's plea for equal rights for women and blacks. Like the Declaration of Independence (pp. 542–45) or Chief Seattle's "Reply to the U.S. Government" (pp. 547–51), "Ain't I a Woman?" is something of a collaboration.

WELL, CHILDREN, where there is so much racket there must be something out of kilter. I think that 'twixt the negroes of the South and the women at the North, all talking about rights, the white men will be in a fix pretty soon. But what's all this here talking about?

That man over there says that women need to be helped into carriages, and lifted over ditches, and to have the best place everywhere. Nobody ever helps me into carriages, or over mud-puddles, or gives me any best place! And ain't I a woman? Look at me! Look at my arm! I have ploughed and planted, and gathered into barns, and no man could head me! And ain't I a woman? I could work as much and eat as much as a man—when I could get it—and bear the lash as well! And ain't I a woman? I have borne thirteen children, and seen most all sold off to slavery, and when I cried out with my mother's grief, none but Jesus heard me! And ain't I a woman?

Then they talk about this thing in the head; what's this they call it? [member of audience whispers, "intellect"] That's it, honey. What's that got to do with women's

SUGGESTED MLA CITATION: Truth, Sojourner. "Ain't I a Woman?" 1851. *Back to the Lake*. Ed. Thomas Cooley. 2nd ed. New York: Norton, 2012. 574–76. Print.

Sojourner Truth in an 1864 carte-de-visite photograph.

See p. 528
for a form of
argument that
treats oppo-
nents as
colleagues.
rights or negroes' rights? If my cup won't hold but a pint, and yours holds a quart, wouldn't you be mean not to let me have my little half measure full?

Then that little man in black there, he says women can't have as much rights as men, 'cause Christ wasn't a woman! Where did your Christ come from? Where did your Christ come from? From God and a woman! Man had nothing to do with Him. 4

If the first woman God ever made was strong enough to turn the world upside down all alone, these women together ought to be able to turn it back, and get it right side up again! And now they is asking to do it, the men better let them. 5

Obliged to you for hearing me, and now old Sojourner ain't got nothing more to say. 6

READING CLOSELY

1. The opening paragraph of Sojourner Truth's speech was added in the 1863 version. What "racket" is it referring to (1)?

2. What is "out of kilter" in the opinion of Truth and the other women who attended the 1851 Women's Convention in Ohio (1)?

3. What solution to the imbalance do Truth and her colleagues propose?

STRATEGIES AND STRUCTURES

1. What EVIDENCE does Truth offer for her contention that women do not "need to be helped into carriages, and lifted over ditches" (2)? How sufficient is that evidence to prove her point?

2. How, and how well, does Truth entertain (and refute) counterarguments to her proposition that women are the equal of men?

3. If women want to set the world right again, Truth's speech concludes, "the men better let them" (5). Does this argument appeal mostly to the listener's intellect ("this thing in the head"), emotions, or sense of ethics (3)? Explain.

4. *Other Methods.* How does Truth DEFINE herself as a woman? How, and how well, does this definition support her argument?

THINKING ABOUT LANGUAGE

1. Truth addresses her audience as "children" (1)? Is this an effective strategy? Why or why not?

2. What is the point of the ANALOGY between Eve and "these women" (5)? Explain.

3. "Ain't I a woman?" is clearly a RHETORICAL QUESTION. What is the effect of repeating it four times in this short speech?

FOR WRITING

1. In the 1851 version, as reported by Marius Robinson in the *Anti-Slavery Bugle*, Truth's speech ends with the following words: "But man is in a tight place, the poor slave is on him, woman is coming on him, he is surely between a hawk and a buzzard." In a paragraph or two, explain which ending you find more effective (and why)—this one or that of the "official" 1863 version (5–6).

2. Marius Robinson's 1851 version of Truth's speech is readily available online. Write a COMPARISON of the two versions that explains how and how well each makes its respective arguments.

3. Write an essay arguing that the power and influence of Truth's celebrated speech was (or was not) the result as much of who the author was—or was perceived to be—as of what the speech actually says.

MICHAEL LEWIS

Buy That Little Girl an Ice Cream Cone

Michael Lewis (b. 1960) is a native of New Orleans and was educated at Princeton University and the London School of Economics. Before becoming a professional writer, he spent four years as a bond salesman on Wall Street, an experience that provided the basis for Lewis' best-selling Liar's Poker *(1989). The author of* Moneyball *(2003) and* The Blind Side *(2006), Lewis also drew on his knowledge of sports and money matters in* The Big Short *(2010), a study of the personalities and gamblers' mentality behind the worst economic crisis in the United States since the Great Depression.*

"Buy That Little Girl an Ice Cream Cone" is a selection from Home Game: An Accidental Guide to Fatherhood *(2009). In the struggle for gender equality, Lewis argues, boys will always be boys; girls, however, are not so predictable.*

W E'RE AT A FANCY HOTEL in Bermuda. Like fancy hotels everywhere, the place 1 is paying new attention to the whims of small children. The baby pool is vast— nearly as big as the pool for the grown-ups, to which it is connected by a slender canal. In the middle of the baby pool is a hot tub, just for little kids. My two daughters, now ages six and three, leap from the hot tub into the baby pool and back again. The pleasure they take in this could not be more innocent or pure.

Then, out of nowhere, come four older boys. Ten, maybe eleven years old. As 2 anyone who has only girls knows, boys add nothing to any social situation but trouble. These four are set on proving the point. Seeing my little girls, they grab the pool noodles—intended to keep three-year-olds afloat—and wield them as weapons. They descend upon Quinn, my six-year-old, whacking the water on either side of her, until she is almost in tears. I'm hovering in the canal between baby pool and grown-up pool, wondering if I should intervene. Dixie beats me to it. She jumps out in front of her older sister and thrusts out her three-year-old chest.

"TEASING BOYS!" she hollers, so loudly that grown-ups around the pool peer 3 over their Danielle Steel novels. Even the boys are taken aback. Dixie, now on stage, raises her voice a notch:

"YOU JUST SHUT UP YOU STUPID MOTHERFUCKING ASSHOLE!" 4

To the extent that all hell can break loose around a baby pool in a Bermuda 5 resort, it does. A John Grisham novel is lowered; several of Danielle Steel's vanish

SUGGESTED MLA CITATION: Lewis, Michael. "Buy That Little Girl an Ice Cream Cone." 2009. *Back to the Lake*. Ed. Thomas Cooley. 2nd ed. New York: Norton, 2012. 578–80. Print.

into beach bags. I remain hovering in the shallows of the grown-up pool where it enters the baby pool, with my entire head above water. My first thought: *Oh . . . my . . . God!* My second thought: *No one knows I'm her father.* I sink lower, like a crocodile, so that just my eyes and forehead are above the waterline; but in my heart a new feeling rises: pride. Behind me a lady on a beach chair shouts, "Kevin! Kevin! Get over here!"

Kevin appears to be one of the noodle-wielding eleven-year-old boys. "But Mooooooommm!" he says.   6

"Kevin! *Now!*"   7

The little monster skulks over to his mother's side while his fellow Orcs await the higher judgment. I'm close enough to hear her ream him out. It's delicious. "Kevin, did you teach that little girl those words?" she asks.   8

"Mooomm! Nooooooo!"   9

"Then where did she learn them?"   10

As it happens, I know the answer to that one: carpool. Months ago! I was driving them home from school, my two girls, plus two other kids—a seven-year-old boy and a ten-year-old girl. They were crammed in the back seat of the Volkswagen Passat, jabbering away; I was alone in the front seat, not especially listening. But then the ten-year-old said, "Deena said a bad word today."   11

"Which one?" asked Quinn.   12

"The S-word," said the ten-year-old.   13

"Ooooooooo," they all said.   14

"What's the S-word?" I asked.   15

"We can't say it without getting in trouble," said the ten-year-old knowingly.   16

"You're safe here," I said.   17

She thought it over for a second, then said, "Stupid."   18

"Ah," I said, smiling.   19

"Wally said the D-word!" said Quinn.   20

"What's the D-word?" I asked.   21

"Dumb!" she shouted, and they all giggled at the sheer illicit pleasure of it. Then the seven-year-old boy chimed in. "I know a bad word, too! I know a bad word, too!" he said.   22

"What's the bad word?" I asked brightly. I didn't see why he should be left out.   23

"Shutupyoustupidmotherfuckingasshole!"   24

I swerved off the road, stopped the car, and hit the emergency lights. I began to deliver a lecture on the difference between bad words and seriously bad words, but the audience was fully consumed with laughter. Dixie, especially, wanted to know the secret of making Daddy stop the car.   25

"Shutupmotherstupid fuck," she said.   26

"Dixie!" I said.   27

"Daddy," said Quinn thoughtfully, "how come you say a bad word when we spill   28
something and when you spill something you just say, 'Oops'?"

"Stupidfuck!" screamed Dixie, and they all laughed.   29

"DIXIE!"   30

She stopped. They all did. For the rest of the drive they whispered.   31

So here we are, months later, in this Bermuda pool, Dixie with her chest thrust   32
out in defiance, me floating like a crocodile and feeling very much different than I
should. I should be embarrassed and concerned. I should be sweeping her out of
the pool and washing her mouth out with soap. I don't feel that way. Actually, I'm
impressed. More than impressed: awed. It's just incredibly heroic, taking out after
this rat pack of boys. Plus she's sticking up for her big sister, which isn't something
you see every day. I don't want to get in her way. I just want to see what happens
next.

Behind me Kevin has just finished being torn what appears to be a new ass-   33
hole by his mother, and is relaunching himself into the baby pool with a real
malice. He's as indignant as a serial killer who got put away on a speeding ticket:
He's guilty of many things but not of teaching a three-year-old girl the art of
cursing. Now he intends to get even. Gathering his fellow Orcs in the hot tub, he
and his companions once again threaten Quinn. Dixie, once again, leaps into the
fray.

"TEASING BOYS!" she shouts. Now she has the attention of an entire Bermuda   34
resort.

"YOU WATCH OUT TEASING BOYS! BECAUSE I PEED IN THIS   35
POOL TWO TIMES! ONCE IN THE HOT POOL AND ONCE IN THE
COLD POOL!"

See p. 526 for
tips on estab-
lishing your
credibility in
an argument.

The teasing boys flee, grossed out and defeated. Various grown-ups say   36
various things to each other, but no one seeks to remove Dixie from the
baby pool. Dixie returns to playing with her sister—who appears far less grateful
than she should be. And the crocodile drops below the waterline, swivels, and vanishes into the depths of the grown-up pool. But he makes a mental note to buy that
little girl an ice-cream cone. Even if her mother disapproves.

READING CLOSELY

1. When his three-year-old daughter hurls grown-up expletives at the boys in
    the hotel swimming pool, says Michael Lewis, he should be "sweeping her out
    of the pool and washing her mouth out with soap" (32). Is he right? Why or
    why not?

2. How well do you think Dixie understands the implications of what she is saying? What does she understand for sure? Explain.

3. Why does Kevin's mother think Dixie learned "those words" from him (8)? Who *did* Dixie learn the profanity from? Was the informant a boy or a girl?

4. In her "Ain't I a Woman?" speech (pp. 574–76), the abolitionist and women's rights activist Sojourner Truth argues that once women have made up their minds to act, "the men better let them." Does young Dixie Lewis' speech in the luxury hotel pool in Bermuda confirm or refute this proposition? Explain.

5. Lewis remains a crocodilian observer throughout the scene in the baby pool. Should he have intervened? Why or why not?

STRATEGIES AND STRUCTURES

1. Lewis argues that his daughter should be rewarded for her behavior "even if her mother disapproves" (35). How, and how well, does he support this conclusion?

2. The boys in the pool, says Lewis, seem bent upon "proving the point" (2). What point? What are the grounds of argument here?

3. If the Orc-like invasion of the baby pool proves a point about the behavior of boys, what point does Dixie's defense of her sister prove about the behavior of girls?

4. In this gendered battle scene, the boys use the pool noodles "as weapons" (2). What weapons do the girls have at their disposal? Explain.

5. Lewis tells a story within a story. What is the purpose of the FLASHBACK, replete with DIALOGUE, to the carpool scene (11–31)?

6. *Other Methods.* Lewis' argument is mostly NARRATIVE. How and how effectively do the events of that narrative prove his fatherly assumptions about the nature of boys versus girls?

THINKING ABOUT LANGUAGE

1. Lewis describes little Dixie as delivering her startling lines from a "stage" (3). Explain the implications of this METAPHOR?

2. Dixie's behavior in standing up for her sister, says Lewis, is nothing short of "heroic" (32). Is the overstatement justified? Why or why not?

3. Before the boys arrive, Lewis' bathing daughters are engaged in a "pleasure" that "could not be more innocent or pure" (1). This is the language of Eden. How and why has the language of Lewis' family fable changed by the end, when the crocodile "drops below the waterline, swivels, and vanishes into the depths" (35)?

For Writing

1. In a paragraph or two, DESCRIBE an occasion when the words of children at play proved to be as potent as sticks or stones—or pool noodles.

2. Write an essay arguing that boys and girls are (or are not) socialized in fundamentally different ways that account (or do not account) for specific differences in adult behaviors—for example, in speech patterns—between males and females. Cite personal experience as appropriate, but also refer to your reading and research in an appropriate academic field, such anthropology, sociology, or linguistics.

Debating the Drinking Age

After the repeal of Prohibition, which outlawed alcohol from 1920 to 1933, most states set the minimal legal drinking age (MLDA) at 21. Between 1969 and 1976, however, as the minimum age for voting and other activities fell, thirty states reduced the MLDA. As a result, some researchers contended, more teenagers were killed or seriously injured in automobile and other accidents. Over the next decade, under pressure from such advocacy groups as Mothers Against Drunk Driving (MADD), sixteen states increased their MLDAs; and in 1984, the federal government enacted the National Minimum Drinking Age Act, which cut federal funding for highways by ten percent to states with an MLDA under 21.

Today, all states comply with this act, which prohibits the purchase and public possession of alcohol by people under 21. The act does not ban the consumption of alcohol by young people, however. And in recent years, some lawmakers and educators have called for a reevaluation of the MLDA. In 2008, for example, the Amethyst Initiative began circulating a statement that "twenty-one is not working," as evidenced by the development of "a culture of dangerous 'binge-drinking.'" By 2011, presidents of more than 125 American colleges and universities had signed that statement.

Should the MLDA be lowered? In the texts presented here, a journalist, a professor, and a research scientist each discuss the legal, medical, and social consequences of the minimum legal age for the purchase and public consumption of alcohol:

Ruth Engs, "Why the Drinking Age Should Be Lowered," p. 584
Jack Hitt, "The Battle of the Binge," p. 587
Robert Voas, "There's No Benefit to Lowering the Drinking Age," p. 591

Questions about this group of readings can be found on p. 594.

RUTH C. ENGS

Why the Drinking Age Should Be Lowered
An Opinion Based on Research

Ruth Clifford Engs is professor emeritus of applied health science at Indiana University, where her work has concentrated on the use, abuse, and regulation of alcohol. In particular, she has written extensively about the drinking patterns and drinking problems of college students.

"Why the Drinking Age Should Be Lowered" appears on Engs' website. The real issue, according to Engs, isn't underage drinking but irresponsible drinking. Elsewhere Engs has described her preferred approach to the problem—drinking permits modeled on driving permits. "How can we expect youth to know how to drink," she writes, "if they are not educated about sensible consumption?"

THE LEGAL DRINKING AGE should be lowered to about 18 or 19 and young adults 1 allowed to drink in controlled environments such as restaurants, taverns, pubs and official school and university functions. In these situations responsible drinking could be taught through role modeling and educational programs. Mature and sensible drinking behavior would be expected. This opinion is based upon research that I have been involved in for over twenty years concerning college-age youth and the history of drinking in the United States and other cultures.

Although the legal purchase age is 21 years of age, a majority of college students 2 under this age consume alcohol but in an irresponsible manner. This is because drinking by these youth is seen as an enticing "forbidden fruit," a "badge of rebellion against authority" and a symbol of adulthood. As a nation we have tried prohibition legislation twice in the past for controlling irresponsible drinking problems. This was during national prohibition in the 1920s and state prohibition during the 1850s. These laws were finally repealed because they were unenforceable and because the backlash towards them caused other social problems. Today we are repeating history and making the same mistakes that occurred in the past. Prohibition did not work then and prohibition for young people under the age of 21 is not working now.

The flouting of the current laws is readily seen among university students. Those 3 under the age of 21 are more likely to be heavy—sometimes called "binge"—

SUGGESTED MLA CITATION: Engs, Ruth C. "Why the Drinking Age Should Be Lowered: An Opinion Based on Research." 1988. *Back to the Lake.* Ed. Thomas Cooley. 2nd ed. New York: Norton, 2012. 584–85. Print.

drinkers (consuming over 5 drinks at least once a week). For example, 22 percent of all students under 21 compared to 18 percent over 21 years of age are heavy drinkers. Among drinkers only, 32 percent of under age compared to 24 percent of legal age are heavy drinkers.

Research from the early 1980s until the present has shown a continuous decrease 4 in drinking and driving related variables which has paralleled the nation's, and also university students', decrease in per capita consumption. However, these declines started in 1980, before the national 1987 law that mandated states to have 21-year-old-alcohol-purchase laws.

The decrease in drinking and driving problems are the result of many factors 5 and not just the rise in purchase age or the decreased per capita consumption. These include: education concerning drunk driving, designated driver programs, increased seat belt and air bag usage, safer automobiles, lower speed limits, free taxi services from drinking establishments, etc.

While there has been a decrease in per capita consumption and motor vehicle 6 crashes, unfortunately, during this same time period there has been an *increase* in other problems related to heavy and irresponsible drinking among college-age youth. Most of these reported behaviors showed little change until *after* the 21-year-old law in 1987. For example from 1982 until 1987 about 46 percent of students reported "vomiting after drinking." This jumped to over 50 percent after the law change. Significant increases were also found for other variables: "cutting class after drinking" jumped from 9 percent to almost 12 percent; "missing class because of hangover" went from 26 percent to 28 percent; "getting lower grades because of drinking" rose from 5 percent to 7 percent; and "been in a fight after drinking" increased from 12 percent to 17 percent. All of these behaviors are indices of irresponsible drinking. This increase in abusive drinking behavior is due to "underground drinking" outside of adult supervision in student rooms and apartments where same-age individuals congregate and because of lack of knowledge of responsible drinking behaviors.

Using statistics and other factual evidence is discussed on p. 516.

Based upon the fact that our current prohibition laws are not working, alternative 7 approaches from the experience of other, and more ancient cultures, who do not have these problems, need to be tried. Groups such as Italians, Greeks, Chinese and Jews, who have few drinking related problems, tend to share some common characteristics. Alcohol is neither seen as a poison or a magic potion, there is little or no social pressure to drink, irresponsible behavior is never tolerated, young people learn at home from their parents and from other adults how to handle alcohol in a responsible manner, there is societal consensus on what constitutes responsible drinking. Because the 21-year-old-drinking-age law is not working, and is counterproductive, it behooves us as a nation to change our current prohibition law and to teach responsible drinking techniques for those who choose to consume alcoholic beverages.

Reading Closely

1. What is Ruth Engs' CLAIM? Where does she state it most clearly and directly?

2. Engs isn't arguing that people under 21 should drink more. So why does she think lowering the MLDA is a good idea? What specific reasons does she give?

3. Why do you think Engs refers to the drinking practices of "more ancient cultures" (7)?

4. Engs states that research has shown that both "drinking and driving related variables" and "per capita consumption" of alcohol have decreased since 1980 (4). Why doesn't she attribute these good results to the MLDA law? To what *does* she attribute these results?

Strategies and Structures

1. How does Engs establish her credibility on the subject of student drinking? Refer to specific places in the text in your response.

2. Who is her intended AUDIENCE? What does Engs want them to do?

3. How and how well does Engs deal with potential objections to her argument?

4. What kind of EVIDENCE does Engs use to support her claim that the drinking age should be lowered?

5. *Other Methods.* Engs COMPARES the MLDA law to the prohibition laws of the 1920s, in which all alcohol was banned in the United States. Do you think this is an effective comparison? Why or why not? Is it a fair one? Explain.

Thinking about Language

1. "Forbidden fruit" (2) is a reference to the Bible—Genesis 2:16–17. How does Engs use this ALLUSION to support her argument?

2. Engs refers to the MLDA laws as "our current prohibition laws" (7). What are the CONNOTATIONS of the word *prohibition* in this context?

3. "Flouting" (3) is frequently confused with *flaunting.* Why is *flouting* the correct choice here?

For Writing

1. Engs claims that "ancient cultures . . . have few drinking related problems" (7). Outline the main points you would make in an argument addressing this claim. You might support it, refute it, or agree with some parts but not others.

2. Write an argument addressing the issue of "how to handle alcohol in a responsible manner" (7).

JACK HITT

The Battle of the Binge

Jack Hitt (b. 1957) is a frequent contributor to such magazines as Harper's, GQ, Rolling Stone, Mother Jones, and Outside. As a reporter for the New York Times Magazine, he has covered everything from the abortion debate and presidential politics to Internet spam and featherless chickens. A familiar voice on National Public Radio's This American Life, Hitt is also the author of Off the Road: A Modern-Day Walk Down the Pilgrim's Route into Spain (1994).

Raised and educated in an era when college students "strained to act intelligently and comfortably while drinking with an elder," Hitt revisits his alma mater in "The Battle of the Binge," first published in the New York Times Magazine in 1999. Largely as a result of laws that raised the legal age to 21, Hitt argues, drinking on campus has changed in ways that he finds both appalling and sobering.

BACK IN THE 70'S—my college time—an English professor I barely knew named 1
Ted Stirling spotted me on the quad and invited me to a small, informal reading
after supper. Maybe he felt sorry for me. I had marooned myself in the French
ghetto of *la litterature comparative*, and had further exiled myself in the cul-de-sac
between Latin and Spanish. So I went that night to sit on stuffed sofas beneath
scowling bishops in gilt frames and to discuss Wallace Stevens's poem "Thirteen
Ways of Looking at a Blackbird." Afterward, Stirling bought the students a pitcher
of beer at the pub, and we strained to act intelligently and comfortably while drinking with an elder. ("Stevens an insurance agent! Surely you jest, Professor. Why,
that would make poets the unacknowledged underwriters of the world, wouldn't
you agree?")

I started thinking about how I learned to drink at college—I went to Sewanee, 2
in Tennessee—when I read about a recent Harvard study that found that 43 percent, nearly half, of all college students today "binge drink," defined as
regularly pounding down four or five stiff ones in a row in order to get See p. 529 for the use of definition to support an argument.
blasted. The pandemic is so severe that 113 college presidents united a
few weeks ago to publicly admit that a generation is in peril. They have
also rolled out a public-service ad, which employs that brand of sarcasm
Madison Avenue thinks young people find amusing. "Binge Beer," it says. "Who
says falling off a balcony is such a bad thing?" See, you're supposed to realize that
falling off a balcony is, in fact, a bad thing.

SUGGESTED MLA CITATION: Hitt, Jack. "The Battle of the Binge." 1999. *Back to the Lake.* Ed.
Thomas Cooley. 2nd ed. New York: Norton, 2012. 587–89. Print.

Other educational tactics include dry rock concerts, abstinent fraternities, 3
"mock 'tail" parties, a Web site of course (www.nasulgc.org/bingedrink) and a new
CD-ROM called "Alcohol 101" and featuring a "virtual party" that segues into an
anatomical lecture about how quickly the bloodstream absorbs alcohol. Look out,
Myst.[1]

What no one seems to have noticed is that the rise in binging has occurred at 4
the very same time that the legal drinking age has been raised everywhere to 21. If
you're 18 to 21, it's the 1920's again and a mini-Prohibition is in full swing. As a
result, moderate drinking has almost vanished among students and, more tellingly,
from school-sponsored events. How anachronistic it feels to describe what used to
be routine college functions, like a Dizzy Gillespie concert or a Robert Penn War-
ren reading, followed by a reception, with drinks and hors d'oeuvres, at which students were expected to at least pretend to be cool about it, i.e., practice drinking.
I frequently received dinner invitations from faculty members like Tom Spaccarelli, a Spanish professor who served up tapas while uncorking a Rioja for a few students. We handled the long stems of our wineglasses as confidently as a colt its legs.

And there was always another occasion. Sewanee had dozens of those inane col- 5
lege societies like Green Ribbon, a group whose invitation to membership I haugh-
tily trashed after Professor Paschall, my sponsor, explained that the point was
nothing more than "getting dressed up and having cocktails with some alumni."

But I began to see the point about 10 years after graduation when I returned to 6
Sewanee to give a little talk. Afterward, I took some students to the pub where they
sheepishly ordered cider. At first, I thought this new college life—clean and sober—
was a good idea.

Then my nephew, a junior there at that time, explained the typical partygoer's 7
schedule: drive off campus or hide in the woods (often alone), guzzle a pint of
bourbon, eat a box of breath mints and then stumble into the dry sorority party
serenely blotto. My nephew knew two students who had died—falling off a cliff,
blood poisoning—and five others who had been paralyzed or seriously injured in
car accidents because of binging. For a college with roughly 1,300 students, this
constitutes a statistical massacre.

We drank wildly in the 70's, too. The Phi's had their seasonal Screaming Bull 8
blowout. Kegs were easy to find on weekends. I have drunk tequila only once in my
life, and this being a family newspaper, my account of that evening can proceed no
further. I was a member of the Sewanee Temperance League, whose annual outdoor party pledged to "rid the world of alcohol by consuming it all ourselves." But
all those events were crowded social occasions, almost always with professors and
their spouses in attendance—not prowling alone in the woods with a pint. After

---

1. *Myst*: A popular computer game that was released in 1993.

college, when you got a job, Screaming Bull opportunities quickly tapered off; the working world was different yet, in time, quite familiar, like an evening with Ted Stirling or a dinner at Tom Spaccarelli's.

This year, Ohio University's zero-tolerance program has proudly outlawed   9
empty beer cans in the dorm. Nearly 7 percent of the entire 16,000-student enroll-ment last year was disciplined for alcohol abuse, often handed over as criminals to the Athens Municipal Court. Despite all the tough bluster, the binge rate among students there hasn't budged from an astounding 60 percent.

For college students, booze has been subsumed into the Manichaean² battle of   10
our drug war. It's either Prohibition or cave into the hippies' legalization schemes. And it seems fairly unreversible. Legislatures raised the drinking minimum in reac-tion to the raw emotion deployed by Mothers Against Drunk Driving. Then col-leges were bullied by insurance companies that threatened to jack up liability rates if administrators didn't take aggressive action. The old days of looking the other way, when the police used to pick up toasted students and quietly drive them to their dorms, seems like collaboration in today's harsh light.

There probably is a way out of this, but it is going to require some larger cultural   11
changes that will make us see the irony, even cruelty, of infantilizing certain young adults. The very people who have urged this situation into existence are too often the people who vent about the increasing lack of "responsibility" in our society (demanding, for example, that juvenile offenders be treated in court as adults). But for middle-class kids in college, they make responsibility an ever-receding ideal, never quite grasped in the pampered ease of an extended adolescence.

In the early 70's, the big political fight among college students was for the right   12
to vote. The argument held that kids who were considered old enough to die for their country and order a drink in a bar should be able to choose their political leaders. It is back to two out of three again. But booze is not like the vote, which can be ignored to no one's immediate peril. Rather, alcohol consumption, like table manners or sexual behavior, is a socialized phenomenon, which if not taught, yields up a kind of wild child. By denying the obvious pleasure of drinking and not teaching it by example, is anyone really surprised that we've loosed upon the world a generation of feral drunks?

---

2. *Manichaean:* A dualistic religion named after a Persian prophet of the third century C.E. In every-day usage, "Manichaean" refers to a conflict of opposites, such as good and evil, light and darkness.

READING CLOSELY

1. When Jack Hitt was in college, how and when did students consume alcohol? In his view, why has "moderate drinking" all but vanished among college students (4)?

2. What is Hitt's explanation for why the MLDA was raised to twenty-one in the first place? Why does he think this trend is "fairly unreversible" (10)?

3. Hitt thinks that a number of changes would have to occur before the MLDA is either lowered or ignored. What are some of those changes?

STRATEGIES AND STRUCTURES

1. Who is Hitt's intended AUDIENCE, and how does he establish his credibility with them?

2. How, and how well, does Hitt deal with potential objections to his argument?

3. Hitt argues that "the rise in binging has occurred at the very same time that the legal drinking age has been raised everywhere to 21" (4). Do you think he effectively demonstrates a CAUSE-AND-EFFECT relationship between the two?

4. *Other Methods.* Hitt's evidence is mainly ANECDOTAL. Cite several examples of his use of personal NARRATIVE, and explain how they support his argument.

THINKING ABOUT LANGUAGE

1. Hitt speaks of the "raw emotion" with which, he claims, Mothers Against Drunk Driving convinced legislators to raise the MLDA (10). What are the CONNOTATIONS of the term "deployed" in the same paragraph? Of "feral" (12)?

2. What are the implications of the SIMILE "as a colt its legs" (4)?

3. When Hitt speaks of cultural changes in paragraph 11, how is he DEFINING culture? How does this definition contribute to his argument?

FOR WRITING

1. Write a paragraph or two arguing that responsible drinking is a moral and ethical issue rather than (or as well as) a "socialized phenomenon" (12).

2. Although Hitt admits a drop in the MLDA is unlikely unless the federal government goes along, he doesn't deal directly with what it would cost individual states if they lowered the MLDA without federal approval—and therefore lost 10 percent of their federal funding for highways. Write an argument that claims the MLDA should or should not be lowered, taking into account the economic aspects of the issue.

ROBERT VOAS

There's No Benefit to Lowering the Drinking Age

Robert Voas is a senior research scientist at the Pacific Institute for Research and Evaluation in Calverton, Maryland. A former astronaut training officer for NASA, he holds a PhD in psychology from the University of California at Los Angeles. After leaving NASA, Voas spent several years in the Peace Corps before joining the U.S. Department of Transportation, where he served as director of the National Highway Traffic Safety Administration's Office of Program Evaluation. A member of the national board of Mothers Against Drunk Driving (MADD), Voas is the author of many articles on motor vehicle accidents and alcohol abuse, particularly among teenagers.

"There's No Benefit to Lowering the Drinking Age" first appeared in the Christian Science Monitor *in 2006.*

AFTER NEARLY FOUR DECADES of exacting research on how to save lives and reduce injuries by preventing drinking and driving, there is a revanchist attempt afoot to roll back one of the most successful laws in generations: the minimum legal drinking age of 21.

This is extremely frustrating. While public health researchers must produce painstaking evidence that's subjected to critical scholarly review, lower-drinking-age advocates seem to dash off remarks based on glib conjecture and self-selected facts.

It's startling that anybody—given the enormous bodies of research and data— would consider lowering the drinking age. And yet, legislation is currently pending in New Hampshire and Wisconsin to lower the drinking age for military personnel and for all residents in Vermont. Just as bad are the arguments from think-tank writers, various advocates, and even academics (including at least one former college president) that ignore or manipulate the real evidence and instead rely on slogans.

I keep hearing the same refrains: "If you're old enough to go to war, you should be old enough to drink," or "the drinking-age law just increases the desire for the forbidden fruit," or "lower crash rates are due to tougher enforcement, not the 21 law," or "Europeans let their kids drink, so they learn how to be more responsible," or finally, "I did it when I was a kid, and I'm OK."

For advice on countering faulty logic, see p. 524. First, I'm not sure what going to war and being allowed to drink have in common. The military takes in youngsters particularly because they are not yet fully developed and can be molded into soldiers. The 21 law is predicated

SUGGESTED MLA CITATION: Voas, Robert. "There's No Benefit to Lowering the Drinking Age." 2006. *Back to the Lake*. Ed. Thomas Cooley. 2nd ed. New York: Norton, 2012. 591–92. Print.

on the fact that drinking is more dangerous for youth because they're still developing mentally and physically, and they lack experience and are more likely to take risks. Ask platoon leaders and unit commanders, and they'll tell you that the last thing they want is young soldiers drinking.

As for the forbidden fruit argument, the opposite is true. Research shows that back when some states still had a minimum drinking age of 18, youths in those states who were under 21 drank more and continued to drink more as adults in their early 20s. In states where the drinking age was 21, teenagers drank less and continue to drink less through their early 20s. 6

And the minimum 21 law, by itself, has most certainly resulted in fewer accidents, because the decline occurred even when there was little enforcement and tougher penalties had not yet been enacted. According to the National Highway Traffic Safety Administration, the 21 law has saved 23,733 lives since states began raising drinking ages in 1975. 7

Do European countries really have fewer youth drinking problems? No, that's a myth. Compared to American youth, binge drinking rates among young people are higher in every European country except Turkey. Intoxication rates are higher in most countries; in Britain, Denmark, and Ireland they're more than twice the U.S. level. Intoxication and binge drinking are directly linked to higher levels of alcohol-related problems, such as drinking and driving. 8

But, you drank when you were a kid, and you're OK. Thank goodness, because many kids aren't OK. An average of 11 American teens die each day from alcohol-related crashes. Underage drinking leads to increased teen pregnancy, violent crime, sexual assault, and huge costs to our communities. Among college students, it leads to 1,700 deaths, 500,000 injuries, 600,000 physical assaults, and 70,000 sexual assaults each year. 9

Recently, New Zealand lowered its drinking age, which gave researchers a good opportunity to study the impact. The result was predictable: The rate of alcohol-related crashes among young people rose significantly compared to older drivers. 10

I've been studying drinking and driving for nearly 40 years and have been involved in public health and behavioral health for 53 years. Believe me when I say that lowering the drinking age would be very dangerous; it would benefit no one except those who profit from alcohol sales. 11

If bars and liquor stores can freely provide alcohol to teenagers, parents will be out of the loop when it comes to their children's decisions about drinking. Age 21 laws are designed to keep such decisions within the family where they belong. Our society, particularly our children and grandchildren, will be immeasurably better off if we not only leave the minimum drinking age law as it is, but enforce it better, too. 12

Reading Closely

1. What is Robert Voas' CLAIM? Where does he articulate it in most clearly?

2. According to Voas, what is the basis for the "21 law" (5)?

3. What other consequences, besides an increase in traffic fatalities among teens, does Voas attribute to "underage drinking" (9)?

4. In Voas' opinion, who are the only people to benefit from a lower MLDA?

5. Why does Voas think that lowering the MLDA would keep parents "out of the loop" (12)?

Strategies and Structures

1. What is the main EVIDENCE that Voas provides to support his claim?

2. Who is Voas' intended AUDIENCE? How does he appeal to their emotions?

3. How and how well does Voas establish his credibility as an expert?

4. Good writers anticipate the arguments that are most likely to be raised by people with different points of view. Voas makes this strategy the main organizing principle of his entire argument. How?

5. *Other Methods.* Voas finds little in common between "going to war and being allowed to drink" (5). Where else (and how effectively) does he use COMPARISON AND CONTRAST to support his argument?

Thinking about Language

1. Look up "revanchist" in a dictionary (1). What does it mean, and how does it fit the context in which it is used here?

2. Why does Voas refer to arguments for lowering the drinking age as "glib conjecture" (2)? How well does he succeed in showing that the phrase is justified?

3. "Refrains" (4) and "myth" (8) have to do with songs and stories. Why (and how effectively) does Voas use these terms?

For Writing

1. To the argument "you drank when you were a kid, and you're OK," Voas replies: "Thank goodness, because many kids aren't OK" (9). Is this retort logical, or does it BEG THE QUESTION? Write a paragraph explaining your view.

2. "Age 21 laws," says Voas, "are designed to keep such decisions [about alcohol consumption] within the family where they belong" (12). Compose an argument refuting or supporting this claim.

Debating the Drinking Age

The following questions refer to the arguments on pp. 584–93.

READING ARGUMENTS

1. Among the participants in this debate on the MLDA, which writer focuses mainly on binge drinking as a form of unsophisticated social behavior? On binge drinking as a form of socially irresponsible behavior? On binge drinking as a form of dangerous behavior? Explain.

2. Which of the arguments in this debate do you think is most likely to appeal to the age group it talks about—that is, those under age 21? to parents and others responsible for the behavior of minors? to academics and health care professionals? Explain why in each case.

3. Which of the participants in this debate makes the most effective use of statistics? How so? Who uses facts and figures the least? Would that person's argument be stronger if it included more numbers? Why or why not?

4. To what extent would you say the language and general style of writing in each of these essays fits the viewpoint and profession of the author (professor of health sciences, journalist, public health researcher)? How would you describe these different prose styles?

FOR WRITING

1. Write a paragraph or two explaining which of the arguments in this debate you find strongest (or weakest)—and why.

2. Write an argument in which you take a position (and support it—with facts, statistics, expert testimony, and other evidence) on some aspect of the MLDA debate not fully covered by Engs, Hitt, or Voas.

Debating Drugs in Sports

In April 2011, home run king Barry Bonds became the last major athlete to be convicted of a crime as a result of the BALCO investigation. The Bay Area Laboratory Cooperative, charged with selling food and health "supplements" that turned out to include steroids and human growth hormone, had included Bonds' name in their client records, along with those of Olympic sprinter Marion Jones, N.F.L defensive tackle Dana Stubblefield, and cyclist Tammy Thomas—all later found guilty of perjury about their dealings with the company.

Even if Bonds' conviction brings an end to the steroid era in baseball, allegations of doping have plagued almost every sport in recent years. Especially hardhit is professional cycling, with the American rider Floyd Landis stripped of his spectacular victory in the 2006 Tour de France as a result of routine drug tests. Evading the questions of a judge or jury, as Bonds did, is a criminal offense. Should it also be a crime to use performance enhancing drugs in sports? Is sports doping morally wrong? Or should there be a don't-ask-don't tell policy in professional athletics? In amateur sports, too, such as the Olympic Games? Should there even be a "gladiator class" of athletes, as in ancient Rome, who are openly permitted to salve their wounds—and overwhelm the competition—with any substance they can get their hands on?

In the following texts, a former competitive athlete and two avid sports bloggers, field these and other tricky questions—legal, moral, and ethical—about the use and misuse of performance-enhancing drugs in today's athletics:

Mark Sisson, "Should We Allow Drugs in Sports?" p. 596
Joe Lindsey, "Why Legalizing Sports Doping Won't Work," p. 602
William Moller, "We, the Public, Place the Best Athletes on Pedestals,"
    p. 607

Questions about this group of readings can be found on p. 613.

MARK SISSON

Should We Allow Drugs in Sports?

Mark Sisson is a health and fitness writer and the founder of Primal Nutrition, a health supplement company. After graduating from Williams College with a major in biology, Sisson was a champion marathon runner, triathlete, and Ironman competitor. He is the former head of the Anti-Doping Commission of the International Triathlon Union (ITU), where he was responsible for the drug testing and education of competitive athletes from around the world. Sisson's blog, Marks Daily Apple, dispenses information and advice on health, nutrition, and fitness.

"Should We Allow Drugs in Sports?" is a blog post from 2008 in which Sisson argues from the viewpoint of a "prosecutor" who sometimes had to suspend young athletes despite drug tests he considered inaccurate and rules of competition he felt were unfair. In his original post, Sisson linked to other websites to provide further information; those links have been replaced with footnotes.

At THE RISK OF SOUNDING a bit brazen, I would suggest that elite and profes- 1 sional sports would be better off allowing athletes to make their own personal decisions regarding the use of so-called "banned substances" and leaving the federations and the IOC[1] out of it entirely. Even the term "banned substance" has a negative connotation, since most of these substances are actually drugs that were developed to enhance health in the general population. The irony here, of course, is that I have always been vehemently against the use of medications when natural remedies are usually better choices. But with sport we have athletes often doing "inhuman" or "unnatural" tasks that might require unnatural remedies. The bottom line is that drug-testing in sports is an extremely complex issue, about which most sports administrators have very little knowledge or understanding.

Expert testimony, p. 517, is a common form of evidence.

First, I should tell you that I was the Anti-doping Commissioner of the 2 International Triathlon Union (ITU)—a relatively new sport within the Olympic family—for nearly 13 years. I had to act as "prosecutor" on many doping cases (doping = drugs in sport). Prior to that, I helped write the first set of "anti-doping" rules for triathlon in 1988. Before that, I was an elite marathoner (2:18) and triathlete (4th Place Ironman Hawaii) in the '70s and '80s, so I

---

1. *IOC:* International Olympic Committee.

SUGGESTED MLA CITATION: Sisson, Mark. "Should We Allow Drugs in Sports?" 2006. *Back to the Lake.* Ed. Thomas Cooley. 2nd ed. New York: Norton, 2012. 596–600. Print.

have accumulated a fair amount of "inside information" regarding drugs in sport at the Olympic level. I also own a supplement company and have done extensive research on performance enhancement in pursuit of natural, legal alternatives.

There are three main points I want to make here: first, that it is impossible to 3 fairly police and adjudicate drugs in sport; second, that the notion of a "level playing field" is a farce; and, finally, that the performance requirements set by the federations at the elite level of sport almost demand access to certain "banned substances" in order to assure the health and vitality of the athlete throughout his or her career and—more importantly—into his or her life after competition.

Impossible to fairly police and adjudicate. Most people think that a positive 4 test is conclusive proof of guilt, but the reality is that almost all these tests are nothing more than GC/MS* quantitative analyses that look for parts per billion of certain metabolites in the urine. They are not black-and-white indicators of guilt. They are wavy lines on a graph subject to interpretation by scientists with varying degrees of expertise. In many cases a "threshold level" is established below which you are "clean" but above which you are "guilty." Test results will vary significantly from one "accredited" lab to another. You can test positive in one lab and, conceivably, have another lab exonerate you using a portion of the very same sample. I have presided over cases where an athlete tested positive for metabolites of nandrolone (a once-popular steroid) at levels of 4 or 5 parts per billion when the cutoff was 2.5 or 3. Even at such disputably low levels, athletes are presumed guilty. Some labs have proven that these metabolites can occur in the body from having consumed certain types of meat, or from other foods, or are even endogenously produced. In my opinion, the threshold levels have always been too low, so a handful of innocent athletes get severely penalized, while others who are dirty but are not tested get cleared to compete and keep whatever money or medal they win.

In the old days if you ate a poppyseed muffin before a race, your urine could 5 easily show above-threshold levels of metabolites of opium and you could be disqualified. It actually happened to a triathlete who was later cleared. There are other similar "false positives" we had to be on the lookout for.

A T/E (testosterone to epitestosterone) higher than 6:1 was considered evidence 6 of a doping violation, yet we had cases of women who scored a T/E of 20, not because testosterone was present in high amounts, but because the epitestosterone was extremely low as a result of birth control pills. In other cases, elite athletes' normal testosterone levels were high enough to exceed the limit, but they were

*Read Frederic Douglas, "GC/MS Analysis," in *Scientific Testimony: An Online Journal*, last modified Nov. 4, 2010 (www.scientific.org/tutorials/articles/gcms.html), for a good description. [Author's note.]

allowed to compete when they showed proof of genetic abnormality. The limit is now 4:1 and produces thousands of "false positives" each year!

In other cases, athletes who have been diagnosed with asthma (now nearing 25   7 percent of the elite athlete population—don't get me started) and who have properly notified the IOC and have a "therapeutic use exemption" on file can use salbutamol, salmeterol, and similar "anabolic-property" drugs which are otherwise banned. But god forbid you are an athlete from a developing nation with asthma whose team physician failed to properly file your papers. Same condition, but now you can be severely penalized for the ignorance of your coaches or doctors.

There are known cases of sabotage where ex-wives have tainted supplements (or   8 even toothpaste) to cause a positive test, and where athletes in races have consumed tainted drinks offered by unscrupulous coaches or fans of rival competitors.

Even when you do get a fairly reliable test result from the lab, a good lawyer can   9 throw doubt on the integrity of the collection process, the chain of custody or a number of other factors, enough to get a truly guilty athlete off on a technicality. All these factors combined lead to the conclusion that it is impossible to fairly police or adjudicate doping in sport.

The notion of a level playing field is a farce. The IOC and many professional   10 leagues suggest that banning doping in sports will create a "level playing field," meaning that all athletes should have access—or not—to the same advantages and disadvantages. Art DeVany's exceptional analysis of home-run distribution* notwithstanding, there are clearly advantages to be had from the use of certain substances specifically within certain sports. Take the use of EPO in cycling and running. EPO (Erythropoetin) is a natural hormone produced by the body. EPO stimulates the production of red blood cells, whose level in the blood is measured by hematocrit. Red blood cells contain the hemoglobin that carries oxygen to muscles where fuel can be burned. The more oxygen you deliver to the muscles, the more energy output you derive from those muscles. So having more red blood cells is a good thing and is a primary goal of many endurance athletes. Hard training raises EPO and hematocrit, but drug companies also make artificial EPO which does the same thing without training (intended medical use is for recovery from chemotherapy, which destroys red blood cells). Artificial EPO is banned. Now here's the irony: research confirms that if you train at sea level and sleep at 14,000 feet, your body makes red blood cells at an impressive rate and amount. Several companies have developed expensive "altitude chambers" for home use where you can now train at sea level and then retire to your room for the night, simulating an

---

*Arthur DeVany, "Steroids and Home Runs," *Economic Inquiry* (in press). PDF: www.arthurdevany .com/downloads/20100226. [Author's note.]

altitude of 14,000 feet or higher. The end result is that you have, within the letter of the law, manipulated your own EPO to artificially raise hematocrit, yet using artificial EPO to do the same thing is punishable by a 2-year suspension. Talk to an endurance athlete from a developing nation with $2 to his name about THAT level playing field.

In the early days of EPO testing, the cycling federation would measure the hema- 11 tocrit of every cyclist before a race. If your hematocrit was above 52 percent, you were not allowed to race and were presumed to have doped. However, there were instances of cyclists from high-mountain regions in South America who had normally high hematocrits (from training AND living at 14,000 feet or higher). Some were not allowed to race because they had achieved a high hematocrit naturally. Meanwhile, others who used artificial EPO to get from, say, 44 percent to 51 percent raced without penalty. Talk to those South Americans about a level playing field.

There are many other idiosyncrasies. Within the IOC, 2 cups of coffee is OK, 12 but 8 cups is illegal. Marijuana will get you suspended by some federations, but not by others. Creatine, one of the best natural performance-enhancing substances, is legal in track and field, while beta-blockers, which have no effect on performance, were not. My point is that the concept of a level playing field is a nice idea, but one that has not been realized in Olympic sport.

Performance requirements almost demand access to certain "banned sub- 13 **stances" in order to assure the health and vitality of the athlete.** World-class athletes tend to die significantly younger than you would predict from heart disease, cancer, diabetes, and early-onset dementia. They also typically suffer premature joint deterioration from the years of pounding, and most endurance athletes look like hell from the years of oxidative damage that has overwhelmed their feeble antioxidant systems. Most people don't realize it, but training at the elite level is actually the antithesis of a healthy lifestyle. The definition of peak fitness means that you are constantly at or near a state of physical breakdown. As a peak performer on a world stage, you have done more work than anyone else, but you have paid a price. It is again ironic that the professional leagues and the IOC, the ones who dangle that carrot of millions of dollars in salary or gold-medalist endorsements, are the same ones who actually create this overtrained, injured, and beat-up army of young people. They don't care. These organizations then deny the athletes the very same drugs and even some natural "health-enhancing" substances that the rest of society can easily receive whenever they feel the least bit uncomfortable.

I had to disqualify and suspend a kid from competition for 90 days because he 14 had a head cold the night before his national championships. His dad had gone to the drugstore and gotten him some Sudafed so he could breathe while he slept. His urine test was positive when he won the race the next day. He forfeited his winnings and he had to sit out the World Championships as a result. I felt terrible, but the rules required that we do it.

I had to suspend a talented and promising young Mexican triathlete because his 15 vitamins contained a tiny amount of a little-known stimulant legal over-the-counter in Mexico. His doctor had prescribed vitamins for him because he had been chronically overtraining and yet had little or no access to decent training foods.

These days many athletes avoid taking high-potency multi-vitamins out of fear 16 that contaminants in their supplements could destroy their careers. Yet these same athletes have nutrient requirements that exceed the RDAs by a factor of 10 or 20 in some cases. It has been said many times that world-class athletes will do anything to win—even if it means risking their lives. If that's the case, then don't let them train so hard that they destroy their health and then deny them the very tools they need to recover!

I could go on, but you get my drift. I believe that with proper supervision, athletes 17 could be healthier and have longer careers (not to mention longer and more productive post-competition lives) using many of these "banned substances." And perhaps the biggest assumption I will make here is that the public just doesn't care. Professional sport has become theater. All the public wants is a good show and an occasional world record.

READING CLOSELY

1. Mark Sisson argues that the fair policing of drugs in sports is "impossible" (3). How and why does he come to this conclusion?

2. In particular, why does he consider a positive reading on a drug test insufficient proof that an athlete has been doping?

3. Sisson characterizes the idea of a level playing field in sports competition as a "farce" (3, 10). Is he right? Why or why not?

4. In Sisson's view, why do some world-class athletes die at a younger age than their less-competitive counterparts? What does he think should be done to prevent great athletes from dying young?

5. Do you agree with Sisson's "biggest assumption" about the use of drugs in sports (17)? Why or why not?

STRATEGIES AND STRUCTURES

1. "Drug-testing in sports," says Sisson, "is an extremely complex issue" (1). Is this the main point of his argument? If not, what is—and where does he state it most directly?

2. Sisson's argument about drugs in sports is made up of three related arguments. Identify each one, and explain how (and how well) it supports his main point about whether or not to allow doping.

3. Does it matter that Sisson was a competitive athlete and anti-doping Commissioner of the International Triathlon Union? That he owns a health supplement company? Explain.

4. What is Sisson's purpose in citing the EXAMPLE of an asthmatic athlete from a "developing nation" (7)? Point out other places where Sisson uses examples to support his argument.

5. *Other Methods.* How do Sisson's DEFINITIONS of "peak fitness" (13) and "professional sport" (17) differ from how these terms are often defined? How, and how well, do Sisson's definitions help to support his argument?

THINKING ABOUT LANGUAGE

1. Explain how Sisson uses the METAPHOR of the "level playing field" (3, 10–12).

2. *Endogenously* means produced or growing from within (4). Should Sisson have explained the meaning of this and other technical terms, such as *metabolites* (4) and *anabolic* (7)? Why or why not?

3. What does Sisson mean by the "chain of custody" in drug testing (9)? Why does he call it a *chain* rather than a rope or thread?

4. "I could go on, but you get my drift" (17). Point out other places in his argument where Sisson uses informal language. Is such language appropriate in a serious debate? Why or why not?

FOR WRITING

1. Sisson divides his argument into three main points in paragraph 3. Choose one of those points and, in a paragraph or two, explain what additional reasons you would give to support (or refute) it.

2. Drawing on Sisson's evidence—but also using evidence from other sources, including your own experience—make an argument in favor of the use of drugs in some sports. Be sure to cite your sources.

JOE LINDSEY

Why Legalizing Sports Doping Won't Work

Joe Lindsey is a freelance sportswriter who lives in Boulder, Colorado. He is a frequent contributor to Bicycling *magazine, sponsor of his regular blog about professional cycling, the* Boulder Report.

"Why Legalizing Sports Doping Won't Work" first appeared as a guest post on the Freakonomics *blog in July 2007. Most of Lindsey's objections to the legalization of drugs in sports are "logistical," but the most serious objection, he implies, is a "moral" one.*

THE IRONY OF THE RECENT REPORT that the Olympics are considering kicking 1
out cycling because of its doping probems is that it was then–International Olympic Committee president Juan Antonio Samaranch who floated the idea in 1997 of a "gladiator class" of sports—where doping was acknowledged and allowed.

It's worth considering, as the Tour de France[1] practically grinds to a halt as one 2
after another top competitor is removed from the race under suspicion of doping, whether we might just throw the doors of the pharmacy wide open and say have at it. "Pure cycling is just an illusion," said Francesco Moser once. Moser is a former top cyclist who now heads the professional riders' union. "There comes a stage when a rider must be told the effects of a medicine. Then if he wants to, let him take it."

Or is that such a good idea? If we play Prometheus[2] to cycling's mortals, what 3
happens?

First, let's set aside two logistical problems. 4

> Convincing readers to accept your premises (p. 520) is half the battle.

One, not all cyclists dope, nor do they want to. Jonathan Vaughters, a 5
former pro who now runs a domestic cycling team called Slipstream Sports, which performs its own anti-doping testing, has characterized the doping dynamic as the dragged and the draggers.* . . . The vast majority of cyclists who would prefer to race clean (the dragged) are instead tempted

---

1. *Tour de France*: Professional cycling's top race.
2. *Prometheus*: In Greek mythology, the Titan who was punished by Zeus for stealing fire from the gods and sharing it with mortals.
The dragged and the draggers: Terms used by *London Times* sportswriter David Walsh in *From Lance to Landis: Inside the American Doping Controversy at the Tour de France* (2007). [Author's note]

SUGGESTED MLA CITATION: Lindsey, Joe. "Why Legalizing Sports Doping Won't Work." 2007. *Back to the Lake*. Ed. Thomas Cooley. 2nd ed. New York: Norton, 2012. 602–05. Print.

Competitors head down the Champs-Élysées at the end of the 2007 Tour de France, from which two entire teams, and the race leader, Michael Rasmussen, withdrew for failing or missing drug tests.

to dope simply to keep up with the small minority who aggressively dope for a competitive advantage (the draggers). Modern oxygen-vector doping is so effective, a rider has two choices: dope and keep up, or stay clean and fall behind. "I guess, after years and years and years of standing on the start line and feeling like I was a mile behind, it finally got to me," said nine-time Tour finisher Frankie Andreu of the experience. Andreu succumbed, temporarily.[*] . . . But it is possible to race and even win clean, if you're smart and work hard. So some racers never dope, even if their careers suffer for it. But if most riders want to race clean, then legalizing doping puts them in an impossible position: dope, or quit the sport.

Second, not all doping techniques are created equal. The most effective regimens are also the most sophisticated and expensive—according to a *der Spiegel* interview, German pro Jorg Jaksche paid 37,000 Euros one year for a "medical program" that was slightly less than comprehensive. Star riders such as Tyler Hamilton and Jan Ullrich are alleged to have paid 50,000 Euros or more, a substantial chunk of the average pro racer's contract but a mere tithe to riders of Hamilton

6

---

[*]"Inside Cycling's Doping Scandal," *Men's Journal*, November 2006. [Author's note]

and Ullrich's salary range. So if doping is legalized, the sport's richest riders and teams will have access to techniques that lesser lights don't. The playing field, never level, would be tilted permanently.

If you can somehow manage to get past those two little hurdles, there is a third, 7 much more formidable one: what to legalize, and how to enforce it?

One of the serious allegations against Michael Rasmussen, who was yanked 8 from the Tour while leading the race, is that in 2002, he attempted to use a synthetic blood substitute called Hemopure.

We can't legalize Hemopure for sporting use. It's only approved for human 9 medical use in one country: South Africa. If you transport it to or use it in France, Italy, the United States or virtually any other country outside of a government-approved clinical trial, you're breaking federal law on the transport and possession of controlled substances. Trenbolone, which *Game of Shadows* authors Mark Fainaru-Wada and Lance Williams say Barry Bonds used, is a veterinary-only product, intended for use in cattle. Don't even mention designer steroids like BALCO's infamous The Clear.[5]

Medical laws and medical ethics prevent us from letting athletes use these sub- 10 stances outside of a clinical trial. But athletes, who eagerly seek out anything that will give them a competitive edge, will still try and get them. H. Lee Sweeney, a professor at the University of Pennsylvania, was shocked when, after publishing research in an obscure scholarly journal on an experimental gene therapy technique to inhibit myostatin (as a therapy for muscular dystrophy), he began receiving inquiries from athletes, and even a high-school wrestling coach, on how to use the technique to boost performance.

Simply put, wherever you draw the line, something, some technique or 11 substance, will always be off-limits. And so you've merely moved the line, not erased it.

Finally, none of that addresses the moral problems involved in legalizing dop- 12 ing. Doping in sports isn't inherently wrong; it's wrong by the value system with which we judge sports. Sports themselves are by their nature civilized: everyone agrees to follow a certain set of rules. If you don't, that's cheating. Legalizing doping doesn't change those rules as much as remove them altogether, and then it's no longer a sport, but merely entertainment. Right or wrong, we look to sports and to athletes for an inspiration that mere entertainment cannot provide—there is an

---

5. *The Clear:* A steroid once distributed by the Bay Area Laboratory Cooperative (BALCO). *Barry Bonds* (b. 1964): Former San Francisco Giants slugger who was convicted of impeding a grand jury investigation into the use of illegal steroids in baseball.

implicit contract that the sweat and effort we see before us is real and natural. Do you want to see who's the best athlete, or just who had the best access to pharmaceutical enhancement?

READING CLOSELY

1. Many competitive athletes, including the "vast majority" of professional cyclists, says Joe Lindsey, would prefer *not* to take performance-enhancing drugs (5). Why do some use them anyway?

2. Lindsey says that "doping in sports isn't inherently wrong" (12). Do you agree that there is no absolute moral standard in sports? Why or why not?

3. If Lindsey thinks sports doping, in and of itself, is not morally wrong, why does he nonetheless conclude that doping shouldn't be legalized?

4. How does Lindsey DEFINE "cheating" in sports (12)? Is this definition adequate? Why or why not?

STRATEGIES AND STRUCTURES

1. In what order does Lindsey present his reasons for opposing the legalization of drugs in sports: most important to least important? Least to most? Some other order? How effective is this arrangement? Explain.

2. Lindsey sums up his first objection by saying that legalizing drugs in sports would present athletes who don't want to dope with an "impossible" choice: "dope, or quit the sport" (5). Is this a valid conclusion to the argument he has just made? Why or why not?

3. Point out other spots in this post where Lindsey summarizes his conclusions in a similar take-away fashion. Is this a good strategy? Explain.

4. Lindsey supports his position with two "logistical" arguments and a "moral" one (4, 12). Are these arguments sufficient to prove his point? Why or why not?

5. *Other Methods.* In the last paragraph, Lindsey distinguishes between sports and "entertainment" (12). How and how well does this COMPARISON serve as a conclusion for Lindsey's entire argument?

THINKING ABOUT LANGUAGE

1. Explain Lindsey's ALLUSION to the myth of Prometheus (3).

2. In what sense is Lindsey using the term "logistical" (4)? Explain.

3. How useful are the terms "dragged" and "draggers" for arguing that doping in sports is attributable to only a small minority of cheaters (5)? Explain.

4. What is the difference in meaning between "infamous" (9) and "famous"?

FOR WRITING

1. In a paragraph or two, summarize one of Lindsey's moral arguments against legalizing drugs in sports.

2. Write an argument explaining why you think the use of performance-enhancing drugs in sports is (or is not) morally wrong.

WILLIAM MOLLER

We, the Public, Place the Best Athletes on Pedestals

William Moller (b. 1983) graduated from Kenyon College in 2006 and lives in New York City, where he works as an analyst in the financial industry. Moller is an avid baseball fan and writes regularly for It's About the Money, *a blog dealing with his hometown team, the New York Yankees.*

In the following post to The Yankee Dollar *blog in May 2009 (originally titled "Those in Glass Houses . . .") Moller responds to the media's reaction to the news that Yankees slugger Alex Rodriguez admitted to using "banned substances" while playing for the Texas Rangers. In his original post, Moller used hyperlinks to other websites to document the sources that support his conclusions; he has replaced those links with footnotes for this book.*

I SPENT MY HIGH SCHOOL YEARS at a boarding school hidden among the apple   1
orchards of Massachusetts. Known for a spartan philosophy regarding the adolescent need for sleep, the school worked us to the bone, regularly slamming us with six hours of homework. I pulled a lot more all-nighters (of the scholastic sort) in my years there than I ever did in college. When we weren't in class, the library, study hall, or formal sit-down meals, we were likely found on a sports field. We also had school on Saturday, beginning at 8 AM just like every other non-Sunday morning.

Adding kindling to the fire, the students were not your laid-back types; every-   2
one wanted that spot at the top of the class, and social life was rife with competition. The type A's that fill the investment banking, legal, and political worlds—those are the kids I spent my high school years with.

And so it was that midway through my sophomore year, I found myself on my   3
third all-nighter in a row, attempting to memorize historically significant pieces of art out of E. H. Gombrich's *The Story of Art*. I had finished a calculus exam the day before, and the day before that had been devoted to world history. And on that one cold night in February, I had had enough. I had hit that point where you've had so little sleep over such a long time that you start seeing spots, as if you'd been staring at a bright light for too long. The grade I would compete for the next day suddenly slipped in importance, and I began daydreaming about how easy the real world would be compared to the hell I was going through.

SUGGESTED MLA CITATION: Moller, William. "We, the Public, Place the Best Athletes on Pedestals." 2009. *Back to the Lake.* Ed. Thomas Cooley. 2nd ed. New York: Norton, 2012. 607–11. Print.

But there was hope. A friend who I was taking occasional study breaks with read   4
the story in the bags beneath my eyes, in the slump of my shoulders, the nervous
drumming of my fingers on the chair as we sipped flat, warm Coke in the common
room. My personal *deus ex machina*,[1] he handed me a small white pill.

I was very innocent. I matured way after most of my peers, and was probably   5
best known for being the kid who took all the soprano solos away from the girls in
the choir as a first-year student. I don't think I had ever been buzzed, much less
drunk. I'd certainly never smoked a cigarette. And knowing full well that what I
was doing could be nothing better than against the rules (and less importantly,
illegal) I did what I felt I needed to do, to accomplish what was demanded of me.
And it worked. I woke up and regained focus like nothing I'd ever experienced.
Unfortunately, it also came with serious side effects: I was a hypersensitized,
stuffed-up, sweaty, wide-eyed mess, but I studied until the birds started chirping.
And I aced my test.

Later I found out the pill was Ritalin, and it was classified as a class 3 drug.[2] I did   6
it again, too—only a handful of times, as the side effects were so awful. But every
time it was still illegal, still against the rules. And as emphasized above, I was much
more worried about the scholastic consequences if I were discovered abusing a
prescription drug than the fact that I was breaking the law. Though I was using it
in a far different manner than the baseball players who would later get caught with
it in their systems, it was still very clearly a "performance-enhancing drug."

Just like every other person on this planet, I was giving in to the incentive   7
scheme that was presented to me. The negative of doing poorly on the test was far
greater than the negative of getting caught, discounted by the anesthetic of low
probability.

I imagine that the same dilemma must have occurred in Alex Rodriguez's sub-   8
conscious before he made the decision to start taking steroids. Alex has been a
phenom in every sense of the word since he was old enough to be labeled an athlete. Who knows if he took steroids in high school—and who cares, really? He did
take them in the major leagues, he almost certainly took them before moving to
Texas, and there's really no compelling argument that he hasn't been taking them
since he moved to New York.

What it really comes down to is that the reason Alex did steroids is you and me.   9
We, the public, place the best athletes on pedestals, gods on high. And Alex is
a prime candidate for such treatment. He's an archetype, carrying the look of

---

1. *Deus ex machina*: Term from ancient Greek drama (literally, "god from the machine"), referring
to an actor playing a god who was mechanically lowered onto the stage in order to intervene on a
character's behalf.

2. *Class 3 drug*: Drug that is illegal to possess without a prescription.

"He's a physical monstrosity, capable of knocking the ball out of Yankee Stadium with only one hand on the bat. And at the deepest level, Alex Rodriguez wants, *craves*, fame."

someone who will one day be cast in bronze. He's a physical monstrosity, capable of knocking the ball out of Yankee Stadium with only one hand on the bat. And at the deepest level Alex Rodriguez wants, *craves*, fame. More than that, really, he wants to be loved. He came to New York wanting to erase the memories of Mantle and DiMaggio and Berra.[3] He wanted to be beautiful and powerful and funny and philanthropic and every other positive adjective he could find.

Really, it was no question whether Alex would take steroids once they were offered. They promised wealth and fame above his wildest dreams. Let's be clear: A-Rod could have been a good player without steroids, maybe even a great player. But he didn't want that. He wanted to be *A-Rod*. 10

And now the cat is out of the bag. Now that we have a test showing us that A-Rod used, we finally stop turning a blind eye to what was patently obvious before. But only for Alex. 11

The entire steroid outcry is pure hypocrisy. Look, you and I both understand that the majority of the best players in baseball are steroid users. And so are a good portion of the less-than-best. And when I say that, I do so without adding the negative connotation added by the self-righteous media types who make a living by 12

---

3. *Yogi Berra* (b. 1925), *Mickey Mantle* (1931–1995), and *Joe DiMaggio* (1914–1999): Record-breaking Yankees players.

drumming up indignation from the masses. If it came out that Mariano Rivera and Derek Jeter[4] were on some sort of designer steroid, I'd be surprised and disappointed, but by no means amazed.

It's why I wasn't surprised in the slightest when Andy Pettitte admitted to using 13
HGH.[5] My only disgust with that situation is that he certainly didn't use it once and then get rid of it, as he said. When Pettitte used HGH (which isn't proven to do anything for athletes, by the way) he did it because he didn't think he'd get caught, not because he thought it was acceptable. And there's no reason to believe he really would have stopped after one use.

This all reeks of the attitude taken toward marijuana by politicians until Barack 14
Obama came around. When asked about marijuana use, Bill Clinton's response was typical: "I didn't inhale." When later asked about marijuana in the context of Clinton's response, Obama replied, "Yes, I did. . . . The point was to inhale, that was the point."

Just as the vast majority of people try marijuana at some point in their lives, the 15
vast majority of baseball players have used steroids, be it HGH, Stanozolol, The Cream, The Clear, or any other BALCO creation.[6] This game is all about getting an edge—whether it be the front offices using BABIP[7] to pick the right players, Sammy Sosa corking a bat, Johnny Damon using maple instead of ash bats, K-Rod putting resin on his baseball cap, Pete Rose mixing Adderall[8] in with a cup of coffee, or Mark McGwire's unabashed andro use. Heck, after Ritalin was outlawed in MLB, the number of baseball players being diagnosed with ADD[9] (for which Ritalin happens to be prescribed) jumped significantly! Is it okay, since they have a doctor's

---

4. *Jeter* (b. 1974) and *Rivera* (b. 1969): Current Yankees stars.

5. *Andy Pettitte . . . HGH*: In 2007, after allegations were leaked to the press following a federal investigation, Yankees pitcher Andy Pettitte (b. 1972) admitted to using human growth hormone (HGH) to enhance his athletic performance.

6. *Bay Area Laboratory Cooperative (BALCO)*: A San Francisco–based company that was at the center of the MLB drug scandal. *Stanozolol* is an anabolic steroid (see http://en.wikipedia.org/wiki/Stanozolol). *The Cream and The Clear*: Steroids created and distributed by BALCO (see http://en.wikipedia.org/wiki/BALCO_Scandal). [Author's note]

7. *Batting average on balls in play (BABIP)*: One statistic used to gauge a player's abilities.

8. *Adderall*: Until 2006, no rules existed to prevent players from using amphetamines such as Adderall to cause a spike in focus and energy level, and such use was rampant. *Resin*: Pitchers are known to sometimes use the brim of their baseball caps to hide banned substances such as pine tar, Vaseline, or resin, which affect the movement of the ball. *Maple instead of ash bats*: In 2008, the use of maple bats, which tend to shatter rather than splinter, came under scrutiny for the danger they posed to fielders and fans alike. *Corking a bat*: Hollowing out a bat and replacing the core with a lighter material to bring the bat beneath regulation weight and gain an advantage. [Author's notes]

9. *Attention deficit disorder (ADD)*: Symptoms include difficulty with staying focused and controlling one's behavior.

scrip? There's a lot of money and fame at stake, and it skews that all-important incentive scheme.

Each and every general manager in the game shares at least three attributes: They're very smart, and they know exactly what's going on—but act as if they don't. And we the public let ourselves be fooled. What's worse, when enough information comes out that we can no longer ignore that a player used, we demonize them relative to their "untainted" peers. By all accounts, Barry Bonds is a real jerk—which is plenty of reason to dislike him. But don't hate him because he's a "cheater." In that sense, he's just one of the gang. 16

For tips on arguing by analogy, see p. 525.

Back in February of 2000, I got to choose between breaking the rules and breaking my grades. I chose the rules, and it wasn't a tough decision. And I'd wager that the lure of being A-Rod is a bit more seductive than an A on that art history test. 17

READING CLOSELY

1. William Moller took Ritalin in high school to stay awake for exams, even though he might have been kicked out if he'd been caught. What "incentive scheme" made this choice attractive (7)? Is he right to say that "every other person on this planet" is subject to such incentives? Explain.

2. According to Moller, athletes break rules for reasons other than money. What are some of them?

3. What does Moller mean when he says that the real reason Alex Rodriguez took illegal steroids was "you and me" (9)? Do you agree? Why or why not?

STRATEGIES AND STRUCTURES

1. Who is the intended AUDIENCE for Moller's argument? How do you know?

2. Moller says he was "giving in" and "breaking the rules" when he took an unprescribed drug in high school (7, 17). If the use of illegal substances in school and sports is not okay in Moller's view, what *is* the point of his argument? Where and how does he state it most directly?

3. Moller argues by ANALOGY, drawing a COMPARISON between his actions as a high school student and those of athletes who take performance-enhancing drugs. Such arguments are only as strong as the analogy is close. By this measure, how strong do you find Moller's argument? Explain?

4. Should Moller have given additional EVIDENCE to support his CLAIM that sports fans are complicit when athletes cheat? What sort of evidence, if any?

5. *Other Methods.* Part of Moller's argument is the confessional NARRATIVE of his own transgressions. How and how well does the guilty aspect of his story support his contentions about athletes and incentives?

Thinking about Language

1. What does Moller mean when he refers to the low probability of getting caught as an "anesthetic" (7)? Why do you think he chose this pharmaceutical METAPHOR?

2. Moller refers to Alex Rodriguez as an "archetype" (9). How does the root meaning of this term suggest someone "cast in bronze" (9)?

3. The root meaning of hypocrisy is "playacting" (12). How might the word apply, in this basic sense, to sports fans and the media as Moller describes them?

For Writing

1. In a paragraph or two, give an example of a star athlete with an incentive to cheat who didn't give in to the temptation.

2. Write an argument attacking (or defending) the proposition that sports fans and the media are at least partially to blame for the doping epidemic in competitive athletics. Feel free to cite personal experience to support your argument, but include other evidence as well.

Debating Drugs in Sports

The following questions refer to the arguments on pages 595–612.

Reading Arguments

1. Among the three writers cited in this debate, Joe Lindsey is the most reluctant to allow the legalization of performance-enhancing drugs in sports. Why? Where do Mark Sisson and William Moller stand on the legalization issue? What are the main reasons for their respective positions?

2. To what extent do the writers in this debate agree that the methods and standards of drug testing used in most sports are ineffective? Who makes the best case for dispensing with drug tests? What are his main reasons?

3. Moller assigns considerable responsibility to fans for the illegal use of drugs in sports. What do the other two writers think about this, and what are their views on the related matter of sports as entertainment? Explain by pointing to specific passages in their arguments.

4. Whether or not you agree with their conclusions, which of the participants in this debate do you think supports his claim most effectively? How? Point to particular evidence and strategies of argument that you find especially convincing.

For Writing

1. In a paragraph, summarize the main reasons you would cite in favor of (or against) legalizing the use of drugs in sports.

2. Write an essay arguing that it is (or is not) morally and ethically wrong for athletes to use performance-enhancing drugs. Cite specific cases and circumstances, and explain what assumptions you're making about the standards of conduct expected from athletes and athletic competition.

Debating Intellectual Property

Intellectual property refers to "labors of the mind"—including books, films, music, software, and architectural or mechanical designs—over which the author may be entitled to certain legal rights of ownership. Intellectual property rights originated with copyright, a legal concept that was established in the United States by the first U.S. Copyright Act, signed into law in 1790 by George Washington. The nation's founders believed that copyright laws encouraged individual creativity, but they also regarded ideas as public goods, and they placed strict limits—fourteen years, with one renewal—on how long authors and inventors could enjoy a monopoly on their own creations.

In 1909, however, Congress doubled the length of copyright. The Copyright Act of 1976 further extended the rights of authors to their own lifetimes plus fifty years. And in 1998, copyrights held by individuals picked up another twenty years under the Sonny Bono Copyright Term Extension Act. This legislation is sometimes referred to as the "Mickey Mouse Protection Act" because it also extended (to almost a hundred years) the term of copyright on works of corporate authorship, including Disney cartoons. Because Mickey made his first appearance in 1928, he was scheduled to enter the public domain in 2003, to be followed soon after by Pluto, Goofy, and Donald Duck. Under the new law, however, early Disney characters—and thousands of other works—will remain private property until at least 2019.

Who should own intellectual property created by individuals? In these texts, a student, two journalists, and a lawyer each explore the conflict between private property rights and the need for public access to intellectual property in the age of the Internet:

Questions about this group of readings can be found on p. 633.

SARAH WILENSKY

Generation Plagiarism

Sarah Wilensky graduated in 2011 from Indiana University, Bloomington, where she was a regular "opinion columnist" for the Indiana Daily Student. *A political science and Jewish studies major, Wilensky was also co-president of the local chapter of STAND, an international, student-led organization devoted to aiding victims of genocide.*

In "Generation Plagiarism," a 2010 column from the Daily Student, *Wilensky argues that plagiarism is still theft—even for a generation of writers brought up on the Internet. The judges for the literary prize to which she refers apparently thought so, too, as the Leipzig Book Fair Prize for 2010 did not go to Helene Hegemann, German author of* Axoltl Roadkill, *who admitted to plagiarizing more than forty passages in the novel.*

I**N SOME WAYS,** it's no surprise that Helene Hegemann, whose first novel was just 1 chosen as a finalist for the Leipzig Book Fair prize for fiction despite serious concerns about plagiarism, is only 17 years old.

While many more mature fiction writers aspire to receive the widespread 2 acclaim that has characterized Hegemann's entrance to the literary world, a shift in generational attitudes and practices around plagiarism are what make it less surprising that the story revolves around such a young woman.

Most mature fiction writers have not stolen entire pages of prose from other 3 authors and then defended their action.

The New York Times reports that Hegemann sees herself as part of "a different 4 generation, one that freely mixes and matches from the whirring flood of information across new and old media, to create something new."

Plagiarism is nothing new, and it may be that as more and more information 5 becomes readily accessible to more people via the Internet, we are simply able to identify plagiarism that would have gone unnoticed in years past.

I think something else is going on—we are the generation of "copy-paste." We 6 write papers with our sources open in neighboring windows on the same laptop screen, and we have access to more of other peoples' ideas than ever before— without even getting off the sofa.

In a 300-level political science class, we spent nearly an entire day of lecture 7 reviewing how to effectively write without any risk of being accused of plagiarism.

SUGGESTED MLA CITATION: Wilensky, Sarah. "Generation Plagiarism." 2010. *Back to the Lake.* Ed. Thomas Cooley. 2nd ed. New York: Norton, 2012. 615–16. Print.

No professor would spend that amount of time nailing home what should be a   8
completely assumed skill, unless her students had shown a desperate need for a
review.

It's tempting to say new technology has created a blurry zone around what used   9
to be a more clear-cut line defining plagiarism. Helene Hegemann certainly seems
to think so.

But technology hasn't changed one relatively non-controversial soci-   10
etally held moral: stealing the words and ideas of others is wrong and
cannot be permitted.

Showing that
you are an eth-
ical person can
bolster your
credibility,
p. 527.

The Leipzig Book Fair should immediately rescind its consideration of   11
Ms. Hegemann's novel, as the literary community should be a leader in
condemning plagiarism. Professors around this University should crack
down on cases of academic dishonesty.

My guess is that if a professor or teaching assistant actually gave the big old F   12
every time they wondered about a very familiar paragraph in a paper, our copy-paste
generation would quickly learn how to write originally and cite appropriately.

Technology, in fact, can be the key to encouraging authentic composition. Easy   13
access to information makes it possible to verify whether that familiar passage is
indeed some other scholar's work, or a case of déjà vu.

Web resources make citations simple, and where all else fails, Turnitin.com   14
inspires exactly the kind of fear that forces students to interact with their sources
appropriately.

Helene Hegemann's defense is indicative of a real problem that must be   15
addressed at every level of the writing community.

In our own university classrooms, ambiguity should not be tolerated, and pla-   16
giarism should be regarded for what it is—not, as Hegemann suggests, "mixing,"
but theft, pure and simple.

READING CLOSELY

1. Is Sarah Wilensky right when she says that the Internet has made it easier for a
   generation of writers to copy from the work of others—whether knowingly or
   unknowingly? Why or why not?

2. Wilensky argues that plagiarism is morally "wrong" (10). What's wrong with it
   in her view?

3. What does Wilensky think should be done each time a professor or teaching assistant finds a "familiar paragraph in a paper" (12)? What do you think of this plan?

4. How can technology be both "the key to encouraging authentic composition" and, at the same time, the means by which writers cut and paste from their sources "without even getting off the sofa" (13, 6)?

STRATEGIES AND STRUCTURES

1. Wilensky's essay was written for the student newspaper at a large state university. Choose several specific passages in her text and explain how (and how well) they address that particular AUDIENCE.

2. To what moral and ethical standard does Wilensky appeal when she argues that plagiarism is wrong and simply "cannot be permitted" (10)? Is this appeal to ethics an effective strategy? Why or why not?

3. Should Wilensky have given additional reasons to support her CLAIM that plagiarism is "theft, pure and simple" (16)? Or is the directness and simplicity of her argument a virtue? Explain.

4. *Other Methods.* In addition to constructing an argument on moral and ethical grounds, Wislensky also examines why an entire generation might be more tempted to plagiarize than ever before. According to her analysis, what are some the main CAUSES of this phenomenon?

THINKING ABOUT LANGUAGE

1. Where did Wilensky get the title of her essay? By ANALOGY with what other sorts of generational labels?

2. According to the *American Heritage Dictionary*, the word *plagiarism* derives from the Latin, *plagiarus*, meaning "plunderer." How might this historical meaning be used to support Wilensky's argument?

3. How (and how accurately) might Helene Hegemann's use of the word "mix" (4, 16) be seen as an example of the logical fallacy of "begging the question"?

FOR WRITING

1. Write a paragraph or two explaining what plagiarism, as you understand it, is- and is not.

2. The Hegemann case is widely discussed online and in printed sources. Write an essay examining the issues in the case. Be sure to address Hegemann's claim that she was not stealing but merely mixing and matching.

TRIP GABRIEL

Plagiarism Lines Blur for Students in Digital Age

Trip Gabriel (b. 1955) is a journalist and former style and fashion editor for the New York Times. *In 2010, Gabriel gave up editing to return to full-time reporting; he writes mostly about schools and such education issues as the importance of "the almighty essay" in college admissions. "Prose in which an author's voice emerges through layers of perfectly correct sentences," Gabriel warns college administrators, "is the hardest kind of writing there is."*

In this essay, which appeared in the Times *in 2010, Gabriel not only reports that easy digital access to the words of others has made plagiarism more widespread than ever on college and university campuses; he also argues that this trend may present a challenge to long-standing Western ideas of authorship and intellectual property. As for the moral aspect of the problem, he concludes by citing, among others, Sarah Wilensky of Indiana University, whose "Generation Plagiarism" (pp. 000–000) he read "in her student newspaper."*

AT RHODE ISLAND COLLEGE, a freshman copied and pasted from a Web site's   1
frequently asked questions page about homelessness—and did not think he needed to credit a source in his assignment because the page did not include author information.

At DePaul University, the tip-off to one student's copying was the purple shade   2
of several paragraphs he had lifted from the Web; when confronted by a writing tutor his professor had sent him to, he was not defensive—he just wanted to know how to change purple text to black.

And at the University of Maryland, a student reprimanded for copying from   3
Wikipedia in a paper on the Great Depression said he thought its entries—unsigned and collectively written—did not need to be credited since they counted, essentially, as common knowledge.

Professors used to deal with plagiarism by admonishing students to give credit   4
to others and to follow the style guide for citations, and pretty much left it at that.

But these cases—typical ones, according to writing tutors and officials respon-   5
sible for discipline at the three schools who described the plagiarism—suggest that many students simply do not grasp that using words they did not write is a serious misdeed.

SUGGESTED MLA CITATION: Gabriel, Trip. "Plagiarism Lines Blur for Students in Digital Age." 2010. *Back to the Lake.* Ed. Thomas Cooley. 2nd ed. New York: Norton, 2012. 618–21. Print.

It is a disconnect that is growing in the Internet age as concepts of intellectual property, copyright and originality are under assault in the unbridled exchange of online information, say educators who study plagiarism.   6

Digital technology makes copying and pasting easy, of course. But that is the least of it. The Internet may also be redefining how students—who came of age with music file-sharing, Wikipedia and Web-linking—understand the concept of authorship and the singularity of any text or image.   7

"Now we have a whole generation of students who've grown up with information that just seems to be hanging out there in cyberspace and doesn't seem to have an author," said Teresa Fishman, director of the Center for Academic Integrity at Clemson University. "It's possible to believe this information is just out there for anyone to take."   8

Professors who have studied plagiarism do not try to excuse it—many are champions of academic honesty on their campuses—but rather try to understand why it is so widespread.   9

Understanding
is the goal of
exploratory
arguments,
p. 514.

In surveys from 2006 to 2010 by Donald L. McCabe, a co-founder of the Center for Academic Integrity and a business professor at Rutgers University, about 40 percent of 14,000 undergraduates admitted to copying a few sentences in written assignments.   10

Perhaps more significant, the number who believed that copying from the Web constitutes "serious cheating" is declining—to 29 percent on average in recent surveys from 34 percent earlier in the decade.   11

Sarah Brookover, a senior at the Rutgers campus in Camden, N.J., said many of her classmates blithely cut and paste without attribution.   12

"This generation has always existed in a world where media and intellectual property don't have the same gravity," said Ms. Brookover, who at 31 is older than most undergraduates. "When you're sitting at your computer, it's the same machine you've downloaded music with, possibly illegally, the same machine you streamed videos for free that showed on HBO last night."   13

Ms. Brookover, who works at the campus library, has pondered the differences between researching in the stacks and online. "Because you're not walking into a library, you're not physically holding the article, which takes you closer to 'this doesn't belong to me,'" she said. Online, "everything can belong to you really easily."   14

A University of Notre Dame anthropologist, Susan D. Blum, disturbed by the high rates of reported plagiarism, set out to understand how students view authorship and the written word, or "texts" in Ms. Blum's academic language.   15

She conducted her ethnographic research among 234 Notre Dame undergraduates. "Today's students stand at the crossroads of a new way of conceiving texts and the people who create them and who quote them," she wrote last year in the book *My Word! Plagiarism and College Culture*, published by Cornell University Press.   16

Ms. Blum argued that student writing exhibits some of the same qualities of   17
pastiche that drive other creative endeavors today—TV shows that constantly reference other shows or rap music that samples from earlier songs.

In an interview, she said the idea of an author whose singular effort creates an   18
original work is rooted in Enlightenment ideas of the individual. It is buttressed by
the Western concept of intellectual property rights as secured by copyright law.
But both traditions are being challenged.

"Our notion of authorship and originality was born, it flourished, and it may be   19
waning," Ms. Blum said.

She contends that undergraduates are less interested in cultivating a unique and   20
authentic identity—as their 1960s counterparts were—than in trying on many different personas, which the Web enables with social networking.

"If you are not so worried about presenting yourself as absolutely unique,   21
then it's O.K. if you say other people's words, it's O.K. if you say things you don't
believe, it's O.K. if you write papers you couldn't care less about because they
accomplish the task, which is turning something in and getting a grade," Ms. Blum
said, voicing student attitudes. "And it's O.K. if you put words out there without
getting any credit."

The notion that there might be a new model young person, who freely borrows   22
from the vortex of information to mash up a new creative work, fueled a brief brouhaha earlier this year with Helene Hegemann, a German teenager whose best-selling novel about Berlin club life turned out to include passages lifted from others.

Instead of offering an abject apology, Ms. Hegemann insisted, "There's no such   23
thing as originality anyway, just authenticity." A few critics rose to her defense,
and the book remained a finalist for a fiction prize (but did not win).

That theory does not wash with Sarah Wilensky, a senior at Indiana University,   24
who said that relaxing plagiarism standards "does not foster creativity, it fosters
laziness."

"You're not coming up with new ideas if you're grabbing and mixing and match-   25
ing," said Ms. Wilensky, who took aim at Ms. Hegemann in a column in her student newspaper headlined "Generation Plagiarism."

"It may be increasingly accepted, but there are still plenty of creative people—   26
authors and artists and scholars—who are doing original work," Ms. Wilensky said
in an interview. "It's kind of an insult that that ideal is gone, and now we're left
only to make collages of the work of previous generations."

In the view of Ms. Wilensky, whose writing skills earned her the role of infor-   27
mal editor of other students' papers in her freshman dorm, plagiarism has nothing
to do with trendy academic theories.

The main reason it occurs, she said, is because students leave high school unpre-   28
pared for the intellectual rigors of college writing.

"If you're taught how to closely read sources and synthesize them into your own 29
original argument in middle and high school, you're not going to be tempted to
plagiarize in college, and you certainly won't do so unknowingly," she said.

At the University of California, Davis, of the 196 plagiarism cases referred to the 30
disciplinary office last year, a majority did not involve students ignorant of the
need to credit the writing of others.

Many times, said Donald J. Dudley, who oversees the discipline office on the 31
campus of 32,000, it was students who intentionally copied—knowing it was
wrong—who were "unwilling to engage the writing process."

"Writing is difficult, and doing it well takes time and practice," he said. 32

And then there was a case that had nothing to do with a younger generation's 33
evolving view of authorship. A student accused of plagiarism came to Mr. Dudley's
office with her parents, and the father admitted that he was the one responsible for
the plagiarism. The wife assured Mr. Dudley that it would not happen again.

READING CLOSELY

1. Professors and school officials who study cases of plagiarism are not looking for
   ways to excuse them, says Trip Gabriel. What are they looking for?

2. The Internet, according to some scholars, may be changing how students view
   "authorship and the written word" (15). What are some of those changes, as
   reported by Gabriel?

3. In addition to blurring traditional distinctions about the ownership of words,
   the Internet, with its potential for "social networking," may be erasing lines
   that have traditionally defined personal identity and the self (20). How?

4. If attitudes toward authorship and the self are changing along the lines Gabriel
   suggests, what implications might those changes have for "concepts of intellectual property" (6)?

STRATEGIES AND STRUCTURES

1. In the opening paragraphs of his argument Gabriel gives EXAMPLES of unrepen-
   tant plagiarism at three different schools. Is this an effective way of introducing
   his topic? Why or why not?

2. Gabriel quotes at some length from the work of Notre Dame anthropologist
   Susan D. Blum. Is this a good strategy? Or should he simply have summarized
   her points himself without attribution? Explain.

3. Gabriel is not debating whether plagiarism is right or wrong—he calls it "a serious misdeed" from the start (5). So what main point is he making about plagiarism, and where does he state it most directly?

4. What effect, if any, does the order in which Gabriel presents his EVIDENCE have upon the substance of his argument? Would it make a difference, for example, if he cited Sarah Wilensky's opinions *before* citing those of Helene Hegemann? Why do you think Gabriel ends with the example of the plagiarizing father?

5. Gabriel does not offer a cure for the problem of blurred visions of ownership in the digital age. Should he have? Why or why not?

6. *Other Methods.* In order to argue that the Internet is changing the way some students regard authorship and their own identities, Gabriel must convince the reader not only that there has been such a change but also that the Internet has the power to produce it. How and how successfully does he establish that a CAUSE-AND-EFFECT relationship is operating here?

Thinking about Language

1. A "disconnect" occurs when a circuit is broken (6). Why might Gabriel have chosen this term to explain the reasons he thinks some students in the digital age "do not grasp" the seriousness of plagiarism (5)?

2. A "brouhaha" is a hubbub (22). Besides having the same meaning, what else do these two ONOMATOPOEIC words have in common?

3. "There's no such thing as originality anyway," says the novelist (and plagiarist) Helene Hegemann, "just authenticity" (23). What distinction is Hegemann making? Is it valid, or merely self-serving? Explain.

4. Gabriel notes that the word texts is "academic language" for "the written word" (15). Is this an accurate translation? What does it tell us about Gabriel's intended AUDIENCE?

For Writing

1. Write a paragraph using the following (or one of Gabriel's opening paragraphs) as a template: "At _____, a student accused of plagiarizing _____ replied that he (or she) was simply _____."

2. "Our notion of authorship and originality" says anthropologist Susan Blum, "was born, it flourished, and it may be waning" (19). Compose an argument addressing the proposition that technology and the Internet has (or has not changed) how today's students view authorship and issues of plagiarism. Draw from your own experience as appropriate, but also cite the expert testimony of scholars like Blum.

ELLEN GOODMAN

Who Owns Dr. King's Words?

Ellen Goodman (b. 1941) joined the Boston Globe *as a columnist in 1967, and readers soon warmed to the quietly serious voice she brought to American political discourse. Her columns are published in nearly four hundred newspapers around the country. Her books include six collections of her columns, most recently* Paper Trail: Common Sense in Uncommon Times *(2004). In 1980 she was awarded a Pulitzer Prize for distinguished commentary.*

In "Who Owns Dr. King's Words?," first published in the Boston Globe *in 1999, Goodman addresses the issue posed by her title: is an important speech a matter of public history, or is it private property? With characteristic even-handedness, she weighs the arguments over the ownership of a dream. The full text of King's famous "I Have a Dream" speech can be found on pages 000–000.*

Aᴛ ꜰɪʀꜱᴛ ɪᴛ ꜱᴏᴜɴᴅꜱ ʟɪᴋᴇ ᴀ ǫᴜᴇꜱᴛɪᴏɴ for a panel of philosophers: Who owns a 1 dream? What happens when a vision that's formed in the words of one person is released like a balloon into the air to be shared with everyone? Whose property is it then?

For tips on narrowing down an argument, see p. 518.

The dream in this case was described by Martin Luther King Jr. Standing 2 before a crowd of 200,000 at the Lincoln Memorial on that August day in 1963, he found the language to match the moment. "I Have a Dream," he told the country in a speech that became a part of our collective eloquence, as much a part of our heritage as the Gettysburg Address.[1]

Dr. King had a gift. Now people are wrangling over the value of that gift. 3

Today the question of dreamers and owners, words and property, history and 4 money, has been set before a panel of three judges in Atlanta. The King family is asking an appeals court to rule that CBS must pay them to use the dream speech in a documentary sold on videotape. They claim that they—not the public—own Dr. King's words.

For years, the King family has been protective or litigious—choose one or the 5 other. They sued and settled with Henry Hampton, who produced the "Eyes on the

---

1. *Gettysburg Address:* One of the most recognized and often-quoted speeches in U.S. history, delivered in 1863 by President Abraham Lincoln.

SUGGESTED MLA CITATION: Goodman, Ellen. "Who Owns Dr. King's Words?" 1999. *Back to the Lake.* Ed. Thomas Cooley. 2nd ed. New York: Norton, 2012. 623–25. Print.

Prize" documentary. They sued and settled with *USA Today*. They regard themselves as keepers of the legacy . . . and the accounting books.

In 1963, no one would have believed there was money to be made from civil 6 rights history. In his lifetime Dr. King was interested in justice, not profit. His family at times lived on the salary of a $6,000-a-year minister. He contributed everything, even his Nobel Prize money, to the Southern Christian Leadership Conference.

When Dr. King was assassinated, the sum total of his estate was a $50,000 7 insurance policy bought for him by Harry Belafonte.[2] That, plus his words.

These words are what the family lawyers call "intellectual property." It's property that will soon be worth an estimated $50 million from multimedia deals, licensing, and real estate. 8

I do not mean to suggest that the family is in the protection racket solely for the 9 money. Schools are granted the use of the "Dream Speech" freely. At the same time, one of the many lawsuits was against a company that wanted to use Dr. King's image on refrigerator magnets.

It's not surprising that the family would resist the trivialization of a man's magnetism into a refrigerator magnet. It's far too easy in our culture to slip from being a martyr on a pedestal to a pop icon on a T-shirt. 10

While we are talking about King and commercialism, it is fair to ask the difference between the family profit—much of which goes to the Center for Nonviolent Social Change in Atlanta—and CBS's profit. 11

But nevertheless there is still the little matter of public history and private property. 12

In the appeals court, the case will not be decided on the grounds of greed but of 13 copyright law and free speech. On the one hand Dr. King gave the press advance copies of the speech; on the other hand, the most eloquent passages were extemporaneous. On the one hand he copyrighted the speech after it was given; on the other hand he characterized it as "a living petition to the public and the Congress."

Those of us who work with words for a living understand the desire to control 14 our ephemeral "product." We are sensitive to the notion of intellectual property and do not take kindly to bootlegged editions of CDs or books or software that show up on black markets.

But Martin Luther King Jr. was not a rock star. Or a software designer. He was 15 a preacher, a leader, a prophet, a martyr. He was, in every sense of the word, a public figure.

One day, 36 years ago, he gave voice to our collective idealism and words to our 16 best collective yearnings: "I have a dream that my four little children will one day

---

2. *Harry Belafonte*: A musician and activist who was a friend of King's.

live in a nation where they will not be judged by the color of their skin but by the content of their character."

This is not a private dream. It doesn't belong to his family estate. It belongs to all of us. 17

READING CLOSELY

1. In Ellen Goodman's view, who owns Martin Luther King's "I Have a Dream" speech, and where does she state her opinion most directly?

2. "There is still the little matter," Goodman says, "of public history and private property" (12). What conflicting interests is she referring to here?

3. How and where does Goodman explain the increase in value of Martin Luther King's "intellectual property" (8)?

4. Why is it "not surprising," according to Goodman, that King's family would be protective of his legacy, including his famous speech (10)?

STRATEGIES AND STRUCTURES

1. Who is Goodman's intended AUDIENCE? How do you know?

2. How, and how well, does Goodman support her CLAIM that King's words belong "to all of us" (17)? Refer to specific passages in the text in your response.

3. Goodman reminds us that she is among those "who work with words for a living" (14). How effective do you find this method of establishing her credibility?

4. Goodman contends that, because Martin Luther King Jr. was a "public figure," his dream "belongs to all of us" (15, 17). Does this argument appeal primarily to the reader's reason or to his or her emotions? Why do you say so?

5. *Other Methods.* Goodman likens "I Have a Dream" to Lincoln's Gettysburg Address (2). How and how well does this COMPARISON support her argument?

THINKING ABOUT LANGUAGE

1. Goodman equates King's speech with a "balloon" released into the air (1). Is this a good ANALOGY? Why or why not?

2. Goodman offers the reader a choice between "protective" and "litigious" (5). Why? What are the CONNOTATIONS of these different terms?

3. Explain the distinction that Goodman is making between being "on a pedestal" and being "on a T-shirt" (10).

FOR WRITING

1. Write a paragraph or two explaining how and why someone's words might (or might not) be considered a form of property.

2. Whom does King's famous speech belong to, in your opinion? Write an argument in which you take (and support) a position on this particular issue—and on the ownership of intellectual property in general.

LAWRENCE LESSIG

Free Culture

Lawrence Lessig (b. 1961), director of the Edmond J. Safra Foundation Center for Ethics at Harvard University and a professor at Harvard Law School, is committed to what he calls "free culture," in which ideas and creative notions freely circulate so that everyone can borrow from and build upon them—particularly in regard to emerging technologies. In The Future of Ideas *(2001), Lessig argued that antiquated notions of intellectual property are a hindrance to technological innovation and the free exchange of ideas, a claim that won him a place on* Scientific American's *list of the world's top fifty visionaries in 2002.*

The following argument is taken from Lessig's Free Culture: How Big Media Uses Technology and the Law to Lock Down Culture and Control Creativity *(2004). It deals with the conflict between an artist's right to get paid for his or her work and the demands of the Internet.*

IF YOU'RE LIKE I WAS A DECADE AGO, or like most people are when they first start thinking about these issues, then just about now you should be puzzled about something you hadn't thought through before.

We live in a world that celebrates "property." I am one of those celebrants. I believe in the value of property in general, and I also believe in the value of that weird form of property that lawyers call "intellectual property." A large, diverse society cannot survive without property; a large, diverse, and modern society cannot flourish without intellectual property.

But it takes just a second's reflection to realize that there is plenty of value out there that "property" doesn't capture. I don't mean "money can't buy you love," but rather, value that is plainly part of a process of production, including commercial as well as noncommercial production. If Disney animators had stolen a set of pencils to draw *Steamboat Willie*,[1] we'd have no hesitation in condemning that taking as wrong—even though trivial, even if unnoticed. Yet there was nothing wrong, at least under the law of the day, with Disney's taking from Buster Keaton or from the

---

1. *Steamboat Willie*: A 1928 Mickey Mouse cartoon, the first to be made with sound.

SUGGESTED MLA CITATION: Lessig, Lawrence. "Free Culture." 2004. *Back to the Lake.* Ed. Thomas Cooley. 2nd ed. New York: Norton, 2012. 627–30. Print.

Brothers Grimm.[2] There was nothing wrong with the taking from Keaton because Disney's use would have been considered "fair." There was nothing wrong with the taking from the Grimms because the Grimms' work was in the public domain.

Thus, even though the things that Disney took—or more generally, the things taken by anyone exercising Walt Disney creativity—are valuable, our tradition does not treat those takings as wrong. Some things remain free for the taking within a free culture, and that freedom is good. . . .   4

It's the same with a thousand examples that appear everywhere once you begin to look. Scientists build upon the work of other scientists without asking or paying for the privilege. ("Excuse me, Professor Einstein, but may I have permission to use your theory of relativity to show that you were wrong about quantum physics?") Acting companies perform adaptations of the works of Shakespeare without securing permission from anyone. (Does *anyone* believe Shakespeare would be better spread within our culture if there were a central Shakespeare rights clearinghouse that all productions of Shakespeare must appeal to first?) And Hollywood goes through cycles with a certain kind of movie: five asteroid films in the late 1990s; two volcano disaster films in 1997.   5

Creators here and everywhere are always and at all times building upon the creativity that went before and that surrounds them now. That building is always and everywhere at least partially done without permission and without compensating the original creator. No society, free or controlled, has ever demanded that every use be paid for or that permission for Walt Disney creativity must always be sought. Instead, every society has left a certain bit of its culture free for the taking—free societies more fully than unfree, perhaps, but all societies to some degree.   6

The hard question is therefore not *whether* a culture is free. All cultures are free to some degree. The hard question instead is "*How* free is this culture?" How much, and how broadly, is the culture free for others to take and build upon? Is that freedom limited to party members? To members of the royal family? To the top ten corporations on the New York Stock Exchange? Or is that freedom spread broadly? To artists generally, whether affiliated with the Met[3] or not? To musicians generally, whether white or not? To filmmakers generally, whether affiliated with a studio or not?   7

2. *Brothers Grimm*: Jakob Grimm (1785–1863) and Wilhelm Grimm (1786–1859), German brothers who collected and published folk tales and fairy tales such as "Snow White and the Seven Dwarfs," "Little Red Riding Hood," and "Hansel and Gretel." *Buster Keaton* (1895–1966): An early comic actor best known for his silent films of the 1920s.

3. *The Met*: Could refer to either the Metropolitan Museum of Art or the Metropolitan Opera, both in New York City.

Free cultures are cultures that leave a great deal open for others to build upon;   8
unfree, or permission, cultures leave much less. Ours was a free culture. It is
becoming much less so.

· · ·

The battle that got this whole [copyright] war going was about music. . . . The   9
appeal of file-sharing music was the crack cocaine of the Internet's growth. It drove
demand for access to the Internet more powerfully than any other single application. It was the Internet's killer app[4]—possibly in two senses of that word. It no
doubt was the application that drove demand for bandwidth. It may well be the
application that drives demand for regulations that in the end kill innovation on
the network.

The aim of copyright, with respect to content in general and music in particu-   10
lar, is to create the incentives for music to be composed, performed, and, most
importantly, spread. The law does this by giving an exclusive right to a composer to
control copies of her performance.

File-sharing networks complicate this model by enabling the spread of content   11
for which the performer has not been paid. Today, file sharing is addictive. In ten
years, it won't be. It is addictive today because it is the easiest way to gain access to
a broad range of content. It won't be the easiest way to get access to a broad range
of content in ten years. Today, access to the Internet is cumbersome and slow—we
in the United States are lucky to have broadband service at 1.5 MBs, and very rarely
do we get service at that speed both up and down.[5] Although wireless access is
growing, most of us still get access across wires. Most only gain access through a
machine with a keyboard. The idea of the always on, always connected Internet is
mainly just an idea.

But it will become a reality, and that means the way we get access to the Inter-   12
net today is a technology in transition. Policy makers should not make policy on
the basis of technology in transition. They should make policy on the basis of where
the technology is going. The question should not be, how should the law regulate
sharing in this world? The question should be, what law will we require when the
network becomes that network it is clearly becoming? That network is one in
which every machine with electricity is essentially on the Net; where everywhere
you are—except maybe the desert or the Rockies—you can instantaneously be

---

4. *Killer app:* Short for "killer application"; a program so desirable that people will pay for the hard-
ware or software it runs on just so they can use the application. In this instance, Lessig believes that
file-sharing—sharing files between computers—is so desirable that people will obtain Internet access
(necessary for file-sharing) just to be able to do it.

5. *Up and down:* Uploading (from computer to Web) and downloading (from Web to computer).

connected to the Internet. Imagine the Internet as ubiquitous as the best cell-phone service, where with the flip of a device, you are connected.

In that world, it will be extremely easy to connect to services that give you   13
access to content on the fly—such as Internet radio, content that is streamed to the user when the user demands. Here, then, is the critical point: When it is *extremely* easy to connect to services that give access to content, it will be *easier* to connect to services that give you access to content than it will be to download and store content *on the many devices you will have for playing content.* It will be easier, in other words, to subscribe than it will be to be a database manager, as everyone in the download-sharing of Napster-like[6] technologies essentially is. Content services will compete with content sharing, even if the services charge money for the content they give access to.

P. 518 gives some tips for stating the point of your argument.

This point about the future is meant to suggest a perspective on the present: It   14
is emphatically temporary. The "problem" with file-sharing—to the extent there is a real problem—is a problem that will increasingly disappear as it becomes easier to connect to the Internet. And thus it is an extraordinary mistake for policy makers today to be "solving" this problem in light of a technology that will be gone tomorrow. . . .

But what if "piracy" doesn't disappear? What if there is a competitive market   15
providing content at a low cost, but a significant number of consumers continue to "take" content for nothing? Should the law do something then?

Yes, it should. But again, what it should do depends upon how the facts develop.   16
The real issue is not whether [the law] eliminates sharing in the abstract. The real issue is its effect on the market. Is it better (a) to have a technology that is 95 percent secure and produces a market of size *x*, or (b) to have a technology that is 50 percent secure but produces a market of five times *x*? Less secure might produce more unauthorized sharing, but it is likely to also produce a much bigger market in authorized sharing. The most important thing is to assure artists' compensation without breaking the Internet. Once that's assured, then it may well be appropriate to find ways to track down the petty pirates.

---

6. *Napster*: An online file-sharing service that allowed users to download music files from other users' computers for free; it is now a legal, pay-per-download service currently owned by Best Buy.

READING CLOSELY

1. Why does Lawrence Lessig think the courts should not impose heavy restrictions on Internet file-sharing?

2. To what extent does Lessig believe in the right of individuals to own property, including intellectual property? Why does he feel this way? Refer to the text in your response.

3. How did the downloading of music stir up a copyright "war" (9)?

4. Why does Lessig think forms of Internet piracy will disappear? How convincing do you find his evidence? Explain.

5. Lessig thinks artists should be compensated for their work, but "without breaking the Internet" (16). In Lessig's view, why is it as important to the cultural life of the nation to have a strong Internet as it is to protect the rights of people whose intellectual property has already contributed to that culture?

STRATEGIES AND STRUCTURES

1. What is Lessig's main point, and where does he state it most directly?

2. Why do you think Lessig begins his argument by saying, "If you're like I was a decade ago" (1)? What assumptions is he making about his AUDIENCE, and why, in particular, does he refer to the reader as "puzzled" (1)?

3. How and how well does Lessig establish his credibility as an ethical person who is looking out for the reader's best interests?

4. How and how well does Lessig justify "Walt Disney creativity" in the early days of animated cartoons (4)? Is his reasoning valid?

5. What general standard does Lessig adopt for judging whether or not the "taking" of intellectual property is ethical (4)? Do you find this argument convincing? Why or why not?

6. *Other Methods.* Lessig DEFINES a free culture as one "that leave[s] a great deal open for others to build upon" (8). How does this definition contribute to his argument about keeping some intellectual property free?

THINKING ABOUT LANGUAGE

1. Point out the different ways in which Lessig uses the word *free*. What are its various meanings at different places in his argument?

2. As applied to the copyright controversy, how appropriate do you find the word "war" (9)? Is this just HYPERBOLE, or is the issue important (and controversial) enough to justify the term? Explain your view.

3. Why does Lessig refer to "Walt Disney creativity" throughout his essay instead of using a phrase like "the limited taking of the intellectual property of others"?

4. What are the implications of Lessig's use of the word "addictive" (11)?

FOR WRITING

1. Write a few paragraphs exploring the idea that intellectual property is a form of private property that must be protected by law. You could defend this claim, challenge it, or agree in some ways but disagree in others.

2. Lessig predicts that file-sharing won't always be "the easiest way to get access to a broad range of content" on the Internet (11). Instead, he argues, it will be easier "to connect to services that give you access to content on the fly"—and to pay for those services (13). Write an argument defending or challenging this position based on your view of where Internet technology is today.

Debating Intellectual Property

The following questions refer to the arguments on pages 615–32.

READING ARGUMENTS

1. Which position, Goodman's on sharing Dr. King's words or Wilensky's on flunking students for plagiarism, is best supported by Lessig's argument for keeping intellectual culture free and open? Explain.

2. Who do you think makes the best use of logical reasoning to support his or her claim? Of facts and figures? Why do you say so?

3. How effective do you find Gabriel's EXAMPLE of the plagiarizing father (33)? How about Lessig's references to Einstein, Shakespeare, and Hollywood (5)? Which is a better use of specific examples to support an argument? Explain.

4. Among the participants in this debate, which one uses the shortest sentences and the least abstract language? To what extent do you think this prose style (and that of the other writers in the debate) is influenced by his or her intended audience? Explain.

FOR WRITING

1. Write a paragraph or two explaining which of the arguments in this debate you find strongest or weakest—and why.

2. Write an argument in which you take a position (and support it—with facts, statistics, expert testimony, and other evidence) on some aspect of the intellectual property debate not fully covered by Wilensky, Gabriel, Goodman, or Lessig.

Debating the Effects of Digital Culture

"Printing, gunpower and the compass. These three," wrote, the English philosopher Francis Bacon in 1620, "have changed the whole face and state of things throughout the world." Gunpower and the compass changed how people dealt with the physical world around them. Printed books, such as Bacon's *Novum Organum* (or "New Instrument"), changed the way human beings explored the interior world of knowledge and ideas. Thanks to more recent technologies, such as the Internet, we can find approximately 371,000 references to Bacon's masterpiece in .22 seconds simply by Googling the original Latin title. Are the electronic technologies of the digital age, like the mechanical ones that preceded them, changing "the whole face and state of things"? Or is the digital revolution simply giving us more efficient ways of communicating with each other and quicker access to new sources of ideas—from Bacon's once obscure but now readily available treatise to *Slate* and the *Huffington Post*?

In the following texts, two writers and a psychologist probe the extent to which today's media and technology are changing not only how we acquire and exchange information but how we define knowledge and the self:

Questions about this group of readings can be found on p. 648.

AMY GOLDWASSER

What's the Matter with Kids Today?

Nothing, actually. Aside from our panic that the Internet is melting their brains.

Amy Goldwasser is the editor of RED: Teenage Girls in America Write on What Fires Up Their Lives Today *(2008; available in paperback), and the social network redthebook.com. Goldwasser recognized the power of such frankly personal essays as a volunteer at the Lower Eastside Girls Club in New York City. She continues to work with the book's young authors nearly every day, adapting their essays for television and theater and editing their personal and political pieces for national publications including* Newsweek, *the* Los Angeles Times *and the* Huffington Post.

"What's the Matter with Kids Today?" was first posted in March 2008 on Salon, *the online arts and culture magazine. For many parents, says Goldwasser—and for such literary luminaries as Doris Lessing, winner of the 2007 Nobel Prize in Literature—the answer to the question posed in her title is   the Internet. As indicated in the subtitle, however, Goldwasser herself argues that what's actually wrong with today's students is nothing but "our panic."*

T HE OTHER WEEK was only the latest takedown of what has become a fashionable   1 segment of the population to bash: the American teenager. A phone (land line!) survey of 1,200 17-year-olds, conducted by the research organization Common Core and released February 26, found our young people to be living in "stunning ignorance" of history and literature.

This furthered the report that the National Endowment for the Arts came out   2 with at the end of 2007, lamenting "the diminished role of voluntary reading in American life," particularly among 13-to-17-year-olds, and Doris Lessing's condemnation, in her acceptance speech for the Nobel Prize in literature, of "a fragmenting culture" in which "young men and women . . . have read nothing, knowing only some specialty or other, for instance, computers."

Kids today—we're telling you!—don't read, don't write, don't care about any-   3 thing farther in front of them than their iPods. The Internet, according to 88-year-old Lessing (whose specialty is sturdy typewriters, or perhaps pens), has "seduced a whole generation into its inanities."

SUGGESTED MLA CITATION: Goldwasser, Amy. "What's the Matter with Kids Today?" 2006. *Back to the Lake.* Ed. Thomas Cooley. 2nd ed. New York: Norton, 2012. 635–37. Print.

Or is it the older generation that the Internet has seduced—into the inanities of ⁴
leveling charges based on fear, ignorance and old-media, multiple-choice testing?
So much so that we can't see that the Internet is only a means of communication,
and one that has created a generation, perhaps the first, of writers, activists, storytellers? When the world worked in hard copy, no parent or teacher ever begrudged
teenagers who disappeared into their rooms to write letters to friends—or a movie
review, or an editorial for the school paper on the first president they'll vote for.
Even 15-year-old boys are sharing some part of their feelings with someone out
there.

We're talking about 33 million Americans who are fluent in texting, e-mailing, ⁵
blogging, IM'ing and constantly amending their profiles on social network sites—
which, on average, 30 of their friends will visit every day, hanging out and writing
for 20 minutes or so each. They're connected, they're collaborative, they're used to
writing about themselves. In fact, they choose to write about themselves, on their
own time, rather than its being a forced labor when a paper's due in school. Regularly, often late at night, they're generating a body of intimate written work. They
appreciate the value of a good story and the power of a speech that moves: Ninety-
seven percent of the teenagers in the Common Core survey connected "I have a
dream" with its speaker—they can watch Dr. King deliver it on demand—and eight
in 10 knew what *To Kill a Mockingbird* is about.

This is, of course, the kind of knowledge we should be encouraging. The Inter- ⁶
net has turned teenagers into honest documentarians of their own lives—reporters
embedded in their homes, their schools, their own heads.

How to appeal
to your reader's
emotions is
discussed on
p. 526.
But this is also why it's dangerous, why we can't seem to recognize ⁷
that it's just a medium. We're afraid. Our kids know things we don't. They
drove the presidential debates onto YouTube and very well may determine the outcome of this election. They're texting at the dinner table and
responsible for pretty much every enduring consumer cultural phenomenon: iPod, iTunes, iPhone; Harry Potter, *High School Musical*; large hot drinks with
gingerbread flavoring. They can sell ads on their social network pages, and they
essentially made MySpace worth $580 million and *Juno* an Oscar winner.

Besides, we're tired of having to ask them every time we need to find Season 2 ⁸
of *Heroes*, calculate a carbon footprint or upload photos to Facebook (now that
we're allowed on).

Plus, they're blogging about us. ⁹

So we've made the Internet one more thing unknowable about the American ¹⁰
teenager, when, really, it's one of the few revelations. We conduct these surveys
and overgeneralize—labeling like the mean girls, driven by the same jealousy and
insecurity.

Common Core drew its multiple-choice questions for teens from a test adminis-   11
tered by the federal government in 1986. Twenty-plus years ago, high school
students didn't have the Internet to store their trivia. Now they know that the specific dates and what-was-that-prince's-name will always be there; they can free
their brains to go a little deeper into the concepts instead of the copyrights, step
back and consider what Scout and Atticus were really fighting for. To criticize
teenagers' author-to-book title matching on the spot, over the phone, is similar to
cold-calling over-40s and claiming their long-division skills or date of *Jaws* recall is
rusty. This is what we all rely on the Internet for.

That's not to say some of the survey findings aren't disturbing. It's crushing to   12
hear that one in four teens could not identify Adolf Hitler's role in world history,
for instance. But it's not because teenagers were online that they missed this. Had
a parent introduced 20 minutes of researching the Holocaust to one month of their
teen's Internet life, or a teacher assigned *The Diary of Anne Frank* (arguably a
13-year-old girl's blog)—if we worked with, rather than against, the way this generation voluntarily takes in information—we might not be able to pick up the
phone and expose tragic pockets of ignorance.

The average teen chooses to spend an average of 16.7 hours a week reading and   13
writing online. Yet the NEA report did not consider this to be "voluntary" reading
and writing. Its findings also concluded that "literary reading declined significantly
in a period of rising Internet use." The corollary is weak—this has as well been a
period of rising franchises of frozen yogurt that doesn't taste like frozen yogurt, of
global warming, of declining rates of pregnancy and illicit drug use among teenagers, and of girls sweeping the country's most prestigious high school science competition for the first time.

Teenagers today read and write for fun; it's part of their social lives. We need to   14
start celebrating this unprecedented surge, incorporating it as an educational tool
instead of meeting it with punishing pop quizzes and suspicion.

We need to start trusting our kids to communicate as they will online—even   15
when that comes with the risk that they'll spill the family secrets or campaign for a
candidate who's not ours.

Once we stop regarding the Internet as a villain, stop presenting it as the enemy   16
of history and literature and worldly knowledge, then our teenagers have the
potential to become the next great voices of America. One of them, 70 years from
now, might even get up there to accept the very award Lessing did—and thank the
Internet for making him or her a writer and a thinker.

READING CLOSELY

1. Many parents, says Amy Goldwasser, think it's "dangerous" for their children to spend a lot of time on the Internet (7). Why? What do they fear, according to her?

2. Is this "suspicion" justified, or is Goldwasser right when she says that such distrust is based on "fear" and "ignorance" (14, 4)? Explain.

3. The average American teenager, says Goldwasser, spends 16.7 hours "reading and writing online" every week (13). Does this fact justify her claim that the Internet "has created a generation, perhaps the first, of writers, activists, storytellers" (4)? Why or why not?

4. Goldwasser says teenagers are reading and writing more than ever, yet the National Endowment for the Arts reports that "literary reading declined significantly in a period of rising Internet use" (13). How does Goldwasser resolve this apparent contradiction?

STRATEGIES AND STRUCTURES

1. Who is Goldwasser's intended AUDIENCE? Telephone researchers who use land lines? Nobel Prize winners? American teenagers? Their parents? Parents who don't use the Internet? Some combination of these? Explain.

2. What is the main point of Goldwasser's argument with regard to teenagers and the Internet? What does she want her readers to do about it? How do you know?

3. Goldwasser's essay was published during the presidential campaign of 2008. How and how well does Goldwasser incorporate this circumstance into her argument? Explain by pointing to specific passages in the text.

4. Goldwasser argues that novelist Doris Lessing's claims about the negative effects of the Internet (as expressed in her acceptance speech for the Nobel Prize in Literature) are false because Lessing was eighty-eight years old when she made the speech and maybe used "sturdy typewriters, or perhaps pens" (3). Is this reasoning valid? Why or why not?

5. *Other Methods.* When she argues that the Internet and other social media have "turned teenagers into honest documentarians of their own lives," Goldwasser is analyzing CAUSE AND EFFECT (6). Are the causes that she cites sufficient to produce the effect she claims for them? Explain.

Thinking about Language

1. In the past, says Goldwasser, parents never "begrudged teenagers" who disappeared into their rooms to write (4). Should she, instead, have said that parents never "begrudged *the time to* teenagers" who disappeared into their rooms? Why or why not?

2. What is a "documentarian," and why might Goldwasser use this term instead of a more familiar one, such as *commentator* or *reporter* (6)?

3. Look up the term "corollary" (13) in your dictionary. Would Goldwasser's logic be strengthened if she had used the term *correlation* instead? Why or why not?

4. Many parents, says Goldwasser, consider the Internet a "villain" (16). Is this HYPERBOLE justified by her argument? Why or why not?

For Writing

1. In her acceptance speech for the 2007 Nobel Prize, Doris Lessing noted that writers are often asked, "How do you write? With a word processor? an electric typewriter? a quill? longhand?" Look up her speech and write a paragraph explaining how she responded to this trivial (in her view) question.

2. Goldwasser's argument assumes that reading and writing online are equivalent, intellectually and aesthetically, to the more traditional kinds. How warranted is this premise? Write an argument agreeing (or disagreeing) with Goldwasser on this aspect of the issue.

STEVEN PINKER

Mind Over Mass Media

Steven Pinker (b. 1954) is a native of Canada and a professor of psychology at Harvard. Pinker specializes in the study of language and cognition, having determined in his freshman year at McGill University in Montreal that for him "language is the key to understanding the human mind." He is the author of numerous books on language and psychology, including The Stuff of Thought: Language as a Window into Human Nature *(2007).*

In "Mind Over Mass Media," an Op-Ed he wrote for the New York Times *in 2010, Pinker examines the relationship between human intelligence and the use (or overuse) of such electronic technologies as PowerPoint, Google, and Twitter. The new media are not turning the human brain to mush, he argues; however, they do require us "to develop strategies of self-control, as we do with every other temptation in life."*

NEW FORMS OF MEDIA have always caused moral panics: the printing press, newspapers, paperbacks and television were all once denounced as threats to their consumers' brainpower and moral fiber. 1

So too with electronic technologies. PowerPoint, we're told, is reducing discourse to bullet points. Search engines lower our intelligence, encouraging us to skim on the surface of knowledge rather than dive to its depths. Twitter is shrinking our attention spans. 2

But such panics often fail basic reality checks. When comic books were accused of turning juveniles into delinquents in the 1950s, crime was falling to record lows, just as the denunciations of video games in the 1990s coincided with the great American crime decline. The decades of television, transistor radios and rock videos were also decades in which I.Q. scores rose continuously. 3

For a reality check today, take the state of science, which demands high levels of brainwork and is measured by clear benchmarks of discovery. These days scientists are never far from their e-mail, rarely touch paper and cannot lecture without PowerPoint. If electronic media were hazardous to intelligence, the quality of science would be plummeting. Yet discoveries are multiplying like fruit flies, and progress is dizzying. Other activities in the life of the mind, like philosophy, history and cultural criticism, are likewise flourishing, as anyone who has lost a morning of work to the Web site Arts & Letters Daily can attest. 4

SUGGESTED MLA CITATION: Pinker, Steven. "Mind Over Mass Media." 2010. *Back to the Lake.* Ed. Thomas Cooley. 2nd ed. New York: Norton, 2012. 640–42. Print.

Critics of new media sometimes use science itself to press their case, citing 5 research that shows how "experience can change the brain." But cognitive neuroscientists roll their eyes at such talk. Yes, every time we learn a fact or skill the wiring of the brain changes; it's not as if the information is stored in the pancreas. But the existence of neural plasticity does not mean the brain is a blob of clay pounded into shape by experience.

Experience does not revamp the basic information-processing capacities of the 6 brain. Speed-reading programs have long claimed to do just that, but the verdict was rendered by Woody Allen after he read *War and Peace* in one sitting: "It was about Russia." Genuine multitasking, too, has been exposed as a myth, not just by laboratory studies but by the familiar sight of an S.U.V. undulating between lanes as the driver cuts deals on his cellphone.

Moreover, as the psychologists Christopher Chabris and Daniel Simons show in 7 their new book *The Invisible Gorilla: And Other Ways Our Intuitions Deceive Us*, the effects of experience are highly specific to the experiences themselves. If you train people to do one thing (recognize shapes, solve math puzzles, find hidden words), they get better at doing that thing, but almost nothing else. Music doesn't make you better at math, conjugating Latin doesn't make you more logical, brain-training games don't make you smarter. Accomplished people don't bulk up their brains with intellectual calisthenics; they immerse themselves in their fields. Novelists read lots of novels, scientists read lots of science.

The effects of consuming electronic media are also likely to be far more limited 8 than the panic implies. Media critics write as if the brain takes on the qualities of whatever it consumes, the informational equivalent of "you are what you eat." As with primitive peoples who believe that eating fierce animals will make them fierce, they assume that watching quick cuts in rock videos turns your mental life into quick cuts or that reading bullet points and Twitter postings turns your thoughts into bullet points and Twitter postings.

For tips on dealing with false analogies and either-or logic, see p. 525.

Yes, the constant arrival of information packets can be distracting or addictive, 9 especially to people with attention deficit disorder. But distraction is not a new phenomenon. The solution is not to bemoan technology but to develop strategies of self-control, as we do with every other temptation in life. Turn off e-mail or Twitter when you work, put away your BlackBerry at dinner time, ask your spouse to call you to bed at a designated hour.

And to encourage intellectual depth, don't rail at PowerPoint or Google. It's not 10 as if habits of deep reflection, thorough research and rigorous reasoning ever came naturally to people. They must be acquired in special institutions, which we call universities, and maintained with constant upkeep, which we call analysis, criticism and debate. They are not granted by propping a heavy encyclopedia on your lap, nor are they taken away by efficient access to information on the Internet.

The new media have caught on for a reason. Knowledge is increasing exponen- 11
tially; human brainpower and waking hours are not. Fortunately, the Internet and
information technologies are helping us manage, search and retrieve our collective
intellectual output at different scales, from Twitter and previews to e-books and
online encyclopedias. Far from making us stupid, these technologies are the only
things that will keep us smart.

READING CLOSELY

1. "Critics of new media," says Steven Pinker, predict that these technologies will
   have dire mental and moral consequences (5, 1). What are some of them? Why
   does Pinker think such predictions are being made?

2. Pinker admits that information overload can be "distracting or addictive" (9).
   What solution does he offer to this problem? Is it a good solution? Why or
   why not?

3. Instead of destroying our "brainpower and moral fiber," what EFFECT does
   Pinker himself think the new electronic technologies will have upon the general population (1)? Why?

4. Human beings, says Pinker, do not naturally and automatically acquire "intellectual depth" and "habits of deep reflection" (10)? According to Pinker, how
   and where—in what kinds of special institutions—do we develop such depth
   and habits?

STRATEGIES AND STRUCTURES

1. Who is more likely to be the intended AUDIENCE for Pinker's argument—
   confirmed critics of the new media, confirmed supporters of it, or people who
   have not yet entirely made up their minds? Explain.

2. "If electronic media were hazardous to intelligence," Pinker argues, "the quality
   of science would be plummeting" (4). How sound is Pinker's logical reasoning
   here? Explain.

3. To make a point about multitasking, Pinker refers to "the familiar sight of an
   S.U.V. undulating between lanes as the driver cuts deals on his cell phone" (6).
   Point out other EXAMPLES of Pinker's use of ANECDOTAL evidence like this. Do
   they provide effective proof for his CLAIMS? Why or why not?

4. Point out specific places in Pinker's argument where he provides more scholarly evidence, such as expert testimony and formal logical reasoning.

5. *Other Methods.* Pinker COMPARES some media critics to "primitive peoples who believe that eating fierce animals will make them fierce" (8). On what basis is he comparing these two groups? Is his comparison logical? Explain.

THINKING ABOUT LANGUAGE

1. Why does Pinker use fruit flies instead of, for example, elephants in his SIMILE about the number of new scientific discoveries (4)?

2. Explain the PUN on *consumer* in Pinker's reference to "the effects of consuming electronic media" (8).

3. Pinker frequently use the word "panic" in his essay (1, 3, 8). Why? Does he justify the use of the term, or could he be accused of the logical fallacy (or strategy) of "begging the question"? Explain?

4. The *American Heritage Dictionary* labels the word *stupid* as "informal." Should Pinker have used a more formal term in stating his thesis that "far from making us stupid, these technologies are the only things that will keep us smart" (11)? Why or why not?

FOR WRITING

1. In a paragraph or two, give an example of an occasion when technology seemed to make the user smarter—or dumber.

2. Compose an essay arguing that there is (or is not) a cause-and-effect relationship between technology and some forms of intelligence. Refer to specific technologies, old or new, in your analysis. For example, you might argue that Kindles and the Internet are (or are not) making us better readers and writers than we would be if we depended solely on older print media, such books and magazines.

PEGGY ORENSTEIN

I Tweet, Therefore I Am

Peggy Orenstein (b. 1961) is a journalist and author of books and essays on gender and family diversity. Born in Minneapolis, Orenstein is a 1983 graduate of Oberlin College. From Schoolgirls *(1994) to* Cinderella Ate My Daughter *(2011), Orenstein's books examine how, in the words of* Bitch *magazine, "the media and popular culture . . . serve up distorted visions of womanhood to girls."*

"I Tweet, Therefore I Am," which appeared in the New York Times Magazine *in 2010, begins with an idyllic scene in which mother and daughter are listening to a downloaded children's book about a mute swan who learns to play the trumpet. In Orenstein's view, however, the media no longer push frankly instructive fairy tales of nature and self-improvement. Instead of helping us to find and express our true selves, Orenstein argues, Twitter, Facebook, and other social media may be encouraging a self-consciousness that causes us to speak in text-bites—not with trumpets but in tweets.*

O**N A RECENT LAZY** S**ATURDAY MORNING,** my daughter and I lolled on a blanket in our front yard, snacking on apricots, listening to a download of E. B. White reading *The Trumpet of the Swan.* Her legs sprawled across mine; the grass tickled our ankles. It was the quintessential summer moment, and a year ago, I would have been fully present for it. But instead, a part of my consciousness had split off and was observing the scene from the outside: this was, I realized excitedly, the perfect opportunity for a tweet. 1

I came late to Twitter. I might have skipped the phenomenon altogether, but I have a book coming out this winter, and publishers, scrambling to promote 360,000-character tomes in a 140-character world, push authors to rally their "tweeps" to the cause. Leaving aside the question of whether that actually boosts sales, I felt pressure to produce. I quickly mastered the Twitterati's unnatural self-consciousness: processing my experience instantaneously, packaging life as I lived it. I learned to be "on" all the time, whether standing behind that woman at the supermarket who sneaked three extra items into the express check-out lane (you know who you are) or despairing over human rights abuses against women in Guatemala. 2

Each Twitter post seemed a tacit referendum on who I am, or at least who I believe myself to be. The grocery-store episode telegraphed that I was tuned in to 3

SUGGESTED MLA CITATION: Orenstein, Peggy. "I Tweet, Therefore I Am." 2010. *Back to the Lake.* Ed. Thomas Cooley. 2nd ed. New York: Norton, 2012. 644–46. Print.

the Seinfeldian absurdities[1] of life; my concern about women's victimization, however sincere, signaled that I also have a soul. Together they suggest someone who is at once cynical and compassionate, petty yet deep. Which, in the end, I'd say, is pretty accurate.

Distilling my personality provided surprising focus, making me feel stripped to   4 my essence. It forced me, for instance, to pinpoint the dominant feeling as I sat outside with my daughter listening to E. B. White. Was it my joy at being a mother? Nostalgia for my own childhood summers? The pleasures of listening to the author's quirky, underinflected voice? Each put a different spin on the occasion, of who I was within it. Yet the final decision ("Listening to E. B. White's 'Trumpet of the Swan' with Daisy. Slow and sweet.") was not really about my own impressions: it was about how I imagined—and wanted—others to react to them. That gave me pause. How much, I began to wonder, was I shaping my Twitter feed, and how much was Twitter shaping me?

See p. 529 for analyzing causes and effects in an argument.

Back in the 1950s, the sociologist Erving Goffman famously argued that all of life is   5 performance: we act out a role in every interaction, adapting it based on the nature of the relationship or context at hand. Twitter has extended that metaphor to include aspects of our experience that used to be considered off-set: eating pizza in bed, reading a book in the tub, thinking a thought anywhere, flossing. Effectively, it makes the greasepaint permanent, blurring the lines not only between public and private but also between the authentic and contrived self. If all the world was once a stage, it has now become a reality TV show: we mere players are not just aware of the camera; we mug for it.

The expansion of our digital universe—Second Life, Facebook, MySpace,   6 Twitter—has shifted not only how we spend our time but also how we construct identity. For her coming book, *Alone Together*, Sherry Turkle, a professor at M.I.T., interviewed more than 400 children and parents about their use of social media and cellphones. Among young people especially she found that the self was increasingly becoming externally manufactured rather than internally developed: a series of profiles to be sculptured and refined in response to public opinion. "On Twitter or Facebook you're trying to express something real about who you are," she explained. "But because you're also creating something for others' consumption, you find yourself imagining and playing to your audience more and more. So those moments in which you're supposed to be showing your true self become a performance. Your *psychology* becomes a performance." Referring to "The Lonely Crowd,"

---

1. *Seinfeldian absurdities*: A reference to a popular TV sitcom (1989–1998) based on a fictionalized version of the lives of comedian Jerry Seinfeld and his friends. The show was notable for being about "nothing" and focusing on the absurdities of everyday situations.

the landmark description of the transformation of the American character from inner- to outer-directed, Turkle added, "Twitter is outer-directedness cubed."

The fun of Twitter and, I suspect, its draw for millions of people, is its infinite   7
potential for connection, as well as its opportunity for self-expression. I enjoy those things myself. But when every thought is externalized, what becomes of insight? When we reflexively post each feeling, what becomes of reflection? When friends become fans, what happens to intimacy? The risk of the performance culture, of the packaged self, is that it erodes the very relationships it purports to create, and alienates us from our own humanity. Consider the fate of empathy: in an analysis of 72 studies performed on nearly 14,000 college students between 1979 and 2009, researchers at the Institute for Social Research at the University of Michigan found a drop in that trait, with the sharpest decline occurring since 2000. Social media may not have instigated that trend, but by encouraging self-promotion over self-awareness, they may well be accelerating it.

None of this makes me want to cancel my Twitter account. It's too late for that   8
anyway: I'm already hooked. Besides, I appreciate good writing whatever the form: some "tweeple" are as deft as haiku masters at their craft. I am experimenting with the art of the well-placed "hashtag" myself (the symbol that adds your post on a particular topic, like #ShirleySherrod, to a stream. You can also use them whimsically, as in, "I am pretending not to be afraid of the humongous spider on the bed. #lieswetellourchildren").

At the same time, I am trying to gain some perspective on the perpetual per-   9
former's self-consciousness. That involves trying to sort out the line between person and persona, the public and private self. It also means that the next time I find myself lying on the grass, stringing daisy chains and listening to E. B. White, I will resist the urge to trumpet about the swan.

READING CLOSELY

1. According to Peggy Orenstein, why is *Twitter* so much "fun," and what accounts for its appeal to so many people (7)?

2. In Orenstein's view, how have *Twitter* and other social media—such as *Second Life*, *Facebook*, and *MySpace*—caused a "blurring [of] lines not only between public and private but also between the authentic and contrived self" (5)?

3. What does Orenstein think we have lost as a result of such blurring? Is she right? Why or why not?

4. Despite her misgivings, Orenstein has no intention of closing her *Twitter* account. Why not?

STRATEGIES AND STRUCTURES

1. If Orenstein is not telling readers to stop tweeting, what *is* the main point of her argument? Where does she state that point most directly?

2. How and how well does Orenstein's tweet—"Listening to E. B. White's 'Trumpet of the Swan' with Daisy. Slow and sweet."—EXEMPLIFY what she says about providing a "surprising focus" to her experience (4)? About "how we construct identity" (6)?

3. What is Orenstein's purpose in referring to the pioneering sociologist Erving Goffman and MIT psychologist Sherry Turkle (5, 6)? Do these references strengthen her argument substantially, or are they just icing on the cake? Explain.

4. "How much . . . was I shaping my Twitter feed, and how much was Twitter shaping me?" (4). How and how well does Orenstein use this key question to sum up her argument? Point to specific passages in the text.

5. *Other Methods.* When Orenstein cites statistics about the decrease in empathy among college students, she is making a CLAIM about CAUSE AND EFFECT (7). How and how well does her EVIDENCE support that claim?

THINKING ABOUT LANGUAGE

1. Orenstein's title is an ALLUSION to "I think, therefore I am," a basic principle of Western philosophy first formulated in French (and later translated into Latin) by René Descartes. How seriously is she drawing the COMPARISON here? Explain.

2. Who are the "Twitterati," and where did Orenstein get this name for them (2)?

3. Why do users of *Twitter* send each other *tweets* instead of *twits*?

4. What is the difference, as Orenstein DEFINES the two terms, between "the authentic and contrived self" (5)?

5. What is a "hashtag," and where does it get its name, #etymologicallyspeaking (8)?

FOR WRITING

1. Write a paragraph summarizing Orenstein's basic claim about the effect of *Twitter* and other social media upon how we define ourselves in the digital age.

2. Based on recent postings (yours or someone else's) on *Twitter, Facebook,* or another social media site, compose an argument of your own in response to Orenstein's. (You can agree with her on some issues, disagree on others, or accept or reject her argument in its entirety.) Be sure to give specific examples of postings.

Debating the Effects of Digital Culture

The following questions refer to the arguments on pages 635–47.

Reading Arguments

1. The Internet is not "the enemy of history and literature and worldly knowledge," says Amy Goldwasser (16). To what extent do Steven Pinker and Peggy Orenstein appear to agree with this position? Explain.

2. Among the three writers cited in this debate, which one is most hesitant to trumpet the virtues of digital culture? Why?

3. On the specific issue of whether the Internet is making us better or worse readers and writers, where do Goldwasser, Pinker, and Orenstein stand, respectively? Point to specific passages that reveal their views most sharply and clearly.

4. Whether or not you agree with the conclusions of their arguments, which of the participants in this debate do you think supports his or her claim most effectively? How? Explain by pointing to particular evidence and strategies of argument that you find especially convincing.

For Writing

1. Write the word *Internet* at the top of a sheet of paper and draw a line down the middle. Label the columns *Pro* and *Con*. Fill in as many reasons and observations on either side as you can think of. Now, outline more or less the same ideas on your computer (or other) screen. Write a paragraph describing the differences between the two experiences.

2. Choose a particular application of digital technology—*Twitter, Second Life, YouTube, Facebook, MySpace,* or other—and write an argument explaining how it works, what its purpose is, and what the benefits (or disadvantages) of using it might be.

CHAPTER 13

Combining the Methods

The web of our life is of a mingled yarn . . . .
—WILLIAM SHAKESPEARE, *All's Well That Ends Well*

When you have a single, clear purpose in mind, you may be able to write a well-organized essay by using a single method of development. The yarns of life, however, are often mingled, as Shakespeare noted, and when you're writing on a complex topic, you might actually end up combining a number of different methods in the same essay. Professional writers do this all the time—as we'll see in the first five pages of best-selling author Michael Lewis' 1989 book *Liar's Poker* (pages 653–56).

Trained in business and finance (as well as in literature), Lewis began his career as a bond salesman on Wall Street—the financial district of New York City—where he spent much of his time on the telephone. After a few years, Lewis decided he wanted to try his hand at a different kind of verbal communication and became a professional writer. In *Liar's Poker*, Lewis compares the economic climate of Wall Street to a high-stakes game.

Lewis isn't simply telling an amusing story about Wall Street and its pastimes. Like an anthropologist studying a strange tribe, he is giving an expert's view of an entire culture. To this more complicated end, Lewis draws on *all* the methods of development discussed in this book. He begins to develop his topic with a NARRATIVE of the day the head of the firm challenged one of the traders to play an office gambling game for a million dollars:

It was sometime early in 1986, the first year of the decline of my firm, Salomon Brothers. Our chairman, John Gutfreund, left his desk at the head of the trading floor and went for a walk. . . . This day in 1986, however, Gutfreund did something strange. Instead of terrifying us all, he walked a straight line to the trading desk of John Meriwether, a member of the board of Salomon Inc. and also one of Salomon's finest bond traders. He whispered a few words. The traders in the vicinity eavesdropped. What Gutfreund said has become a legend at Salomon Brothers and a visceral part of its corporate identity. He said: "One hand, one million dollars, no tears."

Throughout his narrative, Lewis also weaves in a detailed DESCRIPTION of the field of play ("like an epileptic ward"), the spectators ("nerve-racked"), and the key players. First there is the challenger, John Gutfreund:

Gutfreund took the pulse of the place by simply wandering around it and asking questions of the traders. An eerie sixth sense guided him to wherever a crisis was unfolding. Gutfreund seemed able to smell money being lost.

Then there is the champ himself, as Lewis describes him:

John Meriwether had, in the course of his career, made hundreds of millions of dollars for Salomon Brothers. He had an ability, rare among people and treasured by traders, to hide his state of mind. . . . He wore the same blank half-tense expression when he won as he did when he lost. . . . People would say, "He's the best businessman in the place," or "the best risk taker I have ever seen," or "a very dangerous Liar's Poker player."

And what is Liar's Poker? To explain this, Lewis must include a PROCESS ANALYSIS:

In Liar's Poker a group of people—as few as two, as many as ten—form a circle. Each player holds a dollar bill close to his chest. The game is similar in spirit to the card game known as I Doubt It. Each player attempts to fool the others about the serial numbers printed on the face of his dollar bill. . . . The bidding escalates until all the other players agree to challenge a single player's bid. Then, and only then, do the players reveal their serial numbers and determine who is bluffing whom.

Why are Gutfreund, Meriwether, and the other grown men in the office of Salomon Brothers playing what looks, on the surface, like a child's game? Because a good Liar's Poker player was also likely to be a good bond trader. Lewis, it would seem, is using the game as an EXAMPLE of how the trader's mind works:

The questions a Liar's Poker player asks himself are, up to a point, the same questions a bond trader asks himself. Is this a smart risk? Do I feel lucky? How cunning is my opponent? Does he have any idea what he's doing, and if not, how do I exploit his ignorance?

Now we know how Liar's Poker is played and, in general, why the traders played it. We don't, however, know why, on this particular day, Gutfreund challenged Meriwether to play for the unheard-of sum of a million dollars.

To provide this information, Lewis must do a CAUSE-AND-EFFECT analysis, in which he adds a COMPARISON AND CONTRAST of the two men; that comparison, in turn, is based on a CLASSIFICATION of the men according to their functions as managers or traders within the firm:

> Gutfreund was the King of Wall Street, but Meriwether was King of the Game. . . . Gutfreund had once been a trader, but that was as relevant as an old woman's claim that she was once quite a dish. . . . Compared with managing, trading was admirably direct. You made your bets and either you won or you lost. When you won, people—all the way up to the top of the firm—admired you, envied you, and feared you, and with reason: You controlled the loot. When you managed a firm, well, sure you received your quota of envy, fear, and admiration. But for all the wrong reasons. *You did not make the money for Salomon. You did not take the risk.*

Why (the causes) Gutfreund challenged Meriwether (the effect) on this particular day is now clear: "The single rash act of challenging the arbitrage boss to one hand for a million dollars was Gutfreund's way of showing he was a player, too." But it is not yet clear why Meriwether felt obliged to accept the challenge. To explain *this*, Lewis adds a DEFINITION of the player's "code" of conduct:

> The code of the Liar's Poker player was something like the code of the gunslinger. It required a trader to accept all challenges. Because of the code—which was *his* code—John Meriwether felt obliged to play. But he knew it was stupid.

Okay. So now we know how the game is played and why the chief manager of Salomon Brothers challenged the chief bond trader to play a hand of Liar's Poker for a million dollars. We also know why the arbitrage boss felt obliged to accept the challenge. (To see how Meriwether actually met the challenge, you'll have to read the rest of the story.)

But what's the point? The story of the great Liar's Poker challenge may be interesting if you just want to know what happened one day in a big Wall Street firm when people were playing when they should have been working. But what's the significance of these people and their actions? Why should you as a reader want to know about them?

Lewis has already told us the significance of the game for the players. In order to tie all the threads together, however, he must also explain what it might mean to us, his readers and audience. Here's his explanation:

> The game has some of the feel of trading, just as jousting has some of the feel of war. . . . Each player seeks weakness, predictability, and pattern in the others and seeks to avoid it in himself. The bond traders of Goldman, Sachs, First Boston, Morgan Stanley, Merrill Lynch, and other Wall Street firms all play some version of Liar's Poker.

Now we understand the point of Lewis' essay and, indeeed, of the entire book it introduces. He is ARGUING that the nation's financial markets amount to one big game of Liar's Poker. The purpose of all the other methods of narration, description, and exposition that he uses is to support this claim.

You won't always use every method of developing a topic in every essay you write, however. Depending on your main purpose in writing, one or two will usually dominate, as in most of the model essays in this book.

MICHAEL LEWIS

Liar's Poker

IT WAS SOMETIME EARLY IN 1986, the first year of the decline of my firm, Salomon Brothers. Our chairman, John Gutfreund, left his desk at the head of the trading floor and went for a walk. At any given moment on the trading floor billions of dollars were being risked by bond traders.[1] Gutfreund took the pulse of the place by simply wandering around it and asking questions of the traders. An eerie sixth sense guided him to wherever a crisis was unfolding. Gutfreund seemed able to smell money being lost.

He was the last person a nerve-racked trader wanted to see. Gutfreund (pronounced *Good friend*) liked to sneak up from behind and surprise you. This was fun for him but not for you. Busy on two phones at once trying to stem disaster, you had no time to turn and look. You didn't need to. You felt him. The area around you began to convulse like an epileptic ward. People were pretending to be frantically busy and at the same time staring intently at a spot directly above your head. You felt a chill in your bones that I imagine belongs to the same class of intelligence as the nervous twitch of a small furry animal at the silent approach of a grizzly bear. An alarm shrieked in your head: Gutfreund! Gutfreund! Gutfreund!

Often as not, our chairman just hovered quietly for a bit, then left. You might never have seen him. The only trace I found of him on two of these occasions was a turdlike ash on the floor beside my chair, left, I suppose, as a calling card. Gutfreund's cigar droppings were longer and better formed than those of the average Salomon boss. I always assumed that he smoked a more expensive blend than the rest, purchased with a few of the $40 million he had cleared on the sale of Salomon Brothers in 1981 (or a few of the $3.1 million he paid himself in 1986, more than any other Wall Street CEO).

This day in 1986, however, Gutfreund did something strange. Instead of terrifying us all, he walked a straight line to the trading desk of John Meriwether, a member of the board of Salomon Inc. and also one of Salomon's finest bond traders. He whispered a few words. The traders in the vicinity eavesdropped. What Gutfreund said has become a legend at Salomon Brothers and a visceral part of its corporate identity. He said: "One hand, one million dollars, no tears."

1. *Bond traders*: Salespeople who specialize in promissory notes (IOUs) that pay interest.

SUGGESTED MLA CITATION: Lewis, Michael. "Liar's Poker." 1989. *Back to the Lake.* Ed. Thomas Cooley. 2nd ed. New York: Norton, 2012. 653–57. Print.

One hand, one million dollars, no tears. Meriwether grabbed the meaning instantly. The King of Wall Street, as *Business Week* had dubbed Gutfreund, wanted to play a single hand of a game called Liar's Poker for a million dollars. He played the game most afternoons with Meriwether and the six young bond arbitrage[2] traders who worked for Meriwether and was usually skinned alive. Some traders said Gutfreund was heavily outmatched. Others who couldn't imagine John Gutfreund as anything but omnipotent—and there were many—said that losing suited his purpose, though exactly what that might be was a mystery.

The peculiar feature of Gutfreund's challenge this time was the size of the stake. Normally his bets didn't exceed a few hundred dollars. A million was unheard of. The final two words of his challenge, "no tears," meant that the loser was expected to suffer a great deal of pain but wasn't entitled to whine, bitch, or moan about it. He'd just have to hunker down and keep his poverty to himself. But why? You might ask if you were anyone other than the King of Wall Street. Why do it in the first place? Why, in particular, challenge Meriwether instead of some lesser managing director? It seemed an act of sheer lunacy. Meriwether was the King of the Game, the Liar's Poker champion of the Salomon Brothers trading floor.

On the other hand, one thing you learn on a trading floor is that winners like Gutfreund *always* have some reason for what they do; it might not be the best of reasons, but at least they have a concept in mind. I was not privy to Gutfreund's innermost thoughts, but I do know that all the boys on the trading floor gambled and that he wanted badly to be one of the boys. What I think Gutfreund had in mind in this instance was a desire to show his courage, like the boy who leaps from the high dive. Who better than Meriwether for the purpose? Besides, Meriwether was probably the only trader with both the cash and the nerve to play.

The whole absurd situation needs putting into context. John Meriwether had, in the course of his career, made hundreds of millions of dollars for Salomon Brothers. He had an ability, rare among people and treasured by traders, to hide his state of mind. Most traders divulge whether they are making or losing money by the way they speak or move. They are either overly easy or overly tense. With Meriwether you could never, ever tell. He wore the same blank half-tense expression when he won as he did when he lost. He had, I think, a profound ability to control the two emotions that commonly destroy traders—fear and greed—and it made him as noble as a man who pursues his self-interest so fiercely can be. He was thought by many within Salomon to be the best bond trader on Wall Street. Around Salomon

---

2. *Arbitrage*: Buying stocks, bonds, and other securities for immediate resale to profit from price differences in different markets.

no tone but awe was used when he was discussed. People would say, "He's the best businessman in the place," or "the best risk taker I have ever seen," or "a very dangerous Liar's Poker player."

Meriwether cast a spell over the young traders who worked for him. His boys ranged in age from twenty-five to thirty-two (he was about forty). Most of them had Ph.D.'s in math, economics, and/or physics. Once they got onto Meriwether's trading desk, however, they forgot they were supposed to be detached intellectuals. They became disciples. They became obsessed by the game of Liar's Poker. They regarded it as *their* game. And they took it to a new level of seriousness.

John Gutfreund was always the outsider in their game. That *Business Week* put his picture on the cover and called him the King of Wall Street held little significance for them. I mean, that was, in a way, the whole point. Gutfreund was the King of Wall Street, but Meriwether was King of the Game. When Gutfreund had been crowned by the gentlemen of the press, you could almost hear traders thinking: *Foolish names and foolish faces often appear in public places.* Fair enough, Gutfreund had once been a trader, but that was as relevant as an old woman's claim that she was once quite a dish.

At times Gutfreund himself seemed to agree. He loved to trade. Compared with managing, trading was admirably direct. You made your bets and either you won or you lost. When you won, people—all the way up to the top of the firm—admired you, envied you, and feared you, and with reason: You controlled the loot. When you managed a firm, well, sure you received your quota of envy, fear, and admiration. But for all the wrong reasons. *You did not make the money for Salomon. You did not take risk.* You were hostage to your producers. They took risk. They proved their superiority every day by handling risk better than the rest of the risk-taking world. The money came from risk takers such as Meriwether, and whether it came or not was really beyond Gutfreund's control. That's why many people thought that the single rash act of challenging the arbitrage boss to one hand for a million dollars was Gutfreund's way of showing he was a player, too. And if you wanted to show off, Liar's Poker was the only way to go. The game had a powerful meaning for traders. People like John Meriwether believed that Liar's Poker had a lot in common with bond trading. It tested a trader's character. It honed a trader's instincts. A good player made a good trader, and vice versa. We all understood it.

The Game: In Liar's Poker a group of people—as few as two, as many as ten—form a circle. Each player holds a dollar bill close to his chest. The game is similar in spirit to the card game known as I Doubt It. Each player attempts to fool the others about the serial numbers printed on the face of his dollar bill. One trader begins by making "a bid." He says, for example, "Three sixes." He means that all told the serial numbers of the dollar bills held by every player, including himself, contain at least three sixes.

Once the first bid has been made, the game moves clockwise in the circle. Let's say the bid is three sixes. The player to the left of the bidder can do one of two things. He can bid higher (there are two sorts of higher bids: the same quantity of a higher number [three sevens, eights, or nines] and more of any number [four fives, for instance]). Or he can "challenge"—that is like saying, "I doubt it."

The bidding escalates until all the other players agree to challenge a single player's bid. Then, and only then, do the players reveal their serial numbers and determine who is bluffing whom. In the midst of all this, the mind of a good player spins with probabilities. What is the statistical likelihood of there being three sixes within a batch of, say, forty randomly generated serial numbers? For a great player, however, the math is the easy part of the game. The hard part is reading the faces of the other players. The complexity arises when all players know how to bluff and double-bluff.

The game has some of the feel of trading, just as jousting has some of the feel of war. The questions a Liar's Poker player asks himself are, up to a point, the same questions a bond trader asks himself. Is this a smart risk? Do I feel lucky? How cunning is my opponent? Does he have any idea what he's doing, and if not, how do I exploit his ignorance? If he bids high, is he bluffing, or does he actually hold a strong hand? Is he trying to induce me to make a foolish bid, or does he actually have four of a kind himself? Each player seeks weakness, predictability, and pattern in the others and seeks to avoid it in himself. The bond traders of Goldman, Sachs, First Boston, Morgan Stanley, Merrill Lynch, and other Wall Street firms all play some version of Liar's Poker. But the place where the stakes run highest, thanks to John Meriwether, is the New York bond trading floor of Salomon Brothers.

The code of the Liar's Poker player was something like the code of the gunslinger.[3] It required a trader to accept all challenges. Because of the code—which was *his* code—John Meriwether felt obliged to play. But he knew it was stupid. For him, there was no upside. If he won, he upset Gutfreund. No good came of this. But if he lost, he was out of pocket a million bucks. This was worse than upsetting the boss. Although Meriwether was by far the better player of the game, in a

---

3. *Code of the gunslinger:* Code of conduct rooted in the legendary Wild West of the eighteenth- and nineteenth-century United States. The phrase refers to a stoic, warriorlike way of life that required a gunfighter to accept all challenges.

single hand anything could happen. Luck could very well determine the outcome. Meriwether spent his entire day avoiding dumb bets, and he wasn't about to accept this one.

"No, John," he said, "if we're going to play for those kind of numbers, I'd rather play for real money. Ten million dollars. No tears."

Ten million dollars. It was a moment for all players to savor. Meriwether was playing Liar's Poker before the game even started. He was bluffing. Gutfreund considered the counterproposal. It would have been just like him to accept. Merely to entertain the thought was a luxury that must have pleased him well. (It *was* good to be rich.)

On the other hand, ten million dollars was, and is, a lot of money. If Gutfreund lost, he'd have only thirty million or so left. His wife, Susan, was busy spending the better part of fifteen million dollars redecorating their Manhattan apartment (Meriwether knew this). And as Gutfreund *was* the boss, he clearly wasn't bound by the Meriwether code. Who knows? Maybe he didn't even know the Meriwether code. Maybe the whole point of his challenge was to judge Meriwether's response. (Even Gutfreund had to marvel at the king in action.) So Gutfreund declined. In fact, he smiled his own brand of forced smile and said, "You're crazy."

No, thought Meriwether, just very, very good.

A Book Cover

The basic methods that good writers draw upon every day are sometimes used in combination with each other. This cover for a book about human cadavers, for example, employs a number of them all at once. The title, *Stiff*, is a DESCRIPTION of the physical condition of the human body after death; *stiff* is also a slang term for a dead person. Going beyond physical description, Roach's title is a name or label identifying an important aspect of her subject—the sometimes conflicting legal, moral, and medical DEFINITIONS of death itself. Good writers often kill even more than two birds with one stone, however. As you describe and define a subject, you may also tell a story about it, as this book cover does by adding a NARRATIVE element. We see just enough of the person pictured on the cover of Roach's book to know that he or she ended up in the morgue with a tag attached to the big toe. End of story—usually. For the human cadavers in Roach's book, however, death is only the beginning. Simultaneously grim and humorous, the image on the cover captures the first stages of this narrative. The later stages are implied in Roach's subtitle, *The Curious Lives of Human Cadavers*, which tells us that *Stiff* is a book about what happens to our bodies after we die.

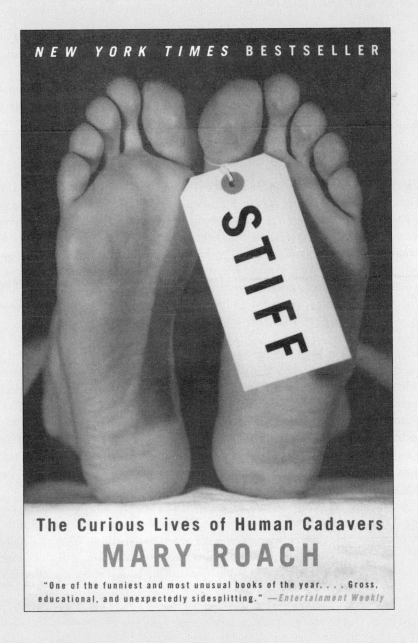

NEW YORK TIMES BESTSELLER

STIFF

The Curious Lives of Human Cadavers
MARY ROACH

"One of the funniest and most unusual books of the year. . . . Gross,
educational, and unexpectedly sidesplitting." —*Entertainment Weekly*

MELISSA HICKS

The High Price of Butter

Melissa Hicks (b. 1979) spent her teenage years in rural Maine and worked in the restaurant business before returning to school to pursue a degree in literature. She lives in Eugene, Oregon, with her cat and seven-year-old son.

Hicks wrote "The High Price of Butter" for an introductory writing course at Lane Community College in Eugene. A narrative essay that uses numerous other methods of development—particularly description and argument—Hicks' piece was runner-up for the 2010 Norton Writer's Prize.

*I*N MY HOUSE we have butter and margarine. The butter is for cooking. The margarine is   1
for macaroni and cheese. I swear that it's the butter that makes everything taste so good.
My favorite foods that remind me of my mother and my own childhood. In the grocery
store aisle, I stand under the harsh white lights of the dairy case, margarine in one hand
and butter in the other. I weigh them in my hand and compare the price; I weigh them in

> Combining
> NARRATIVE
> and ARGUMENT
> is discussed
> on p. 562.

my mind, thinking of the high cost of butter. No matter how long I stand and
weigh, I always put the butter in my cart. I remember the times when I was a
girl—the taste of sweet, fresh butter melting on my tongue. I remember the work
it took, and I know the price is more than fair.

For my fourteenth birthday, I got a cow. I did not ask for a cow. I had very   2
clearly asked for a horse. While every girl-child wants a horse, I felt that I had
earned mine. I had worked at a farm down the road for the last two summers.
I rode my bike to the stables. I would shovel the manure, feed the horses, ride for
hours, and then pedal home exhausted. I knew how to take care of a horse. The life
my family had worked and sweated for, clearing our own little spot in the Maine
woods, was as well suited to horse-raising as any of our other pursuits. Even more,
my father had dropped hints here and there. While he would not definitively say
it was a horse, he did say I could ride it. The fact was, I didn't know beans
about cows.

We had a small farm in rural Maine. We cleared the land to put our trailer   3
there. We hauled the brush and burned it. We pulled stumps, sometimes with the
help of a tractor or a friendly neighbor with access to dynamite. We had a well and
a septic tank dug. Onto the trailer we built a two-room addition with clean lumber
and tongue-and-groove walls. My father's handmade bookshelves separated it into

SUGGESTED MLA CITATION: Hicks, Melissa. "The High Price of Butter." 2010. *Back to the Lake.* Ed. Thomas Cooley. 2nd ed. New York: Norton, 2012. 660–66. Print.

halves, one half being my parents' bedroom. A door led into the trailer, where my sisters and I slept.

We had to apply to the town office to put up new cedar poles for the power lines 4
to our lot. On our two acres we raised chickens, rabbits, and sometimes a pig. We had room for so many animals that turned into dinner, but in all the years I'd begged, we had never had room for a horse.

Down the hill from our house sat our barn. Like everything else we'd worked so 5
hard on during the summer leading up to my fourteenth birthday, it was a sure sign of horses to come. The barn had one stall. It was built so that the back door opened into the rabbits' shed, and as soon as you entered, you could see their red eyes through the black doorway in the rear. It smelled like clean hay and fresh ammonia, and when the days were cold (as they were in September), the smells seemed to bite my cheeks with the cold.

The barn was built around a huge cedar tree with white-ringed wounds where 6
my father's chainsaw had slid through thick branches. Nailed to its furry brown bark were sections of two-by-four, rising parallel to the loft. Its roots gripped the floor tightly, still growing. One side of the square hole that framed the loft entrance was nailed to the tree with thick spikes. We avoided picturing the consequences of its either growing or dying, but it was sure to do both eventually.

The main door into the barn was aligned diagonally with the door to the rabbits' 7
shed on the opposite wall. To the right was the stall, and to the left a large open window of the kind that horses stick their heads through. On the floor below it was a massive water tank, more than bathtub size; above it was a recently installed spigot. In a corner were a stack of green poles and pegs, and loops of wire to install an electric fence. These were all signs of impending horses.

The cow actually arrived about a week before my birthday. She was a small, 8
brown cow—a Guernsey. She was a heifer that would soon birth a calf, and we would get to milk her. My father had gotten her from a farmers' co-operative program. After the calf was weaned, we would donate it back to them. We would have butter and cheese and fresh milk from my cow.

School had just started. Despite the farm, my parents both had day jobs, like 9
everyone else I knew. This was making ends meet. It was another reason to get up early in the morning, and another chore to be done when I got home. The most bitter part though, was that the heifer was still not a horse.

This is not the butter I knew as a girl. I hear the crinkle as I pull it from its plastic shop- 10
ping bag and place it, still in its perfect slick cardboard packaging, on the counter to soften.
I bang through the kitchen, leaving a trail of open cabinets in my wake as I thrust goodies
onto shelves. I pull out my cutting board before I twirl around to twist the knobs on my stove.
I set my oven to 425° and bend low to grab my casserole dish from under the sink. I plunk
it on the cutting board before whirling again to dig through the cupboards for filling.

I think to myself, it's a shame to use canned filling with the real butter, but even my 11
mother couldn't do scratch every time. The oven is not yet heated, and I am thinking of
my cobbler. I pull out a mixing bowl and measuring cup. I think of my mother and how
she prepared everything in advance so she could just add and mix when the right time
came. I break the seal on the butter's box, setting two sticks inside the blue Pyrex dish.
The remaining two are sent to the fridge.

I named her Francis Mary. It suited her. She had large brown eyes that always 12
seemed sadly pensive, with soft cream-colored hair rimming them. The fur around
her eyes ended abruptly in the deep reddish-brown of her fur. For spite and for
pretend, I decided I would ride her. I sat on her after milking-time one day. My
sneakers bumped the rough wood planks on either side of the stall when she
shifted. Our breaths blew mightily, visibly—twin streams in autumn air. The milk
steamed quietly in its bucket. On a shelf sat my tape player. I sang "Faith" with
George Michael and whispered encouragement to Francis Mary while I tugged on
the rope I'd tied to her halter. When the tape ended, I picked up the milk and
headed up to our house.

Melissa Hicks (left) and her sister Angela in an old photograph taken at their home in
Maine, where Melissa learned to make butter from her parents and received a cow as a
present on her fourteenth birthday.

The back steps crossed over a muddy trench. Our main trailer sat up on a little 13
ledge. The steps were wooden and rickety, with sticky, abrasive tar paper stapled to
the wooden planks; the handrails were sturdy two-by-fours and there were no
fronts or sides. Between the holes, you saw the muddy gully, unless you saw cold
white snow and muddy footprints.

Dirty barn clothes meant using these steps. We left our dirty boots outside the 14
door. Here were windows of plastic sheeting, empty seed pots and trays, old watering dishes, and big plastic outdoor toys, outgrown and overused, left dirty in various corners. It was a greenhouse in the spring, and a den for hairy spiders all year
long.

After dinner, usually twilight—sometimes in the dark—I'd lift heavy buckets of 15
milk up the stairs into the warmth of the kitchen. A wooden sign says "Willkom-
men" above the stove. I step outside to take off my rubber-toed boots; jacket and
gloves were hung in the barn. My cheeks pink, I step back inside in wool socks and
hang my hat on the peg.

My father is standing by the sink. He takes the aluminum buckets and pours 16
them through a large metal sieve into precooled pitchers, waiting in the sink. In
the clear plastic we can see the cream at it cools and separates from the milk. My
father covers the pitchers and puts them in the fridge. My mother watches the
news as I start my homework. My sisters disappear, whispering about Barbies and
coloring books. I draw pictures of princesses and half-heartedly pretend to do my
algebra. If we weren't making butter, I could disappear into my room. I could wrap
myself in jackets and blankets, and put on thick gloves. I could pull curls from the
kitchen phone-chord and run it under the back door, huddling and whispering to
girlfriends, or worse even, boys.

Thanks to my mother, I don't need a recipe for anything. But for cobbler, one must 17
measure. I pull the waxy paper off the butter, letting the sticks fall whole into my pan.
Sturdy long rectangles of solidified cream bounce sullenly as they hit. They leave a mark
as they tumble, a visible trail of clean grease and flavor. These go into the oven. I melt
them whole and let them bubble and simmer until the butter turns brown.

"No matter how long you cook it, margarine will never brown," my mother said while 18
preparing some supper or other. "That's how you know the difference." It seemed awfully
silly to me at the time. I couldn't imagine why I would want butter brown, or even how
brown was any different from burnt. I remember the words, and wonder if anyone else
gets such a thrill from waiting for their butter to bubble.

Hours later, the milk is cold. It is quiet as we gather around the kitchen table, a 19
last task before bedtime—not every day, but often. Washcloths lie on warm wood,
wet and ready for the occasional drop. My parents have put the pitchers of milk
back on the table and are skimming with clean, cold, metal ladles. They are large
and gleaming. They look medicinal against the whiteness of the milk. They are

cold next to the pictures of fruit in happy bowls, the small glories hanging from refrigerator magnets, and the homey dark wood of the table.

The cream sings and tinkles as it rushes into waiting Ball jars. It is thick and deep-sounding for a liquid. A white line runs around the top of each pitcher, a line of fat where the cream has bubbled up from the depths of the comparatively thin milk. Each jar is filled about halfway before being topped with a rubber ring, copper top, and screw ring by my mother.

She hands me a jar. I feel the coldness as the milk sloshes inside the glass, cooling the tips of my fingers and palms. I raise it about level with my head and begin shaking. My arms and shoulders warm as I shake the jar. Time seems to slow down, and it's no time before my arms start to burn. By this time, a second jar is ready, handed to the next eldest, Emily. Her hair is brown like mine, but thicker. Sometimes there is a third jar—often not.

As my arms tire, I alter the motion. Instead of shaking the jar up and down, I go side to side. My youngest sister has the darkest hair, in long braids. She asks for the jar. My mother, setting the milk back in the fridge, tells her to wait her turn.

I shake, and I shake. My face feels red and there is always a greasy strand of hair in my eyes. Everything is stupid and embarrassing, especially cows and shit-kicker boots. I don't want to make my own butter or weed gardens. I don't want meat from little white packages, made of the animals I fed all last year. I want some food with a price tag. I feel self-conscious; my fat shakes with the jar. I worry about my bra. I know that soon I will sweat, and I feel like that would make me shrivel and die. My father is heading down to the barn one more time, to check on the water and the rabbits. He tells us to switch jars.

I give mine to my mother, and Emily passes hers to Angela, the youngest. I link my fingers, stretch out my arms and push. We giggle and talk as the constant sloshing grows thicker, audible lumps under the warm yellow lightbulbs in the kitchen. In the mirror, we are reflected, dark heads bent as we shake and talk. When the second team tires, we alternate rolling and shaking the jars. Emily rolls her jar back and forth across the table to my mother. A yellow lump rolls in whitish liquid, slowly growing larger; waxen and heavy, it thuds and rolls inside the Ball jar, one beat behind.

I shake, slower now. A dull golden lump is heavy in my jar too. Up and down three times: Shake, shake, shake. Side to side again. I pass it to my sister. Soon we will roll our jar, too. My mother rolls the jar to Emily who picks it up and shakes. Now the table is empty; Angela and I begin to roll our jar automatically to each other over the smooth wood. We see brown whirls of wood flash by under the speeding, tumbling butter.

My mother is putting store-bought rolls into the preheated oven. She takes the jar from Emily, after washing her hands, and scrapes the butter with a spatula into cold, heavy, cast-iron molds from the fridge. They are cold even on the counter in the daytime. The molds are shaped like ripened ears of corn with their husks spread out behind them. We will sell this butter.

She puts the molds back into the refrigerator and takes the last jar from me. She 27 scrapes that into a large ball with her hands on a cutting board, and cuts it square with a knife. She collects the scraps into a longer oval with her hands again, and cuts away a stick. She cuts the larger block in pieces twice as my sisters and I wipe the table. Finally, my mother wraps the butter in white wax paper.

Now the kitchen is quiet, without the rolling and thudding. I silently fantasize 28 about flaky biscuits melting on my tongue. My sisters and I are yawning, but our stomachs growl at the smell. On the cutting board are the scraps from the last block of butter. They are not grocery-store squares, but long strips, thick and round on one side. The image of a delightfully buttery slug comes to mind, slithering onto a hot roll before leaving a slick buttery trail down my throat. The best part of the butter is that there was plenty.

The butter melts, forming first a slowly oozing lump, then a golden liquid coating, 29 *bubbling delicately inside the stove. I know this because my nose tells me. I could look inside the oven, but there is no need. I open the lids on my counter bins: Two cups flour (into the measuring cup out to the bowl), two cups sugar; I get two cups of milk, which I pour before closing the door. Last I grab a spoon, and dip it twice into the baking powder. Now I whisk, smoothing the lumpy ooze into a thick, creamy batter.*

I run my can opener across two cans of filling and smile. 30

"It's two of everything, so you can't ever forget!" I can see my mother smiling through 31 *the phone as she guides me.*

By this time the butter is bubbling quicker, brown crispy bunches collecting on the top 32 *of the hot yellow liquid. I pull it out of the oven and put it on the stovetop. I turn back to the counter to take off my oven mitts and pour half of the batter from the bowl, straight into the boiling butter. It sizzles, and the batter rises immediately. The butter rushes up around the edges of the pan, and rises over the batter, to settle in yellow pools in its center.*

I spoon out the filling, amber apples smelling of cinnamon, sitting on a fluffy bed of 33 *clouds and sweet molten butter. The other half of the batter goes on top, and quickly I put the pan back into the oven. I smile, leaning on the counter, and wait. Soon I will have my cobbler. My tongue prepares for the first bite of sweet dough and apple, and the little rush of butter in every bite, that will drip, softly onto its buds. Like every time before and every time to come, I will pull it from the oven and proudly say to my son,*

"Look Cy, I made it from scratch. And I used real butter, too." 34

To me the cost of butter is more than a price tag. The cost of butter reminds me 35 of my childhood, and how my family struggled to be pioneers in the twentieth century. The cost of butter reminds me of the value of hard work, and how that work brought my family together. I always think of Francis Mary, who never was a horse, but allowed me to ride her anyway. I think of cold fingers, frozen noses, and sloshing warm milk on my pants. Yet the cost of butter is more than a symbol of hard work and quality. The fact that I buy it is an affirmation of my own choices in life. Because of my childhood, I know the cost in sweat of butter. As an adult, I chose to pay that price in cash.

READING WITH AN EYE FOR THE METHODS

1. "The High Price of Butter" is constructed around two NARRATIVES—one about Melissa Hicks as a teenager in rural Maine, the other about her as an adult making a cobbler. How and how well does Hicks weave them together? Point out places where the two come together that you find particularly effective—and explain why.

2. Along with the narrative elements of her essay, Hicks frequently blends in DESCRIPTIVE passages, like that of the barn "built so that the back door opened into the rabbits' shed, and as soon as you entered, you could see their red eyes through the black doorway in the rear" (5). Cite several other descriptions and explain what they contribute to Hicks' essay.

3. Hicks uses PROCESS ANALYSIS to explain how she makes a cobbler like her mother's. Where else does she use this method? For what purpose(s)?

4. Real butter may be expensive, Hicks argues, but "the price is more than fair" (1). This is the main point in an ARGUMENT that threads through the narrative, descriptive, and other elements of Hicks' essay. How, and how well, does she use the various methods of development to prove this point? Explain.

USING THE METHODS

1. Write out one of your favorite recipes and—as you analyze the process—tell the story of where the recipe came from and how you learned it.

2. Using various methods of development, write an essay about an expensive product or service that you think is (or is not) worth the price. Explain why you think so; tell how you came to use (or reject) the product or service; and describe what it is good for (or not).

ERIC SCHLOSSER

What We Eat

Eric Schlosser (b. 1959) earned a bachelor's degree in American history from Princeton University and later studied the history of the British monarchy at Oxford University. He is an investigative reporter for the Atlantic Monthly *and other magazines. On assignment for* Rolling Stone, *he began to look into a different kind of history—that of consumer culture, particularly fast food, as represented in the American marketplace by McDonald's and other franchises. The result was* Fast Food Nation: The Dark Side of the All-American Meal *(2001). Schlosser is also the author of* Reefer Madness: Sex, Drugs, and Cheap Labor in the American Black Market *(2003).*

"What We Eat," a selection from Fast Food Nation, *argues not only that the fast food industry has changed the way Americans eat, but that its methods and values have become the country's chief export. Schlosser supports this argument with a host of examples, stories, and statistics. "In trying to tie together all these different threads,"he told an interviewer for* Powell's, *"there was a huge risk that it would be a total mess." Actually, this selection, like the rest of Schlosser's book, is tightly organized. The secret of combining many topics and methods at once, he says, is "balance"—something he finds lacking in the American meal and in consumer culture as a whole.*

OVER THE LAST THREE DECADES, fast food has infiltrated every nook and cranny 1
of American society. An industry that began with a handful of modest hot dog and hamburger stands in southern California has spread to every corner of the nation, selling a broad range of foods wherever paying customers may be found. Fast food is now served at restaurants and drive-throughs, at stadiums, airports, zoos, high schools, elementary schools, and universities, on cruise ships, trains, and airplanes, at K-Marts, Wal-Marts, gas stations, and even at hospital cafeterias. In 1970, Americans spent about $6 billion on fast food; in 2001, they spent more than $110 billion. Americans now spend more money on fast food than on higher education, personal computers, computer software, or new cars. They spend more on fast food than on movies, books, magazines, newspapers, videos, and recorded music—combined.

e p. 560 tips on roducing CRIPTION your text.

Pull open the glass door, feel the rush of cool air, walk in, get on line, study 2
the backlit color photographs above the counter, place your order, hand over a few dollars, watch teenagers in uniforms pushing various buttons, and moments

SUGGESTED MLA CITATION: Schlosser, Eric. "What We Eat." 2001. *Back to the Lake*. Ed. Thomas Cooley. 2nd ed. New York: Norton, 2012. 667–74. Print.

later take hold of a plastic tray full of food wrapped in colored paper and cardboard. The whole experience of buying fast food has become so routine, so thoroughly unexceptional and mundane, that it is now taken for granted, like brushing your teeth or stopping for a red light. It has become a social custom as American as a small, rectangular, hand-held, frozen, and reheated apple pie.

. . . Fast food has proven to be a revolutionary force in American life; I am interested in it both as a commodity and as a metaphor. What people eat (or don't eat) has always been determined by a complex interplay of social, economic, and technological forces. The early Roman Republic was fed by its citizen-farmers; the Roman Empire, by its slaves. A nation's diet can be more revealing than its art or literature. On any given day in the United States about one-quarter of the adult population visits a fast food restaurant. During a relatively brief period of time, the fast food industry has helped to transform not only the American diet, but also our landscape, economy, workforce, and popular culture. Fast food and its consequences have become inescapable, regardless of whether you eat it twice a day, try to avoid it, or have never taken a single bite.

The extraordinary growth of the fast food industry has been driven by fundamental changes in American society. Adjusted for inflation, the hourly wage of the average U.S. worker peaked in 1973 and then steadily declined for the next twenty-five years. During that period, women entered the workforce in record numbers, often motivated less by a feminist perspective than by a need to pay the bills. In 1975, about one-third of American mothers with young children worked outside the home; today almost two-thirds of such mothers are employed. As the sociologists Cameron Lynne Macdonald and Carmen Sirianni have noted, the entry of so many women into the workforce has greatly increased demand for the types of services that housewives traditionally perform: cooking, cleaning, and child care. A generation ago, three-quarters of the money used to buy food in the United States was spent to prepare meals at home. Today about half of the money used to buy food is spent at restaurants—mainly at fast food restaurants.

The McDonald's Corporation has become a powerful symbol of America's service economy, which is now responsible for 90 percent of the country's new jobs. In 1968, McDonald's operated about one thousand restaurants. Today it has about thirty thousand restaurants worldwide and opens almost two thousand new ones each year. An estimated one out of every eight workers in the United States has at some point been employed by McDonald's. The company annually hires about one million people, more than any other American organization, public or private. McDonald's is the nation's largest purchaser of beef, pork, and potatoes—and the second largest purchaser of chicken. The McDonald's Corporation is the largest owner of retail property in the world. Indeed, the company earns the majority of its profits not from selling food but from collecting rent. McDonald's spends more

"The Golden Arches are now more widely recognized than the Christian cross."

money on advertising and marketing than any other brand. As a result it has replaced Coca-Cola as the world's most famous brand. McDonald's operates more playgrounds than any other private entity in the United States. It is responsible for the nation's bestselling line of children's clothing (McKids) and is one of the largest distributors of toys. A survey of American schoolchildren found that 96 percent could identify Ronald McDonald. The only fictional character with a higher degree of recognition was Santa Claus. The impact of McDonald's on the way we live today is hard to overstate. The Golden Arches are now more widely recognized than the Christian cross.

In the early 1970s, the farm activist Jim Hightower warned of "the McDonald- 6 ization of America." He viewed the emerging fast food industry as a threat to independent businesses, as a step toward a food economy dominated by giant corporations, and as a homogenizing influence on American life. In *Eat Your Heart Out* (1975), he argued that "bigger is *not* better." Much of what Hightower feared has come to pass. The centralized purchasing decisions of the large restaurant chains and their demand for standardized products have given a handful of corporations an unprecedented degree of power over the nation's food supply. Moreover, the tremendous success of the fast food industry has encouraged other industries to adopt similar business methods. The basic thinking behind fast food has become the operating system of today's retail economy, wiping out small businesses, obliterating regional differences, and spreading identical stores throughout the country like a self-replicating code.

America's main streets and malls now boast the same Pizza Huts and Taco Bells, 7 Gaps and Banana Republics, Starbucks and Jiffy-Lubes, Foot Lockers, Snip N' Clips, Sunglass Huts, and Hobbytown USAs. Almost every facet of American life has now been franchised or chained. From the maternity ward at a Columbia/HCA hospital to an embalming room owned by Service Corporation International—"the world's largest provider of death care services," based in Houston, Texas, which since 1968 has grown to include 3,823 funeral homes, 523 cemeteries, and 198 crematoriums, and which today handles the final remains of one out of every nine Americans—a person can now go from the cradle to the grave without spending a nickel at an independently owned business.

The key to a successful franchise, according to many texts on the subject, can be 8 expressed in one word: "uniformity." Franchises and chain stores strive to offer exactly the same product or service at numerous locations. Customers are drawn to familiar brands by an instinct to avoid the unknown. A brand offers a feeling of reassurance when its products are always and everywhere the same. "We have found out . . . that we cannot trust some people who are nonconformists," declared Ray Kroc, one of the founders of McDonald's, angered by some of his franchisees. "We will make conformists out of them in a hurry. . . . The organization cannot trust the individual; the individual must trust the organization."

One of the ironies of America's fast food industry is that a business so dedicated 9 to conformity was founded by iconoclasts and self-made men, by entrepreneurs willing to defy conventional opinion. Few of the people who built fast food empires ever attended college, let alone business school. They worked hard, took risks, and followed their own paths. In many respects, the fast food industry embodies the best and the worst of American capitalism at the start of the twenty-first century— its constant stream of new products and innovations, its widening gulf between rich and poor. The industrialization of the restaurant kitchen has enabled the fast food chains to rely upon a low-paid and unskilled workforce. While a handful of workers manage to rise up the corporate ladder, the vast majority lack full-time employment, receive no benefits, learn few skills, exercise little control over their workplace, quit after a few months, and float from job to job. The restaurant industry is now America's largest private employer, and it pays some of the lowest wages. During the economic boom of the 1990s, when many American workers enjoyed their first pay raises in a generation, the real value of wages in the restaurant industry continued to fall. The roughly 3.5 million fast food workers are by far the largest group of minimum wage earners in the United States. The only Americans who consistently earn a lower hourly wage are migrant farm workers.

A hamburger and french fries became the quintessential American meal in the   10
1950s, thanks to the promotional efforts of the fast food chains. The typical American now consumes approximately three hamburgers and four orders of french fries every week. But the steady barrage of fast food ads, full of thick juicy burgers and long golden fries, rarely mentions where these foods come from nowadays or what ingredients they contain. The birth of the fast food industry coincided with Eisenhower-era glorifications of technology, with optimistic slogans like "Better Living through Chemistry" and "Our Friend the Atom." The sort of technological wizardry that Walt Disney promoted on television and at Disneyland eventually reached its fulfillment in the kitchens of fast food restaurants. Indeed, the corporate culture of McDonald's seems inextricably linked to that of the Disney empire, sharing a reverence for sleek machinery, electronics, and automation. The leading fast food chains still embrace a boundless faith in science—and as a result have changed not just what Americans eat, but also how their food is made.

The current methods for preparing fast food are less likely to be found in cook-   11
books than in trade journals such as *Food Technologist* and *Food Engineering*. Aside from the salad greens and tomatoes, most fast food is delivered to the restaurant already frozen, canned, dehydrated, or freeze dried. A fast food kitchen is merely the final stage in a vast and highly complex system of mass production. Foods that may look familiar have in fact been completely reformulated. What we eat has changed more in the last forty years than in the previous forty thousand. Like Cheyenne Mountain,[1] today's fast food conceals remarkable technological advances behind an ordinary-looking façade. Much of the taste and aroma of American fast food, for example, is now manufactured at a series of large chemical plants off the New Jersey Turnpike.

In the fast food restaurants of Colorado Springs, behind the counters, amid the   12
plastic seats, in the changing landscape outside the window, you can see all the virtues and destructiveness of our fast food nation. I chose Colorado Springs as a focal point . . . because the changes that have recently swept through the city are emblematic of those that fast food—and the fast food mentality—have encouraged throughout the United States. Countless other suburban communities, in every part of the country, could have been used to illustrate the same points. The extraordinary growth of Colorado Springs neatly parallels that of the fast food industry: during the last few decades, the city's population has more than doubled. Subdivisions, shopping malls, and chain restaurants are appearing in the foothills of

---

1. *Cheyenne Mountain*: A bi-national (United States and Canada) military operations center and high-level command post near Colorado Springs, Colorado, containing missile sensors and other high-tech equipment. The center is built inside a mountain and is entered through a 540-meter tunnel; it is designed to withstand direct nuclear attack.

Cheyenne Mountain and the plains rolling to the east. The Rocky Mountain region as a whole has the fastest-growing economy in the United States, mixing high-tech and service industries in a way that may define America's workforce for years to come. And new restaurants are opening there at a faster pace than anywhere else in the nation.

Fast food is now so commonplace that it has acquired an air of inevitability, as though it were somehow unavoidable, a fact of modern life. And yet the dominance of the fast food giants was no more preordained than the march of colonial split-levels, golf courses, and manmade lakes across the deserts of the American West. The political philosophy that now prevails in so much of the West—with its demand for lower taxes, smaller government, an unbridled free market—stands in total contradiction to the region's true economic underpinnings. No other region of the United States has been so dependent on government subsidies for so long, from the nineteenth-century construction of its railroads to the twentieth-century financing of its military bases and dams. One historian has described the federal government's 1950s highway-building binge as a case study in "interstate socialism"—a phrase that aptly describes how the West was really won. The fast food industry took root alongside that interstate highway system, as a new form of restaurant sprang up beside the new off-ramps. Moreover, the extraordinary growth of this industry over the past quarter-century did not occur in a political vacuum. It took place during a period when the inflation-adjusted value of the minimum wage declined by about 40 percent, when sophisticated mass marketing techniques were for the first time directed at small children, and when federal agencies created to protect workers and consumers too often behaved like branch offices of the companies that were supposed to be regulated. Ever since the administration of President Richard Nixon, the fast food industry has worked closely with its allies in Congress and the White House to oppose new worker safety, food safety, and minimum wage laws. While publicly espousing support for the free market, the fast food chains have quietly pursued and greatly benefited from a wide variety of government subsidies. Far from being inevitable, America's fast food industry in its present form is the logical outcome of certain political and economic choices. 13

In the potato fields and processing plants of Idaho, in the ranchlands east of Colorado Springs, in the feedlots and slaughterhouses of the High Plains, you can see the effects of fast food on the nation's rural life, its environment, its workers, and its health. The fast food chains now stand atop a huge food-industrial complex that has gained control of American agriculture. During the 1980s, large multinationals—such as Cargill, ConAgra, and IBP—were allowed to dominate one commodity market after another. Farmers and cattle ranchers are losing their independence, essentially becoming hired hands for the agribusiness giants or being forced off the land. Family farms are now being replaced by gigantic corporate farms with absen- 14 tee owners. Rural communities are losing their middle class and becoming socially stratified, divided between a small, wealthy elite and large numbers of the working poor. Small towns that seemingly belong in a Norman Rockwell painting are being turned into rural ghettos. The hardy, independent farmers whom Thomas Jefferson considered the bedrock of American democracy are a truly vanishing breed. The United States now has more prison inmates than full-time farmers.

The fast food chains' vast purchasing power and their demand for a uniform 15 product have encouraged fundamental changes in how cattle are raised, slaughtered, and processed into ground beef. These changes have made meatpacking— once a highly skilled, highly paid occupation—into the most dangerous job in the United States, performed by armies of poor, transient immigrants whose injuries often go unrecorded and uncompensated. And the same meat industry practices that endanger these workers have facilitated the introduction of deadly pathogens, such as *E. coli* O157:H7, into America's hamburger meat, a food aggressively marketed to children. Again and again, efforts to prevent the sale of tainted ground beef have been thwarted by meat industry lobbyists and their allies in Congress. The federal government has the legal authority to recall a defective toaster oven or stuffed animal—but still lacks the power to recall tons of contaminated, potentially lethal meat.

I do not mean to suggest that fast food is solely responsible for every social prob- 16 lem now haunting the United States. In some cases (such as the malling and sprawling of the West) the fast food industry has been a catalyst and a symptom of larger economic trends. In other cases (such as the rise of franchising and the spread of obesity) fast food has played a more central role. By tracing the diverse influences of fast food I hope to shed light not only on the workings of an important industry, but also on a distinctively American way of viewing the world.

Elitists have always looked down at fast food, criticizing how it tastes and regard- 17 ing it as another tacky manifestation of American popular culture. The aesthetics of fast food are of much less concern to me than its impact upon the lives of ordinary Americans, both as workers and consumers. Most of all, I am concerned about its impact on the nation's children. Fast food is heavily marketed to children and prepared by people who are barely older than children. This is an industry that both feeds and feeds off the young. During the two years spent researching this book, I ate an enormous amount of fast food. Most of it tasted pretty good. That is one of the main reasons people buy fast food; it has been carefully designed to taste good. It's also inexpensive and convenient. But the value meals, two-for-one deals, and free refills of soda give a distorted sense of how much fast food actually costs. The real price never appears on the menu.

The sociologist George Ritzer has attacked the fast food industry for celebrating 18 a narrow measure of efficiency over every other human value, calling the triumph of McDonald's "the irrationality of rationality." Others consider the fast food industry proof of the nation's great economic vitality, a beloved American institution that appeals overseas to millions who admire our way of life. Indeed, the values, the culture, and the industrial arrangements of our fast food nation are now being exported to the rest of the world. Fast food has joined Hollywood movies, blue jeans, and pop music as one of America's most prominent cultural exports. Unlike other commodities, however, fast food isn't viewed, read, played, or worn. It enters the body and becomes part of the consumer. No other industry offers, both literally and figuratively, so much insight into the nature of mass consumption.

Reading with an Eye for the Methods

1. The fast food industry in America, says Eric Schlosser, has seen "extraordinary growth" in recent decades (4). What are some of the main CAUSES of this phenomenon, according to his analysis?

2. Where else in his essay does Schlosser analyze causes and effects? What are some of them, especially in rural areas?

3. Why does Schlosser choose Colorado Springs as a "focal point" for his essay and the book that it introduces (12)? What does the town EXEMPLIFY and why is it, in his opinion, a good example?

4. What other methods, such as NARRATIVE and ARGUMENT, does Schlosser use in this selection? How and where does he combine them to help explain "the nature of mass consumption" (18)?

Using the Methods

1. "Pull open the glass door, feel the rush of cool air, walk in," and DESCRIBE in a paragraph what you see inside a familiar fast food restaurant (2).

2. Write an essay in which you attack or agree with Schlosser's thesis that "fast food has proven to be a revolutionary force in American life" (3). Give numerous examples.

MALCOLM GLADWELL

The Tipping Point

Hush Puppies, Crime, Yawning, and Other Contagions

Malcolm Gladwell (b. 1963) grew up in Canada and produced his first prize-winning story at the age of 16—an interview with God. After graduating from the University of Toronto in 1984, he became a science and business writer and a bureau chief for the Washington Post. In 1996, Gladwell joined the writing staff of the New Yorker. Drawing on research in sociology, psychology, and social psychology, Gladwell's articles and books—including the best-selling The Tipping Point (2000), Blink (2005), and Outliers (2008)—deal with the large-scale implications of apparently insignificant events.

In The Tipping Point, Gladwell studies the structure of epidemics, taking the field of epidemiology well beyond the realm of disease to show "how little things can make a big difference" in all aspects of life. In the following chapter from that book, Gladwell illustrates this principle with a number of specific examples, notably a sudden rise in the sales of Hush Puppies ("the classic American brushed-suede shoes with the light-weight crepe sole") and the sudden decrease in the rate of violent crime on the streets of New York.

FOR HUSH PUPPIES—the classic American brushed-suede shoes with the light-weight crepe sole—the Tipping Point came somewhere between late 1994 and early 1995. The brand had been all but dead until that point. Sales were down to 30,000 pairs a year, mostly to backwoods outlets and small-town family stores. Wolverine, the company that makes Hush Puppies, was thinking of phasing out the shoes that made them famous. But then something strange happened. At a fashion shoot, two Hush Puppies executives—Owen Baxter and Geoffrey Lewis—ran into a stylist from New York who told them that the classic Hush Puppies had suddenly become hip in the clubs and bars of downtown Manhattan. "We were being told," Baxter recalls, "that there were resale shops in the Village, in Soho, where the shoes were being sold. People were going to the Ma and Pa stores, the little stores that still carried them, and buying them up." Baxter and Lewis were baffled at first. It made no sense to them that shoes that were so obviously out of fashion could make a comeback. "We were told that Isaac Mizrahi[1] was wearing

---

1. *Isaac Mizrahi:* Well-known fashion designer.

SUGGESTED MLA CITATION: Gladwell, Malcolm. "The Tipping Point." 2000. *Back to the Lake.* Ed. Thomas Cooley. 2nd ed. New York: Norton, 2012. 675–81. Print.

the shoes himself," Lewis says. "I think it's fair to say that at the time we had no idea who Isaac Mizrahi was."

By the fall of 1995, things began to happen in a rush. First the designer John Bartlett called. He wanted to use Hush Puppies in his spring collection. Then another Manhattan designer, Anna Sui, called, wanting shoes for her show as well. In Los Angeles, the designer Joel Fitzgerald put a twenty-five-foot inflatable basset hound—the symbol of the Hush Puppies brand—on the roof of his Hollywood store and gutted an adjoining art gallery to turn it into a Hush Puppies boutique. While he was still painting and putting up shelves, the actor Pee-wee Herman walked in and asked for a couple of pairs. "It was total word of mouth," Fitzgerald remembers.

In 1995, the company sold 430,000 pairs of the classic Hush Puppies, and the next year it sold four times that, and the year after that still more, until Hush Puppies were once again a staple of the wardrobe of the young American male. In 1996, Hush Puppies won the prize for best accessory at the Council of Fashion Designers awards dinner at Lincoln Center, and the president of the firm stood up on the stage with Calvin Klein and Donna Karan and accepted an award for an achievement that—as he would be the first to admit—his company had almost nothing to do with. Hush Puppies had suddenly exploded, and it all started with a handful of kids in the East Village and Soho.

How did that happen? Those first few kids, whoever they were, weren't deliberately trying to promote Hush Puppies. They were wearing them precisely because no one else would wear them. Then the fad spread to two fashion designers who used the shoes to peddle something else—haute couture. The shoes were an incidental touch. No one was trying to make Hush Puppies a trend. Yet, somehow, that's exactly what happened. The shoes passed a certain point in popularity and they tipped. How does a thirty-dollar pair of shoes go from a handful of downtown Manhattan hipsters and designers to every mall in America in the space of two years?

1.

There was a time, not very long ago, in the desperately poor New York City neighborhoods of Brownsville and East New York, when the streets would turn into ghost towns at dusk. Ordinary working people wouldn't walk on the sidewalks. Children wouldn't ride their bicycles on the streets. Old folks wouldn't sit on stoops and park benches. The drug trade ran so rampant and gang warfare was so ubiquitous in that part of Brooklyn that most people would take to the safety of their apartment at nightfall. Police officers who served in Brownsville in the 1980s and early 1990s say that, in those years, as soon as the sun went down their radios exploded with chatter between beat officers and their dispatchers over every conceivable kind of violent and dangerous crime. In 1992, there were 2,154 murders in New York City and 626,182 serious crimes, with the weight of those crimes falling hardest in places like Brownsville and East New York. But then something strange happened. At some mysterious and critical point, the crime rate began to turn. It tipped. Within five years, murders had dropped 64.3 percent to 770 and total crimes had fallen by almost half to 355,893. In Brownsville and East New York, the sidewalks filled up again, the bicycles came back, and old folks reappeared on the stoops. "There was a time when it wasn't uncommon to hear rapid fire, like you would hear somewhere in the jungle in Vietnam," says Inspector Edward Messadri, who commands the police precinct in Brownsville. "I don't hear the gunfire anymore."

The New York City police will tell you that what happened in New York was 6 that the city's policing strategies dramatically improved. Criminologists point to the decline of the crack trade and the aging of the population. Economists, meanwhile, say that the gradual improvement in the city's economy over the course of the 1990s had the effect of employing those who might otherwise have become criminals. These are the conventional explanations for the rise and fall of social problems, but in the end none is any more satisfying than the statement that kids in the East Village caused the Hush Puppies revival. The changes in the drug trade, the population, and the economy are all long-term trends, happening all over the country. They don't explain why crime plunged in New York City so much more than in other cities around the country, and they don't explain why it all happened in such an extraordinarily short time. As for the improvements made by the police, they are important too. But there is a puzzling gap between the scale of the changes in policing and the size of the effect on P. 651 suggests when to weave in an analysis of CAUSE-AND-EFFECT. places like Brownsville and East New York. After all, crime didn't just slowly ebb in New York as conditions gradually improved. It plummeted. How can a change in a handful of economic and social indices cause murder rates to fall by two-thirds in five years?

2.

· · ·

The rise of Hush Puppies and the fall of New York's crime rate are textbook exam- 7 ples of epidemics in action. Although they may sound as if they don't have very much in common, they share a basic, underlying pattern. First of all, they are clear examples of contagious behavior. No one took out an advertisement and told people that the traditional Hush Puppies were cool and they should start wearing them. Those kids simply wore the shoes when they went to clubs or cafes or walked the streets of downtown New York, and in so doing exposed other people to their fashion sense. They infected them with the Hush Puppies "virus."

The crime decline in New York surely happened the same way. It wasn't that   8
some huge percentage of would-be murderers suddenly sat up in 1993 and decided
not to commit any more crimes. Nor was it that the police managed magically to
intervene in a huge percentage of situations that would otherwise have turned
deadly. What happened is that the small number of people in the small number of
situations in which the police or the new social forces had some impact started
behaving very differently, and that behavior somehow spread to other would-be
criminals in similar situations. Somehow a large number of people in New York
got "infected" with an anti-crime virus in a short time.

The second distinguishing characteristic of these two examples is that in both   9
cases little changes had big effects. All of the possible reasons for why New York's
crime rate dropped are changes that happened at the margin; they were incremen-
tal changes. The crack trade leveled off. The population got a little older. The police
force got a little better. Yet the effect was dramatic. So too with Hush Puppies.
How many kids are we talking about who began wearing the shoes in downtown
Manhattan? Twenty? Fifty? One hundred—at the most? Yet their actions seem to
have single-handedly started an international fashion trend.

Finally, both changes happened in a hurry. They didn't build steadily and slowly.   10
It is instructive to look at a chart of the crime rate in New York City from, say, the
mid-1960s to the late 1990s. It looks like a giant arch. In 1965, there were 200,000
crimes in the city and from that point on the number begins a sharp rise, doubling
in two years and continuing almost unbroken until it hits 650,000 crimes a year in
the mid-1970s. It stays steady at that level for the next two decades, before plung-
ing downward in 1992 as sharply as it rose thirty years earlier. Crime did not taper
off. It didn't gently decelerate. It hit a certain point and jammed on the brakes.

These three characteristics—one, contagiousness; two, the fact that little causes   11
can have big effects; and three, that change happens not gradually but at one dramatic moment—are the same three principles that define how measles moves
through a grade-school classroom or the flu attacks every winter. Of the three, the
third trait—the idea that epidemics can rise or fall in one dramatic moment—is the
most important, because it is the principle that makes sense of the first two and
that permits the greatest insight into why modern change happens the way it does.
The name given to that one dramatic moment in an epidemic when everything can
change all at once is the Tipping Point.

3.

A world that follows the rules of epidemics is a very different place from the world   12
we think we live in now. Think, for a moment, about the concept of contagiousness. If I say that word to you, you think of colds and the flu or perhaps something

very dangerous like HIV or Ebola. We have, in our minds, a very specific, biological notion of what contagiousness means. But if there can be epidemics of crime or epidemics of fashion, there must be all kinds of things just as contagious as viruses. Have you ever thought about yawning, for instance? Yawning is a surprisingly powerful act. Just because you read the word "yawning" in the previous two sentences—and the two additional "yawns" in this sentence—a good number of you will probably yawn within the next few minutes. Even as I'm writing this, I've yawned twice. If you're reading this in a public place, and you've just yawned, chances are that a good proportion of everyone who saw you yawn is now yawning too, and a good proportion of the people watching the people who watched you yawn are now yawning as well, and on and on, in an ever-widening, yawning circle.

Yawning is incredibly contagious. I made some of you reading this yawn simply ₁₃ by writing the word "yawn." The people who yawned when they saw you yawn, meanwhile, were infected by the sight of you yawning—which is a second kind of contagion. They might even have yawned if they only heard you yawn, because yawning is also aurally contagious: if you play an audiotape of a yawn to blind people, they'll yawn too. And finally, if you yawned as you read this, did the thought cross your mind—however unconsciously and fleetingly—that you might be tired? I suspect that for some of you it did, which means that yawns can also be emotionally contagious. Simply by writing the word, I can plant a feeling in your mind. Can the flu virus do that? Contagiousness, in other words, is an unexpected property of all kinds of things, and we have to remember that, if we are to recognize and diagnose epidemic change.

The second of the principles of epidemics—that little changes can somehow ₁₄ have big effects—is also a fairly radical notion. We are, as humans, heavily socialized to make a kind of rough approximation between cause and effect. If we want to communicate a strong emotion, if we want to convince someone that, say, we love them, we realize that we need to speak passionately and forthrightly. If we want to break bad news to someone, we lower our voices and choose our words carefully. We are trained to think that what goes into any transaction or relationship or system must be directly related, in intensity and dimension, to what comes out. Consider, for example, the following puzzle. I give you a large piece of paper, and I ask you to fold it over once, and then take that folded paper and fold it over again, and then again, and again, until you have refolded the original paper 50 times. How tall do you think the final stack is going to be? In answer to that question, most people will fold the sheet in their mind's eye, and guess that the pile would be as thick as a phone book or, if they're really courageous, they'll say that it would be as tall as a refrigerator. But the real answer is that the height of the stack would approximate the distance to the sun. And if you folded it over one more time, the stack would be as high as the distance to the sun and back. This is an example of what in mathematics is called a geometric progression. Epidemics are another example of geometric progression: when a virus spreads through a population, it doubles and doubles again, until it has (figuratively) grown from a single sheet of paper all the way to the sun in fifty steps. As human beings we have a hard time with this kind of progression, because the end result—the effect—seems far out of proportion to the cause. To appreciate the power of epidemics, we have to abandon this expectation about proportionality. We need to prepare ourselves for the possibility that sometimes big changes follow from small events, and that sometimes these changes can happen very quickly.

This possibility of sudden change is at the center of the idea of the Tipping Point and might well be the hardest of all to accept. The expression first came into popular use in the 1970s to describe the flight to the suburbs of whites living in the older cities of the American Northeast. When the number of incoming African Americans in a particular neighborhood reached a certain point—20 percent, say—sociologists observed that the community would "tip": most of the remaining whites would leave almost immediately. The Tipping Point is the moment of critical mass, the threshold, the boiling point. There was a Tipping Point for violent crime in New York in the early 1990s, and a Tipping Point for the reemergence of Hush Puppies, just as there is a Tipping Point for the introduction of any new technology. Sharp introduced the first low-priced fax machine in 1984, and sold about 80,000 of those machines in the United States in that first year. For the next three years, businesses slowly and steadily bought more and more faxes, until, in 1987, enough people had faxes that it made sense for everyone to get a fax. Nineteen eighty-seven was the fax machine Tipping Point. A million machines were sold that year, and by 1989 two million new machines had gone into operation. Cellular phones have followed the same trajectory. Through the 1990s, they got smaller and cheaper, and service got better until 1998, when the technology hit a Tipping Point and suddenly everyone had a cell phone. . . .

All epidemics have Tipping Points. Jonathan Crane, a sociologist at the University of Illinois, has looked at the effect the number of role models in a community—the professionals, managers, teachers whom the Census Bureau has defined as "high status"—has on the lives of teenagers in the same neighborhood. He found little difference in pregnancy rates or school drop-out rates in neighborhoods of between 40 and 5 percent of high-status workers. But when the number of professionals dropped below 5 percent, the problems exploded. For black schoolchildren, for example, as the percentage of high-status workers falls just 2.2 percentage points—from 5.6 percent to 3.4 percent—drop-out rates more than double. At the same Tipping Point, the rates of child-bearing for teenaged girls—which barely move at all up to that point—nearly double. We assume, intuitively, that neighborhoods and social problems decline in some kind of steady progression. But sometimes they may not decline steadily at all; at the Tipping Point, schools can lose control of their students, and family life can disintegrate all at once.

I remember once as a child seeing our family's puppy encounter snow for the   17
first time. He was shocked and delighted and overwhelmed, wagging his tail nervously, sniffing about in this strange, fluffy substance, whimpering with the mystery of it all. It wasn't much colder on the morning of his first snowfall than it had been the evening before. It might have been 34 degrees the previous evening, and now it was 31 degrees. Almost nothing had changed, in other words, yet—and this was the amazing thing—everything had changed. Rain had become something entirely different. Snow! We are all, at heart, gradualists, our expectations set by the steady passage of time. But the world of the Tipping Point is a place where the unexpected becomes expected, where radical change is more than possibility. It is—contrary to all our expectations—a certainty.

Two simple questions . . . lie at the heart of what we would all like to accom-   18
plish as educators, parents, marketers, business people, and policymakers. Why is it that some ideas or behaviors or products start epidemics and others don't? And what can we do to deliberately start and control positive epidemics of our own?

READING WITH AN EYE FOR THE METHODS

1. Besides giving specific EXAMPLES of epidemics, Malcolm Gladwell is analyzing CAUSES for why epidemics occur. What are some of the causes?

2. How does Gladwell DEFINE a Tipping Point, and how does this definition contribute to his analysis of how and why epidemics take place?

3. Where does Gladwell use other methods of development, such as NARRATION, DESCRIPTION, or PROCESS ANALYSIS? Point out several instances, and explain how they support his analysis.

USING THE METHODS

1. In a paragraph, explain how, according to Gladwell, the sales of Hush Puppies exemplify an epidemic in action.

2. Write an essay in which you use (and give full credit to) Gladwell's Tipping Point theory to analyze the causes of one of the following: an emerging trend in fashion, the ascension of a top-ten tune, the spread of a rumor, the sale of a product or idea by word-of-mouth advertising, or the spread of a disease.

The Checklist Manifesto

Atul Gawande (b. 1965) is a surgeon, professor of medicine, and award-winning writer. A native of Brooklyn and the son of doctors from India who ultimately transplanted the family to Athens, Ohio, Gawande attended Stanford University, Oxford University, and Harvard Medical School. He received a MacArthur Fellowship in 2006 for his medical research and writing, collected in Complications: A Surgeon's Notes on an Imperfect Science *(2002) and* Better: A Surgeon's Notes on Performance *(2007). He is the director of the World Health Organization's Global Challenge for Safer Surgical Care.*

"The Checklist Manifesto," a selection from Gawande's eponymous 2009 bestseller, is an extended argument about the need to manage extreme complexity in medicine and other fields. Gawande supports this main point with numerous examples using both description and narration—and with process analysis, cause-and-effect analysis, and other methods. One hero of the piece is Dr. Peter Pronovost of the Johns Hopkins Hospital, whom Gawande describes as "an odd mixture of the nerdy and the messianic. . . . He hated the laboratory—with all those micropipettes and cell cultures, and no patients around—but he had that scientific 'How can I solve this unsolved problem?' turn of mind."

SOME TIME AGO I read a case report in the *Annals of Thoracic Surgery*. It was, in 1 the dry prose of a medical journal article, the story of a nightmare. In a small Austrian town in the Alps, a mother and father had been out on a walk in the woods with their three-year-old daughter. The parents lost sight of the girl for a moment and that was all it took. She fell into an icy fishpond. The parents frantically jumped in after her. But she was lost beneath the surface for thirty minutes before they finally found her on the pond bottom. They pulled her to the surface and got her to the shore. Following instructions from an emergency response team reached on their cell phone, they began cardiopulmonary resuscitation.

Rescue personnel arrived eight minutes later and took the first recordings of the 2 girl's condition. She was unresponsive. She had no blood pressure or pulse or sign of breathing. Her body temperature was just 66 degrees. Her pupils were dilated and unreactive to light, indicating cessation of brain function. She was gone.

SUGGESTED MLA CITATION: Gawande, Atul. "The Checklist Manifesto." 2009. *Back to the Lake.* Ed. Thomas Cooley. 2nd ed. New York: Norton, 2012. 682–95. Print.

But the emergency technicians continued CPR anyway. A helicopter took her   3
to the nearest hospital, where she was wheeled directly into an operating room,
a member of the emergency crew straddling her on the gurney, pumping her chest.
A surgical team got her onto a heart-lung bypass machine as rapidly as it
could. . . .

Between the transport time and the time it took to plug the machine into her,   4
she had been lifeless for an hour and a half. By the two-hour mark, however, her
body temperature had risen almost ten degrees, and her heart began to beat. It was
her first organ to come back.

After six hours, the girl's core reached 98.6 degrees, normal body temperature.   5
The team tried to shift her from the bypass machine to a mechanical ventilator, but
the pond water and debris had damaged her lungs too severely for the oxygen
pumped in through the breathing tube to reach her blood. So they switched her
instead to an artificial-lung system known as ECMO—extracorporeal membrane
oxygenation. To do this, the surgeons had to open her chest down the middle with
a power saw and sew the lines to and from the portable ECMO unit directly into
her aorta and her beating heart.

The ECMO machine now took over. The surgeons removed the heart-lung   6
bypass machine tubing. They repaired the vessels and closed her groin incision.
The surgical team moved the girl into intensive care, with her chest still open and
covered with sterile plastic foil. Through the day and night, the intensive care unit
team worked on suctioning the water and debris from her lungs with a fiberoptic
bronchoscope. By the next day, her lungs had recovered sufficiently for the team to
switch her from ECMO to a mechanical ventilator, which required taking her back
to the operating room to unplug the tubing, repair the holes, and close her chest.

Over the next two days, all the girl's organs recovered—her liver, her kidneys,   7
her intestines, everything except her brain. A CT scan showed global brain swell-
ing, which is a sign of diffuse damage, but no actual dead zones. So the team esca-
lated the care one step further. It drilled a hole into the girl's skull, threaded a
probe into the brain to monitor the pressure, and kept that pressure tightly controlled through constant adjustments in her fluids and medications. For more than
a week, she lay comatose. Then, slowly, she came back to life.

First, her pupils started to react to light. Next, she began to breathe on her own.   8
And, one day, she simply awoke. Two weeks after her accident, she went home.
Her right leg and left arm were partially paralyzed. Her speech was thick and
slurry. But she underwent extensive outpatient therapy. By age five, she had recovered her faculties completely. Physical and neurological examinations were normal. She was like any little girl again.

What makes this recovery astounding isn't just the idea that someone could be   9
brought back after two hours in a state that would once have been considered

death. It's also the idea that a group of people in a random hospital could manage to pull off something so enormously complicated. Rescuing a drowning victim is nothing like it looks on television shows, where a few chest compressions and some mouth-to-mouth resuscitation always seem to bring someone with water-logged lungs and a stilled heart coughing and sputtering back to life. To save this one child, scores of people had to carry out thousands of steps correctly: placing the heart-pump tubing into her without letting in air bubbles; maintaining the sterility of her lines, her open chest, the exposed fluid in her brain; keeping a temperamental battery of machines up and running. The degree of difficulty in any one of these steps is substantial. Then you must add the difficulties of orchestrating them in the right sequence, with nothing dropped, leaving some room for improvisation, but not too much.

For every drowned and pulseless child rescued, there are scores more who don't   10 make it—and not just because their bodies are too far gone. Machines break down; a team can't get moving fast enough; someone fails to wash his hands and an infection takes hold. Such cases don't get written up in the *Annals of Thoracic Surgery*, but they are the norm, though people may not realize it.

. . .

On any given day in the United States alone, some ninety thousand people are   11 admitted to intensive care. Over a year, an estimated five million Americans will be, and over a normal lifetime nearly all of us will come to know the glassed bay of an ICU from the inside. Wide swaths of medicine now depend on the life support systems that ICUs provide: care for premature infants; for victims of trauma, strokes, and heart attacks; for patients who have had surgery on their brains, hearts, lungs, or major blood vessels. Critical care has become an increasingly large portion of what hospitals do. Fifty years ago, ICUs barely existed. Now, to take a recent random day in my hospital, 155 of our almost 700 patients are in intensive care. The average stay of an ICU patient is four days, and the survival rate is 86 percent. Going into an ICU, being put on a mechanical ventilator, having tubes and wires run into and out of you, is not a sentence of death. But the days will be the most precarious of your life.

Fifteen years ago, Israeli scientists published a study in which engineers   12 observed patient care in ICUs for twenty-four-hour stretches. They found that the average patient required 178 individual actions per day, ranging from administering a drug to suctioning the lungs, and every one of them posed risks. Remarkably, the nurses and doctors were observed to make an error in just 1 percent of these actions—but that still amounted to an average of two errors a day with every patient. Intensive care succeeds only when we hold the odds of doing harm low enough for the odds of doing good to prevail. This is hard. There are dangers simply in lying unconscious in bed for a few days. Muscles atrophy. Bones lose mass.

Pressure ulcers form. Veins begin to clot. You have to stretch and exercise patients' flaccid limbs daily to avoid contractures; you have to give subcutaneous injections of blood thinners at least twice a day, turn patients in bed every few hours, bathe them and change their sheets without knocking out a tube or a line, brush their teeth twice a day to avoid pneumonia from bacterial buildup in their mouths. Add a ventilator, dialysis, and the care of open wounds, and the difficulties only accumulate.

. . .

Here, then, is the fundamental puzzle of modern medical care: you have a desper- 13
ately sick patient and in order to have a chance of saving him you have to get the knowledge right and then you have to make sure that the 178 daily tasks that follow are done correctly—despite some monitor's alarm going off for God knows what reason, despite the patient in the next bed crashing, despite a nurse poking his head around the curtain to ask whether someone could help "get this lady's chest open." There is complexity upon complexity. And even specialization has begun to seem inadequate. So what do you do?

The medical profession's answer has been to go from specialization to super- 14
specialization. . . . In the past decade, training programs focusing on critical care have opened in most major American and European cities, and half of American ICUs now rely on superspecialists.

Expertise is the mantra of modern medicine. In the early twentieth century, you 15
needed only a high school diploma and a one-year medical degree to practice med-
icine. By the century's end, all doctors had to have a college degree, a four-year medical degree, and an additional three to seven years of residency training in an individual field of practice—pediatrics, surgery, neurology, or the like. In recent years, though, even this level of preparation has not been enough for the new complexity of medicine. After their residencies, most young doctors today are going on to do fellowships, adding one to three further years of training in, say, laparoscopic surgery, or pediatric metabolic disorders, or breast radiology, or critical care. A young doctor is not so young nowadays; you typically don't start in independent practice until your midthirties.

We live in the era of the superspecialist—of clinicians who have taken the time 16
to practice, practice, practice at one narrow thing until they can do it better than anyone else. They have two advantages over ordinary specialists: greater knowl-
edge of the details that matter and a learned ability to handle the complexities of the particular job. There are degrees of complexity, though, and medicine and other fields like it have grown so far beyond the usual kind that avoiding daily mistakes is proving impossible even for our most superspecialized. . . .

Medicine, with its dazzling successes but also frequent failures, therefore poses a 17
significant challenge: What do you do when expertise is not enough? What do you

do when even the superspecialists fail? We've begun to see an answer, but it has come from an unexpected source—one that has nothing to do with medicine at all.

. . .

On October 30, 1935, at Wright Air Field in Dayton, Ohio, the U.S. Army Air Corps held a flight competition for airplane manufacturers vying to build the military's next-generation long-range bomber. It wasn't supposed to be much of a competition. In early evaluations, the Boeing Corporation's gleaming aluminum-alloy Model 299 had trounced the designs of Martin and Douglas. Boeing's plane could carry five times as many bombs as the army had requested; it could fly faster than previous bombers and almost twice as far. A Seattle newspaperman who had glimpsed the plane on a test flight over his city called it the "flying fortress," and the name stuck. The flight "competition," according to the military historian Phillip Meilinger, was regarded as a mere formality. The army planned to order at least sixty-five of the aircraft.

A small crowd of army brass and manufacturing executives watched as the Model 299 test plane taxied onto the runway. It was sleek and impressive, with a 103-foot wingspan and four engines jutting out from the wings, rather than the usual two. The plane roared down the tarmac, lifted off smoothly, and climbed sharply to three hundred feet. Then it stalled, turned on one wing, and crashed in a fiery explosion. Two of the five crew members died, including the pilot, Major Ployer P. Hill.

B-17 bomber and ground crew.

An investigation revealed that nothing mechanical had gone wrong. The crash 20 had been due to "pilot error," the report said. Substantially more complex than previous aircraft, the new plane required the pilot to attend to the four engines, each with its own oil-fuel mix, the retractable landing gear, the wing flaps, electric trim tabs that needed adjustment to maintain stability at different airspeeds, and constant-speed propellers whose pitch had to be regulated with hydraulic controls, among other features. While doing all this, Hill had forgotten to release a new locking mechanism on the elevator and rudder controls. The Boeing model was deemed, as a newspaper put it, "too much airplane for one man to fly." The army air corps declared Douglas's smaller design the winner. Boeing nearly went bankrupt.

Still, the army purchased a few aircraft from Boeing as test planes, and some 21 insiders remained convinced that the aircraft was flyable. So a group of test pilots got together and considered what to do.

What they decided *not* to do was almost as interesting as what they actually did. 23 They did not require Model 299 pilots to undergo longer training. It was hard to imagine having more experience and expertise than Major Hill, who had been the air corps' chief of flight testing. Instead, they came up with an ingeniously simple approach: they created a pilot's checklist. Its mere existence indicated how far aeronautics had advanced. In the early years of flight, getting an aircraft into the air might have been nerve-racking but it was hardly complex. Using a checklist for

Cockpit of a B-17.

takeoff would no more have occurred to a pilot than to a driver backing a car out of the garage. But flying this new plane was too complicated to be left to the memory of any one person, however expert.

The test pilots made their list simple, brief, and to the point—short enough to   23
fit on an index card, with step-by-step checks for takeoff, flight, landing, and taxiing. It had the kind of stuff that all pilots know to do. They check that the brakes are released, that the instruments are set, that the door and windows are closed, that the elevator controls are unlocked—dumb stuff. You wouldn't think it would make that much difference. But with the checklist in hand, the pilots went on to fly the Model 299 a total of 1.8 million miles without one accident. The army ultimately ordered almost thirteen thousand of the aircraft, which it dubbed the B-17. And, because flying the behemoth was now possible, the army gained a decisive air advantage in the Second World War, enabling its devastating bombing campaign across Nazi Germany.

Much of our work today has entered its own B-17 phase. Substantial parts of   24
what software designers, financial managers, firefighters, police officers, lawyers, and most certainly clinicians do are now too complex for them to carry out reliably from memory alone. Multiple fields, in other words, have become too much airplane for one person to fly.

Yet it is far from obvious that something as simple as a checklist could be of   25
substantial help. We may admit that errors and oversights occur—even devastating ones. But we believe our jobs are too complicated to reduce to a checklist. Sick people, for instance, are phenomenally more various than airplanes. A study of forty-one thousand trauma patients in the state of Pennsylvania—just trauma patients—found that they had 1,224 different injury-related diagnoses in 32,261 unique combinations. That's like having 32,261 kinds of airplane to land. Mapping out the proper steps for every case is not possible, and physicians have been skeptical that a piece of paper with a bunch of little boxes would improve matters.

. . .

In 2001, though, a critical care specialist at Johns Hopkins Hospital named Peter   26
Pronovost decided to give a doctor checklist a try. He didn't attempt to make the checklist encompass everything ICU teams might need to do in a day. He designed it to tackle just one of their hundreds of potential tasks . . . : central line infections.

On a sheet of plain paper, he plotted out the steps to take in order to avoid infec-   27
tions when putting in a central line. Doctors are supposed to (1) wash their hands with soap, (2) clean the patient's skin with chlorhexidine antiseptic, (3) put sterile drapes over the entire patient, (4) wear a mask, hat, sterile gown, and gloves, and (5) put a sterile dressing over the insertion site once the line is in. Check, check, check, check, check. These steps are no-brainers; they have been known and taught for years. So it seemed silly to make a checklist

See p. 650 for combining NARRATIVE and PROCESS ANALYSIS.

for something so obvious. Still, Pronovost asked the nurses in his ICU to observe the doctors for a month as they put lines into patients and record how often they carried out each step. In more than a third of patients, they skipped at least one.

The next month, he and his team persuaded the Johns Hopkins Hospital admin- 28 istration to authorize nurses to stop doctors if they saw them skipping a step on the checklist; nurses were also to ask the doctors each day whether any lines ought to be removed, so as not to leave them in longer than necessary. This was revolutionary. Nurses have always had their ways of nudging a doctor into doing the right thing, ranging from the gentle reminder ("Um, did you forget to put on your mask, doctor?") to more forceful methods (I've had a nurse bodycheck me when she thought I hadn't put enough drapes on a patient). But many nurses aren't sure whether this is their place or whether a given measure is worth a confrontation. (Does it really matter whether a patient's legs are draped for a line going into the chest?) The new rule made it clear: if doctors didn't follow every step, the nurses would have backup from the administration to intervene.

For a year afterward, Pronovost and his colleagues monitored what happened. 29 The results were so dramatic that they weren't sure whether to believe them: the ten-day line-infection rate went from 11 percent to zero. So they followed patients for fifteen more months. Only two line infections occurred during the entire period. They calculated that, in this one hospital, the checklist had prevented forty-three infections and eight deaths and saved two million dollars in costs.

Pronovost recruited more colleagues, and they tested some more checklists in 30 his Johns Hopkins ICU. One aimed to ensure that nurses observed patients for pain at least once every four hours and provided timely pain medication. This reduced from 41 percent to 3 percent the likelihood of a patient's enduring untreated pain. They tested a checklist for patients on mechanical ventilation, making sure, for instance, that doctors prescribed antacid medication to prevent stomach ulcers and that the head of each patient's bed was propped up at least thirty degrees to stop oral secretions from going into the windpipe. The proportion of patients not receiving the recommended care dropped from 70 percent to 4 percent, the occurrence of pneumonias fell by a quarter, and twenty-one fewer patients died than in the previous year. The researchers found that simply having the doctors and nurses in the ICU create their own checklists for what they thought should be done each day improved the consistency of care to the point that the average length of patient stay in intensive care dropped by half.

These checklists accomplished what checklists elsewhere have done, Pronovost 31 observed. They helped with memory recall and clearly set out the minimum necessary steps in a process. He was surprised to discover how often even experienced personnel failed to grasp the importance of certain precautions. In a survey of ICU staff taken before introducing the ventilator checklists, he found that half hadn't

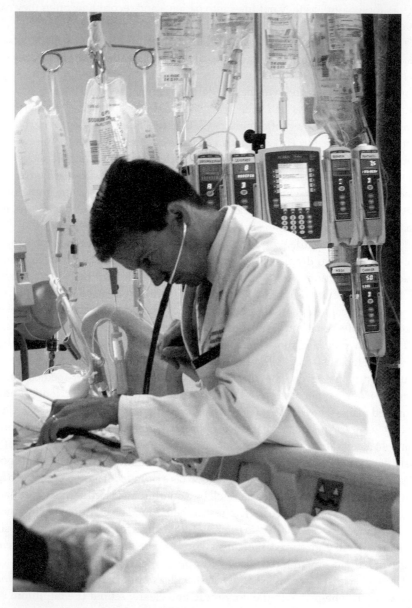

Dr. Peter Pronovost attends a patient.

realized that evidence strongly supported giving ventilated patients antacid medication. Checklists, he found, established a higher standard of baseline performance.

These seem, of course, ridiculously primitive insights. Pronovost is routinely 32
described by colleagues as "brilliant," "inspiring," a "genius." He has an M.D. and
a Ph.D. in public health from Johns Hopkins and is trained in emergency medicine, anesthesiology, and critical care medicine. But, really, does it take all that
to figure out what anyone who has made a to-do list figured out ages ago? Well,
maybe yes.

Despite his initial checklist results, takers were slow to come. He traveled 33
around the country showing his checklists to doctors, nurses, insurers, employers—
anyone who would listen. He spoke in an average of seven cities a month. But few
adopted the idea.

There were various reasons. Some physicians were offended by the suggestion 34
that they needed checklists. Others had legitimate doubts about Pronovost's evidence. So far, he'd shown only that checklists worked in one hospital, Johns
Hopkins, where the ICUs have money, plenty of staff, and Peter Pronovost walking
the hallways to make sure that the idea was being properly implemented. How
about in the real world—where ICU nurses and doctors are in short supply, pressed
for time, overwhelmed with patients, and hardly receptive to the notion of filling
out yet another piece of paper?

In 2003, however, the Michigan Health and Hospital Association approached 35
Pronovost about testing his central line checklist throughout the state's ICUs. It
would be a huge undertaking. But Pronovost would have a chance to establish
whether his checklists could really work in the wider world.

I visited Sinai-Grace Hospital, in inner-city Detroit, a few years after the project 36
was under way, and I saw what Pronovost was up against. Occupying a campus of
redbrick buildings amid abandoned houses, check-cashing stores, and wig shops on
the city's West Side, just south of Eight Mile Road, Sinai-Grace is a classic urban
hospital. It employed at the time eight hundred physicians, seven hundred nurses,
and two thousand other medical personnel to care for a population with the lowest
median income of any city in the country. More than a quarter of a million residents were uninsured; 300,000 were on state assistance. That meant chronic
financial problems. Sinai-Grace is not the most cash-strapped hospital in the city—
that would be Detroit Receiving Hospital, where more than a fifth of the patients
have no means of payment. But between 2000 and 2003, Sinai-Grace and eight
other Detroit hospitals were forced to cut a third of their staff, and the state had to
come forward with a $50 million bailout to avert their bankruptcy.

Sinai-Grace has five ICUs for adult patients and one for infants. Hassan Makki, 37
the director of intensive care, told me what it was like there in 2004, when
Pronovost and the hospital association started a series of mailings and conference

calls with hospitals to introduce checklists for central lines and ventilator patients. "Morale was low," he said. "We had lost lots of staff, and the nurses who remained weren't sure if they were staying." Many doctors were thinking about leaving, too. Meanwhile, the teams faced an even heavier workload because of new rules limiting how long the residents could work at a stretch. Now Pronovost was telling them to find the time to fill out some daily checklists?

Tom Piskorowski, one of the ICU physicians, told me his reaction: "Forget the paperwork. Take care of the patient." [38]

I accompanied a team on 7:00 a.m. rounds through one of the surgical ICUs. It had eleven patients. Four had gunshot wounds (one had been shot in the chest; one had been shot through the bowel, kidney, and liver; two had been shot through the neck and left quadriplegic). Five patients had cerebral hemorrhaging (three were seventy-nine years and older and had been injured falling down stairs; one was a middle-aged man whose skull and left temporal lobe had been damaged by an assault with a blunt weapon; and one was a worker who had become paralyzed from the neck down after falling twenty-five feet off a ladder onto his head). There was a cancer patient recovering from surgery to remove part of his lung, and a patient who had had surgery to repair a cerebral aneurysm. [39]

The doctors and nurses on rounds tried to proceed methodically from one room to the next but were constantly interrupted: a patient they thought they'd stabilized began hemorrhaging again; another who had been taken off the ventilator developed trouble breathing and had to be put back on the machine. It was hard to imagine that they could get their heads far enough above the daily tide of disasters to worry about the minutiae on some checklist. [40]

Yet there they were, I discovered, filling out those pages. Mostly, it was the nurses who kept things in order. Each morning, a senior nurse walked through the unit, clipboard in hand, making sure that every patient on a ventilator had the bed propped at the right angle and had been given the right medicines and the right tests. Whenever doctors put in a central line, a nurse made sure that the central line checklist had been filled out and placed in the patient's chart. Looking back through the hospital files, I found that they had been doing this faithfully for more than three years. [41]

Pronovost had been canny when he started. In his first conversations with hospital administrators, he hadn't ordered them to use the central line checklist. Instead, he asked them simply to gather data on their own line infection rates. In early 2004, they found, the infection rates for ICU patients in Michigan hospitals were higher than the national average, and in some hospitals dramatically so. Sinai-Grace experienced more central line infections than 75 percent of American hospitals. Meanwhile, Blue Cross Blue Shield of Michigan agreed to give hospitals small bonus payments for participating in Pronovost's program. A checklist suddenly seemed an easy and logical thing to try. [42]

In what became known as the Keystone Initiative, each hospital assigned a   43
project manager to roll out the checklist and participate in twice-monthly conference calls with Pronovost for troubleshooting. Pronovost also insisted that
the participating hospitals assign to each unit a senior hospital executive who
would visit at least once a month, hear the staff's complaints, and help them solve
problems.

The executives were reluctant. They normally lived in meetings, worrying about   44
strategy and budgets. They weren't used to venturing into patient territory and
didn't feel they belonged there. In some places, they encountered hostility, but
their involvement proved crucial. In the first month, the executives discovered that
chlorhexidine soap, shown to reduce line infections, was available in less than a
third of the ICUs. This was a problem only an executive could solve. Within weeks,
every ICU in Michigan had a supply of the soap. Teams also complained to the
hospital officials that, although the checklist required patients be fully covered
with a sterile drape when lines were being put in, full-size drapes were often
unavailable. So the officials made sure that drapes were stocked. Then they persuaded Arrow International, one of the largest manufacturers of central lines, to
produce a new kit that had both the drape and chlorhexidine in it.

In December 2006, the Keystone Initiative published its findings in a landmark   45
article in the *New England Journal of Medicine*. Within the first three months of the
project, the central line infection rate in Michigan's ICUs decreased by 66 percent.
Most ICUs—including the ones at Sinai-Grace Hospital—cut their quarterly infection rate to zero. Michigan's infection rates fell so low that its average ICU outper-
formed 90 percent of ICUs nationwide. In the Keystone Initiative's first eighteen
months, the hospitals saved an estimated $175 million in costs and more than fif-
teen hundred lives. The successes have been sustained for several years now—all
because of a stupid little checklist.

It is tempting to think this might be an isolated success. Perhaps there is some-   46
thing unusual about the strategy required to prevent central line infections. After
all, the central line checklist did not prevent any of the other kinds of complications that can result from sticking these foot-long plastic catheters into people's
chests—such as a collapsed lung if the needle goes in too deep or bleeding if a
blood vessel gets torn. It just prevented infections. In this particular instance, yes,
doctors had some trouble getting the basics right—making sure to wash their
hands, put on their sterile gloves and gown, and so on—and a checklist proved
dramatically valuable. But among the myriad tasks clinicians carry out for patients,
maybe this is the peculiar case.

I started to wonder, though.   47

Around the time I learned of Pronovost's results, I spoke to Markus Thalmann, the   48
cardiac surgeon who had been the lead author of the case report on the extraordinary

rescue of the little girl from death by drowning. Among the many details that intrigued me about the save was the fact that it occurred not at a large cutting-edge academic medical center but at an ordinary community hospital. This one was in Klagenfurt, a small provincial Austrian town in the Alps nearest to where the girl had fallen in the pond. I asked Thalmann how the hospital had managed such a complicated rescue.

He told me he had been working in Klagenfurt for six years when the girl came   49
in. She had not been the first person whom he and his colleagues had tried to revive from cardiac arrest after hypothermia and suffocation. His hospital received between three and five such patients a year, he estimated, mostly avalanche victims, some of them drowning victims, and a few of them people attempting suicide by taking a drug overdose and then wandering out into the snowy Alpine forests to fall unconscious. For a long time, he said, no matter how hard the hospital's medical staff tried, they had no survivors. Most of the victims had been without a pulse and oxygen for too long when they were found. But some, he was convinced, still had a flicker of viability in them, yet he and his colleagues had always failed to sustain it.

He took a close look at the case records. Preparation, he determined, was the   50
chief difficulty. Success required having an array of people and equipment at the ready—trauma surgeons, a cardiac anesthesiologist, a cardiothoracic surgeon, bio-engineering support staff, a cardiac perfusionist, operating and critical care nurses, intensivists. Almost routinely, someone or something was missing.

He tried the usual surgical approach to remedy this—yelling at everyone to get   51
their act together. But still they had no saves. So he and a couple of colleagues decided to try something new. They made a checklist.

They gave the checklist to the people with the least power in the whole   52
process—the rescue squads and the hospital telephone operator—and walked them through the details. In cases like these, the checklist said, rescue teams were to tell the hospital to prepare for possible cardiac bypass and rewarming. They were to call, when possible, even before they arrived on the scene, as the preparation time could be significant. The telephone operator would then work down a list of people to notify them to have everything set up and standing by.

With the checklist in place, the team had its first success—the rescue of the   53
three-year-old girl. Not long afterward, Thalmann left to take a job at a hospital in Vienna. The team, however, has since had at least two other such rescues, he said. In one case, a man had been found frozen and pulseless after a suicide attempt. In another, a mother and her sixteen-year-old daughter were in an accident that sent them and their car through a guardrail, over a cliff, and into a mountain river. The mother died on impact; the daughter was trapped as the car rapidly filled with icy water. She had been in cardiac and respiratory arrest for a prolonged period of time when the rescue team arrived.

From that point onward, though, everything moved like clockwork. By the time   54
the rescue team got to her and began CPR, the hospital had been notified. The
transport team delivered her in minutes. The surgical team took her straight to the
operating room and crashed her onto heart-lung bypass. One step followed right
after another. And, because of the speed with which they did, she had a chance.

As the girl's body slowly rewarmed, her heart came back. In the ICU, a mechan-   55
ical ventilator, fluids, and intravenous drugs kept her going while the rest of her
body recovered. The next day, the doctors were able to remove her lines and tubes.
The day after that, she was sitting up in bed, ready to go home.

READING WITH AN EYE FOR THE METHODS

1. Gawande often makes a point by telling a story, as when he writes about the girl
   rescued from drowning in the Austrian Alps. Of the many NARRATIVE elements
   in his essay, which do you find particularly effective? Why?

2. "The medical profession's answer" to the problem of the increasing complexity
   of modern medical care, says Atul Gawande, is "to go from specialization to
   superspecialization" (14). How does Gawande DEFINE this term, and how does
   this definition help to organize and support his argument about checklists?

3. Gawande likens the practice of medicine to flying an airplane. What is the purpose of this COMPARISON? Why does he go on to point out that "sick people . . .
   are phenomenally more various than airplanes" (25)?

4. A checklist is usually the result of a PROCESS ANALYSIS. Point out places in his
   essay where Gawande effectively uses this and other methods of development,
   such as DESCRIPTION or CAUSE-AND-EFFECT analysis. How do these additional
   methods help to support his ARGUMENT?

USING THE METHODS

1. Draw up a checklist of the objects and actions required for one of the following:
   studying for an exam, preparing to take a trip, riding a horse, flying a small
   plane, administering some form of first aid or other emergency medical service.

2. Write an essay about using a checklist, or other relatively simple device, to manage a complex procedure or situation. Explain how the procedure works, why
   understanding it is important, and how it was (or could be) improved by following a checklist or some other simple measure. Illustrate your point with a brief
   narrative or two. Use other methods as appropriate.

BILLY COLLINS

Fishing on the Susquehanna in July

Billy Collins (b. 1941) grew up in New York, the son of an electrician and a nurse. He studied at Holy Cross College and the University of California, Riverside, where he earned a PhD in romantic poetry. The poet laureate of the United States from 2001 to 2003, Collins teaches English at Lehman College of New York University.

"Fishing on the Susquehanna in July" is from Collins' poetry collection Picnic, Lightning *(1998). The poem is a description of "American scenes"—particularly of a man fishing on a river in Maryland—as depicted in paintings that Collins once viewed in a Philadelphia art gallery. As Collins looks at the fisherman, however, he goes beyond merely describing the tranquil scene to demonstrate how art, including the art of writing, "manufactures" experience.*

I have never been fishing on the Susquehanna   1
or on any river for that matter
to be perfectly honest.

Not in July or any month
have I had the pleasure—if it is a pleasure—   5
of fishing on the Susquehanna.

I am more likely to be found
in a quiet room like this one—
a painting of a woman on the wall,

a bowl of tangerines on the table—   10
trying to manufacture the sensation
of fishing on the Susquehanna.

There is little doubt
that others have been fishing
on the Susquehanna,   15

SUGGESTED MLA CITATION: Collins, Billy. "Fishing on the Susquehanna in July." 1998. *Back to the Lake.* Ed. Thomas Cooley. 2nd ed. New York: Norton, 2012. 696–97. Print.

rowing upstream in a wooden boat,
sliding the oars under the water
then raising them to drip in the light.

But the nearest I have ever come to
fishing on the Susquehanna   20
was one afternoon in a museum in Philadelphia,

when I balanced a little egg of time
in front of a painting
in which that river curled around a bend

under a blue cloud-ruffled sky,   25
dense trees along the banks,
and a fellow with a red bandana

sitting in a small, green
flat-bottom boat
holding the thin whip of a pole.   30

That is something I am unlikely
ever to do, I remember
saying to myself and the person next to me.

Then I blinked and moved on
to other American scenes   35
of haystacks, water whitening over rocks,

even one of a brown hare
who seemed so wired with alertness
I imagined him springing right out of the frame.

READING WITH AN EYE FOR THE METHODS

1. In stanzas 7–13 (lines 19–39), Billy Collins is DESCRIBING what he saw "one afternoon in a museum in Philadelphia" (21). What place is he describing in stanzas 3 and 4 (lines 7–12)? Why is Collins more likely to be found in places like these than in a boat on a lake or river?

2. Of all the five senses—sight, sound, touch, smell, and taste—which one is most important in Collins' description? What DOMINANT IMPRESSION does he create by exercising it?

3. Among other methods of development, Collins draws heavily on NARRATION. What are some of the narrative elements of his poem, and what story do they help him to tell?

USING THE METHODS

1. Write a paragraph describing the objects or scene depicted in a painting or photograph that has captured your imagination.

2. In an essay, describe that painting or photograph *and* how it makes you think and feel as you observe and examine it.

3. In an essay, ANALYZE THE PROCESS of "trying to manufacture" the sensation of fishing (or any other experience) as that process is depicted in Collins' poem.

Using Sources in Your Writing

Research is formalized curiosity. It is poking and prying with a purpose.
—ZORA NEALE HURSTON

Whatever your purpose, academic research requires "poking and prying" into sources of information that go well beyond your own immediate knowledge of a subject. If you're examining the student loan controversy of 2007, for example, you'll consult news stories and blog commentary published at that time. Or if you're analyzing a poem by Rita Dove, you'll study Dove's other poetry and read critical interpretations of her work in literary journals. This appendix shows how to find reliable sources, use what you learn in your own writing, and document your sources accurately.

Finding and Evaluating Sources

As you do your research, you will encounter a wide range of potential sources—print and online, general and specialized, published and firsthand. You'll need to evaluate these sources carefully, choose the ones that best support your THESIS, and decide how to incorporate each source into your own paper.

Finding Appropriate Sources

The kinds of sources you turn to will depend on your topic. If you're doing research on a literary or historical topic, you might consult scholarly books and articles and standard reference works such as *The Dictionary of American Biography* or the *Literary History of the United States*. If your research is aimed at a current issue, you would likely consult newspapers and other periodicals, websites, and recent books.

Check your assignment to see if you are required to use primary or secondary sources—or both. *Primary sources* are original works, such as historical documents, literary works, eyewitness accounts, diaries, letters, and lab studies, as well as any original field research you do. *Secondary sources* include books and articles, reviews, biographies, and other works that interpret or discuss primary sources. For example, novels and poems are primary sources; articles interpreting them are secondary sources.

Whether a work is considered primary or secondary often depends on your topic and purpose. If you're analyzing a poem, a critic's article analyzing the poem is a secondary source—but if you're investigating the critic's work, the article would be a primary source.

LIBRARY-BASED SOURCES

When you conduct academic research, it is often better to start with your library's website rather than with a commercial search engine such as *Google*. Library websites provide access to a range of well-organized resources, including scholarly databases through which you can access authoritative articles that have been screened by librarians or specialists in a particular field. In general, there are three kinds of sources you'll want to consult: reference works, books, and periodicals.

- *Reference works.* The reference section of your school's library is the place to find encyclopedias, dictionaries, atlases, almanacs, bibliographies, and other reference works. Remember, though, that reference works are only a starting point, a place where you can get an overview of your topic or basic facts about it. Some reference works are *general*, such as *The New Encyclopaedia Britannica* or the *Statistical Abstract of the United States*. Others are *specialized*, providing in-depth information on a single field or topic.

- *Books.* The library catalog is your main source for finding books. Most catalogs are computerized and can be accessed through the library's website. You can search by author, title, subject, or keyword. When you click on a specific source, you'll find more bibliographic data about author, title, and publication; the call number (which identifies the book's location on the library's shelves); related subject headings (which may lead to other useful materials in the library)—and more.

- *Periodicals.* To find journal and magazine articles, you will need to search periodical indexes and databases. Indexes (such as the *New York Times Index*) provide listings of articles organized by topics; databases (such as LexisNexis) provide the full texts. Although some databases are available for free, many can be accessed by subscription through your library.

WEB-BASED SOURCES

The Web offers countless sites sponsored by governments, educational institutions, organizations, businesses, and individuals. Because it is so vast and dynamic, however, finding useful information can be a challenge. There are several ways to search the Web:

- *Keyword searches. Google, Bing, Ask.com, Yahoo!, AltaVista,* and *Lycos* all scan the Web looking for the keywords you specify.

- *Metasearches. Copernic Agent, SurfWax,* and *Dogpile* let you use several search engines simultaneously.

- *Academic searches.* For peer-reviewed academic writing in many disciplines, try *Google Scholar*; or use *Scirus* for scientific, technical, and medical documents.

Although many websites provide authoritative information, keep in mind that Web content varies greatly in its stability and reliability: what you see on a site today may be different (or gone) tomorrow. So save or make copies of pages you plan to use, and carefully evaluate what you find. Here are just a few of the many resources available on the Web.

- *Indexes, databases, and directories.* Information put together by specialists and grouped by topics can be especially helpful. You may want to consult *Librarians' Internet Index* (an annotated subject directory of more than 20,000 websites selected by librarians); *Infomine* (a huge collection of databases, mailing lists, catalogs, articles, directories, and more); or *The World Wide Web Virtual Library* (a catalog of websites on numerous subjects, compiled by experts).

- *News sites.* Many newspapers, magazines, and radio and TV stations have websites that provide both up-to-the-minute information and also archives of older news articles. Through *Google News* and *NewsLink,* for example, you can access current news worldwide, whereas *Google News Archive Search* has files going back to the 1700s.

- *Government sites.* Many government agencies and departments maintain websites where you can find government reports, statistics, legislative information, and other resources. *USA.gov* offers information, services, and other resources from the U.S. government.

- *Digital archives.* These sites collect and organize materials from the past—including drawings, maps, recordings, speeches, and historic documents—often focusing on a particular subject or country. For example, the National Archives and Records Administration and the Library of Congress both archive items relevant to the culture and history of the United States.

• *Discussion lists and forums.* Online mailing lists, newsgroups, discussion groups, and forums let members post and receive messages from other members. To join a discussion with people who are knowledgeable about your topic, try searching for your topic—for example, for "E. B. White discussion forum." Or consult a site such as *Google Groups.*

SEARCHING ELECTRONICALLY

When you search for subjects on the Web or in library catalogs, indexes, or databases, you'll want to come up with keywords that will lead to the information you need. Specific commands vary among search engines and databases, but most search engines now offer "Advanced Search" options that allow you to narrow your search by typing keywords into text boxes labeled as follows:

• All of these words
• The exact phrase
• Any of these words
• None of these words

In addition, you may filter the results to include only full-text articles (articles that are available in full online); only certain domains (such as *.edu,* for educational sites; *.gov,* for government sites; or *.org,* for nonprofit sites); and, in library databases, only scholarly, peer-reviewed sites. Type quotation marks around words to search for an exact phrase: "Twitter revolution" or "Neil Gaiman."

Some databases may require you to limit searches through the use of various symbols or Boolean operators (AND, OR, NOT). See the Advanced Search instructions for help with such symbols, which may be called *field tags.*

If a search turns up too many sources, be more specific (*homeopathy* instead of *medicine*). If your original keywords don't generate good results, try synonyms (*home remedy* instead of *folk medicine*). Keep in mind that searching requires flexibility, both in the words you use and the methods you try.

Evaluating Sources

Searching the *Health Source* database for information on the incidence of meningitis among college students, you find seventeen articles. An "exact words" *Google* search yields thirty-seven. How do you decide which sources to read? The following questions can help you select reliable and useful sources.

- *Is the source relevant?* Look at the title and at any introductory material to see what it covers. Does the source appear to relate directly to your purpose? What will it add to your work?

- *What are the author's credentials?* Has the author written other works on this subject? Is he or she known for taking a particular position on it? If the author's credentials are not stated, you might do a Web search to see what else you can learn about him or her.

- *What is the stance?* Does the source cover various points of view or advocate only one perspective? Does its title suggest a certain slant? If you're evaluating a website, check to see whether it includes links to sites expressing other perspectives.

- *Who is the publisher?* Books published by university presses and articles in scholarly journals are peer-reviewed by experts in the field before they are published. Those produced for a general audience do not always undergo such rigorous review and factchecking. At well-established publishing houses, however, submissions are usually vetted by experienced editors or even editorial boards.

- *If the source is a website, who is the sponsor?* Is the site maintained by an organization, interest group, government agency, or individual? If the site doesn't give this information on its homepage, look for clues in the URL domain: *.edu* is used mostly by colleges and universities, *.gov* by government agencies, *.org* by nonprofit organizations, *.mil* by the military, and *.com* by commercial organizations. Be aware that the sponsor may have an agenda—to argue a position, present biased information, or sell a product—and that text on the site does not necessarily undergo rigorous review or factchecking.

- *What is the level of the material?* Texts written for a general audience might be easier to understand but may not be authoritative enough for academic work. Scholarly texts will be more authoritative but may be harder to comprehend.

- *How current is the source?* Check to see when books and articles were published and when websites were last updated. (If a site lists no date, see if links to other sites still work; if not, the site is probably too dated to use.) A recent publication date or updating, however, does not necessarily mean the source is better—some topics require current information whereas others call for older sources.

- *Does the source include other useful information?* Is there a bibliography that might lead you to additional materials? How current or authoritative are the sources it cites?

Taking Notes

When you find material that will be useful to your argument, take careful notes.

- *Use index cards, a computer file, or a notebook,* labeling each entry with information that will allow you to keep track of where it comes from—author, title, the pages or the URL, and (for online sources) the date of access.

- *Take notes in your own words and use your own sentence patterns.* If you make a note that is a detailed paraphrase, label it as such so that you'll know to provide appropriate documentation if you use it.

- *If you find wording that you'd like to quote,* be sure to enclose the exact words in quotation marks to distinguish your source's words from your own.

- *Label each note with a subject heading* so you can organize your notes easily when constructing an outline for your paper.

Incorporating Source Materials into Your Text

There are many ways to incorporate source materials into your own text. Three of the most common are quoting, paraphrasing, or summarizing. Let's look at the differences between these three forms of reference, and then consider when to use each one and how to work these references into your text.

Quoting

When you quote someone else's words, you reproduce their language exactly, in quotation marks—though you can add your own words in brackets or omit unnecessary words in the original by using ellipsis marks (. . .). This example from Mary Roach's "How to Know If You Are Dead" uses all of these conventions:

> In her analysis of the life-saving role of human cadavers, Mary Roach notes that "a gurney with a [newly deceased] cadaver commands no urgency. It is wheeled by a single person, . . . like a shopping cart" (167).

Paraphrasing

When you paraphrase, you restate information from a source in your own words, using your own sentence structures. Because a paraphrase includes all the main points of the source, it is usually about the same length as the original.

Here is a paragraph from Diane Ackerman's essay "Why Leaves Turn Color in the Fall," followed by two sample paraphrases. The first demonstrates some of the challenges of paraphrasing.

ORIGINAL SOURCE

Where do the colors come from? Sunlight rules most living things with its golden edicts. When the days begin to shorten, soon after the summer solstice on June 21, a tree reconsiders its leaves. All summer it feeds them so they can process sunlight, but in the dog days of summer the tree begins pulling nutrients back into its trunk and roots, pares down, and gradually chokes off its leaves. A corky layer of cells forms at the leaves' slender petioles, then scars over. Undernourished, the leaves stop producing the pigment chlorophyll, and photosynthesis ceases. Animals can migrate, hibernate, or store food to prepare for winter. But where can a tree go? It survives by dropping its leaves, and by the end of autumn only a few fragile threads of fluid-carrying xylem hold leaves to their stems.

UNACCEPTABLE PARAPHRASE

Ackerman tells us where the colors of leaves come from. The amount of sunlight is the trigger, as is true for most living things. At the end of June, as daylight lessens, a tree begins to treat its leaves differently. It feeds them all summer so they can turn sunlight into food, but in August a tree begins to redirect its food into its trunk and roots, gradually choking the leaves. A corky group of cells develops at the petioles, and a scar forms. By autumn, the leaves don't have enough food, so they stop producing chlorophyll, and photosynthesis also stops. Although animals are able to migrate, hibernate, or stow food for the winter, a tree cannot go anywhere. It survives only by dropping its leaves, and by the time winter comes only a few leaves remain on their stems.

This first paraphrase borrows too much of the language of the original or changes it only slightly. It also follows the original sentence structure too closely. The following paraphrase avoids both of these pitfalls.

ACCEPTABLE PARAPHRASE

Ackerman explains why leaves change color. Diminishing sunlight is the main instigator. A tree nourishes its leaves—and encourages photosynthesis—for most of the summer. By August, however, as daylight continues to lessen, a tree starts to reroute its food to the roots and trunk, a process that saves the tree but eventually kills the leaves. In autumn, because the leaves are almost starving, they can neither manufacture chlorophyll to stay green nor carry out photosynthesis. By this time, the base of the petiole, or leaf's stem, has hardened, in preparation for the final drop. Unlike animals, who have many ways to get ready for winter—hiding food ahead of time, moving to a warm climate, sleeping through winter—a tree is immobile. It can make it through the winter only by losing its leaves (257).

Summarizing

Unlike a paraphrase, a summary does not present all the details in the original source, so it is generally as brief as possible. Summaries may boil down an entire book or essay into a single sentence, or they may take a paragraph or more to present the main ideas. Here, for example, is a summary of the Ackerman paragraph:

> In late summer and fall, Ackerman explains, trees put most of their food into their roots and trunk, which causes leaves to change color and die but enables trees to live through the winter (257).

Deciding Whether to Quote, Paraphrase, or Summarize

Follow these rules of thumb to determine whether you should quote a source directly, paraphrase it in detail, or merely summarize the main points.

- *Quote* a text when the exact wording is critical to making your point (or that of an authority you wish to cite), or when the wording itself is part of what you're analyzing.
- *Paraphrase* when the meaning of a text is important to your argument but the original language is not essential, or when you're clarifying or interpreting the ideas (not the words) in the text.
- *Summarize* when the main points of the text are important to your argument but the details can be left out in the interest of conciseness.

Using Signal Phrases

When you quote, paraphrase, or summarize a source, identify your source clearly and use a signal phrase ("she says," "he thinks") to distinguish the words and ideas of your source from your own. Consider this example:

> Professor and textbook author Elaine Tyler May claims that many high school history textbooks are too bland to interest young readers (531).

This sentence summarizes a general position about the effectiveness of certain textbooks ("too bland"), and it attributes that view to a particular authority (Elaine

Tyler May), citing her credentials (professor, textbook author) for speaking as an authority on the subject. By using the signal phrase "claims that," the sentence also distinguishes the words and ideas of the source from those of the writers.

The verb you use in a signal phrase can be neutral (*says* or *thinks*), or it can indicate your (or your source's) stance toward the subject. In this case, the use of the verb *claims* suggests that what the source says is arguable (or that the writer of the sentence believes it is). The signal verb you choose can influence your reader's understanding of the sentence and of your attitude toward what it says.

Acknowledging Sources and Avoiding Plagiarism

As a writer, you must acknowledge any words and ideas that come from others. There are numerous reasons for doing so: to give credit where credit is due, to recognize the various authorities and many perspectives you have considered, to show readers where they can find your sources, and to situate your own arguments in the ongoing academic conversation. Using other people's words and ideas without acknowledgment is plagiarism, a serious academic and ethical offense.

MATERIAL THAT DOESN'T HAVE TO BE ACKNOWLEDGED

- Facts that are common knowledge, such as the name of the current president of the United States
- Well-known statements accompanied by a signal phrase: "As John F. Kennedy said, 'Ask not what your country can do for you; ask what you can do for your country.'"

MATERIAL THAT REQUIRES ACKNOWLEDGMENT

- Direct quotations, paraphrases, and summaries
- Arguable statements and any information that is not commonly known (statistics and other data)
- The personal or professional opinions and assertions of others
- Visuals that you did not create yourself (charts, photographs, and so on)
- Collaborative help you received from others

Plagiarism is (1) using another writer's exact words without quotation marks, (2) using another writer's words or ideas without in-text citation or other documentation, (3) paraphrasing or summarizing someone else's ideas using language or sentence structure that is close to the original. The following practices will help you avoid plagiarizing:

- *Take careful notes*, clearly labeling quotations and using your own phrasing and sentence structure in paraphrases and summaries.

- *Check all paraphrases and summaries* to be sure they are stated in *your* words and sentence structures—and that you put quotation marks around any of the source's original phrasing.

- *Know what sources you must document*, and identify them both in the text and in a works-cited list.

- *Check to see that all quotations are documented;* it is not enough just to include quotation marks or indent a block quotation.

- *Be especially careful with online material*—copying source material directly into a document you are writing invites plagiarism. Like other sources, information from the Web must be acknowledged.

- *Recognize that plagiarism has consequences.* A scholar's work will be discredited if it too closely resembles the work of another scholar. Journalists who plagiarize lose their jobs, and students routinely fail courses or are dismissed from school when they are caught cheating—all too often by submitting essays that they have purchased from online "research" sites.

So, don't take the chance. If you're having trouble with an assignment, ask your instructor for assistance. Or visit your school's writing center. Writing centers can help with advice on all aspects of your writing, including acknowledging sources and avoiding plagiarism.

Documentation

Taken collectively, all the information you provide about sources is your *documentation.* Many organizations and publishers—for example, the American Psychological Association (APA), the University of Chicago Press, and the Council of Science Editors (CSE)—have their own documentation styles. The focus here is on the documentation system of the Modern Language Association (MLA) because it is one of the most common systems used in college courses, especially in the liberal arts.

See pp. 725–34 for a sample paper with MLA-style citations. The MLA's documentation system has two basic parts (1) brief in-text references for quotations, paraphrases, or summaries and (2) more-detailed information for each in-text reference in a list of works cited at the end of the text. MLA style requires that each item in your works-cited list include the following information: author, editor, or organization; title of work; place of publication; publisher; date of publication; medium of publication; and, for online sources, date when you accessed the source. Here is an example of how the two parts work together. Note that you can identify the author either in a signal phrase or in parentheses:

IN-TEXT CITATIONS (WITH AND WITHOUT SIGNAL PHRASE)

As Lester Faigley puts it, "The world has become a bazaar from which to shop for an individual 'lifestyle'" (12).

As one observer suggests, "The world has become a bazaar from which to shop for an individual 'lifestyle'" (Faigley 12).

CORRESPONDING WORKS-CITED REFERENCE

Faigley, Lester. *Fragments of Rationality: Postmodernity and the Subject of Composition.* Pittsburgh: U of Pittsburgh P, 1992. Print.

MLA In-Text Documentation

Brief documentation in your text makes clear to your reader what you took from a source and where within the source you found the information. As you cite each source, you will need to decide whether or not to name the author in a signal phrase—"as Toni Morrison writes"—or in parentheses—"(Morrison 24)." For either style of reference, try to put the parenthetical citation at the end of the sentence or as close as possible to the material you've cited without awkwardly interrupting the sentence. When citing a direct quotation (as in no. 1), note that the parenthetical reference comes after the closing quotation marks but before the period at the end of the sentence.

1. AUTHOR NAMED IN A SIGNAL PHRASE

If you mention the author in a signal phrase, put only the page number(s) in parentheses. Do not write *page* or *p.*

> McCullough describes John Adams as having "the hands of a man accustomed to pruning his own trees, cutting his own hay, and splitting his own firewood" (18).

2. AUTHOR NAMED IN PARENTHESES

If you do not mention the author in a signal phrase, put his or her last name in parentheses along with the page number(s). Do not use punctuation between the name and the page number(s).

> One biographer describes John Adams as someone who was not a stranger to manual labor (McCullough 18).

3. AFTER A BLOCK QUOTATION

When quoting more than three lines of poetry, more than four lines of prose, or dialogue between two or more characters from a drama, set off the quotation from the rest of your text, indenting it one inch (or ten spaces) from the left margin. Do not use quotation marks, and place any parenthetical documentation *after* the final punctuation.

> In *Eastward to Tartary*, Kaplan captures ancient and contemporary Antioch:
>
>> At the height of its glory in the Roman-Byzantine age, when it had an amphitheater, public baths, aqueducts, and sewage pipes, half a million people lived in Antioch. Today the population is only 125,000. With sour relations between Turkey and Syria, and unstable politics throughout the Middle East, Antioch is now a backwater—seedy and tumbledown, with relatively few tourists. I found it altogether charming. (123)

4. TWO OR MORE AUTHORS

For a work by two or three authors, name all the authors, either in a signal phrase or in parentheses.

> Carlson and Ventura's stated goal is to introduce Julio Cortázar, Marjorie Agosín, and other Latin American writers to an audience of English-speaking adolescents (5).

For a work with four or more authors, you can mention all their names *or* just the name of the first author followed by *et al.*, which means "and others."

> One popular survey of American literature breaks the contents into sixteen thematic groupings (Anderson, Brinnin, Leggett, Arpin, and Toth 19–24).

> One popular survey of American literature breaks the contents into sixteen thematic groupings (Anderson et al. 19–24).

5. ORGANIZATION OR GOVERNMENT AS AUTHOR

Cite the organization either in a signal phrase or in parentheses. It's acceptable to shorten long names.

> The U.S. government can be direct when it wants to be. For example, it sternly warns, "If you are overpaid, we will recover any payments not due you" (Social Security Administration 12).

6. AUTHOR UNKNOWN

If you can't determine an author, use the work's title or a shortened version of the title in the parentheses.

> A powerful editorial in last week's paper asserts that healthy liver donor Mike Hurewitz died because of "frightening" faulty postoperative care ("Every Patient's Nightmare").

7. LITERARY WORKS

When referring to literary works that are available in many different editions, you need to cite additional information so that readers of any edition can locate the text you are citing.

Novels: Give the page and chapter number of the edition you are using.

> In *Pride and Prejudice*, Mrs. Bennett shows no warmth toward Jane and Elizabeth when they return from Netherfield (105; ch. 12).

Verse plays: Give the act, scene, and line numbers; separate them with periods.

> Macbeth develops the vision theme when he addresses the Ghost with "Thou hast no speculation in those eyes / Which thou dost glare with" (3.3.96–97).

Poems: Give the part and line numbers (separated by periods). If a poem has only line numbers, use the word *line(s)* in the first reference.

The mere in *Beowulf* is described as "not a pleasant place!" (line 1372). Later, it is called "the awful place" (1378).

8. TWO OR MORE WORKS CITED TOGETHER

If you cite the works in the same parentheses, separate the references with a semicolon.

> Critics have looked at both *Pride and Prejudice* and *Frankenstein* from a cultural perspective (Tanner 7; Smith viii).

9. SOURCE QUOTED IN ANOTHER SOURCE

When you are quoting text that you found quoted in another source, use the abbreviation *qtd. in* in the parenthetical reference.

> Charlotte Brontë wrote to G. H. Lewes: "Why do you like Miss Austen so very much? I am puzzled on that point" (qtd. in Tanner 7).

10. WORK WITHOUT PAGE NUMBERS

For works without page numbers, including many online sources, identify the source using the author or other information either in a signal phrase or in parentheses. If the source has paragraph or section numbers, use them with the abbreviations *par.* or *sec.*

> Studies reported in *Scientific American* and elsewhere show that music training helps children to be better at multitasking later in life ("Hearing the Music," par. 2).

11. AN ENTIRE WORK

If you refer to an entire work rather than a part of it, there's no need to include page numbers.

> At least one observer considers Turkey and Central Asia to be explosive (Kaplan).

MLA List of Works Cited

A works-cited list provides full bibliographic information for every source cited in your text. Here's some general advice to help you format your list:

- Start the list on a new page.
- Center the title (Works Cited) one inch from the top of the page.
- Double-space the whole list.
- Begin each entry flush with the left-hand margin and indent subsequent lines one-half inch or five spaces.
- Alphabetize entries by the author's last name. If a work has no identifiable author, use the first major word of the title (disregard *A, An, The*).
- If you cite more than one work by a single author, list them all alphabetically by title, and use three hyphens in place of the author's name after the first entry (see no. 3 for an example).

Books

For most books, you'll need to list the author; the title and any subtitle; and the place of publication, publisher, date, and the medium—*Print*. A few details to note when citing books:

- *Authors*: List the primary author last-name-first, and include any middle name or initial after the first name.
- *Titles*: Capitalize all principal words in titles and subtitles, including short verbs such as *is* and *are*. Do not capitalize *a, an, the, to,* or any preposition or conjunction unless they begin a title or subtitle. Italicize book titles, but place quotation marks around works within books.
- *Publication place and publisher*: If there's more than one city listed on the title page, use only the first. Use a shortened form of the publisher's name (Norton for W. W. Norton & Company; Princeton UP for Princeton University Press).
- *Dates*: If more than one year is given, use the most recent one.

1. ONE AUTHOR

Miller, Susan. *Assuming the Positions: Cultural Pedagogy and the Politics of Commonplace Writing*. Pittsburgh: U of Pittsburgh P, 1998. Print.

2. TWO OR MORE WORKS BY THE SAME AUTHOR(S)

Give the author's name in the first entry, and then use three hyphens in the author slot for each of the subsequent works, listing them alphabetically by the first important word of each title.

Kaplan, Robert D. *The Coming Anarchy: Shattering the Dreams of the Post Cold War.* New York: Random, 2000. Print.

———. *Eastward to Tartary: Travels in the Balkans, the Middle East, and the Caucasus.* New York: Random, 2000. Print.

3. TWO OR THREE AUTHORS

Follow the order of names on the book's title page. List the second and third authors first-name-first.

Malless, Stanley, and Jeffrey McQuain. *Coined by God: Words and Phrases That First Appear in the English Translations of the Bible.* New York: Norton, 2003. Print.

Sebranek, Patrick, Verne Meyer, and Dave Kemper. *Writers INC: A Guide to Writing, Thinking, and Learning.* Burlington: Write Source, 1990. Print.

4. FOUR OR MORE AUTHORS

You may give each author's name or the name of the first author only, followed by *et al.* (Latin for "and others").

Anderson, Robert, et al. *Elements of Literature: Literature of the United States.* Austin: Holt, 1993. Print.

5. ORGANIZATION OR GOVERNMENT AS AUTHOR

Diagram Group. *The Macmillan Visual Desk Reference.* New York: Macmillan, 1993. Print.

For a government publication, give the name of the government first, followed by the names of any department and agency.

United States. Dept. of Health and Human Services. Natl. Inst. of Mental Health. *Autism Spectrum Disorders.* Washington: GPO, 2004. Print.

6. ANTHOLOGY

Use this model only when you are citing the whole anthology or the contributions of the editor(s).

Kitchen, Judith, and Mary Paumier Jones, eds. *In Short: A Collection of Brief Creative Nonfiction.* New York: Norton, 1996. Print.

7. WORK(S) IN AN ANTHOLOGY

Give the inclusive page numbers of the selection you are citing.

> Achebe, Chinua. "Uncle Ben's Choice." *The Seagull Reader: Literature*. Ed.
>   Joseph Kelly. New York: Norton, 2005. 23–27. Print.

To document two or more selections from one anthology, list each selection by author and title, followed by the editors' names and the pages of the selection. In addition, include in your works-cited list an entry for the anthology itself (no. 6).

> Hiestand, Emily. "Afternoon Tea." Kitchen and Jones 65–67.

> Ozick, Cynthia. "The Shock of Teapots." Kitchen and Jones 68–71.

8. AUTHOR AND EDITOR

Start with the author if you've cited the text itself.

> Austen, Jane. *Emma*. Ed. Stephen M. Parrish. New York: Norton, 2000. Print.

Start with the editor if you've cited his or her contribution.

> Parrish, Stephen M., ed. *Emma*. By Jane Austen. New York: Norton, 2000.
>   Print.

9. TRANSLATION

> Dostoevsky, Fyodor. *Crime and Punishment*. Trans. Richard Pevear and
>   Larissa Volokhonsky. New York: Vintage, 1993. Print.

10. FOREWORD, INTRODUCTION, PREFACE, OR AFTERWORD

> Tanner, Tony. Introduction. *Pride and Prejudice*. By Jane Austen. London:
>   Penguin, 1972. 7–46. Print.

11. MULTIVOLUME WORK

If you cite all the volumes, give the number of volumes after the title.

> Sandburg, Carl. *Abraham Lincoln: The War Years*. 4 vols. New York:
>   Harcourt, 1939. Print.

If you cite only one volume, give the volume number after the title.

> Sandburg, Carl. *Abraham Lincoln: The War Years*. Vol. 2. New York:
>   Harcourt, 1939. Print.

12. EDITION OTHER THAN THE FIRST

> Gibaldi, Joseph. *MLA Handbook for Writers of Research Papers*. 6th ed. New York: MLA, 2003. Print.

13. ARTICLE IN A REFERENCE BOOK

Provide the author's name if the article is signed. If a reference book is well known, give only the edition and the year of publication.

> "Iraq." *The New Encyclopaedia Brittanica*. 15th ed. 2007. Print.

If a reference book is less familiar, give complete publication information.

> Benton-Cohen, Katherine. "Women in the Reform and Progressive Era." *A History of Women in the United States*. Ed. Doris Weatherford. 4 vols. Danbury, CT: Grolier, 2004. Print.

Periodicals

For most articles, you'll need to list the author, the article title and any subtitle, the periodical title, any volume and issue number, the date, inclusive page numbers, and the medium—*Print*. A few details to note when citing periodicals:

- *Authors*: Format authors as you would for a book.
- *Titles*: Capitalize titles and subtitles as you would for a book. Omit any initial *A*, *An*, or *The*. Italicize periodical titles; place article titles within quotation marks.
- *Dates*: Abbreviate the names of months except for May, June, and July: Jan., Feb., Mar., Apr., Aug., Sept., Oct., Nov., Dec. Journals paginated by both volume and issue need only the year (in parentheses).
- *Pages*: If an article does not fall on consecutive pages, give the first page with a plus sign (55+).

14. ARTICLE IN A JOURNAL

> Bartley, William. "Imagining the Future in *The Awakening*." *College English* 62.6 (2000): 719–46. Print.

For journals that do not have volume numbers, give the issue number after the title, followed by the year of publication and inclusive page numbers.

> Flynn, Kevin. "The Railway in Canadian Poetry." *Canadian Literature* 174 (2002): 70–95. Print.

15. ARTICLE IN A MAGAZINE

> Cloud, John. "Should SATs Matter?" *Time* 12 Mar. 2001: 62+. Print.

For a monthly magazine, include only the month and year.

> Fellman, Bruce. "Leading the Libraries." *Yale Alumni Magazine* Feb. 2002:
> 26–31. Print.

16. ARTICLE IN A DAILY NEWSPAPER

> Springer, Shira. "Celtics Reserves Are Whizzes vs. Wizards." *Boston Globe*
> 14 Mar. 2005: D4+. Print.

If you are documenting a particular edition of a newspaper, specify the edition (*late ed.*, *natl. ed.*, and so on) after the date.

> Margulius, David L. "Smarter Call Centers: At Your Service?" *New York
> Times* 14 Mar. 2002, late ed.: G1+. Print.

17. UNSIGNED ARTICLE

> "Coal Mine Inspections Fall Short." *Atlanta Journal-Constitution* 18 Nov.
> 2007: A7. Print.

18. EDITORIAL OR LETTER TO THE EDITOR

> "Gas, Cigarettes Are Safe to Tax." Editorial. *Lakeville Journal* 17 Feb. 2005:
> A10. Print.

> Festa, Roger. "Social Security: Another Phony Crisis." Letter. *Lakeville
> Journal* 17 Feb. 2005: A10. Print.

19. BOOK REVIEW

> Frank, Jeffrey. "Body Count." Rev. of *The Exception*, by Christian Jungersen.
> *New Yorker* 30 July 2007: 86–87. Print.

Online Sources

Not every online source gives you all the data that the MLA would like to see in a works-cited entry. Ideally, you'll be able to list the author's name, the title, information about print publication (if applicable), information about electronic publication (title of site, editor, date of first electronic publication and/or most recent revision, name of publisher or sponsoring institution), the publication medium, date of access, and, if necessary, a URL. Here are a few details to note when citing online sources:

- *Authors or editors and title*: Format authors and titles as you would for a print book or periodical.

- *Publisher*: If the name of the publisher or sponsoring institution is unavailable, use *N.p.*

- *Dates*: Abbreviate the months as you would for a print periodical. Although MLA asks for the date when materials were first posted or most recently updated, you won't always be able to find that information; if it's unavailable, use *n.d.* Be sure to include the date on which you accessed the source.

- *Pages*: If the citation calls for page numbers but the source is unpaginated, use *n. pag.* in place of page numbers.

- *Medium*: Indicate the medium—Web, email, PDF, MP3, jpeg, and so on.

- *URL*: MLA assumes that readers can locate most sources on the Web by searching for the author, title, or other identifying information, so they don't require a URL for most online sources. When readers cannot locate the source without a URL, give the address of the website in angle brackets. When a URL won't fit on one line, break it only after a slash (and do not add a hyphen). If a URL is very long, consider using the one from the site's homepage or search page instead.

20. ENTIRE WEBSITE OR PERSONAL WEBSITE

Zalta, Edward N., ed. *Stanford Encyclopedia of Philosophy*. Metaphysics Research Lab, Center for the Study of Language and Information, Stanford U, 2007. Web. 14 Nov. 2010.

Nunberg, Geoffrey. Home page. School of Information, U of California, Berkeley, 2009. Web. 3 Apr. 2009.

21. WORK FROM A WEBSITE

Buff, Rachel Ida. "Becoming American." *Immigration History Research Center*. U of Minnesota, 24 Mar. 2008. Web. 4 Apr. 2008.

22. ONLINE BOOK OR PART OF A BOOK

Cite a book you access online as you would a print book, adding the name of the site or database, the medium, and the date of access. (See next page for examples.)

Anderson, Sherwood. *Winesburg, Ohio.* New York: B. W. Huebsch, 1919. *Bartleby.com.* Web. 7 Apr. 2008.

If you are citing a part of a book, put the part in quotation marks before the book title. If the online book is paginated, give the pages; if not, use *N. pag.*

Anderson, Sherwood. "The Philosopher." *Winesburg, Ohio.* New York: B. W. Huebsch, 1919. N. pag. *Bartleby.com.* Web. 7 Apr. 2008.

To cite a book you've downloaded onto a Kindle, Nook, or other digital device, follow the setup for a print book, but indicate the ebook format at the end of your citation.

Larson, Erik. *The Devil in the White City: Murder, Mayhem, and Madness at the Fair That Changed America.* New York: Vintage, 2004. Kindle.

23. ARTICLE IN AN ONLINE JOURNAL

If a journal does not number pages or if it numbers each article separately, use *n. pag.* in place of page numbers.

Moore, Greggory. "The Process of Life in *2001: A Space Odyssey.*" *Images: A Journal of Film and Popular Culture* 9 (2000): n. pag. Web. 12 May 2009.

24. ARTICLE IN AN ONLINE MAGAZINE

Landsburg, Steven E. "Putting All Your Potatoes in One Basket: The Economic Lessons of the Great Famine." *Slate.* Slate, 13 Mar. 2001. Web. 8 Dec. 2007.

25. ARTICLE ACCESSED THROUGH DATABASE

For articles accessed through a library's subscription services, such as InfoTrac and EBSCOhost, cite the publication information for the source, followed by the name of the database.

Bowman, James. "Moody Blues." *American Spectator* June 1999: 64–65. *Academic Search Premier.* Web. 15 Mar. 2005.

26. ARTICLE IN AN ONLINE NEWSPAPER

Mitchell, Dan. "Being Skeptical of Green." *New York Times.* New York Times, 24 Nov. 2007. Web. 26 Nov. 2007.

27. ONLINE EDITORIAL

"Outsourcing Your Life." Editorial. *ChicagoTribune.com*. Chicago Tribune, 24 Nov. 2004. Web. 3 Jan. 2008.

28. BLOG ENTRY

If the entry has no title, use "Blog entry" (without quotation marks). Cite a whole blog as you would a personal website (no. 20). If the publisher or sponsor is unavailable, use *N.p.*

Gladwell, Malcolm. "Underdogs." N.p., 13 May 2009. Web. 11 Aug. 2011.

29. EMAIL CORRESPONDENCE

Smith, William. "Teaching Grammar—Some Thoughts." Message to the author. 15 Feb. 2008. Email.

30. POSTING TO AN ELECTRONIC FORUM

Mintz, Stephen H. "Manumission During the Revolution." H-Net List on Slavery. Michigan State U, 14 Sept. 2006. Web. 18 Apr. 2009.

31. ARTICLE IN AN ONLINE REFERENCE WORK OR WIKI

"Dubai." *MSN Encarta*. Microsoft Corporation, 2008. Web. 20 June 2008.

For a wiki, cite the date of the last modification or update as the publication date.

"Pi." *Wikipedia*. Wikimedia Fundation, 6 Aug. 2011. Web. 11 Aug. 2011.

32. PODCAST

Blumberg, Alex, and Adam Davidson. "The Giant Pool of Money." Host Ira Glass. *This American Life*. Chicago Public Radio, 9 May 2008. Web. 18 Sept. 2008.

Other Kinds of Sources

Many of the sources in this section can be found online. If there is no Web model here, start with the guidelines most appropriate for the source you need to cite, omit the original medium, and end your citation with the title of the website, italicized; the medium (Web); and the day, month, and year of access.

33. ART (PRINT AND ONLINE)

Van Gogh, Vincent. *The Potato Eaters*. 1885. Oil on canvas. Van Gogh
  Museum, Amsterdam.

Warhol, Andy. *Self-Portrait*. 1979. Polaroid Polacolor print. J. Paul Getty
  Museum, Los Angeles. *The Getty*. Web. 5 Jan. 2008.

34. CARTOON OR COMIC STRIP (PRINT AND ONLINE)

Chast, Roz. "The Three Wise Men of Thanksgiving." Cartoon. *New Yorker* 1
  Dec. 2003: 174. Print.

Adams, Scott. "Dilbert." Comic strip. *Dilbert.com*. United Features Syndicate,
  9 Nov. 2007. Web. 26 Nov. 2007.

35. CD-ROM OR DVD-ROM

Cite like a book, but indicate any pertinent information about the edition or version.

Othello. Princeton: Films for the Humanities and Sciences, 1998. CD-ROM.

36. FILM, DVD, OR VIDEO CLIP

Super 8. Dir. J. J. Abrams. Perf. Joel Courtney, Kyle Chandler, and Elle
  Fanning. Paramount, 2011. Film.

To cite a particular person's work, start with that name.

Cody, Diablo, scr. *Juno*. Dir. Jason Reitman. Perf. Ellen Page, Nichael Cera,
  Jennifer Garner, and Jason Bateman. Fox Searchlight, 2007. DVD.

Cite a video clip from YouTube or a similar site as you would a short work from a
website.

PivotMasterDX, dir. "Storaged." *YouTube*. YouTube, 29 Apr. 2009. Web.
  11 Aug. 2011.

37. BROADCAST, PUBLISHED, AND PERSONAL INTERVIEW

Gates, Henry Louis, Jr. Interview. *Fresh Air*. NPR. WNYC, New York. 9 Apr.
  2002. Radio.

Brzezinski, Zbigniew. "Against the Neocons." *American Prospect* Mar. 2005:
  26–27. Print.

Berra, Yogi. Personal interview. 17 June 2001.

38. PUBLISHED LETTER

White, E. B. Letter to Carol Angell. 28 May 1970. *Letters of E. B. White*. Ed. Dorothy Lobarno Guth. New York: Harper, 1976. 600. Print.

39. MAP (PRINT AND ONLINE)

Toscana. Map. Milan: Touring Club Italiano, 1987. Print.

"Austin, TX." Map. *Google Maps*. Google, 11 Aug. 2011. Web. 11 Aug. 2011.

40. MUSICAL SCORE

Beethoven, Ludwig van. *String Quartet No. 13 in B Flat, Op. 130*. 1825. New York: Dover, 1970. Print.

41. SOUND RECORDING (WITH ONLINE VERSION)

Whether you list the composer, conductor, or performer first depends on where you want to place the emphasis.

Beethoven, Ludwig van. *Missa Solemnis*. Perf. Westminster Choir and New York Philharmonic. Cond. Leonard Bernstein. Sony, 1992. CD.

The Beatles. "Can't Buy Me Love." *A Hard Day's Night*. United Artists, 1964. MP3 file.

Davis, Miles. "So What." *Birth of the Cool*. Columbia, 1959. *Miles Davis*. Web. 14 Feb. 2009.

42. TELEVISION OR RADIO PROGRAM (WITH ONLINE VERSION)

"Stirred." *The West Wing*. Writ. Aaron Sorkin, Dir. Jeremy Kagan. Perf. Martin Sheen. NBC. WPTV, West Palm Beach, 3 Apr. 2002. Television.

"Bush's War." *Frontline*. Writ. and Dir. Michael Kirk. *PBS.org*. PBS, 24 Mar. 2008. Web. 10 Apr. 2009.

43. MP3, JPEG, PDF, OR OTHER DIGITAL FILE

For downloaded songs, photographs, PDFs, and other documents stored on your computer or another digital device, follow the guidelines for the type of work you are citing (art, journal article, and so on) and give the file type as the medium. (See next page for examples.)

Talking Heads. "Burning Down the House." *Speaking in Tongues.* Sire, 1983. Digital file.

Taylor, Aaron. "Twilight of the Idols: Performance, Melodramatic Villainy, and *Sunset Boulevard." Journal of Film and Video* 59 (2007): 13–31. PDF file.

Citing Sources Not Covered by MLA

To cite a source that isn't covered by the MLA guidelines, look for models similar to the source you're citing. Give any information readers will need in order to find the source themselves—author, title, subtitle; publisher and/or sponsor; medium; dates; and any other pertinent information. You might want to try out the citation yourself, to be sure it will lead others to your source.

Sample Student Research Paper

Dylan Borchers wrote the following research paper for a first-year writing class. He used MLA style for his essay, but documentation styles vary from discipline to discipline, so ask your instructor if you're not sure which style you should use.

Dylan Borchers

Professor Bullock

English 102, Section 4

31 March 2009

Heading includes your full name and identifies the teacher, course, and date.

Against the Odds:

Center the title.

Harry S. Truman and the Election of 1948

"Thomas E. Dewey's Election as President Is a Foregone

Double-space throughout.

Conclusion," read a headline in the *New York Times* during the

presidential election race between incumbent Democrat Harry S.

Truman and his Republican challenger, Thomas E. Dewey. Earlier,

Life magazine had put Dewey on its cover with the caption "The

Next President of the United States" (qtd. in "1948 Truman-Dewey

Election"). In a *Newsweek* survey of fifty prominent political writers,

each one predicted Truman's defeat, and *Time* correspondents

declared that Dewey would carry 39 of the 48 states (Donaldson

210). Nearly every major media outlet across the United States

endorsed Dewey and lambasted Truman. As historian Robert H.

Ferrell observes, even Truman's wife, Bess, thought he would be

beaten (270).

If you name the author of a source in a signal phrase, give the page numbers in parentheses.

The results of an election are not so easily predicted, as the

famous photograph on page 2 shows. Not only did Truman win the

election, but he won by a significant margin, with 303 electoral

votes and 24,179,259 popular votes, compared to Dewey's 189

electoral votes and 21,991,291 popular votes (Donaldson 204–07). In

fact, many historians and political analysts argue that Truman

Fig. 1. President Harry S. Truman holds up an Election Day edition of the *Chicago Daily Tribune*, which mistakenly announced "Dewey Defeats Truman." St. Louis, 4 Nov. 1948 (Rollins).

would have won by an even greater margin had third-party Progressive candidate Henry A. Wallace not split the Democratic vote in New York State and Dixiecrat Strom Thurmond not won four states in the South (McCullough 711). Although Truman's defeat was heavily predicted, those predictions themselves, Dewey's passiveness as a campaigner, and Truman's zeal turned the tide for a Truman victory.

    In the months preceding the election, public opinion polls predicted that Dewey would win by a large margin. Pollster Elmo Roper stopped polling in September, believing there was no reason to continue, given a seemingly inevitable Dewey landslide. Although the margin narrowed as the election drew near, the other pollsters

Put your last name and the page number in the upper-right corner of each page.

Put illustrations close to the text they relate to. Label with figure number, caption, and parenthetical source citation.

Indent first line of paragraph 5 spaces or $\frac{1}{2}$ inch.

predicted a Dewey win by at least 5 percent (Donaldson 209). Many historians believe that these predictions aided the president in the long run. First, surveys showing Dewey in the lead may have prompted some of Dewey's supporters to feel overconfident about their candidate's chances and therefore to stay home from the polls on Election Day. Second, these same surveys may have energized Democrats to mount late get-out-the-vote efforts ("1948 Truman-Dewey Election"). Other analysts believe that the overwhelming predictions of a Truman loss also kept at home some Democrats who approved of Truman's policies but saw a Truman loss as inevitable. According to political analyst Samuel Lubell, those Democrats may have saved Dewey from an even greater defeat (Hamby, *Man of the People* 465). Whatever the impact on the voters, the polling numbers had a decided effect on Dewey.

Historians and political analysts alike cite Dewey's overly cautious campaign as one of the main reasons Truman was able to achieve victory. Dewey firmly believed in public opinion polls. With all indications pointing to an easy victory, Dewey and his staff believed that all he had to do was bide his time and make no foolish mistakes. Dewey himself said, "When you're leading, don't talk" (qtd. in McCullough 672). Each of Dewey's speeches was well-crafted and well-rehearsed. As the leader in the race, he kept his remarks faultlessly positive, with the result that he failed to deliver a solid message or even mention Truman or any of Truman's policies. Eventually, Dewey began to be perceived as aloof and stuffy. Once

> Give the author and page in parentheses when there's no signal phrase.

> If you quote text that's quoted in another source, cite that source in a parenthetical reference.

If you cite two or more works closely together, give a parenthetical citation for each one.

observer compared him to the plastic groom on top of a wedding cake (Hamby, "Harry S. Truman"), and others noted his stiff, cold demeanor (McCullough 671–74).

As his campaign continued, observers noted that Dewey seemed uncomfortable in crowds, unable to connect with ordinary people. And he made a number of blunders. One took place at a train stop when the candidate, commenting on the number of children in the crowd, said he was glad they had been let out of school for his arrival. Unfortunately for Dewey, it was a Saturday ("1948: The Great Truman Surprise"). Such gaffes gave voters the feeling that Dewey was out of touch with the public.

Again and again through the autumn of 1948, Dewey's campaign speeches failed to address the issues, with the candidate declaring that he did not want to "get down in the gutter" (qtd. in McCullough 701). When told by fellow Republicans that he was losing ground, Dewey insisted that his campaign not alter its course. Even *Time* magazine, though it endorsed and praised him, conceded that his speeches were dull (McCullough 696). According to historian Zachary Karabell, they were "notable only for taking place, not for any specific message" (244). Dewey's numbers in the polls slipped in the weeks before the election, but he still held a comfortable lead over Truman. It would take Truman's famous whistle-stop campaign to make the difference.

Few candidates in U.S. history have campaigned for the presidency with more passion and faith than Harry Truman. In the autumn of 1948, he wrote to his sister, "It will be the greatest campaign any President ever made. Win, lose, or draw, people will know where I stand" (91). For thirty-three days, Truman traveled the nation, giving hundreds of speeches from the back of the *Ferdinand Magellan* railroad car. In the same letter, he described the pace: "We made about 140 stops and I spoke over 147 times, shook hands with at least 30,000 and am in good condition to start out again tomorrow for Wilmington, Philadelphia, Jersey City, Newark, Albany and Buffalo" (91). McCullough writes of Truman's campaign:

> No President in history had ever gone so far in quest of support from the people, or with less cause for the effort, to judge by informed opinion. . . . As a test of his skills and judgment as a professional politician, not to say his stamina and disposition at age sixty-four, it would be like no other experience in his long, often difficult career, as he himself understood perfectly. More than any other event in his public life, or in his presidency thus far, it would reveal the kind of man he was. (655)

He spoke in large cities and small towns, defending his policies and attacking Republicans. As a former farmer and relatively late bloomer, Truman was able to connect with the public. He developed an energetic style, usually speaking from notes rather than from a prepared speech, and often mingled with the crowds that met his train. These crowds grew larger as the campaign

Set off quotations of four or more lines by indenting 1 inch (or 10 spaces).

Put parenthetical references after final punctuation in a block quotation.

progressed. In Chicago, over half a million people lined the streets as he passed, and in St. Paul the crowd numbered over 25,000. When Dewey entered St. Paul two days later, he was greeted by only 7,000 supporters ("1948 Truman-Dewey Election"). Reporters brushed off the large crowds as mere curiosity seekers wanting to see a president (McCullough 682). Yet Truman persisted, even if he often seemed to be the only one who thought he could win. By going directly to the American people and connecting with them, Truman built the momentum needed to surpass Dewey and win the election.

The legacy and lessons of Truman's whistle-stop campaign continue to be studied by political analysts, and politicians today often mimic his campaign methods by scheduling multiple visits to key states, as Truman did. He visited California, Illinois, and Ohio 48 times, compared with 6 visits to those states by Dewey. Political scientist Thomas M. Holbrook concludes that his strategic campaigning in those states and others gave Truman the electoral votes he needed to win (61, 65).

The 1948 election also had an effect on pollsters, who, as Elmo Roper admitted, "couldn't have been more wrong" (qtd. in Karabell 255). *Life* magazine's editors concluded that pollsters as well as reporters and commentators were too convinced of a Dewey victory to analyze the polls seriously, especially the opinions of undecided voters (Karabell 256). Pollsters assumed that undecided voters would vote in the same proportion as decided voters—and that

If you cite a work with no known author, use the title in your parenthetical reference.

turned out to be a false assumption (Karabell 258). In fact, the lopsidedness of the polls might have led voters who supported Truman to call themselves undecided out of an unwillingness to associate themselves with the losing side, further skewing the polls' results (McDonald, Glynn, Kim, and Ostman 152). Such errors led pollsters to change their methods significantly after the 1948 election.

In a work by four or more authors, either cite them all or name the first one followed by *et al.*

After the election, many political analysts, journalists, and historians concluded that the Truman upset was in fact a victory for the American people, who, the *New Republic* noted, "couldn't be ticketed by the polls, knew its own mind and had picked the rather unlikely but courageous figure of Truman to carry its banner" (qtd. in McCullough 715). How "unlikely" is unclear, however; Truman biographer Alonzo Hamby notes that "polls of scholars consistently rank Truman among the top eight presidents in American history" (*Man of the People* 641). But despite Truman's high standing, and despite the fact that the whistle-stop campaign is now part of our political landscape, politicians have increasingly imitated the style of the Dewey campaign, with its "packaged candidate who ran so as not to lose, who steered clear of controversy, and who made a good show of appearing presidential" (Karabell 266). The election of 1948 shows that voters are not necessarily swayed by polls, but it may have presaged the packaging of candidates by public relations experts, to the detriment of public debate on the issues in future presidential elections.

Works Cited

Donaldson, Gary A. *Truman Defeats Dewey*. Lexington: UP of
    Kentucky, 1999. Print.

Ferrell, Robert H. *Harry S. Truman: A Life*. Columbia: U of Missouri P,
    1994. Print.

Hamby, Alonzo L., ed. "Harry S. Truman (1945–1953)."
    AmericanPresident.org. Miller Center of Public Affairs,
    U of Virginia, 11 Dec. 2003. Web. 17 Mar. 2009.

———. *Man of the People: A Life of Harry S. Truman*. New York:
    Oxford UP, 1995. Print.

Holbrook, Thomas M. "Did the Whistle-Stop Campaign Matter?" *PS:
    Political Science and Politics* 35.1 (2002): 59–66. Print.

Karabell, Zachary. *The Last Campaign: How Harry Truman Won the
    1948 Election*. New York: Knopf, 2000. Print.

McCullough, David. *Truman*. New York: Simon & Schuster, 1992. Print.

McDonald, Daniel G., Carroll J. Glynn, Sei-Hill Kim, and Ronald E.
    Ostman. "The Spiral of Silence in the 1948 Presidential
    Election." *Communication Research* 28.2 (2001): 139–55. Print.

"1948: The Great Truman Surprise." *Media and Politics Online
    Projects: Media Coverage of Presidential Campaigns*. Dept. of
    Political Science and International Affairs, Kennesaw State U,
    29 Oct. 2003. Web. 20 Mar. 2009.

"1948 Truman-Dewey Election." *Electronic Government Project:
    Eagleton Digital Archive of American Politics*. Eagleton Inst. of
    Politics, Rutgers, State U of New Jersey, 2004. Web. 19 Mar. 2009.

Center the
heading.

Alphabetize the
list by authors'
last names or by
title for works
with no author.

Begin each
entry at the left
margin; indent
subsequent
lines $\frac{1}{2}$ inch or
five spaces.

If you cite more
than one work
by a single
author, list them
alphabetically
by title, and use
three hyphens
in place of the
author's name.

Rollins, Byron. Untitled photograph. "The First 150 Years: 1948." AP
    History. Associated Press, n.d. Web. 23 Mar. 2009.

Truman, Harry S. "Campaigning, Letter, October 5, 1948." *Harry S.
    Truman*. Ed. Robert H. Ferrell. Washington: CQ P, 2003. 91.
    Print.

Check to be
sure that every
source you use
is in the works
cited list.

Credits

Text

DIANE ACKERMAN: "Why Leaves Turn Color in the Fall" copyright © 1990 by Diane Ackerman, from *A Natural History of the Senses* by Diane Ackerman. Used by permission of Random House, Inc.

GAIL BABILONIA: "The Celebrity Chef" is reprinted from *Dialogues*, Vol. 3, Spring 2004, by permission of the Writing Program, Rutgers, The State University of New Jersey.

DAVID BARBOZA: "Piling on the Cookies," published as "Permutations Push Oreo Far Beyond Cookie Aisle" from *The New York Times*, Oct. 4, 2003. Copyright © 2003 The New York Times. All rights reserved. Used by permission and protected by the Copyright Laws of the United States. The printing, copying, redistribution or retransmission of the Material without express written permission is prohibited.

DAN BARRY: "Cancer's Oddest Effect" Originally published as "My Brain on Chemo: Alive and Alert" from *The New York Times*, Sept. 1, 2009. Copyright © 2009 The New York Times. All rights reserved. Used by permission and protected by the Copyright Laws of the United States. The printing, copying, redistribution or retransmission of the Material without express written permission is prohibited.

DAVE BARRY: "I Will Survive . . . Or at Least I'll be Delayed" from *The Miami Herald*, Aug. 8, 2004. Reprinted with the permission of the author.

LYNDA BARRY: "The Sanctuary of School" by Lynda Barry, originally published in *The New York Times*, Jan. 5, 1992, and used courtesy of Darhansoff & Verrill Literary Agents. Copyright © 1992 by Lynda Barry.

ANNE BERNAYS: "Warrior Day" from *The New York Times*, July 5, 2009. Copyright © 2009 The New York Times. All rights reserved. Used by permission and protected by the Copyright Laws of the United States. The printing, copying, redistribution or retransmission of the Material without express written permission is prohibited.

DYLAN BORCHERS: "Against the Odds: Harry S. Truman and the Election of 1948." Reprinted by permission of the author.

734

JOHN BRANCH: "Perfection in the Horseshoe Pit as the Best Ever Takes His Turn" from *The New York Times*, July 21, 2010. Copyright © 2010 The New York Times. All rights reserved. Used by permission and protected by the Copyright Laws of the United States. The printing, copying, redistribution or retransmission of the Material without express written permission is prohibited.

DAVID BROOKS: "People Like Us" first appeared in *The Atlantic Monthly*, Sept. 2003. Reprinted by permission of the author.

BRUCE CATTON: "Grant and Lee: A Study in Contrasts" by Bruce Catton is reprinted by permission of William B. Catton.

ROGER COHEN: "The Meaning of Life" from *The New York Times*, July 16, 2009. Copyright © 2009 The New York Times. All rights reserved. Used by permission and protected by the Copyright Laws of the United States. The printing, copying, redistribution or retransmission of the Material without express written permission is prohibited.

BILLY COLLINS: "Fishing on the Susquehanna in July" from *Picnic, Lightning* by Billy Collins, copyright © 1998. Reprinted by permission of the University of Pittsburgh Press.

ROBERT CONNORS: "How in the World Do You Get a Skunk Out of a Bottle?" from *Selected Essays of Robert J. Connors*. Every effort has been made to contact the copyright holder of this selection. If you have information that can help us locate this rights holder, please contact Permissions Department, W. W. Norton & Company, Inc., 500 5th Avenue, New York, NY 10110.

EMILY DICKINSON: "The Way I Read a Letter's—this—" is reprinted by the permission of the publishers and the Trustees of Amherst College from *The Poems of Emily Dickinson*, Thomas H. Johnson, ed., Cambridge, Mass.: The Belknap Press of Harvard University Press. Copyright © 1951, 1955, 1979, 1983 by the President and Fellows of Harvard College.

ANNIE DILLARD: From *An American Childhood* by Annie Dillard. Copyright © 1987 by Annie Dillard. Reprinted by permission of HarperCollins Publishers.

MICHAEL DIRDA: "Commencement Advice" was originally published as "Readings," copyright © 1999 The Washington Post. Reprinted with permission.

MATTHEW DOUGLAS: "The Evil Empire?" Reprinted by permission of the author.

RITA DOVE: "American Smooth" from *American Smooth* by Rita Dove. Copyright © 2004 by Rita Dove. Used by permission of W. W. Norton & Company, Inc.

RUTH C. ENGS: "Why the Drinking Age Should Be Lowered," copyright © 1988 by Ruth C. Engs is reprinted by permission of the author.

STEPHANIE ERICSSON: "The Ways We Lie" copyright © 1992 by Stephanie Ericsson. Originally published by *The Utne Reader*. Reprinted by permission of Dunham Literary Inc., as agent for the author.

TRIP GABRIEL: "Plagiarism Lines Blur for Students in Digital Age." Originally published as "For Students in Internet Age, No Shame in Copy and Paste" from *The New York Times*, August 2, 2010 The New York Times. All rights reserved. Used by permission and protected by the Copyright Laws of the United States. The printing, copying, redistribution or retransmission of the Material without express written permission is prohibited.

HENRY LOUIS GATES JR.: "The Way to Reduce Black Poverty" published as "Breaking the Silence" from *The New York Times*, Aug. 1, 2004. Copyright © 2004 The New York Times. All rights reserved. Used by permission and protected by the Copyright Laws of the United States. The printing, copying, redistribution or retransmission of the Material without express written permission is prohibited.

ATUL GAWANDE: "The Checklist" from *The Checklist Manifesto: How to Get Things Right* by Atul Gawande. Copyright © 2009 by Atul Gawande. Reprinted by permission of Henry Holt and Company, LLC.

MALCOLM GLADWELL: From *The Tipping Point* by Malcolm Gladwell. Copyright © 2000 by Malcolm Gladwell. Reprinted by permission of Little Brown & Company.

AMY GOLDWASSER: "What's the Matter with Kids Today?" from *Salon*, March 14, 2008. Copyright © 2008 by Amy Goldwasser. Reprinted by permission of the author.

ELLEN GOODMAN: "Who Owns Dr. King's Words?" by Ellen Goodman. Copyright © 1999 Globe Newspaper Company. Republished with permission.

JEFF GREMMELS: "The Clinic" is reprinted by permission of the author.

JAMIE GULLEN: "The Danish Way of Life." Reprinted by The Danish Institute for Study Abroad and the author.

MELISSA HICKS: "The High Price of Butter." Reprinted with permission of the author.

JACK HITT: "The Battle of the Binge" is reprinted from *The New York Times* magazine, Oct. 24, 1999 by permission of the author.

PHIL HOLLAND: "Render Unto Larry's" from *The New York Times*, July 17, 2009. Copyright © 2009 The New York Times. All rights reserved. Used by permission and protected by the Copyright Laws of the United States. The printing, copying, redistribution or retransmission of the Material without express written permission is prohibited.

JACK HORNER: "The Extraordinary Characteristics of Dyslexia" from *Perspectives on Language and Literacy*, Summer 2008 Issue. Reprinted by permission of the International Dyslexia Association.

ALEX HORTON: "On Getting By" from *Army of Dude*, January 13, 2010. Reprinted by permission of Alex Horton.

DEBRA HOUCHINS: "Treat Yourself to Tiramisu on a Student Budget" from *The Collegiate Times*, July 14, 2010. Reprinted by permission of the author.

ZORA NEALE HURSTON: From *How It Feels to Be Colored Me* is used with permission of the estate of Zora Neale Hurston.

SHIRLEY JACKSON: "The Lottery" From *The Lottery* by Shirley Jackson. Copyright © 1948, 1949 by Shirley Jackson. Copyright renewed 1976, 1977 by Laurence Hyman, Barry Hyman, Mrs. Smith Webster and Mrs. Joanne Schnurer. Reprinted by permission of Farrar, Straus and Giroux.

PAULA T. KELSO: "Behind the Curtain," copyright © 2003 Edwardsville Journal of Sociology is reprinted by permission from *Edwardsville Journal of Sociology* Volume 3.2. http://siue.edu/sociology/sociology/EJS/

MARTIN LUTHER KING JR.: "I Have a Dream" is reprinted by arrangement with The Heirs to the Estate of Martin Luther King Jr., c/o Writers House as agent for the proprietor, New York, NY.

NICHOLAS D. KRISTOF: "Food for the Soul" from *The New York Times*, August 23, 2009. Copyright © 2009 The New York Times. All rights reserved. Used by permission and protected by the Copyright Laws of the United States. The printing, copying, redistribution or retransmission of the Material without express written permission is prohibited.

LAWRENCE LESSIG: "Liberate the Music—Again" from *Free Culture* by Lawrence Lessig. Copyright © 2004 by Lawrence Lessig. Used by permission of The Penguin Press, a division of Penguin Group (USA) Inc.

MICHAEL LEWIS: From *Liar's Poker* by Michael Lewis. Copyright © 1989 by Michael Lewis. "Buy That Little Girl an Ice Cream Cone" from *Home Game: An Accidental Guide to Fatherhood*. Copyright © 2009 by Michael Lewis. Used by permission of W. W. Norton & Company.

JOE LINDSEY: "Why Legalizing Sports Doping Won't Work" from *The New York Times*, July 27, 2010. Reprinted by permission of the author.

BOBBIE ANN MASON: "Being Country" from *Clear Springs* by Bobbie Ann Mason. Copyright © 1999 by Bobbie Ann Mason. Used by permission of Random House, Inc.

ERIN MCKEAN: "Verbed! Not Every Noun Wants to Stay That Way" from Wordnik.com. Originally published in *The Boston Globe*, July 25, 2010. Reprinted by permission of the author.

FATEMA MERNISSI: From *Dreams of Trespass*, copyright © 1994 by Fatema Mernissi. Reprinted by permission of Basic Books, a member of the Perseus Books Group.

JIM MILLER: "The Natural Order of a Small Town." Reprinted with permission from the November 23, 2009 issue of *The Nation*. For subscription information, call 1-800-333-8536. Portions of each week's Nation magazine can be accessed at http://thenation.com.

WILLIAM MOLLER: "Those Who Live in Glass Houses . . ." from *Yankees Dollar* blog, May 5, 2009. Reprinted by permission of the author.

TONI MORRISON: "Strangers" by Toni Morrison is reprinted by permission of International Creative Management, Inc. Copyright © 1998 by Toni Morrison.

MICHAEL C. MUNGER: "10 Tips on How to Write Less Badly" from *The Chronicle of Higher Education*, Sept. 6, 2010. Reprinted by permission of the author.

GEOFFREY NUNBERG: "The War of Words" published as "The -Ism Schism" from *The New York Times*, July 11, 2004. Copyright © 2004 The New York Times. All rights reserved. Used by permission and protected by the Copyright Laws of the United States. The printing, copying, redistribution or retransmission of the Material without express written permission is prohibited.

BARACK OBAMA: The speech "A More Perfect Union" was delivered by Senator Barack Obama at the Constitution Center, Philadelphia, PA, March 18, 2008.

FLANNERY O'CONNOR: "A Good Man Is Hard to Find" from *A Good Man Is Hard to Find and Other Stories*. Copyright © 1953 by Flannery O'Connor and renewed 1981 by Regina O'Connor. Reprinted by permission of Harcourt, Inc.

THE ONION: "All Seven Deadly Sins Committed at Church Bake Sale" from Vol. 37 no., 45 is reprinted with permission of *The Onion*. Copyright © 2007 by Onion, Inc. www.theonion.com.

PEGGY ORENSTEIN: "I Tweet, Therefore I Am" from *The New York Times*, August 1, 2010. Copyright © 2010 The New York Times. All rights reserved. Used by permission and protected by the Copyright Laws of the United States. The printing, copying, redistribution or retransmission of the Material without express written permission is prohibited.

JUDITH ORTIZ COFER: "More Room" from *Silent Dancing* by Judith Ortiz Cofer. Copyright © 1990 Arte Publico Press-University of Houston. Reprinted with permission.

STEVEN PINKER: "Mind Over Mass Media" from *The New York Times*, June 11, 2010. Copyright © 2010 The New York Times. All rights reserved. Used by permission and protected by the Copyright Laws of the United States. The printing, copying, redistribution or retransmission of the Material without express written permission is prohibited.

JOSHUA PIVEN, DAVID BORGENICHT AND JENNIFER WORICK: From *The Worst-Case Scenario Survival Handbook: College* by Joshua Piven et al., illustrated by Brenda Brown, copyright © 2004 by Quirk Productions, Inc. Used with permission of Chronicle Books LLC, San Francisco, visit ChronicleBooks.com.

SYLVIA PLATH: From "Mirror" from *Crossing the Water* by Sylvia Plath. Reprinted by permission of HarperCollins Publishers and Faber and Faber Ltd. Copyright © 1963 by Ted Hughes. Originally appeared in *The New Yorker*. Published in Great Britain in *Collected Poems*.

ANNA QUINDLEN: From *How Reading Changed My Life* by Anna Quindlen. Copyright © 1998 by Anna Quindlen. Used by permission of Ballantine Books, a division of Random House, Inc.

ADRIENNE RICH: Part vi of "Ritual Acts" from *The School Among the Ruins: Poems 2000–2004* by Adrienne Rich. Copyright © 2004 by Adrienne Rich. Used by permission of the author and W. W. Norton & Company.

MARY ROACH: From *Stiff: The Curious Lives of Human Cadavers* by Mary Roach. Copyright © 2003 by Mary Roach. Used by permission of W. W. Norton & Company.

HENRY L. ROEDIGER III: "Why Are Textbooks So Expensive?" by Henry L. Roediger III. Reprinted by permission of the Association for Psychological Science from the *American Psychological Society Observer*.

RICHARD RUSSO: From *Straight Man* by Richard Russo. Copyright © 1997 by Richard Russo. Used by permission of Random House, Inc.

ZAINAB SALBI: "Little House in the War Zone" from *The New York Times*, Sept. 5, 2009. Copyright © 2009 The New York Times. All rights reserved. Used by permission and protected by the Copyright Laws of the United States. The printing, copying, redistribution or retransmission of the Material without express written permission is prohibited.

GITANGELI SAPRA: "I'm Happy With an Arranged Marriage—The Risk of Failure Is Lower." Copyright © 2003 NI Syndication, London. Reprinted by permission.

ERIC SCHLOSSER: "What We Eat" from *Fast Food Nation* by Eric Schlosser. Copyright © 2001 by Eric Schlosser. Reprinted by permission of Houghton Mifflin Company. All right reserved.

DAVID SEDARIS: From *Me Talk Pretty One Day* by David Sedaris. Copyright © 2000 by David Sedaris. Used by permission of Little Brown & Company.

CHRIS SEGUIN: Excerpts from www.juggling.org/programs/java/seguin/index/html. Reprinted by permission of the author.

ANNE SEXTON: "Her Kind" from *To Bedlam and Part Way Back* by Anne Sexton. Copyright © 1960 by Anne Sexton, renewed 1988 by Linda G. Sexton. Reprinted by permission of Houghton Mifflin Harcourt Publishing Company. All rights reserved.

SAIRA SHAH: "Longing to Belong" was first published in *The New York Times*, Sept. 21, 2003. Reprinted by permission of Fletcher & Parry LLC.

ZOE SHEWER: "Ready, Willing, and Able." Reprinted by permission of the author.

MARK SISSON: "Should We Allow Drugs in Sports?" from *Mark's Daily Apple* blog, 2006. Reprinted by permission of the author.

CAROLYN STONEHILL: "Modern Dating, Prehistoric Style." Reprinted by permission of the author.

AMY TAN: "Mother Tongue" first appeared in *The Threepenny Review*. Copyright © 1990 by Amy Tan. Reprinted by permission of the author and the Sandra Dijkstra Literary Agency.

DEBORAH TANNEN: "But What Do You Mean?" by Deborah Tannen, *Redbook*, October 1994. Copyright © 1994 by Deborah Tannen. Reprinted by permission of HarperCollins Publishers.

LAUREL THATCHER ULRICH: "The Slogan" from *Well-Behaved Women Seldom Make History* by Laurel Thatcher Ulrich. Copyright © 2007 by Laurel Thatcher Ulrich. Used by permission of Alfred K. Knopf, a division of Random House, Inc.

HAL R. VARIAN: "Analyzing the Marriage Gap" published as "Economic Scene; Ask Not What You Can Do For Marriage; Ask What Marriage Can Do For Your Bottom Line" from *The New York Times*, July 29, 2004. Copyright © 2004 The New York Times. All rights reserved. Used by permission and protected by the Copyright Laws of the United States. The printing, copying, redistribution or retransmission of the Material without express written permission is prohibited.

ROBERT VOAS: "There's No Benefit to Lowering the Drinking Age" from *The Christian Science Monitor*, Jan. 12, 2006. Reprinted by permission of the author.

MICHELLE WATSON: "Shades of Character" by Michelle Watson is used by permission of the author, Michelle Watson DeBord.

JOANNA WEISS: "Happy Meals and Old Spice Guy" from *The Boston Globe*, July 25, 2010. Copyright © The Boston Globe. All rights reserved. Used by permission and protected by the Copyright Laws of the United States. The printing, copying, redistribution or retransmission of the Material without express written permission is prohibited.

E. B. WHITE: "Once More to the Lake" from *One Man's Meat*. Text copyright © 1941 by E. B. White. Copyright renewed. Reprinted by permission of Tilbury House Publishers, Gardiner, Maine.

SARAH WILENSKY: "Generation Plagiarism" from *Indiana Daily Student*, Feb. 5, 2010. Used by permission of Indiana Daily Student.

MONICA WUNDERLICH: "My Technologically Challenged Life" first appeared in *Delta Winds* 2004. Reprinted by permission of the author.

Illustrations

p. 6: Anna Quindlen, *How Reading Changed My Life*. Copyright 1998. Reprinted with permission of Ballantine Books, Random House. **p. 35:** Doug Steley B / Alamy. **p. 43:** David M Grossman / The Image Works. **p. 83:** Gordon Marshal, Canada. **p. 86:** © Lynda Barry. **p. 100:** Picture Contact BV / Alamy. **p. 124:** Lake County Museum / Corbis. **p. 125:** http://www.belgradelakesmaine.com/. **p. 141:** From *Sneakers: The Complete Collector's Guide*, written and designed by Unorthodox Styles, Thames & Hudson Inc., New York. Text and layout © 2005 Thames & Hudson Ltd., London. Photograph © 2005 Unorthodox Styles. Reprinted by kind permission of Thames & Hudson. **p. 148:** Doug Benz / The New York Times / Redux. **p. 160:** Corbis. **p. 189:** Courtesy of Peak Fulfillment, a service of Gavan Burke Enterprises, Inc. **p. 191:** "All Seven Deadly Sins Committed at Church Bake Sale," courtesy of The Onion. **p. 195:** Naum Kazhdan / The New York Times. **p. 208:** Image Courtesy of The Advertising Archives. **p. 214:** John Springer Collection / Corbis. **p. 216:** Associated Press. **p. 238:** Rebecca Homiski. **p. 241:** Bettmann / Corbis. **p. 244:** From *The Worst-Case Scenario Survival Handbook: College* by Joshua Piven et al., illustrated by Brenda Brown, copyright © 2004 by Quirk Productions, Inc. Used with permission of Chronicle Books LLC, San Francisco, visit ChronicleBooks.com. **p. 258:** First Light / Alamy. **p. 287:** Courtesy of Junenoire Photography. **p. 292:** Jeff Miller / University of

Wisconsin-Madison. **p. 308:** Heritage Images / Corbis. **p. 324:** Data from Bureau of Labor Statistics, U.S. Department of Labor, 2009. **p. 335:** Photos 12 / Alamy. **p. 401:** © The New Yorker Collection, 1998, Roz Chast from Cartoonbank.com. All Rights Reserved. **p. 411:** Getty Images / Axiom RM. **p. 425:** Jack Delano / Corbis. **p. 426:** Graves County, Kentucky Archives. **p. 459:** Courtesy of Aeroports de Paris. **p. 461:** Wikimedia. **p. 468:** William Davis / Hulton Archive / Getty Images. **p. 469:** STOCK4B / Getty Images. **p. 483:** © Rube Goldberg, Inc. **p. 541:** Courtesy of the Life Is Good Company. **p. 548:** PoodlesRock / Corbis. **p. 555:** Hulton-Deutsch Collection / Corbis. **p. 575:** The Granger Collection, New York. **p. 603:** NRT-Sports / Alamy. **p. 609:** Saed Hindash / Star Ledger / Corbis. **p. 659:** Mary Roach, *Stiff.* New York: Norton. Photo by Mark Atkins / Panoptika.net. **p. 662:** Courtesy of Melissa Hicks. **p. 669:** James Leynse / Corbis. **p. 686:** Corbis. **p. 687:** George D. Lepp / Corbis. **p. 690:** 2005 Crosskeys Media®. **p. 726:** Bettmann / Corbis.

Glossary / Index

A

ABSTRACT, 18, 122, 135, 174 Intangible; having to do with essences and ideas rather than specific instances. *Liberty, truth,* and *beauty* are abstract concepts. To make such abstractions more CONCRETE in your writing, DEFINE them clearly and provide lots of specific EXAMPLES and DESCRIPTIVE details.

academic searches, 701

ACADEMIC WRITING, 48–61 In a sense, all the writing you do in school is "academic." However, academic writing is better defined not by location but by PURPOSE, which is to engage the writer in the ongoing human conversation about ideas and to contribute, however modestly, to the advancement of knowledge.

considering other views, 53–54
finding out what's been said about your topic, 49
responding to ideas of others, 50–53

This glossary / index defines key terms and concepts and directs you to pages in the book where they are used or discussed. Terms set in SMALL CAPITAL LETTERS are defined elsewhere in the glossary / index.

templates for structuring your response, 52–53
saying why your ideas matter, 54
student example, "Modern Dating, Prehistoric Style" (Stonehill), 51–52, 55–61
synthesizing ideas, 50
using the methods of development, 54

Ackerman, Diane, "Why Leaves Turn Color in the Fall," 228

AD HOMINEM, **525** A FALLACY that attacks the person making an ARGUMENT instead of addressing the actual issue.

adjectives, 135, 327
affect, 465
"Against the Odds" (Borchers), 724–33
agreement, 52–53
"Ain't I a Woman?" (Truth), 34, 574–77
All Over But the Shoutin' (Bragg), 24
"All Seven Deadly Sins Committed at Church Bake Sale" (*The Onion*), 181, 190–93

ALLUSION A passing reference, especially to a work of literature. For example, the title of Barack Obama's speech "A More Perfect Union" is an allusion to a phrase in the preamble to the U.S. Constitution.

An American Childhood (Dillard), 66–68, 72–73, 90–94

American Psychological Association (APA), 708

"American Smooth" (Dove), 170–72

among, 280

ANALOGY, 525 A COMPARISON that points out similarities between otherwise dissimilar things, or ones not usually compared. Analogies can help you to DESCRIBE, EXEMPLIFY, DEFINE, or ANALYZE an unfamiliar subject (the flow of electrons along a wire) by likening it to a more familiar one (the flow of water through a pipe). Drawing analogies is also a useful strategy in ARGUMENT, where you claim that what is true in one, usually simpler case (family finances) is true in another, more complicated case (national fiscal policy).

ANALYSIS The mental act of taking something apart to understand and explain how the pieces fit together, such as the steps in a PROCESS or the chain of events leading from a CAUSE to a particular EFFECT.

"Analyzing the Marriage Gap" (Varian), 500–503

and, 46

ANECDOTE, 30–31, 63, 517 A brief NARRATIVE, often told for the purpose of attracting a reader's interest or leading into a larger point.

Angelou, Maya, 132

Angier, Natalie, "Intolerance of Boyish Behavior," 27, 34

ANNOTATE, 3–4, 5, 6 To make notations about a text by writing questions and comments in the margins and by highlighting, underlining, circling, or otherwise marking specific words and phrases.

ANTONYM A word whose meaning is opposite to that of another word, as *weak* is the antonym of *strong.* Antonyms and SYN-ONYMS are especially useful in establishing and extending a DEFINITION.

APA (American Psychological Association), 708

apostrophes, with possessives, 46–47

APPEAL TO DOUBTFUL AUTHORITY, 525 A FALLACY of citing as expert testimony the opinions of people who do not necessarily have special knowledge of the issue.

ARGUMENT, 9, 37, 54, 513–648 Writing that takes a position on an issue and seeks to convince its AUDIENCE to act in a certain way, to believe in the truth or validity of a statement, or simply to listen with an open mind.

    anticipating other arguments, 527, 529, 530

    appealing to readers' emotions, 526

    audience and, 515, 529–30

    cause-and-effect analysis and, 529, 530

    claim and, 530

    classification and division and, 325

    common errors in, 530–32

    comparison and contrast and, 279, 529

    composing an, 514–15

    connectors and, 531

    credibility and, 530

    defining, 514

    definition and, 382–83, 384, 530

    drafting an, 517–29

    emotional appeals and, 530

    ending with recommendations, 33

    establishing credibility, 526–27

    evidence and, 515–16, 530

    example and, 174, 530

    generating ideas, 515–16

    logical fallacies, 524–25

    logical reasoning, 530

    organizing an, 517–29

    with other methods, 529, 530, 652

    process analysis and, 234, 529

AUDIENCE, 36, 65, 66, 74   The actual or intended readers of a piece of writing.

B

BASIS FOR COMPARISON, 271, 273, 278, 282   The common ground, usually of shared characteristics, on which two subjects can be **COMPARED**. Ulysses S. Grant and Robert E. Lee, for instance, can be compared on the basis that both were Civil War generals.

"The Battle of the Binge" (Hitt), 587–90

because, 464, 465, 531

BEGGING THE QUESTION, 525 A FAL-
LACY of taking for granted what the ARGU-
MENT is supposed to prove.

"Behind the Curtain" (Kelso), 465–81

"Being Country" (Mason), 46, 126–27,
    130–31, 422–31

Bernays, Anne, "Warrior Day," 46, 69,
    104–7

Bernstein, Richard, "The Growing
    Cowardice of Online Anonymity,"
    179

Berry, Wendell, "Conservation Is Good
    Work," 26, 34

better, 280

between, 280

Birkenstein, Cathy, *"They Say / I Say,"*
    50–51

"Black Men and Public Space" (Staples),
    30–31

Blink (Gladwell), 173–74

blog entries, citing MLA-style, 721

body paragraphs, 31–32

book reviews, citing MLA-style, 718

books, as sources, 700
    citing MLA-style, 714–17, 719

books, citing MLA-style, 700, 713–16,
    719–20

Boolean operators, 702

Borchers, Dylan, "Against the Odds,"
    724–33

Borgenicht, David, "How to Pull an All-
    Nighter," 242–45

Boyle, T. C., *Talk Talk*, 132

Bragg, Rick, *All Over But the Shoutin'*, 24

**BRAINSTORMING, 19, 176, 226, 273,
379, 454–55, 515–16** A way of GENER-
ATING IDEAS, individually or with others, in
which you LIST thoughts and ideas on a par-

ticular topic as they come to mind during a
short time period.

Branch, John, "Perfection in the Horseshoe
    Pit," 146–51

Briggs, Joe Bob, "Get in Touch with Your
    Ancient Spear," 227

Brooks, David, "People Like Us," 352–58

Burke, Kenneth, 48

but, 46

"But What Do You Mean?" (Tannen), 320,
    363–70

"Buy That Little Girl an Ice Cream Cone"
    (Lewis), 578–82

C

"Cancer's Oddest Effect" (Barry), 495–99

capitalization, 45

"Car Talk," 188–89

Carroll, Lewis, *Alice in Wonderland*, 271

cartoons or comic strips, citing MLA-style,
    722

Catton, Bruce, "Grant and Lee," 277, 307–12

CAUSAL CHAIN, 458 A series of events
in which one event CAUSES another, which
in turn causes another event, all leading to
an ultimate EFFECT. A row of dominoes on
end is a classic example: the fall of one domino causes another to tip over, which in turn
pushes over another domino, until the entire
row has toppled.

**CAUSE-AND-EFFECT ANALYSIS, 9, 24,
37, 55, 73, 451–512** Writing that explains
why something happened (a CAUSE) and
examines what might happen as a result (an
EFFECT).

    argument and, 529, 530
    audience and, 463
    causal chain, 458
    chronological order and, 457, 463
    classification and division and, 325, 326
    common errors in, 464–65
    composing a, 452–63

CAUSES   Conditions or events necessary to produce an **EFFECT**. The *immediate cause* of an effect is the one closest to it in time and most directly responsible for producing the effect. *Remote causes* are further in time from an effect and less direct in producing it. The *main cause* of an effect is the most important cause; it is not only necessary to produce the effect but sufficient to do so. *Contributing causes* are less important but still contribute to the effect; they are not, however, sufficient to produce it on their own. *See also* **CAUSE-AND-EFFECT ANALYSIS**

CHRONOLOGICAL ORDER, 68 The sequence of events in time, particularly important in a **NARRATIVE** or **PROCESS ANALYSIS.**

CLAIM, 23, 514, 518, 523 The main point you make or position you take on an issue in an **ARGUMENT.**

DENOTATION The literal meaning of a word; its dictionary definition. *See also* CONNOTATION

DESCRIPTION, 9, 21, 24, 25, 33, 37, 41, 54, 121–72 Writing that appeals to the senses: it tells how something looks, feels, sounds, smells, or tastes. An *objective description* describes the subject factually, without the intrusion of the writer's own feelings, whereas a *subjective description* includes the writer's feelings about the subject.

DIALOGUE, 72–73, 74, 75 Direct speech, especially between two or more speakers in a NARRATIVE, quoted word for word. Dialogue is an effective way of introducing the views of others into a FIRST-PERSON narrative.

emotional appeals, 526, 530

Engs, Ruth, "Why the Drinking Age Should Be Lowered," 584–86

Environmental Protection Agency, "Make Way for Salmon in Duck Creek," 123

Ericsson, Stephanie, "The Ways We Lie," 336–44

essays, parts of, 28–33
    body paragraphs, 31–32
    conclusions, 32–33
    introductions, 29–31

etc., 182

ETYMOLOGY, 376, 382, 386   A word history, or the practice of tracing such histories, often used to extend a **DEFINITION**. The modern English word *march*, for example, is derived from the French *marcher* ("to walk"), which in turn is derived from the Latin word *marcus* ("a hammer"). A march is thus a measured walk or movement, as if to the steady beat of a hammer. In most dictionaries, the etymology of a word is explained in parentheses or brackets before the first definition.

EVIDENCE, 32, 37, 523   Proof; the facts and figures, examples, expert testimony, or personal experience that a writer uses to support a **THESIS** or other **CLAIMS** of an **ARGUMENT**.
    argument and, 530
    effective, 515–16

"The Evil Empire?" (Douglas), 532–39

EXAMPLE, 9, 25, 31, 33, 55, 173–222, 516, 523   A specific instance or illustration of a general idea. Among "things that have given males a bad name," for example, humorist Dave Barry cites "violent crime, war, spitting, and ice hockey."
    abstract and, 174
    argument and, 174, 530
    audience and, 175–76, 181

cause-and-effect analysis and, 180

composing an exemplification essay, 175–80

concrete, 181

defining, 173–74

definition and, 376, 377

description and, 180, 181

drafting an exemplification essay, 177–80

editing for common errors in examples, 182

finding good examples, 176–77

generating ideas by finding good examples, 176

narration and, 180, 181

organization and, 177–80, 181

with other methods, 180, 181, 650–51

parallelism and, 182

process analysis and, 232, 234

providing sufficient examples, 177, 179, 181

purpose and, 175–76, 181

reading with a critical eye, 181

readings
    "All Seven Deadly Sins Committed at Church Bake Sale" (*The Onion*), 190–93
    "Commencement Advice" (Dirda), 178, 199–206
    "Happy Meals and Old Spice Guy" (Weiss), 207–10
    "Piling on the Cookies" (Barboza), 178, 194–98
    "Ritual Acts vi" (Rich), 221–22
    "Well-Behaved Women Seldom Make History" (Ulrich), 211–20

specific, 181

stating the point, 177, 181

student example, "My Technologically Challenged Life" (Wunderlich), 182–87

templates for drafting, 178

thesis and, 177, 181

transitional words and phrases, 34

HYPERBOLE A **FIGURE OF SPEECH** that uses intentional exaggeration, often in a **DESCRIPTION** or to make a point: "The professor explained it to us for two weeks one afternoon." *See also* **UNDERSTATEMENT**

I

INDUCTION, 520–24 A form of logical reasoning that proceeds from particular evidence to a general conclusion, useful in persuading others that an **ARGUMENT** is valid. *See also* **DEDUCTION**

IRONY The use of words to suggest a meaning or condition different from, and often directly opposed to, those conveyed by taking the words literally: "When Congress finishes the serious business of trading insults, per-

LISTING, 19, 176, 226, 273, 319, 379, 515–16 GENERATING IDEAS by making lists of specific words, phrases, topics, examples, and other details as they occur to you, either while working by yourself or with others.

LOOPING, 17–19, 319 A directed form of FREEWRITING in which you GENERATE IDEAS by narrowing your focus—and summarizing what you have just written—each time you freewrite.

METAPHOR, 132 A FIGURE OF SPEECH—
often used in DESCRIPTIVE writing—that
compares one thing with another, without
the use of a stated connecting word: *Throughout the battle, Sergeant Phillips was a rock.*

MLA-STYLE DOCUMENTATION, 47, 709–
33 A two-part DOCUMENTATION system
created by the Modern Language Association that consists of brief in-text parenthetical citations and a list of sources at the
end of the text. This documentation style,
explained fully in the Appendix, is often
used in literature and writing classes.

MODE A form or manner of discourse. In classical rhetoric, the four basic modes of speaking or writing are NARRATION, DESCRIPTION, EXPOSITION, and ARGUMENT.

N

NARRATION, 9, 21, 33, 37, 54, 62–120 An account of actions and events that happen to someone or something in a particular place and time. Because narration is essentially storytelling, it is often used in fiction; however, it is also an important element in almost all writing and speaking. The opening of Lincoln's Gettysburg Address, for example, is in the narrative mode: "Fourscore and seven years ago our fathers bought forth on this continent a new nation."

NARRATOR, 72–73 The person (or thing) telling a story. A **FIRST-PERSON** narrator (*I, we*) is both an observer of the scene and a participant in the action, but is limited by what he or she knows or imagines. A **THIRD-PERSON** narrator (*he, she, it they*) is limited to the role of observer, though sometimes an all-knowing one. *See also* **POINT OF VIEW**

NAYSAYER, 53, 58, 59 A potential opponent, especially in an academic argument. *Planting a naysayer* in a piece of academic writing is a rhetorical move that allows you to anticipate and disarm possible arguments against your **THESIS**.

NON SEQUITUR, 525 Latin for "does not follow"; a **FALLACY** of using a statement that has little or no logical connection to the preceding statement.

O

RHETORIC, 49, 53, 79, 138, 186, 238, 283, 331, 397, 479, 537 The art of using language effectively in speech and in writing. The term originally belonged to oratory, and it implies the presence of both a speaker (or writer) and a listener (or reader).

RHETORICAL QUESTION, 180, 185 A question for which the speaker already has an answer in mind; used in **ARGUMENT** and other writing to introduce a statement as if it were the reader's own answer to the writer's question.

ROGERIAN ARGUMENT, 528–29 A strategy of **ARGUMENT** developed by the psychologist Carl Rogers that seeks common ground among opposing points of view and that treats the participants on all sides as colleagues rather than adversaries.

SETTING, 8, 74 The physical place and time in which an action or event occurs, especially important in NARRATIVE and DESCRIPTIVE writing.

SIMILE, 132 A FIGURE OF SPEECH, often used in DESCRIPTIVE WRITING, that compares one thing to another using *like* or *as*: *He stood like an oak.*

SUBJECT-BY-SUBJECT COMPARISON, 274–75, 279 A way of organizing a comparison (or contrast) in which two or more subjects are discussed individually, making a number of points about one subject and then covering more or less the same points about the other subject. A subject-by-subject comparison of London and New York would address first London, examining its nightlife, museums, theater, and history, and then look at New York in all these aspects. *See also* POINT-BY-POINT COMPARISON

SUMMARY, 5, 35, 51–52, 706, 708 A restatement, in your own words, of the main substance and most important points of a text—useful for reading critically, GENERATING IDEAS by LOOPING, serving as a TRANSITION between ideas in your writing, and (when DOCUMENTED) incorporating ideas from other sources.

THIRD PERSON, 72 The grammatical
and NARRATIVE point of view—expressed
by the personal pronouns *he, she, it,* and
they—that limits the narrator to the role of
observer, though sometimes an all-knowing
one. *See also* FIRST PERSON

TONE, 2, 4, 5, 6, 378, 527 A writer's
attitude toward his or her subject or AUDI-
ENCE: sympathy, longing, amusement, shock,
sarcasm, awe—the range is endless.

TOPIC SENTENCE, 33, 34 A sentence
that gives readers the main point of a paragraph, making a clear statement about the
topic.

TOULMIN ARGUMENT, 523 A practical
form of ARGUMENT, developed by the British philosopher Stephen Toulmin, that supports a CLAIM by presenting facts and other
data (the grounds) and a logical basis (the
warrant) on which the grounds are said to
justify the claim.

TRANSITIONS, 34, 35, 37, 74 Connecting words or phrases that guide the reader
from one idea or statement to another.
Transitions can help to establish a CHRONO-
LOGICAL sequence in NARRATIVE writing,
to connect EXAMPLES, and to move between
steps in a PROCESS.

U

UNDERSTATEMENT A FIGURE OF SPEECH
that deliberately makes something out to be
weaker, smaller, or less important than it
really is—often for purposes of humor. A
classic example is Mark Twain's "The report
of my death was an exaggeration." *See also*
HYPERBOLE

MENU OF READINGS

*student writing